INSIDE OF WALL SURROUNDING CITY OF PEKING, CHINA

Peking has 16 gates of which this gives a view of the most interesting. The walls of the outer city are 30 miles in circumference and are kept in perfect order. They are 50 feet high with a width of 60 feet at the base and 40 feet at the top. Each of the 16 gates is surmounted with a high tower built in galleries provided with countless loopholes, all of which makes the taking of the city a most difficult operation.

THE MARVELOUS PROGRESS OF THE 19TH CENTURY

The above symbolic picture, after the master painting of Paul Sinibaldi, explains the secret of the wonderful progress of the past 100 years. The genius of Industry stands in the centre. To her right sits Chemistry; to the left the geniuses of Electricity with the battery, the telephone, the electric light; there also are the geniuses of Navigation with the propeller, and of Literature and Art, all bringing their products to Industry who passes them through the hands of Labor in the foreground to be fashioned for the use of mankind.

THE ACHIEVEMENTS OF ONE HUNDRED YEARS

THE CIRCLE
—OF THE—
CENTURY

Embracing Descriptions of the Decisive Battles of the Century and the Great Soldiers Who
Fought Them; the Rise and Fall of Nations; the Changes in the Map of the World, and the
Causes Which Contributed to Political and Social Revolutions; Discoverers and Discoveries;
Explorers of the Tropics and Arctics; Inventors and Their Inventions; the Growth of Liter-
ature, Science and Art; the Progress of Religion, Morals and Benevolence in All Civilized Nations.

1833

By CHARLES MORRIS, LL. D.

Author of "The Aryan Race," "Civilization, Its History, Etc.," "The Greater Republic," Etc.

Embellished With Nearly 100 Full-Page Half-Tone Engravings, Illus-
trating the Greatest Events of the Century, and 100 Portraits of the
Most Famous Men in the World.

INTERNATIONAL PUBLISHING CO.
PHILADELPHIA, PA.

LIST OF CHAPTERS AND SUBJECTS

Introduction

CHAPTER I
The Threshold of the Century

CHAPTER II
Napoleon Bonaparte; The Man of Destiny

CHAPTER III
Europe in the Grasp of the Iron Hand

CHAPTER IV

The Decline and Fall of Napoleon's Empire

CHAPTER V

Nelson and Wellington, the Champions of England

CHAPTER VI

From the Napoleonic Wars to the Revolution of 1830

PAGE

LIST OF FULL-PAGE ILLUSTRATIONS

ALPHABETICAL LIST OF PORTRAITS

THE DUKE OF CHARTRES AT THE BATTLE OF JEMAPPES—(FROM THE ORIGINAL PAINTING BY A. LE DRES)

At Jemappes, in November, 1792, a battle was fought between the French and Austrians. The Duke of Chartres was Chief Lieutenant under General Dumouriez and commanded the centre of attack. In 1830 the Duke was made King of France, and on account of his peaceful reign was known as the "Citizen's King." In 1848 he abdicated the throne and soon after Napoleon III became President of the new Republic.

BATTLE OF CHATEAU-GONTIER (REIGN OF TERROR, 1792)

INTRODUCTION.

IT is the story of a hundred years that we propose to give ; the record of the noblest and most marvelous century in the annals of mankind. Standing here, at the dawn of the Twentieth Century, as at the summit of a lofty peak of time, we may gaze far backward over the road we have traversed, losing sight of its minor incidents, but seeing its great events loom up in startling prominence before our eyes ; heedless of its thronging millions, but proud of those mighty men who have made the history of the age and rise like giants above the common throng. History is made up of the deeds of great men and the movements of grand events, and there is no better or clearer way to tell the marvelous story of the Nineteenth Century than to put upon record the deeds of its heroes and to describe the events and achievements in which reside the true history of the age.

First of all, in this review, it is important to show in what the greatness of the century consists, to contrast its beginning and its ending, and point out the stages of the magnificent progress it has made. It is one thing to declare that the Nineteenth has been the greatest and most glorious of the centuries ; it is another and more arduous task to trace the development of this greatness and the culmination of this career of glory. This it is that we shall endeavor to do in the pages of this work. All of us have lived in the century here described, many of us through a great part of it, some of us, possibly, through the whole of it. It is in the fullest sense our own century, one of which we have a just right to feel proud, and in whose career all of us must take a deep and vital interest.

Before entering upon the history of the age it is well to take a bird's-eye view of it, and briefly present its claims to greatness. They are many and mighty, and can only be glanced at in these introductory pages ; it would need volumes to show them in full. They cover every field of human effort. They have to do with political development, the relations of capital and labor, invention, science, literature, production, commerce, and a dozen other life interests, all of which will be considered in this work. The greatness of the world's progress can be most clearly shown by pointing out the state of affairs in the several

A Bird's-
Eye View

branches of human effort at the opening and closing of the century and
placing them in sharp contrast.   This it is proposed to do in this introductory sketch.

A hundred years ago the political aspect of the world was remarkably
different from what it is now.   Kings, many of them, were tyrants ; peoples,
as a rule, were slaves—in fact, if not in name.   The absolute government
of the Middle Ages had been in a measure set aside, but the throne had
Tyranny and still immense power, and between the kings and the nobles
Oppression in the people were crushed like grain between the upper and
the Eighteenth nether millstones.   Tyranny spread widely ; oppression was
Century rampant ; poverty was the common lot ; comfort was confined
to the rich ; law was merciless ; punishment for trifling offences was swift
and cruel ; the broad sentiment of human fellowship had just begun to
develop ; the sun of civilization shone only on a narrow region of the earth,
beyond which barbarism and savagery prevailed.

In 1800, the government of the people had just fairly begun.   Europe
had two small republics, Switzerland and the United Netherlands, and in
the West the republic of the United States was still in its feeble youth.
The so-called republic of France was virtually the kingdom of Napoleon
the autocratic First Consul, and those which he had founded elsewhere
were the slaves of his imperious will.   Government almost everywhere. was
autocratic and arbitrary.   In Great Britain, the freest of the monarchies,
the king's will could still set aside law and justice in many instances and
parliament represented only a tithe of the people.   Not only was universal
suffrage unknown, but some of the greatest cities of the kingdom had no
voice in making the laws.

Government and In 1900, a century later, vast changes had taken place
the Rights of in the political world.   The republic of the United States
Man in 1900 had grown from a feeble infant into a powerful giant, and its
free system of government had spread over the whole great continent of
America.   Every independent nation of the West had become a republic
and Canada, still a British colony, was a republic in almost everything but
the name.   In Europe, France was added to the list of firmly-founded
republics, and throughout that continent, except in Russia and Turkey, the
power of the monarchs had declined, that of the people had advanced.   In
1800, the kings almost everywhere seemed firmly seated on their thrones.
In 1900, the thrones everywhere were shaking, and the whole moss-grown
institution of kingship was trembling over the rising earthquake of the
popular will.

The influence of the people in the government had made a marvelous lvance. The right of suffrage, greatly restricted in 1800, had become niversal in most of the civilized lands at the century's end. Throughout he American continent every male citizen had the right of voting. The ame was the case in most of western Europe, and even in far-off Japan hich a century before had been held under a seemingly help- **Suffrage and** ss tyranny. Human slavery, which held captive millions **Human** pon millions of men and women in 1800, had vanished from **Freedom** he realms of civilization in 1900, and a vigorous effort was being made to anish it from every region of the earth. As will be seen from this hasty etrospect, the rights of man had made a wonderful advance during the entury, far greater than in any other century of human history.

In the feeling of human fellowship, the sentiment of sympathy and enevolence, the growth of altruism, or love for mankind, there had been n equal progress. At the beginning of the century law was stern, justice evere, punishment frightfully cruel. Small offences met with severe retri- ution. Men were hung for a dozen crimes which now call for only a light unishment. Thefts which are now thought severely punished **Criminal Law** y a year or two in prison then often led to the scaffold. **and Prison** Men are hung now, in the most enlightened nations, only for **Discipline in** murder. Then they were hung for fifty crimes, some so slight **1800** s to seem petty. A father could not steal a loaf of bread for his starving hildren except at peril of a long term of imprisonment, or, possibly, of leath on the scaffold.

And imprisonment then was a different affair from what it is now. The risons of that day were often horrible dens, noisome, filthy, swarming with ermin, their best rooms unfit for human residence, their worst dungeons hell upon earth. This not only in the less advanced nations, but even in enlightened England. Newgate Prison, in London, for instance, was a sink of niquity, its inmates given over to the cruel hands of ruthless gaolers, orced to pay a high price for the least privilege, and treated worse than rute cattle if destitute of money and friends. And these were not alone elons who had broken some of the many criminal laws, but men whose ruilt was not yet proved, and poor debtors whose only crime was their mis- ortune. And all this in England, with its boast of high civilization. The eople were not ignorant of the condition of the prisons; Parliament was ppealed to a dozen times to remedy the horrors of the jails; yet many ears passed before it could be induced to act.

Compare this state of criminal law and prison discipline with that of he present day. Then cruel punishments were inflicted for small offences; low the lightest punishments compatible with the well-being of the com

munity are the rule.   The sentiment of human compassion has become stro
and compelling ; it is felt in the courts as well as among the people ; pub
opinion has grown powerful, and a punishment to-day too severe for t

Prisons and crime would be visited with universal condemnation.   T
Punishment treatment of felons has been remarkably ameliorated.   T
in 1900 modern prison is a palace as compared with that of a centu
ago.   The terrible jail fever which swept through the old-time prisons like
pestilence, and was more fatal to their inmates than the gallows, has bee
stamped out.   The idea of sanitation has made its way into the cell ar
the dungeon, cleanliness is enforced, the frightful crowding of the pa
is not permitted, prisoners are given employment, they are not permitted
infect one another with vice or disease, kindness instead of cruelty is th
rule, and in no direction has the world made a greater and more radic
advance.

A century ago labor was sadly oppressed.   The factory system ha
recently begun.   The independent hand and home work of the earlier ce
The Factory turies was being replaced by power and machine work.   Th
System and the steam-engine and the labor-saving machine, while bringin
Oppression of blessings to mankind, had brought curses also.   Workme
the Working- were crowded into factories and mines, and were poor
man paid, ill-treated, ill-housed, over-worked.   Innocent little chi
dren were forced to perform hard labor when they should have been at pla
or at school.   The whole system was one of white slavery of the mos
oppressive kind.

To-day this state of affairs no longer exists.   Wages have risen, th
hours of labor have decreased, the comfort of the artisan has grown, wha
were once luxuries beyond his reach have now become necessaries of life
Young children are not permitted to work, and older ones not beyond thei
strength.   With the influences which have brought this about we are no
here concerned.   Their consideration must be left to a later chapter.   It i
enough here to state the important development that has taken place.

Perhaps the greatest triumph of the nineteenth century has been in the
domain of invention.   For ages past men have been aiding the work o
their hands with the work of their brains.   But the progress of inventio
continued slow and halting, and many tools centuries old were in commo
use until the nineteenth century dawned.   The steam-engine came earlier,
and it is this which has stimulated all the rest.   A power was given to man
enormously greater than that of his hands, and he at once began to devise
means of applying it.   Several of the important machines used in manufac
ture were invented before 1800, but it was after that year that the great era

of invention began, and words are hardly strong enough to express the marvelous progress which has since taken place.

To attempt to name all the inventions of the nineteenth century would be like writing a dictionary. Those of great importance might be named by the hundreds; those which have proved epoch-making by the dozens. To manufacture, to agriculture, to commerce, to all fields of human labor, they extend, and their name is legion. Standing on the summit of this century and looking backward, its beginning appears pitifully poor and meager. Around us to-day are hundreds of busy workshops, filled with machinery, pouring out finished products with extraordinary speed, men no longer makers of goods, but waiters upon machines. In the fields the grain is planted and harvested, the grass cut and gathered, the ground ploughed and cultivated, everything done by machines. Looking back for a century, what do we see? Men in the fields with the scythe and the sickle, in the barn with the flail, working the ground with rude old ploughs and harrows, doing a hundred things painfully by hand which now they do easily and rapidly by machines. Verily the rate of progress on the farm has been marvelous.

The Era of Wonderful Inventions

The above are only a few of the directions of the century's progress. In some we may name, the development has been more extraordinary still. Let us consider the remarkable advance in methods of travel. In the year 1800, as for hundreds and even thousands of years before, the horse was the fastest means known of traveling by land, the sail of traveling by sea. A hundred years more have passed over our heads, and what do we behold? On all sides the powerful and swift locomotive, well named the iron-horse, rushes onward, bound for the ends of the earth, hauling men and goods to right and left with a speed and strength that would have seemed magical to our forefathers. On the ocean the steam engine performs the same service, carrying great ships across the Atlantic in less than a week, and laughing at the puny efforts of the sail. The horse, for ages indispensible to man, is threatened with banishment. Electric power has been added to that of steam. The automobile carriage is coming to take the place of the horse carriage. The steam plough is replacing the horse plough. The time seems approaching when the horse will cease to be seen in our streets, and may be relegated to the zoological garden.

The Fate of the Horse and the Sail

In the conveyance of news the development is more like magic than fact. A century ago news could not be transported faster than the horse could run or the ship could sail. Now the words of men can be carried through space faster than one can breathe. By the aid of the telephone a man can speak to his friend a thousand miles away. And with the phono-

graph we can, as it were, bottle up speech, to be spoken, if desired, a thous-
and years in the future.　Had we whispered those things to our forefathers
of a century past we should have been set down as wild romancers or insane
fools, but now they seem like every-day news.

These are by no means all the marvels of the century.　At its beginning the constitution of the atmosphere had been recently discovered
In the preceding period it was merely known as a mysterious gas called air
To-day we can carry this air about in buckets like so much water, or freeze
it into a solid like ice.　In its gaseous state it has long been used as the
power to move ships and windmills.　In its liquid state it may also soon
become a leading source of power, and in a measure replace steam, the great
power of the century before.

In what else does the beginning of the twentieth stand far in advance
of that of the nineteenth century?　We may contrast the tallow candle
with the electric light, the science of to-day with that of a century
Education, Dis=　ago, the methods and the extension of education and the
covery and　dissemination of books with those of the year 1800.　Discovery
Commerce　and colonization of the once unknown regions of the world
have gone on with marvelous speed.　The progress in mining has been
enormous, and the production of gold in the nineteenth century perhaps
surpasses that of all previous time.　Production of all kinds has enormously
increased, and commerce now extends to the utmost regions of the earth,
bearing the productions of all climes to the central seats of civilization, and
supplying distant and savage tribes with the products of the loom and the
mine.

Such is a hasty review of the condition of affairs at the end of the
nineteenth century as compared with that existing at its beginning.　No
effort has been made here to cover the entire field, but enough has been
said to show the greatness of the world's progress, and we may fairly speak
of this century as the Glorious Nineteenth.

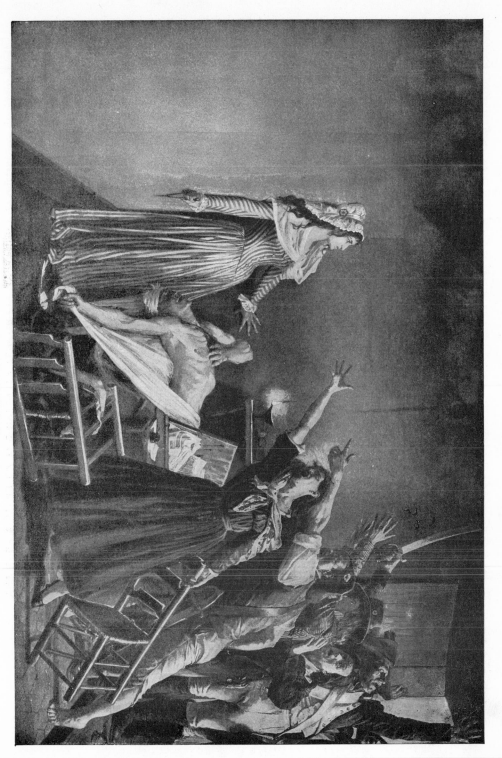

DEATH OF MARAT

Never was there a more excusable act of murder than that of the monster Marat, the most savage of the leaders of the Reign of Terror, by the knife of the devoted maiden Charlotte Corday. She boldly avowed her guilt and its purpose, and suffered death by the guillotine, July 17, 1793.

THE LAST VICTIMS OF THE REIGN OF TERROR—(FROM THE PAINTING BY MULLER)

CHAPTER I.

The Threshold of the Century.

AFTER its long career of triumph and disaster, glory and shame, the world stands to-day at the end of an old and the beginning of a new century, looking forward with hope and backward with pride, for it has just completed the most wonderful hundred years it has ever known, and has laid a noble foundation for the twentieth century, now at its dawn. There can be no more fitting time than this to review the marvelous progress of the closing century, through a portion of which *The Age we Live* all of us have lived, many of us through a great portion of *in and its* it. Some of the greatest of its events have taken place before *Great Events* our own eyes; in some of them many now living have borne a part; to picture them again to our mental vision cannot fail to be of interest and profit to us all.

When, after a weary climb, we find ourselves on the summit of a lofty mountain, and look back from that commanding altitude over the ground we have traversed, what is it that we behold? The minor details of the scenery, many of which seemed large and important to us as we passed, are now lost to view, and we see only the great and imposing features of the landscape, the high elevations, the town-studded valleys, the deep and winding streams, the broad forests. It is the same when, from the summit of an age, we gaze backward over the plain of time. The myriad of petty happenings are lost to sight, and we see only the striking events, the critical epochs, the mighty crises through which the world has passed. *True History* These are the things that make true history, not the daily *and the Things* doings in the king's palace or the peasant's hut. What we *which Make it* should seek to observe and store up in our memories are the turning points in human events, the great thoughts which have ripened into noble deeds, the hands of might which have pushed the world forward in its career; not the trifling occurrences which signify nothing, the passing actions which have borne no fruit in human affairs. It is with such turning points, such critical periods in the history of the nineteenth century, that this work proposes to deal; not to picture the passing bubbles on the stream of time, but to point out the great ships which have sailed up that stream laden deep

3   (33)

with a noble freight.   This is history in its deepest and best aspect, and we have set our camera to photograph only the men who have made and the events which constitute this true history of the nineteenth century.

On the threshold of the century with which we have to deal two grand events stand forth ; two of those masterpieces of political evolution which mold the world and fashion the destiny of mankind.   These are, in the Eastern hemisphere, the French Revolution ; in the Western hemisphere, the American Revolution and the founding of the republic of the United

Two of the World's Great- est Events States.   In the whole history of the world there are no events that surpass these in importance, and they may fitly be dwelt upon as main foundation stones in the structure we are seek- ing to build.   The French Revolution shaped the history of Europe for nearly a quarter century after 1800.   The American Revolution shaped the history of America for a still longer period, and is now beginning to shape the history of the world.   It is important therefore that we dwell on those two events sufficiently to show the part they have played in the history of the age.   Here, however, we shall confine our attention to the Revolution in France.   That in America must be left to the American section of our work.

The Mediæval Age was the age of Feudalism, that remarkable system of government based on military organization which held western Europe

The Feudal Sys- tem and Its Abuses captive for centuries.   The State was an army, the nobility its captains and generals, the king its commander-in-chief, the people its rank and file.   As for the horde of laborers, they were hardly considered at all.   They were the hewers of wood and drawers of water for the armed and fighting class, a base, down-trodden, enslaved multitude, destitute of rights and privileges, their only mission in the world to provide food for and pay taxes to their masters, and often doomed to starve in the midst of the food which their labor produced.

France, the country in which the Feudal system had its birth, was the country in which it had the longest lease of life.   It came down to the verge of the nineteenth century with little relief from its terrible exactions.   We see before us in that country the spectacle of a people steeped in misery, crushed by tyranny, robbed of all political rights, and without a voice to make their sufferings known ; and of an aristocracy lapped in luxury, proud, vain, insolent, lavish with the people's money, ruthless with the people's blood, and blind to the spectre of retribution which rose higher year by year before their eyes.

One or two statements must suffice to show the frightful injustice that prevailed.   The nobility and the Church, those who held the bulk of the wealth of the community, were relieved of all taxation, the whole burden of which fell upon the mercantile and laboring classes—an unfair exaction that threatened to crush industry out of existence. And to picture the condition of the peasantry, the tyranny of the feudal customs, it will serve to repeat the oft-told tale of the peasants who, after their day's hard labor in the fields, were forced to beat the ponds all night long in order to silence the croaking of the frogs that disturbed some noble lady's slumbers. Nothing need be added to these two instances to show the oppression under which the people of France lay during the long era of Feudalism.

This era of injustice and oppression reached its climax in the closing years of the eighteenth century, and went down at length in that hideous nightmare of blood and terror known **The Climax of Feudalism in France** as the French Revolution. Frightful as this was, it was unavoidable. The pride and privilege of the aristocracy had the people by the throat, and only the sword or the guillotine could loosen their hold. In this terrible instance the guillotine did the work.

It was the need of money for the spendthrift throne that precipitated the Revolution. For years the indignation of the people had been growing and spreading ; for years the authors of the nation had been adding fuel to the flame. The voices of Voltaire, Rousseau and a dozen others had been heard in advocacy of the rights of man, and the people were growing daily more restive under their load. But still the lavish waste of money wrung from the hunger and sweat of the people went on, until the king and his advisers found their coffers empty and were without hope of filling them without a direct appeal to the nation at large.

It was in 1788 that the fatal step was taken. Louis XVI, King of France, called a session of the States General, the Parliament **The States General is Convened** of the kingdom, which had not met for more than a hundred years. This body was composed of three classes, the representatives of the nobility, of the church, and of the people. In all earlier instances they had been docile to the mandate of the throne, and the monarch, blind to the signs of the times, had no thought but that this assembly would vote him the money he asked for, fix by law a system of taxation for his future supply, and dissolve at his command.

He was ignorant of the temper of the people. They had been given a voice at last, and were sure to take the opportunity to speak their mind. Their representatives, known as the Third Estate, were made up of bold, earnest, indignant men, who asked for bread and were not to be put off with a crust. They were twice as numerous as the representatives of the nobles and the clergy, and thus held control of the situation. They were ready to support the throne, but refused to vote a penny until the crying evils of the State were reformed. They broke loose from the other two Estates, established a separate parliament under the name of the National Assembly, and begun that career of revolution which did not cease until it had brought monarchy to an end in France and set all Europe aflame.

The court sought to temporize with the engine of destruction which it had called into existence, prevaricated, played fast and loose, and with every false move riveted the fetters of revolution more tightly round its neck. In July, 1789, the people of Paris took a hand in the game. They

The Fall of the Bastille

rose and destroyed the Bastille, that grim and terrible State prison into which so many of the best and noblest of France had been cast at the pleasure of the monarch and his ministers, and which the people looked upon as the central fortress of their oppression and woe.

With the fall of the Bastille discord everywhere broke loose, the spirit of the Revolution spread from Paris through all France, and the popular Assembly, now the sole law-making body of the State, repealed the oppressive laws of which the people complained, and with a word overturned abuses many of which were a thousand years old. It took from the nobles their titles and privileges, and reduced them to the rank of simple citizens. It confiscated the vast landed estates of the church, which embraced nearly one-third of France. It abolished the tithes and the unequal taxes, which had made the clergy and nobles rich and the people poor. At a later date, in the madness of reaction, it enthroned the Goddess of Reason and sought to abolish religion and all the time-honored institutions of the past.

The Revolution grew, month by month and day by day. New and more radical laws were passed; moss-grown abuses were swept away in an hour's sitting; the king, who sought to escape, was seized and held as a hostage; and war was boldly declared against Austria and Prussia, which showed a disposition to interfere. In November, 1792, the French army gained a brilliant victory at Jemmapes, in Belgium, which eventually led to the conquest of that kingdom by France. It was the first important event in the career of victory which in the coming years was to make France glorious in the annals of war.

King and Queen Under the Guillotine

The hostility of the surrounding nations added to the revolutionary fury in France. Armies were marching to the rescue of the king, and the unfortunate monarch was seized, reviled and insulted by the mob, and incarcerated in the prison called the Temple. The queen, Marie Antoinette, daughter of the Emperor of Austria, was likewise haled from the palace to the prison. In the following year 1793, king and queen alike were taken to the guillotine and their

NAPOLEON AND THE MUMMY OF PHARAOH

Strange thoughts must have passed through the mind of him soon to be Emperor of France, in gazing on the shriveled form of one of the great monarchs of old Egypt. Did he not ask himself then : what are glory and power worth, if this is the end of kingly greatness ?

NAPOLEON CROSSING THE ALPS

The renowned exploit of Hannibal leading an army across the lofty and frozen passes of the Alps was emulated by Napoleon in 1800, when he led his army across the St. Bernard Pass, descended like a torrent on the Austrians in Italy, and defeated them in the great battle of Marengo royal heads fell into the fatal basket. The Revolution was consummated, the monarchy was at an end, France had fallen into the hands of the people, and from them it descended into the hands of a ruthless and blood-thirsty mob.

At the head of this mob of revolutionists stood three men, Danton, Marat, and Robespierre, the triumvirate of the Reign of Terror, under which all safety ceased in France, and all those against whom the least breath of suspicion arose were crowded into **The Reign of Terror** prison, from which hosts of them made their way to the dreadful knife of the guillotine. Multitudes of the rich and noble had fled from France, among them Lafayette, the friend and aid of Washington in the American Revolution, and Talleyrand, the acute statesman who was to play a prominent part in later French history.

Marat, the most savage of the triumvirate, was slain in July, 1793, by the knife of Charlotte Corday, a young woman of pious training, who offered herself as the instrument of God for the removal of this infamous monster. His death rather added to than stayed the tide of blood, and in April, 1794, Danton, who sought to check its flow, fell a victim to his ferocious associate. But the Reign of Terror was nearing its end. In July the Assembly awoke from its stupor of fear, Robespierre was denounced, seized, and executed, and the frightful carnival of bloodshed came to an end. The work of the National Assembly had been fully consummated, Feudalism was at an end, monarchy in France had ceased and a republic had taken its place, and a new era for Europe had dawned.

Meanwhile a foreign war was being waged. England had **The Wars of the French Revolution** formed a coalition with most of the nations of Europe, and France was threatened by land with the troops of Holland, Prussia, Austria, Spain and Portugal, and by sea with the fleet of Great Britain. The incompetency of her assailants saved her from destruction. Her generals who lost battles were sent to prison or to the guillotine, the whole country rose as one man in defence, and a number of brilliant victories drove her enemies from her borders and gave the armies of France a position beyond the Rhine.

These wars soon brought a great man to the front, Napoleon Bonaparte, a son of Corsica, with whose nineteenth century career we shall deal at length in the following chapters, but of whose earlier exploits something must be said here. His career fairly began in 1794, when, under the orders of the National Convention—the successor of the National Assembly —he quelled the mob in the streets of Paris with loaded cannon and put a final end to the Terror which had so long prevailed.

Placed at the head of the French army in Italy, he quickly astonished the world by a series of the most brilliant victories, defeating the Austrians and the Sardinians wherever he met them, seizing Venice, the city of the lagoon, and forcing almost all Italy to submit to his arms. A republic was established here and a new one in Switzerland, while Belgium and the left bank of the Rhine were held by France.

Napoleon in Italy and Egypt. His wars here at an end, Napoleon's ambition led him to Egypt, inspired by great designs which he failed to realize. In his absence anarchy arose in France. The five Directors, then at the head of the Government, had lost all authority, and Napoleon, who had unexpectedly returned, did not hesitate to overthrow them and the Assembly which supported them. A new government, with three Consuls at its head, was formed, Napoleon as First Consul holding almost royal power. Thus France stood in 1800, at the end of the Eighteenth Century.

In the remainder of Europe there was nothing to compare with the momentous convulsion which had taken place in France. England had gone through its two revolutions more than a century before, and its people were the freest of any in Europe. Recently it had lost its colonies in America, but it still held in that continent the broad domain of Canada, and was building for itself a new empire in India, while founding colonies in twenty other lands. In commerce and manufactures it entered the nine-

England as a Centre of Industry and Commerce. teenth century as the greatest nation on the earth. The hammer and the loom resounded from end to end of the island, mighty centres of industry arose where cattle had grazed a century before, coal and iron were being torn in great quantities from the depths of the earth, and there seemed everywhere an endless bustle and whirr. The ships of England haunted all seas and visited the most remote ports, laden with the products of her workshops and bringing back raw material for her factories and looms. Wealth accumulated, London became the money market of the world, the riches and prosperity of the island kingdom were growing to be a parable among the nations of the earth.

On the continent of Europe, Prussia, which has now grown so great, had recently emerged from its mediæval feebleness, mainly under the powerful hand of Frederick the Great, whose reign extended until 1786, and whose ambition, daring, and military genius made him a fitting predecessor of Napoleon the Great, who so soon succeeded him in the annals of war. Unscrupulous in his aims, this warrior king had torn Silesia from Austria, added to his kingdom a portion of unfortunate Poland, annexed the principality of East Friesland, and lifted Prussia into a leading position among the European states.

Germany, now—with the exception of Austria—a compact empire, was then a series of disconnected states, variously known as kingdoms, principalities, margravates, electorates, and by other titles, the whole forming the so-called Holy Empire, though it was " neither holy nor an empire." It had drifted down in this fashion from the Middle Ages, and the work of consolidation had but just begun, in the conquests of Frederick the Great. A host of petty potentates ruled the land, whose states, aside from Prussia and Austria, were too weak to have a voice in the councils of Europe. Joseph II., the titular emperor of Germany, made an earnest and vigorous effort to combine its elements into a powerful unit; but he signally failed, and died in 1790, a disappointed and embittered man.

The Condition of the German States

Austria, then far the most powerful of the German states, was from 1740 to 1780 under the reign of a woman, Maria Theresa, who struggled in vain against her ambitious neighbor, Frederick the Great, his kingdom being extended ruthlessly at the expense of her imperial dominions. Austria remained a great country, however, including Bohemia and Hungary among its domains. It was lord of Lombardy and Venice in Italy, and was destined to play an important but unfortunate part in the coming Napoleonic wars.

The peninsula of Italy, the central seat of the great Roman Empire, was, at the opening of the nineteenth century, as sadly broken up as Germany, a dozen weak states taking the place of the one strong one that the good of the people demanded. The independent cities of the mediæval period no longer held sway, and we hear no more of wars between Florence, Genoa, Milan, Pisa and Rome ; but the country was still made up of minor states—Lombardy, Venice and Sardinia in the north, Naples in the south, Rome in the centre, and various smaller kingdoms and dukedoms between. The peninsula was a prey to turmoil and dissension. Germany and France had made it their fighting ground for centuries, Spain had filled the south with her armies, and the country had been miserably torn and rent by these frequent wars and those between state and state, and was in a condition to welcome the coming of Napoleon, whose strong hand for the time promised the blessing of peace and union.

Dissension in Italy and Decay in Spain

Spain, not many centuries before the greatest nation in Europe, and, as such, the greatest nation on the globe, had miserably declined in power and place at the opening of the nineteenth century. Under the emperor Charles I.

it had been united with Germany, while its colonies embraced two-thirds of the great continent of America. Under Philip II. it continued powerful in Europe, but with his death its decay set in. Intolerance checked its growth in civilization, the gold brought from America was swept away by more enterprising states, its strength was sapped by a succession of feeble monarchs, and from first place it fell into a low rank among the nations of Europe. It still held its vast colonial area, but this proved a source of weakness rather than of strength, and the people of the colonies, exasperated by injustice and oppression, were ready for the general revolt which was soon to take place. Spain presented the aspect of a great nation ruined by its innate vices, impoverished by official venality and the decline of industry, and fallen into the dry rot of advancing decay.

Of the nations of Europe which had once played a prominent part, one **The Partition of Poland by the Robber Nations.** was on the point of being swept from the map. The name of Poland, which formerly stood for a great power, now stands only for a great crime. The misrule of the kings, the turbulence of the nobility, and the enslavement of the people had brought that state into such a condition of decay that it lay like a rotten log amid the powers of Europe.

The ambitious nations surrounding—Russia, Austria, and Prussia—took advantage of its weakness, and in 1772 each of them seized the portion of Poland that bordered on its own territories. In the remainder of the kingdom the influence of Russia grew so great that the Russian ambassador at Warsaw became the real ruler in Poland. A struggle against Russia began in 1792, Kosciusko, a brave soldier who had fought under Washington in America, being at the head of the patriots. But the weakness of the king tied the hands of the soldiers, the Polish patriots left their native land in despair, and in the following year Prussia and Russia made a further division of the state, Russia seizing a broad territory with more than 3,000,-000 inhabitants.

In 1794 a new outbreak began. The patriots returned and a desperate struggle took place. But Poland was doomed. Suvoroff, the greatest of the Russian generals, swept the land with fire and sword. Kosciusko fell wounded, crying, "Poland's end has come," and Warsaw was taken and desolated by its assailants. The patriot was right; the end had come. What remained of Poland was divided up between Austria, Prussia, and Russia, and only a name remained.

There are two others of the powers of Europe of which we must speak, Russia and Turkey. Until the seventeenth century Russia had been a domain of barbarians, weak and disunited, and for a long period the vassal of the savage Mongol conquerors of Asia. Under Peter the Great (1689-1725) it rose into power and prominence, took its place among civilized states, and began that career of conquest and expansion which is still going on. At the end of the eighteenth **Russia and Turkey.** century it was under the rule of Catharine II., often miscalled Catharine the Great, who died in 1796, just as Napoleon was beginning his career. Her greatness lay in the ability of her generals, who defeated Turkey and conquered the Crimea, and who added the greater part of Poland to her empire. Her strength of mind and decision of character were not shared by her successor, Paul I., and Russia entered the nineteenth century under the weakest sovereign of the Romanoff line.

Turkey, once the terror of Europe, and sending its armies into the heart of Austria, was now confined within the boundaries it had long before won, and had begun its long struggle for existence with its powerful neighbor, Russia. At the beginning of the nineteenth century it was still a powerful state, with a wide domain in Europe, and continued to defy the Christians who coveted its territory and sought its overthrow. But the canker-worm of a weak and barbarous government was at its heart, while its cruel treatment of its Christian subjects exasperated the strong powers of Europe and invited their armed interference.

As regards the world outside of Europe and America, no part of it had yet entered the circle of modern civilization. Africa was an almost unknown continent; Asia was little better known; and the islands of the Eastern seas were still in process of discovery. Japan, which was approaching its period of manumission from barbarism, was still closed to the world, and China lay like a huge and helpless bulk, fast in the fetters of conservatism and blind self-sufficiency.

CHAPTER II.

Napoleon Bonaparte; The Man of Destiny.

THE first fifteen years of the nineteenth century in Europe yield us the history of a man, rather than of a continent. France was the centre of Europe; Napoleon, the Corsican, was the centre of France. All the affairs of all the nations seemed to gather around this genius of war. He was respected, feared, hated; he had risen with the suddenness of a thunder-cloud on a clear horizon, and flashed the lightnings of victory in the dazzled eyes of the nations. All the events of the period were concentrated into one great event, and the name of that event was Napoleon. He seemed incarnate war, organized destruction; sword in hand he dominated the nations, and victory sat on his banners with folded wings. He was, in a full sense, the man of destiny, and Europe was his prey.

Never has there been a more wonderful career. The earlier great conquerors began life at the top; Napoleon began his at the

A Remarkable Man and a Wonderful Career

bottom. Alexander was a king; Cæsar was an aristocrat of the Roman republic; Napoleon rose from the people, and was not even a native of the land which became the scene of his exploits. Pure force of military genius lifted him from the lowest to the highest place among mankind, and for long and terrible years Europe shuddered at his name and trembled beneath the tread of his marching legions. As for France, he brought it glory, and left it ruin and dismay.

We have briefly epitomized Napoleon's early career, his doings in the Revolution, in Italy, and in Egypt, unto the time that France's worship of his military genius raised him to the rank of First Consul, and gave him in effect the power of a king. No one dared question his word, the army was at his beck and call, the nation lay prostrate at his feet—not in fear but in admiration. Such was the state of affairs in France in the closing year of the eighteenth century. The Revolution was at an end; the Republic existed only as a name; Napoleon was the autocrat of France and the terror of Europe. From this point we resume the story of his career.

The First Consul began his reign with two enemies in the field,

The Enemies and Friends of France.

England and Austria. Prussia was neutral, and he had won the friendship of Paul, the emperor of Russia, by a shrewd move. While the other nations refused to exchange the Russian prisoners they held, Napoleon sent home 6,000 of these captives,

(44)

newly clad and armed, under their own leaders, and without demanding ransom.   This was enough to win to his side the weak-minded Paul, whose delight in soldiers he well knew.

Napoleon now had but two enemies in arms to deal with.   He wrote letters to the king of England and the emperor of Austria, offering peace. The answers were cold and insulting, asking France to take back her Bourbon kings and return to her old boundaries.   Nothing remained but war. Napoleon prepared for it with his usual rapidity, secrecy, and keenness of judgment.

There were two French armies in the field in the spring of 1800, Moreau commanding in Germany, Massena in Italy.   Switzerland, which was occupied by the French, divided the armies of the enemy, and Napoleon determined to take advantage of the separation of their forces, and strike an overwhelming blow.   He sent word to Moreau and Massena to keep the enemy in check at any cost, and secretly gathered a third army, whose corps were dispersed here and there, while the powers of Europe were aware only of the army of reserve at Dijon, made up of conscripts and invalids.

Meanwhile the armies in Italy and Germany were doing their best to obey orders.   Massena was attacked by the Austrians before he could concentrate his troops, his army was cut in two, and he was forced to fall back upon Genoa, in which city he was closely besieged, with a fair prospect of being conquered by starvation if not soon relieved.   Moreau was more fortunate.   He defeated the Austrians in a series of battles and drove them back on Ulm, where he blockaded them in their camp.   All was ready for the great movement which Napoleon had in view.

Movements of the Armies in Germany and Italy

Twenty centuries before Hannibal had led his army across the great mountain barrier of the Alps, and poured down like an avalanche upon the fertile plains of Italy.   The Corsican determined to repeat this brilliant achievement and emulate Hannibal's career.   Several passes across the mountains seemed favorable to his purpose, especially those of the St. Bernard, the Simplon and Mont Cenis.   Of these the first was the most difficult ; but it was much the shorter, and Napoleon determined to lead the main body of his army over this ice-covered mountain pass, despite its dangers and difficulties.   The enterprise was one to deter any man less bold than Hannibal or Napoleon, but it was welcome to the hardihood and daring of these men, who rejoiced in the seemingly impossible and spurned at hardships and perils.

The task of the Corsican was greater than that of the Carthaginian.

He had cannon to transport, while Hannibal's men carried only swords and
spears.   But the genius of Napoleon was equal to the task.

Napoleon Crosses the Alps at St. Bernard Pass

The cannon were taken from their carriages and placed in the
hollowed-out trunks of trees, which could be dragged with
ropes over the ice and snow.   Mules were used to draw the
gun-carriages and the wagon-loads of food and munitions of war.   Stores
of provisions had been placed at suitable points along the road.

Thus prepared, Napoleon, on the 16th of May, 1800, began his remarkable march, while smaller divisions of the army were sent over the Simplon,
the St. Gothard and Mont Cenis passes.   It was an arduous enterprise.
The mules proved unequal to the task given to them ; the peasants refused
to aid in this severe work ; the soldiers were obliged to harness themselves
to the cannon, and drag them by main strength over the rocky and ice-
covered mountain path.   The First Consul rode on a mule at the head of
the rear-guard, serene and cheerful, chatting with his guide as with a friend,
and keeping up the courage of the soldiers by his own indomitable spirit.

A few hours' rest at the hospice of St. Bernard, and the descent was
begun, an enterprise even more difficult than the ascent.   For five days the
dread journey continued, division following division, corps succeeding corps.
The point of greatest peril was reached at Aosta, where, on a precipitous
rock, stood the little Austrian fort of Bard, its artillery commanding the
narrow defile.

It was night when the vanguard reached this threatening spot.   It was
passed in dead silence, tow being wrapped round the wheels of the carriages
and a layer of straw and refuse spread on the frozen ground, while the
troops followed a narrow path over the neighboring mountains.   By daybreak the passage was made and the danger at an end.

The sudden appearance of the French in Italy was an utter surprise to
the Austrians.   They descended like a torrent into the valley, seized Ivry,
and five days after reaching Italy met and repulsed an Austrian force.   The

The Situation in Italy

divisions which had crossed by other passes one by one joined
Napoleon.   Melas, the Austrian commander, was warned of
the danger that impended, but refused to credit the seemingly
preposterous story.   His men were scattered, some besieging Massena, in
Genoa, some attacking Suchet on the Var.   His danger was imminent, for
Napoleon, leaving Massena to starve in Genoa, had formed the design of
annihilating the Austrian army at one tremendous blow.

The people of Lombardy, weary of the Austrian yoke, and hoping for
liberty under the rule of France, received the new-comers with transport,
and lent them what aid they could.   On June 9th, Marshall Lannes met

THE BATTLE OF RIVOLI

Rivoli is a village of Venetia, Italy, on the western bank of the Adige ; population, about 1,000. On January 14 and 15, 1797, Napoleon Bonaparte here, in his first campaign as commander-in-chief, gained a great victory over the Austrians commanded by Alvinczy, who lost 20,000 prisoners.

MARIE ANTOINETTE LED TO EXECUTION

The hapless wife of Louis XVI, of France, imprisoned during the Revolution in the prisons of the Temple and Conciergerie, separated from her family and friends, and treated to great indignities, died at length under the knife of the guillotine, October 16, 1793.

and defeated the Austrians at Montebello, after a hot engagement. "I heard the bones crackle like a hailstorm on the roofs," he said. On the 14th, the two armies met on the plain of Marengo, and one of the most famous of Napoleon's battles began.

Napoleon was not ready for the coming battle, and was taken by surprise. He had been obliged to break up his army in order to guard all the passages open to the enemy. When he entered, on the 13th, the plain between the Scrivia and the Bormida, near the little village of Marengo, he was ignorant of the movements of the Austrians, and was not expecting the onset of Melas, who, on the **The Famous Field of Marengo** following morning, crossed the Bormida by three bridges, and made a fierce assault upon the divisions of generals Victor and Lannes. Victor was vigorously attacked and driven back, and Marengo was destroyed by the Austrian cannon. Lannes was surrounded by overwhelming numbers, and, fighting furiously, was forced to retreat. In the heat of the battle Bonaparte reached the field with his guard and his staff, and found himself in the thick of the terrific affray and his army virtually beaten.

The retreat continued. It was impossible to check it. The enemy pressed enthusiastically forward. The army was in imminent danger of being cut in two. But Napoleon, with obstinate persistance, kept up the fight, hoping for some change in the perilous situation. Melas, on the contrary,—an old man, weary of his labors, and confident in the seeming victory,—withdrew to his headquarters at Alessandria, whence he sent off despatches to the effect that the terrible Corsican had at length met defeat.

He did not know his man. Napoleon sent an aide-de-camp in all haste after Desaix, one of his most trusted generals, who had just returned from Egypt, and whose corps he had detached towards Novi. All depended upon his rapid return. Without Desaix the battle was lost. Fortunately the alert general did not wait for the messenger. His ears caught the sound of distant cannon and, scenting danger, he marched back with the utmost speed.

Napoleon met his welcome officer with eyes of joy and hope. "You see the situation," he said, rapidly explaining the state of affairs. "What is to be done?"

"It is a lost battle," Desaix replied. "But there are some hours of daylight yet. We have time to win another." **A Great Battle Lost and Won**

While he talked with the commander, his regiments had hastily formed, and now presented a threatening front to the Austrians. Their presence gave new spirit to the retreating troops.

"Soldiers and friends," cried Napoleon to them, "remember that it is my custom to sleep upon the field of battle."

Back upon their foes turned the retreating troops, with new animation, and checked the victorious Austrians. Desaix hurried to his men and placed himself at their head.

"Go and tell the First Consul that I am about to charge," he said to an aide. "I need to be supported by cavalry."

A few minutes afterwards, as he was leading his troops irresistibly forward, a ball struck him in the breast, inflicting a mortal wound. "I have been too long making war in Africa; the bullets of Europe know me no more," he sadly said. "Conceal my death from the men; it might rob them of spirit."

The soldiers had seen him fall, but, instead of being dispirited, they were filled with fury, and rushed forward furiously to avenge their beloved leader. At the same time Kellermann arrived with his dragoons, impetuously hurled them upon the Austrian cavalry, broke through their columns, and fell upon the grenadiers who were wavering before the troops of Desaix. It was a death-stroke. The cavalry and infantry together swept them back in a disorderly retreat. One whole corps, hopeless of escape, threw down its arms and surrendered. The late victorious army was everywhere in retreat. The Austrians were crowded back upon the Bormida, here block-ing the bridges, there flinging themselves into the stream, on all sides flying from the victorious French. The cannon stuck in the muddy stream and were left to the victors. When Melas, apprised of the sudden change in the aspect of affairs, hurried back in dismay to the field, the battle was irretriev-ably lost, and General Zach, his representative in command, was a prisoner in the hands of the French. The field was strewn with thousands of the dead. The slain Desaix and the living Kellermann had turned the Austrian victory into defeat and saved Napoleon.

The Result of the Victory of Marengo A few days afterwards, on the 19th, Moreau in Germany won a brilliant victory at Hochstadt, near Blenheim, took 5,000 prisoners and twenty pieces of cannon, and forced from the Austrians an armed truce which left him master of South Germany. A still more momentous armistice was signed by Melas in Italy, by which the Aus-trians surrendered Piedmont, Lombardy, and all their territory as far as the Mincio, leaving France master of Italy. Melas protested against these severe terms, but Napoleon was immovable.

"I did not begin to make war yesterday," he said. "I know your situa-tion. You are out of provisions, encumbered with the dead, wounded, and sick, and surrounded on all sides. I could exact everything. I ask only what the situation of affairs demands. I have no other terms to offer."

During the night of the 2d and 3d of July, Napoleon re-entered Paris, which he had left less than two months before. Brilliant ova- **Napoleon Returns to France** tions met him on his route, and all France would have pros- trated itself at his feet had he permitted. He came crowned with the kind of glory which is especially dear to the French, that gained on the field of battle.

Five months afterwards, Austria having refused to make peace without the concurrence of England, and the truce being at an end, another famous victory was added to the list of those which were being inscribed upon the annals of France. On the 3d of December the veterans under Moreau met an Austrian army under the Archduke John, on the plain of Hohenlinden, across which ran the small river Iser.

The Austrians marched through the forest of Hohen- **Moreau and the Great Battle of Hohen= linden** linden, looking for no resistance, and unaware that Moreau's army awaited their exit. As they left the shelter of the trees and debouched upon the plain, they were attacked by the French in force. Two divisions had been despatched to take them in the rear, and Moreau held back his men to give them the necessary time. The snow was falling in great flakes, yet through it his keen eyes saw some signs of confusion in the hostile ranks.

" Richepanse has struck them in the rear," he said. " the time has come to charge."

Ney rushed forward at the head of his troops, driving the enemy in confusion before him. The centre of the Austrian army was hemmed in between the two forces. Decaen had struck their left wing in the rear and forced it back upon the Inn. Their right was driven into the valley. The day was lost to the Austrians, whose killed and wounded numbered 8,000, while the French had taken 12,000 prisoners and eighty-seven pieces of cannon.

The victorious French advanced, sweeping back all opposition, until Vienna, the Austrian capital, lay before them, only a few leagues away. His staff officers urged Moreau to take possession of the city.

" That would be a fine thing to do, no doubt," he said; " but to my fancy to dictate terms of peace will be a finer thing still."

The Austrians were ready for peace at any price. On Christmas day, 1800, an armistice was signed which delivered to the French **The Peace of Luneville** the valley of the Danube, the country of the Tyrol, a number of fortresses, and immense magazines of war materials. The war continued in Italy till the end of December, when a truce was signed there and the conflict was at an end.

Thus the nineteenth century dawned with France at truce with all her foes except Great Britain. In February, 1801, a treaty of peace between Austria and France was signed at Luneville, in which the valley of the Etsch and the Rhine was acknowledged as the boundary of France. Austria was forced to relinquish all her possessions in Italy, except the city of Venice and a portion of Venetia ; all the remainder of North Italy falling into the hands of France. Europe was at peace with the exception of the hostile relations still existing between England and France.

The war between these two countries was mainly confined to Egypt, where remained the army which Napoleon had left in his hasty return to France. As it became evident in time that neither the British land forces nor the Turkish troops could overcome the French veterans in the valley of the Nile, a treaty was arranged which stipulated that the French soldiers, 24,000 in all, should be taken home in English ships, with their arms and ammunition, Egypt being given back to the rule of the Sultan. This was followed by the peace of Amiens (March 27, 1802), between England and France, and the long war was, for the time, at an end. Napoleon had conquered peace.

The Peace of Amiens

During the period of peaceful relations that followed Napoleon was by no means at rest. His mind was too active to yield him long intervals of leisure. There was much to be done in France in sweeping away the traces of the revolutionary insanity. One of the first cares of the Consul was to restore the Christian worship in the French churches and to abolish the Republican festivals. But he had no intention of giving the church back its old power and placing another kingship beside his own. He insisted that the French church should lose its former supremacy and sink to the position of a servant of the Pope and of the temporal sovereign of France.

Establishing his court as First Consul in the Tuileries, Napoleon began to bring back the old court fashions and etiquette, and attempted to restore the monarchical customs and usages. The elegance of royalty reappeared, and it seemed almost as if monarchy had been restored.

A further step towards the restoration of the kingship was soon taken. Napoleon, as yet Consul only for ten years, had himself appointed Consul for life, with the power of naming his successor. He was king now in everything but the name. But he was not suffered to wear his new honor in safety. His ambition had aroused the anger of the republicans, conspiracies rose around him, and more than once his life was in danger. On his way to the opera house an infernal machine was exploded, killing several persons but leaving him unhurt.

NAPOLEON BONAPARTE

MEETING OF TWO SOVEREIGNS

Pope Pius VII, at the request, almost the command, of Napoleon, came from Rome to France in 1804, to crown the great conqueror Emperor of the French. He was very ceremoniously received by Napoleon, and treated with every outward show of honor. Years afterwards he was brought to France and forced to reside there, as the virtual captive of the Emperor.

Other plots were organized, and Fouché, the police-agent of the time, was kept busy in seeking the plotters, for whom there was brief mercy when found. Even Moreau, the victor at Hohenlinden, accused of negotiating with the conspirators, was disgraced, and exiled himself from France. Napoleon dealt with his secret enemies with the same ruthless energy as he did with his foes in the field of battle.

The Punishment of the Conspirators and the Assassination of the Duke d'Enghien

His rage at the attempts upon his life, indeed, took a form that has been universally condemned. The Duke d'Enghien, a royalist French nobleman, grandson of the Prince of Condé, who was believed by Napoleon to be the soul of the royalist conspiracies, ventured too near the borders of France, and was seized in foreign territory, taken in haste to Paris, and shot without form of law or a moment's opportunity for defence. The outrage excited the deepest indignation throughout Europe. No name was given it but murder, and the historians of to-day speak of the act by no other title.

The opinion of the world had little effect upon Napoleon. He was a law unto himself. The death of one man or of a thousand men weighed nothing to him where his safety or his ambition was concerned. Men were the pawns he used in the great game of empire, and he heeded not how many of them were sacrificed so that he won the game.

The culmination of his ambition came in 1804, when the hope he had long secretly cherished, that of gaining the imperial dignity, was realized. He imitated the example of Cæsar, the Roman conqueror, in seeking the crown as a reward for his victories, and was elected emperor of the French by an almost unanimous vote. That the sanction of the church might be obtained for the new dignity, the Pope was constrained to come to Paris, and there anointed him emperor on December 2, 1804.

Napoleon Crowned Emperor of the French

The new emperor hastened to restore the old insignia of royalty. He surrounded himself with a brilliant court, brought back the discarded titles of nobility, named the members of his family princes and princesses, and sought to banish every vestige of republican simplicity. Ten years before he had begun his career in the streets of Paris by sweeping away with cannon-shot the mob that rose in support of the Reign of Terror. Now he had swept away the Republic of France and founded a French empire, with himself at its head as Napoleon I.

But though royalty was restored, it was not a royalty of the old type. Feudalism was at an end. The revolution had destroyed the last relics of that effete and abominable system and it was an empire on new and modern lines which Napoleon had founded, a royalty voted into existence by a free people, not resting upon a nation of slaves.

The new emperor did not seek to enjoy in leisure his new dignity. His restless mind impelled him to broad schemes of public improvement. He **The Great** sought glory in peace as actively as in war. Important **Works Devised** changes were made in the management of the finances in order **By the New** to provide the great sums needed for the government, the **Emperor** army, and the state. Vast contracts were made for road and canal building, and ambitious architectural labors were set in train. Churches were erected, the Pantheon was completed, triumphal arches were built, two new bridges were thrown over the Seine, the Louvre was ordered to be finished, the Bourse to be constructed, and a temple consecrated to the exploits of the army (now the church of the Madeleine) to be built. Thousands of workmen were kept busy in erecting these monuments to his glory, and all France resounded with his fame.

Among the most important of these evidences of his activity of intellect was the formation of the *Code Napoleon*, the first organized code of French law, and still the basis of jurisprudence in France. First promulgated in 1801, as the Civil Code of France, its title was changed to the *Code Napoleon* in 1804, and as such it stands as one of the greatest monuments raised by Napoleon to his glory. Thus the Consul, and subsequently the Emperor, usefully occupied himself in the brief intervals between his almost incessant wars.

CHAPTER III.

Europe in the Grasp of the Iron Hand.

THE peace of Amiens, which for an interval left France without an open enemy in Europe, did not long continue. England failed to carry out one of the main provisions of this treaty, holding on to the island of Malta in despite of the French protests. The feeling between the two nations soon grew bitter, and in 1803 England again declared war against France. William Pitt, the unyielding foe of Napoleon, came again to the head of the ministry in 1804, and displayed all his old activity in organizing coalitions against the hated Corsican. **England Declares War** The war thus declared was to last, so far as England was concerned, until Napoleon was driven from his throne. It was conducted by the English mainly through the aid of money paid to their European allies and the activity of their fleet. The British Channel remained an insuperable obstacle to Napoleon in his conflict with his island foe, and the utmost he could do in the way of revenge was to launch his armies against the allies of Great Britain, and to occupy Hanover, the domain of the English king on the continent. This he hastened to do.

The immunity of his persistent enemy was more than the proud conqueror felt disposed to endure. Hitherto he had triumphed over all his foes in the field. Should these haughty islanders contemn his power and defy his armies? He determined to play the role of William of Normandy, centuries before, and attack them on their own shores. This design he had long entertained, and began actively to prepare for as soon as war was declared. An army was encamped at Boulogne, and a great flotilla prepared to convey it across the narrow sea. The war **Great Preparations for the Invasion of England** material gathered was enormous in quantity; the army numbered 120,000 men, with 10,000 horses; 1,800 gunboats of various kinds were ready; only the support of the fleet was awaited to enable the crossing to be achieved in safety.

We need not dwell further upon this great enterprise, since it failed to yield any result. The French admiral whose concurrence was depended upon took sick and died, and the great expedition was necessarily postponed. Before new plans could be laid the indefatigable Pitt had succeeded in organizing a fresh coalition in Europe, and Napoleon found full employment for his army on the continent.

In April, 1805, a treaty of alliance was made between England and Russia. On the 9th of August, Austria joined this alliance. Sweden subsequently gave in her adhesion, and Prussia alone remained neutral among the great powers. But the allies were mistaken if they expected to take the astute Napoleon unawares. He had foreseen this combination, and, while keeping the eyes of all Europe fixed upon his great preparations at Boulogne, he was quietly but effectively laying his plans for the expected campaign.

The Austrians had hastened to take the field, marching an army into Bavaria and forcing the Elector, the ally of Napoleon, to fly from his capital. The French emperor was seemingly taken by surprise, and apparently was in no haste, the Austrians having made much progress before he left his palace at Saint Cloud. But meanwhile his troops were quietly but

Rapid March on Austria

rapidly in motion, converging from all points towards the Rhine, and by the end of September seven divisions of the army, commanded by Napoleon's ablest Generals,—Ney, Murat, Lannes, Soult and others,—were across that stream and marching rapidly upon the enemy. Bernadotte led his troops across Prussian territory in disdain of the neutrality of that power, and thereby gave such offence to King Frederick William as to turn his mind decidedly in favor of joining the coalition.

Early in October the French held both banks of the Danube, and before the month's end they had gained a notable triumph. Mack, one of the Austrian commanders, with remarkable lack of judgment, held his army in the fortress of Ulm while the swiftly advancing French were cutting off every avenue of retreat, and surrounding his troops. An extraordinary result followed. Ney, on the 14th, defeated the Austrians at Elchingen, cutting off Mack from the main army and shutting him up hopelessly in

The Surrender of General Mack

Ulm. Five days afterwards the desparing and incapable general surrendered his army as prisoners of war. Twenty-three thousand soldiers laid their weapons and banners at Napoleon's feet and eighteen generals remained as prisoners in his hands. It was a triumph which in its way atoned for a great naval disaster which took place on the succeeding day, when Nelson, the English admiral, attacked and destroyed the whole French fleet at Trafalgar.

The succeeding events, to the great battle that closed the campaign, may be epitomized. An Austrian army had been dispatched to Italy under the brave and able Archduke Charles. Here Marshal Massena commanded the French and a battle took place near Caldiero on October 30th. The Austrians fought stubbornly, but could not withstand the impetuosity of the French, and were forced to retreat and abandon northern Italy to Massena and his men.

DEATH OF LORD NELSON—BATTLE OF TRAFALGAR, OCTOBER 21, 1805

The greatest sea fight in history is represented by the above engraving. It was off Cape Trafalgar, southern coast of Spain, that Lord Nelson met and defeated the combined French and Spanish fleets, vastly his superior in number of vessels and men. This victory sounded the keynote in the decline of Napoleon's power and changed the destiny of Europe. Nelson fell and died as he heard the words telling him that the naval power of France and Spain was destroyed. "It is glorious to die in the moment of victory."

MURAT AT BATTLE OF JENA

General Murat was the Sheridan of France, the most dashing and daring cavalry leader in Napoleon's armies. Napoleon said of him: "It was really a magnificent sight to see him in battle, heading the cavalry." At Jena he played an efficient part in breaking the ranks of the Prussians.

In the north the king of Prussia, furious at the violation of his neutral territory by the French under Bernadotte, gave free passage to the Russian and Swedish troops, and formed a league of friendship with the Czar Alexander. He then dispatched his minister Haugwitz to Napoleon, with a demand that concealed a threat, requiring him, as a basis of peace, to restore the former treaties in Germany, Switzerland, Italy and Holland.

With utter disregard of this demand Napoleon advanced along the Danube towards the Austrian states, meeting and defeating the Austrians and Russians in a series of sanguinary conflicts. The Russian army was the most ably commanded, and its leader Kutusoff led it backward in slow but resolute retreat, fighting only when attacked. The French under Mortier were caught isolated on the left bank of the Danube, and fiercely assailed by the Russians, losing heavily before they could be reinforced.

Despite all resistance, the French continued to advance, Murat soon reaching and occupying Vienna, the Austrian capital, from which the emperor had hastily withdrawn. Still **The Advance on Vienna** the retreat and pursuit continued, the allies retiring to Moravia, whither the French, laden with an immense booty from their victories, rapidly followed. Futile negotiations for peace succeeded, and on the 1st of December, the two armies, both concentrated in their fullest strength (92,000 of the allies to 70,000 French) came face to face on the field of Austerlitz, where on the following day was to be fought one of the memorable battles in the history of the world.

The Emperor Alexander had joined Francis of Austria, and the two monarchs, with their staff officers, occupied the castle and village of Austerlitz. Their troops hastened to occupy the plateau of Pratzen, which Napoleon had designedly left free. His plans of battle **The Eve Before Austerlitz** was already fully made. He had, with the intuition of genius, foreseen the probable manœuvers of the enemy, and had left open for them the position which he wished them to occupy. He even announced their movement in a proclamation to his troops.

"The positions that we occupy are formidable," he said, "and while the enemy march to turn my right they will present to me their flank."

This movement to the right was indeed the one that had been decided upon by the allies, with the purpose of cutting off the road to Vienna by isolating numerous corps dispersed in Austria and Styria. It had been shrewdly divined by Napoleon in choosing his ground.

The fact that the 2d of December was the anniversary of the coronation of their emperor filled the French troops with ardor. They celebrated it by making great torches of the straw which formed their beds and illuminating their camp.   Early the next morning the allies began their projected movement.   To the joy of Napoleon his prediction was fulfilled, they were advancing towards his right. He felt sure that the victory was in his hands.

He held his own men in readiness while the line of the enemy deployed. The sun was rising, its rays gleaming through a mist, which dispersed as it **The Greatest of** rose higher.   It now poured its brilliant beams across the **Napoleon's** field, the afterward famous "sun of Austerlitz."   The move-**Victories** ment of the allies had the effect of partly withdrawing their troops from the plateau of Pratzen.   At a signal from the emperor the strongly concentrated centre of the French army moved forward in a dense mass, directing their march towards the plateau, which they made all haste to occupy.   They had reached the foot of the hill before the rising mist revealed them to the enemy.

The two emperors watched the movement without divining its intent. " See how the French climb the height without staying to reply to our fire," said Prince Czartoryski, who stood near them.

The emperors were soon to learn why their fire was disdained.   Their marching columns, thrown out one after another on the slope, found them-selves suddenly checked in their movement, and cut off from the two wings of the army.   The allied force had been pierced in its centre, which was flung back in disorder, in spite of the efforts of Kutusoff to send it aid.   At the same time Davout faced the Russians on the right, and Murat and Lannes attacked the Russian and Austrian squadrons on the left, while Kel-lermann's light cavalry dispersed the squadrons of the Uhlans.

The Russian guard, checked in its movement, turned towards Pratzen, in a desperate effort to retrieve the fortune of the day.   It was incautiously pursued by a French battalion, which soon found itself isolated and in danger.   Napoleon perceived its peril and hastily sent Rapp to its sup-port, with the Mamelukes and the chasseurs of the guard.   They rushed forward with energy and quickly drove back the enemy, Prince Repnin remaining a prisoner in their hands.

The day was lost to the allies.   Everywhere disorder prevailed and their troops were in retreat.   An isolated Russian division threw down its arms and surrendered.   Two columns were forced back beyond the marshes. The soldiers rushed in their flight upon the ice of the lake, which the intense cold had made thick enough to bear their weight.

                     And now a terrible scene was witnessed.   War is merci **The Dreadful** less ; death is its aim ; the slaughter of an enemy by any **Lake Horror** means is looked upon as admissible.   By Napoleon's order the French cannon were turned upon the lake.   Their plunging balls rent and splintered the ice under the feet of the crowd of fugitives. Soon it broke with a crash, and the unhappy soldiers, with shrill cries of despair, sunk to death in the chilling waters beneath, thousands of them perishing. It was a frightful expedient—one that would be deemed a crime in any other code than the merciless one of war.

A portion of the allied army made a perilous retreat along a narrow embankment which separated the two lakes of Melnitz and Falnitz, their exposed causeway swept by the fire of the French batteries. Of the whole army, the corps of Prince Bagration alone withdrew in order of battle.

All that dreadful day the roar of battle had resounded. At its close the victorious French occupied the field ; the allied army was pouring back in disordered flight, the dismayed emperors in its midst ; thousands of dead covered the fatal field, the groans of thousands of wounded men filled the air. More than 30,000 prisoners, including twenty generals, remained in Napoleon's hands, and with them a hundred and twenty pieces of cannon and forty flags, including the standards of the Imperial Guard of Russia.

The defeat was a crushing one. Napoleon had won the most famous of his battles. The Emperor Francis, in deep depression, **Treaty of** asked for an interview and an armistice. Two days afterward **Peace with** the emperors,—the conqueror and the conquered,—met and **Austria** an armistice was granted. While the negotiations for peace continued Napoleon shrewdly disposed of the hostility of Prussia by offering the state of Hanover to that power and signing a treaty with the king. On December 26th a treaty of peace between France and Austria was signed at Presburg. The Emperor Francis yielded all his remaining possessions in Italy, and also the Tyrol, the Black Forest, and other districts in Germany, which Napoleon presented to his allies, Bavaria, Wurtemberg, and Baden ; whose monarchs were still more closely united to Napoleon by marriages between their children and relatives of himself and his wife Josephine. Bavaria and Wurtemberg were made kingdoms, and Baden was raised in rank to a grand-duchy; The three months' war was at an end. Austria had paid dearly for her subserviency to England. Of the several late enemies of France, only two remained in arms, Russia and England. And in the latter Pitt, Napoleon's greatest enemy, died during the next month, leaving the power in the hands of Fox, an admirer of the Corsican. Napoleon was at the summit of his glory and success.

Napoleon's political changes did not end with the partial dismemberment of Austria. His ambition to become supreme in Europe and to rule everywhere lord paramount, inspired him to exalt his family, raising his relatives to the rank of kings, but keeping them the servants of his imperious will. Holland lost its independence, Louis Bonaparte being named its king.

Napoleon Awards Kingdoms to His Brothers and Adherents

Joachim Murat, brother-in-law of the emperor, was given a kingdom on the lower Rhine, with Düsseldorf as its capital. A stroke of Napoleon's pen ended the Bourbon monarchy in Naples, and Joseph Bonaparte was sent thither as king, with a French army to support him. Italy was divided into dukedoms, ruled over by the marshals and adherents of the emperor, whose hand began to move the powers of Europe as a chess-player moves the pieces upon his board.

The story of his political transformations extends farther still. By raising the electors of Bavaria and Wurtemberg to the rank of kings, he had practically brought to an end the antique German Empire—which indeed had long been little more than a name. In July, 1806, he completed this work. The states of South and West Germany were organized into a league named the Confederation of the Rhine, under the protection of Napoleon. Many small principalities were suppressed and their territories added to the larger ones, increasing the power of the latter, and winning the gratitude of their rulers for their benefactor. The empire of France was in this manner practically extended over Italy, the Netherlands, and the west and south of Germany. Francis II., lord of the " Holy Roman Empire," now renounced the title which these radical changes had made a mockery, withdrew his states from the imperial confederation of Germany, and assumed the title of Francis I. of Austria. The Empire of Germany, once powerful, but long since reduced to a shadowy pretence, finally ceased to exist.

These autocratic changes could not fail to arouse the indignation of the monarchs of Europe and imperil the prevailing peace. Austria was in no

The Hostile Irritation of Prussia

condition to resume hostilities, but Prussia, which had maintained a doubtful neutrality during the recent wars, grew more and more exasperated as these high-handed proceedings went on. A league which the king of Prussia sought to form with Saxony and Hesse-Cassel was thwarted by Napoleon ; who also, in negotiating for peace with England, offered to return Hanover to that country, without consulting the Prussian King, to whom this electorate had been ceded. Other causes of resentment existed, and finally Frederick William of Prussia, irritated beyond control, sent a so-called " ultimatum " to Napoleon, demanding the evacuation of South Germany by the French. As might have been expected, this proposal was rejected with scorn, whereupon Prussia broke off all communication with France and began preparations for war.

The Prussians did not know the man with whom they had to deal. It was an idle hope that this state could cope alone with the power of Napoleon and his allies, and while Frederick William was slowly **The Prussian** preparing for the war which he had long sought to avoid, the **Armies in** French troops were on the march and rapidly approaching the **the Field** borders of his kingdom. Saxony had allied itself with Prussia under compulsion, and had added 20,000 men to its armies. The elector of Hesse-Cassel had also joined the Prussians, and furnished them a contingent of troops. But this hastily levied army, composed of men few of whom had ever seen a battle, seemed hopeless as matched with the great army of war-worn veterans which Napoleon was marching with his accustomed rapidity against them. Austria, whom the Prussian King had failed to aid, now looked on passively at his peril. The Russians, who still maintained hostile relations with France, held their troops immovable upon the Vistula. Frederick William was left to face the power of Napoleon alone.

The fate of the campaign was quickly decided. Through **March of the** the mountain passes of Franconia Napoleon led his forces **French Upon** against the Prussian army, which was divided into two corps, **Prussia** under the command of the Duke of Brunswick and the Prince of Hohenlohe. The troops of the latter occupied the road from Weimar to Jena. The heights which commanded the latter town were seized by Marshal Lannes on his arrival. A second French corps, under Marshals Davout and Bernadotte, marched against the Duke of Brunswick and established themselves upon the left bank of the Saale.

On the morning of the 4th of October, 1806, the conflict at Jena, upon which hung the destiny of the Prussian Kingdom, began. The troops under the Prince of Hohenlohe surpassed in number those of Napoleon, but were unfitted to sustain the impetuosity of the French assault. Soult and Augereau, in command of the wings of the French army, advanced rapidly, enveloping the Prussian forces and driving them back by the vigor of their attack. Then on the Prussian center the guard and the reserves fell in a compact mass whose tremendous impact the enemy found it impossible to endure. The retreat became a rout. The Prussian army broke into a mob of fugitives, flying in terror before Napoleon's irresistible veterans.

They were met by Marshal Biechel with an army of 20,000 men advancing in all haste to the aid of the Prince of Hohenlohe. **Defeat of the** Throwing his men across the line of flight, he did his utmost **Prussians at** to rally the fugitives. His effort was a vain one. His men **Jena and** were swept away by the panic-stricken mass and pushed back **Auerstadt** by the triumphant pursuers. Weimar was reached by the French and the

Germans simultaneosly, the former seizing prisoners in such numbers as seriously to hinder their pursuit.

While this battle was going on, another was in progress near Auerstadt, where Marshal Davout had encountered the forces of the Duke of Brunswick, with whom was Frederick William, the king. Bernadotte, ordered by the emperor to occupy Hamburg, had withdrawn his troops, leaving Davout much outnumbered by the foe. But heedless of this, he threw himself across their road in the defile of Kœsen, and sustained alone the furious attack made upon him by the duke. Throwing his regiments into squares, he poured a murderous fire on the charging troops, hurling them back from his immovable lines. The old duke fell with a mortal wound. The king and his son led their troops to a second, but equally fruitless, attack. Davout, taking advantage of their repulse, advanced and seized the heights of Eckartsberga, where he defended himself with his artillery. Frederick William, discouraged by this vigorous resistance, retired towards Weimar with the purpose of joining his forces with those of the Prince of Hohenlohe and renewing the attack.

Davout's men were too exhausted to pursue, but Bernadotte was encountered and barred the way, and the disaster at Jena was soon made evident by the panic-stricken mass of fugitives, whose flying multitude, hotly pursued by the French, sought safety in the ranks of the king's corps, which they threw into confusion by their impact. It was apparent that the battle was irretrievably lost. Night was approaching. The king marched hastily away, the disorder in his ranks increasing as the darkness fell. In that one fatal day he had lost his army and placed his kingdom itself in jeopardy. "They can do nothing but gather up the *débris*," said Napoleon.

The French lost no time in following up the defeated army, which had **The Demoriliza-** broken into several divisions in its retreat. On the 17th, **tion of the** Duke Eugene of Wurtemberg and the reserves under his **Prussian** command were scattered in defeat. On the 28th, the Prince **Forces** of Hohenlohe, with the 12,000 men whom he still held together, was forced to surrender. Blucher, who had seized the free city of Lübeck, was obliged to follow his example. On all sides the scattered *débris* of the army was destroyed, and on October 27th Napoleon entered in triumph the city of Berlin, his first entry into an enemy's capital.

Napoleon The battle ended, the country occupied, the work of **Divides the** revenge of the victor began. The Elector of Hesse was driven **Spoils of** from his throne and his country stricken from the list of the **Victory** powers of Europe. Hanover and the Hanseatic towns were occupied by the French. The English merchandise found in ports and warehouses was seized and confiscated. A heavy war contribution was laid upon the defeated state. Severe taxes were laid upon Hamburg, Bremen and Leipzig, and from all the leading cities the treasures of art and science were carried away to enrich the museums and galleries of France.

Saxony, whose alliance with Prussia had been a forced one, was alone spared. The Saxon prisoners were sent back free to their sovereign, and the elector was granted a favorable peace and honored with the title of king. In return for these favors he joined the Confederation of the Rhine, and such was his gratitude to Napoleon that he remained his friend and ally in the trying days when he had no other friend among the powers of Europe.

The harsh measures of which we have spoken were not the only ones taken by Napoleon against his enemies. England, the most implacable of his foes, remained beyond his reach, mistress of the seas as he was lord of the land. He could only meet the islanders upon their favorite element, and in November 21, 1806, he sent from Berlin to Talleyrand, his Minister of Foreign Affairs, a decree establishing a continental embargo against Great Britain.

"The British Islanders," said this famous edict of reprisal, "are declared in a state of blockade. All commerce and all correspondence with them are forbidden." All letters or packets addressed to an Englishman or written in English were to be seized; every English subject found in **The Embargo** any country controlled by France was to be made a prisoner **on British** of war; all commerce in English merchandise was forbidden, **Commerce** and all ships coming from England or her colonies were to be refused admittance to any port.

It is hardly necessary to speak here of the distress caused, alike in Europe and elsewhere, by this war upon commerce, in which England did not fail to meet the harsh decrees of her opponent by others equally severe. The effect of these edicts upon American commerce is well known. The commerce of neutral nations was almost swept from the seas. One result was the American war of 1812, which for a time seemed as likely to be directed against France as Great Britain.

Meanwhile Frederick William of Prussia was a fugitive king. He refused to accept the harsh terms of the armistice **Frederick** offered by Napoleon, and in despair resolved to seek, with the **William a** remnant of his army, some 25,000 in number, the Russian **Fugitive in** camp, and join his forces with those of Alexander of Russia, **the Russian** still in arms against France. **Camp**

Napoleon, not content while an enemy remained in arms, with inflexible resolution resolved to make an end of all his adversaries, and meet in battle the great empire of the north.   The Russian armies then occupied Poland, whose people, burning under the oppression and injustice to which they had been subjected, gladly welcomed Napoleon's specious offers to bring them back their lost liberties, and rose in his aid when he marched his armies into their country.

Here the French found themselves exposed to unlooked-for privations. They had dreamed of abundant stores of food, but discovered that the country they had invaded was, in this wintry season, a desert; a series of frozen solitudes incapable of feeding an army, and holding no reward for them other than that of battle with and victory over the hardy Russians.

Napoleon advanced to Warsaw, the Polish capital.   The Russians were entrenched behind the Narew and the Ukra.   The French continued to advance.   The Russians were beaten and forced back in every battle, several furious encounters took place, and Alexander's army fell back upon the Pregel, intact and powerful still, despite the French successes.   The wintry chill and the character of the country seriously interfered with Napoleon's plans, the troops being forced to make their way through thick and rain-soaked forests, and march over desolate and marshy plains.   The winter of

The French in the Dreary Plains of Poland
the north fought against them like a strong army and many of them fell dead without a battle.   Warlike movements became almost impossible to the troops of the south, though the hardy northeners, accustomed to the climate, continued their military operations.

By the end of January the Russian army was evidently approaching in force, and immediate action became necessary.   The cold increased.   The mud was converted into ice.   On January 30, 1807, Napoleon left Warsaw and marched in search of the enemy.   General Benningsen retreated, avoiding battle, and on the 7th of February entered the small town of Eylau, from which his troops were pushed by the approaching French.   He encamped outside the town, the French in and about it; it was evident that a great battle was at hand.

The weather was cold.   Snow lay thick upon the ground and still fell in great flakes.   A sheet of ice covering some small lakes formed part of the country upon which the armies were encamped, but was thick enough to bear their weight.   It was a chill, inhospitable country to which the demon of war had come.

Before daybreak on the 8th Napoleon was in the streets of Eylau, forming his line of battle for the coming engagement.   Soon the artillery of both armies opened, and a rain of cannon balls began to decimate the opposing ranks.   The Russian fire was concentrated on the town, which

BATTLE OF EYLAU

The battle fought at Eylau, in East Prussia, February 8, 1807, between the Russians and French, was the most indecisive engagement in Napoleon's career. Both sides claimed victory, but the Russians retreated in the night. A dense snowfall occurred during the battle, and nearly led to the defeat of the French.

BATTLE OF FRIEDLAND

A sanguinary engagement at Friedland, a small town in East Prussia, fought on June 14, 1807, ended in the defeat of the Russians under Bennigsen by Napoleon's army. It lead to the Peace of Tilsit, and the end of a long and desperate war.

was soon in flames. That of the French was directed against a hill which the emperor deemed it important to occupy. The two armies, **The Frightful** nearly equal in numbers,—the French having 75,000 to the **Struggle at** Russian 70,000,—were but a short distance apart, and the **Eylau** slaughter from the fierce cannonade was terrible.

A series of movements on both sides began, Davout marching upon the Russian flank and Augereau upon the centre, while the Russians manœuvred as if with a purpose to outflank the French on the left. At this interval an unlooked-for obstacle interfered with the French movements, a snow-fall beginning, which grew so dense that the armies lost sight of each other, and vision was restricted to a few feet. In this semi-darkness the French columns lost their way, and wandered about uncertainly. For half an hour the snow continued to fall. When it ceased the French army was in a critical position. Its cohesion was lost; its columns were straggling about and incapable of supporting one another; many of its superior officers were wounded. The Russians, on the contrary, were on the point of executing a vigorous turning movement, with 20,000 infantry, supported by cavalry and artillery.

"Are you going to let me be devoured by these people?" cried Napoleon to Murat, his eagle eye discerning the danger.

He ordered a grand charge of all the cavalry of the army, consisting of eighty squadrons. With Murat at their head, they rushed **Murat's** like an avalanche on the Russian lines, breaking through the **Mighty** infantry and dispersing the cavalry who came to its support. **Charge** The Russian infantry suffered severely from this charge, its two massive lines being rent asunder, while the third fell back upon a wood in the rear. Finally Davout, whose movement had been hindered by the weather, reached the Russian rear, and in an impetuous charge drove them from the hilly ground which Napoleon wished to occupy.

The battle seemed lost to the Russians. They began a retreat, leaving the ground strewn thickly with their dead and wounded. But at this critical moment a Prussian force, some 8,000 strong, which was being pursued by Marshal Ney, arrived on the field and checked the French advance and the Russian retreat. Benningsen regained sufficient confidence to prepare for final attack, when he was advised of the approach of Ney, who was two or three hours behind the Prussians. At this discouraging news a final retreat was ordered.

The French were left masters of the field, though little attempt was made to pursue the menacing columns of the enemy, who withdrew in military array. It was a victory that came near being a defeat, and which,

indeed, both sides claimed.   Never before had Napoleon been so stubbornly withstood.   His success had been bought at a frightful cost, and

**The Cost of
Victory
Frightful**

Königsberg, the old Prussian capital, the goal of his march,
was still covered by the compact columns of the allies.   The
men were in no condition to pursue.   Food was wanting, and
they were without shelter from the wintry chill.   Ney surveyed the terrible
scene with eyes of gloom.   " What a massacre," he exclaimed ; " and without result."

So severe was the exhaustion on both sides from this great battle that
it was four months before hostilities were resumed.   Meanwhile Danzig,
which had been strongly besieged, surrendered, and more than 30,000 men
were released to reinforce the French army.   Negotiations for peace went
slowly on, without result, and it was June before hostilities again became
imminent.

Eylau, which now became Napoleon's headquarters, presented a very
different aspect at this season from that of four months before.   Then all
was wintry desolation ; now the country presented a beautiful scene of green
woodland, shining lakes, and attractive villages.   The light corps of the army
were in motion in various directions, their object being to get between the
Russians and their magazines and cut off retreat to Königsberg.   On June
13th Napoleon, with the main body of his army, marched towards Friedland, a town on the River Alle, in the vicinity of Königsberg, towards which
the Russians were marching.   Here, crossing the Alle, Benningsen drove
from the town a regiment of French hussars which had occupied it, and fell
with all his force on the corps of Marshal Lannes, which alone had reached
the field.

Lannes held his ground with his usual heroic fortitude, while sending

**Napoleon on
the Field of
Friedland**

successive messengers for aid to the emperor.   Noon had
passed when Napoleon and his staff reached the field at full
gallop, far in advance of the troops.   He surveyed the field
with eyes of hope.   " It is the 14th of June, the anniversary of Marengo,"
he said ; " it is a lucky day for us."

" Give me only a reinforcement," cried Oudinot, " and we will cast all
the Russians into the water."

This seemed possible.   Benningsen's troops were perilously concentrated within a bend of the river.   Some of the French generals advised de-
ferring the battle till the next day, as the hour was late, but Napoleon was
too shrewd to let an advantage escape him.

" No," he said, " one does not surprise the enemy twice in such a blunder."   He swept with his field-glass the masses of the enemy before him,

then seized the arm of Marshal Ney. " You see the Russians and the town of Friedland," he said. " March straight forward ; seize the town ; take the bridges, whatever it may cost. Do not trouble yourself with what is taking place around you. Leave that to me and the army."

The troops were coming in rapidly, and marching to the places assigned them. The hours moved on. It was half-past five in the afternoon when the cannon sounded the signal of the coming fray.

Meanwhile Ney's march upon Friedland had begun. A terrible fire from the Russians swept his ranks as he advanced. Aided by cavalry and artillery, he reached a stream defended by the Russian Imperial Guard. Before those picked troops the French recoiled in temporary disorder ; but the division of General Dupont, marching briskly up, broke the Russian guard, and the pursuing French rushed into the town. In a short time it was in flames and the fugitive Russians were cut off from the bridges, which were seized and set on fire. *The Assault of the Indomitable Ney*

The Russians made a vigorous effort to recover their lost ground, General Gortschakoff endeavoring to drive the French from the town, and other corps making repeated attacks on the French centre. All their efforts were in vain. The French columns continued to advance. By ten o'clock the battle was at an end. Many of the Russians had been drowned in the stream, and the field was covered with their dead, whose numbers were estimated by the boastful French bulletins at 15,000 or 18,000 men, while they made the improbable claim of having lost no more than 500 dead. Königsberg, the prize of victory, was quickly occupied by Marshal Soult, and yielded the French a vast quantity of food, and a large store of military supplies which had been sent from England for Russian use. The King of Prussia had lost the whole of his possessions with the exception of the single town of Memel. *The Total Defeat of the Russians*

Victorious as Napoleon had been, he had found the Russians no contemptible foes. At Eylau he had come nearer defeat than ever before in his career. He was quite ready, therefore, to listen to overtures for peace, and early in July a notable interview took place between him and the Czar of Russia at Tilsit, on the Niemen, the two emperors meeting on a raft in the centre of the stream. What passed between them is not known. Some think that they arranged for a division of Europe between their respective empires, Alexander taking all the east and Napoleon all the west. However that was, the treaty of peace, signed July 8th, was a disastrous one for the defeated Prussian king, who was punished for his temerity in seeking to fight *The Emperors at Tilsit and the Fate of Prussia*

Napoleon alone by the loss of more than half his kingdom, while in addition a heavy war indemnity was laid upon his depleted realms.

He was forced to yield all the countries between the Rhine and the Elbe, to consent to the establishment of a Dukedom of Warsaw, under the supremacy of the king of Saxony, and to the loss of Danzig and the surrounding territory, which were converted into a free State. A new kingdom, named Westphalia, was founded by Napoleon, made up of the territory taken from Prussia and the states of Hesse, Brunswick and South Hanover. His younger brother, Jerome Bonaparte, was made its king. It was a further step in his policy of founding a western empire.

Louisa, the beautiful and charming queen of Frederick William, sought Tilsit, hoping by the seduction of her beauty and grace of address to induce Napoleon to mitigate his harsh terms. But in vain she brought to bear upon him all the resources of her intellect and her attractive charm of manner. He continued cold and obdurate, and she left Tilsit deeply mortified and humiliated.

In northern Europe only one enemy of Napoleon remained. Sweden retained its hostility to France, under the fanatical enmity of Gustavus IV., who believed himself the instrument appointed by Providence to reinstate the Bourbon monarchs upon their thrones. Denmark, which refused to ally
Denmark and Sweden itself with England, was visited by a British fleet, which bombarded Copenhagen and carried off all the Daaish ships of war, an outrage which brought this kingdom into close alliance with France. The war in Sweden must have ended in the conquest of that country, had not the people revolted and dethroned their obstinate king. Charles XIII., his uncle was placed on the throne, but was induced to adopt Napoleon's marshal Bernadotte as his son. The latter, as crown prince, practically succeeded the incapable king in 1810.

Events followed each other rapidly. Napoleon, in his desire to add kingdom after kingdom to his throne, invaded Portugal and interfered in the affairs of Spain, from whose throne he removed the last of the Bourbon kings, replacing him by his brother, Joseph Bonaparte. The result was a revolt of the Spanish people which all his efforts proved unable to quell, aided, as they were eventually, by the power of England. In Italy his intrigues continued. Marshal Murat succeeded Joseph Bonaparte on the throne of Naples. Eliza, Napoleon's sister, was made queen of Tuscany.
The Pope a Captive at Fontainebleau The temporal sovereignty of the Pope was seriously interfered with and finally, in 1800, the pontiff was forcibly removed from Rome and the states of the Church were added to the French territory, Pius VII., the pope, was eventually brought to

France and obliged to reside at Fontainebleau, where he persistently refused to yield to Napoleon's wishes or perform any act of ecclesiastical authority while held in captivity.

These various arbitrary acts had their natural result, that of active hostility. The Austrians beheld them with growing indignation, and at length grew so exasperated that, despite their many defeats, they decided again to dare the power and genius of the conqueror. In April, 1809, the Vienna Cabinet once more declared war against France and made all haste to put its armies in the field. Stimulated by this, a revolt broke out in the Tyrol, the simple-minded but brave and sturdy mountaineers gathering under the leadership of Andreas Hofer, a man of authority among them, and welcoming the Austrian troops sent to their aid.

As regards this war in the Tyrol, there is no need here to go into details. It must suffice to say that the bold peasantry, aided **Andreas Hofer** by the natural advantages of their mountain land, for a time **and the War** freed themselves from French dominion, to the astonishment **in the Tyrol** and admiration of Europe. But their freedom was of brief duration, fresh troops were poured into the country, and though the mountaineers won more than one victory, they proved no match for the power of their foes. Their country was conquered, and Hofer, their brave leader, was taken by the French and remorselessly put to death by the order of Napoleon.

The struggle in the Tyrol was merely a side issue in the new war with Austria, which was conducted on Napoleon's side with his usual celerity of movement. The days when soldiers are whisked forward at locomotive speed had not yet dawned, yet the French troops made extraordinary progress on foot, and war was barely declared before the army of Napoleon covered Austria. This army was no longer made up solely of Frenchmen. The Confederation of the Rhine practically formed part of Napoleon's empire, and Germans now fought side by side with Frenchmen ; Marshal Lefebvre leading the Bavarians, Bernadotte the Saxons, Au- **The Army of** gereau the men of Baden, Wurtemberg, and Hesse. On the **Napoleon** other hand, the Austrians were early in motion, and by the 10th **Marches** of April the Archduke Charles had crossed the Inn with his **Upon Austria** army and the King of Bavaria, Napoleon's ally, was in flight from his capital.

The quick advance of the Austrians had placed the French army in danger. Spread out over an extent of twenty-five leagues, it ran serious risk of being cut in two by the rapidly marching troops of the Archduke. Napoleon, who reached the front on the 17th, was not slow to perceive the peril and to take steps of prevention. A hasty concentration of his forces was ordered and vigorously begun.

5

' Never was there need for more rapidity of movement than now," he wrote to Massena. " Activity, activity, speed !"

Speed was the order of the day. The French generals ably seconded the anxious activity of their chief. The soldiers fairly rushed together.

A Grave Peril Overcome

A brief hesitation robbed the Austrians of the advantage which they had hoped to gain. The Archduke Charles, one of the ablest tacticians ever opposed to Napoleon, had the weakness of over-prudence, and caution robbed him of the opportunity given him by the wide dispersion of the French.

He was soon and severely punished for his slowness. On the 19th Davout defeated the Austrians at Fangen and made a junction with the Bavarians. On the 20th and 21st Napoleon met and defeated them in a series of engagements. Meanwhile the Archduke Charles fell on Ratisbon, held by a single French regiment, occupied that important place, and attacked Davout at Eckmühl. Here a furious battle took place. Davout, outnumbered, maintained his position for three days. Napoleon, warned of the peril of his marshal, bade him to hold on to the death, as he was hastening to his relief with 40,000 men. The day was well advanced when the emperor came up and fell with his fresh troops on the Austrians, who, still bravely fighting, were forced back upon Ratisbon. During the night the Archduke wisely withdrew and marched for Bohemia, where a large reinforcement awaited him. On the 23d Napoleon attacked the town, and

The Battle of Eckmühl and the Capture of Ratisbon

carried it in spite of a vigorous defence. His proclamation to his soldiers perhaps overestimated the prizes of this brief but active campaign, which he declared to be a hundred cannon, forty flags, all the enemy's artillery, 50,000 prisoners, a large number of wagons, etc. Half this loss would have fully justified the Archduke's retreat.

In Italy affairs went differently. Prince Eugene Beauharnais, for the first time in command of a French army, found himself opposed by the

The Campaign In Italy

Archduke John, and met with a defeat. On April 16th, seeking to retrieve his disaster, he attacked the Archduke, but the Austrians bravely held their positions, and the French were again obliged to retreat. General Macdonald, an officer of tried ability, now joined the prince, who took up a defensive position on the Adige, whither the Austrians marched. On the 1st of May Macdonald perceived among them indications of withdrawal from their position.

"Victory in Germany !" he shouted to the prince. " Now is our time for a forward march !"

He was correct, the Archduke John had been recalled in haste to aid his brother in the defence of Vienna, on which the French were advancing in force.

The campaign now became a race for the capital of Austria. During its progress several conflicts took place, in each of which the French won. The city was defended by the Archduke Maximilian with an army of over 15,000 men, but he found it expedient to withdraw, and on the 13th the troops of Napoleon occupied the place. Meanwhile Charles had concentrated his troops and was marching hastily towards the opposite side of the Danube, whither his brother John was advancing from Italy.

It was important for Napoleon to strike a blow before this junction could be made. He resolved to cross the Danube in the suburbs of the capital itself, and attack the Austrians before they were reinforced. In the vicinity of Vienna the channel of the river is broken by many islets. At the island of Lobau, the point chosen for the attempt, the river is broad and deep, but Lobau is separated from the opposite bank by only a narrow branch, while two smaller islets offered themselves as aids in the construction of bridges, there being four channels, over each of which a bridge was thrown.

The work was a difficult one. The Danube, swollen by **The Bridges** the melting snows, imperilled the bridges, erected with diffi- **over the** culty and braced by insufficient cordage. But despite this **Danube** peril the crossing began, and on May 20th Marshal Massena reached the other side and posted his troops in the two villages of Aspern and Essling, and along a deep ditch that connected them.

As yet only the vanguard of the Austrians had arrived. Other corps soon appeared, and by the afternoon of the 21st the entire army, from 70,000 to 80,000 strong, faced the French, still only half their number, and in a position of extreme peril, for the bridge over the main channel of the river had broken during the night, and the crossing was cut off in its midst.

Napoleon, however, was straining every nerve to repair the bridge, and Massena and Lannes, in command of the advance, fought like men fighting for their lives. The Archduke Charles, the ablest soldier Napoleon had yet encountered, hurled his troops in masses upon Aspern, which covered the bridge to Lobau. Several times it was taken and retaken, but the French held on with a death grip, all the strength of the Austrians seeming insufficient to break the hold of Lannes upon Essling. An advance in force, which nearly cut the communication between the two villages, was checked by an impetuous cavalry charge, and night fell, leaving the situation unchanged.

At dawn of the next day more than 70,000 French had crossed the stream; Marshal Davout's corps, with part of the artillery and most of the ammunition, being still on the right bank. At this critical moment the large bridge, against which the Austrians had sent fireships, boats laden with stone and other floating missiles, broke for the third time, and the engineers of the French army were again forced to the most strenuous and hasty exertions for its repair.

The struggle of the day that had just begun was one of extraordinary **The Great Struggle of Essling and Aspern** valor and obstinacy. Men went down in multitudes; now the Austrians, now the French, were repulsed; the Austrians, impetuously assailed, slowly fell back; and Lannes was preparing for a vigorous movement designed to pierce their centre, when word was brought Napoleon that the great bridge had again yielded to the floating *débris*, carrying with it a regiment of cuirassiers, and cutting off the supply of ammunition. Lannes was at once ordered to fall back upon the villages, and simultaneously the Austrians made a powerful assault on the French centre, which was checked with great difficulty. Five times the charge was renewed, and though the enemy was finally repelled, it became evident that Napoleon, for the first time in his career, had met with a decided check. Night fell at length, and reluctantly he gave the order to retreat. He had lost more than a battle, he had lost the brilliant soldier Lannes, who fell with a mortal wound. Back to the **Napoleon Forced to his First Retreat** island of Lobau marched the French; Massena, in charge of the rear-guard, bringing over the last regiments in safety. More than 40,000 men lay dead and wounded on that fatal field, which remained in Austrian hands. Napoleon, at last, was obliged to acknowledge a repulse, if not a defeat, and the nations of Europe held up their heads with renewed hope. It had been proved that the Corsican was not invincible.

Some of Napoleon's generals, deeply disheartened, advised an immediate retreat, but the emperor had no thought of such a movement. It would have brought a thousand disasters in its train. On the contrary, he held the island of Lobau with a strong force, and brought all his resources to bear on the construction of a bridge that would defy the current of the stream. At the same time reinforcements were hurried forward, until by the 1st of July, he had around Vienna an army of 150,000 men. The Austrians had probably from 135,000 to 140,000. The archduke had, morever, strongly fortified the positions of the recent battle, expecting the attack upon them to be resumed.

THE ORDER TO CHARGE AT FRIEDLAND

At the decisive battle of Friedland, the Russian army was incautiously drawn up within a loop of the river. Napoleon was quick to perceive their mistake, and in a terrible charge he carried the town, burned the bridges, and then used his whole army to drive the Russians into the stream.

NAPOLEON AND THE QUEEN OF PRUSSIA AT TILSIT (FROM THE PAINTING BY GROS)

Tilsit is a city of about 25,000 inhabitants in Eastern Prussia. Here the Treaty of Peace between the French and Russian Emperors and also between France and Prussia was signed in July, 1807

Napoleon had no such intention. He had selected the heights ranging from Neusiedl to Wagram, strongly occupied by the Austrians, **The Second** but not fortified, as his point of attack, and on the night of **Crossing of the Danube** July 4th bridges were thrown from the island of Lobau to the mainland, and the army which had been gathering for several days on the island began its advance. It moved as a whole against the heights of Wagram, occupying Aspern and Essling in its advance.

The great battle began on the succeeding day. It was hotly contested at all points, but attention may be confined to the movement against the plateau of Wagram, which had been entrusted to Marshal Davout. The height was gained after a desperate struggle; the key of the battlefield was held by the French; the Austrians, impetuously **The Victory at Wagram** assailed at every point, and driven from every point of vantage, began a retreat. The Archduke Charles had anxiously looked for the coming of his brother John, with the army under his command. He waited in vain, the laggard prince failed to appear, and retreat became inevitable. The battle had already lasted ten hours, and the French held all the strong points of the field; but the Austrians withdrew slowly and in battle array, presenting a front that discouraged any effort to pursue. There was nothing resembling a rout.

The Archduke Charles retreated to Bohemia. His forces were dispersed during the march, but he had 70,000 men with him when Napoleon reached his front at Znaim, on the road to Prague, on the 11th of July. Further hostilities were checked by a request for a truce, preliminary to a peace. The battle, already begun, was stopped, and during the night an armistice was signed. The vigor of the Austrian resistance and the doubtful attitude of the other powers made Napoleon willing enough to treat for terms.

The peace, which was finally signed at Vienna, October 14, 1809, took from Austria 50,000 square miles of territory and 3,000,000 inhabitants, together with a war contribution of $85,000,000, **The Peace of Vienna** while her army was restricted to 150,000 men. The overthrow of the several outbreaks which had taken place in north Germany, the defeat of a British expedition against Antwerp, and the suppression of the revolt in the Tyrol, ended all organized opposition to Napoleon, who was once more master of the European situation.

Raised by this signal success to the summit of his power, lord paramount of Western Europe, only one thing remained to trouble the mind of the victorious emperor. His wife, Josephine, was childless; his throne threatened to be left without an heir. Much as he had seemed to love his wife, the companion of his early days, when he was an unknown and uncon-sidered subaltern, seeking humbly enough for military employment in Paris, yet ambition and the thirst for glory were always the ruling passions in his nature, and had now grown so dominant as to throw love and wifely devo-tion utterly into the shade.   He resolved to set aside his wife and seek a new bride among the princesses of Europe, hoping in this way to leave an heir of his own blood as successor to his imperial throne.

Negotiations were entered into with the courts of Europe to obtain a daughter of one of the proud royal houses as the spouse of the plebeian emperor of France.   No maiden of less exalted rank than a princess of the imperial families of Russia or Austria was high enough to meet the ambitious aims of this proud lord of battles, and negotiations were entered into with both, ending in the selection of Maria Louisa, daughter of the Emperor Francis of Austria, who did not venture to refuse a demand for his daughter's hand from the master of half his dominions.

The Divorce of Josephine and Marriage of Maria Louisa   Napoleon was not long in finding a plea for setting aside the wife of his days of poverty and obscurity.   A defect in the marriage was alleged, and the transparent farce went on. The divorce of Josephine has awakened the sympathy of a century.   It was, indeed, a piteous example of state-craft, and there can be no doubt that Napoleon suffered in his heart while yielding to the dictates of his unbridled ambition.   The marriage with Maria Louisa, on the 2d of April, 1810, was conducted with all possible pomp and display, no less than five queens carrying the train of the bride in the august ceremony.   The purpose of the marriage did not fail; the next year a son was born to Napoleon.   But this imperial youth, who was dignified with the title of King of Rome, was destined to an inglorious life, as an unconsidered te'iant of the gilded halls of his imperial grandfather of Austria.

CHAPTER IV.

The Decline and Fall of Napoleon's Empire.

AMBITION, unrestrained by caution, uncontrolled by moderation, has its inevitable end. An empire built upon victory, trusting solely to military genius, prepares for itself the elements of its overthrow. This fact Napoleon was to learn. In the outset of his career he opposed a new art of war to the obsolete one of his enemies, and his path to empire was over the corpses of slaughtered armies and the ruins of fallen kingdoms. But year by year they learned his art, in war after war their resistance grew more stringent, each successive victory was won with more difficulty and at greater cost, and finally, at the crossing of the Danube, the energy and genius of Napoleon met their equal, and the standards of France went back in defeat. It was the tocsin of fate. His career of victory had culminated. From that day its decline began.

The Causes of the Rise and Decline of Napoleon's Power

It is interesting to find that the first effective check to Napoleon's victorious progress came from one of the weaker nations of Europe, a power which the conqueror contemned and thought to move as one of the minor pieces in his game of empire. Spain at that time had reached almost the lowest stage of its decline. Its king was an imbecile ; the heir to the throne a weakling ; Godoy, the " Prince of the Peace," the monarch's favorite, an ambitious intriguer. Napoleon's armies had invaded Portugal and forced its monarch to embark for Brazil, his American domain. A similar movement was attempted in Spain. This country the base Godoy betrayed to Napoleon, and then, frightened by the consequences of his dishonorable intrigues,

Aims and Intrigues in Portugal and Spain

sought to escape with the king and court to the Spanish dominions in America. His scheme was prevented by an outbreak of the people of Madrid, and Napoleon, ambitiously designing to add the peninsula to his empire, induced both Charles IV. and his son Ferdinand to resign from the throne. He replaced them by his brother, Joseph Bonaparte, who, on June 6, 1808, was named King of Spain.

Hitherto Napoleon had dealt with emperors and kings, whose overthrow carried with it that of their people. In Spain he had a new element, the people itself, to deal with. The very weakness of Spain proved its strength. Deprived of their native monarchs, and given a king not of their own choice,

The Bold Defiance of the People of Spain

the whole people rose in rebellion and defied Napoleon and his armies. An insurrection broke out in Madrid in which 1,200 French soldiers were slain. Juntas were formed in different cities, which assumed the control of affairs and refused obedience to the new king. From end to end of Spain the people sprang to arms and began a guerilla warfare which the troops of Napoleon sought in vain to quell. The bayonets of the French were able to sustain King Joseph and his court in Madrid, but proved powerless to put down the people. Each city, each district, became a separate centre of war, each had to be conquered separately, and the strength of the troops was consumed in petty contests with a people who avoided open warfare and dealt in surprises and scattered fights, in which victory counted for little and needed to be repeated a thousand times.

The Spanish did more than this. They put an army in the field which

Spain's Brilliant Victory and King Joseph's Flight

was defeated by the French, but they revenged themselves brilliantly at Baylen, in Andalusia, where General Dupont, with a corps 20,000 strong, was surrounded in a position from which there was no escape, and forced to surrender himself and his men as prisoners of war.

This undisciplined people had gained a victory over France which none of the great powers of Europe could match. The Spaniards were filled with enthusiasm; King Joseph hastily abandoned Madrid; the French armies retreated across the Ebro. Soon encouraging news came from Portugal. The English, hitherto mainly confining themselves to naval warfare and to aiding the enemies of Napoleon with money, had landed an army in that country under Sir Arthur Wellesley (afterwards Lord Wellington) and other generals, which would have captured the entire French army had it not capitulated on the terms of a free passage to France. For the time being the peninsula of Spain and Portugal was free from Napoleon's power.

The humiliating reverse to his arms called Napoleon himself into the field. He marched at the head of an army into Spain, defeated the insur-

The Heroic Defence of Saragossa

gents wherever met, and reinstated his brother on the throne. The city of Saragossa, which made one of the most heroic defences known in history, was taken, and the advance of the British armies was checked. And yet, though Spain was widely overrun, the people did not yield. The junta at Cadiz defied the French, the guerillas continued in the field, and the invaders found themselves baffled by an enemy who was felt oftener than seen.

The Austrian war called away the emperor and the bulk of his troops, but after it was over he filled Spain with his veterans, increasing the strength of the army there to 300,000 men, under his ablest generals, Soult, Massena, Ney, Marmont, Macdonald and others. They marched through Spain from end to end, yet, though they held all the salient points, the people refused to submit, but from their mountain fastnesses kept up a petty and annoying war.

Massena, in 1811, invaded Portugal, where Wellington with an English army awaited him behind the strong lines of Torres Vedras, **Wellington's** which the ever-victorious French sought in vain to carry by **Career in** assault. Massena was compelled to retreat, and Soult, by **Portugal and** whom the emperor replaced him, was no more successful **Spain** against the shrewd English general. At length Spain won the reward of her patriotic defence. The Russian campaign of 1812 compelled the emperor to deplete his army in that country, and Wellington came to the aid of the patriots, defeated Marmont at Salamanca, entered Madrid, and forced King Joseph once more to flee from his unquiet throne.

For a brief interval he was restored by the French army under Soult and Suchet, but the disasters of the Russian campaign brought the reign of King Joseph to a final end, and forced him to give up the pretence of reigning over a people who were unflinchingly determined **The Reward** to have no king but one of their own choice. The story of **of Patriotic** the Spanish war ends in 1813, when Wellington defeated the **Valor** French at Vittoria, pursued them across the Pyrenees, and set foot upon the soil of France.

While these events were taking place in Spain the power of Napoleon was being shattered to fragments in the north. On the banks of the Niemen, a river that flows between Prussia and Poland, there gath- **A Record of** ered near the end of June, 1812, an immense army of more **Disaster** than 600,000 men, attended by an enormous multitude of non-combatants, their purpose being the invasion of the empire of Russia. Of this great army, made up of troops from half the nations of Europe, there reappeared six months later on that broad stream about 16,000 armed men, almost all that were left of that stupendous host. The remainder had perished on the desert soil or in the frozen rivers of Russia, few of them surviving as prisoners in Russian hands. Such was the character of the dread catastrophe that broke the power of the mighty conqueror and delivered Europe from his autocratic grasp.

The breach of relations between Napoleon and Alexander was largely due to the arbitrary and high-handed proceedings of the French emperor, who was accustomed to deal with the map of Europe as if it represented his private domain.   He offended Alexander by enlarging the duchy of Warsaw —one of his own creations—and deeply incensed him by extending the French empire to the shores of the Baltic, thus robbing of his dominion the Duke of Oldenburg, a near relative of Alexander.   On the other hand the Czar declined to submit the commercial interests of his country to the rigor of Napoleon's "continental blockade," and made a new tariff, which interfered with the importation of French and favored that of English goods.   These and other acts in which Alexander chose to place his own interests in advance of those of Napoleon were as wormwood to the haughty soul of the latter, and he determined to punish the Russian autocrat as he had done the other monarchs of Europe who refused to submit to his dictation.

Napoleon and the Czar at Enmity

For a year or two before war was declared Napoleon had been preparing for the greatest struggle of his life, adding to his army by the most rigorous methods of conscription and collecting great magazines of war material, though still professing friendship for Alexander.   The latter, however, was not deceived.   He prepared, on his part, for the threatened struggle, made peace with the Turks, and formed an alliance with Bernadotte, the crown prince of Sweden, who had good reason to be offended with his former lord and master.   Napoleon, on his side, allied himself with Prussia and Austria, and added to his army large contingents of troops from the German states.   At length the great conflict was ready to begin between the two autocrats, the Emperors of the East and the West, and Europe resounded with the tread of marching feet.

In the closing days of June the grand army crossed the Niemen, its last regiments reaching Russian soil by the opening of July.   Napoleon, with the advance, pressed on to Wilna, the capital of Lithuania.   On all sides the Poles rose in enthusiastic hope, and joined the ranks of the man whom they looked upon as their deliverer. Onward went the great army, marching with Napoleon's accustomed rapidity, seeking to prevent the concentration of the divided Russian forces, and advancing daily deeper into the dominions of the czar.

The Invasion of Russia by the Grand Army

The French emperor had his plans well laid.   He proposed to meet the Russians in force on some interior field, win from them one of his accustomed brilliant victories, crush them with his enormous columns, and force the dismayed czar to sue for peace on his own terms.   But plans need two sides for their consummation, and the Russian leaders did not propose to lose the advantage given them by nature.   On and on went Napoleon, deeper and deeper into that desolate land, but the great army he was to crush failed to loom up before him, the broad plains still spread onward empty of soldiers, and disquiet began to assail his imperious soul as he found the Russian hosts keeping constantly beyond his reach, luring **The French** him ever deeper into their vast territory.   In truth Barclay de **Baffled by** Tolly, the czar's chief in command, had adopted a policy **the Russian** which was sure to prove fatal to Napoleon's purpose, that of **Policy** persistently avoiding battle and keeping the French in pursuit of a fleeting will-of-the-wisp, while their army wasted away from natural disintegration in that inhospitable clime.

He was correct in his views.   Desertion, illness, the death of young recruits who could not endure the hardships of a rapid march in the severe heat of midsummer, began their fatal work.   Napoleon's plan of campaign proved a total failure.   The Russians would not wait to be defeated, and each day's march opened a wider circle of operations before the advancing host, whom the interminable plain filled with a sense of hopelessness.   The heat was overpowering, and men dropped from the ranks as rapidly as though on a field of battle.   At Vitebsk the army was inspected, and the emperor was alarmed at the rapid decrease in his forces.   Some of the divisions had lost more than a fourth of their men, in every corps the ranks were depleted, and reinforcements already had to be set on the march.

Onward they went, here and there bringing the Russians to bay in a minor engagement, but nowhere meeting them in numbers.   Europe waited in vain for tidings of a great battle, and Napoleon began to look upon his proud army with a feeling akin to despair.   He was not alone in his eagerness for battle.   Some of the high-spirited Russians, among them Prince Bagration, were as eager, but as yet the prudent policy of Barclay de Tolly prevailed.

On the 14th of August, the army crossed the Dnieper, and marched, now 175,000 strong, upon Smolensk, which was reached on the 16th.   This ancient and venerable town was dear to the Russians, and **Smolensk Cap-** they made their first determined stand in its defence, fighting **tured and in** behind its walls all day of the 17th.   Finding that the assault **Flames** was likely to succeed, they set fire to the town at night and withdrew, leaving to the French a city in flames.   The bridge was cut, the Russian army was beyond pursuit on the road to Moscow, nothing had been gained by the struggle but the ruins of a town.

The situation was growing desperate.   For two months the army had advanced without a battle of importance, and was soon in the heart of Russia, reduced to half its numbers, while the hoped-for victory seemed as far off as ever.   And the short summer of the north was nearing its end.

The severe winter of that climate would soon begin. Discouragement everywhere prevailed. Efforts were made by Napoleon's marshals to induce him to give up the losing game and retreat, but he was not to be moved from his purpose. A march on Moscow, the old capital of the empire, he felt sure would bring the Russians to bay. Once within its walls he hoped to dictate terms of peace

Napoleon was soon to have the battle for which his soul craved. Barclay's prudent and successful policy was not to the taste of many of the Russian leaders, and the czar was at length induced to replace him by fiery old Kutusoff, who had commanded the Russians at Austerlitz. A change in the situation was soon apparent. On the 5th of September the French army debouched upon the plain of Borodino, on the road to Moscow, and the emperor saw with joy the Russian army drawn up to dispute the way to the "Holy City" of the Muscovites. The dark columns of troops were strongly intrenched behind a small stream, frowning rows of guns threatened the advancing foe, and hope returned to the emperor's heart.

The Battle of Borodino
Battle began early on the 7th, and continued all day long, the Russians defending their ground with unyielding stubborness, the French attacking their positions with all their old impetuous dash and energy. Murat and Ney were the heroes of the day. Again and again the emperor was implored to send the imperial guard and overwhelm the foe, but he persistently refused. "If there is a second battle to-morrow," he said, "what troops shall I fight it with? It is not when one is eight hundred leagues from home that he risks his last resource."

The guard was not needed. On the following day Kutusoff was obliged to withdraw, leaving no less than 40,000 dead or wounded on the field. Among the killed was the brave Prince Bagration. The retreat was an orderly one. Napoleon found it expedient not to pursue. His own losses aggregated over 30,000, among them an unusual number of generals, of whom ten were killed and thirty-nine wounded. Three days proved a brief time to attend to the burial of the dead and the needs of the wounded. Napoleon named the engagement the Battle of the Moskwa, from the river that crossed the plain, and honored Ney, as the hero of the day, with the title of Prince of Moskwa.

The First Sight of the Holy City of Russia
On the 15th the Holy City was reached. A shout of "Moscow! Moscow!" went up from the whole army as they gazed on the gilded cupolas and magnificent buildings of that famous city, brilliantly lit up by the afternoon sun. Twenty miles in circumference, dazzling with the green of its copper domes and

MARSHAL NEY RETREATING FROM RUSSIA

Marshal Ney, who commanded the rear-guard of Napoleon's army during the retreat from Russia, won imperishable fame by his brilliant and daring deeds. Had it not been for his courage and military skill it is doubtful if a man of that great army would have escaped from the frozen soil of the north.

GENERAL BLÜCHER'S FALL AT LIGNY

General Blücher, "Marshal Forward," as he was called, from his intrepid boldness, was a veteran of over seventy years of age at the date of the battle of Waterloo. He was defeated at Ligny, and during the battle was unhorsed and charged over by the French and Prussian cavalry. He reached with his troops the field of Waterloo in time to decide the battle against the French.

its minarets of yellow stone, the towers and walls of the famous Kremlin rising above its palaces and gardens, it seemed like some fabled city of the Arabian Nights. With renewed enthusiasm the troops rushed towards it. while whole regiments of Poles fell on their knees, thanking God for delivering this stronghold of their oppressors into their hands.

It was an empty city into which the French marched; its streets deserted, its dwellings silent, Its busy life had vanished like a morning mist. Kutusoff had marched his army through it and left it to his foes. The inhabitants were gone, with what they could carry of their treasures. The city, like the empire, seemed likely to be a barren conquest, for here, as elsewhere, the **The Grand Army in the Old Russian Capital** policy of retreat, so fatal to Napoleon's hopes, was put into effect. The emperor took up his abode in the Kremlin, within whose ample precincts he found quarters for the whole imperial guard. The remainder of the army was stationed at chosen points about the city. Provisions were abundant, the houses and stores of the city being amply supplied. The army enjoyed a luxury of which it had been long deprived, while Napoleon confidently awaited a triumphant result from his victorious progress.

A terrible disenchantment awaited the invader. Early on the following morning word was brought him that Moscow was on fire. Flames arose from houses that had not been opened. It was evidently a premeditated conflagration. The fire burst out at once in a dozen quarters, and a high wind carried the flames from street to street, from house to house, from church to church. Russians were captured who boasted that they had fired the town under orders and who met death unflinchingly. The governor had left them behind for this fell purpose. The poorer people, many of whom had remained hidden in their huts, now fled in terror, taking with them what cherished **The Burning of the Great City of Moscow.** possessions they could carry. Soon the city was a seething mass of flames.

The Kremlin did not escape. A tower burst into flames. In vain the imperial guard sought to check the fire. No fire-engines were to be found in the town. Napoleon hastily left the palace and sought shelter outside the city, where for three days the flames ran riot, feeding on ancient palaces and destroying untold treasures. Then the wind sank and rain poured upon the smouldering embers. The great city had become a desolate heap of smoking ruins, into which the soldiers daringly stole back in search of valuables that might have escaped the flames.

This frightful conflagration was not due to the czar, but to Count Rostopchin, the governor of Moscow, who was subsequently driven from Russia by the execrations of those he had ruined. But it served as a proclamation to Europe of the implacable resolution of the Muscovites and their determination to resist to the bitter end.

Napoleon, sadly troubled in soul, sent letters to Alexander, suggesting the advisability of peace. Alexander left his letters unanswered. Until October 18th the emperor waited, hoping against hope, willing to grant almost any terms for an opportunity to escape from the fatal trap into which his overweening ambition had led him. No answer came from the czar. He was inflexible in his determination not to treat with these invaders of his country. In deep dejection Napoleon at length gave the order to retreat—too late, as it was to prove, since the terrible Russian winter was ready to descend upon them in all its frightful strength.

The army that left that ruined city was a sadly depleted one. It had **The Grand Army Begins Its Retreat** been reduced to 103,000 men. The army followers had also become greatly decreased in numbers, but still formed a host, among them delicate ladies, thinly clad, who gazed with terrified eyes from their traveling carriages upon the dejected troops. Articles of plunder of all kinds were carried by the soldiers, even the wounded in the wagons lying amid the spoil they had gathered. The Kremlin was destroyed by the rear guard, under Napoleon's orders, and over the drear Russian plains the retreat began.

It was no sooner under way than the Russian policy changed. From retreating, they everywhere advanced, seeking to annoy and cut off the enemy, and utterly to destroy the fugitive army if possible. A stand was made at the town of Maloi-Yaroslavitz, where a sanguinary combat took place. The French captured the town, but ten thousand men lay dead or wounded on the field, while Napoleon was forced to abandon his projected line of march, and to return by the route he had followed in his advance on Moscow. From the bloody scene of contest the retreat continued, the battlefield of Borodino being crossed, and, by the middle of November, the ruins of Smolensk reached.

Winter was now upon the French in all its fury. The food brought from Moscow had been exhausted. Famine, frost, and fatigue had proved more fatal than the bullets of the enemy. In fourteen days after reaching **The Sad Remnant of the Army of Invasion** Moscow the army lost 43,000 men, leaving it only 60,000 strong. On reaching Smolensk it numbered but 42,000, having lost 18,000 more within eight days. The unarmed followers are said to have still numbered 60,000. Worse still, the supply of arms and provisions ordered to be ready at Smolensk was in great part lacking, only rye-flour and rice being found. Starvation threatened to aid the winter cold in the destruction of the feeble remnant of the "Grand Army."

Onward went the despairing host, at every step harassed by the Russians, who followed like wolves on their path. Ney, in command of the rear-guard, was the hero of the retreat. Cut off by the Russians from the main column, and apparently lost beyond hope, he made a wonderful escape by crossing the Dnieper on the ice during the night and rejoining his companions, who had given up the hope of ever seeing him again.

On the 26th the ice-cold river Beresina was reached, destined to be the most terrible point on the whole dreadful march. Two bridges **The Dreadful** were thrown in all haste across the stream, and most of the **Crossing of** men under arms crossed, but 18,000 stragglers fell into the **the Beresina** hands of the enemy. How many were trodden to death in the press or were crowded from the bridge into the icy river cannot be told. It is said that when spring thawed the ice 30,000 bodies were found and burned on the banks of the stream. A mere fragment of the great army remained alive. Ney was the last man to cross that frightful stream.

On the 3d of December Napoleon issued a bulletin which has become famous, telling the anxious nations of Europe that the grand army was annihilated, but the emperor was safe. Two days afterwards he surrendered the command of the army to Murat and set out at all speed for Paris, where his presence was indispensibly necessary. On the 13th of December some 16,000 haggard and staggering men, almost too weak to hold the arms to which they still despairingly clung, recrossed the Niemen, which the grand army had passed in such magnificent strength and with such abounding resources less than six months before. It was the greatest and most astounding disaster in the military history of the world.

This tale of terror may be fitly closed by a dramatic story told by General Mathieu Dumas, who, while sitting at breakfast in Gumbinnen, saw enter a haggard man, with long beard, blackened face, and red and glaring eyes.

"I am here at last," he exclaimed. "Don't you know me?"

"No," said the general. "Who are you?"

"I am the rear-guard of the Grand Army. I have fired the last musket-shot on the bridge of Kowno. I have thrown the last of our arms into the Niemen, and came hither through the woods. I am Marshal Ney."

"This is the beginning of the end," said the shrewd Talleyrand, when Napoleon set out on his Russian campaign. The remark proved true, the disaster in Russia had loosened the grasp of the Corsican on the throat of Europe, and the nations, which hated as much as they feared their ruthless enemy, made active preparations for his overthrow. While he was in France, actively gathering men and materials for a renewed struggle, signs of an implacable hostility began to manifest themselves on all sides in the surrounding states.   Belief in the invincibility of Napoleon had vanished, and little fear was entertained of the raw conscripts whom he was forcing

Europe in Arms into the ranks to replace his slaughtered veterans.
Against
Napoleon   Prussia was the first to break the bonds of alliance with France, to ally itself with Russia, and to call its people to arms against their oppressor.   They responded with the utmost enthusiasm, men of all ranks and all professions hastened to their country's defence, and the noble and the peasant stood side by side as privates in the same regiment.   In March, 1813, the French left Berlin, which was immediately occupied by the Russian and Prussian allies.   The king of Saxony, however, refused to desert Napoleon, to whom he owed many favors and whose anger he feared; and his State, in consequence, became the theatre of the war.

Across the opposite borders of this kingdom poured the hostile hosts,

The Opening meeting in battle at Lützen and Buntzen.   Here the French
of the held the field, driving their adversaries across the Oder, but
Final Struggle not in the wild dismay seen at Jena.   A new spirit had been aroused in the Prussian heart, and they left thousands of their enemies dead upon the field, among whom Napoleon saw with grief his especial friend and favorite Duroc.

A truce followed, which the French emperor utilized in gathering fresh levies.   Prince Metternich, the able chancellor of the Austrian empire, sought to make peace, but his demands upon Napoleon were much greater than the proud conqueror was prepared to grant, and he decisively refused to cede the territory held by him as the spoils of war.   His refusal brought upon him another powerful foe, Austria allied itself with his enemies, formally declaring war on August 12, 1813, and an active and terrible struggle began.

Napoleon's army was rapidly concentrated at Dresden, upon whose

The Battle of works of defence the allied army precipitated itself in a vigor-
Dresden, Na- ous assault on August 26th.   Its strength was wasted against
poleon's Last the vigorously held fortifications of the city, and in the end
Great Victory the gates were flung open and the serried battalions of the
Old Guard appeared in battle array.   From every gate of the city these tried soldiers poured, and rushed upon the unprepared wings of the hostile host.   Before this resistless charge the enemy recoiled, retreating with heavy loss to the heights beyond the city, and leaving Napoleon master of the field.

On the next morning the battle was resumed.   The allies, strongly posted, still outnumbered the French, and had abundant reason to expect victory. But Napoleon's eagle eye quickly saw that their left wing lacked the strength of the remainder of the line, and upon this he poured the bulk of his forces, while keeping their centre and right actively engaged. The result justified the instinct of his genius, the enemy was driven back in disastrous defeat, and once again a glorious victory was inscribed upon the banners of France—the final one in Napoleon's career of fame.

Yet the fruits of this victory were largely lost in the events of the remainder of the month. On the 26th Blücher brilliantly defeated Marshal Macdonald on the Katzbach, in Silesia; on the 30th General **A Series of** Vandamme, with 10,000 French soldiers, was surrounded and **French** captured at Culm, in Bohemia; and on the 27th Hirschfeld, at **Disasters** Hagelsberg, with a corps of volunteers, defeated Girard. The Prussian-Swedish army similarly won victories on August 25th and September 6th, and a few weeks afterward the Prussian general, Count York, supported by the troops of General Horn, crossed the Elbe in the face of the enemy, and gained a brilliant victory at Wartenburg. Where Napoleon was present victory inclined to his banner. Where he was absent his lieutenants suffered defeat. The struggle was everywhere fierce and desperate, but the end was at hand.

The rulers of the Rhine Confederation now began to desert Napoleon and all Germany to join against him. The first to secede was Bavaria, which allied itself with Austria and joined its forces to those of the allies. During October the hostile armies concentrated in front of **The Fatal** Leipzig, where was to be fought the decisive battle of the war. **Meeting of** The struggle promised was the most gigantic one in which **the Armies** Napoleon had ever been engaged. Against his 100,000 men **at Leipzig** was gathered a host of 300,000 Austrians, Prussians, Russians, and Swedes.

We have not space to describe the multitudinous details of this mighty struggle, which continued with unabated fury for three days, October 16th, 17th, and 18th. It need scarcely be said that the generalship shown by Napoleon in this famous contest lacked nothing of his usual brilliancy, and that he was ably seconded by Ney, Murat, Augereau, and others of his famous generals, yet the overwhelming numbers of the enemy enabled them to defy all the valor of the French and the resources of their great leader, and at evening of the 18th the armies still faced each other in battle array, the fate of the field yet undecided.

Napoleon was in no condition to renew the combat. During the long affray the French had expended no less than 250,000 cannon balls. They had but 16,000 left, which two hours' firing would exhaust. Reluctantly he gave the order to retreat, and all that night the wearied and disheartened troops filed through the gates of Leipzig, leaving a rear-guard in the city, who defended it bravely against the swarming multitude of the foe. A disastrous blunder terminated their stubborn defence. Orders had been left to blow up the bridge across the Elster, but the mine was, by mistake, set off too soon, and the gallant garrison, 12,000 in number, with a multitude of sick and wounded, was forced to surrender as prisoners of war.

The end was drawing near. Vigorously pursued, the French reached the Rhine by forced marches, defeating with heavy loss the army of Austrians and Bavarians which sought to block their way. The stream was crossed and the French were once more upon their own soil. After years of contest, Germany was finally freed from Napoleon's long-victorious hosts.

Marked results followed. The carefully organized work of Napoleon's policy quickly fell to pieces. The kingdom of Westphalia was dissolved. **The Break-up** The elector of Hesse and the dukes of Brunswick and Olden- **of Napoleon's** burg returned to the thrones from which they had been driven. **European** The Confederation of the Rhine ceased to exist, and its states **Empire** allied themselves with Austria. Denmark, long faithful to France, renounced its alliance in January, 1814. Austria regained possession of Lombardy, the duke of Tuscany returned to his capital, and the Pope, Pius VII., long held captive by Napoleon, came back in triumph to Rome. A few months sufficed to break down the edifice of empire slowly reared through so many years, and almost all Europe outside of France united itself in hostility to its hated foe.

Napoleon was offered peace if he would accept the Rhine as the French frontier, but his old infatuation and trust in his genius prevailed over the dictates of prudence, he treated the offer in his usual double-dealing way, and the allies, convinced that there could be no stable peace while he remained on the throne, decided to cross the Rhine and invade France.

Blücher led his columns across the stream on the first day of 1814, Schwarzenberg marched through Switzerland into France, and Wellington **The War in** crossed the Pyrenees. Napoleon, like a wolf brought to bay, **France and** sought to dispose of his scattered foes before they would unite, **the Abdica-** and began with Blücher, whom he defeated five times within **tion of the** as many days. The allies, still in dread of their great **Emperor** opponent, once more offered him peace, but his success robbed him of wisdom, he demanded more than they were willing to give, and his enemies, encouraged by a success gained by Blücher, broke off the negotiations and marched on Paris, now bent on the dethronement of their dreaded antagonist.

A few words will bring the story of this contest to an end. France was exhausted, its army was incapable of coping with the serried battalions marshalled against it, Paris surrendered before Napoleon could come to its defence, and in the end the emperor, vacillating and in despair, was obliged, on April 7, 1814, to sign an unconditional act of abdication. The powers of Europe awarded him as a kingdom the diminutive island of Elba, in the Mediterranean, with an annual income of 2,000,000 francs and an army composed of 400 of his famous guard. The next heir to the throne returned as Louis XVIII. France was given back its old frontier of 1492, the foreign armies withdrew from her soil, and the career of the great Corsican seemed at an end.

In spite of their long experience with Napoleon, the event proved that the powers of Europe knew not all the audacity and mental resources of the man with whom they had to deal. They had made what might have proved a fatal error in giving him an asylum so near the coast of France, whose people, intoxicated with the dream of glory through which he had so long led them, would be sure to respond enthusiastically to an appeal to rally to his support.

The powers were soon to learn their error. While the Congress of Vienna, convened to restore the old constitution of Europe, was deliberating and disputing, its members were startled by the news that the dethroned emperor was again upon the soil of France, and that Louis XVIII. was in full flight for the frontier. Napoleon had landed on March 1, 1815, and set out on his return to Paris, the army and the people rapidly gathering to his support. On the 30th he entered the Tuileries in a blaze of triumph, the citizens, thoroughly dissatisfied with their brief experience of Bourbon rule, going mad with enthusiasm in his welcome.

Thus began the famous period of the "Hundred Days." The powers declared Napoleon to be the "enemy of nations," and armed a half million of men for his final overthrow. The fate of his desperate attempt was soon decided. For the first time he was to meet the British in battle, and in Wellington to encounter the only man who had definitely made head against his legions. A British army was dispatched in all haste to Belgium, Blücher with his Prussians hastened to the same region, and the mighty final struggle was at hand. The persistent and unrelenting enemies of the Corsican conqueror, the British islanders, were destined to be the agents of his overthrow.

The little kingdom of Belgium was the scene of the momentous contest that brought Napoleon's marvelous career to an end. Thither he led his army, largely made up of new conscripts ; and thither the English and the Prussians hastened to meet him. On June 16, 1815, the prelude to the **The Gathering** great battle took place. Napoleon met Blücher at Ligny and **of the Armies** defeated him ; then, leaving Grouchy to pursue the Prussians, **in Belgium** he turned against his island foes. On the same day Ney encountered the forces of Wellington at Quatre Bras, but failed to drive them back. On the 17th Wellington took a new position at Waterloo, and awaited there his great antagonist.

June 18th was the crucial day in Napoleon's career, the one in which his power was to fall, never to rise again. Here we shall but sketch in outline this famous battle, reserving a fuller account of it for our next chapter, **The Terrible** under the story of Wellington, the victor in the fray. The **Defeat at** stupendous struggle, as Wellington himself described it, **Waterloo** was "a battle of giants." Long the result wavered in the balance. All day long the British sustained the desperate assaults of their antagonists. Terrible was the contest, frightful the loss of life. Hour after hour passed, charge after charge was hurled by Napoleon against the British lines, which still closed up over the dead and stood firm ; and it seemed as if night would fall with the two armies unflinchingly face to face, neither of them victor in the terrible fray.

The arrival of Blücher with his Prussians turned the scale. To Napoleon's bitter disappointment Grouchy, who should have been close on the heels of the Prussians, failed to appear, and the weary and dejected French were left to face these fresh troops without support. Napoleon's Old Guard in vain flung itself into the gap, and the French nation long repeated in pride the saying attributed to the commander of this famous corps "The guard dies, but it never surrenders."

In the end the French army broke and fled in disastrous rout, three-fourths of the whole force being left dead, wounded, or prisoners, while all its artillery became the prize of the victors. Napoleon, pale and confused, was led by Soult from the battlefield. It was his last fight. **Napoleon Meets** His abdication was demanded, and he resigned the crown in **His Fate** favor of his son. A hopeless and unnerved fugitive, he fled from Paris to Rochefort, hoping to escape to America. But the British fleet held that port, and in despair he went on board a vessel of the fleet, trusting himself to the honor of the British nation. But the statesmen of England had no sympathy with the vanquished adventurer, from whose ambition Europe had suffered so terribly. He was sent as a state prisoner to the island of St. Helena, there to end his days. His final hour of glory came in 1842, when his ashes were brought in pomp and display to Paris.

THE EVE OF WATERLOO

No more impressive scene could be imagined than this peaceful slumber of an army on the eve of what was to prove one of the most famous battles of history. On the succeeding night many of these slumberers slept the sleep of death, but their hands had brought to an end the career of Napoleon.

WELLINGTON AT WATERLOO GIVING THE WORD TO ADVANCE

his spirited illustration figures the final event in the mighty struggle at Waterloo, when the French, after hurling themselves a dozen times against the unyielding British ranks, like storm waves upon a rock-bound shore, staggered back in despair, and Wellington

CHAPTER V.

Nelson and Wellington. the Champions of England.

FOR nearly twenty years went on the stupendous struggle between Napoleon the Great and the powers of Europe, but in all that time, and among the multitude of men who met the forces of France in battle, only two names emerge which the world cares to remember, those of Horatio Nelson, the most famous of the admirals of England, and Lord Wellington, who alone seemed able to overthrow the greatest military genius of modern times. On land the efforts of Napoleon were seconded by the intrepidity of a galaxy of heroes, Ney, Murat, Moreau, Massena, and other men of fame. At sea the story reads differently. That era of stress and strain raised no great admiral in the service of France; her ships were feebly commanded, and the fleet of Great Britain, under the daring Nelson, kept its proud place as mistress of the sea. **England and France on Land and Sea**

The first proof of this came before the opening of the century, when Napoleon, led by the ardor of his ambition, landed in Egypt, with vague hopes of rivaling in the East the far-famed exploits of Alexander the Great. The fleet which bore him thither remained moored in Aboukir Bay, where Nelson, scouring the Mediterranean in quest of it, first came in sight of its serried line of ships on August 1, 1798. One alternative alone dwelt in his courageous soul, that of a heroic death or a glorious victory. **Nelson Discovers the French Fleet in Aboukir Bay** "Before this time to-morrow I shall have gained a victory or Westminster Abbey," he said.

In the mighty contest that followed, the French had the advantage in numbers, alike of ships, guns, and men. They were drawn up in a strong and compact line of battle, moored in a manner that promised to bid defiance to a force double their own. They lay in an open roadstead, but had every advantage of situation, the British fleet being obliged to attack them in a position carefully chosen for defence. Only the genius of Nelson enabled him to overcome those advantages of the enemy. "If we succeed, what will the world say?" asked Captain Berry, on hearing the admiral's plan of battle. "There is no if in the case," answered the admiral. "That we shall succeed is certain : who may live to tell the story is a very different question."

The story of the "Battle of the Nile" belongs to the record of

The Glorious Battle of the Nile. eighteenth century affairs. All we need say here is that it ended in a glorious victory for the English fleet. Of thirteen ships of the line in the French fleet, only two escaped. Of four frigates, one was sunk and one burned. The British loss was 895 men Of the French, 5,225 perished in the terrible fray. Nelson sprang, in a moment, from the position of a man without fame into that of the naval hero of the world—as Dewey did in as famous a fray almost exactly a century later. Congratulations and honors were showered upon him, the Sultan of Turkey rewarded him with costly presents, valuable testimonials came from other quarters, and his own country honored him with the title of Baron Nelson of the Nile, and settled upon him for life a pension of £2,000.

The first great achievement of Nelson in the nineteenth century was the result of a daring resolution of the statesmen of England, in their desperate contest with the Corsican conqueror. By his exploit at the Nile the admiral had very seriously weakened the sea-power of France. But there were powers then in alliance with France—Russia, Sweden and Denmark—which had formed a confederacy to make England respect their naval rights, and whose combined fleet, if it should come to the aid of France, might prove sufficient to sweep the ships of England from the seas.

The weakest of these powers, and the one most firmly allied to France, was Denmark, whose fleet, consisting of twenty-three ships of the line and about thirty-one frigates and smaller vessels, lay at Copenhagen. At any moment this powerful fleet might be put at the disposal of Napoleon. This possible danger the British cabinet resolved to avoid. A plan was laid to destroy the fleet of the Danes, and on the 12th of March, 1801, the British fleet sailed with the purpose of putting this resolution into effect.

The Fleet Sails for Copenhagen Nelson, then bearing the rank of vice-admiral, went with the fleet, but only as second in command. To the disgust of the English people, Sir Hyde Parker, a brave and able seaman, but one whose name history has let sink into oblivion, was given chief command—a fact which would have insured the failure of the expedition if Nelson had not set aside precedent, and put glory before duty. Parker, indeed, soon set Nelson chafing by long drawn-out negotiations, which proved useless, wasted time, and saved the Danes from being taken by surprise. When, on the morning of April 30th, the British fleet at length advanced through the Sound and came in sight of the Danish line of defence, they beheld formidable preparations to meet them.

Eighteen vessels, including full-rigged ships and hulks, were moored in a line nearly a mile and a half in length, flanked to the northward by two artificial islands mounted with sixty-eight heavy cannon and supplied with furnaces for heating shot. Near by lay two large block-ships. The Danish Line of Defence Across the harbor's mouth extended a massive chain, and shore batteries commanded the channel. Outside the harbor's mouth were moored two 74-gun ships, a 40-gun frigate, and some smaller vessels. In addition to these defences, which stretched for nearly four miles in length, was the difficulty of the channel, always hazardous from its shoals, and now beaconed with false buoys for the purpose of luring the British ships to destruction.

With modern defences—rapid-fire guns and steel-clad batteries—the enterprise would have been hopeless, but the art of defence was then at a far lower level. Nelson, who led the van in the 74-gun ship *Elephant*, gazed on these preparations with admiration, but with no evidence of doubt as to the result. The British fleet consisted of eighteen line of battle ships, with a large number of frigates and other craft, and with this force, and his indomitable spirit, he felt confident of breaking these formidable lines.

At ten o'clock on the morning of April 2d the battle began, two of the British ships running aground almost before a gun was fired. The Attack on the Danish Fleet At sight of this disaster Nelson instantly changed his plan of sailing, starboarded his helm, and sailed in, dropping anchor within a cable's length of the *Dannebrog*, of 62 guns. The other ships followed his example, avoiding the shoals on which the *Bellona* and *Russell* had grounded, and taking position at the close quarters of 100 fathoms from the Danish ships.

A terrific cannonade followed, kept up by both sides with unrelenting fury for three hours, and with terrible effect on the contesting ships and their crews. At this juncture took place an event that has made Nelson's name immortal among naval heroes. Admiral Parker, whose flag-ship lay at a distance from the hot fight, but who heard the incessant and furious fire and saw the grounded ships flying signals of distress, began to fear that Nelson was in serious danger, from which it was his duty to withdraw him. At about one o'clock he reluctantly hoisted a signal for the action to cease.

At this moment Nelson was pacing the quarter-deck of the *Elephant*, inspired with all the fury of the fight. "It is a warm business," he said to Colonel Stewart, who was on the ship with him; "and any moment may be the last of either of us; but, mark you, I would not for thousands be anywhere else."

As he spoke the flag-lieutenant reported that the signal to cease action was shown on the mast-head of the flag-ship *London*, and asked if he should report it to the fleet.

"No," was the stern answer; "merely acknowledge it. Is our signal for 'close action' still flying?"

"Yes," replied the officer.

How Nelson Answered the Signal to Cease Action "Then see that you keep it so," said Nelson, the stump of his amputated arm working as it usually did when he was agitated. "Do you know," he asked Colonel Stewart, "the meaning of signal No. 39, shown by Parker's ships?"

"No. What does it mean?"

"To leave off action!" He was silent a moment, then burst out, "Now damn me if I do!"

Turning to Captain Foley, who stood near him, he said: "Foley, you know I have only one eye; I have a right to be blind sometimes." He raised his telescope, applied it to his blind eye, and said: "I really do not see the signal."

On roared the guns, overhead on the *Elephant* still streamed the signal for "close action," and still the torrent of British balls rent the Danish ships. In half an hour more the fire of the Danes was fast weakening. In an hour it had nearly ceased. They had suffered frightfully, in ships and lives, and only the continued fire of the shore batteries now kept the contest alive. It was impossible to take possession of the prizes, and Nelson sent a flag of truce ashore with a letter in which he threatened to burn the vessels, with all on board, unless the shore fire was stopped. This threat proved effective, the fire ended, the great battle was at an end.

At four o'clock Nelson went on board the *London*, to meet the admiral. He was depressed in spirit, and said: "I have fought contrary to orders, and may be hanged; never mind, let them."

There was no danger of this; Parker was not that kind of man. He had raised the signal through fear for Nelson's safety, and now gloried in his success, giving congratulations where his subordinate looked for blame. The Danes had fought bravely and stubbornly, but they had no commander of the spirit and genius of Nelson, and were forced to yield to British pluck and endurance. Until June 13th, Nelson remained in the Baltic, watching the Russian fleet which he might still have to fight. Then came orders for his return home, and word reached him that he had been created Viscount Nelson for his services.

There remains to describe the last and most famous of Nelson's exploits, that in which he put an end to the sea-power of France, by destroying the remainder of her fleet at Trafalgar, and met death at the moment of victory. Four years had passed since the fight at Copenhagen. During much of that time Nelson had kept his fleet on guard off Toulon, impatiently waiting until the enemy should venture from that port of refuge. At length, the combined fleet of France and Spain, now in alliance, escaped his vigilance, and sailed to the West Indies to work havoc in the **Nelson in Chase** British colonies. He followed them thither in all haste ; and **of the French** subsequently, on their return to France, he chased them back **Fleet** across the seas, burning with eagerness to bring them to bay.

On the 19th of October, 1805, the allied fleet put to sea from the harbor of Cadiz, confident that its great strength would enable it to meet any force the British had upon the waves. Admiral De Villeneuve, with thirty-three ships of the line and a considerable number of smaller craft, had orders to force the straits of Gibraltar, land troops at Naples, sweep British cruisers and commerce from the Mediterranean, and then seek the port of Toulon to refit. As it turned out, he never reached the straits, his fleet meeting its fate before it could leave the Atlantic waves. Nelson had reached the coast of Europe again, and was close at hand when the doomed ships of the allies appeared. Two swift ocean scouts saw **The Allied** the movements, and hastened to Lord Nelson with the wel- **Fleet Leaves** come news that the long-deferred moment was at hand. On **Cadiz** the 21st, the British fleet came within view, and the following signal was set on the mast-head of the flag-ship:

" The French and Spaniards are out at last ; they outnumber us in ships and guns and men ; we are on the eve of the greatest sea-fight in history."

On came the ships, great lumbering craft, strangely unlike the war-vessels of to-day. Instead of the trim, grim, steel-clad, steam-driven modern battle-ship, with its revolving turret, and great frowning, breech-loading guns, sending their balls through miles of air, those were bluff-bowed, ungainly hulks, with bellying sides towering like black walls above the sea as if to make the largest mark possible for hostile shot, with a great show of muzzle-loading guns of small range, while overhead rose lofty spars and spreading sails. Ships they were that to-day would be sent to the bottom in five minutes of fight, but which, mated against others of the same build, were capable of giving a gallant account of themselves.

It was off the shoals of Cape Trafalgar, near the southern extremity of Spain, that the two fleets met, and such a tornado **Off Cape** of fire as has rarely been seen upon the ocean waves was poured **Trafalgar** from their broad and lofty sides. As they came together there floated from the masthead of the *Victory*, Nelson's flagship, that signal which has become the watchword of the British isles : " England expects that every man will do his duty."

We cannot follow the fortunes of all the vessels in that stupendous fray, the most famous sea-fight in history. It must serve to follow the *Victory* in her course, in which Nelson eagerly sought to thrust himself into The "Victory" and Her Brilliant Fight the heart of the fight and dare death in his quest for victory. He was not long in meeting his wish. Soon he found himself in a nest of enemies, eight ships at once pouring their fire upon his devoted vessel, which could not bring a gun to bear in return, the wind having died away and the ship lying almost motionless upon the waves.

Before the *Victory* was able to fire a shot fifty of her men had fallen killed or wounded, and her canvas was pierced and rent till it looked like a series of fishing nets. But the men stuck to their guns with unyielding tenacity, and at length their opportunity came. A 68-pounder carronade, loaded with a round shot and 500 musket balls, was fired into the cabin windows of the *Bucentaure*, with such terrible effect as to disable 400 men and 20 guns, and put the ship practically out of the fight.

The *Victory* next turned upon the *Neptune* and the *Redoubtable*, of the enemy's fleet. The *Neptune*, not liking her looks, kept off, but she collided and locked spars with the *Redoubtable*, and a terrific fight began. On the opposite side of the *Redoubtable* came the British ship *Temeraire*, and opposite it again a second ship of the enemy, the four vessels lying bow to bow, and rending one another's sides with an incessant hail of balls. On the *Victory* the gunners were ordered to depress their pieces, that the balls should not go through and wound the *Temeraire* beyond. The muzzles of their cannon fairly touched the enemy's side, and after each shot a bucket of water was dashed into the rent, that they may not set fire to the vessel which they confidently expected to take as a prize.

In the midst of the hot contest came the disaster already spoken of. Brass swivels were mounted in the French ship's tops to sweep with their fire the deck of their foe, and as Nelson and Captain Hardy paced together their poop deck, regardless of danger, the admiral suddenly fell. A ball from one of these guns had reached the noblest mark on the fleet.

The Great Battle and its Sad Disaster "They have done for me at last, Hardy," the fallen man said.

"Don't say you are hit!" cried Hardy in dismay.

"Yes, my backbone is shot through."

His words were not far from the truth. He never arose from that fatal shot. Yet, dying as he was, his spirit survived.

"I hope none of our ships have struck, Hardy," he feebly asked, in a later interval of the fight.

"No, my lord. There is small fear of that,"

"I'm a dead man, Hardy, but I'm glad of what you say. Whip them now you've got them. Whip them as they've never been whipped before."

Another hour passed. Hardy came below again to say that fourteen or fifteen of the enemy's ships had struck.

"That's better, though I bargained for twenty," said the dying man. "And now, anchor, Hardy—anchor."

"I suppose, my lord, that Admiral Collingwood will now take the direction of affairs."

"Not while I live," exclaimed Nelson, with a momentary return of energy. "Do *you* anchor, Hardy."

"Then shall *we* make the signal, my lord."

"Yes, for if I live, I'll anchor."

That was the end. Five minutes later Horatio Nelson, England's greatest sea champion, was dead. He had won —not "Victory and Westminster Abbey"—but victory and a noble resting place in St. Paul's Cathedral.

Victory for England and Death for Her Famous Admiral

Collingwood did not anchor, but stood out to sea with the eighteen prizes of the hard fought fray. In the gale that followed many of the results of victory were lost, four of the ships being retaken, some wrecked on shore, some foundering at sea, only four reaching British waters in Gibraltar Bay. But whatever was lost, Nelson's fame was secure, and the victory at Trafalgar is treasured as one of the most famous triumphs of British arms.

The naval battle at Copenhagen, won by Nelson, was followed, six years later, by a combined land and naval expedition in which Wellington, England's other champion, took part. Again inspired by the fear that Napoleon might use the Danish fleet for his own purposes, the British government, though at peace with Denmark, sent a fleet to Copenhagen, bombarded and captured the city, and seized the Danish ships. A battle took place on land in which Wellington (then Sir Arthur Wellesley) won an easy victory and, captured 10,000 men. The whole business was an inglorious one, a dishonorable incident in a struggle in which the defeat of Napaleon stood first, honor second. Among the English themselves some defended it on the plea of policy, some called it piracy and murder.

Not long afterwards England prepared to take a serious part on land in the desperate contest with Napoleon, and sent a British force to Portugal, then held by the French army of invasion under Marshal Junot. This force, 10,000 strong, was commanded by Sir Arthur Wellesley, and landed July 30, 1808, at Mondego Bay. He was soon joined by General Spencer from Cadiz, with 13,000 men.

The British in Portugal

The French, far from home and without support, were seriously alarmed at this invasion, and justly so, for they met with defeat in a sharp battle at Vimeira, and would probably have been forced to surrender as prisoners of war had not the troops been called off from pursuit by Sir Harry Burrard, who had been sent out to supersede Wellesley in command. The end of it all was a truce, and a convention under whose terms the French troops were permitted to evacuate Portugal with their arms and baggage and return to France. This release of Junot from a situation which precluded escape so disgusted Wellesley that he threw up his command and returned to

The Death of Sir John Moore

England. Other troops sent out under Sir John Moore and Sir David Baird met a superior force of French in Spain, and their expedition ended in disaster. Moore was killed while the troops were embarking to return home, and the memory of this affair has been preserved in the famous ode, " The burial of Sir John Moore," from which we quote :

> " We buried him darkly at dead of night,
> The sod with our bayonets turning,
> By the glimmering moonbeams' misty light
> And the lanterns dimly burning. "

In April, 1809, Wellesley returned to Portugal, now chief in command, to begin a struggle which was to continue until the fall of Napoleon. There were at that time about 20,000 British soldiers at Lisbon, while the French had in Spain more than 300,000 men, under such generals as Ney, Soult, and Victor. The British, indeed, were aided by a large number of natives in arms. But these, though of service as guerillas, were almost useless in regular warfare.

Wellesley was at Lisbon. Oporto, 170 miles north, was held by Marshal Soult, who had recently taken it. Without delay Wellington marched

The Gallant Crossing of the Douro

thither, and drove the French outposts across the river Douro. But in their retreat they burned the bridge of boats across the river, seized every boat they could find, and rested in security, defying their foes to cross. Soult, veteran officer though he was, fancied that he had disposed of Wellesley, and massed his forces on the sea-coast side of the town, in which quarter alone he looked for an attack.

He did not know his antagonist. A few skiffs were secured, and a small party of British was sent across the stream. The French attacked them, but they held their ground till some others joined them, and by the time Soult was informed of the danger Wellesley had landed a large force and controlled a good supply of boats. A battle followed in which the French were routed and forced to retreat. But the only road by which their

RETREAT OF NAPOLEON FROM WATERLOO

In the slaughter of his Old Guard on the field of Waterloo, Napoleon recognized the tocsin of fate. Pale, distressed, despairing, he was led by Marshal Soult from the scene of slaughter. It was the last of his many fields of battle and death, and his career would have had a nobler ending if he had died there rather than fled.

THE REMNANT OF AN ARMY

The defeat of the French in the battle of Waterloo was so complete that all organization was lost, many of the soldiers fleeing singly from the field. This state of affairs is here strikingly depicted.

artillery or baggage could be moved had been seized by General Beresford, and was strongly held. In consequence Soult was forced to abandon all his wagons and cannon and make his escape by bye-roads into Spain.

This signal victory was followed by another on July 27, 1809, when Wellesley, with 20,000 British soldiers and about 40,000 Spanish allies, met a French army of 60,000 men at Talavera in Spain. The battle that succeeded lasted two days. The brunt of it fell upon the British, the Spaniards proving of little use, **The Victory at Talavera and the Victor's Reward** yet it ended in the defeat of the French, who retired unmolested, the British being too exhausted to pursue.

The tidings of this victory were received with the utmost enthusiasm in England. It was shown by it that British valor could win battles against Napoleon's on land as well as on sea. Wellesley received the warmest thanks of the king, and, like Nelson, was rewarded by being raised to the peerage, being given the titles of Baron Douro of Wellesley and Viscount Wellington of Talavera. In future we shall call him by his historic title of Wellington.

Men and supplies just then would have served Wellington better than titles. With strong support he could have marched on and taken Madrid. As it was, he felt obliged to retire upon the fortress of Badajoz, near the frontier of Portugal. Spain was swarming with French soldiers, who were gradually collected there until they exceeded 350,000 men. Of these 80,000, under the command of Massena, were sent to act against the British. Before this strong force Wellington found it necessary to draw back, and the frontier fortresses of Almeida and Ciudad Rodrigo were taken by the French. Wellington's first stand was on the heights of Busaco, September, 1810. Here, with 30,000 men, he withstood all the attacks of the French, who in the end were forced to withdraw. Massena then tried to gain the road between Lisbon and Oporto, whereupon Wellington quickly retreated towards Lisbon.

The British general had during the winter been very usefully employed. The road by which Lisbon must be approached passes the village of Torres Vedras, and here two strong lines of earthworks were constructed, some twenty-five miles in length, stretching from the sea to the Tagus, and effectually securing Lisbon against attack. These works had been built with such secrecy and **Wellington's Impregnable Lines at Torres Vedras** despatch that the French were quite ignorant of their existence, and Massena, marching in confidence upon the Portuguese capital, was amazed and chagrined on finding before him this formidable barrier.

It was strongly defended, and all his efforts to take it proved in vain. He then tried to reduce the British by famine, but in this he was equally baffled, food being poured into Lisbon from the sea. He tried by a feigned retreat to draw the British from their works, but this stratagem failed of effect, and for four months more the armies remained inactive. At length the exhaustion of the country of provisions made necessary a real retreat, and Massena withdrew across the Spanish frontier, halting near Salamanca. Of the proud force with which Napoleon proposed to "drive the British leopards into the sea," more than half had vanished in this luckless campaign.

But though the French army had withdrawn from Portugal, the frontier fortresses were still in French hands, and of these Almeida, near the

The Siege and Capture of the Portuguese Fortresses

borders, was the first to be attacked by Wellington's forces. Massena advanced with 50,000 men to its relief, and the two armies met at Fuentes-de-Onoro, May 4, 1811. The French made attacks on the 5th and 6th, but were each time repulsed, and on the 7th Massena retreated, sending orders to the governor of Almeida to destroy the fortifications and leave the place.

Another battle was fought in front of Badajoz of the most sanguinary character, the total loss of the two armies being 15,000 killed and wounded. For a time the British seemed threatened with inevitable defeat, but the fortune of the day was turned into victory by a desperate charge. Subsequently Ciudad Rodrigo was attacked, and was carried by storm, in January, 1812. Wellington then returned to Badajoz, which was also taken by storm, after a desperate combat in which the victors lost 5,000 men, a number exceeding that of the whole French garrison.

These continued successes of the British were seriously out of consonance with the usual exploits of Napoleon's armies. He was furious with his marshals, blaming them severely, and might have taken their place in the struggle with Wellington but that his fatal march to Russia was about

Wellington Wins at Salamanca and Enters Madrid

to begin. The fortress taken, Wellington advanced into Spain, and on July 21st encountered the French army under Marmont before the famous old town of Salamanca. The battle, one of the most stubbornly contested in which Wellington had yet been engaged, ended in the repulse of the French, and on August 12th the British army marched into Madrid, the capital of Spain, from which King Joseph Bonaparte had just made his second flight.

Wellington's next effort was a siege of the strong fortress of Burgos. This proved the one failure in his military career, he being obliged to raise the siege after several weeks of effort. In the following year he was strongly reinforced, and with an army numbering nearly 200,000 men he marched on the retreating enemy, meeting them at Vittoria, near the boundary of

France and Spain, on June 21, 1813. The French were for the first time in this war in a minority. They were also heavily encumbered with baggage, the spoils of their occupation of Spain. The battle ended in a complete victory for Wellington, who captured 157 cannon and a vast quantity of plunder, including the spoils of Madrid and of the palace of the kings of Spain. The specie, of which a large sum was taken, quickly disappeared among the troops, and failed to reach the treasure chests of the army.

Vittoria and the Pyrenees

The French were now everywhere on the retreat. Soult, after a vigorous effort to drive the British from the passes of the Pyrenees, withdrew, and Wellington and his army soon stood on the soil of France. A victory over Soult at Nivelle, and a series of successes in the following spring, ended the long Peninsular War, the abdication of Napoleon closing the long and terrible drama of battle. In the whole six years of struggle Wellington had not once been defeated on the battlefield.

His military career had not yet ended. His great day of glory was still to come, that in which he was to meet Napoleon himself in the field, and, for the first time in the history of the great Corsican, drive back his army in utter rout.

A year or more had passed since the events just narrated. In June, 1815, Wellington found himself at the head of an army some 100,000 strong, encamped around Brussels, the capital of Belgium. It was a mingled group of British, Dutch, Belgian, Hanoverian, German, and other troops, hastily got together, and many of them not safely to be depended upon. Of the British, numbers had never been under fire. Marshal Blücher, with an equal force of Prussian troops, was near at hand; the two forces prepared to meet the rapidly advancing Napoleon.

The Gathering of the Forces at Brussels

We have already told of the defeat of Blücher at Ligny, and the attack on Wellington at Quatre Bras. On the evening of the 17th the army, retreating from Quatre Bras, encamped on the historic field of Waterloo in a drenching rain, that turned the roads into streams, the fields into swamps. All night long the rain came down, the soldiers enduring the flood with what patience they could. In the morning it ceased, fires were kindled, and active preparations began for the terrible struggle at hand.

Here ran a shallow valley, bounded by two ridges, the northern of which was occupied by the British, while Napoleon posted his army on its arrival along the southern ridge. On the slope before the British centre was the white-walled farm house of La Haye Sainte, and in front of the right wing the chateau of Hougoumont

The Battlefield of Waterloo

with its various stout stone buildings. Both of these were occupied by men of Wellington's army, and became leading points in the struggle of the day.

It was nine o'clock in the morning before the van-guard of the French army made its appearance on the crest of the southern ridge. By half-past ten 61,000 soldiers,—infantry, cavalry, and artillery—lay encamped in full sight. About half-past eleven came the first attack of that remarkable day, during which the French waged an aggressive battle, the British stood on the defensive.

This first attack was directed against Hougoumont, around which there **The Desperate Charges of the French** was a desperate contest. At this point the affray went on, in successive waves of attack and repulse, all day long; yet still the British held the buildings, and all the fierce valor of the French failed to gain them a foothold within.

About two o'clock came a second attack, preceded by a frightful cannonade upon the British left and centre. Four massive columns, led by Ney, poured steadily forward straight for the ridge, sweeping upon and around the farm-stead of La Haye Sainte, but met at every point by the sabres and bayonets of the British lines. Nearly 24,000 men took part in this great movement, the struggle lasting more than an hour before the French staggered back in repulse. Then from the French lines came a stupendous cavalry charge, the massive columns composed of no less than forty squadrons of cuirassiers and dragoons, filling almost all the space between Hougoumont and La Haye Sainte as they poured like a torrent upon the British lines. Torn by artillery, rent by musketry; checked, reformed; charging again, and again driven back; they expended their strength and their lives on the infantry squares that held their ground with the grimmest obstinacy. Once more, now strengthened by the cavalry of the Imperial Guard, they came on to carnage and death, shattering themselves against those unyielding squares, and in the end repulsed with frightful loss.

The day was now well advanced, it being half-past four in the afternoon; the British had been fearfully shaken by the furious efforts of the **Blücher's Prussians and the Charge of Napoleon's Old Guard** French; when, emerging from the woods at St. Lambert, appeared the head of a column of fresh troops. Who were they? Blücher's Prussians, or Grouchy's pursuing French? On the answer to this question depended the issue of that terrible day. The question was soon decided; they were the Prussians; no sign appeared of the French; the hearts of the British beat high with hope and those of the French sank low in despair, for these fresh troops could not fail to decide the fate of that mighty field of battle. Soon the final struggle came. Napoleon, driven to desperation, launched his grand reserve corps, the far-famed Imperial Guard, upon his enemies. On they come, with Ney at their head; on them pours a terrible torrent of flame; from a distance the front ranks appear stationary, but only because they meet a death-line as they come, and fall in bleeding rows. Then on them, in a wild charge, rush the British Foot Guards, take them in flank, and soon all is over. "The Guard dies, but never surrenders," says their commander. Die they do, few of them surviving to take part in that mad flight which swept Napoleon from the field and closed the fatal day of Waterloo. England has won the great victory, now nearly a century old, and Wellington from that day of triumph takes rank with the greatest of British heroes.

7

CHAPTER VI.

From the Napoleonic Wars to the Revolution of 1830

THE terrific struggle of the "Hundred Days," which followed Napoleon's return from Elba and preceded his exile to St. Helena, made a serious break in the deliberations of the Congress of Vienna, convened for the purpose of recasting the map of Europe, which Napoleon had so sadly transformed, of setting aside the radical work of the French

A Quarter Century of Revolution

Revolution, and, in a word, of turning back the hands of the clock of time. Twenty-five years of such turmoil and volcanic disturbance as Europe had rarely known were at an end; the ruling powers were secure of their own again; the people, worn-out with the long and bitter struggle, welcomed eagerly the return of rest and peace; and the emperors and kings deemed it a suitable time to throw overboard the load of new ideas under which the European "ship of state" seemed to them likely to founder.

The Congress of Vienna was, in its way, a brilliant gathering. It included, mainly as handsome ornaments, the emperors of Russia and Austria, the kings of Prussia, Denmark, Bavaria and Wurtemberg; and, as its working element, the leading statesmen of Europe, including the Eng-

The Congress of Vienna

lish Castlereagh and Wellington, the French Talleyrand, the Prussian Hardenberg, and the Austrian Metternich. Checked in its deliberations for a time by Napoleon's fierce hundred days' death struggle, it quickly settled down to work again, having before it the vast task of undoing the mighty results of a quarter of a century of revolution. For the French Revolution had broadened into an European revolution, with Napoleon and his armies as its great instruments. The whole continent had been sown thickly during the long era of war with the Napoleonic ideas, and a crop of new demands and conditions had grown up not easily to be uprooted.

Reaction was the order of the day in the Vienna Congress. The shaken power of the monarchs was to be restored, the map of Europe to be readjusted, the people to be put back into the submissive condition which they occupied before that eventful 1789, when the States-General of France began its momentous work of overturning the equilibrium of the world.

As for the people, deeply infected as they were with the new ideas of liberty and the rights of man, which had made their way **Europe After** far beyond the borders of France, they were for the time worn- **Napoleon's** out with strife and turmoil, and settled back supinely to **Fall** enjoy the welcome era of rest, leaving their fate in the hands of the astute plenipotentiaries who were gathered in their wisdom at Vienna.

These worthy tools of the monarchs had an immense task before them—too large a one, as it proved. It was easy to talk about restoring to the nations the territory they had possessed before Napoleon began his career as a map-maker; but it was not easy to do so except at the cost of new wars. The territories of many of the powers had been added to by the French emperor, and they were not likely to give up their new posses- sions without a vigorous protest. In Germany the changes had been enormous. Napoleon had found there more than three hundred separate states, some no larger than a small American county, yet each possessed of the paraphernalia of a court and sovereign, a capital, an army and a public debt. And these were feebly combined into the phantasm known as the Holy Roman Empire. When Napoleon had finished his work this empire had ceased to exist, except as a tradition, and the great galaxy of sovereign states was reduced to thirty-nine. These included the great dominions of Austria and Prussia; the smaller states of Bavaria, Saxony, Hanover and Wurtemberg, which Napoleon had raised into kingdoms; and a vastly reduced group of minor states. The work done here it was somewhat dangerous to meddle with. The small potentates of Germany were like so many bull-dogs, glaring jealously across their new borders, and ready to fly at one another's throats at any suggestion of a change. The utmost they would yield was to be united into a confederacy **The Work of** called the *Bund*, with a Diet meeting at Frankfurt. But **the Congress** as the delegates to the Diet were given no law-making power, the *Bund* became an empty farce.

The great powers took care to regain their lost possessions, or to replace them with an equal amount of territory. Prussia and Austria spread out again to their old size, though they did not cover quite the old ground. Most of their domains in Poland were given up, Prussia getting new terri- tory in West Germany and Austria in Italy. Their provinces in Poland were ceded to Alexander of Russia, who added to them some of his own Polish dominions, and formed a new kingdom of Poland, he being its king. So in a shadowy way Poland was brought to life again. England got for her share in the spoils a number of French and Dutch colonies, including Malta and the Cape Colony in Africa. Thus each of the great powers repaid itself for its losses.

In Italy a variety of changes were made. The Pope got back the States of the Church; Tuscany was restored to its king; the same was the

Italy, France, and Spain

case with Naples, King Murat being driven from his throne and put to death. Piedmont, increased by the Republic of Genoa, was restored to the king of Sardinia. Some smaller states were formed, as Parma, Modena, and Lucca. Finally, Lombardy and Venice, much the richest regions of Italy, were given to Austria, which country was made the dominant power in the Italian peninsula.

Louis XVIII., the Bourbon king, brother of Louis XVI., who had reigned while Napoleon was at Elba, came back to the throne of France. The title of Louis XVII. was given to the poor boy, son of Louis XVI., who died from cruel treatment in the dungeons of the Revolution. In Spain the feeble Ferdinand returned to the throne which he had given up without a protest at the command of Napoleon. Portugal was given a monarch of its old dynasty. All seemed to have floated back into the old conditions again.

As for the rights of the people, what had become of them? Had they been swept away and the old wrongs of the people been brought back? Not quite. The frenzied enthusiasm for liberty and human rights of the past

The Rights of Man

twenty-five years could not go altogether for nothing. The lingering relics of feudalism had vanished, not only from France but from all Europe, and no monarch or congress could bring them back again. In its place the principles of democracy had spread from France far among the peoples of Europe. The principle of class privilege had been destroyed in France, and that of social equality had replaced it. The principle of the liberty of the individual, especially in his religious opinions, and the doctrine of the sovereignty of the people, had been proclaimed. These had still a battle before them. They needed to fight their way. Absolutism and the spirit of feudalism were arrayed against them. But they were too deeply implanted in the minds of the people to be eradicated, and their establishment as actual conditions has been the most important part of the political development of the nineteenth century.

Revolution was the one thing that the great powers of Europe feared and hated; this was the monster against which the Congress of Vienna directed its efforts. The cause of quiet and order, the preservation of the established state of things, the authority of rulers, the subordination of peoples, must be firmly maintained, and revolutionary disturbers must be put down with a strong hand. Such was the political dogma of the Congress. And yet, in spite of its assembled wisdom and the principles it promul-

LORD HORATIO NELSON

ARTHUR WELLESLEY, DUKE OF WELLINGTON

ILLUSTRIOUS LEADERS OF ENGLAND'S NAVY AND ARMY

JAMES WATT—THE FATHER OF THE STEAM ENGINE

It is to the steam engine that the wonderful productive progress of recent times is largely due, and
to the famous Scotch engineer, James Watt, belongs the honor of inventing the first
effective steam engine. His idea of condensing the steam from his engine in
a separate vessel came to him in 1765, and with this fortunate conception began the wonderful series of improvements which have
given us the magnificent engine of to-day.

gated, the nineteenth century has been especially the century of revolutions, actual or virtual, the result being an extraordinary growth in the liberties and prerogatives of the people.

The plan devised by the Congress for the suppression of revolution was the establishment of an association of monarchs, which became known as the Holy Alliance. Alexander of Russia, Francis of Austria, and Frederick William of Prussia formed a cove- **The Holy Alliance** nant to rule in accordance with the precepts of the Bible, to stand by each other in a true fraternity, to rule their subjects as loving parents, and to see that peace, justice, and religion should flourish in their dominions. An ideal scheme it was, but its promulgators soon won the name of hypocrites and the hatred of those whom they were to deal with on the principle of love and brotherhood. Reaction was the watchword, absolute sovereignty the purpose, the eradication of the doctrine of popular sovereignty the sentiment, which animated these powerful monarchs ; and the Holy Alliance meant practically the determination to unite their forces against democracy and revolution wherever they should show themselves.

It was not long before the people began to move. The attempt to re-establish absolute governments shook them out of their sluggish quiet. Revolution lifted its head again in the face of the Holy **Revolution in** Alliance, its first field being Spain. Ferdinand VII., on **Spain and** returning to his throne, had but one purpose in his weak **Naples** mind, which was to rule as an autocrat, as his ancestors had done. He swore to govern according to a constitution, and began his reign with a perjury. The patriots had formed a constitution during his absence, and this he set aside and never replaced by another. On the contrary, he set out to abolish all the reforms made by Napoleon, and to restore the monasteries, to bring back the inquisition, and to prosecute the patriots. Five years of this reaction made the state of affairs in Spain so intolerable that the liberals refused to submit to it any longer. In 1820 they rose in revolt, and the king, a coward under all his show of bravery, at once gave way and restored the constitution he had set aside.

The shock given the Holy Alliance by the news from Spain was quickly followed by another coming from Naples. The Bourbon king who had been replaced upon the throne of that country, another Ferdinand, was one of the most despicable men of his not greatly esteemed race. His government, while weak, was harshly oppressive. But it did not need a revolution to frighten this royal dastard. A mere general celebration of the victory of the liberals in Spain was enough, and in his alarm he hastened to give his people a constitution similar to that which the Spaniards had gained.

These awkward affairs sadly disturbed the equanimity of those statesmen who fancied that they had fully restored the divine right of kings.
Metternich, the Austrian advocate of reaction, hastened to call a new Con-

**Metternich
and His Con-
gresses**

gress, in 1820, and another in 1821. The question he put to
these assemblies was, Should revolution be permitted, or should
Europe interfere in Spain and Naples, and pledge herself to
uphold everywhere the sacred powers of legitimate monarchs? His old
friends of the Holy Alliance backed him up in this suggestion, both Con-
gresses adopted it, a policy of repression of revolutions became the pro-
gramme, and Austria was charged to restore what Metternich called
"order" in Naples.

He did so. The liberals of Naples were far too weak to oppose the
power of Austria. Their government fell to pieces as soon as the Austrian
army appeared, and the impotent but cruel Ferdinand was made an absolute
king again. The radicals in Piedmont started an insurrection which was
quickly put down, and Austria became practically the lord and master of Italy.

Proud of his success, Metternich called a new Congress in 1822, in
which it was resolved to repeat in Spain what had been done in Naples.

**How Order was
Restored in
Spain**

France was now made the instrument of the absolutists. A
French army marched across the Pyrenees, put down the government of the liberals, and gave the king back his despotic
rule. He celebrated his return to power by a series of cruel executions. The
Holy Alliance was in the ascendant, the liberals had been bitterly repaid for
their daring, terror seized upon the liberty-loving peoples, and Europe
seemed thrown fully into the grasp of the absolute kings

Only in two regions did the spirit of revolt triumph during this period

**The Revolution
in Greece**

of reaction. These were Greece and Spanish America. The
historic land of Greece had long been in the hands of a despotism with which even the Holy Alliance was not in sympathy—that of Turkey. Its very name, as a modern country, had almost vanished, and Europe heard with astonishment in 1821 that the descendants of
the ancient Greeks had risen against the tyranny under which they had been
crushed for centuries.

The struggle was a bitter one. The sultan was atrocious in his cruelties. In the island of Chios alone he brutally murdered 20,000 Greeks. But
the spirit of the old Athenians and Spartans was in the people, and they
kept on fighting in the face of defeat. For four years this went on, while
the powers of Europe looked on without raising a hand. Some of their
people indeed took part, among them Lord Byron, who died in Greece in
1824 ; but the governments failed to warm up to their duty.

Their apathy vanished in 1825, when the sultan, growing weary of the struggle, and bent on bringing it to a rapid end, called in the aid of his powerful vassal, Mehemed Ali, Pasha of Egypt. Mehemed responded by sending a strong army under his son Ibrahim, who landed in the Morea (the ancient Peloponnesus), where he treated the people with shocking cruelty.

A year of this was as much as Christian Europe could stand. England first aroused herself. Canning, the English prime minister, persuaded Nicholas, who had just succeeded Alexander as Czar of Russia, to join with him in stopping this horrible business. France also lent her aid, and the combined powers **The Powers Come to the Rescue of Greece** warned Ibrahim to cease his cruel work. On his refusal, the fleets of England and France attacked and annihilated the Turkish-Egyptian fleet in the battle of Navarino.

The Sultan still hesitated, and the czar, impatient at the delay, declared war and invaded with his army the Turkish provinces on the Danube. The next year, 1829, the Russians crossed the Balkans and descended upon Constantinople. That city was in such imminent danger of capture that the obstinacy of the sultan completely disappeared and he humbly consented to all the demands of the powers. Servia, Moldavia and Wallachia, the chief provinces of the Balkan peninsula, were put under the rule of Christian governors, and the independence of Greece was fully acknowledged. Prince Otto of Bavaria was made king, and ruled until 1862. In Greece liberalism had conquered, but elsewhere in Europe the reaction established by the Congress of Vienna still held sway.

The people merely bided their time. The good seed sown could not fail to bear fruit in its season. The spirit of revolution was in the air, and any attempt to rob the people of the degree of liberty which they enjoyed was very likely to precipitate a revolt against **The Spirit of Revolution** the tyranny of courts and kings. It came at length in France, that country the ripest among the nations for revolution. Louis XVIII. an easy, good-natured old soul, of kindly disposition towards the people, passed from life in 1824, and was succeeded by his brother, Count of Artois, as Charles X.

The new king had been the head of the ultra-royalist faction, an advocate of despotism and feudalism, and quickly doubled the hate which the people bore him. Louis XVIII. had been liberal in his policy, and had given increased privileges to the people. **Charles X. and His Attempt at Despotism** Under Charles reaction set in. A vast sum of money was voted to the nobles to repay their losses during the Revolution. Steps were taken to muzzle the press and gag the universities. This was more than the Chamber of Deputies was willing to do, and it was dissolved. But the tyrant at the head of the government went on, blind to the signs in the air, deaf to the people's voice. If he could not get laws from the Chamber, he would make them himself in the old arbitary fashion, and on July 26, 1830, he issued, under the advice of his prime minister, four decrees, which limited the list of voters and put an end to the freedom of the press. Practically the constitution was set aside, the work of the Revolution ignored, and absolutism re-established in France.

King Charles had taken a step too far. He did not know the spirit of the French. In a moment Paris blazed into insurrection. Tumult arose on every side. Workmen and students paraded the streets with enthusiastic cheers for the constitution. But under their voices there were soon heard deeper and more ominous cries. "Down with the ministers!" came the demand. And then, as the throng increased and grew more violent, arose the revolutionary slogan, "Down with the Bourbons!" The infatu-

The Revolution in Paris ated old king was amusing himself in his palace of St. Cloud, and did not discover that the crown was tottering upon his head. He knew that the people of Paris had risen, but looked upon it as a passing ebullition of French temper. He did not awake to the true significance of the movement until he heard that there had been fighting between his troops and the people, that many of the citizens lay dead in the streets, and that the soldiers had been driven from the city which remained in the hands of the insurrectionists.

Then the old imbecile, who had fondly fancied that the Revolution of 1789 could be set aside by a stroke of his pen, made frantic efforts to lay the demon he had called into life. He hastily cancelled the tyrannical decrees. Finding that this would not have the desired effect, he abdicated the throne in favor of his grandson. But all was of no avail. France had had enough of him and his house. His envoys were turned back from the gates of Paris unheard. Remembering the fate of Louis XVI., his unhappy brother, Charles X., turned his back upon France and hastened to seek a refuge in England.

Meanwhile a meeting of prominent citizens had been held in Paris, the result of their deliberations being that Charles X. and his heirs should be deposed and the crown offered to Louis Philippe, duke of Orleans. There

Louis Philippe Chosen as King had been a Louis Philippe in the Revolution of 1789, a radical member of the royal house of Bourbon, who, under the title of Egalité, had joined the revolutionists, voted for the death of Louis XVI., and in the end had his own head cut off by the guillotine. His son as a young man had served in the revolutionary army and had been one of its leaders in the important victory of Jemappes. But when the terror came he hastened from France, which had become a very unsafe place for one of his blood. He had the reputation of being liberal in his views, and was the first man thought of for the vacant crown. When the Chamber of Deputies met in August and offered it to him, he did not hesitate to accept. He swore to observe and reign under the constitution, and took the throne under the title of Louis Philippe, king of the French. Thus speedily and happily ended the second Revolution in France.

But Paris again proved itself the political centre of Europe. The deposition of Charles X. was like a stone thrown into the seething waters of European politics, and its effects spread far and wide be- **Effect in Europe** yond the borders of France. The nations had been bound **of the Revo-** hand and foot by the Congress of Vienna. The people had **lution** writhed uneasily in their fetters, but now in more than one locality they rose in their might to break them, here demanding a greater degree of liberty, there overthrowing the government.

The latter was the case in Belgium. Its people had suffered severely from the work of the Congress of Vienna. Without even a pretence of consulting their wishes, their country had been incorporated with Holland as the kingdom of the Netherlands, the two countries being fused into one under a king of the old Dutch House of Orange. The idea was good enough in itself. It was intended to make a kingdom strong enough to help keep France in order. But an attempt to fuse these two states was like an endeavor to mix oil and water. The people of the two countries had long since drifted apart from each other, and had irreconcilable ideas and interests. Holland was a colonizing and commercial country, Belgium an industrial country ; Holland was Protestant, Belgium was Catholic ; Holland was Teutonic in blood, Belgium was a mixture of the Teutonic and French, but wholly French in feeling and customs.

The Belgians, therefore, were generally discontented with the act of fusion, and in 1830 they imitated the French by a revolt against **The Belgian** King William of Holland. A tumult followed in Brussels, **Uprising and** which ended in the Dutch soldiers being driven from the city. **Its Result** King William, finding that the Belgians insisted on independence, decided to bring them back to their allegiance by force of arms. The powers of Europe now took the matter in hand, and, after some difference of opinion, decided to grant the Belgians the independence they demanded. This was a meddling with his royal authority to which King William did not propose to submit, but when the navy of Great Britain and the army of France approached his borders he changed his mind, and since 1833 Holland and Belgium have gone their own way under separate kings. A limited monarchy, with a suitable constitution, was organized for Belgium by the powers, and Prince Leopold, of the German house of Saxe-Coburg, was placed upon the throne.

The Movements in Germany and Italy   The spirit of revolution extended into Germany and Italy, but only with partial results. Neither in Austria nor Prussia did the people stir, but in many of the smaller states a demand was made for a constitution on liberal lines, and in every instance the princes had to give way. Each of these states gained a representative form of government, the monarchs of Prussia and Austria alone retaining their old despotic power.

In Italy there were many signs of revolutionary feeling; but Austria still dominated that peninsula, and Metternich kept a close watch upon the movements of its people. There was much agitation. The great secret society of the Carbonari sought to combine the patriots of all Italy in a grand stroke for liberty and union, but nothing came of their efforts. In the States of the Church alone the people rose in revolt against their rulers, but they were soon put down by the Austrians, who invaded their territory, dispersed their weak bands, and restored the old tyranny. The hatred of the Italians for the Austrians grew more intense, but their time had not yet come; they sank back in submission and awaited a leader and an opportunity.

There was one country in which the revolution in France called forth a more active response, though, unhappily, only to double the weight of the chains under which its people groaned. This was unfortunate **The Condition of Poland**   Poland; once a great and proud kingdom, now dismembered and swallowed up by the land-greed of its powerful neighbors. It had been in part restored by Napoleon, in his kingdom of Warsaw, and his work had been in a measure recognized by the Congress of Vienna. The Czar Alexander, kindly in disposition and moved by pity for the unhappy Poles, had re-established their old kingdom, persuading Austria and Prussia to give up the bulk of their Polish territory in return for equal areas elsewhere. He gave Poland a constitution, its own army, and its own administration, making himself its king, but promising to rule as a constitutional monarch.

This did not satisfy the Poles. It was not the independence they craved. They could not forget that they had been a great power in Europe when Russia was still the weak and frozen duchy of Muscovy. **The Revolt of the Poles**   When the warm-hearted Alexander died and the cold-hearted Nicholas took his place, their discontent grew to dangerous proportions. The news of the outbreak in France was like a firebrand thrown in their midst. In November, 1830, a few young hot-heads sounded the note of revolt, and Warsaw rose in insurrection against the Russians.

For a time they were successful. Constantine, the czar's brother governor of Poland, was scared by the riot, and deserted the capital leaving the revolutionists in full control. Towards the frontier he hastened, winged by alarm, while the provinces rose in rebellion behind him as he passed Less than a week had passed before the Russian power was with-drawn from Poland, and its people were once more lords of their own land They set up a provisional government in Warsaw, and prepared to defend themselves against the armies that were sure to come.

What was needed now was unity. A single fixed and resolute purpose, under able and suitable leaders, formed the only conceivable condition of success. But Poland was, of all countries, the least capable **A Fatal Lack** of such unity. The landed nobility was full of its old feudal **of Unity** notions; the democracy of the city was inspired by modern sentiments. They could not agree ; they quarreled in castle and court, while their hasty levies of troops were marching to meet the Russians in the field. Under such conditions success was a thing beyond hope.

Yet the Poles fought well. Kosciusko, their former hero, would have been proud of their courage and willingness to die for their country. But against the powerful and ably led Russian armies their gallantry was of no avail, and their lack of unity fatal. In May, 1831, they were overwhelmed at Ostrolenka by the Russian hosts. In September a traitor betrayed Warsaw, and the Russian army entered its gates The revolt was at an end, and Poland again in fetters.

Nicholas the Czar fancied that he had spoiled these people by kindness and clemency. They should not be spoiled in that way any longer. Under his harsh decrees the Kingdom of Poland vanished. He **The Fate of** ordered that it should be made a Russian province, and held **Poland** by a Russian army of occupation The very language of the Poles was forbidden to be spoken, and their religion was to be replaced by the Orthodox Russian faith. Those brief months of revolution and inde-pendence were fatal to the liberty-loving people. Since then, except during their brief revolt in 1863, they have lain in fetters at the feet of Russia, nothing remaining to them but their patriotic memories and their undying aspiration for freedom and independence.

CHAPTER VII.

Bolivar, the Liberator of Spanish America.

IN the preceding chapter mention was made of two regions in which the spirit of revolt triumphed during the period of reaction after the Napoleonic wars—Greece and Spanish America. The revolt in Greece was there described; that in Spanish America awaits description. It had its hero, one of the great soldiers of the Spanish race, perhaps the greatest and ablest of guerilla leaders; "Bolivar the Liberator," as he was known on his native soil.

Spain had long treated her colonists in a manner that was difficult for a high-spirited people to endure. Only two thoughts seemed to rule in their management, the one being to derive from the colonies all possible profit for the government at home, the other to make use of them as a means by which the leaders in Spain could pay their political debts. The former purpose was sought to be carried out by severe taxation, commercial restriction, and the other methods in which a short-sighted country seeks to enrich itself by tying the hands and checking the industries of its colonists. To achieve the latter purpose all important official positions in the colonies were held by natives of Spain. Posts in the government, in the customs, in all salaried offices were given to strangers, who knew nothing of the work they were to do or the conditions of the country to which they were sent, and whose single thought was to fill their purses as speedily as possible and return to enjoy their wealth in Spain.

How Spain Treated Her Colonies

All this was galling to the colonists, who claimed to be loyal Spaniards, and they rebelled in spirit against this swarm of human locusts which descended annually upon them, practicing every species of extortion and fraud in their eagerness to grow rich speedily and carrying much of the wealth of the country back to the mother land. Add to this the severe restrictions on industry and commerce, the prohibition of trade except with Spain, the exactions of every kind, legal and illegal, to which the people were forced to submit, and their deep-seated dissatisfaction is easy to understand

The Oppression of the People

FROUDE.

CARLYLE.

RUSKIN.

GIBBON.

MACAULAY.

GREAT
ENGLISH
HISTORIANS
· AND ·
PROSE WRITERS

LEO XIII.

PIUS IX.

FAMOUS POPES OF THE CENTURY

The war for independence in the United States had no apparent influence upon the colonies of Spanish America. They remained loyal to Spain. The French Revolution seemed also without effect. But during the long Napoleonic wars, when Spain remained for years in the grip of the Corsican, and the people of Spanish America were left largely to govern themselves, a thirst for liberty arose, and a spirit of revolt showed itself about 1810 throughout the length and breadth of the colonies.

Chief among the revolutionists was Simon Bolivar, a native of Caracas, the capital of Venezuela. In 1810 we find him in London, **Bolivar, the** seeking the aid of the British government in favor of the **Revolutionary** rebels against Spain. In 1811 he served as governor of **Leader** Puerto Cabello, the strongest fortress in Venezuela. He was at that time subordinate to General Miranda, whom he afterwards accused of treason, and who died in a dungeon in Spain. In the year named Venezuela proclaimed its independence, but in 1813, Bolivar, who had been entitled its " Liberator," was a refugee in Jamaica, and his country again a vassal of Spain.

The leaders of affairs in Spain knew well where to seek the backbone of the insurrection. Bolivar was the one man whom they feared. He removed, there was not a man in sight capable of leading the rebels to victory. To dispose of him, a spy was sent to Jamaica, his purpose being to take the Liberator's life. This man, after **An Attempt at** gaining a knowledge of Bolivar's habits and movements, **Assassination** bribed a negro to murder him, and in the dead of night the assassin stole up to Bolivar's hammock and plunged his knife into the sleeper's breast. As it proved, it was not Bolivar, but his secretary, who lay there, and the hope of the American insurrectionists escaped.

Leaving Jamaica, Bolivar proceeded to San Domingo, where he found a warm supporter in the president, Petion. Here, too, he met Luis Brion, a Dutch shipbuilder of great wealth. His zeal for the principles of liberty infused Brion with a like zeal. The result was that Brion fitted out seven schooners and placed them at Bolivar's disposal, supplied 3,500 muskets to arm recruits who should join Bolivar's standard, and devoted his own life and services to the sacred cause. Thus slenderly equipped, Bolivar commenced operations in 1816 at the port of Cayos de San Luis, where the leading refugees from Cartagena, New Granada, and Venezuela **Bolivar Re-** had sought sanctuary. By them he was accepted as leader, **turns to** and Brion, with the title of " Admiral of Venezuela," was given **Venezuela** command of the squadron he had himself furnished. The growing expedition now made for the island of Margarita, which Arismendi had wrested from the Spanish governor; and here, at a convention of officers, Bolivar was named "Supreme Chief," and the third Venezuelan war began. It was marked by many a disaster to the patriot arms, and so numerous vicissitudes that, until the culminating triumph of Boyaca on August 7th, 1819, it remained doubtful upon which side victory would ultimately rest.

The war was conducted on the part of the Spaniards with the most fiendish cruelty, prisoners taken in war and the unarmed people of the country alike being tortured and murdered under circumstances of revolting barbarity. "The people of Margarita," writes an English officer who served in Venezuela, "saw their liberties threatened and endangered; their

The Savage Cruelty of the Spaniards wives, children, and kindred daily butchered and murdered; and the reeking members of beings most dear to them exposed to their gaze on every tree and crag of their native forests and mountains; nor was it until hundreds had been thus slaughtered that they pursued the same course. The result was that the Spaniards were routed. I myself saw upwards of seven thousand of their skulls, dried and heaped together in one place, which is not inaptly termed 'Golgotha,' as a trophy of victory."

Another writer tells us: "I saw several women whose ears and noses had been cut off, their eyes torn from their sockets, their tongues cut out, and the soles of their feet pared by the orders of Monteverde, a Spanish brigadier-general." The result of these excesses of cruelty was an implacable hatred of the Spaniard, and a determination to carry on the war unto death.

In 1815 Ferdinand of Spain determined to put an end once for all to the movement for independence that, in varying forms, had been agitating for five years the whole of Spanish America. Accordingly, strong reinforcements to the royalist armies were sent out, under General Morillo. These arrived at Puerto Cabello, and, besides ships of war, comprised 12,000 troops—a force in itself many times larger than all the scattered bands of patriots then under arms put together. Morillo soon had Venezuela under his thumb, and, planting garrisons throughout it, proceeded to lay siege to

The Methods of General Morillo Cartagena. Capturing this city in four months, he marched unopposed to Santa Fe de Bogota, the capital of New Granada, ruin and devastation marking his progress. In a despatch to Ferdinand, which was intercepted, he wrote: "Every person of either sex who was capable of reading and writing was put to death. By thus cutting off all who were in any way educated, I hoped to effectually arrest the spirit of revolution."

An insight into Morillo's methods of coping with the "spirit of revolution" is furnished by his treatment of those he found in the opulent city of Maturin on its capture. Dissatisfied with the treasure he found there, he suspected the people of wealth to have anticipated his arrival by burying their property. To find out the supposed buried treasure, he had all those whom he regarded as likely to know where it was hidden collected together and, to make them confess, had the soles of their feet cut off, and then had them driven over hot sand. Many of the victims of this horrid piece of cruelty survived, and were subsequently seen by those that have narrated it.

At the commencement of the war, with the exception of the little band on the island of Margarita, the patriotic cause was represented by a few scattered groups along the banks of the Orinoco, on the plains of Barcelona and of Casanare. These groups pursued a kind of guerilla warfare, quite independently of one another, and without any plan to achieve. They were kept together by the fact that submission meant death. The leader of one of these groups, Paez by name, presents one of the most pic- **Paez the Guer-**
turesque and striking characters that history has produced. **illa and His**
He was a Llanero, or native of the elevated plains of Barinas, **Exploits**
and quite illiterate. As owner of herds of half-wild cattle, he became chief of a band of herdsmen, which he organized into an army, known as the "Guides of the Apure," a tributary of the Orinoco, and whose banks were the base of Paez's operations. Only one of his many daring exploits can be here recorded. That occurred on the 3rd of June, 1819, when Paez was opposing the advance of Morillo himself. With 150 picked horsemen, he swam the river Orinoco and galloped towards the Spanish camp. "Eight hundred of the royalist cavalry," writes W. Pilling, General Mitre's trans- lator, "with two small guns, sallied out to meet him. He slowly retreated, drawing them on to a place called Las Queseras del Medio, where a bat- talion of infantry lay in ambush by the river. Then, splitting his men into groups of twenty, he charged the enemy on all sides, forcing them under the fire of the infantry, and recrossed the river with two killed and a few wounded, leaving the plain strewn with the dead of the enemy."

While Paez's dashing exploits were inspiring the revolutionary leaders with fresh courage, which enabled them at least to hold their own, a system of enlisting volunteers was instituted in London by Don Luis Lopes Mendez, representative of the republic. The Napoleonic wars being over, the European powers were unable to reduce their swollen armaments, and English and German officers entered into contracts with Mendez to take out to Venezuela organized corps of artillery, lancers, hussars, and rifles. On enlisting, soldiers received a bounty of £20; their pay was 2s. a day and rations, and at the end of the war they were promised £125 and an allot- ment of land. The first expedition to leave England comprised 120 hussars and lancers, under Colonel Hippisley; this body became the basis of a corps of regular cavalry.   The nucleus of a battalion of riflemen was taken out

British Soldiers Join the Insurgents
by Colonel Campbell ; and a subaltern, named Gilmour, with the title of colonel, formed with 90 men the basis of a brigade of artillery.   General English, who had served in the Peninsular War under Wellington, contracted with Mendez to take out a force of 1,200 Englishmen ; 500 more went out under Colonel Elsom, who also brought out 300 Germans under Colonel Uzlar.   General MacGregor took 800, and General Devereux took out the Irish Legion, in which was a son of the Irish tribune, Daniel O'Connell.   Smaller contingents also went to the seat of war ; these mentioned, however, were the chief, and without their aid Bolivar was wont to confess that he would have failed.

Now it was that a brilliant idea occurred to Bolivar.   He had already sent 1,200 muskets and a group of officers to General Santander, who was the leader of the patriots on the plains of Casanare.   This enabled Santander to increase his forces from amongst the scattered patriots in that neighborhood.   He thereupon began to threaten the frontier of New Granada, with the result that General Barreiro, who had been left in command of that province by Morillo, deemed it advisable to march against him and crush his growing power.   Santander's forces, however, though inferior in number, were too full of enthusiasm for Barreiro's soldiers—reduced to a half-hearted condition from being forced to take part in cruelties that they gained nothing from, except the odium of the people they moved amongst.

Bolivar's Plan to Invade New Granada
Barreiro, accordingly, was diiven back ; and, on receiving the news of Santander's success, Bolivar at once formed the conception of crossing the Andes and driving the Spaniards out of New Granada.   The event proved that this was the true plan of campaign for the patriots.   Already they had lost three campaigns through endeavoring to dislodge the Spaniards from their strongest positions, which were in Venezuela ; now, by gaining New Granada, they would win prestige and consolidate their power there for whatever further efforts circumstances might demand.

Thus, as it has been described, did the veil drop from Bolivar's eyes ; and so confident was he of ultimate success, that he issued to the people of New Granada this proclamation : " The day of America has come ; no human power can stay the course of Nature guided by Providence.   Before the sun has again run his annual course, altars to Liberty will arise throughout your land."

Bolivar immediately prepared to carry out his idea, and on the 11th of June, 1819, he joined Santander at the foot of the Andes, bringing with him four battalions of infantry, of which one—the "Albion"—was composed entirely of English soldiers—two squadrons of lancers, one of carabineers, and a regiment called the "Guides of the Apure," part of which were English—in all 2,500 men. To join Santander was no easy task, for it involved the crossing of an immense plain covered with water at this season of the year, and the swimming of seven deep rivers—war materials, of course, having to be taken along as well. This, however, was only a foretaste of the still greater difficulties that lay before the venturesome band.

General Santander led the van with his Casanare troops, and entered the mountain defiles by a road leading to the centre of the province of Tunja, which was held by Colonel Barreiro with 2,000 infantry **The Crossing** and 400 horse. The royalists had also a reserve of 1,000 **of the Andes** troops at Bogota, the capital of New Granada; at Cartagena, and in the valley of Cauca were other detachments, and there was another royalist army at Quito. Bolivar, however, trusted to surprise and to the support of the inhabitants to overcome the odds that were against him. As the invading army left the plains for the mountains the scene changed. The snowy peaks of the eastern range of the Cordillera appeared in the distance, while, instead of the peaceful lake through which they had waded, they were met by great masses of water tumbling from the heights. The roads ran along the edge of precipices and were bordered by gigantic trees, upon whose tops rested the clouds, which dissolved themselves in incessant rain. After four days' march the horses were foundered; an entire squadron of Llaneros deserted on finding themselves on foot. The torrents were crossed on narrow trembling bridges formed of trunks of trees, or by means of the aerial "taravitas."* Where they were fordable, the current was so strong that the infantry had to pass two by two with their arms thrown round each other's shoulders; and woe to him who lost his footing—he lost his life too. Bolivar frequently passed and re-passed these torrents on horseback, carrying behind him the sick and weakly, or the women who accompanied his men.

The temperature was moist and warm; life was supportable with the aid of a little firewood; but as they ascended the mountain the scene changed again. Immense rocks piled one upon another, and hills of snow, bounded the view on every side; below lay the clouds, veiling the depths of the abyss; an ice-cold wind cut through the stoutest clothing. At these heights no other noise is heard save that of the roaring torrents left behind, and the

---

* Bridges made of several thongs of hide twisted into a stout rope well greased and secured to trees on opposite banks. On the rope is suspended a cradle or hammock to hold two, and drawn backwards and forwards by long lines. Horses and mules were also thus conveyed, suspended by long girths round their bodies.

scream of the condor circling round the snowy peaks above. Vegetation disappears ; only lichens are to be seen clinging to the rock, and a tall plant, bearing plumes instead of leaves, and crowned with yellow flowers, resembling a funeral torch. To make the scene more dreary yet, the path was marked out by crosses erected in memory of travellers who had perished by the way.

On entering this glacial region the provisions gave out ; the cattle they had brought with them as their chief resource could go no farther. They reached the summit by the Paya pass, where a battalion could hold an army in check. It was held by an outpost of 300 men, who were dislodged by the vanguard under Santander without much difficulty.

The Terror of the Mountains Now the men began to murmur, and Bolivar called a council of war, to which he showed that still greater difficulties lay before them, and asked if they would persevere or return. All were of opinion that they should go on, a decision which infused fresh spirit into the weary troops.

In this passage more than one hundred men died of cold, fifty of whom were Englishmen ; no horse had survived. It was necessary to leave the spare arms, and even some of those that were carried by the soldiers. It was a mere skeleton of an army which reached the beautiful valley of Sagamoso, in the heart of the province of Tunja, on the 6th of July, 1819 From this point Bolivar sent back assistance to the stragglers left behind, collected horses, and detached parties to scour the country around and communicate with some few guerillas who still roamed about.

Meanwhile, Barreiro was still in ignorance of Bolivar's arrival. Indeed, he had supposed the passage of the Cordillera at that season impossible. As soon, however, as he did learn of his enemy's proximity, he collected his forces and took possession of the heights above the plains of Vargas, thus interposing between the patriots and the town of Tunja, which, being attached to the independent cause, Bolivar was anxious to enter. The opposing armies met on the 25th of July, and engaged in battle for five hours. The patriots won, chiefly through the English infantry, led by Colonel James Rooke, who was himself wounded and had an arm shot off. Still, the action had been indecisive, and the royalist power remained unbroken.

Bolivar's Methods of Fighting Bolivar now deceived Barreiro by retreating in the daytime, rapidly counter-marching, and passing the royalist army in the dark through by-roads. On August 5th he captured Tunja, where he found an abundance of war material, and by holding which he cut Barreiro's communication with Bogota, the capital. It was in rapid movements like these that the strength of Bolivar's generalship lay. Freed from the shackles of military routine that enslaved the Spanish officers, he astonished them by forced marches over roads previously deemed impracticable to a regular army. While they were manœuvring, hesitating, calculating, guarding the customary avenues of approach, he surprised them by concentrating a superior force upon a point where they least expected an attack, threw them into confusion, and cut up their troops in detail. Thus it happens that Bolivar's actions in the field do not lend themselves to the same impressive exposition as do those of less notable generals.

Barreiro, finding himself shut out from Tunja, fell back upon Venta Quemada, where a general action took place. The country was mountainous and woody, and well suited to Bolivar's characteristic tactics. He placed a large part of his troops in ambush, got his cavalry in the enemy's rear, and presented only a small front. This the enemy attacked furiously, and with apparent success. It was only a stratagem, however, for as they drove back Bolivar's front, the troops in ambush sallied forth and attacked them in the flanks, while the cavalry attacked them in the rear. Thus were the Spaniards surrounded. General Barreiro was taken prisoner on the field of battle. On finding his capture to be inevitable, he threw away his sword that he might not have the mortification of surrendering it to Bolivar. His second in command, Colonel Ximenes, was also taken, as were also almost all the commandants and majors of the corps, a multitude of inferior officers, and more than 1,600 men. All their arms, ammunition, artillery, horses, etc., likewise fell into the patriots' hands. Hardly fifty men escaped, and among these were some chiefs and officers of cavalry, who fled before **The Victory of Boyaca** the battle was decided. Those who escaped, however, had only the surrounding country to escape into, and there they were captured by the peasantry, who bound them and brought them in as prisoners. The patriot loss was incredibly small—only 13 killed and 53 wounded.

At Boyaca the English auxiliaries were seen for the first time under fire, and so gratified was Bolivar with their behavior, that he made them all members of the Order of the Liberator.

Thus was won Boyaca, which, after Maypu, is the great battle of South America. It gave the preponderance to the patriot arms in the north of the continent, as Maypu had done in the south. It gave New Granada to the patriots, and isolated Morillo in Venezuela.

Nothing now remained for Bolivar to do but to reach Bogota, the capital, and assume the reins of government, for already the Spanish officials, much to the relief of the inhabitants, had fled. So, with a small escort, he rode forward, and entered the city on August 10th, amid the acclamations of the populace.

The final battle in this implacable war took place in 1821 at Carabobo, where the Spaniards met with a total defeat, losing more than 6,000 men. This closed the struggle, the Spaniards withdrew, and a republic was organized with Bolivar as president. In 1823 he aided the Peruvians in gaining their independence, and was declared their liberator and given supreme authority. For two years he ruled as dictator, and then resigned, giving the country a republican constitution. The people of the upper section of Peru organized a commonwealth of their own, which they named Bolivia, in honor of their liberator, while the congress of Lima elected him president for life.

Meanwhile Chili had won its liberty in 1817 as a result of the victory of Maypu, above mentioned, and Buenos Ayres had similarly fought for and gained independence. In North America a similar struggle for liberty had gone on, and with like result, Central America and Mexico winning their freedom after years of struggle and scenes of devastation and cruelty such as those above mentioned. At the opening of the nineteenth century Spain held a dominion of continental dimensions in America. At the close of the first quarter of the century, as a result of her mediæval methods of administration, she had lost all her possessions on the western continent except the two islands of Cuba and Porto Rico. Yet, learning nothing from her losses, she pursued the same methods in these fragments of her dominions, and before the close of the century these also were torn from her hands. Cruelty and oppression had borne their legitimate fruits, and Spain, solely through her own fault, had lost the final relics of her magnificent colonial empire.

WILLIAM EWART GLADSTONE

JOHN BRIGHT

BENJAMIN DISRAELI

WILLIAM PITT

GREAT ENGLISH STATESMEN

ALBERT EDWARD, PRINCE OF WALES.

QUEEN VICTORIA.

BRITAIN'S SOVEREIGN AND HEIR APPARENT TO THE THRONE.

CHAPTER VIII.

Great Britain as a World Empire.

ON the western edge of the continent of Europe lies the island of Great Britain, in the remote past a part of the continent, but long ages ago cut off by the British Channel. Divorced from the mainland, left like a waif in the western sea, peopled by men with their own interests and aims, it might naturally be expected to have enough to attend to at home and to take no part in continental affairs.

Such was the case originally. The island lay apart, almost unknown, and was, in a sense, "discovered" by the Roman conquerors. But new people came to it, the Anglo-Saxons, and subsequently the Normans, both of them scions of that stirring race of Vikings who made the seas their own centuries ago and descended in conquering inroads on all the shores of Europe, while their **The Adventurous Disposition of the British People** darings keels cut the waters of far-off Greenland and touched upon the American coast. This people—stirring, aggressive, fearless—made a new destiny for Great Britain. Their island shores were too narrow to hold them, and they set out on bold ventures in all seas. Their situation was a happy one for a nation of daring navigators and aggressive warriors. Europe lay to the east, the world to the west. As a result the British islands have played a leading part alike in the affairs of Europe and of the world.

France, the next door neighbor of Great Britain, was long its prey. While, after the memorable invasion of William of Normandy, France never succeeded in transporting an army to the island shores, and even Napoleon failed utterly in his stupendous expedition, **Hostility of England to France** the islanders sent army after army to France, defeated its chivalry on many a hard-fought field, ravaged its most fertile domains, and for a time held it as a vassal realm of the British King.

All this is matter of far-past history. But the old feeling was prominently shown again in the Napoleonic wars, when Great Britain resumed her attitude of enmity to France, and pursued the conqueror with an unrelenting hostility that finally ended in his overthrow. Only for this aggressive island Europe might have remained the bound slave of Napoleon's whims.   He could conquer his enemies on land, but the people of England lay beyond his reach.   Every fleet he sent to sea was annihilated by his island foes.   They held the empire of the waters as he did that of the land.   Enraged against these ocean hornets, he sought to repeat the enterprise of William of Normany, but if his mighty Boulogne expedition had put to sea it would probably have met the fate of the Armada of Spain. Great Britain was impregnable.   The conqueror of Europe chafed against its assaults in vain.   This little island of the west was destined to be the main agent in overthrowing the great empire that his military genius had built.

The Vast Industries of Great Britain   Great Britain, small as it was, had grown, by the opening of the nineteenth century, to be the leading power in Europe.   Its industries, its commerce, its enterprise had expanded enormously.   It had become the great workshop and the chief distributor of the world.   The raw material of the nations flowed through its ports, the finished products of mankind poured from its looms, London became the great money centre of the world, and the industrious and enterprising islanders grew enormously rich, while few steps of progress and enterprise showed themselves in any of the nations of the continent.

It was with its money-bags that England fought against the conqueror. It could not conveniently send men, but it could send money and supplies to the warring nations, and by its influence and aid it formed coalition after coalition against Napoleon, each harder to overthrow than the last.   Every peace that the Corsican won by his victories was overthrown by England's influence.   Her envoys haunted every court, whispering hostility in the

How England Fought Against Napoleon   ears of monarchs, planning, intriguing, instigating, threatening, in a thousand ways working against his plans, and unrelentingly bent upon his overthrow.   It was fitting, then, that an English general should give Napoleon the *coup de grace*, and that he should die a prisoner in English hands.

Chief among those to whom Napoleon owes his overthrow was William Pitt, prime minister of England during the first period of his career of conquest, and his unrelenting enemy.   It was Pitt that organized Europe against him, that kept the British fleet alert and expended the British revenues without stint against this disturber of the peace of the nations, and that formed the policy which Great Britain, after the short interval of the ministry of Fox, continued to pursue until his final defeat was achieved.

Whether this policy was a wise one is open to question.   It may be that Great Britain caused more harm than it cured.   Only for its persistant hostility the rapid succession of Napoleonic wars might not have taken place, and much of the terrible bloodshed and misery caused by them might have been obviated. It seems to have been, in its way, disastrous to the interests of mankind. Napoleon, it is true, had no regard for the stability of dynasties and kingdoms, but he wrought for the overthrow of the old-time tyranny, and his marches and campaigns had the effect of stirring up the dormant peoples of Europe, and spreading far and wide that doctrine of human equality and the rights of man which was the outcome of the French Revolution. Had he been permitted to die in peace upon the throne and transmit his crown to his descendant, the long era of reaction would doubtless have been avoided and the people of Europe have become the freer and happier as a result of Napoleon's work.

Was England's Policy a Wise One

The people of Great Britain had no reason to thank their ministers for their policy. The cost of the war, fought largely with the purse, had been enormous, and the public debt of the kingdom was so greatly increased that its annual interest amounted to $150,000,000. But the country emerged from the mighty struggle with a vast growth in power and prestige. It was recognized as the true leader in the great contest and had lifted itself to the foremost position in European politics. On land it had waged the only successful campaign against Napoleon previous to that of the disastrous Russian expedition. At sea it had destroyed all opposing fleets, and reigned the unquestioned mistress of the ocean except in American waters, where alone its proud ships had met defeat.

The Prestige Gained by Great Britain

The islands of Great Britain and Ireland had ceased to represent the dominions under the rule of the British king. In the West Indies new islands had been added to his colonial possessions. In the East Indies he had become master of an imperial domain far surpassing the mother country in size and population, and with untold possibilities of wealth. In North America the great colony of Canada was growing in population and prosperity. Island after island was being added to his possessions in the Eastern seas. Among these was the continental island of Australia, then in its early stage of colonization. The possession of Gibraltar and Malta, the protectorate over the Ionian Islands, and the right of free navigation on the Dardanells gave Great Britain the controlling power in the Mediterranean. And Cape Colony, which she received as a result of the Treaty of Vienna, was the entering wedge for a great dominion in South Africa.

Great Extension of England's Colonies

Thus Great Britain had attained the position and dimensions of a world-empire.   Her colonies lay in all continents and spread through all

seas, and they were to grow during the century until they enormously excelled the home country in dimensions, popu-lation, and natural wealth.   The British Islands were merely the heart, the vital centre of the great system, while the body and limbs lay afar, in Canada, India, South Africa, Australia and elsewhere.

But the world-empire of Great Britain was not alone one of peaceful trade and rapid accumulation of wealth, but of wars spread through all the continents, war becoming a permanent feature of its history in the nine-teenth century.   After the Napoleonic period England waged only one war in Europe, the Crimean ; but elsewhere her troops were almost con-stantly engaged.   Now they were fighting with the Boers and the Zulus of South Africa, now with the Arabs on the Nile, now with the wild tribes of the Himalayas, now with the natives of New Zealand, now with the half savage Abyssinians.   Hardly a year has passed without a fight of some sort, far from the centre of this vast dominion, while for years England and Russia have stood face to face on the northern borders of India, threatening at any moment to become involved in a terrible struggle for dominion.

And the standing of Great Britain as a world power lay not alone in her vast colonial dominion and her earth-wide wars, but also in the extra-ordinary enterprise that carried her ships to all seas, and made her the commercial emporium of the world.   Not only to her own colonies, but to all lands, sailed her enormous fleet of merchantmen, gathering the products of the earth, to be consumed at home or distributed again to the nations of Europe and America.   She had assumed the position of the purveyor and carrier for mankind.

This was not all.   Great Britain was in a large measure, the producer for mankind.   Manufacturing enterprise and industry had grown im-mensely on her soil, and countless factories, forges and other workshops turned out finished goods with a speed and profusion undreamed of before. The preceding century had been one of active invention, its vital product being the steam engine, that wonder-worker which at a touch was to over-turn the old individual labor system of the world, and replace it with the congregate, factory system that has revolutionized the industries of man-kind.   The steam engine stimulated invention extraordinarily.   Machines for

spinning, weaving, iron-making, and a thousand other pur-poses came rapidly into use, and by their aid one of the greatest steps of progress in the history of mankind took place, the grand nineteenth century revolution in methods of production

Great Britain did not content herself with going abroad for the materials of her active industries. She dug her way into the bowels of the earth, tore from the rock its treasures of coal and iron, and thus obtained the necessary fuel for her furnaces and metal for her machines. The whole island resounded with the ringing of hammers and rattle of wheels, goods were produced very far beyond the capacity of the island for their consumption, and the vast surplus was sent abroad to all quarters of the earth, to clothe savages in far-off regions and to furnish articles of use and luxury to the most enlightened of the nations. To the ship as a carrier was soon added the locomotive and its cars, conveying these products inland with unprecedented speed from a thousand ports. And **Commercial Enterprise** from America came the parallel discovery of the steamship, signalling the close of the long centuries of dominion of the sail. Years went on and still the power and prestige of Great Britain grew, still its industry and commerce spread and expanded, still its colonies increased in population and new lands were added to the sum, until the island-empire stood foremost in industry and enterprise among the nations of the world, and its people reached the summit of their prosperity. From this lofty elevation was to come, in the later years of the century, a slow but inevitable decline, as the United States and the leading European nations developed in industry, and rivals to the productive and commercial supremacy of the British islanders began to arise in various quarters of the earth.

It cannot be said that the industrial prosperity of Great Britain, while of advantage to her people as a whole, was necessarily so to individuals. While one portion of the nation amassed enormous wealth, the bulk of the people sank into the deepest poverty. The factory system brought with it oppression and misery which it would need a century of industrial revolt to overcome. The costly wars, the crushing taxation, the oppressive corn-laws, which forbade the importation of foreign corn, the extravagant expenses of the court and salaries of officials, all conspired to depress the people. Manufactures fell into the hands of the few, and a vast number of artisans were **Disastrous Effect on the People of the New Conditions** forced to live from hand to mouth, and to labor for long hours on pinching wages. Estates were similarly accumulated in the hands of the few, and the small land-owner and trader tended to disappear. Everything was taxed to the utmost it would bear, while government remained blind to the needs and sufferings of the people and made no effort to decrease the prevailing misery.

Thus it came about that the era of Great Britain's greatest prosperity and supremacy as a world-power was the one of greatest industrial oppression and misery at home, a period marked by rebellious uprisings among the people, to be repressed with cruel and bloody severity. It was a period of industrial transition, in which the government flourished and the people suffered, and in which the seeds of revolt and revolution were widely spread on every hand.

This state of affairs cannot be said to have ended. In truth the present condition of affairs is one that tends to its aggravation. Neither the manufacturing nor commercial supremacy of Great Britain are what they once were. In Europe, Germany has come into the field as a formidable competitor, and is gaining a good development in manufacturing industry. The same must be said of the United States, the products of whose workshops have increased to an enormous extent, and whose commerce has grown to surpass that of any other nation on the earth. The laboring population of Great Britian has severely felt the effects of this active rivalry, and is but slowly adapting itself to the new conditions which it has brought about, the slow but sure revolution in the status of the world's industries.

CHAPTER IX

The Great Reform Bill and the Corn Laws.

AT the close of the last chapter we depicted the miseries of the people of Great Britain, due to the revolution in the system of industry, the vast expenses of the Napoleonic wars, the extravagance of the government, and the blindness of Parliament to the condition of the working classes. The situation had grown intolerable; it was widely felt that something must be done; if affairs were allowed to go on as they were the people might rise in a revolt that would widen into revolution. A general outbreak seemed at hand. To use the language of **A Period of Riot and Tumult** the times, the "Red Cock" was crowing in the rural districts. That is, incendiary fires were being kindled in a hundred places. In the centres of manufacture similar signs of discontent appeared. Tumultuous meetings were held, riots broke out, bloody collisions with the troops took place. Daily and hourly the situation was growing more critical. The people were in that state of exasperation that is the preliminary stage of insurrection.

Two things they strongly demanded, reform in Parliament and repeal of the Corn Laws. It is with these two questions, reform and repeal, that we propose to deal in this chapter.

The British Parliament, it is scarcely necessary to say, is composed of two bodies, the House of Lords and the House of Commons. The former represents the aristocratic element of the nation;—in short, it **The Parliament of Great Britain** represents simply its members, since they hold their seats as a privilege of their titles, and have only their own interests to consider, though the interests of their class go with their own. The latter are supposed to represent the people, but up to the time with which we are now concerned they had never fully done so, and they did so now less than ever, since the right to vote for them was reserved to a few thousands of the rich.

In the year 1830, indeed, the House of Commons had almost ceased to represent the people at all. Its seats were distributed in accordance with a system that had scarcely changed in the least for two hundred years.

The idea of distributing the members in accordance with the population was scarcely thought of, and a state of affairs had arisen which was as absurd as it was unjust.   For during these two hundred years great changes

Two Centuries of Change

had taken place in England.   What were mere villages or open plains had become flourishing commercial or manufacturing cities.   Manchester, Leeds, Sheffield, Liverpool, and other centres of industry had become seats of great and busy populations. On the other hand, flourishing towns had decayed, ancient boroughs had become practically extinct.   Thus there had been great changes in the distribution of population, but the distribution of seats in Parliament remained the same.

As a result of this state of affairs the great industrial towns, Manchester, Birmingham, Sheffield, Leeds, and others, with their hundreds of thousands of people, did not send a single member to Parliament, while places with only a handful of voters were duly represented, and even places with

Disfranchised Cities and Rotten Boroughs

no voters at all sent members to Parliament.   Land-holding lords nominated and elected those, generally selecting the younger sons of noble families, and thus a large number of the "representatives of the people" really represented no one but the gentry to whom they owed their places.   "Rotten" boroughs these were justly called, but they were retained by the stolid conservatism with which the genuine Briton clings to things and conditions of the past.

The peculiar state of affairs was picturesquely pointed out by Lord John Russell in a speech in 1831.   "A stranger," he said, "who was told that this country is unparalleled in wealth and industry, and more civilized and enlightened than any country was before it—that it is a country which prides itself upon its freedom, and which once in seven years elects representatives from its population to act as the guardians and preservers of that freedom—would be anxious and curious to see how that representation is formed, and how the people choose their representatives.

"Such a person would be very much astonished if he were taken to a ruined mound and told that that mound sent two representatives to Parlia-

The Case Presented by Lord John Russell

ment; if he were taken to a stone wall and told that these niches in it sent two representatives to Parliament; if he were taken to a park, where no houses were to be seen' and told that that park sent two representatives to Parliament.   But he would be still more astonished if he were to see large and opulent towns, full of enterprise and industry and intelligence, containing vast magazines of every species of manufacture, and were then told that these towns sent no representatives to Parliament.

RUDYARD KIPLING.   T. HALL CAINE.   A. CONAN DOYLE.

ROBERT LOUIS STEVENSON.   GEORGE DU MAURIER.   JAMES M. BARRIE.

WILLIAM BLACK.   WALTER BESANT.   GEORGE MACDONALD.

POPULAR WRITERS OF FICTION.

JUSTIN McCARTHY

JAMES BRYCE.

JOHN MORLEY

A J. BALFOUR

ENGLISH STATESMEN IN LITERATURE.

"Such a person would be still more astonished if he were taken to Liverpool, where there is a large constituency, and told, 'Here you will have a fine specimen of a popular election.' He would see bribery employed to the greatest extent and in the most unblushing manner; he would see every voter receiving a number of guineas in a bag as the price of his corruption; and after such a spectacle he would be, no doubt, much astonished that a nation whose representatives are thus chosen, could perform the functions of legislation at all, or enjoy respect in any degree."

Such was the state of affairs when there came to England the news of the quiet but effective French Revolution of 1830. Its effect in England was a stern demand for the reform of this mockery miscalled House of Commons, of this lie that claimed to represent the English people. We have not told the whole story of the transparent falsehood. Two years before no man could be a member of Parliament who did not belong to the Church of England. No Dissenter could hold any public office in the kingdom. The multitudes of Methodists, Presbyterians, Baptists, and other dissenting sects were excluded from any share in the government. The same was the case with the Catholics, few in England, but forming the bulk of the population of Ireland. This evil, so far as all but the Catholics were con-

Dissenters and Catholics Admitted to Parliament

cerned, was removed by Act of Parliament in 1828. The struggle for Catholic liberation was conducted in Ireland by Daniel O'Connell, the most eloquent and patriotic of its orators. He was sneered at by Lord Wellington, then prime minister of Great Britain. But when it was seen that all Ireland was backing her orator the Iron Duke gave way, and a Catholic Relief Bill was passed in 1829, giving Catholics the right to hold all but the highest offices of the realm. In 1830, instigated by the revolution in France, the great fight for the reform of Parliamentary representation began.

The question was not a new one. It had been raised by Cromwell, nearly two hundred years before. It had been brought forward a number of times during the eighteenth century. It was revived in 1809 and again in 1821, but public opinion did not come strongly to its support until 1830 George IV., its strong opponent, died in that year; William IV., a king more in its favor, came to the throne; the government of the bitterly conservative Duke of Wellington was defeated and Earl Grey, a Liberal minister, took his place; the time was evidently ripe for reform, and soon the great fight was on.

The people of England looked upon the reform of Parliament as a restoring to them of their lost liberties, and their feelings were deeply enlisted in the event. When, on the 1st of March, 1831, the bill was

brought into the House of Commons, the public interest was intense.   For
hours eager crowds waited in the streets, and when the doors of the
The Reform Bill   Parliament house were opened every inch of room in the
Introduced   galleries was quickly filled, while for hundreds of others no
room was to be had.

The debate opened with the speech by Lord John Russell from which
we have quoted.   In the bill offered by him he proposed to disfranchise
entirely sixty-two of the rotten boroughs, each of which had less than 2,000
inhabitants ; to reduce forty-seven others, with less than 4,000 inhabitants,
to one member each ; and to distribute the 168 members thus unseated
among the populous towns, districts, and counties which either had no
members at all, or a number out of all proportion to their population.
Also the suffrage was to be extended, the hours for voting shortened, and
other reforms adopted.

The bill was debated, pro and con, with all the eloquence then in Parliament.   Vigorously as it was presented, the opposing elements were too
strong, and its consideration ended in defeat by a majority of eight.   Par-
The Fate of   liament was immediately dissolved by the premier, and an
Reform in   appeal was made to the people.   The result showed the
Parliament   strength of the public sentiment, limited as the suffrage then
was.   The new Parliament contained a large majority of reformers, and
when the bill was again presented it was carried by a majority of 106.   On
the evening of its passage it was taken by Earl Grey into the House of
Lords, where it was eloquently presented by the prime minister and bitterly
attacked by Lord Brougham, who declared that it would utterly overwhelm the aristocratic part of the House.   His view was that of his
fellows, and the Reform Bill was thrown out by a majority·of forty-one.

Instantly, on the news of this action of the Lords, the whole country
blazed into a state of excitement and disorder only surpassed by that of
civil war.   The people were bitterly in earnest in their demand for reform,
England on the   their feelings being wrought up to an intense pitch of excite-
Verge of   ment.   Riots broke out in all sections of the country.
Revolution   London seethed with excitement.   The peers were mobbed
in the streets and hustled and assaulted wherever seen.   They made their
way to the House only through a throng howling for reform.   Those
known to have voted against the bill were in peril of their lives, some being
forced to fly over housetops to escape the fury of the people.   Angry
debates arose in the House of Lords in which even the Bishops took an
excited part.   The Commons was like a bear-pit, a mass of furiously

wrangling opponents. England was shaken to the centre by the defeat of the bill, and Parliament reflected the sentiment of the people.

On December 12th, Russell presented a third Reform Bill to the House, almost the same in its provisions as those which had been defeated. The debate now was brief, and the result certain. It was felt to be no longer safe to juggle with the people. On the 18th the bill was passed, with a greatly increased majority, now amounting to 162. To the Lords again it went, where the Tories, led by Lord Wellington, were in a decided majority against it. It had no chance of passage, unless the king would create enough new peers to outvote the opposition. This King William refused to do, and Earl Grey resigned the ministry, leaving the Tories to bear the brunt of the situation they had produced.

The result was one barely short of civil war. The people rose in fury determined upon reform or revolution. Organized unions sprang up in every town. Threats of marching an army upon London were made. Lord Wellington was mobbed in the streets and was in peril of his life. The maddened populace went so far as to curse and stone the king himself, one stone striking him in the forehead. The country was indeed on the verge of insurrection against the government, and unless quick action was taken it was impossible to foresee the result. *How the Reform Bill Was Passed*

William IV., perhaps with the recent experience of Charles X. of France before his eyes, gave way, and promised to create enough new peers to insure the passing of the bill. To escape this unwelcome necessity Wellington and others of the Tories agreed to stay away from Parliament. and the Lords, pocketing their dignity as best they could, passed the bill by a safe majority, and reform was attained. Similar bills were passed for Scotland and Ireland, and thus was achieved the greatest measure of reform in the history of the British Parliament. It was essentially a revolution, the first great step in the evolution of a truly representative assembly in Great Britain.

The second great step was taken in 1867, in response to a popular demonstration almost as great and threatening as that of 1830. The Tories themselves, under their leader Mr. Disraeli, were obliged to bring in this bill, which extended the suffrage to millions of the people, and made it almost universal among the commercial and industrial classes. Nearly twenty years later, in 1884, a new *The Extension of the Suffrage* crusade was made in favor of the extension of the suffrage to agricultural laborers, previously disfranchised. The accomplishment of this reform ended the great struggle, and for the first time in their history the people of Great Britain were adequately represented in their Parliament, which had ceased to be the instrument of a class and at last stood for the whole commonwealth.

The question of Parliamentary reform settled, a second great question, that of the Corn Laws, rose up prominently before the people. It was one that appealed more immediately to them than that of representation. The benefits to come from the latter were distant and problematical; those to come from a repeal of the Corn Laws were evident and immediate. Every poor man and woman felt each day of his life the crushing effect of these laws, which bore upon the food on their tables, making still more scarce and high-priced their scanty means of existence.

For centuries commerce in grain had been a subject of legislation. In 1361 its exportation from England was forbidden, and in 1463 its importation was prohibited unless the price of wheat was greater than 6s. 3d. per quarter. As time went on changes were made in these laws, but the tariff charges kept up the price of grain until late in the nineteenth century, and added greatly to the miseries of the working classes.

The Corn Laws

The farming land of England was not held by the common people, but by the aristocracy, who fought bitterly against the repeal of the Corn Laws, which, by laying a large duty on grain, added materially to their profits. But while the aristocrats were benefited, the workers suffered, the price of the loaf being decidedly raised and their scanty fare correspondingly diminished.

More than once they rose in riot against these laws, and occasional changes were made in them, but many years passed after the era of parliamentary reform before public opinion prevailed in this second field of effort. Richard Cobden, one of the greatest of England's orators, was the apostle of the crusade against these misery-producing laws. He advocated their repeal with a power and influence that in time grew irresistible. He was not affiliated with either of the great parties, but stood apart as an independent Radical, a man with a party of his own, and that party, Free Trade. For the crusade against the Corn Laws widened into one against the whole principle of protection. Backed by the public demand for cheap food, the movement went on, until in 1846 Cobden brought over to his side the government forces under Sir Robert Peel, by whose aid the Corn Laws were swept away and the ports of England thrown open to the free entrance of food from any part of the world. The result was a serious one to English agriculture, but it was of great benefit to the English people in their status as

Cobden and the Anti-Corn Law Crusade

the greatest of manufacturing and commercial nations. Supplying the world with goods, as they did, it was but just that the world should supply them with food. With the repeal of the duties on grain **Great Britain** the whole system of protection was dropped and in its place **Adopts Free** was adopted that system of free trade in which Great Britain **Trade** stands alone among the nations of the world. It was a system especially adapted to a nation whose market was the world at large, and under it British commerce spread and flourished until it became one of the wonders of the world.

9

CHAPTER X.

Turkey, the "Sick Man" of Europe.

AMONG the most interesting phases of nineteenth-century history is that of the conflict between Russia and Turkey, a struggle for dominion that came down from the preceding centuries, and still seems only temporarily laid aside for final settlement in the years to come. In the eighteenth century the Turks proved quite able to hold their own against all the power of Russia and all the armies of Catharine the Great, and they entered the nineteenth century with their ancient do-

The "Sick Man" of Europe minion largely intact. But they were declining in strength while Russia was growing, and long before 1900 the empire of the Sultan would have become the prey of the Czar had not the other powers of Europe come to the rescue. The Czar Nicholas designated the Sultan as "the sick man" of Europe, and such he and his empire have truly become.

The ambitious designs of Russia found abundant warrant in the cruel treatment of the Christian people of Turkey. A number of Christian kingdoms lay under the Sultan's rule, in the south inhabited by Greeks, in the north by Slavs; their people treated always with harshness and tyranny; their every attempt at revolt repressed with savage cruelty. We have seen how the Greeks rebelled against their oppressors in 1821, and, with the aid

The Result of the War of 1829 of Europe, won their freedom in 1829. Stirred by this struggle, Russia declared war against Turkey in 1828, and in the treaty of peace signed at Adrianople in 1829 secured not only the independence of Greece, but a large degree of home-rule for the northern principalities of Servia, Moldavia, and Wallachia. Turkey was forced in a measure to loosen her grip on Christian Europe. But the Russians were not satisfied with this. They had got next to nothing for themselves. England and the other Western powers, fearful of seeing Russia in possession of Constantinople, had forced her to release the fruits of her victory. It was the first step in that jealous watchfulness of England over Constantinople which was to have a more decided outcome in later years. The newborn idea of maintaining the balance of power in Europe stood in Russia's way, the nations of the West viewing in alarm the threatening growth of the great Muscovite Empire.

The ambitious Czar Nicholas looked upon Turkey as his destined prey, and waited with impatience a sufficient excuse to send his armies again to the Balkan Peninsula, whose mountain barrier formed the great natural bulwark of Turkey in the north. Though the Turkish government at this time avoided direct oppression of its Christian subjects, the fanatical Mohammedans were difficult to restrain, and the robbery and murder of Christians was of common occurrence. A source of hostility at length arose from the question of protecting these ill-treated peoples. By favor of old treaties the czar claimed a certain right to protect the Christians of the Greek faith. France assumed a similar protectorate over the Roman Catholics of Palestine, but the greater number of Greek Christians in the Holy Land, and the powerful support of the czar, gave those the advantage in the frequent quarrels which arose in Jerusalem between the pilgrims from the East and the West.

Oppression of the Christians of Turkey

Nicholas, instigated by his advantage in this quarter, determined to declare himself the protector of all the Christians in the Turkish Empire, a claim which the sultan dared not admit if he wished to hold control over his Mohammedan subjects. War was in the air, and England and France, resolute to preserve the "balance of power," sent their fleets to the Dardanelles as useful lookers-on.

The Balance of Power in Europe

The sultan had already rejected the Russian demand, and Nicholas lost no time in sending an army, led by Prince Gortchakoff, with orders to cross the Pruth and take possession of the Turkish provinces on the Danube. The gauntlet had been thrown down. War was inevitable. The English newspapers demanded of their government a vigorous policy. The old Turkish party in Constantinople was equally urgent in its demand for hostilities. At length, on October 4, 1853, the sultan declared war against Russia unless the Danubian principalities were at once evacuated. Instead of doing so, Nicholas ordered his generals to invade the Balkan territory, and on the other hand France and England entered into alliance with the Porte and sent their fleets to the Bosporus. Shortly afterwards the Russian Admiral Nachimoff surprised a Turkish squadron in the harbor of Sinope, attacked it, and—though the Turks fought with the greatest courage—the fleet was destroyed and nearly the whole of its crews were slain.

The Sultan Declares War Against Russia

This turned the tide in England and France, which declared war in March, 1854, while Prussia and Austria maintained a waiting attitude. No event of special importance took place early in the war. In April Lord Raglan, with an English army of 20,000 men, landed in Turkey and the siege of the Russian city of Odessa was begun.   Meanwhile the Russians, who had crossed the Danube, found it advisable to retreat and withdraw across the Pruth, on a threat of hostilities from Austria and Prussia unless the principalities were evacuated.

England and France Come to the Aid of Turkey

The French had met with heavy losses in an advance from Varna, and the British fleet had made an expedition against St. Petersburg, but had been checked before the powerful fortress of Cronstadt.   Such was the state of affairs in the summer of 1854, when the allies determined to carry the war into the enemy's territory, attack the maritime city of Sebastopol in the Crimea, and seek to destroy the Russian naval power in the Black Sea.

Of the allied armies 15,000 men had already perished.   With the remaining forces, rather more than 50,000 British and French and 6,000 Turks, the fleet set sail in September across the Black Sea, and landed near Eupatoria on the west coast of the Crimean peninsula, on the 4th of September, 1854.   Southwards of Eupatoria the sea forms a bay, into which, near the ruins of the old town of Inkermann, the little river Tschernaja pours itself.   On its southern side

The War in the Crimea

lies the fortified town of Sebastopol, on its northern side strong fortifications were raised for the defence of the fleet of war which lay at anchor in the bay.   Farther north the western mountain range is intersected by the river Alma, over which Prince Menzikoff, governor of the Crimea, garrisoned the heights with an army of 30,000 men.   Against the latter the allies first directed their attack, and, in spite of the strong position of the Russians on the rocky slopes, Menzikoff was compelled to retreat, owing his escape from entire destruction only to the want of cavalry in the army of the allies. This dearly bought and bloody battle on the Alma gave rise to hopes of a speedy termination of the campaign ; but the allies, weakened and wearied by the fearful struggle, delayed a further attack, and Menzikoff gained time to strengthen his garrison, and to surround Sebastopol with strong fortifications.   When the allies approached the town they were soon convinced that any attack on such formidable defences would be fruitless, and that they must await the arrival of fresh reinforcements and ammunition.   The English took up their position on the Bay of Balaklava, and the French to the west, on the Kamiesch.

There now commenced a siege such as has seldom occurred in the history of the world.   The first attempt to storm by a united attack of the land army and the fleet showed the resistance to be much more formidable than had been expected by the allies.   Eight days later the English were surprised in their strong **position** near Balaklava by General Liprandi.

THE SULTAN OF TURKEY

POTENTATES OF THE EAST

THE SHAH OF PERSIA

LANDING IN THE CRIMEA AND THE BATTLE OF ALMA

On the landing of the allied British, French and Turks in the Crimea in September, 1854, Prince Menshikoff occupied the adjacent heights with an army of 30,000 men. He was attacked by the allies and driven from his position in the battle of Alma. From that point the invaders marched to the siege of Sebastopol.

The battle of Balaklava was decided in favor of the allies, and on the 5th of November, when Menzikoff had obtained fresh reinforce- **The Battle of** ments, the murderous battle of Inkermann was fought under **Balaklava** the eyes of the two Grand Princes Nicholas and Michael, and after a mighty struggle was won by the allied armies. Fighting in the ranks were two other princely personages, the Duke of Cambridge and Prince Napoleon, son of Jerome, former King of Westphalia.

Of the engagements here named there is only one to which special attention need be directed, the battle of Balaklava, in which occurred that mad but heroic "Charge of the Light Brigade," which has become famous in song and story. The purpose of this conflict on the part of the Russians was to cut the line of communication of the allies, by capturing the redoubts that guarded them, and thus to enforce a retreat by depriving the enemy of supplies.

The day began with a defeat of the Turks and the capture by the Russians of several of the redoubts. Then a great body of **The Highland-** Russian cavalry, 3,000 strong, charged upon the 93d High- **ers' "Thin,** landers, who were drawn up in line to receive them. There **Red Line"** was comparatively but a handful of these gallant Scotchmen, 550 all told, but they have made themselves famous in history as the invincible "thin, red line."

Sir Colin Campbell, their noble leader, said to them : "Remember, lads, there is no retreat from here. You must die where you stand."

"Ay, ay, Sir Colin," shouted the sturdy Highlanders, "we will do just that."

They did not need to. The murderous fire from their "thin, red line" was more than the Russians cared to endure, and they were driven back in disorder.

The British cavalry completed the work of the infantry. On the serried mass of Russian horsemen charged Scarlett's Heavy Brigade, vastly inferior to them in number, but inspired with a spirit and courage that carried its bold horsemen through the Russian columns with such resistless energy that the great body of Muscovite cavalry broke and fled—3,000 completely routed by 800 gallant dragoons.

And now came the unfortunate but world-famous event of the day. It was due to a mistaken order. Lord Raglan, thinking that the Russians intended to carry off the guns captured in the Turkish redoubts, sent an order to the brigade of light cavalry to "advance rapidly to the front and prevent the enemy from carrying off the guns."

Lord Lucan, to whom the command was brought, did not understand
Captain Nolan it. Apparently, Captain Nolan, who conveyed the order, did
and the Order not clearly explain its purport.
to Charge "Lord Raglan orders that the cavalry shall attack immediately," he said, impatient at Lucan's hesitation.

"Attack, sir ; attack what ?" asked Lucan.

"There, my lord, is your enemy ; there are your guns," said Nolan,
with a wave of his hand towards the hostile lines.

The guns he appeared to indicate were those of a Russian battery at
the end of the valley, to attack which by an unsupported cavalry charge
was sheer madness.   Lucan rode to Lord Cardigan, in command of the
cavalry, and repeated the order.

"But there is a battery in front of us and guns and riflemen on either
flank," said Cardigan.

"I know it," answered Lucan.   "But Lord Raglan will have it.   We
have no choice but to obey."

"The brigade will advance," said Cardigan, without further hesitation.

In a moment more the "gallant six hundred" were in motion—going in
the wrong direction, as Captain Nolan is thought to have percieved.   At
all events he spurred his horse across the front of the brigade, waving his
sword as if with the intention to set them right.   But no one understood
him, and at that instant a fragment of shell struck him and hurled him dead
to the earth.   There was no further hope of stopping the mad charge.

On and on went the devoted Light Brigade, their pace increasing at
every stride, headed straight for the Russian battery half a league away.
The Charge As they went fire was opened on them from the guns in flank.
of the Light Soon they came within range of the guns in front, which
Brigade also opened a raking fire.   They were enveloped in "a zone
of fire, and the air was filled with the rush of shot, the bursting of shells,
and the moan of bullets, while amidst the infernal din the work of death
went on, and men and horses were incessantly dashed to the ground."

But no thought of retreat seems to have entered the minds of those
brave dragoons and their gallant leader.   Their pace increased ; they
reached the battery and dashed in among the guns ; the gunners were cut
down as they served their pieces.   Masses of Russian cavalry standing near
were charged and forced back.   The men fought madly in the face of death
until the word came to retreat.

Then, emerging from the smoke of the battle, a feeble remnant of the
" gallant six hundred " appeared upon the plain, comprising one or two large
groups, though the most of them were in scattered parties of two or three.

One group of about seventy men cut their way through three squadrons of Russian lancers. Another party of equal strength broke through a second intercepting force. Out of some 647 men in all, 247 were killed and wounded, and nearly all the horses were slain. Lord Cardigan, the first **The Sad End** to enter the battery, was one of those who came back alive. **of a Deed** The whole affair had occupied no more than twenty minutes. **of Glory** But it was a twenty minutes of which the British nation has ever since been proud, and which Tennyson has made famous by one of the most spirit-stirring of his odes. The French General Bosquet fairly characterized it by his often quoted remark : "C'est magnifique, mais ce n'est pas la guerre." (It is magnificent, but it is not war.)

These battles in the field brought no changes in the state of affairs. The siege of Sebastopol went on through the winter of 1854–55, during which the allied army suffered the utmost misery and privation, partly the effect of climate, largely the result of fraud and incompetency at home. Sisters of Mercy and self-sacrificing English ladies—chief among them the noble Florence Nightingale—strove to assuage the sufferings brought on the soldiers by cold, hunger, and disease, but these enemies proved more fatal than the sword.

In the year 1855 the war was carried on with increased energy. Sardinia joined the allies and sent them an army of 15,000 men. Austria broke with Russia and began preparations for war. And in March the obstinate czar Nicholas died and his milder son Alexander took his place. Peace was demanded in Russia, yet 25,000 of her sons had fallen and the honor of the nation seemed involved. The war went on, both sides increasing their forces. Month by month the allies more closely invested the besieged city. After the middle of August the assault became almost incessant, cannon balls dropping like an unceasing storm of hail in forts and streets.

On the 5th of September began a terrific bombardment, continuing day and night for three days, and sweeping down more than 5,000 Russians on the ramparts. At length, as the hour of noon struck on **The Assault on** September 8th, the attack of which this play of artillery was **and Capture** the prelude began, the French assailing the Malakoff, the **of Sebastop** British the Redan, these being the most formidable of the defensive works of the town. The French assault was successful and Sebastopol became untenable. That night the Russians blew up their remaining forts, sunk their ships of war, and marched out of the town, leaving it as the prize of victory to the allies. Soon after Russia gained a success by capturing the Turkish fortress of Kars, in Asia Minor, and, her honor satisfied with this success, a treaty of peace was concluded. In this treaty the Black Sea was

made neutral and all ships of war were excluded from its waters, while the
safety of the Christians of Wallachia, Moldavia and Servia was assured by
making these principalities practically independent, under the protection of
the powers of Europe.

Turkey came out of the war weakened and shorn of territory. But
the Turkish idea of government remained unchanged, and in twenty years'

The Revolt in Bosnia

time Russia was fairly goaded into another war. In 1875
Bosnia rebelled in consequence of the insufferable oppression
of the Turkish tax-collectors. The brave Bosnians maintained
themselves so sturdily in their mountain fastnesses that the Turks almost
despaired of subduing them, and the Christian subjects of the Sultan in all
quarters became so stirred up that a general revolt was threatened.

The Turks undertook to prevent this in their usual fashion. Irregular
troops were sent into Christian Bulgaria with orders to kill all they met. It
was an order to the Mohammedan taste. The defenceless villages of Bulgaria were entered and their inhabitants slaughtered in cold blood, till
thousands of men, women. and children had been slain.

When tidings of these atrocities reached Europe the nations were
filled with horror. The Sultan made smooth excuses, and diplomacy

The "Bulgarian Horror" and Its Effect

sought to settle the affair, but it became evident that a massacre so terrible as this could not be condoned so easily.
Disraeli, then prime minister of Great Britain, sought to
dispose of these reports as matters for jest; but Gladstone, at that time in
retirement, arose in his might, and by his pamphlet on the "Bulgarian
Horrors" so aroused public sentiment in England that the government
dared not back up Turkey in the coming war.

Hostilities were soon proclaimed. The Russians, of the same race and religious sect as the Bulgarians, were excited beyond control, and in April, 1877,
Alexander II. declared war against Turkey The outrages of the Turks had
been so flagrant that no allies came to their aid, while the rottenness of
their empire was shown by the rapid advance of the Russian armies.

They crossed the Danube in June. In a month later they had
occupied the principal passes of the Balkan mountains and were in position to descend on the broad plain that led to Constantinople. But at this
point in their career they met with a serious check. Osman Pasha, the
single Turkish commander of ability that the war developed, occupied the
town of Plevna with such forces as he could gather, fortified it as strongly
as possible, and from behind its walls defied the Russians.

They dared not advance and leave this stronghold in their rear. For
five months all the power of Russia and the skill of its generals were held in

check by this brave man and his few followers, until Europe and America alike looked on with admiration at his remarkable defence, in view of which the cause of the war was almost forgotten. The Russian Osman Pacha general Krüdener was repulsed with the loss of 8,000 men. and the De- The daring Skobeleff strove in vain to launch his troops over fence of Plevna Osman's walls. At length General Todleben undertook the siege, adopting the slow but safe method of starving out the defenders. Osman Pacha now showed his courage, as he had already shown his endurance. When hunger and disease began to reduce the strength of his men, he resolved on a final desperate effort. At the head of his brave garrison the "Lion of Plevna" sallied from the city, and fought with desperate courage to break through the circle of his foes. He was finally driven back into the city and compelled to surrender.

Osman had won glory, and his fall was the fall of the Turkish cause. The Russians crossed the Balkan, capturing in the Schipka Pass a Turkish army of 30,000 men. Adrianople was taken, and the Turk- The Total De- ish line of retreat cut off. The Russians marched to the feat of the Bosporus, and the Sultan was compelled to sue for peace to Turks save his capital from falling into the hands of the Christians, as it had fallen into those of the Turks four centuries before.

Russia had won the game for which she had made so long a struggle. The treaty of San Stefano practically decreed the dissolution of the Turkish Empire. But at this juncture the other nations of Europe took part. They were not content to see the balance of power destroyed by Russia becoming master of Constantinople, and England demanded that the treaty should be revised by the European powers. Russia protested, but Disraeli threatened war, and the czar gave way.

The Congress of Berlin, to which the treaty was referred, settled the question in the following manner : Montenegro, Roumania, and Servia were declared independent, and Bulgaria became free, except that The Congress it had to pay an annual tribute to the sultan. The part of of Berlin old Bulgaria that lay south of the Balkan Mountains was named East Roumelia and given its own civil government, but was left under the military control of Turkey. Bosnia and Herzegovina were placed under the control of Austria. All that Russia obtained for her victories were some provinces in Asia Minor. Turkey was terribly shorn, and since then her power has been further reduced, for East Roumelia has broken loose from her control and united itself again to Bulgaria.

Another twenty years passed, and Turkey found itself at war again. It was the old story, the oppression of the Christians This time the trouble began in Armenia, a part of Turkey in Asia, where in 1895 and 1896 terrible massacres took place. Indignation reigned in Europe, but fears

The Turks in Armenia and Crete

of a general war kept them from using force, and the sultan paid no heed to the reforms he promised to make.

In 1896 the Christians of the island of Crete broke out in revolt against the oppression and tyranny of Turkish rule. Of all the powers of Europe little Greece was the only one that came to their aid, and the great nations, still inspired with the fear of a general war, sent their fleet and threatened Greece with blockade unless she would withdraw her troops.

The result was one scarcely expected. Greece was persistant, and gathered a threatening army on the frontier of Turkey, and war broke out in 1897 between the two states. The Turks now, under an able commander, showed much of their ancient valor and intrepidity, crossing the frontier, defeating the Greeks in a rapid series of engagements, and occupying Thessaly, while the Greek army was driven back in a state of utter demoralization. At this juncture, when Greece lay at the mercy of Turkey, as Turkey had

The War Between Turkey and Greece

lain at that of Russia twenty years before, the powers, which had refused to aid Greece in her generous but hopeless effort, stepped in to save her from ruin. Turkey was bidden to call a halt, and the sultan reluctantly stopped the march of his army. He demanded the whole of Thessaly and a large indemnity in money. The former the powers refused to grant, and reduced the indemnity to a sum within the power of Greece to pay. Thus the affair ended, and such is the status of the Eastern Question to-day. But it may be merely a question of time when Russia shall accomplish her long-cherished design, and become master of Constantinople; possibly by the way of Asia, in which her power is now so rapidly and widely extending.

CHAPTER XI.

The European Revolution of 1848.

THE revolution of 1830 did not bring peace and quiet to France nor to Europe. In France the people grew dissatisfied with their new monarch; in Europe generally they demanded a greater share of liberty. Louis Philippe delayed to extend the suffrage; he used his high position to add to his great riches; he failed to win the hearts of the French, and was widely accused of selfishness and greed. There were risings of legitimists in favor of the Bourbons, while the republican element was opposed to monarchy. No less than eight attempts were made to remove the king by assassination—all of them failures, but they showed **Opposition in** the disturbed state of public feeling. Liberty, equality, fra- **France to** ternity became the watchwords of the working classes, social- **Louis Philippe** istic ideas arose and spread, and the industrial element of the various nations became allied in one great body of revolutionists known as the " Internationalists."

In Germany the demand of the people for political rights grew until it reached a crisis. The radical writings of the " Young Germans," the stirring songs of their poets, the bold utterances of the press, the doctrines of the " Friends of Light " among the Protestants and of the " German Catholics " among the Catholics, all went to show that the people were deeply dissatisfied alike with the state and the church. They were rapidly arousing from their sluggish acceptance of the work of the Congress of Vienna of 1815, and the spirit of liberty was in the air.

The King of Prussia, Frederick William IV., saw danger ahead. He became king in 1840 and lost no time in trying to make his **Revolutionary** rule popular by reforms. An edict of toleration was issued, **Sentiment in** the sittings of the courts were opened to the public, and the **Germany and** Estates of the provinces were called to meet in Berlin. In **Italy** the convening of a Parliament he had given the people a voice. The Estates demanded freedom of the press and of the state with such eloquence and energy that the king dared not resist them. The people had gained a great step in their progress towards liberty.

In Italy also the persistent demands of the people met with an encouraging response. The Pope, Pius IX., extended the freedom of the press, gave a liberal charter to the City of Rome, and began the formation of an Italian confederacy. In Sicily a revolutionary outbreak took place, and the King of Naples was compelled to give his people a constitution and a parliament. His example was followed in Tuscany and Sardinia. The tyrannical Duke of Modena was forced to fly from the vengeance of his people, and the throne of Parma became vacant by the death in 1847 of Maria Louisa, the widow of Napoleon Bonaparte, a woman little loved and less respected.

The Italians were filled with hope by these events. Freedom and the unity of Italy loomed up before their eyes. Only two obstacles stood in their way, the Austrians and the Jesuits, and both of these were bitterly hated. Gioberti, the enemy of the Jesuits, was greeted with cheers, under which might be heard harsh cries of " Death to the Germans."

Such was the state of affairs at the beginning of 1848. The measure of liberty granted the people only whetted their appetite for more, and over all Western Europe rose an ominous murmur, the voice of the people demanding the rights of which they had so long been deprived. In France this demand was growing dangerously insistent; in Paris, the centre of European revolution, it threatened an outbreak. Reform banquets were the order of the day in France, and one was arranged for in Paris to signalize the meeting of the Chambers.

Guizot, the historian, who was then minister of foreign affairs, had deeply offended the liberal party of France by his reactionary policy. The government threw fuel on the fire by forbidding the banquet and taking

The Outbreak in Paris

steps to suppress it by military force. The people were enraged by this false step and began to gather in excited groups. Throngs of them—artisans, students, and tramps—were soon marching through the streets, with shouts of "Reform! Down with Guizot!" The crowds rapidly increased and grew more violent. The people were too weak to cope with them; the soldiers were loath to do so; soon barricades were erected and fighting began.

For two days this went on. Then the king, alarmed at the situation, dimissed Guizot and promised reform, and the people, satisfied for the time and proud of their victory, paraded the streets with cheers and songs. All now might have gone well but for a hasty and violent act on the part of the troops. About ten o'clock at night a shouting and torch-bearing throng marched through the Boulevards, singing and waving flags. Reaching the Ministry of Foreign Affairs, they halted and called for its illumination.

THE CONGRESS AT BERLIN, JUNE 13, 1878

After the close of the Russo-Turkish War of 1877, a Congress of the European Powers was held at Berlin to decide on the status of Turkey, its purpose being largely to prevent Russia from taking possession of Constantinople. One of its results was to give Great Britain control of the island of Cyprus.

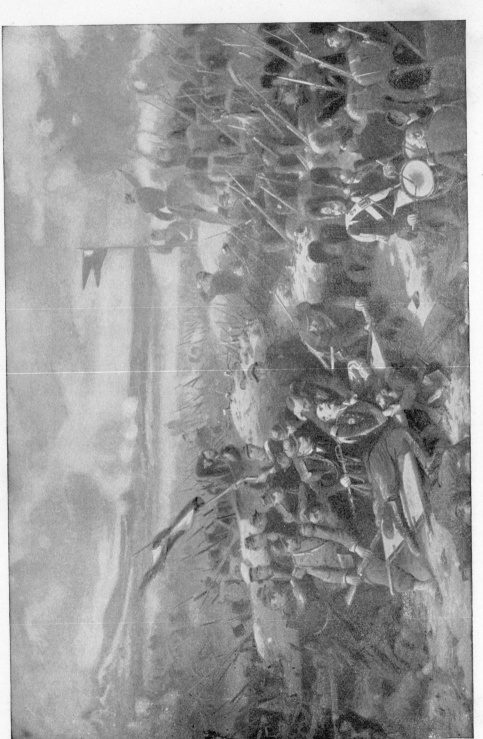

THE WOUNDING OF GENERAL BOSQUET—(FROM THE PAINTING BY YVON)

One of the most successful French Marshals in the Crimean War was Pierre Francois Joseph Bosquet. Parliament voted him England's thanks for the part he played in winning the battle of Inkermann. He also took a leading part in the capture of the Malakoff, Siege of Sebastopol, September 8, 1855, where he was seriously wounded.

The troops on duty there interfered, and, on an insult to their colonel and the firing of a shot from the mob, they replied with a volley, before which fifty-two of the people fell killed and wounded.

This reckless and sanguinary deed was enough to turn revolt into revolution. The corpses were carried on biers through the streets by the infuriated people, the accompanying torch-bearers shouting: **Revolt Becomes Revolution** "To arms! they are murdering us!" At midnight the tocsin call rang from the bells of Notre Dame; the barricades, which had been partly removed, were restored; and the next morning, February 24, 1848, Paris was in arms. In the struggle that followed they were quickly victorious, and the capital was in their hands.

Louis Philippe followed the example of Charles X., abdicated his throne and fled to England. After the fate of Louis XVI. no monarch was willing to wait and face a Paris mob. The kingdom was overthrown, and a republic, the second which France had known, was established, the aged Dupont de l'Eure being chosen president. The poet Lamartine, the socialist Louis Blanc, the statesmen Ledru-Rollin and Arago became members of the Cabinet, and all looked forward to a reign **The Second French Republic** of peace and prosperity. The socialists tried the experiment of establishing national workshops in which artisans were to be employed at the expense of the state, with the idea that this would give work to all.

Yet the expected prosperity did not come. The state was soon deeply in debt, many of the people remained unemployed, and the condition of industry grew worse day by day. The treasury proved incapable of paying the state artisans, and the public workshops were closed. In June the trouble came to a crisis and a new and sanguinary outbreak began, instigated by the hungry and disappointed workmen, and led by the advocates of the "Red Republic," who acted with ferocious brutality. General Brea and the Archbishop of Paris were murdered, and the work of slaughter grew so horrible that the National Assembly, to put an end to it, made General Cavaignac dictator and commissioned him to put down the revolt. A terrible struggle ensued between the mob and the troops, ending in the suppression of the revolt and the arrest and banishment of many of its ringleaders. Ten or twelve thousand people had been killed. The National Assembly adopted a republican constitution, under which a single legislative chamber and a president to be elected every four years were provided for. The assembly wished to make General Cavaignac president, but the nation, blinded by their faith in the name of the great conqueror, elected by an almost unanimous vote his nephew, Louis Napoleon, a man who had suffered a long term of imprisonment for his several attempts against the reign of the late king. The revolution, for the time being, was at an end, and France was a republic again.

The effect of this revolution in France spread far and wide through Europe. Outbreaks occurred in Italy, Poland, Switzerland and Ireland, and in Germany the revolutionary fever burned hot. Baden was the first state to yield to the demands of the people for freedom of the press, a parliament and other reforms, and went so far as to abolish the imposts still remaining from feudal times. The other minor states followed its example. In Saxony, Würtemberg and other states class abuses were abolished, liberals given prominent positions under government, the suffrage and the legislature reformed, and men of liberal sentiment summoned to discuss the formation of new constitutions.

Effect of the Revolution of 1848 in Europe

But it was in the great despotic states of Germany—Prussia and Austria—that the liberals gained the most complete and important victory, and went farthest in overthrowing autocratic rule and establishing constitutional government. The great Austrian statesman who had been a leader in the Congress of Vienna and who had suppressed liberalism in Italy, Prince Metternich, was still, after more than thirty years, at the head of affairs in Vienna. He controlled the policy of Austria; his word was law in much of Germany; time had cemented his authority, and he had done more than any other man in Europe in maintaining despotism and building a dam against the rising flood of liberal sentiment.

Metternich and His System

But the hour of the man who had destroyed the work of Napoleon was at hand. He had failed to recognize the spirit of the age or to perceive that liberalism was deeply penetrating Austria. To most of the younger statesmen of Europe the weakness of his policy and the rottenness of his system were growing apparent, and it was evident that they must soon fall before the onslaught of the advocates of freedom.

An incitement was needed, and it came in the news of the Paris revolution. At once a hot excitement broke out everywhere in Austria. From Hungary came a vigorous demand for an independent parliament, reform of the constitution, decrease of taxes, and relief from the burden of the national debt of Austria. From Bohemia, whose rights and privileges had been seriously interfered with in the preceding year, came similar demands. In Vienna itself the popular outcry for increased privileges grew insistant.

The excitement of the people was aggravated by their distrust of the paper money of the realm and by a great depression in commerce and indus try. Daily more workmen were thrown out of employment, and soon throngs of the hungry and discontented gathered in the streets. Students, as usual, led away by their boyish love of excitement, were the first to create a disturbance, but others soon joined in, **The Outbreak in Vienna** and the affair quickly became serious.

The old system was evidently at an end. The policy of Metternich could restrain the people no longer. Lawlessness became general, excesses were committed by the mob, the dwellings of those whom the populace hated were attacked and plundered, the authorities were resisted with arms, and the danger of an overthrow of the government grew imminent. The press, which had gained freedom of utterance, added to the peril of the situation by its inflammatory appeals to the people, and by its violence checked the progress of the reforms which it demanded. Metternich, by his system of restraint, had kept the people in ignorance of the first principles of political affairs, and the liberties which they now asked for showed them to be unadapted to a liberal government. The old minister, whose system was falling in ruins about him, fled from the country and sought a refuge in England, that haven of political failures.

In May, 1848, the emperor, alarmed at the threatening state of affairs, left his capital and withdrew to Innsbruck. The tidings of his withdrawal stirred the people to passion, and the outbreak of mob **Flight and Return of the Emperor** violence which followed was the fiercest and most dangerous that had yet occurred. Gradually, however, the tumult was appeased, a constitutional assembly was called into being and opened by the Archduke John, and the Emperor Ferdinand re-entered Vienna amid the warm acclamations of the people. The outbreak was at an end. Austria had been converted from an absolute to a constitutional monarchy.

In Berlin the spirit of revolution became as marked as in Vienna. The King resisted the demands of the people, who soon came into conflict with the soldiers, a fierce street fight breaking out which continued with violence for two weeks. The revolutionists demanded the removal of the troops and the formation of a citizen militia, and the king, alarmed **Revolt in Prussia and the German Union** at the dangerous crisis in affairs, at last assented. The troops were accordingly withdrawn, the obnoxious ministry was dismissed, and a citizen-guard was created for the defence of the city. Three days afterwards the king promised to govern as a constitutional monarch, an assembly was elected by universal suffrage, and to it was given the work of preparing a constitution for the Prussian state. Here, as in Austria, the revolutionists had won the day and irresponsible government was at an end.

Elsewhere in Germany radical changes were taking place. King Louis of Bavaria, who had deeply offended his people, resigned in favor of his son. The Duke of Hesse-Darmstadt did the same. Everywhere the liberals were in the ascendant, and were gaining freedom of the press and constitutional government. The formation of Germany into a federal empire was proposed and adopted, and a National Assembly met at Frankfort on May 18, 1848. It included many of the ablest men of Germany. Its principal work was to organize a union under an irresponsible executive, who was to be surrounded by a responsible ministry. The Archduke John of Austria was selected to fill this new, but brief imperial position, and made a solemn entry into Frankfort on the 11th of July.

All this was not enough for the ultra radicals. They determined to found a German republic, and their leaders, Hecker and Struve, called the people to arms. An outreak took place in Baden, but it was quickly suppressed, and the republican movement came to a speedy end. In the north

The Schleswig-Holstein Affair war broke out between Denmark and Schleswig-Holstein, united duchies which desired to be freed from Danish rule and annexed to Germany, and called for German aid. But just then the new German Union was in no condition to come to their assistance, and Prussia preferred diplomacy to war, with the result that Denmark came out victorious from the contest. As will be seen in a later chapter, Prussia, under the energetic leadership of Bismarck, came, a number of years afterwards, to the aid of these discontented duchies, and they were finally torn from Danish control.

While these exciting events were taking place in the north, Italy was swept with a storm of revolution from end to end. Metternich was no longer at hand to keep it in check, and the whole peninsula seethed with revolt. Sicily rejected the rule of the Bourbon king of Naples, chose the

War in Sicily and Sardinia Duke of Genoa, son of Charles Albert of Sardinia, for its king, and during a year fought for liberty. This patriotic effort of the Sicilians ended in failure. The Swiss mercenaries of the Neapolitan king captured Syracuse and brought the island into subjection, and the tyrant hastened to abolish the constitution which he had been frightened into granting in his hour of extremity.

In the north of Italy war broke out between Austria and Sardinia. Milan and Venice rose against the Austrians and drove out their garrisons, throughout Lombardy the people raised the standard of independence, and Charles Albert of Sardinia called his people to arms and invaded that country, striving to free it and the neighboring state of Venice from Austrian rule. For a brief season he was successful, pushing the Austrian troops to the frontiers, but the old Marshal Radetzky defeated him at Verona and compelled him to seek safety in flight. The next year he renewed his attempt, but with no better success. Depressed by his failure, he resigned the crown to his son Victor Emmanuel, who made a disadvantageous peace with Austria. Venice held out for several months, but was finally subdued, and Austrian rule was restored in the north.

Meanwhile the pope, Pius IX., offended his people by his unwillingness to aid Sardinia against Austria. He promised to grant a constitutional government and convened an Assembly in Rome, but the **The Revolution in Rome** Democratic people of the state were not content with feeble concessions of this kind. Rossi, prime minister of the state, was assassinated, and the pope, filled with alarm, fled in disguise, leaving the Papal dominion to the revolutionists, who at once proclaimed a republic and confiscated the property of the Church.

Mazzini, the leader of "Young Italy," the ardent revolutionist who had long worked in exile for Italian independence, entered the Eternal City, and with him Garibaldi, long a political refugee in America and a gallant partisan leader in the recent war with Austria The arrival of these celebrated revolutionists filled the democratic party in Rome with the greatest enthusiasm, and it was resolved to defend the States of the Church to the last extremity, viewing them as the final asylum of Italian liberty.

In this extremity the pope called on France for aid. That country responded by sending an army, which landed at Civita-Vecchia and marched upon and surrounded Rome. The new-comers declared that they came as friends, not as foes; it was not their purpose to overthrow the republic, but to defend the capital from Austria and Naples. The leaders of the insurgents in Rome did not trust their professions and promises and refused them admittance. A fierce struggle followed. The republicans **Capture of** defended themselves stubbornly. For weeks they defied the **Rome by the** efforts of General Oudinot and his troops. But in the end **French Army** they were forced to yield, a conditional submission was made, and the French soldiers occupied the city. Garibaldi, Mazzini, and others of the leaders took to flight, and the old conditions were gradually resumed under the controlling influence of French bayonets. For years afterwards the French held the city as the allies and guard of the pope.

The revolutionary spirit, which had given rise to war in Italy, yielded a still more resolute and sanguinary conflict in Hungary, **The Outbreak** whose people were divided against themselves. The Magyars, **in Hungary** the descendants of the old Huns, who demanded governmental institutions of their own, separate from these of Austria, though

10

under the Austrian monarch, were opposed by the Slavonic part of the population, and war began between them. Austrian troops were ordered to the aid of Jellachich, the ruler of the Slavs of Croatia in South Hungary, but their departure was prevented by the democratic people of Vienna, who rose in violent insurrection, induced by their sympathy with the Magyars.

The whole city was quickly in tumult, an attack was made on the arsenals, and the violence became so great that the emperor again took to flight. War in Austria followed. A strong army was sent to subdue the rebellious city, which was stubbornly defended, the students' club being the centre of the revolutionary movement. Jellachich led his Croatians to the aid of the emperor's troops, the city was surrounded and besieged, sallies and assaults were of daily occurrence, and for a week and more a bloody conflict continued day and night. Vienna was finally taken by storm, the **Vienna Captured by Storm** troops forcing their way into the streets, where shocking scenes of murder and violence took place. On November 21, 1848, Jellachich entered the conquered city, martial law was proclaimed, the houses were searched, the prisons filled with captives, and the leaders of the insurrection put to death.

Shortly afterwards the Emperor Ferdinand abdicated the throne in favor of his youthful nephew, Francis Joseph, who at once dissolved the constitutional assembly and proclaimed a new constitution and a new code of laws. Hungary was still in arms, and offered a desperate resistance to the Austrians, who now marched to put down the insurrection. They found it no easy task. The fiery eloquence of the orator Kossuth roused the Magyars to a desperate resistance, Polish leaders came to their support, foreign volunteers strengthened their ranks, Gorgey, their chief leader, showed great military skill, and the Austrians were driven out and the fortresses taken. The independence of Hungary was now proclaimed, and a government established under Kossuth as provisional president.

The repulse of the Austrians nerved the young emperor to more **The Hungarian Revolt and Its Suppression** strenuous exertions. The aid of Russia was asked, and the insurgent state invaded on three sides, by the Croatians from the south, the Russians from the north, and the Austrians, under the brutal General Haynau, from the west.

The conflict continued for several months, but quarrels between the Hungarian leaders weakened their armies, and in August, 1849, Gorgey, who had been declared dictator, surrendered to the invaders, Kossuth and the other leaders seeking safety in flight. Haynau made himself infamous by his cruel treatment of the Hungarian people, particularly by his use of the lash upon women. His conduct raised such wide-spread indignation that he was roughly handled by a party of brewers, on his visit to London in 1850.

With the fall of Hungary the revolutionary movement of 1848 came to an end. The German Union had already disappeared. There were various other disturbances, besides those we have recorded, but finally all the states settled down to peace and quiet. Its results had been great in increasing the political privileges of the people of Western Europe, and with it the reign of despotism in that section of the continent came to an end.

The greatest hero of the war in Hungary was undoubtedly Louis Kossuth, whose name has remained familiar among those of the patriots of his century. From Hungary he made his way to Turkey, where he was imprisoned for two years at Kutaieh, being finally released through the intervention of the governments of Great Britain and the United States. He then visited England, where he was received with enthusiastic, popular demonstrations and made several admirable speeches in the English language, of which he had excellent command. In the autumn of 1851 he came to the United States, where he had a flattering reception and spoke on the wrongs of Hungary to enthusiastic audiences in the principal cities.

CHAPTER XII

Louis Napoleon and the Second French Empire.

THE name of Napoleon is a name to conjure with in France. Two generations after the fall of Napoleon the Great, the people of that country had practically forgotten the misery he had brought them, and remembered only the glory with which he had crowned the name of France. When, then, a man whom we may fairly designate as Napoleon the Small offered himself for their suffrages, they cast their votes almost unanimously in his favor.

Charles Louis Napoleon Bonaparte, to give this personage his full name, was a son of Louis Bonaparte, once king of Holland, and Hortense de Beauharnais, and had been recognized by Napoleon as, after his father, **Louis Napoleon** the direct successor to the throne. This he made strenuous **and His Claim** efforts to obtain, hoping to dethrone Louis Philippe and in-**to the Throne** stall himself in his place. In 1836, with a few followers, he made an attempt to capture Strasbourg. His effort failed and he was arrested and transported to the United States. In 1839 he published a work entitled " Napoleonic Ideas," which was an apology for the ambitious acts of the first Napoleon.

The growing unpopularity of Louis Philippe tempted him at this time to make a second attempt to invade France. He did it in a rash way almost certain to end in failure. Followed by about fifty men, and bringing with him a tame eagle, which was expected to perch upon his banner as the harbinger of victory, he sailed from England in August, 1840, and landed at Boulogne. This desperate and foolish enterprise proved a complete **A Rash and** failure. The soldiers whom the would-be usurper expected **Unsuccessful** to join his standard arrested him, and he was tried for treason **Invasion** by the House of Peers. This time he was not dealt with so leniently as before, but was sentenced to imprisonment for life and was confined in the Castle of Ham. From this fortress he escaped in disguise in May, 1846, and made his way to England.

The revolution of 1848 gave the restless and ambitious adventurer a more promising opportunity. He returned to France, was elected to the National Assembly, and on the adoption of the republican constitution

BATTLE OF CHAMPIGNY

On November 30, 1870, the French besieged in Paris made a desperate effort to break through the investing lines of the Germans at Champigny, on the River Marne. The struggle continued for two days and ended in the repulse of the French. This defeat sealed the fate of Paris and of France.

THADDEUS KOSCIUSKO   LOUIS KOSSUTH

NOBLE SONS OF POLAND AND HUNGARY

offered himself as a candidate for the Presidency of the new republic. And now the magic of the name of Napoleon told. General Cavaignac, his chief competitor, was supported by the solid men of the country, who distrusted the adventurer; but the people rose almost solidly in his support, and he was elected president for four years by 5,562,834 votes, against 1,469,166 for Cavaignac.

The new President of France soon showed his ambition. He became engaged in a contest with the Assembly and aroused the distrust of the Republicans by his autocratic tones. In 1849 he still further offended the Democratic party by sending an army to Rome, which put an end to the republic in that city. He sought to make his Cabinet officers the pliant instruments of his will, and thus caused De Tocqueville, the celebrated author, who was minister for foreign affairs, to resign. "We were not the men to serve him on those terms," said De Tocqueville, at a later time.

An Autocratic President of France

The new-made president was feeling his way to imperial dignity. He could not forget that his illustrious uncle had made himself emperor, and his ambition instigated him to the same course. A violent controversy arose between him and the Assembly, which body passed a law restricting universal suffrage, and thus reducing the popular support of the president. In June, 1850, it increased his salary at his request, but granted the increase only for one year—an act of distrust which proved a new source of discord.

Louis Napoleon meanwhile was preparing for a daring act. He secretly obtained the support of the army leaders and prepared covertly for the boldest stroke of his life. On the 2d of December, 1851,— the anniversary of the establishment of the first empire and of the battle of Austerlitz,—he got rid of his opponents by means of the memorable *coup d'etat*, and seized the supreme power of the state.

The Coup d'etat of Louis Napoleon

The most influential members of the Assembly had been arrested during the preceding night, and when the hour for the session of the House came the men most strongly opposed to the usurper were in prison. Most of them were afterwards exiled, some for life, some for shorter terms. This act of outrage and violation of the plighted faith of the president roused the Socialists and Republicans to the defence of their threatened liberties, insurrections broke out in Paris, Lyons, and other towns, street barricades were built, and severe fighting took place. But Napoleon had secured the army, and the revolt was suppressed with blood and slaughter. Baudin, one of the deposed deputies, was shot on the barricade in the Faubourg St. Antoine, while waving in his hand the decree of the constitution. He was afterwards honored as a martyr to the cause of republicanism in France.

The usurper had previously sought to gain the approval of the people by liberal and charitable acts, and to win the goodwill of the civic authori-

How Napoleon Won Popular Support

ties by numerous progresses through the interior.   He posed as a protector and promoter of national prosperity and the rights of the people, and sought to lay upon the Assembly all the defects of his administration.   By these means, which aided to awaken the Napoleonic fervor in the state, he was enabled safely to submit his acts of violence and bloodshed to the approval of the people.   The new constitution offered by the president was put to vote, and was adopted by the enormous majority of more than seven million votes.   By its terms Louis Napoleon was to be president of France for ten years, with the power of a monarch, and the Parliament was to consist of two bodies, a Senate and a Legislative House, which were given only nominal power.

This was as far as Napoleon dared to venture at that time.   A year

Louis Napoleon is Elected Emperor

later, on December 1, 1852, having meanwhile firmly cemented his power, he passed from president to emperor, again by a vote of the people, of whom, according to the official report, 7,824,189 cast their votes in his favor.

Thus ended the second French republic, an act of usurpation of the basest and most unwarranted character.   The partisans of the new emperor were rewarded with the chief offices of the state ; the leading republicans languished in prison or in exile for the crime of doing their duty to their constituents ; and Armand Marrest, the most zealous champion of the republic, died of a broken heart from the overthrow of all his efforts and aspirations.   The honest soldier and earnest patriot, Cavaignac, in a few years followed him to the grave.   The cause of liberty in France seemed lost.

The crowning of a new emperor of the Napoleonic family in France naturally filled Europe with apprehensions.   But Napoleon III., as he styled himself, was an older man than Napoleon I., and seemingly less likely to be carried away by ambition.   His favorite motto, " The Empire is peace," aided to restore quietude, and gradually the nations began to trust in his words, " France wishes for peace ; and when France is satisfied the world is quiet."

Warned by one of the errors of his uncle, he avoided seeking a wife in the royal families of Europe, but allied himself with a Spanish lady of noble

Marriage of the Emperor

rank, the young and beautiful Eugenie de Montijo, duchess of Teba.   At the same time he proclaimed that, "A sovereign raised to the throne by a new principle should remain faithful to that principle, and in the face of Europe frankly accept the position of a parvenu, which is an honorable title when it is obtained by the public suffrage of a great people. For seventy years all princes' daughters married to rulers of France have been unfortunate ; only one, Josephine, was remembered with affection by the French people, and she was not born of a royal house."

The new emperor sought by active public works and acts of charity to win the approval of the people. He recognized the necessity of aiding the working classes as far as possible, and protecting them from poverty and wretchedness. During a dearth in 1853 a "baking fund" was organized in Paris, the city contributing funds to enable bread to be sold at a low price. Dams and embankments were built along the rivers to overcome the effects of floods. New streets were opened, bridges built, railways constructed, to increase internal traffic. Splendid buildings were erected for **Public Works** municipal and government purposes. Paris was given a new **in Paris and** aspect by pulling down its narrow lanes, and building wide **France** streets and magnificent boulevards—the latter, as was charged, for the purpose of depriving insurrection of its lurking places. The great exhibition of arts and industries in London was followed in 1854 by one in France, the largest and finest seen up to that time. Trade and industry were fostered by a reduction of tariff charges, joint stock companies and credit associations were favored, and in many ways Napoleon III. worked wisely and well for the prosperity of France, the growth of its industries, and the improvement of the condition of its people.

But the new emperor, while thus actively engaged in labors of peace, by no means lived up to the spirit of his motto, "The Empire is peace." An empire founded upon the army needs to give employment to that army. A monarchy sustained by the votes of a people athirst for **The Ambition** glory needs to do something to appease that thirst. A throne **of the Em-** filled by a Napoleon could not safely ignore the "Napo- **peror** leonic Ideas," and the first of these might be stated as "The Empire is war." And the new emperor was by no means satisfied to pose simply as the "nephew of his uncle." He possessed a large share of the Napoleonic ambition, and hoped by military glory to surround his throne with some of the lustre of that of Napoleon the First.

Whatever his private views, it is certain that France under his reign became the most aggressive nation of Europe, and the overweening ambition and self-confidence of the new emperor led him to the same end as his great uncle, that of disaster and overthrow.

The very beginning of Louis Napoleon's career of greatness, as president of the French Republic, was signalized by an act of military aggression, in sending his army to Rome and putting an end to the new Italian republic. These troops were kept there until 1866, and the aspirations of the Italian patriots were held in check until that year. Only when United Italy stood menacingly at the gates of Rome were these foreign troops withdrawn.

In 1854 Napoleon allied himself with the British and the Turks against Russia, and sent an army to the Crimea, which played an effective part in the great struggle in that peninsula. The troops of France had the honor of rendering Sebastopol untenable, carrying by storm one of its two great fortresses and turning its guns upon the city.

The French in the Crimea

The next act of aggression of the French emperor was against Austria. As the career of conquest of Napoleon I. had begun with an attack upon the Austrians in Italy, Napoleon III. attempted a similar enterprise, and with equal success. He had long been cautiously preparing in secret for hostilities with Austria, but lacked a satisfactory excuse for declaring war. This came in 1858 from an attempt at assassination. Felice Orsini, a fanatical Italian patriot, incensed at Napoleon from his failing to come to the aid of Italy, launched three explosive bombs against his carriage. The effect was fatal to many of the people in the street, though the intended victim escaped. Orsini won sympathy while in prison by his patriotic sentiments and the steadfastness of his love for his country. " Remember that the Italians shed their blood for Napoleon the great," he wrote to the emperor. " Liberate my country, and the blessings of twenty-five millions of people will follow you to posterity."

Orsini's Attempt at Assassination

Louis Napoleon had once been a member of a secret political society of Italy; he had taken the oath of initiation; his failure to come to the aid of that country when in power constituted him a traitor to his oath and one doomed to death ; the act of Orsini seemed the work of the society. That he was deeply moved by the attempted assassination is certain, and the result of his combined fear and ambition was soon to be shown.

On New Year's Day, 1859, while receiving the diplomatic corps at the Tuileries, Napoleon addressed the following significant words to the Austrian ambassador : " I regret that our relations are not so cordial as I could wish, but I beg you to report to the Emperor that my personal sentiments towards him remain unaltered."

Such is the masked way in which diplomats announce an intention of war. The meaning of the threatening words was soon shown, when Victor Emmanuel, shortly afterwards, announced at the opening of the Chambers in Turin that Sardinia could no longer remain indifferent to the cry for help which was

The Warlike Attitude of France and Sardinia

rising from all Italy. Ten years had passed since the defeat of the Sardinians on the plains of Lombardy. During that time they had cherished a hope of retribution, and it was now evident that an alliance had been made with France and that the hour of vengeance was at hand.

Austria was ready for the contest. Her finances, indeed, were in a serious state, but she had a large army in Lombardy. This was increased, Lombardy was declared in a state of siege, and every step was taken to guard against assault from Sardinia. Delay was disadvantageous to Austria, as it would permit her enemies to complete their preparations, and on April 23, 1859, an ultimatum came from Vienna, demanding that Sardinia should put her army on a peace footing or war would ensue,

A refusal came from Turin. Immediately field-marshal Gyulai received orders to cross the Ticino. Thus, after ten years of peace, the beautiful plains of Northern Italy were once more to endure the ravages of war. This act of Austria was severely criticised by the neutral powers, which had been seeking to allay the trouble. Napoleon took advantage of it, accusing Austria of breaking the peace by invading the territory of his ally, the king of Sardinia. **Advance of the Austrian Army**

The real fault committed by Austria, under the circumstances, was not in precipitating war, which could not well be avoided in the temper of her antagonists, but in putting, through court favor and privileges of rank, an incapable leader at the head of the army. Old Radetzky, the victor in the last war, was dead, but there were other able leaders who were thrust aside in favor of the Hungarian noble Franz Gyulai, a man without experience as commander-in-chief of an army.

By his uncertain and dilatory movements Gyulai gave the Sardinians time to concentrate an army of 80,000 men around the fortress of Alessandria, and lost all the advantage of being the first in the field. In early May the French army reached Italy, partly by way of the St. Bernard Pass, partly by sea ; and Garibaldi, with his mountaineers, took up a position that would enable him to attack the right wing of the Austrians.

Later in the month Napoleon himself appeared, his presence and the name he bore inspiring the soldiers with new valor, while his first order of the day, in which he recalled the glorious deeds which their fathers had done on those plains under his great uncle, roused them to the highest enthusiasm. While assuming the title of commander-in-chief, he left the conduct of the war to his able subordinates, MacMahon, Niel, Canrobert, and others. **The French in Italy and the March on Milan**

The Austrian general, having lost the opportunity to attack, was now put on the defensive, in which his incompetence was equally manifested.

Being quite ignorant of the position of the foe, he sent Count Stadion, with 12,000 men, on a reconnoisance.   An encounter took place at Montebello on May 20th, in which, after a sharp engagement, Stadion was forced to retreat.   Gyulai directed his attention to that quarter, leaving Napoleon to march unmolested from Alessandria to the invasion of Lombardy.   Gyulai now, aroused by the danger of Milan, began his retreat across the Ticino, which he had so uselessly crossed.

The road to Milan crossed the Ticino River and the Naviglio Grande, a broad and deep canal a few miles east of the river.   Some distance farther on lies the village of Magenta, the seat of the first great battle of the war. Sixty years before, on those Lombard plains, Napoleon the Great had first

A Campaign of Blunders   lost, and then, by a happy chance, won the famous battle of Marengo.   The Napoleon now in command was a very different man from the mighty soldier of the year 1800, and the French escaped a disastrous rout only because the Austrians were led by a worse general still.   Some one has said that victory comes to the army that makes the fewest blunders.   Such seems to have been the case in the battle of Magenta, where military genius was the one thing wanting.

The French pushed on, crossed the river without finding a man to dispute the passage,—other than a much-surprised customs official,—and reached an undefended bridge across the canal.   The high road to Milan seemed deserted by the Austrians.   But Napoleon's troops were drawn out in a preposterous line, straddling a river and a canal, both difficult to cross, and without any defensive positions to hold against an attack in force.   He supposed that the Austrians were stretched out in a similar long line. This was not the case.   Gyulai had all the advantages of position, and might have concentrated his army and crushed the advanced corps of the French if he had known his situation and his business.   As it was, between ignorance on the one hand and indecision on the other, the battle was fought with about equal forces on either hand.

The first contest took place at Buffalora, a village on the canal where

Buffalora and Magenta   the French encountered the Austrians in force.   Here a bloody struggle went on for hours, ending in the capture of the place by the Grenadiers of the Guard, who held on to it afterwards with stubborn courage.

General MacMahon, in command of the advance, had his orders to march forward, whatever happened, to the church-tower of Magenta, and, in strict obedience to orders, he pushed on, leaving the grenadiers to hold their own as best they could at Buffalora, and heedless of the fact that the reserve troops of the army had not yet begun to cross the river.   It was the 5th of June, and the day was well advanced when MacMahon came in contact with the Austrians at Magenta, and the great contest of the day began.

It was a battle in which the commanders on both sides, with the exception of MacMahon, showed lack of military skill and the soldiers on both sides the staunchest courage. The Austrians seemed devoid of plan or system, and their several divisions were beaten in detail by the French. On the other hand, General Camou, in command of the second division of MacMahon's corps, acted as Desaix had done at the battle of Marengo, marched at the sound of the distant cannon. But, **Camou's Deliberate March** unlike Desaix, he moved so deliberately that it took him six hours to make less than five miles. He was a tactician of the old school imbued with the idea that every march should be made in perfect order.

At half-past four MacMahon, with his uniform in disorder and followed by a few officers of his staff, dashed back to hurry up this deliberate reserve. On the way thither he rode into a body of Austrian sharpshooters. Fortune favored him. Not dreaming of the presence of the French general, they saluted him as one of their own commanders. On his way back he made a second narrow escape from capture by the Uhlans.

The drums now beat the charge, and a determined attack was made by the French, the enemy's main column being taken between two fires. Desperately resisting, it was forced back step by step upon Magenta. Into the town the columns rolled, and the fight became fierce around the church. High in the tower of this edifice stood the Austrian general and his staff, watching the fortunes of the fray; and from this point he caught sight of the four regiments of Camou, advancing as regularly as if on parade. They were not given the chance to fire a shot or receive a scratch, eager as they were to take part in the fight. At sight of them the **The French Victory at Magenta** Austrian general ordered a retreat and the battle was at an end. The French owed their victory largely to General Mellinet and his Grenadiers of the Guard, who held their own like bull-dogs at Buffalora while Camou was advancing with the deliberation of the old military rules. MacMahon and Mellinet and the French had won the day. Victor Emmanuel and the Sardinians did not reach the ground until after the battle was at end. For his services on that day of glory for France MacMahon was made Marshal of France and Duke of Magenta.

The prize of the victory of Magenta was the possession of Lombardy. Gyulai, unable to collect his scattered divisions, gave orders for a general retreat. Milan was evacuated with precipitate haste, and the garrisons were withdrawn from all the towns, leaving them to be occupied by the

French and Italians.   On the 8th of June Napoleon and Victor Emmanuel rode into Milan side by side, amid the loud acclamations of the people, who looked upon this victory as an assurance of Italian freedom and unity.

Milan and the Quadrilateral   Meanwhile the Austrians retreated without interruption, not halting until they arrived at the Mincio, where they were protected by the famous Quadrilateral, consisting of the four powerful fortresses of Peschiera, Mantua, Verona, and Leguano, the mainstay of the Austrian power in Italy.

The French and Italians slowly pursued the retreating Austrians, and on the 23d of June bivouacked on both banks of the Chiese River, about fifteen miles west of the Mincio.   The Emperor Francis Joseph had recalled the incapable Gyulai, and, in hopes of inspiring his soldiers with new spirit, himself took command.   The two emperors, neither of them soldiers, were thus pitted against each other, and Francis Joseph, eager to retrieve the disaster at Magenta, resolved to quit his strong position of defence in the Quadrilateral and assume the offensive.

At two o'clock in the morning of the 24th the allied French and Italian army resumed its march, Napoleon's orders for the day being based upon the reports of his reconnoitering parties and spies.   These led him to believe that, although a strong detachment of the enemy might be encountered west of the Mincio, the main body of the Austrians was awaiting him on the eastern side of the river.   But the French intelligence department was badly served.   The Austrians had stolen a march upon Napoleon.   Undetected by the French scouts, they had re-

The Armies on the Mincio   crossed the Mincio, and by nightfall of the 23d their leading columns were occupying the ground on which the French were ordered to bivouac on the evening of the 24th.   The intention of the Austrian emperor, now commanding his army in person, had been to push forward rapidly and fall upon the allies before they had completed the passage of the river Chiese.   But this scheme, like that of Napoleon, was based on defective information.   The allies broke up from their bivouacs many hours before the Austrians expected them to do so, and when the two armies came in contact early in the morning of the 24th of June the Austrians were quite as much taken by surprise as the French.

The Austrian army, superior in numbers to its opponents, was posted in a half-circle between the Mincio and Chiese, with the intention of pressing forward from these points upon a centre.   But the line was extended too far, and the centre was comparatively weak and without reserves. Napoleon, who that morning received complete intelligence of the position of the Austrian army, accordingly directed his chief strength against the

VICTOR HUGO

NOTED FRENCH AUTHORS

ALEXANDER DUMAS

NAPOLEON III AT THE BATTLE OF SOLFERINO, 1859—(FROM THE ORIGINAL PAINTING BY YVON)

The village of Solferino in Northern Italy is made historic by two notable battles which occurred there. In 1796 the French conquered the Austrians; and in 1859 the allied French and Sardinians, commanded by their respective monarchs, gained here another great victory over the Austrians commanded by their Emperor.

enemy's centre, which rested upon a height near the village of Solferino. Here, on the 24th of June, after a murderous conflict, in which the French commanders hurled continually renewed masses against the decisive position, while on the other side the Austrian reinforcements failed through lack of unity of plan and decision of action, the heights were at length won by the French troops in spite of heroic resistance on the part of the Austrian soldiers; the Austrian line of battle being cut through, and the army thus divided into two separate masses. A second attack which Napoleon promptly directed against Cavriano had a similar result; for the commands given by the Austrian generals were confused and had no general and definite aim. The fate of the battle was already in a great measure decided, when a tremendous storm broke forth that **The Battle of Solferino** put an end to the combat at most points, and gave the Austrians an opportunity to retire in order. Only Benedek, who had twice beaten back the Sardinians at various points, continued the struggle for some hours longer. On the French side Marshal Niel had pre-eminently distinguished himself by acuteness and bravery. It was a day of bloodshed, on which two great powers had measured their strength against each other for twelve hours. The Austrians had to lament the loss of 13,000 dead and wounded, and left 9,000 prisoners in the enemy's hands; on the side of the French and Sardinians the number of killed and wounded was even greater, for the repeated attacks had been made upon well-defended heights, but the number of prisoners was not nearly so great.

The victories in Italy filled the French people with the warmest admiration for their emperor, they thinking, in their enthusiasm, that a true successor of Napoleon the great had come to bring glory **The Feeling in** to their arms. Italy also was full of enthusiatic hope, fancying **France and** that the freedom and unity of the Italians was at last assured. **Italy** Both nations were, therefore, bitterly disappointed in learning that the war was at an end, and that a hasty peace had been arranged between the emperors, which left the hoped-for work but half achieved.

Napoleon estimated his position better than his people. Despite his victories, his situation was one of danger and difficulty. The army had suffered severely in its brief campaign, and the Austrians were still in possession of the Quadrilateral, a square of powerful fortresses which he might seek in vain to reduce. And a threat of serious trouble had arisen in Germany. The victorious career of a new Napoleon in Italy was alarming. It was not easy to forget the past. The German powers, though they had declined to come to the aid of Austria, were armed and ready, and at any moment might begin a hostile movement upon the Rhine.

Napoleon, wise enough to secure what he had won, without hazarding its loss, arranged a meeting with the Austrian emperor, whom he found quite as ready for peace. The terms of the truce arranged between them were that Austria should abandon Lombardy to the line of the Mincio, almost its eastern boundary, and that Italy should form a confederacy under the presidency of the pope. In the treaty subsequently made only the first of these conditions was maintained, Lombardy passing to the king of Sardinia. He received also the small states of Central Italy, whose tyrants had fled, ceding to Napoleon, as a reward for his assistance, the realm of Savoy and the city and territory of Nice.

A Meeting of the Emperors and Treaty of Peace

Napoleon had now reached the summit of his career. In the succeeding years the French were to learn that they had put their faith in a hollow emblem of glory, and Napoleon to lose the prestige he had gained at Magenta and Solferino. His first serious mistake was when he yielded to the voice of ambition, and, taking advantage of the occupation of the Americans in their civil war, sent an army to invade Mexico.

The ostensible purpose of this invasion was to collect a debt which the Mexicans had refused to pay, and Great Britain and Spain were induced to take part in the expedition. But their forces were withdrawn when they found that Napoleon had other purposes in view, and his army was left to fight its battles alone. After some sanguinary engagements the Mexican army was broken into a series of guerilla bands, incapable of facing his well-drilled troops, and Napoleon proceeded to reorganize Mexico as an empire, placing the Archduke Maximilian of Austria on the throne.

The Invasion of Mexico

All went well while the people of the United States were fighting for their national union, but when their war was over the ambitious French emperor was soon taught that he had committed a serious error. He was given plainly to understand that the French troops could only be kept in Mexico at the cost of a war with the United States, and he found it convenient to withdraw them early in 1867. They had no sooner gone than the Mexicans were in arms against Maximilian, and his rash determination to remain quickly led to his capture and execution as a usurper.

The inaction of Napoleon during the wars which Prussia fought with Denmark and Austria gave further blows to his prestige in France, and the opposition to his policy of personal government grew so strong that he felt himself obliged to submit his policy to a vote of the people. He was sustained by a large majority. Yet he perceived that his power was sinking. He was obliged to loosen the

Napoleon Loses Prestige in France

reins of government at home, though knowing that the yielding of increased liberty to the people would weaken his own control. Finally, finding himself failing in health, confidence, and reputation, he yielded to advisers who told him that the only hope for his dynasty lay in a successful war, and undertook the war of 1870 against Prussia.

The origin and events of this war will be considered in a subsequent chapter. It will suffice to say here that its events proved Napoleon's incapacity as a military emperor, he being utterly deceived in the condition of the French army and unwarrantably ignorant of that of the Germans. He believed that the army of France was in the highest condition of organization and completely supplied, when the very contrary was the case ; and was similarly deceived concerning the state of the military force of Prussia. The result was that which might have been expected. The German troops, admirably organized and excellently commanded, defeated the French in a series of engagments that fairly took the breath of the world by their rapidity and completeness, ending in the capture of Napoleon and his army. As a consequence the second empire of France came to an end and Napoleon lost his throne. He died two years afterwards an exile in England, that place of shelter for French royal refugees.

CHAPTER XIII.

Garibaldi and the Unification of Italy.

FROM the time of the fall of the Roman Empire until late in the nineteenth century, a period of some fourteen hundred years, Italy remained disunited, divided up between a series of states, small and large, hostile and peaceful, while its territory was made the battlefield of the surrounding powers, the helpless prey of Germany, France, and Spain. Even

Lack of Italian Unity

the strong hand of Napoleon failed to bring it unity, and after his fall its condition was worse than before, for Austria held most of the north and exerted a controlling power over the remainder of the peninsula, so that the fair form of liberty fled in dismay from its shores.

But the work of Napoleon had inspired the patriots of Italy with a new sentiment, that of union. Before the Napoleonic era the thought of a united Italy scarcely existed, and patriotism meant adherence to Sardinia, Naples, or some other of the many kingdoms and duchies. After that era union became the watchword of the revolutionists, who felt that the only hope of giving Italy a position of dignity and honor among the nations

Italian Unity and Its Heroes

lay in making it one country under one ruler. The history of the nineteenth century in Italy is the record of the attempt to reach this end, and its successful accomplishment.

And on that record the names of two men most prominently appear, Mazzini, the indefatigable conspirator, and Garibaldi, the valorous fighter; to whose names should be added that of the eminent statesmen, Count Cavour, and that of the man who reaped the benefit of their patriotic labors, Victor Emmanuel, the first king of united Italy.

The basis of the revolutionary movements in Italy was the secret political association known as the Carbonari, formed early in the nineteenth century and including members of all classes in its ranks. In 1814 this powerful society projected a revolution in Naples, and in 1820 it was

The Carbonari

strong enough to invade Naples with an army and force from the king an oath to observe the new constitution which it had prepared. The revolution was put down in the following year by the Austrians, acting as the agents of the "Holy Alliance,"—the compact of Austria, Prussia, and Russia.

An ordinance was passed, condemning any one who should attend a meeting of the Carbonari to capital punishment.   But the society continued to exist, despite this severe enactment, and has been at the basis of many of the outbreaks that have taken place in Italy since 1820.   Mazzini, Garibaldi, and all the leading patriots were members of this powerful organization, which was daring enough to condemn Napoleon III. to death, and almost to succeed in his assassination, for his failure to live up to his obligations as a member of the society.

Giuseppe Mazzini, a native of Genoa, became a member of the Carbonari in 1830.   His activity in revolutionary movements caused him soon after to be proscribed, and in 1831 he sought Marseilles, where he organized a new political society called " Young Italy," whose watchword was " God and the People," and whose basic principle was the union of the several states and kingdoms into one nation, as *Mazzini the Patriot* the only true foundation of Italian liberty.   This purpose he avowed in his writings and pursued through exile and adversity with inflexible constancy, and it is largely due to the work of this earnest patriot that Italy to-day is a single kingdom instead of a medley of separate states.   Only in one particular did he fail.   His persistent purpose was to establish a republic, not a monarchy.

While Mazzini was thus working with his pen, his compatriot, Giuseppe Garibaldi, was working as earnestly with his sword.   This daring soldier, a native of Nice and reared to a life on the *Early Career of Garibaldi* sea, was banished as a revolutionist in 1834, and the succeeding fourteen years of his life were largely spent in South America, in whose wars he played a leading part.

The revolution of 1848 opened Italy to these two patriots, and they hastened to return, Garibaldi to offer his services to Charles Albert of Sardinia, by whom, however, he was treated with coldness and distrust. Mazzini, after founding the Roman republic in 1849, called upon Garibaldi to come to its defence, and the latter displayed the greatest heroism in the contest against the Neapolitan and French invaders.   He escaped from Rome on its capture by the French, and, after many desperate conflicts and adventures with the Austrians, was again driven into exile, and in 1850 became a resident of New York.   For some time he worked in a manufactory of candles on Staten Island, and afterwards made several voyages on the Pacific.

The war of 1859 opened a new and promising channel for the devotion of Garibaldi to his native land.   Being appointed major-general and commissioned to raise a volunteer corps, he *The Hunters of the Alps* organized the hardy body of mountaineers called the " Hunters of the Alps," and with them performed prodigies of valor on the plains of Lombardy, winning victories over the Austrians at Varese, Como and other places. In his ranks was his fellow-patriot Mazzini.

The success of the French and Sardinians in Lombardy during this war stirred Italy to its centre. The grand duke of Tuscany fled to Austria. The duchess of Parma sought refuge in Switzerland. The duke of Modena found shelter in the Austrian camp. Everywhere the brood of tyrants took to flight. Bologna threw off its allegiance to the pope, and proclaimed the king of Sardinia dictator. Several other towns in the states of the Church did the same. In the terms of the truce between Louis Napoleon and Francis Joseph the rulers of these realms were to resume their reigns if the people would permit. But the people would not permit, and they were all annexed to Sardinia, which country was greatly expanded as a result of the war.

It will not suffice to give all the credit for these revolutionary movements to Mazzini, the organizer, Garibaldi, the soldier, and the ambitious monarchs of France and Sardinia. More important than king and emperor was the eminent statesman, Count Cavour, prime minister of Sardinia from 1852. It is to this able man that the honor of the unification of Italy most **Count Cavour** fully belongs, though he did not live to see it. He sent a **the Brain of** Sardinian army to the assistance of France and England in **Italy** the Crimea in 1855, and by this act gave his state a standing among the powers of Europe. He secured liberty of the press and favored toleration in religion and freedom of trade. He rebelled against the dominion of the papacy, and devoted his abilities to the liberation and unity of Italy, undismayed by the angry fulminations from the Vatican. The war of 1859 was his work, and he had the satisfaction of seeing Sardinia increased by the addition of Lombardy, Tuscany, Parma and Modena. A great step had been taken in the work to which he had devoted his life.

The next step in the great work was taken by Garibaldi, who now struck at the powerful kingdom of Naples and Sicily in the south. It **Garibaldi's In-** seemed a difficult task. Francis II., the son and successor of **vasion of** the infamous "King Bomba," had a well-organized army of **Sicily** 150,000 men. But his father's tyranny had filled the land with secret societies, and fortunately at this time the Swiss mercenaries were recalled home, leaving to Francis only his unsafe native troops. This was the critical interval which Mazzini and Garibaldi chose for their work.

At the beginning of April, 1860, the signal was given by separate insurrections in Messina and Palermo. These were easily suppressed by the troops in garrison ; but though both cities were declared in a state of siege, they gave occasion for demonstrations by which the revolutionary chiefs excited the public mind. On the 6th of May, Garibaldi started with two steamers from Genoa with about a thousand Italian volunteers, and on the 11th landed near Marsala, on the west coast of Sicily. He proceeded to the mountains, and near Salemi gathered round him the scattered bands of the free corps. By the 14th his army had increased to 4,000 men. He now issued a proclamation, in which he took upon himself the dictatorship of Sicily, in the name of Victor Emmanuel, king of Italy. After waging various successful combats under the most difficult circumstances, Garibaldi advanced upon the capital, announcing his arrival by beacon-fires kindled at night. On the 27th he was in front of the Porta Termina of Palermo, and at once gave the signal for the attack. The people rose in mass, and assisted the operations of the besiegers by Capture of Palermo barricade-fighting in the streets. In a few hours half the town was in Garibaldi's hands. But now General Lanza, whom the young king had dispatched with strong reinforcements to Sicily, furiously bombarded the insurgent city, so that Palermo was reduced almost to a heap of ruins. At this juncture, by the intervention of an English admiral, an armistice was concluded, which led to the departure of the Neapolitan troops and war vessels and the surrender of the town to Garibaldi, who thus, with a band of 5,000 badly armed followers, had gained a signal advantage over a regular army of 25,000 men. This event had tremendous consequences, for it showed the utter hollowness of the Neapolitan government, while Garibaldi's fame was everywhere spread abroad. The glowing fancy of the Italians beheld in him the national hero before whom every enemy would bite the dust. This idea seemed to extend even to the Neapolitan court itself, where all was doubt, confusion and dismay. The king hastily summoned a liberal ministry, and offered to restore the constitution of 1848, but the general verdict was, "too late," and his proclamation fell flat on a people who had no trust in Bourbon faith.

The arrival of Garibaldi in Naples was enough to set in blaze all the combustible materials in that state. His appearance there was not long delayed. Six weeks after the surrender of Messina is Taken Palermo he marched against Messina. On the 21st of July the fortress of Melazzo was evacuated, and a week afterwards all Messina except the citadel was given up.

Europe was astounded at the remarkable success of Garibaldi's handful of men. On the mainland his good fortune was still more astonishing. He had hardly landed—which he did almost in the face of the Neapolitan fleet —than Reggio was surrendered and its garrison withdrew. His progress through the south of the kingdom was like a triumphal procession. At the **Flight of Francis II. and Conquest of Naples** end of August he was at Cosenza; on the 5th of September at Eboli, near Salerno. No resistance appeared. His very name seemed to work like magic on the population. The capital had been declared in a state of siege, and on September 6th the king took flight, retiring, with the 4,000 men still faithful to him, behind the Volturno. The next day Garibaldi, with a few followers, entered Naples, whose populace received him with frantic shouts of welcome.

The remarkable achievements of Garibaldi filled all Italy with overmastering excitement. He had declared that he would proclaim the kingdom of Italy from the heart of its capital city, and nothing less than this would content the people. The position of the pope had become serious. He refused to grant the reforms suggested by the **The Army of the Pope** French emperor, and threatened with excommunication any one who should meddle with the domain of the Church. Money was collected from faithful Catholics throughout the world, a summons was issued calling for recruits to the holy army of the pope, and the exiled French General Lamoricière was given the chief command of the troops, composed of men who had flocked to Rome from many nations. It was hoped that the name of the celebrated French leader would have a favorable influence on the troops of the French garrison of Rome.

The settlement of the perilous situation seemed to rest with Louis Napoleon. If he had let Garibaldi have his way the latter would, no doubt, have quickly ended the temporal sovereignty of the pope and made Rome the capital of Italy. But Napoleon seems to have arranged with Cavour to leave the king of Sardinia free to take possession of Naples, Umbria and the other provinces, provided that Rome and the "patrimony of St. Peter" were left intact.

At the beginning of September two Sardinian army corps, under Fanti and Cialdini, marched to the borders of the states of the church. Lamoricière advanced against Cialdini with his motley troops, but **Victor Emmanuel in Naples** was quickly defeated, and on the following day was besieged in the fortess of Ancona. On the 29th he and the garrison surrendered as prisoners of war. On the 9th of October Victor Emmanuel arrived and took command. There was no longer a papal army to oppose him, and the march southward proceeded without a check.

The object of the king in assuming the chief command was to complete the conquest of the kingdom of Naples, in conjunction with Garibaldi. For though Garibaldi had entered the capital in triumph, the progress on the line of the Volturno had been slow; and the expectation that the

GUISEPPE GARIBALDI

GREAT ITALIAN PATRIOTS

VICTOR EMMANUEL

THE ZOUAVES CHARGING THE BARRICADES AT MENTANA

In 1867 Garibaldi made a final effort to take the city of Rome, it being one of the cherished objects of his life to make it the capital of United Italy. He would have succeeded in capturing the famous city had not the French come to the aid of the papal troops. The allied forces were too strong, and he was defeated at Mentana. The illustration shows the French Zouaves in a dashing bayonet charge against the barricades of the revolutionists.

Neapolitan army would go over to the invaders in a mass had not been realized. The great majority of the troops remained faithful to the flag, so that Garibaldi, although his irregular bands amounted to more than 25,000 men, could not hope to drive away King Francis, or to take the fortresses of Capua and Gaeta, without the help of Sardinia. Against the diplomatic statesman Cavour, who fostered no illusions, and saw the conditions of affairs in its true light, the simple, honest Garibaldi cherished a deep aversion. He could never forgive Cavour for having given up Nice, Garibaldi's native town, to the French. On the other hand, he felt attracted toward the king, who in his opinion seemed to be the man raised up by Providence for the liberation of Italy. **Garibaldi Yields His Conquests** Accordingly, when Victor Emmanuel entered Sessa, at the head of his army, Garibaldi was easily induced to place his dictatorial power in the hands of the king, to whom he left the completion of the work of the union of Italy. After greeting Victor Emmanuel with the title of King of Italy, and giving the required resignation of his power, with the words, "Sire, I obey," he entered Naples, riding beside the king; and then, after recommending his companions in arms to his majesty's special favor, he retired to his home on the island of Caprera, refusing to receive a reward, in any shape or form, for his services to the state and its head.

The progress of the Sardinian army compelled Francis to give up the line of the Volturno, and he eventually took refuge, with his best troops, in the fortress of Gaeta. On the maintenance of this fortress hung the fate of the kingdom of Naples. Its defence is the only bright point in the career of the feeble Francis, whose courage was aroused by the heroic resolution of his young wife, the Bavarian Princess Mary. **Capture of Gaeta** For three months the defence continued. But no European power came to the aid of the king, disease appeared with scarcity of food and of munitions of war, and the garrison was at length forced to capitulate. The fall of Gaeta was practically the completion of the great work of the unification of Italy. Only Rome and Venice remained to be added to the united kingdom. On February 18, 1861, Victor Emmanuel assembled at Turin the deputies of all the states that acknowledged his supremacy, and in their presence assumed the title of King of Italy, which he was the first to bear. In four **Victor Emmanuel Made King of Italy** months afterwards Count Cavour, to whom this great work was largely due, died. He had lived long enough to see the purpose of his life practically accomplished.

Great as had been the change which two years had made, the patriots of Italy were not satisfied. "Free from the Alps to the Adriatic!" was their cry; "Rome and Venice!" became the watchword of the revolutionists. Mazzini, who had sought to found a republic, was far from content, and the agitation went on.   Garibaldi was drawn into it, and made bitter complaint of the treatment his followers had received.   In 1862, disheartened at the inaction of the king, he determined to undertake against Rome an expedition like that which he had led against Naples two years before.

In June he sailed from Genoa and landed at Palermo, where he was **Garibaldi's Ex-** quickly joined by an enthusiastic party of volunteers.   They **pedition** supposed that the government secretly favored their design, **Against Rome** but the king had no idea of fighting against the French troops in Rome and arousing international complications, and he energetically warned all Italians against taking part in revolutionary enterprises.

But Garibaldi persisted in his design.   When his way was barred by the garrison of Messina he turned aside to Catania, where he embarked with 2,000 volunteers, declaring he would enter Rome as a victor, or perish beneath its walls.   He landed at Melito on the 24th of August, and threw himself at once, with his followers, into the Calabrian mountains.   But his enterprise was quickly and disastrously ended.   General Cialdini despatched a division of the regular army, under Colonel Pallavicino, against the volunteer bands.   At Aspromonte, on the 28th of August, the two forces came into collision.   A chance shot was followed by several volleys from the regulars.   Garibaldi forbade his men to return the fire of their fellow-subjects of the Italian kingdom.   He was wounded, and taken **Sent Back to** prisoner with his followers, a few of whom had been slain **Caprera** in the short combat.   A government steamer carried the wounded chief to Varignano, where he was held in a sort of honorable imprisonment, and was compelled to undergo a tedious and painful operation for the healing of his wound.   He had at least the consolation that all Europe looked with sympathy and interest upon the unfortunate hero ; and a general sense of relief was felt when, restored to health, he was set free, and allowed to return to his rocky island of Caprera.

Victor Emmanuel was seeking to accomplish his end by safer means. The French garrison of Rome was the obstacle in his way, and this was finally removed through a treaty with Louis Napoleon in September, 1864, **Florence the** the emperor agreeing to withdraw his troops during the succeed-**Capital of** ing two years, in which the pope was to raise an army large **Italy** enough to defend his dominions.   Florence was to replace Turin as the capital of Italy.   This arrangement created such disturbances in Turin that the king was forced to leave that city hastily for his new capital.   In December, 1866, the last of the French troops departed from Rome, in despite of the efforts of the pope to retain them. By their withdrawal Italy was freed from the presence of foreign soldiers for the first time probably in a thousand years.

In 1866 came an event which reacted favorably for Italy, though her part in it was the reverse of triumphant. This was the war between Prussia and Austria. Italy was in alliance with Prussia, and Victor Emmanuel hastened to lead an army across the Mincio to **The War of 1866** the invasion of Venetia, the last Austrian province in Italy. Garibaldi at the same time was to invade the Tyrol with his volunteers. The enterprise ended in disaster. The Austrian troops, under the Archduke Albert, encountered the Italians at Custozza and gained a brilliant victory, despite the much greater numbers of the Italians.

Fortunately for Italy, the Austrians had been unsuccessful in the north, and the emperor, with the hope of gaining the alliance of France and breaking the compact between Italy and Prussia, decided to cede Venetia to Louis Napoleon. His purpose failed. All Napoleon did in response was to act as a peacemaker, while the Italian king refused to recede from his alliance. Though the Austrians were retreating from a country which no longer belonged to them, the invasion of Venetia by the Italians continued, and several conflicts with the Austrian army took place.

But much the most memorable event of this brief war occurred on the sea, in the most striking contest of ironclad ships between the American civil war and the Japan-China contest. Both countries concerned had fleets on the Adriatic. Italy was the strongest in naval vessels, possessing ten ironclads and a considerable number of wooden ships. Austria's ironclad fleet was seven in number, plated with thin iron and **The Fleets in the Adriatic** with no very heavy guns. In addition there was a number of wooden vessels and gunboats. But in command of this fleet was an admiral in whose blood was the iron which was lacking on his ships, Tegethoff, the Dewey of the Adriatic. Inferior as his ships were, his men were thoroughly drilled in the use of the guns and the evolutions of the ships, and when he sailed it was with the one thought of victory.

Persano, the Italian admiral, as if despising his adversary, engaged in siege of the fortified island of Lissa, near the Dalmatian coast, leaving the Austrians to do what they pleased. What they pleased was to attack him with a fury such as has been rarely seen. Early on July 20, 1866, when the Italians were preparing for a combined assault of the island by land and sea, their movement was checked by the signal displayed on a scouting frigate: "Suspicious-looking ships are in sight." Soon afterwards the Austrian fleet appeared, the ironclads leading, the wooden ships in the rear.

The battle that followed has had no parallel before or since. The whole Austrian fleet was converted into rams. Tegethoff gave one final order to his captains: "Close with the enemy and ram everything grey." Grey was the color of the Italian ships. The Austrian were painted black, so as to prevent any danger of error.

Fire was opened at two miles distance, the balls being wasted in the waters between the fleets, "Full steam ahead," signalled Tegethoff. On came the fleets, firing steadily, the balls now beginning to tell. "Ironclads will ram and sink the enemy," signalled Tegethoff. It was the last order he gave until the battle was won.

Soon the two lines of ironclads closed amid thick clouds of smoke. Tegethoff, in his flagship, the *Ferdinand Max*, twiced rammed a grey ironclad without effect. Then, out of the smoke, loomed up the tall masts of **The Sinking** the *Re d'Italia*, Persano's flagship in the beginning of the **of the "Re** fray. Against this vessel the *Ferdinand Max* rushed at full **d'Italia"** speed, and struck her fairly amidships. Her sides of iron were crushed in by the powerful blow, her tall masts toppled over, and down beneath the waves sank the great ship with her crew of 600 men. The next minute another Italian ship came rushing upon the Austrian, and was only avoided by a quick turn of the helm.

One other great disaster occurred to the Italians. The *Palestro* was set on fire, and the pumps were put actively to work to drown the magazine. **The "Palestro"** The crew thought the work had been successfully performed, **is Blown Up** and that they were getting the fire under control, when there suddenly came a terrible burst of flame attended by a roar that drowned all the din of the battle. It was the death knell of 400 men, for the *Palestro* had blown up with all on board.

The great ironclad turret ship and ram of the Italian fleet, the *Affondatore*, to which Admiral Persano had shifted his flag, far the most powerful vessel in the Adriatic, kept outside of the battle-line, and was of little service in the fray. It was apparently afraid to encounter Tegethoff's terrible rams. The battle ended with the Austrian fleet, wooden vessels and all, passing practically unharmed through the Italian lines into the harbor of Lissa, leaving death and destruction in their rear. Tegethoff was the one Austrian who came out of that war with fame. Persano on his return home **Venetia Ceded** was put on trial for cowardice and incompetence. He was con- **to Italy** victed of the latter and dismissed from the navy in disgrace.

But Italy, though defeated by land and sea, gained a valuable prize from the war, for Napoleon ceded Venetia to the Italian king, and soon afterwards Victor Emmanuel entered Venice in triumph, the solemn act of homage being performed in the superb Place of St. Marks. Thus was completed the second act in the unification of Italy.

The national party, with Garibaldi at its head, still aimed at the possession of Rome, as the historic capital of the peninsula. In 1867 he made a second attempt to capture Rome, but the papal army, strengthened with a a new French auxiliary force, defeated his badly armed volunteers, and he was taken prisoner and held captive for a time, after which he was sent back to Caprera. This led to the French army of occupation being returned to Civita Vecchia, where it was kept for several years.

The final act came as a consequence of the Franco-German war of 1870, which rendered necessary the withdrawal of the French troops from Italy. The pope was requested to make a peaceful abdica- **Rome Becomes** tion. As he refused this, the States of the Church were occu- **the Capital** pied up to the walls of the capital, and a three hours' cannon- **of Italy** ade of the city sufficed to bring the long strife to an end. Rome became the capital of Italy, and the whole peninsula, for the first time since the fall of the ancient Roman empire, was concentrated into a single nation, under one king.

CHAPTER XIV.

Bismarck and the New Empire of Germany.

WHAT was for many centuries known as "The Holy Roman Empire of the German Nation" was a portion of the great imperial domain of Charlemagne, divided between his sons on his death in 814. It became an elective monarchy in 911, and from the reign of Otho the Great was confined to Germany, which assumed the title above given. This great empire survived until 1804, when the imperial title, then held by Francis I. of Austria, was given up, and Francis styled himself Emperor of Austria. It is an interesting coincidence that this empire ceased to exist in the same year that Napoleon, who in a large measure restored the empire of Charlemagne, assumed the imperial crown of France. The restoration of the Empire of Germany, though not in its old form, was left to Prussia, after the final overthrow of the Napoleonic imperial dynasty in 1871.

The Empires of Germany and France

Prussia, originally an unimportant member of the German confederation, rose to power as Austria declined, its progress upward being remarkably rapid. Frederick William, the "Great Elector" of Brandenburg, united the then minor province of Prussia to his dominions, and at his death in 1688 left it a strong army and a large treasure. His son, Frederick I., was the first to bear the title of King of Prussia. Frederick the Great, who became king in 1740, had under him a series of disjointed provinces and a population of less than 2,500,000. His genius made Prussia a great power, which grew until, in 1805, it had a population of 9,640,000 and a territory of nearly 6,000 square miles.

The Rapid Growth of Prussia

We have seen the part this kingdom played in the Napoleonic wars. Dismembered by Napoleon and reduced to a mere fragment, it regained its old importance by the Treaty of Vienna. The great career of this kingdom began with the accession, in 1862, of King William I., and the appointment, in the same year, of Count Otto von Bismarck as Minister of the King's House and of Foreign Affairs. It was not King William, but Count Bismarck, who raised Prussia to the exalted position it has since assumed.

Bismarck began his career by an effort to restore the old despotism, setting aside acts of the legislature with the boldness of an autocrat, and seeking to make the king supreme over the representatives of the people

Bismarck's Despotic Acts and Warlike Aggressions
He disdained the protest of the Chamber of Deputies in concluding a secret treaty with Russia. He made laws and decreed budget estimates without the concurrence of the Chambers. And while thus busily engaged at home in altercations with the Prussian Parliament, he was as actively occupied with foreign affairs.

In 1864 Austria reluctantly took part with Prussia in the occupation of the duchy of Schleswig-Holstein, claimed by Denmark. A war with Denmark followed, which ultimately resulted in the annexation to Prussia of the disputed territory. In this movement Bismarck was carrying out a project which he had long entertained, that of making Prussia the leading power in Germany. A second step in this policy was taken in 1866, when the troops of Prussia occupied Hanover and Saxony. This act of aggression led to a war, in which Austria, alarmed at the ambitious movements of Prussia, came to the aid of the threatened states.

Bismarck was quite ready. He had strengthened Prussia by an alliance with Italy, and launched the Prussian army against that of Austria with a rapidity that overthrew the power of the allies in a remarkably brief and most brilliant campaign. At the decisive battle of Sadowa fought July 3, 1866, King William commanded the Prussian army and Field-marshal Benedek the Austrian. But back of the Prussian king was General Von Moltke one of the most brilliant strategists of modern times, to whose skillful combinations, and distinguished services in organizing the army of Prussia, that state owed its rapid series of successes in war.

At Sadowa the newly-invented needle-gun played an effective part in bringing victory to the Prussian arms. The battle continued actively from 7.30 A.M. to 2.30 P.M., at which hour the Prussians carried the centre of the

Austria Overthrown at Sadowa
Austrian position. Yet, despite this, the advantage remained with the Austrians until 3.30, at which hour the Crown Prince Frederick drove their left flank from the village of Lipa. An hour more sufficed to complete the defeat of the Austrians, but it was 9 P.M. before the fighting ceased. In addition to their losses on the field, 15,000 of the Austrians were made prisoners and their cause was lost beyond possibility of recovery.

There seemed nothing to hinder Bismarck from overthrowing and dismembering the Austrian empire, as Napoleon had done more than once, but there is reason to believe that the dread of France coming to the aid of the defeated realm made him stop short in his career of victory. Napoleon III. boasted to the French Chambers that he had stayed the conqueror at the

WILLIAM I. EMPEROR OF UNITED GERMANY.

NOTED GERMAN EMPERORS.

WILLIAM II. PRESENT EMPEROR.

OTTO VON BISMARCK

H. KARL B. VON MOLTKE

RENOWNED SONS OF GERMANY

gates of Vienna. However that be, a treaty of peace was signed, in which Austria consented to withdraw from the German Confederation. Bismarck had gained one great point in his plans, in removing a formidable rival from his path. The way was cleared for making Prussia the supreme power in Germany. The German allies of Austria suffered severely for their assistance to that power. Saxony kept its king, but fell under Prussian control; and Hanover, Hesse-Cassel, Nassau, and the free city of Frankfurt-on-the-Main were absorbed by Prussia.

The States of South Germany had taken part on the side of Austria in the war, and continued the struggle after peace had been made between the main contestants. The result was the only one that could have been expected under the circumstances. Though the Bavarians and Würtembergers showed great bravery in the several conflicts, the **South German** Prussians were steadily successful, and the South German **States in the** army was finally obliged to retire beyond the Main, while **War** Würzburg was captured by the Prussians. In this city a truce was effected which ultimately led to a treaty of peace. Würtemberg, Bavaria, and Baden were each required to pay a war indemnity, and a secret measure of the treaty was an offensive and defensive alliance with Prussia for common action in case of a foreign war.

Mention was made in the last chapter of the long disunion of Italy, its division into a number of separate and frequently hostile states from the fall of the Roman Empire until its final unification in 1870. A similar condition had for ages existed in Germany. The so-called Ger- **Disunion of** man Empire of the mediæval period was little more than a **Germany** league of separate states, each with its own monarch and distinct government. And the authority of the emperor decreased with time until it became but a shadow. It vanished in 1804, leaving Germany composed of several hundred independent states, small and large.

Several efforts were made in the succeeding years to restore the bond of union between these states. Under the influence of Napoleon they were organized into South German and North German Confederacies, and the effect of his interference with their internal affairs was such that they became greatly reduced in number, many of the minor states being swallowed up by their more powerful neighbors.

The subsequent attempts at union proved weak and ineffective. The *Bund*, or bond of connection between these states, formed after **Efforts at** the Napoleonic period, was of the most shadowy character, **Union** its congress being destitute of power or authority. The National Assembly, convened at Frankfurt after the revolution of 1848, with the Archduke John of Austria as administrator of the empire, proved equally powerless. It made a vigorous effort to enforce its authority, but without avail; Prussia refused to be bound by its decisions; and the attitude of opposition assumed by this powerful state soon brought the new attempt at union to an end.

In 1886 the war between the two great powers of Germany, in which most of the smaller powers were concerned, led to more decided measures, in the absorption by Prussia of the states above named, the formation of a North German League among the remaining states of the north, and the offensive and defensive alliance with Prussia of the South German states. By the treaty of peace with Austria, that power was excluded from the German League, and Prussia remained the dominant power in Germany. A constitution for the League was adopted in 1867, providing for a Diet, or legislative council of the League, elected by the direct votes of the people, and an army, which was to be under the command of the Prussian king and subject to the military laws of Prussia. Each state in the League bound itself to supply a specified sum for the support of the army.

Here was a union with a backbone—an army and a budget—and Bismarck had done more in the five years of his ministry in forming an united Germany than his predecessors had done in fifty years. **The Feeling for Unity** But the idea of union and alliance between kindred states was then widely in the air. Such a union had been practically completed in Italy, and Hungary in 1867 regained her ancient rights, which had been taken from her in 1849, being given a separate government, with Francis Joseph, the emperor of Austria, as its king. It was natural that the common blood of the Germans should lead them to a political confederation, and equally natural that Prussia, which so overshadowed the smaller states in strength, should be the leading element in the alliance.

The great increase in the power and importance of Prussia, as an outcome of the war with Austria, was viewed with jealousy in France. The Emperor Napoleon sought, by a secret treaty with Holland, to obtain possession of the state of Luxemburg, for which a sum of money was to be paid. This negotiation became known and was defeated by Bismarck, the King of Holland shrinking from the peril of war and the publicity of a disgraceful transaction. But the interference of Prussia with this underhand scheme added to the irritation of France.

The Position of Louis Napoleon And thus time passed on until the eventful year 1870. By that year Prussia had completed its work among the North German states and was ready for the issue of hostilities, if this should be necessary. On the other hand, Napoleon, who had found his prestige in France from various causes decreasing, felt obliged in 1870 to depart from his policy of personal rule and give that country a constitutional government. This proposal was submitted to a vote of the people and was sustained by an immense majority. He also took occasion to state that "peace was never more assured than at the present time." This assurance gave satisfaction to the world, yet it was a false one, for war was probably at that moment assured.

There were alarming signs in France. The opposition to Napoleonism was steadily gaining power. A bad harvest was threatened—a serious source of discontent. The Parliament was discussing the reversal of the sentence of banishment against the Orleans family. These indications of a change in public sentiment appeared to call for some act that would aid in restoring the popularity of the emperor. And of all the acts that could be devised a national war seemed the most promising. If the Rhine frontier, which every French regarded as the natural boundary of the empire, could be regained by the arms of the nation, discontent and opposition would vanish, the name of Napoleon would win back its old prestige, and the reign of Bonapartism would be firmly established.

Acts speak louder than words, and the acts of Napoleon were not in accord with his assurances of peace. Extensive military preparations began, and the forces of the empire were strengthened by land and sea, while great trust was placed in a new weapon, **Preparations for Hostilities** of murderous powers, called the *mitrailleuse*, the predecessor of the machine gun, and capable of discharging twenty-five balls at once.

On the other hand, there were abundant indications of discontent in Germany, where a variety of parties inveighed against the rapacious policy of Prussia, and where Bismarck had sown a deep crop of hate. It was believed in France that the minor states would not support Prussia in a war. In Austria the defeat in 1866 rankled, and hostilities against Prussia on the part of France seemed certain to win sympathy and support in that composite empire. Colonel Stoffel, the French military envoy at Berlin, declared that Prussia would be found abundantly prepared for a struggle; but his warnings went unheeded in the French Cabinet, and the warlike preparations continued.

Napoleon did not have to go far for an excuse for the war upon which he was resolved. One was prepared for him in that potent source of trouble, the succession to the throne of Spain. In **The Revolution in Spain** that country there had for years been no end of trouble, revolts, Carlist risings, wars and rumors of wars. The government of Queen Isabella, with its endless intrigues. plots, and alternation of despotism and anarchy, and the pronounced immorality of the queen, had become so distasteful to the people that finally, after several years of revolts and armed risings, she was driven from her throne by a revolution, and for a time Spain was without a monarchy and ruled on republican principles.

But this arrangement did not prove satisfactory. The party in opposition looked around for a king, and negotiations began with a distant relative of the Prussian royal family, Leopold of Hohenzollern. Prince Leopold accepted the offer, and informed the king of Prussia of his decision.

The news of this event caused great excitement in Paris, and the Prussian government was advised of the painful feeling to which the incident had given rise. The answer from Berlin that the Prussian **The Spanish** government had no concern in the matter, and that Prince **Succession** Leopold was free to act on his own account, did not allay the excitement. The demand for war grew violent and clamorous, the voices of the feeble opposition in the Chambers were drowned, and the journalists and war partisans were confident of a short and glorious campaign and a triumphant march to Berlin.

The hostile feeling was reduced when King William of Prussia, though he declined to prohibit Prince Leopold from accepting the crown, expressed his concurrence with the decision of the prince when he withdrew his acceptance of the dangerous offer. This decision was regarded as **Napoleon's De-** sufficient, even in Paris; but it did not seem to be so in the **mand and** palace, where an excuse for a declaration of war was ardently **William's** **Refusal** desired. The emperor's hostile purpose was enhanced by the influence of the empress, and it was finally declared that the Prussian king had aggrieved France in permitting the prince to become a candidate for the throne without consulting the French Cabinet.

Satisfaction for this shadowy source of offence was demanded, but King William firmly refused to say any more on the subject and declined to stand in the way of Prince Leopold if he should again accept the offer of the Spanish throne. This refusal was declared to be an offence to the honor and a threat to the safety of France. The war party was so strongly in the ascendant that all opposition was now looked upon as lack of **The Declaration** patriotism, and on the 15th of July the Prime Minister Ollivier **of War** announced that the reserves were to be called out and the necessary measures taken to secure the honor and security of France. When the declaration of war was hurled against Prussia the whole nation seemed in harmony with it, and public opinion appeared for once to have become a unit throughout France.

Rarely in the history of the world has so trivial a cause given rise to such stupendous military and political events as took place in France in a brief interval following this blind leap into hostilities. Instead of a triumphant march to Berlin and the dictation of peace from its palace, France was to find itself in two months' time without an emperor or an army, and in a few months more completely subdued and occupied by foreign troops, while Paris had been made the scene of a terrible siege and a frightful communistic riot, and a republic had succeeded the empire. It was such a series of events as have seldom been compressed within the short interval of half a year.

In truth Napoleon and his advisers were blinded by their hopes to the true state of affairs. The army on which they depended, and which they assumed to be in a high state of efficiency and discipline, was lacking in almost every requisite of an efficient force. The first Napoleon was his own minister of war. The third Napoleon, when told by his war minister that "not a single button was wanting on a single gaiter," took the words for the fact, and hurled an army without supplies and organization against the most thoroughly organized army the world had ever known. That the French were as brave as the Germans goes without saying ; they fought desperately, but from the first confusion reigned in their movements, while military science of the highest kind dominated those of the Germans.

State of the French and German Armies

Napoleon was equally mistaken as to the state of affairs in Germany. The disunion upon which he counted vanished at the first threat of war. All Germany felt itself threatened and joined hands in defence. The declaration of war was received there with as deep an enthusiasm as in France and a fervent eagerness for the struggle. The new popular song, *Die Wacht am Rhein* ("The Watch on the Rhine") spread rapidly from end to end of the country, and indicated the resolution of the German people to defend to the death the frontier stream of their country.

The French looked for a parade march to Berlin, even fixing the day of their entrance into that city—August 15th, the emperor's birthday. On the contrary, they failed to set their foot on German territory, and soon found themselves engaged in a death struggle with the invaders of their own land. In truth, while the Prussian diplomacy was conducted by Bismarck, the ablest statesman Prussia had ever known, the movements of the army were directed by far the best tactician Europe then possessed, the famous Von Moltke, to whose strategy the rapid success of the war against Austria had been due. In the war with France Von Moltke, though too old to lead the armies in per-

Bismarck and Von Moltke

son, was virtually commander-in-chief, and arranged those masterly combinations which overthrew all the power of France in so remarkably brief a period. Under his directions, from the moment war was declared, everything worked with clocklike precision. It was said that Von Moltke had only to touch a bell and all went forward. As it was, the Crown Prince Frederick fell upon the French while still unprepared, won the first battle, and steadily held the advantage to the end, the French being beaten by the strategy that kept the Germans in superior strength at all decisive points.

But to return to the events of war. On July 23, 1870, the Emperor Napoleon, after making his wife Eugenie regent of France, set out with his son at the head of the army, full of high hopes of victory and triumph. By the end of July King William had also set out from Berlin to join the armies that were then in rapid motion towards the frontier.

The emperor made his way to Metz, where was stationed his main army, about 200,000 strong, under Marshals Bazaine and Canrobert and General Bourbaki. Further east, under Marshal MacMahon, **Strength of the Armies** the hero of Magenta, was the southern army, of about 100,000 men. A third army occupied the camp at Chalons, while a well-manned fleet set sail for the Baltic, to blockade the harbors and assail the coast of Germany. The German army was likewise in three divisons, the first, of 61,000 men, under General Steinmetz; the second, of 206,000 men, under Prince Frederick Charles; and the third, of 180,000 men, under the crown prince and General Blumenthal. The king, commander-in-chief of the whole, was in the centre, and with him the general staff under the guidance of the alert Von Moltke. Bismarck and the minister of war Von Roon were also present, and so rapid was the movement of these great forces that in two weeks after the order to march was given 300,000 armed Germans stood in rank along the Rhine.

The two armies first came together on August 2d, near Saarbrück, on **Battles of Saar-brück and Weissenburg** the frontier line of the hostile kingdoms. It was the one success of the French, for the Prussians, after a fight in which both sides lost equally, retired in good order. This was proclaimed by the French papers as a brilliant victory, and filled the people with undue hopes of glory. It was the last favorable report, for they were quickly overwhelmed with tidings of defeat and disaster.

Weissenburg, on the borders of Rhenish Bavaria, had been invested by a division of MacMahon's army. On August 4th the right wing of the army of the Crown Prince Frederick attacked and repulsed this investing force after a hot engagement, in which its leader, General Douay, was killed, and the loss on both sides was heavy. Two days later occurred a battle which decided the fate of the whole war, that of Worth-Reideshofen, where the army of the crown prince met that of MacMahon, and after a desperate struggle, which continued for fifteen hours, completely defeated him, with very heavy losses on both sides.   MacMahon retreated in haste towards the army at Chalons, while the crown prince took possession of Alsace, and prepared for the reduction of the fortresses on the Rhine, from Strasburg to Belfort.   On the same day as that of the battle of Worth, General Steinmetz stormed the heights of Spicheren, and, though at great loss of life, drove Frossard from those heights and back upon Metz.

The occupation of Alsace was followed by that of Lorraine, by the Prussian army under King William, who took possession of Nancy and the country surrounding on August 11th.   These two provinces had formerly belonged to Germany, and it was the aim of the Prussians to **Occupation of** retain them as the chief anticipated prize of the war.   Mean- **Alsace and** while the world looked on in amazement at the extraordinary **Lorraine** rapidity of the German success, which, in two weeks after Napoleon left Paris, had brought his power to the verge of overthrow.

Towards the Moselle River and the strongly fortified town of Metz, 180 miles northeast of Paris, around which was concentrated the main French force, all the divisions of the German army now advanced, and on the 14th of August they gained a victory at Colombey-Neuvilly which drove their opponents back from the open field towards the fortified city.

It was Moltke's opinion that the French proposed to make their stand before this impregnable fortress, and fight there desperately for victory. But, finding less resistance than he expected, he concluded, **The Situation** on the 15th, that Bazaine, in fear of being cooped up within **at Metz** the fortress, meant to march towards Verdun, there to join his forces with those of MacMahon and give battle to the Germans in the plain.

The astute tactician at once determined to make every effort to prevent this concentration of his opponents, and by the evening of the 15th a cavalry division had crossed the Moselle and reached the village of Mars-la-Tour, where it bivouacked for the night.   It had seen troops in motion towards Metz, but did not know whether these formed the rear-guard or the vanguard of the French army in its march towards Verdun.

In fact, Bazaine had not yet got away with his army.   All the roads from Metz were blocked with heavy baggage, and it was impossible to move so large an army with expedition.   The time thus lost by Bazaine was diligently improved by Frederick Charles, and on the morning of the 16th the Brandenburg army corps, one of the best and bravest in the German army, had followed the cavalry and come within sight of the Verdun road.

It was quickly perceived that a French force was before them, and some preliminary skirmishing developed the enemy in such strength as to convince the leader of the corps that he had in his front the whole or the greater part of Bazaine's army, and that its escape from Metz had not been achieved.

They were desperate odds with which the brave Brandenburgers had to contend, but they had been sent to hold the French until reinforcements could arrive, and they were determined to resist to the death.

The Battle of Mars-la-Tour For nearly six hours they resisted, with unsurpassed courage, the fierce onslaughts of the French, though at a cost in life that perilously depleted the gallant corps. Then, about four o'clock in the afternoon, Prince Frederick Charles came up with reinforcements to their support and the desperate contest became more even.

Gradually fortune decided in favor of the Germans, and by the time night had come they were practically victorious, the field of Mars-la-Tour, after the day's struggle, remaining in their hands. But they were utterly exhausted, their horses were worn out, and most of their ammunition was spent, and though their impetuous commander forced them to

Defeat of the French a new attack, it led to a useless loss of life, for their powers of fighting were gone. They had achieved their purpose, that of preventing the escape of Bazaine, though at a fearful loss, amounting to about 16,000 men on each side. "The battle of Vionville [Mars-la-Tour] is without a parallel in military history," said Emperor William, "seeing that a single army corps, about 20,000 men strong, hung on to and repulsed an enemy more than five times as numerous and well equipped. Such was the glorious deed done by the Brandenburgers, and the Hohenzollerns will never forget the debt they owe to their devotion."

Two days afterwards (August 16th), at Gravelotte, a village somewhat nearer to Metz, the armies, somewhat recovered from the terrible struggle of the 14th, met again, the whole German army being now brought up, so

Great Victory of the Germans at Gravelotte that over 200,000 men faced the 140,000 of the French. It was the great battle of the war. For four hours the two armies stood fighting face to face, without any special result, neither being able to drive back the other. The French held their ground and died. The Prussians dashed upon them and died. Only late in the evening was the right wing of the French army broken, and the victory, which at five o'clock remained uncertain, was decided in favor of the Germans. More than 40,000 men lay dead and wounded upon the field, the terrible harvest of those nine hours of conflict. That night Bazaine withdrew his army behind the fortifications at Metz. His effort to join MacMahon had ended in failure.

THE STORMING OF THE GEISBURG, AUGUST 4, 1870

An incident of the Franco-Prussian War; 1,200 Frenchmen and 1,500 Germans were killed and wounded in this charge; the latter were victorious

CROWN PRINCE FREDERICK AT THE BATTLE OF FROSCHWILLER, AUGUST 6, 1870

In this battle the French under Marshal MacMahon were defeated by the Prussians. The French maintained for some time a fierce but helpless struggle in the streets of Frosch-willer, but by 5 P.M., it came to an end. The dead and wounded lay thick and the gutters ran with blood, and 9,000 French soldiers and 200 officers as prisoners stood sombre and downcast in the streets of the town from which their army had fled. The Germans' victory cost them 489 officers and 10,153 men.

It was the fixed purpose of the Prussians to detain him in that stronghold, and thus render practically useless to France its largest army. A siege was to be prosecuted, and an army of 150,000 men was extended around the town. The fortifications were far too strong to **The Siege** be taken by assault, and all depended on a close blockade. **of Metz** On August 31st Bazaine made an effort to break through the German lines, but was repulsed. It became now a question of how long the provisions of the French would hold out.

The French emperor, who had been with Bazaine, had left his army before the battle of Mars-la-Tour, and was now with MacMahon at Chalons. Here lay an army of 125,000 infantry and 12,000 cavalry. On it the Germans were advancing, in doubt as to what movement it would make, whether back towards Paris or towards Metz for the relief of Bazaine. They sought to place themselves in a position to check either. The latter movement was determined on by the French, but was carried out in a dubious **MacMahon** and uncertain manner, the time lost giving abundant opportu- **Marches to** nity to the Germans to learn what was afoot and to prepare to **Relieve** prevent it. As soon as they were aware of MacMahon's inten- **Bazaine** tion of proceeding to Metz they made speedy preparations to prevent his relieving Bazaine. By the last days of August the army of the crown prince had reached the right bank of the Aisne, and the fourth division gained possession of the line of the Maas. On August 30th the French under General de Failly were attacked by the Germans at Beaumont and put to flight with heavy loss. It was evident that the hope of reaching Metz was at an end, and MacMahon, abandoning the attempt, concentrated his army around the frontier fortress of Sedan.

This old town stands on the right bank of the Meuse, in an angle of territory between Luxemburg and Belgium, and is surrounded by meadows, gardens, ravines, ditches and cultivated fields ; the castle rising on a cliff-like eminence to the southwest of the place. MacMahon **The French** had stopped here to give his weary men a rest, not to fight, **Surrounded** but Von Moltke decided, on observing the situation, that Sedan should be the grave-yard of the French army. "The trap is now closed, and the mouse in it," he said, with a chuckle of satisfaction.

Such proved to be the case. On September 1st the Bavarians won the village of Bazeille, after hours of bloody and desperate struggle. During this severe fight Marshal MacMahon was so seriously wounded that he was obliged to surrender the chief command, first to Ducrot, and then to General Wimpffen, a man of recognized bravery and cold calculation.

Fortune soon showed itself in favor of the Germans.   To the north-west of the town, the North German troops invested the exits from St. Meuges and Fleigneux, and directed a fearful fire of artillery against the French forces, which, before noon, were so hemmed in the valley that only two insufficient outlets to the south and north remained open.   But Gen-

The Battle of Sedan

eral Wimpffen hesitated to seize either of these routes, the open way to Illy was soon closed by the Prussian guard corps, and a murderous fire was now directed from all sides upon the French, so that, after a last energetic struggle at Floing, they gave up all attempts to force a passage, and in the afternoon beat a retreat towards Sedan.   In this small town the whole army of MacMahon was collected by evening, and there prevailed in the streets and houses an unprecedented disorder and confusion, which was still further increased when the German troops from the surrounding heights began to shoot down upon the fortress, and the town took fire in several places.

That an end might be put to the prevailing misery, Napoleon now commanded General Wimpffen to capitulate.   The flag of truce already waved on the gates of Sedan when Colonel Bronsart appeared, and in the name of the king of Prussia demanded the surrender of the army and fortress.   He soon returned to headquarters, accompanied by the French General Reille, who presented to the king a written message from Napoleon : "As I may not die in the midst of my army, I lay my sword in the hands of your majesty."   King William accepted it with an expression of sympathy for the hard fate of the emperor and of the French army which had fought so bravely under his own eyes.   The conclusion of the treaty of capitulation was placed in the hands of Wimpffen, who, accompanied by General Castelnau, set out for Doncherry to negotiate with Moltke and Bismarck.   No attempts, however, availed to move Moltke from his stipulation for the surrender of the whole army at discretion ; he granted a short respite, but if this expired without surrender, the bombardment of the town was to begin anew.

At six o'clock in the morning the capitulation was signed, and was ratified by the king at his headquarters at Vendresse (2d September).   Thus the world heheld the incredible spectacle of an army of 83,000 men surrendering themselves and their weapons to the victor, and being carried off as prisoners of war to Germany.   Only the officers who gave their written word of honor to take no further part in the present war with Germany were permitted to retain their arms and personal property.   Probably the assurance of Napoleon, that he had sought death on the battlefield but had not found it, was literally true ; at any rate, the fate of the unhappy man, bowed down as he was both by physical and mental suffering, was so solemn and tragic, that there was no room for hypocrisy, and that he had exposed himself to personal danger was admitted on all sides. Ac- **Surrender of** companied by Count Bismarck, he stopped at a small and **Napoleon and** mean-looking laborer's inn on the road to Doncherry, where, **His Army** sitting down on a stone seat before the door, with Count Bismarck, he declared that he had not desired the war, but had been driven to it through the force of public opinion ; and afterwards the two proceeded to the little castle of Bellevue, near Frenois, to join King William and the crown prince. A telegram to Queen Augusta thus describes the interview : "What an impressive moment was the meeting with Napoleon ! He was cast down, but dignified in his bearing. I have granted him Wilhelmshöhe, near Cassel, as his residence. Our meeting took place in a little castle before the western glacis of Sedan."

The locking up of Bazaine in Metz and the capture of MacMahon's army at Sedan were fatal events to France. The struggle continued for months, but it was a fight against hope. The subsequent events of the war consisted of a double siege, that of Metz and that of Paris, with various minor sieges, and a desperate but hopeless effort of France in the field. As for the empire of Napoleon III., it was at an end. The tidings of the terrible catastrophe at Sedan filled the people with a fury that soon became revolutionary. While Jules Favre, the republican deputy, was offering a motion in the Assembly that the emperor had forfeited the crown, and that a provisional government should be established, the people were thronging the streets of Paris with cries of "Deposition ! Republic !" **Revolution** On the 4th of September the Assembly had its final meeting. **and the Third** Two of its prominent members, Jules Favre and Gambetta, **Republic** sustained the motion for deposition of the emperor, and it was carried after a stormy session. They then made their way to the senate-chamber, where, before a thronging audience, they proclaimed a republic and named a government for the national defence. At its head was General Trochu, military commandant at Paris. Favre was made minister of foreign affairs ; Gambetta, minister of the interior ; and other prominent members of the Assembly filled the remaining cabinet posts. The legislature was dissolved, the Palais de Bourbon was closed, and the Empress Eugenie quitted the Tuileries and made her escape with a few attendants to Belgium, whence she sought a refuge in England. Prince Louis Napoleon made his way to Italy, and the swarm of courtiers scattered in all directions ; some faithful followers of the deposed monarch seeking the castle of Wilhelmshöhe, where the unhappy Louis Napoleon occupied as a prison the same beautiful palace and park in which his uncle Jerome Bonaparte had once passed six years in a life of pleasure. The second French Empire was at an end; the third French Republic had begun—one that had to pass through many changes and escape many dangers before it would be firmly established.

"Not a foot's breadth of our country nor a stone of our fortresses shall be surrendered," was Jules Favre's defiant proclamation to the

**Jules Favre's
Defiance**

invaders, and the remainder of the soldiers in the field were collected in Paris, and strengthened with all available rein-forcements. Every person capable of bearing arms was en-rolled in the national army, which soon numbered 400,000 men. There was need of haste, for the victors at Sedan were already marching upon the capital, inspired with high hopes from their previous astonishing success. They knew that Paris was strongly fortified, being encircled by powerful lines of defence, but they trusted that hunger would soon bring its garrison to terms. The same result was looked for at Metz, and at Strasburg, which was also besieged.

Thus began at three main points and several minor ones a military siege the difficulties, dangers, and hardships of which surpassed even those of the winter campaign in the Crimea. Exposed at the fore-posts to the enemy's balls, chained to arduous labor in the trenches and redoubts, and suffering from the effects of bad weather, and insufficient food and clothing, the German soldiers were compelled to undergo great privations and sufferings before the fortifications; while many fell in the frequent skirmishes and sallies, many succumbed to typhus and epidemic disease, and many returned home mutilated, or broken in health.

No less painful and distressing was the condition of the besieged. While the garrison soldiers on guard were constantly compelled to face death in nocturnal sallies, or led a pitiable existence in damp huts, having

**Hardships of
the Conflict**

inevitable surrender constantly before their eyes, and disarma-ment and imprisonment as the reward of all their struggles and exertions, the citizens in the towns, the women and chil-dren, were in constant danger of being shivered to atoms by the fearful shells, or of being buried under falling walls and roofs; and the poorer part of the population saw with dismay the gradual diminution of the necessa-ries of life, and were often compelled to pacify their hunger with the flesh of horses, and disgusting and unwholesome food.

The republican government possessed only a usurped power, and none but a freely elected national assembly could decide as to the fate of the French nation. Such an assembly was therefore summoned for the 16th of October. Three members of the government—Crémieux, Fourichon, and Glais-Vizoin—were despatched before the entire blockade of the town had been effected, to Tours, to maintain communication with the provinces.   An attempt was also made at the same time to induce the great powers which had not taken part in the war to organize an intervention, as hitherto only America, Switzerland, and Spain had sent official recognition.   For this important and delicate mission the old statesman and historian Thiers was selected, and, in spite of his three-and-seventy years, immediately set out on the journey to London, St. Petersburg, Vienna, and Florence.   Count Bismarck, however, in the name of Prussia, refused any intervention in internal affairs.   In two despatches to the ambassadors of foreign courts, the chancellor declared that the war, begun by the Emperor Napoleon, had been approved by the representatives of the nation, and that thus all France was answerable for the result.   Germany was obliged, therefore, to demand guarantees which should secure her in future against attack, or, at any rate, render attack more difficult.   Thus a cession of territory on the part of France was laid down as the basis of a treaty of peace.   The neutral powers were also led to the belief that if they fostered in the French any hope of intervention, peace would only be delayed.   The mission of Thiers, therefore, yielded no useful result, while the direct negotiation which Jules Favre conducted with Bismarck proved equally unavailing.

Thiers and Bismarck

Soon the beleaguered fortresses began to fall.   On the 23d of September the ancient town of Toul, in Lorraine, was forced to capitulate, after a fearful bombardment; and on the 27th Strasburg, in danger of the terrible results of a storming, after the havoc of a dreadful artillery fire, hoisted the white flag, and surrendered on the following day.   The supposed impregnable fortress of Metz held out little longer.   Hunger did what cannon were incapable of doing.   The successive sallies made by Bazaine proved unavailing, though, on October 7th, his soldiers fought with desperate energy, and for hours the air was full of the roar of cannon and mitrailleuse and the rattle of musketry.   But the Germans withstood the attack unmoved, and the French were forced to withdraw into the town.

Bazaine then sought to negotiate with the German leaders at Versailles, offering to take no part in the war for three months if permitted to withdraw.   But Bismarck and Moltke would listen to no terms other than unconditional surrender, and these terms were finally accepted, the besieged army having reached the brink of starvation.   It was with horror and despair that France learned, on the 30th of October, that the citadel of Metz, with its fortifications and arms of defence, had been yielded to the Germans, and its army of more than 150,000 men had surrendered as prisoners of war.

Siege and Surrender of Metz

This hasty surrender at Metz, a still greater disaster to France than that of Sedan, was not emulated at Paris, which for four months held out against all the efforts of the Germans.   On the investment of the great city, King William removed his headquarters to the historic palace of Versailles,

The Germans at Versailles

setting up his homely camp-bed in the same apartments from which Louis XIV. had once issued his despotic edicts and commands.   Here Count Bismarck conducted his diplomatic labors and Moltke issued his directions for the siege, which, protracted from week to week and month to month, gradually transformed the beautiful neighborhood, with its prosperous villages, superb country houses, and enchanting parks and gardens, into a scene of sadness and desolation.

In spite of the vigorous efforts made by the commander-in-chief Trochu, both by continuous firing from the forts and by repeated sallies, to prevent Paris from being surrounded, and to force a way through the trenches, his enterprises were rendered fruitless by the watchfulness and strength of the Germans.   The blockade was completely accomplished; Paris was surrounded and cut off from the outer world; even the underground telegraphs, through which communication was for a time secretly maintained with the provinces, were by degrees discovered and destroyed. But to the great astonishment of Europe, which looked on with keenly pitched excitement at the mighty struggle, the siege continued for months

The Siege of Paris

without any special progress being observable from without or any lessening of resistance from within.   On account of the extension of the forts, the Germans were compelled to remain at such a distance that a bombardment of the town at first appeared impossible; a storming of the outer works would, moreover, be attended with such sacrifices, that the humane temper of the king revolted from such a proceeding.   The guns of greater force and carrying power which were needed from Germany, could only be procured after long delay on account of the broken lines of railway.   Probably also there was some hesitation on the German side to expose the beautiful city, regarded by so many as the " metropolis of civilization," to the risk of a bombardment, in which works of art, science, and a historical past would meet destruction.   Nevertheless, the declamations of the French at the Vandalism of the northern barbarians met with assent and sympathy from most of the foreign powers.

Determination and courage falsified the calculations at Versailles of a quick cessation of the resistance.   The republic offered a far more energetic and determined opposition to the Prussian arms than the empire had done. The government of the national defence still declaimed with stern reiteration: " Not a foot's breadth of our country; not a stone of our fortresses!"

and positively rejected all proposals of treaty based on territorial concessions.   Faith in the invincibility of the republic was rooted as an indisputable dogma in the hearts of the French people.   The victories and the commanding position of France from 1792 to 1799 were regarded as so entirely
the necessary result of the Revolution, that a conviction prevailed that the
formation of a republic, with a national army for its defence, would have an
especial effect on the rest of Europe.   Therefore, instead of summoning a
constituent Assembly, which, in the opinion of Prussia and **The Energy of**
the other foreign powers, would alone be capable of offering **Resistance**
security for a lasting peace, it was decided to continue the
revolutionary movements, and to follow the same course which, in the years
1792 and 1793, had saved France from the coalition of the European powers
—a revolutionary dictatorship such as had once been exercised by the Convention and the members of the Committee of Public Safety, must again
be revived, and a youthful and hot-blooded leader was alone needed to stir
up popular feeling and set it in motion.   To fill such a part no one was better adapted than the advocate Gambetta, who emulated the career of the
leaders of the Revolution, and whose soul glowed with a passionate ardor
of patriotism.   In order to create for himself a free sphere of action, and
to initiate some vigorous measure in place of the well-rounded phrases and
eloquent proclamations of his colleagues Trochu and Jules Favre, he quitted
the capital in an air-balloon and entered into communication with the Government delegation at Tours, which through him soon obtained a fresh impetus.   His next most important task was the liberation of the capital from
the besieging German army, and the expulsion of the enemy from the
" sacred " soil of France.   For this purpose he summoned, **Gambetta and**
with the authority of a minister of war, all persons capable of **His Work**
bearing arms up to forty years of age to take active service,
and despatched them into the field ; he imposed war-taxes, and terrified the
tardy and refractory with threats of punishment.   Every force was put in
motion ; all France was transformed into a great camp.   A popular war was
now to take the place of a soldiers' war, and what the soldiers had failed to
effect must be accomplished by the people ; France must be saved, and the
world freed from despotism.   To promote this object, the whole of France,
with the exception of Paris, was divided into four general governments, the
headquarters of the different governors being Lille, Le Mans, Bourges, and
Besançon.   Two armies, from the Loire and from the Somme, were to
march simultaneously towards Paris, and, aided by the sallies of Trochu and
his troops, were to drive the enemy from the country.   Energetic attacks
were now attempted from time to time, in the hope that when the armies of

relief arrived from the provinces, it might be possible to effect a coalition; but all these efforts were constantly repulsed after a hot struggle by the besieging German troops. At the same time, during the month of October, the territory between the Oise and the Lower Seine was scoured by reconnoitering troops, under Prince Albrecht, the south-east district was protected by a Würtemberg detachment through the successful battle near Nogent on the Seine, while a division of the third army advanced towards the south **The Southward** accompanied by two cavalry divisions. A more unfortunate **Advance of** circumstance, however, for the Parisians was the cutting off of **the Germans** all communication with the outer world, for the Germans had destroyed the telegraphs. But even this obstacle was overcome by the inventive genius of the French. By means of pigeon letter-carriers and air-balloons, they were always able to maintain a partial though one-sided and imperfect communication with the provinces, and the aërostatic art was developed and brought to perfection on this occasion in a manner which had never before been considered possible.

The whole of France, and especially the capital, was already in a state of intense excitement when the news of the capitulation of Metz came to **Gambetta's** add fresh fuel to the flame. Outside the walls Gambetta was **Army of** using heroic efforts to increase his forces, bringing Bedouin **Defence** horsemen from Africa and inducing the stern old revolutionist Garibaldi to come to his aid; and Thiers was opening fresh negotiations for a truce. Inside the walls the Red Republic raised the banners of insurrection and attempted to drive the government of national defence from power.

This effort of the dregs of revolution to inaugurate a reign of terror failed, and the provisional government felt so elated with its victory that it determined to continue at the head of affairs and to oppose the calling of a chamber of national representatives. The members proclaimed oblivion for what had passed, broke off the negotiations for a truce begun by Thiers, **The Negotia-** and demanded a vote of confidence. The indomitable spirit **tions Are** shown by the French people did not, on the other hand, in- **Broken Off** spire the Germans with a very lenient or conciliatory temper. Bismarck declared in a despatch the reasons why the negotiations had failed: "The incredible demand that we should surrender the fruits of all our efforts during the last two months, and should go back to the conditions which existed at the beginning of the blockade of Paris, only affords fresh proof that in Paris pretexts are sought for refusing the nation the right of election." Thiers mournfully declared the failure of his undertaking, but in Paris the popular voting resulted in a ten-fold majority in favor of the government and the policy of postponement.

KING OSCAR II. OF SWEDEN AND NORWAY.

KING CHRISTIAN IX. OF DENMARK.

EMPEROR FRANCIS JOSEPH OF AUSTRIA.

KING VICTOR EMMANUEL III., OF ITALY

RULERS OF SWEDEN AND NORWAY, DENMARK, AUSTRIA AND ITALY

LEON GAMBETTA

LOUIS ADOLPHE THIERS

FERDINAND DeLESSEPS

PRESIDENT LOUBET

GREAT MEN OF MODERN FRANCE

After the breaking off of the negotiations, the world anticipated some energetic action towards the besieged city. The efforts of the enemy were, however, principally directed to drawing the iron girdle still tighter, enclosing the giant city more and more closely, and cutting off every means of communication, so that at last a surrender might be brought about by the stern necessity of starvation. That this object would not be accomplished as speedily as at Metz, that the city of pleasure, enjoyment, and luxury would withstand a siege of four months, had never been contemplated for a moment. It is true that, as time went on, all fresh meat disappeared from the market, with the exception of horse-flesh; that white bread, on which Parisians place such value, was replaced by a baked compound of meal and bran; that the stores of dried and salted food began to decline, until at last rats, dogs, cats, and even animals from the zoological gardens were prepared for consumption at restaurants. Yet, to the **Famine and** amazement of the world, all these miseries, hardships, and **Misery in** sufferings were courageously borne, nocturnal watch was kept, **Paris** sallies were undertaken, and cold, hunger, and wretchedness of all kinds were endured with an indomitable steadfastness and heroism. The courage of the besieged Parisians was also animated by the hope that the military forces in the provinces would hasten to the aid of the hard-pressed capital, and that therefore an energetic resistance would afford the rest of France sufficient time for rallying all its forces, and at the same time exhibit an elevating example. In the carrying out of this plan, neither Trochu nor Gambetta was wanting in the requisite energy and circumspection. The former organized sallies from time to time, in order to reconnoitre and discover whether the army of relief was on its way from the provinces; the latter exerted all his powers to bring the Loire army up to the Seine. But both erred in undervaluing the German war forces; they did not believe that the hostile army would be able to keep Paris in a state of blockade, and at the same time engage the armies on the south and north, east and west. They had no conception of the hidden, inexhaustible strength of the Prussian army organization—of a nation in arms which could send forth constant reinforcements of battalions and recruits, and fresh bodies of disciplined troops to fill the gaps left in the ranks by the wounded and fallen. There could be no doubt as to the termination of this terrible war, or the final victory of German energy and discipline.

Throughout the last months of the eventful year 1870, the northern part of France, from the Jura to the Channel, from the Belgian frontier to the Loire, presented the aspect of a wide battlefield. Of the troops that had been set free by the capitulation of Metz, a part remained behind in garrison, another division marched northwards in order to invest the provinces of Picardy and Normandy, to restore communication with the sea, and to bar the road to Paris, and a third division joined the second army, whose commander-in-chief, Prince Frederick Charles, set up his headquarters at Troyes.   Different detachments were despatched against the northern fortresses, and by degrees Soissons, Verdun, Thionville, Ham, where Napoleon had once been a prisoner, Pfalzburg and Montmedy, all fell into the hands of the Prussians, thus opening to them a free road for the supplies of provisions.   The garrison troops were all carried off as prisoners to Germany ; the towns—most of them in a miserable condition—fell into the enemy's hands ; many houses were mere heaps of ruins and ashes, and the larger part of the inhabitants were suffering severely from poverty, hunger and disease.

The Fall of the Fortresses

The greatest obstacles were encountered in the northern part of Alsace and the mountainous districts of the Vosges and the Jura, where irregular warfare, under Garibaldi and other leaders, developed to a dangerous extent, while the fortress of Langres afforded a safe retreat to the guerilla bands.   Lyons and the neighboring town of St. Etienne became hotbeds of excitement, the red flag being raised and a despotism of terror and violence established.   Although many divergent elements made up this army of the east, all were united in hatred of the Germans and the desire to drive the enemy back across the Rhine.

Guerilla Warfare in the East

Thus, during the cold days of November and December, when General Von Treskow began the siege of the important fortress of Belfort, there burst forth a war around Gray and Dijon marked by the greatest hardships, perils and privations to the invaders.   Here the Germans had to contend with an enemy much superior in number, and to defend themselves against continuous firing from houses, cellars, woods and thickets, while the impoverished soil yielded a miserable subsistence, and the broken railroads cut off freedom of communication and of reinforcement.

The whole of the Jura district, intersected by hilly roads as far as the plateau of Langres, where, in the days of Cæsar, the Romans and Gauls were wont to measure their strength with each other, formed during November and December the scene of action of numerous encounters which, in conjunction with sallies from the garrison at Belfort, inflicted severe injury on Werder's troops.   Dijon had repeatedly to be evacuated ; and the nocturnal attack at Chattillon, 20th November, by Garibaldians, when one hundred and twenty Landwehrmen and Hussars perished miserably, and seventy horses were lost, affording a striking proof of the dangers to which the German army was

In the Jura District

exposed in this hostile country ; although the revolutionary excesses of the turbulent population of the south diverted to a certain extent the attention of the National Guard, who were compelled to turn their weapons against an internal enemy.

By means of the revolutionary dictatorship of Gambetta the whole French nation was drawn into the struggle, the annihilation of the enemy being represented as a national duty, and the war assuming a steadily more violent character. The indefatigable patriot continued his exertions to increase the army and unite the whole south and west against **Gambetta and** the enemy, hoping to bring the army of the Loire to such **the Army** dimensions that it would be able to expel the invaders from **of the Loire** the soil of France. But these raw recruits were poorly fitted to cope with the highly disciplined Germans, and their early successes were soon followed by defeat and discouragement, while the hopes entertained by the Paris garrison of succor from the south vanished as news of the steady progress of the Germans were received.

During these events the war operations before Paris continued un-interruptedly. Moltke had succeeded, in spite of the difficulties of trans-port, in procuring an immense quantity of ammunition, and the long-delayed bombardment of Paris was ready to begin. Having stationed with all secrecy twelve batteries with seventy-six guns around Mont Avron, on Christmas-day the firing was directed with such success against the forti-fied eminences, that even in the second night the French, after great losses, evacuated the important position, the "key of Paris," which was immedi-ately taken possession of by the Saxons. Terror and dismay spread throughout the distracted city when the eastern forts, Rosny, Nogent and Noisy, were stormed amid a tremendous volley **The Bombard-** of firing. Vainly did Trochu endeavor to rouse the failing **ment of Paris** courage of the National Guard ; vainly did he assert that the government of the national defence would never consent to the humiliation of a capitu-lation ; his own authority had already waned ; the newspapers already accused him of incapacity and treachery, and began to cast every aspersion on the men who had presumptuously seized the government, and yet were not in a position to effect the defence of the capital and the country. After the new year the bombardment of the southern forts began, and the terror in the city daily increased, though the violence of the radical journals kept in check any hint of surrender or negotiation. Yet in spite of fog and snow-storms the bombardment was systematically continued, and with every day the destructive effect of the terrible missiles grew more pronounced.

Trochu was blamed for having undertaken only small sallies, which could have no result. The commander-in-chief ventured no opposition to the party of action. With the consent of the mayors of the twenty *arrondissements* of Paris a council of war was held. The threatening famine, the firing of the enemy, and the excitement prevailing among the adherents of the red republic rendered a decisive step necessary. Consequently, on the 19th of January, a great sally was decided on, and the entire armed forces of the capital were summoned to arms. Early in the morning, a body of 100,000 men marched in the direction of Meudon, Sevres and St. Cloud for the decisive conflict. The left wing was commanded by General Vinoy, the right by Ducrot, while Trochu from the watch-tower directed the entire

The Last Great Sally from Paris struggle. With great courage Vinoy dashed forward with his column of attack towards the fifth army corps of General Kirchbach, and succeeded in capturing the Montretout entrenchment, through the superior number of his troops, and in holding it for a time. But when Ducrot, delayed by the barricades in the streets, failed to come to his assistance at the appointed time, the attack was driven back after seven hours' fierce fighting by the besieging troops. Having lost 7,000 dead and wounded, the French in the evening beat a retreat, which almost resembled a flight. On the following day Trochu demanded a truce, that the fallen National Guards, whose bodies strewed the battlefield, might be interred. The victors, too, had to render the last rites to many a brave soldier. Thirty-nine officers and six hundred and sixteen soldiers were given in the list of the slain.

Entire confidence had been placed by the Parisians in the great sally. When the defeat, therefore, became known in its full significance, when the number of the fallen was found to be far greater even than had been stated in the first accounts, a dull despair took possession of the famished city, which next broke forth into violent abuse against Trochu, "the traitor." Capitulation now seemed imminent; but as the commander-in-chief had declared that he would never countenance such a disgrace, he resigned his post to Vinoy. Threatened by bombardment from without, terrified within by the pale spectre of famine, paralysed and distracted by the violent dissensions among the people, and without prospect of effective aid from the

A Truce at Paris provinces, what remained to the proud capital but to desist from a conflict the continuation of which only increased the unspeakable misery, without the smallest hope of deliverance? Gradually, therefore, there grew up a resolution to enter into negotiations with the enemy; and it was the minister Jules Favre, who had been foremost with the cry of "no surrender" four months before, who was now compelled to take the first step to deliver his country from complete ruin. It was probably the bitterest hour in the life of the brave man, who loved France and liberty with such a sincere affection, when he was conducted through the German outposts to his interview with Bismarck at Versailles. He brought the proposal for a convention, on the strength of which the garrison was to be permitted to retire with military honors to a part of France not hitherto invested, on promising to abstain for several months from taking part in the struggle. But such conditions were positively refused at the Prussian headquarters, and a surrender was demanded as at Sedan and Metz. Completely defeated, the minister returned to Paris. At a second meeting on the following day, it was agreed that from the 27th, at twelve o'clock at night, the firing on both sides should be discontinued. This was the preliminary to the conclusion of a three weeks' truce, to await the summons of a National Assembly, with which peace might be negotiated.

The war was at an end so far as Paris was concerned. But it continued in the south, where frequent defeat failed to depress Gambetta's indomitable energy, and where new troops constantly replaced those put to rout. Garibaldi, at Dijon, succeeded in doing what the French had not done during the war, in the capture of a Prussian banner. But the progress of the Germans soon rendered his position untenable, and, finding his exertions unavailing, he resigned his command and retired to his island of Caprera. Two disasters completed the overthrow of France. Bourbaki's army, 85,000 strong, became shut in, with scanty food and ammunition, among the snow-covered valleys of the **Bourbaki's Army and the Siege of Belfort** Jura, and to save the disgrace of capitulation it took refuge on the neutral soil of Switzerland; and the strong fortress of Belfort, which had been defended with the utmost courage against its besiegers, finally yielded, with the stipulation that the brave garrison should march out with the honors of war. Nothing now stood in the way of an extension of the truce. On the suggestion of Jules Favre, the National Assembly elected a commission of fifteen members, which was to aid the chief of the executive, and his ministers, Picard and Favre, in the negotiations for peace. That cessions of territory and indemnity of war expenses would have to be conceded had long been acknowledged in principle; but protracted and excited discussions took place as to the extent of the former and the amount of **The Harsh Terms of Peace** the latter, while the demanded entry of the German troops into Paris met with vehement opposition. But Count Bismarck resolutely insisted on the cession of Alsace and German Lorraine, including Metz and Diedenhofen Only with difficulty were the Germans persuaded to separate Belfort from the rest of Lorraine, and leave it still in the possession of the French. In respect to the expenses of the war, the sum of five milliards of francs ($1,000,000,000) was agreed upon, of which the first milliard was to be paid in the year 1871, and the rest in a stated period. The stipulated entry into Paris also—so bitter to the French national pride—was only partially carried out; the western side only of the city was to be traversed in the march of the Prussian troops, and again evacuated in two days. On the basis of these conditions, the preliminaries of the Peace of Versailles were concluded on the 26th of February between the Imperial Chancellor and Jules Favre. Intense excitement prevailed when the terms of the treaty became known; they were dark days in the annals of French history. But in spite of the opposition of the extreme Republican party, led by Quinet and Victor Hugo, the Assembly recognized by an overpowering majority the necessity for the Peace, and the preliminaries were accepted by 546 to 107 votes. Thus ended the mighty war between France and Germany—a war which has had few equals in the history of the world.

Had King William received no indemnity in cash or territory from France, he must still have felt himself amply repaid for the cost of the brief but sanguinary war, for it brought him a power and prestige with which the astute diplomatist Bismarck had long been seeking to invest his name. Political changes move slowly in times of peace, rapidly in times of war. The whole of Germany, with the exception of Austria, had sent troops to the conquest of France, and every state, north and south alike,

The Glory of Germany   shared in the pride and glory of the result. South and North Germany had marched side by side to the battlefield, every difference of race or creed forgotten, and the honor of the German fatherland the sole watchword. The time seemed to have arrived to close the breach between north and south, and obliterate the line of the Main, which had divided the two sections. North Germany was united under the leadership of Prussia, and the honor in which all alike shared now brought South Germany into line for a similar union.

The first appeal in this direction came from Baden. Later in the year plenipotentiaries sought Versailles from the kingdoms of Bavaria and Würtemberg and the grand duchies of Baden and Hesse, their purpose being to arrange for and define the conditions of union between the South and the North German states. For weeks this momentous question filled all Germany with excitement and public opinion was in a state of high tension. The scheme of union was by no means universally approved, there being a large party in opposition, but the majority in its favor in Chambers proved sufficient to enable Bismarck to carry out his plan.

This was no less than to restore the German Empire, or rather to estab-lish a new empire of Germany, in which Austria, long at the head of the former empire, should have no part, the imperial dignity being conferred upon the venerable King William of Prussia, a monarch whose birth dated back to the eighteenth century, and who had lived throughout the Napoleonic wars.

Restoration of the German Empire

Near the close of 1870 Bismarck concluded treaties with the ambassa-dors of the Southern States, in which they agreed to accept the constitution of the North German Union. These treaties were ratified, after some op-position from the "patriots" of the lower house, by the legislatures of the four states involved. The next step in the proceeding was a suggestion from the king of Bavaria to the other princes that the imperial crown of Germany should be offered to King William of Prussia.

When the North German Diet at Berlin had given its consent to the new constitution, congratulatory address was despatched to the Pruss-ian monarch at Versailles. Thirty members of the Diet, with the president Simson at their head, announced to the aged hero-king the nation's wish that he should accept the new dignity. He replied to the deputation in sol-emn audience that he accepted the imperial dignity which the German nation and its princes had offered him. On the 1st of January, 1871, the new con-stitution was to come into operation. The solemn assumption of the im-perial office did not take place, however, until the 18th of January, the day on which, one hundred and seventy years before, the new em-peror's ancestor, Frederick I., had placed the Prussian crown on his head at Königsberg, and thus laid the basis of the growing greatness of his house. It was an ever-memorable coincidence, that in the superb-mirrored hall of the Versailles palace, where, since the days of Richelieu, so many plans had been concerted for the humiliation of Ger-many, King William should now proclaim himself German Emperor. After the reading of the imperial proclamation to the German people by Count Bismarck, the Grand Duke led a cheer, in which the whole assembly joined amid the singing of national hymns. Thus the important event had taken place which again summoned the German Empire to life, and made over the imperial crown with renewed splendor to another royal house. Barbarossa's old legend, that the dominion of the empire was, after long tribulation, to pass from the Hohenstaufen to the Hohenzollern, was now fulfilled; the dream long aspired after by German youth had now become a reality and a living fact.

The Crowning of William I. at Versailles

The tidings of the conclusion of peace with France, whose prelimi-naries were completed at Frankfurt on the 10th of May, 1871, filled all Germany with joy, and peace festivals on the most splendid scale extended from end to end of the new empire, in all parts of which an earnest spirit of patriotism was shown, while Germans from all regions of the world sent home expressions of warm sympathy with the new national organization of their fatherland.

The decade just completed had been one of remarkable political changes in Europe, unsurpassed in significance during any other period of

A Decade of Remarkable Changes

equal length. The temporal dominion of the pope had vanished and all Italy had been united under the rule of a single king. The empire of France had been overthrown and a republic established in its place, while that country had sunk greatly in prominence among the European states. Austria had been utterly defeated in war, had lost its last hold on Italy and its position of influence among the German states. And all the remaining German lands had united into a great and powerful empire, of such extraordinary military strength that the surrounding nations looked on in doubt, full of vague fears of trouble from this new and potent power introduced into their midst.

Bismarck, however, showed an earnest desire to maintain international peace and good relations, seeking to win the confidence of foreign governments, while at the same time improving and increasing that military force which had been proved to be so mighty an engine of war.

In the constitution of the new empire two legislative bodies were provided for, the *Bundesrath* or Federal Council, whose members are annually

The Legislature of the Empire

appointed by the respective state governments, and the *Reichstag* or Representative body, whose members are elected by universal suffrage for a period of three years, an annual session being required. Germany, therefore, in its present organization, is practically a federal union of states, each with its own powers of internal government, and with a common legislature approximating to our Senate and House of Representatives.

The remaining incidents of Bismarck's remarkable career may be briefly given. It consisted largely in a struggle with the Catholic Church organization, which had attained to great power in Germany, and was aggressive to an extent that roused the vigorous opposition of the chancellor of the empire, who was not willing to acknowledge any

The Power of the Catholic Church in Prussia

power in Germany other than that of the emperor.

King Frederick William IV., the predecessor of the reigning monarch, had made active efforts to strengthen the Catholic Church in Prussia, its clergy gaining greater privileges in that Protestant state than they possessed in any of the Catholic states. They had established everywhere in North Germany their congregations and monasteries, and, by their control of public education, seemed in a fair way to eventually make Catholicism supreme in the empire.

This state of affairs Bismarck set himself energetically to reform. The minister of religious affairs was forced to resign, and his place was taken by Falk, a sagacious statesman, who introduced a new school law, bringing the whole educational system under state control, and carefully regulating the power of the clergy over religious and moral education. This law met with such violent opposition that all the personal influence of Bismarck and Falk were needed to carry it, and it gave such deep offence to the pope that he refused to receive the German ambassador. He declared the Falk law invalid, and the German bishops united in a declaration against the chancellor. Bismarck retorted by a law expelling the Jesuits from the empire.

The New Laws Against Church Power

In 1873 the state of affairs became so embittered that the rights and liberties of the citizens seemed to need protection against a priesthood armed with extensive powers of discipline and excommunication. In consequence Bismarck introduced, and by his eloquence and influence carried, what were known as the May Laws. These provided for the scientific education of the Catholic clergy, the confirmation of clerical appointments by the state, and a tribunal to consider and revise the conduct of the bishops.

These enactments precipitated a bitter contest between church and state, while the pope declared the May Laws null and void and threatened with excommunication all priests who should submit to them. The state retorted by withdrawing its financial support from the Catholic church and abolishing those clauses of the constitution under which the church claimed independence of the state. Pope Pius IX. died in 1878, and on the election of Leo XIII. attempts were made to reconcile the existing differences. The reconciliation was a victory for the church, the May Laws ceasing to be operative, the church revenues being restored and the control of the clergy over education in considerable measure regained. New concessions were granted in 1886 and 1887, and Bismarck felt himself beaten in his long conflict with his clerical opponents, who had proved too strong and deeply entrenched for him.

The Triumph of the Church

Economic questions became also prominent, the revenues of the empire requiring some change in the system of free trade and the adoption of protective duties, while the railroads were acquired by the various states of the empire. Meanwhile the rapid growth of socialism excited apprehension, which was added to when two attempts were made on the life of the emperor. These were attributed to the Socialists, and severe laws for the suppression of socialism were enacted. Bismarck also sought to cut the

The Socialists and the Insurance Laws

ground from under the feet of the Socialists by an endeavor to improve the condition of the working classes. In 1881 laws were passed compelling employers to insure their work-men in case of sickness or accident, and in 1888 a system of compulsory insurance against death and old age was introduced. None of these measures, however, checked the growth of socialism, which very actively continued.

In 1882 a meeting was arranged by the chancellor between the emper-ors of Germany, Russia, and Austria, which was looked upon in Europe as a political alliance. In 1878 Russia drifted somewhat apart from Ger-many, but in the following year an alliance of defence and offence was con-cluded with Austria, and a similar alliance at a later date with Italy. This, which still continues, is known as the Triple Alliance. In 1877 Bismarck announced his intention to retire, being worn out with the great labors of his position. To this the emperor, who felt that his state rested on the shoulders of the " Iron Chancellor," would not listen, though he gave him indefinite leave of absence.

On March 9, 1888, Emperor William died. He was ninety years of age, having been born in 1797. He was succeeded by his son Frederick, then incurably ill from a cancerous affection of the throat, which carried him to the grave after a reign of ninety-nine days. His oldest son, William, succeeded on June 15, 1888, as William II.

The liberal era which was looked for under Frederick was checked by his untimely death, his son at once returning to the policy of William I. and

William II. and the Dismissal of Bismarck

Bismarck. He proved to be far more positive and dictatorial in disposition than his grandfather, with decided and vigorous views of his own, which soon brought him into conflict with the equally positive chancellor. The result was a rupture with Bismarck, and his dismissal from the premiership in 1890. The young emperor subse-quently devoted himself in a large measure to the increase of the army and navy, a policy which brought him into frequent conflicts with the Reichstag, whose rapidly growing socialistic membership was in strong opposition to this development of militarism.

The old statesman, to whom Germany owed so much, was deeply ag-grieved by this lack of gratitude on the part of the self-opinionated young emperor. Subsequently a reconciliation took place. But the political career of the great Bismarck was at an end, and he died on July 30, 1898. It is an interesting coincidence that almost at the same time died the equally great, but markedly different, statesman of England, William Ewart Gladstone. Count Cavour, the third great European statesman of the last half of the nineteenth century, had completed his work and passed away nearly forty years before.

The career of William II. has been one of much interest and some alarm to the other nations of Europe. His eagerness for the development of the army and navy, and the energy with which he pushed forward its organization and sought to add to its strength, seemed significant of warlike intentions, and there was dread that this energetic young monarch might break the peace of Europe, if only to prove the irresistible strength of the military machine he had formed. But as years went on the **The Development of the German Army** apprehensions to which his early career and expressions gave rise were quieted, and the fear that he would plunge Europe into war vanished. The army and navy began to appear rather a costly plaything of the active young man than an engine of destruction, while it tended in considerable measure to the preservation of peace by rendering Germany a power dangerous to go to war with.

The speeches with which the emperor began his reign showed an exaggerated sense of the imperial dignity, though his later career indicated far more judgment and good sense than the early display of overweening self-importance promised, and the views of William II. now command far more respect than they did at first. He has shown himself a man of exuberant energy. Despite a permanent weakness of his left arm and a serious affection of the ear, he early became a skilful horseman and an untiring hunter, as well as an enthusiastic yachtsman, and there are few men in the empire more active and enterprising to-day than the Kaiser.

A principal cause of the break between William and Bismarck was the imperial interference with the laws for the suppression of Social- **State Socialism** ism. As already stated, the old chancellor had established a system of compulsory old age insurance, through which workmen and their employers—aided by the state—were obliged to provide for the support of artisans after a certain age. The system seems to have worked satisfactorily, but socialism of a more radical kind has grown in the empire far more rapidly than the emperor has approved of, and he has vigorously, though unsuccessfully, endeavored to prevent its increase. Another of his favorite measures, a religious education bill, he was obliged to withdraw on account of the opposition it excited. On more than one occasion he has come into sharp conflict with the Reichstag concerning increased taxation for the army and navy, and a strong party against his autocratic methods has sprung up, and has forced him more than once to recede from warmly-cherished measures.

It may be of interest here to say something concerning the organization of the existing German empire.   The constitution of this empire, as **Constitution of the German Empire** adopted April 16, 1871, proposes to "form an eternal union for the protection of the realm and the care of the welfare of the German people," and places the supreme direction of military and political affairs in the King of Prussia, under the title of Deutscher Kaiser (German emperor).   The war-making powers of the emperor, however, are restricted, since he is obliged to obtain the consent of the Bundesrath (the Federal Council) before he can declare war otherwise than for the defence of the realm.   His authority as emperor, in fact, is much less than that which he exercises as King of Prussia, since the imperial legislature is independent of him, he having no power of veto over the laws passed by it.

This legislature consists of two bodies, the Bundesrath, representing the states of the union, whose members, 58 in number, are chosen for each session by the several state governments ; and the Reichstag, representing the people, whose members, 397 in number, are elected by universal suffrage for periods of five years.   The German union, as now constituted, comprises four kingdoms, six grand duchies, five duchies, seven principalities, three cities, and the Reichsland of Alsace-Lorraine ; twenty-six separate states in all.   It includes all the German peoples with the exception of those of Austria.

The progress of Germany within the century under review has been very great.   The population of the states of the empire, 24,831,000 at the end of the Napoleonic wars, is now over 52,000,000, having more than doubled in number.   The wealth of the country has grown in a far greater **The Progress of Germany** ratio, and Germany to-day is the most active manufacturing nation on the continent of Europe.   Agriculture has similarly been greatly developed, and one of its products, the sugar beet, has become a principal raw material of manufacture, the production of beet-root sugar having increased enormously.   The commerce of the empire has similarly augmented, it having become one of the most active commercial nations of the earth.   Its imports, considerable in quantity, consist largely of raw materials and food stuffs, while it vies with Great Britain and the United States in the quantity of finished products sent abroad.   In short, Germany has taken its place to-day as one of the most energetic of productive and commercial nations, and its wealth and importance have increased correspondingly.

CHAPTER XV.

Gladstone, the Apostle of Liberalism in England.

IT is a fact of much interest, as showing the growth of the human mind, that William Ewart Gladstone, the great advocate of English Liberalism, made his first political speech in vigorous opposition to the Reform Bill of 1831. He was then a student at Oxford University, but this boyish address had such an effect upon his hearers, that Bishop Wordsworth felt sure the speaker "would one day rise to be Prime Minister of England." This prophetic utterance may be mated with another one, **Gladstone's** by Archdeacon Denison, who said: "I have just heard the **First Political** best speech I ever heard in my life, by Gladstone, against the **Address** Reform Bill. But, mark my words, that man will one day be a Liberal, for he argued against the Bill on liberal ground."

Both these far-seeing men hit the mark. Gladstone became Prime Minister and the leader of the Liberal Party in England. Yet he had been reared as a Conservative, and for many years he marched under the banner of Conservatism. His political career began in the first Reform Parliament, in January, 1833. Two years afterward he was made an under-secretary in Sir Robert Peel's Cabinet. It was under the same **Gladstone in** Premier that he first became a full member of the Cabinet, in **Parliament** 1845, as Secretary of State for the Colonies. He was still a **and the** Tory in home politics, but had become a Liberal in his com- **Cabinet** mercial ideas, and was Peel's right-hand man in carrying out his great commercial policy.

The repeal of the Corn-laws was the work for which his Cabinet had been formed, and Gladstone, as the leading Free-trader in the Tory ranks, was called to it. As for Cobden, the apostle of Free-trade, Gladstone admired him immensely. "I do not know," he said in later years, "that there is in any period a man whose public career and life were nobler or more admirable. Of course, I except Washington. Washington, to my mind, is the purest figure in history." As an advocate of Free-trade Gladstone first came into connection with another noble figure, that of John Bright, who was to remain associated with him during most of his career. In 1857 he first took rank as one of the great moral forces of modern times.   In that year he visited Naples, where he saw the barbarous treatment of political prisoners under the government of the infamous King Bomba, and described them in letters whose indignation was breathed in

The Letters from Naples such tremendous tones that England was stirred to its depths and all Europe awakened.   These thrilling epistles gave the cause of Italian freedom an impetus that had much to do with its subsequent success, and gained for Gladstone the warmest veneration of patriotic Italians.

In 1852 he first came into opposition with the man against whom he was to be pitted during the remainder of his career, Benjamin Disraeli, who had made himself a power in Parliament, and in that year became Chancellor of the Exchequer in Lord Derby's Cabinet and leader of the House of Commons.   The revenue Budget introduced by him showed a sad lack of financial ability, and called forth sharp criticisms, to which he replied in a speech made up of scoffs, gibes and biting sarcasms, so daring and audacious in character as almost to intimidate the House.   As he sat down Mr. Gladstone rose and launched forth into an oration which became historic. He gave voice to that indignation which lay suppressed beneath the cowed feeling which for the moment the Chancellor of the Exchequer's perform-

First Contest Between Gladstone and Disraeli ance had left among his hearers.   In a few minutes the House was wildly cheering the intrepid champion who had rushed into the breach, and when Mr. Gladstone concluded, having torn to shreds the proposals of the Budget, a majority followed him into the division lobby, and Mr. Disraeli found his government beaten by nineteen votes.   Such was the first great encounter between the two rivals.

Lord Derby resigned at once, and politics were plunged into a condition of the wildest excitement and confusion.   Mr. Gladstone was the butt of Protectionist execration.   He was near being thrown out of the window at the Carlton Club by twenty extreme Tories, who, coming upstairs after dinner, found him alone in the drawing-room.   They did not quite go this length, though they threatened to do so, but contented themselves with insulting him.

In the Cabinet that followed, headed by Lord Aberdeen, Gladstone succeeded Disraeli as Chancellor of the Exchequer, a position in which he was to make a great mark.   In April, 1853, he introduced his first Budget, a marvel of ingenious statemanship, in its highly successful effort to equalize taxation.   It remitted various taxes which had pressed hard upon the poor and restricted business, and replaced them by applying the succession duty to real estate, increasing the duty on spirits, and extending the income tax. The latter Gladstone spoke of as an emergency tax, only to be applied in times of national danger, and presented a plan to extinguish it in 1860. His plan failed to work. Nearly fifty years have passed since then, and the income tax still remains, seemingly a fixed element of the British revenue system.

Taken altogether, and especially in its expedients to equalize taxation, this first Budget of Mr. Gladstone may be justly called the greatest of the century. The speech in which it was introduced and expounded created an extraordinary impression on the House and the country. For the first time in Parliament figures were made as interesting as a fairy tale ; the dry bones of statistics were invested with a new and potent life, and it was shown how the yearly balancing of the national accounts might be directed by and made to promote the profoundest and most fruitful principles of statesmanship. With such lucidity and picturesqueness was this financial oratory rolled forth that the dullest intellect could follow with pleasure the complicated scheme ; and for five hours the House of Commons sat as if it were under the sway of a magician's wand. When Mr. Gladstone resumed his seat, it was felt that the career of the coalition Ministry was assured by the genius that was discovered in its Chancellor of the Exchequer. *Gladstone's Great Budget Speech*

It was, indeed, to Gladstone's remarkable oratorical powers that much of his success as a statesman was due. No man of his period was his equal in swaying and convincing his hearers. His rich and musical voice, his varied and animated gestures, his impressive and vigorous delivery, great fluency, and wonderful precision of statement, gave him a power over an audience which few men of the century have enjoyed. His sentences, indeed, were long and involved, *Gladstone's Powers as an Orator* growing more so as his years advanced, but their fine choice of words, rich rhetoric, and eloquent delivery carried away all that heard him, as did his deep earnestness, and intense conviction of the truth of his utterances.

We must pass rapidly over a number of years of Gladstone's career, through most of which he continued to serve as Chancellor of the Exchequer, and to amaze and delight the country by the financial reforms effected in his annual Budgets. Between 1853 and 1866 those reforms represented a decrease in the weight of the burden of the national revenue amounting to £13,000,000.

Meanwhile his Liberalism had been steadily growing, and reached its culmination in 1865, when the great Tory university of Oxford, which he had long represented, rejected him as its member. At once he offered himself as a candidate for South Lancashire, in which his native place was situated, saying, in the opening of his speech at Manchester: "At last, my friends, I am come among you; to use an expression which has become very famous and is not likely to be forgotten, 'I am come among you unmuzzled.'"

Unmuzzled he was, as his whole future career was to show. Oxford had, in a measure, clipped his wings. Now he was free to give the fullest

Gladstone the Liberal Leader of the House

expression to his liberal faith, and to stand before the country as the great apostle of reform. In 1866 he became, for the first time in his career, leader of the House of Commons— Lord Russel, the Prime Minister, being in the House of Lords. Many of his friends feared for him in this difficult position; but the event proved that they had no occasion for alarm, he showing himself one of the most successful leaders the House had ever had.

His first important duty in this position was to introduce the new suffrage Reform Bill, a measure to extend the franchise in counties and boroughs that would have added about 400,000 voters to the electorate. In the debate that followed Gladstone and Disraeli were again pitted against each other in a grand oratorical contest. Disraeli taunted him with his

The Suffrage Reform Bill

youthful speech at Oxford against the Reform Bill of 1831. Gladstone replied in a burst of vigorous eloquence, in which he scored his opponent for lingering in a conservatism from which the speaker gloried in having been strong enough to break. He and the Cabinet were pledged to stand or fall with the Bill But, if it fell, the principle of right and justice which it involved would not fall. It was sure to survive and triumph in the future. He ended with this stirring prediction:

" You cannot fight against the future. Time is on our side. The great social forces which move onwards in their might and majesty, and which the tumult of our debates does not for a moment impede or disturb, those great social forces are against you: they are marshalled on our side; and the banner which we now carry into this fight, though perhaps at some moment it may droop over our sinking heads, yet it soon again will float in the eye of Heaven, and it will be borne by the firm hands of the united people of the three kingdoms, perhaps not to an easy, but to a certain, and to a not far distant, victory."

Disraeli and his party won. The Bill was defeated. But its defeat roused the people almost as they had been roused in 1832. A formidable riot broke out in London. Ten thousand people marched in procession past Gladstone's residence, singing odes in honor of "the People's William." There were demonstrations in his favor and in support of the

Bill throughout the country. The agitation continued during the winter, its fire fed by the eloquence of another of the great orators of the century, the "tribune of the people," John Bright. This distingu- **England** ished man and powerful public speaker, through all his **Agitated on** life a strenuous advocate of moral reform and political **Reform** progress, had begun his parliamentary career as an advocate of the Reform Bill of 1831–32. He now became one of the great leaders in the new campaign and through his eloquence and that of Gladstone the force of public opinion rose to such a height that the new Derby-Disraeli ministry found itself obliged to bring in a Bill similar to that which it had worked so hard to overthrow.

And now a striking event took place. The Tory Reform Bill was satisfactory to Gladstone in its general features, but he proposed many improvements—lodger franchise, educational and savings-bank franchises, enlargement of the redistribution of seats, etc.—every one of which was yielded in committee, until, as one lord remarked, nothing of the original Bill remained but the opening word, "Whereas." This bill, really the work of Gladstone, and more liberal than the one which had been defeated, was passed, and Toryism, in the very success of its measure, suffered a crushing defeat. To Gladstone, as the people perceived, their right to vote was due.

But Disraeli was soon to attain to the exalted office for which he had long been striving. In February, 1868, failing health caused **Disraeli Be-** Lord Derby to resign, and Disraeli was asked to form a **comes Prime** new administration. Thus the "Asian Mystery," as he had **Minister** been entitled, reached the summit of his ambition, in becoming Prime Minister of England.

He was not to hold this position long. Gladstone was to reach the same high eminence before the year should end. Disraeli's government, beginning in February, 1868, was defeated on the question of the disestablishment of the Irish Church; an appeal to the country resulted in a large Liberal gain; and on December 4th the Queen sent for Mr. Gladstone and commissioned him to form a new ministry. The task was completed by the 9th, Mr. Bright, who had aided so greatly in the triumph of the Liberals, entering the new cabinet as President of the Board of Trade. Thus at last, after thirty-five years of active public life, Mr. Glad- **Gladstone is** stone was at the summit of power—Prime Minister of Great **Made Prime** Britain with a strong majority in Parliament in his support. **Minister**

Bishop Wilberforce, who met him in this hour of triumph, wrote of him thus in his journal: "Gladstone as ever great, earnest, and honest; as unlike the tricky Disraeli as possible. He is so delightfully true and the same; just as full of interest in every good thing of every kind."

The period which followed the election of 1868—the period of the Gladstone Administration of 1868–74—has been called "the golden age of Liberalism." It was certainly a period of great reforms. The first, the most heroic, and probably—taking all the results into account—the most completely successful of these, was the disestablishment of the Irish Church.

Though Mr. Gladstone had a great majority at his back, the difficulties which confronted him were immense. In Ireland the wildest protests emanated from the friends of the Establishment. The "loyal minority" declared that their loyalty would come to an end if the measure were passed. One synod, speaking with a large assumption, even for a synod, of inspired knowledge, denounced it as "highly offensive to the Almighty God." The Orangemen threatened to rise in insurrection. A martial clergyman proposed to "kick the Queen's crown into the Boyne" if she assented to such a Bill. Another announed his intention of fighting with the Bible in one hand and the sword in the other. These appeals and these threats of civil war, absurd as they proved to be in reality, were not without producing some effect in Great Britain, and it was amid a din of warnings, of misgiving counsels, and of hostile cries, that Mr. Gladstone proceeded to carry out the mandate of the nation which he had received at the polls.

On the first of March, 1869, he introduced his Disestablishment Bill.

Disestablishment of the Irish Church His speech was one of the greatest marvels amongst his oratorical achievements. His chief opponent declared that, though it lasted three hours, it did not contain a redundant word. The scheme which it unfolded—a scheme which withdrew the temporal establishment of a Church in such a manner that the Church was benefited, not injured, and which lifted from the backs of an oppressed people an intolerable burden—was a triumph of creative genius. Leaving aside his Budgets, which stand in a different category, it seems to us there is no room to doubt that in his record of constructive legislation this measure for the disestablishment of the Irish Church is Mr. Gladstone's most perfect masterpiece.

Disraeli's speech in opposition to this measure was referred to by the *London Times* as "flimsiness relieved by spangles." After a debate in which Mr. Bright made one of his most famous speeches, the bill was carried by a majority of 118. Before this strong manifestation of the popular will the House of Lords, which deeply disliked the Bill, felt obliged to give way, and passed it by a majority of seven.

In 1870 Mr. Gladstone introduced his Irish Land Bill, a measure of reform which Parliament had for years refused to grant. By it the tenant was given the right to hold his farm as long as he paid his rent, and received a claim upon the improvement made by himself and his predecessors—a tenant-right which he could sell. This bill was triumphantly carried; and another important Liberal measure, Mr. Forster's Education Bill, became law.

The Irish Land Bill Enacted

In the following sessions the tide of Liberal reform continued on its course. Among the reforms adopted was that of vote by ballot. A measure was introduced abolishing purchase in the Army; and on this question Mr. Gladstone had his third notable conflict with the Lords. The Lords threw out the Bill. The imperious Premier, having found that purchase in the Army existed only by royal sanction, advised the Queen to issue a Royal Warrant cancelling the regulation. By a single act of executive authority he carried out a reform to which Parliament had, through one of its branches, refused its assent. This was a high-handed, not to say autocratic, step, and it afforded a striking revelation of the capacities in boldness and resolution of Mr. Gladstone's character. It was denounced as Cæsarism and Cromwellism in some quarters; in others as an unconstitutional invocation of the royal prerogative.

But the career of reform at length proved too rapid for the country to follow. The Government was defeated in 1873 on a bill for University Education in Ireland. Gladstone at once resigned, but, as Disraeli declined to form a Government, he was obliged to resume office. In 1874 he took the bold step of dissolving Parliament and appealing to the country for support. If he were returned to power he promised to repeal the income tax. He was not returned. The Tory party gained a majority of 46. Gladstone at once resigned, not only the Premiership, but the leadership of the Liberal party, and retired to private life—a much needed rest after his many years of labor. Disraeli succeeded him as Prime Minister, and two years afterwards was raised to the peerage by the Queen as the Earl of Beaconsfield.

Defeat of Gladstone and the Liberals

Mr. Gladstone was never idle. The intervals of his public duties were filled with tireless studies and frequent literary labors. Chief among the latter were his "Homeric Studies," works which showed great erudition and active mental exercise, though not great powers of critical discrimination. They adopted views which were then becoming obsolete, and their conclusions have been rejected by Homeric scholars. Gladstone's greatness was as an orator and a moral reformer, not as a great logician and brilliant thinker.

In the period at which we have arrived his moral greatness and literary fervor were both called into exercise in an international cause. The Bulgarian atrocities of 1876—spoken of in Chapter X—called the aged

Gladstone on the Bulgarian Horrors

statesman from his retirement, and his pamphlet entitled "Bulgarian Horrors and the Question of the East," rang through England like a trumpet-call. "Let the Turks now carry away their abuses in the only possible manner—by carrying off themselves," he wrote. "Their Zaptiehs and their Mudirs, their Bimbashis and their Yuzbachis, their Kaimakams and their Pashas, one and all, bag and baggage, shall, I hope, clear out from the province they have desolated and profaned."

He followed up this pamphlet by a series of speeches, delivered to great meetings and to the House of Commons, with which for four years he sought, as he expressed it, "night and day to counterwork the purpose of Lord Beaconsfield." He succeeded; England was prevented by his

His Second Great Contest with Disraeli

eloquence from joining the Turks in the war; but he excited the fury of the war party to such an extent that at one time it was not safe for him to appear in the streets of London. Nor was he quite safe in the House of Commons, where the Conservatives hated him so bitterly as to jeer and interrupt him whenever he spoke, and a party of them went so far as to mob him in the House.

Yet the sentiment he had aroused saved the country from the greatest of the follies by which it was threatened; and, if it failed to stop the lesser adventures in which Lord Beaconsfield found an outlet for the passions he had unloosed,—an annexation of Cyprus, an interference in Egypt, an annexation of the Transvaal, a Zulu war which Mr. Gladstone denounced as "one of the most monstrous and indefensible in our history," an Afghan war which he described as a national crime,—it nevertheless was so true an interpretation of the best, the deliberate, judgment of the nation, that it sufficed eventually to bring the Liberal party back to power.

This took place in 1880. In the campaign for the Parliament elected in that year Gladstone took a most active part, and had much to do with the great Liberal victory that followed. In the face of the overwhelming

Gladstone Again Made Premier

majority that was returned Lord Beaconsfield resigned office, and Gladstone a second time was called to the head of the government.

As in the previous, so in the present, Gladstone administration the question of Ireland loomed up above all others. While Beaconsfield remained Premier Ireland was lost sight of, quite dwarfed by the Eastern question upon which the two life-long adversaries measured their strength.

But as Turkey went down in public interest Ireland rose. The Irish people were gaining a vivid sense of their power under the Constitution. And another famine came to put the land laws and government of Ireland to a severe test. Still more, Ireland gained a leader, a man of remarkable ability, who was to play as great a part in its history as O'Connell had done half a century before. This was Charles Stewart Parnell, the founder of the Irish Land League—a powerful trade-union of tenant farmers—and for many years the leader of the Irish party in Parliament. In the Parliament of 1880 his **Parnell Becomes the Leader of the Irish Party** followers numbered sixty-eight, enough to make him a power to be dealt with in legislation.

Gladstone, in assuming control of the new government, was quite unaware of the task before him. When he had completed his work with the Church and the Land Bills ten years before, he fondly fancied that the Irish question was definitely settled. The Home Rule movement, which was started in 1870, seemed to him a wild delusion which would die away of itself. In 1884 he said : " I frankly admit that I had had much upon my hands connected with the doings of the Beaconsfield Government in every quarter of the world, and I did not know—no one knew—the severity of the crisis that was already swelling upon the horizon, and that shortly after rushed upon us like a flood."

He was not long in discovering the gravity of the situation, of which the House had been warned by Mr. Parnell. The famine had brought its crop of misery, and, while the charitable were seeking to relieve the distress, many of the landlords were turning adrift their tenants **The Famine and the Bill for Irish Relief** for non-payment of rents. The Irish party brought in a Bill for the Suspension of Evictions, which the government replaced by a similar one for Compensation for Disturbance. This was passed with a large majority by the Commons, but was rejected by the Lords, and Ireland was left to face its misery without relief.

The state of Ireland at that moment was too critical to be dealt with in this manner. The rejection of the Compensation for Disturbance Bill was, to the peasantry whom it had been intended to protect, a message of despair, and it was followed by the usual symptom of despair in Ireland, an outbreak of agrarian crime. On the one hand over 17,000 persons were evicted ; on the other there was a dreadful crop of murders and outrages. The Land League sought to do what Parliament did not ; but in doing so it came in contact with the law. Moreover, the revolution—for revolution it seemed to be—grew too formidable for its control ; the utmost it succeeded in doing was in some sense to ride without directing the storm. The first decisive step of Mr. Forster, the chief secretary for Ireland, was to strike a blow at the Land League. In November he ordered the prosecution of

Mr. Forster's Policy of Coercion

Mr. Parnell, Mr. Biggar, and several of the officials of the organization, and before the year was out he announced his intention of introducing a Coercion Bill. This step threw the Irish members under Mr. Parnell and the Liberal Government into relations of definitive antagonism.

Mr. Forster introduced his Coercion Bill on January 24, 1881. It was a formidable measure, which enabled the chief secretary, by signing a warrant, to arrest any man on suspicion of having committed a given offence, and to imprison him without trial at the pleasure of the government. It practically suspended the liberties of Ireland. The Irish members exhausted every resource of parliamentary action in resisting it, and their tactics resulted in several scenes unprecedented in parliamentary history. In order to pass the Bill it was necessary to suspend them in a body several times. Mr. Gladstone, with manifest pain, found himself, as leader of the House, the agent by whom this extreme resolve had to be executed.

The Coercion Bill passed, Mr. Gladstone introduced his Land Bill of

Gladstone's New Land Bill

1881, which was the measure of conciliation intended to balance the measure of repression. This was really a great and sweeping reform, whose dominant feature was the introduction of the novel and far-reaching principle of the State stepping in between landlord and tenant and fixing the rents. The Bill had some defects, as a series of amending acts, which were subsequently passed by both Liberal and Tory Governments, proved; but, apart from these, it was on the whole the greatest measure of land reform ever passed for Ireland by the Imperial Parliament.

But Ireland was not yet satisfied. Parnell had no confidence in the good intentions of the government, and took steps to test its honesty, which so angered Mr. Forster that he arrested Mr. Parnell and several other leaders and pronounced the Land League an illegal body. Forster was well meaning but mistaken. He fancied that by locking up the ringleaders he could bring quiet to the country. On the contrary, affairs were

Stirring Events in Ireland

soon far worse than ever, crime and outrage spreading widely. In despair, Mr. Forster released Parnell and resigned. All now seemed hopeful; coercion had proved a failure; peace and quiet were looked for; when, four days afterward, the whole country was horrified by a terrible crime. The new secretary for Ireland, Lord Cavendish, and the under-secretary, Mr. Burke, were attacked and hacked to death with knives in Phœnix Park.

Everywhere panic and indignation arose. A new Coercion Act was passed without delay. It was vigorously put into effect, and a state of virtual war between England and Ireland again came into existence.

Trouble also arose in the East. Great Britain, in its usual fashion of seeking to carry the world on its shoulders, had made the control of the Suez Canal an excuse for an annoying interference in the government of Egypt. The result was a revolution that drove Ismail Pasha from his throne. As the British still held control, a revolt broke out among the people, headed by an ambitious leader named Arabi Pasha, and Alexandria was seized, the British being driven out and many of them killed. Much as Gladstone deprecated war, he felt himself forced into it. John Bright, to whom war was a crime that nothing could warrant, resigned from the cabinet, but the Government acted vigorously, the British fleet being ordered to bombard Alexandria. This was done effectively. The city, half reduced to ashes, was occupied by the British, Arabi and his army withdrawing in haste. Soon afterwards he was defeated by General Wolseley and the insurrection was at an end. Egypt remained a vassal of Great Britain. An unfortunate sequel to this may be briefly stated. A formidable insurrection

The Bombardment of Alexandria and Death of Gordon

broke out in the Soudan, under El Mahdi, a Mohammedan fanatic, who captured the city of Khartoum and murdered the famous General Gordon. For years Upper Egypt was lost to the state, it being recovered only at the close of the century by a military expedition.

In South Africa the British were less successful. Here a war had been entered into with the Boers, in which the British forces suffered a severe defeat at Majuba Hill. Gladstone did not adopt the usual fashion of seeking revenge by the aid of a stronger force, but made peace, the Boers gaining what they had been fighting for.

Disasters like this weakened the administration. Parnell and his followers joined hands with the Tories, and a vigorous assault was made upon the government. Slowly its majority fell

The Defeat of the Liberals

away, and at length, in May, 1885, it was defeated.

The scene which followed was a curious one. The Irish raised cries of "No Coercion," while the Tories delivered themselves up to a frenzy of jubilation, waving hats and handkerchiefs, and wildly cheering. Lord Randolph Churchill jumped on a bench, brandished his hat madly above his head, and altogether behaved as if he were beside himself. Mr. Gladstone calmly resumed the letter to the Queen which he had been writing on his knee, while the clerk at the table proceeded to run through the orders of the day, as if nothing particular had happened. When in a few moments the defeated Premier moved the adjournment, he did so still holding his letter in one hand and the pen in the other, and the Conservatives surged through the doorway, tumultuously cheering.

Gladstone's great opponent was no longer on earth to profit by his defeat. Beaconsfield had died in 1881, and Lord Salisbury became head of the new Tory Government, one which owed its existence to Irish votes. It had a very short life. Parnell and his fellows soon tired of their unnatural alliance, turned against and defeated the Government, and Gladstone was sent for to form a new government. On February 1, 1886, he became Prime Minister of Great Britain for the third time.

During the brief interval his opinions had suffered a great revolution. He no longer thought that Ireland had all it could justly demand. He returned to power as an advocate of a most radical measure, that of Home
Gladstone a Rule for Ireland, a restoration of that separate Parliament
Convert to which it had lost in 1800. He also had a scheme to buy out
Home Rule the Irish landlords and establish a peasant proprietary by state aid. His new views were revolutionary in character, but he did not hesitate —he never hesitated to do what his conscience told him was right. On April 8, 1886, he introduced to Parliament his Home Rule Bill.

The scene that afternoon was one of the most remarkable in Parliamentary history. Never before was such interest manifested in a debate by either the public or the members of the House. In order to secure their places, members arrived at St. Stephen's at six o'clock in the morning, and spent the day on the premises ; and, a thing quite unprecedented, members
A Remarkable who could not find places on the benches filled up the floor of
Scene in Par- the House with rows of chairs. The strangers', diplomats',
liament peers', and ladies' galleries were filled to overflowing. Men begged even to be admitted to the ventilating passages beneath the floor of the Chamber that they might in some sense be witnesses of the greatest feat in the lifetime of an illustrious old man of eighty. Around Palace Yard an enormous crowd surged, waiting to give the veteran a welcome as he drove up from Downing Street.

Mr. Gladstone arrived in the House, pale and still panting from the excitement of his reception in the streets. As he sat there the entire Liberal party—with the exception of Lord Hartington, Sir Henry James, Mr. Chamberlain and Sir George Trevelyan—and the Nationalist members, by a spontaneous impulse, sprang to their feet and cheered him again and again. The speech which he delivered was in every way worthy of the occasion. It expounded, with marvelous lucidity and a noble eloquence, a tremendous scheme of constructive legislation—the re-establishment of a legislature in

Ireland, but one subordinate to the Imperial Parliament, and hedged round with every safeguard which could protect the unity of the Empire. It took three hours in delivery, and was listened to throughout with the utmost attention on every side of the House. At its close all parties united in a tribute of admiration for the genius which had astonished them with such an exhibition of its powers.

Yet it is one thing to cheer an orator, another thing to vote for a revolution. The Bill was defeated—as it was almost sure to be. Mr. Gladstone at once dissolved Parliament and appealed to the country in a new election, with the result that he was decisively defeated. His bold declaration that the contest was one between the classes and the masses turned the aristocracy against him, while he had again roused the bitter hatred of his opponents.

But the "Grand Old Man" bided his time. The new Salisbury ministry was one of coercion carried to the extreme in Ireland, wholesale eviction, arrest of members of Parliament, suppression of public meetings by force of arms, and other measures of violence which in the end wearied the British public and doubled the support of Home Rule. In 1892 Mr. Gladstone returned to power with a majority of more than thirty Home Rulers in his support.

It was one of the greatest efforts in the career of the old Parliamentary hero when he brought his new Home Rule Bill before the House. Never in his young days had he worked more earnestly and incessantly. He disarmed even his bitterest enemies, none of whom now dreamed of treating him with disrespect. Mr. Balfour spoke of the delight and fascination with which even his **Gladstone's Last and Greatest Triumph** opponents watched his leading of the House and listened to his unsurpassed eloquence. Old age had come to clothe with its pathos, as well as with its majesty, the white-haired, heroic figure. The event proved one of the greatest triumphs of his life. The Bill passed with a majority of thirty-four. That it would pass in the House of Lords no one looked for. It was defeated there by a majority of 378 out of 460.

With this great event the public career of the Grand Old Man came to an end. The burden had grown too heavy for his reduced strength. In March, 1894, to the consternation of his party, he announced his intention of retiring from public life. The Queen offered, **The Close of a Great Career** as she had done once before, to raise him to the peerage as an earl, but he declined the proffer. His own plain name was a title higher than that of any earldom in the kingdom.

On May 19, 1898 William Ewart Gladstone laid down the burden of his life as he had already done that of labor. The greatest and noblest figure in legislative life of the nineteenth century had passed away from earth.

NICHOLAS II. AND FAMILY

RUSSIA'S ROYAL FAMILY AND HER LITERARY LEADER

COUNT LYOF NIKOLAIEVITCH TOLSTOÏ

CHARLES STEWART PARNELL.

WILLIAM O'BRIEN.

MICHAEL DAVITT

T. M. HEALY.

FOUR GREAT MODERN IRISH LEADERS

CHAPTER XVI.

Ireland the Downtrodden.

TIME was when Ireland was free. But it was a barbarian freedom. The island had more kings than it had counties, each petty chief bearing the royal title, while their battles were as frequent as those of our Indian tribes of a past age. The island, despite the fact that it had an active literature reaching back to the early centuries of the Christian era, was in a condition of endless turmoil. This state of affairs was gradually put an end to after the English conquest; but the civilization which was introduced into the island was made bitter by an injustice and oppression which has filled the Irish heart with an undying hatred of the English nation and a ceaseless desire to break loose from its bonds. **Ireland in the Past Centuries.**

For centuries, indeed, the rule of England was largely a nominal one, the English control being confined to a few coast districts in the east. In the interior the native tribes continued under the rule of their chiefs, were governed by their own laws, and remained practically independent.

It was not until the reign of James I. that England became master of all Ireland. In the last days of the reign of Elizabeth a great rising against the English had taken place in Ulster, under a chief named O'Neill. The Earl of Essex failed to put it down and was disgraced by the queen in consequence. The armies of James finally suppressed the rebellion, and the unruly island, now, for the first time, came fully under the control of an English king. It had given the earlier monarchs nothing but trouble, and James determined to weaken its power for mischief. To do so he took possession of six counties of Ulster and filled them with Scotch and English colonists. As for the Irish, they were simply crowded out, and left to seek a living where they could. There was no place left for them but the marshes. **The O'Neill Rebellion and the Confiscation of Ulster**

This act of ruthless violence filled the Irish with an implacable hatred of their oppressors which had not vanished in the years since it took place. They treasured up their wrongs for thirty years, but in 1641, when England was distracted by its civil war, they rose in their wrath, fell upon the colonists and murdered all who could not save themselves by flight. For eight years, while the English had their hands full at home, the Irish held their reconquered lands in triumph, but in 1649 Cromwell fell upon them with his invincible Ironsides, and took such a cruel revenge that he himself confessed that he had imbued his hands in blood like a common butcher. In truth, the Puritans looked upon the Papists as outside the pale of

Cromwell's Bloody Severity and the Fate of the Irish

humanity, and no more to be considered than a herd of wild beasts, and they dealt with them as hunters might with noxious animals.

The severity of Cromwell was threefold greater than that of James, for he drove the Irish out of three provinces, Ulster, Leinster and Munster, bidding them go and find bread or graves in the wilderness of Connaught. Again the Irish rose, when James II., the dethroned king, came to demand their aid; and again they were overthrown, this time in the memorable Battle of the Boyne. William III. now completed the work of confiscation. The greater part of the remaining province of Connaught was taken from its holders and given to English colonists. The natives of the island became a landless people in their own land.

To complete their misery and degradation, William and the succeeding monarchs robbed them of all their commerce and manufactures, by forbidding them to trade with other countries. Their activity in this direction interfered with the profits of English producers and merchants. By these

The Cause of Irish Hatred of England

merciless and cruel methods the Irish were reduced to a nation of tenants, laborers and beggars, and such they still remain, downtrodden, oppressed, their most lively sentiment being their hatred of the English, to whom they justly impute their degradation.

The time came when England acknowledged with shame and sorrow the misery to which she had reduced a sister people—but it was then too late to retrieve the wrong. English landlords owned the land, manufacturing industry had been irretrievably crowded out, the evil done was past mending.

With these preliminary statements we come to the verge of the nineteenth century. America had rebelled against England and gained independence. This fact stirred up a new desire for liberty in the Irish. The island had always possessed a legislature of its own, but it was of no value to the natives. It represented only the great Protestant landowners, and could pass no act without the consent of the Privy Council of England.

A demand for a national Parliament was made, and the English government, having its experience in America before its eyes, granted it, an act being passed in 1782 which made Ireland independent of England in legislation, a system such as is now called Home Rule. **Home Rule and the Act of Union** It was not enough. It did not pacify the island. The religious animosity between the Catholics and Protestants continued, and in 1798 violent disturbances broke out, with massacres on both sides.

The Irish Parliament was a Protestant body, and at first was elected solely by Protestant votes. Grattan, the eminent Irish statesman, through whose efforts this body had been made an independent legislature,—" The King, Lords, and Commons of Ireland, to make laws for the people of Ireland,"—carried an act to permit Catholics to vote for its members. He then strove for a measure to permit Catholics to sit as members in the Irish Parliament. This was too much for George III. He recalled Lord Fitzwilliam, the viceroy of Ireland, who had encouraged and assisted Grattan and blighted the hopes of the Irish Catholics.

The revolt that followed was the work of a society called the United Irishmen, organized by Protestants, but devoted to the interests of Ireland. Wolfe Tone, one of its leading members, went to France and induced Napoleon to send an expedition to Ireland. A fleet was dispatched, but this, like the Spanish Armada, was dispersed by a storm, and the few Frenchmen who landed were soon captured. **The United Irishmen and Act of Union** The rebellion was as quickly crushed, and was followed by deeds of remorseless cruelty, so shameful that they were denounced by the commander-in chief himself. With this revolt the independence of Ireland ended. An act of union was offered and carried through the Irish Parliament by a very free use of money among the members, and the Irish Legislature was incorporated with the British one. Since January 1, 1801, all laws for Ireland have been made in London.

Among the most prominent members of the United Irishmen Society were two brothers named Emmet, the fate of one of whom has ever since been remembered with sympathy, Thomas A. Emmet, one of these brothers, was arrested in 1798 as a member of this society, and was imprisoned until 1802, when he was released on condition that he should spend the remainder of his life on foreign soil. He eventually reached New York, at whose bar he attained eminence. The fate of his more famous brother, Robert Emmet, was tragical. This young man, a school-fellow of Thomas Moore, the poet, was expelled from Trinity College in 1798, when twenty years of age, as a member of the United Irishmen. He went to the continent, interviewed Napoleon on behalf of the Irish cause, and returned in 1802 with a wild idea of freeing Ireland by his own efforts from English rule.

Organizing a plan for a revolution, and expending his small fortune in the purchase of muskets and pikes, he formed a plot to seize Dublin Castle, capture the viceroy, and dominate the capital. At the head of a small body

The Fate of Robert Emmet of followers he set out on this hopeless errand, which ended at the first volley of the guards, before which his confederates hastily dispersed. Emmet, who had dressed himself for the occassion in a green coat, white breeches and cocked hat, was deeply morti-fied at the complete failure of his scheme. He fled to the Wicklow moun-tains, whence, perceiving that success in his plans was impossible, he resolved to escape to the continent. But love led him to death. He was deeply attached to the daughter of Curran, the celebrated orator, and, in despite of the advice of his friends, would not consent to leave Ireland until he had seen her. The attempt was a fatal one. On his return from the interview with his lady-love he was arrested and imprisoned on a charge of high treason. He was condemned to death September 19, 1803, and was hanged the next day.

Before receiving sentence he made an address to the court of such noble and pathetic eloquence that it still thrills the reader with sympathetic emotion. It is frequently reprinted among examples of soul-stirring oratory. The disconsolate woman, Sarah Curran, perished of a broken heart after his untimely death. This event is the theme of one of Moore's finest poems: " She is far from the land where her young hero lies."

The death of Emmet and the dispersal of the United Irishmen by no means ended the troubles in Ireland, but rather added to their force. Ire-land and England, unlike in the character and religion of their people and in their institutions, continued in a state of hostility, masked or active, the

Landlords, Tenants and Clergy old feuds being kept alive on the one side by the landlords, on the other by the peasantry and the clergy. The country was divided into a great number of small farms, thousands of them being less than five acres each in size. For these the landlords—many of whom the tenants never saw and some of whom had never seen Ireland—often exacted extravagant rents. Again, while the great majority of the people was Catholic, the Catholic clergy had to be supported by the voluntary contributions of the poverty-stricken people, while tithes, or church taxes, were exacted by law for the payment of clergymen of the English Church, who remained almost without congregations. Finally, the Catholics were disfranchised. After the abolishment of the Irish

Parliament they were without representation in the government under which they lived. No Catholic could be a member of Parliament. It is not surprising that their protest was vigorous, and that the British government had many rebellious outbreaks to put down.

It was the disfranchisement of the Catholics that first roused opposition. Grattan brought up a bill for "Catholic Emancipation"—that is, the admission of Catholics to the British Parliament and the repeal of certain ancient, and oppressive edicts—in 1813. The *O'Connell and Catholic Emancipation* bill was lost, but a new and greater advocate of Irish rights now arose, Daniel O'Connell, the "Liberator," the greatest of Irish orators and patriots, who for many years was to champion the cause of downtrodden Ireland.

The "counsellor"—a favorite title of O'Connell among his Irish admirers—was a man of remarkable powers, noted for his boisterous Irish wit and good humor, his fearlessness and skill as a counsel, his constant tact and readiness in reply, his unrivalled skill in the cross-examination of Irish witnesses, and the violent language which he often employed in court. This man, of burly figure, giant strength, inexhaustible energy and power of work, a voice mighty enough to drown the noise of a *The "Counsellor" and His Oratory* crowd, a fine command of telling language, coarse but effective humor, ready and telling retort, and master of all the artillery of vituperation, was just the man to control the Irish people, passing with the ease of a master from bursts of passion and outbreaks of buffoonery to passages of the tenderest pathos. Thoroughly Irish, he seemed made by nature to sustain the cause of Ireland.

O'Connell was shrewd enough to deter revolt, and, while awakening in the Irish the spirit of nationality, he taught them to keep political agitation within constitutional limits, and seek by legislative means what they had no hope of gaining by force of arms. His legal practice was enormous, yet amid it he found time for convivial relaxation and for a deep plunge into the whirlpool of politics.

The vigorous advocate was not long in rising to the chiefship of the Irish party, but his effective work in favor of Catholic emancipation began in 1823, when he founded the "Irish Association," a gigantic system of organization which Ireland had nothing similar to before. The *The Irish Association* clergy were disinclined to take part in this movement, but O'Connell's eloquence brought them in before the end of the year, and under their influence it became national, spreading irresistibly throughout the land and rousing everywhere the greatest enthusiasm. To obtain funds for its support the "Catholic Rent" was established—one penny a month—which yielded as much as £500 per week.

In alarm at the growth of this association, the government brought in a bill for its suppression, but O'Connell, too shrewd to come into conflict with the authorities, forstalled them by dissolving it in 1825. He had set the ball rolling. The Irish forty-shilling freeholders gained courage to oppose their landlords in the elections. In 1826 they carried Waterford. In 1828 O'Connell himself stood as member of parliament for Clare, and was elected amid the intense enthusiasm of the people.

This triumph set the whole country in a flame. The lord-lieutenant looked for an insurrection, and even Lord Wellington, prime minister of England, was alarmed at the threatening outlook. But O'Connell, knowing that an outbreak would be ruinous to the Catholic cause, used his marvelous powers to still the agitation and to induce the people to wait for parliamentary relief.

This relief came the following year. A bill was passed which admitted Catholics to parliament, and under it O'Connell made his appearance in the House of Commons May 15, 1829. He declined to take the old oaths,

O'Connell in Parliament which had been repealed by the bill. The House refused to admit him on these conditions, and he went down to Clare again, which sent him back like a conqueror. At the beginning of 1830 he took his seat unopposed.

O'Connell's career in parliament was one of persistent labor for the repeal of the "Act of Union" with Great Britain, and Home Rule for Ireland, in the advocacy of which he kept the country stirred up for years. The abolition of tithes for the support of the Anglican clergy was another of his great subjects of agitation, and this one member had the strength of a host as an advocate of justice and freedom for his country.

The agitation on the Catholic question had quickened the sense of the wrongs of Ireland, and the Catholics were soon engaged in a crusade against tithes and the established Church, which formed the most offensive symbols of their inferior position in the state. In 1830 the potato crop in Ireland was very poor, and wide-spread misery and destitution prevailed. O'Connell advised the people to pay no tithes, but in this matter they passed

The Tithe Troubles beyond his control, and for months crime ran rampant. The farmers refused to pay tithes or rents, armed bands marched through the island, and murder and incendiarism visited the homes of the rich. A stringent coercion bill was enacted and the troubles were put down by the strong hand of the law. Subsequently the Whig party, then in power, practically abolished tithes, cutting down the revenue of the Established Church, and using the remainder for secular purposes, and the agitation subsided.

In 1832 O'Connell became member for Dublin, and nominated most of the Irish candidates, with such effect that he had in the next Parliament a following of forty-five members, known sarcastically as his "tail." He gradually attained a position of great eminence in the House of Commons, standing in the first rank of parliamentary orators as a debater.

When a Tory ministry came into power, in 1841, O'Connell began a vigorous agitation in favor of repeal of the Act of Union and of Home Rule for Ireland, advocating the measure with all his wonder- **The Home Rule** ful power of oratory. In 1843 he travelled 5,000 miles through **Crusade** Ireland, speaking to immense meetings, attended by hundreds of thousands of people, and extending to every corner of the island. But thanks to his great controlling power, and the influence of Father Mathew, the famous temperance advocate, these audiences were never unruly mobs, but remained free from crime and drunkenness. The greatest was that held on the Hill of Tara, at which, according to the *Nation*, three-quarters of a million persons were present.

O'Connell wisely deprecated rebellion and bloodshed. "He who commits a crime adds strength to the enemy," was his favorite motto. Through a whole generation, with wonderful skill, he kept the public mind at the highest pitch of political excitement, yet restrained it from violence. But with all his power the old chief began to lose control of the enthuisastic Young Ireland party and, confident that the government must soon yield to the impassioned appeal from a whole nation, he allowed himself in his speeches to outrun his sober judgment.

Fearful of an outbreak of violence, the government determined to put an end to these enormous meetings, and a force of 35,000 men was sent to Ireland. A great meeting had been called for Clantarf on October 5, 1843, but it was forbidden the day before by the authorities, and O'Connell, fearing bloodshed, abandoned it. He was arrested, however, tried for a conspiracy to arouse sedition, and sentenced to a year's imprison- **O'Connell** ment and a fine of £2,000. This sentence was set aside by **Imprisoned** the House of Lords some months afterward as erroneous, and at once bonfires blazed across Ireland from sea to sea. But the three months he passed in prison proved fatal to the old chief, then nearly seventy years old. He contracted a disease which carried him to the grave three years afterwards.

During his withdrawal the Young Ireland party began to advocate resistance to the government. In 1846 and 1847 came the potato famine, the most severe visitation Ireland had known during the century, and in 1848 the revolutionary movement in Europe made itself felt on Irish soil.

In the latter year the ardent Young Ireland party carried the country into rebellion ; but the outbreak was easily put down, hardly a drop of blood be-

The Young Ireland Rebellion ing shed in its suppression. The popular leader, Smith O'Brien, was banished to Australia, but was eventually pardoned. John Mitchell, editor of the *Nation* and the *United Irishman*, was also banished, but subsequently escaped from Australia to the United States.

The wrongs of Ireland remained unredeemed, and as long as this was the case quiet could not be looked for in the island. In 1858 a Phœnix conspiracy was discovered and suppressed. Meanwhile John O'Mahony, one of the insurgents of 1848, organized a formidable secret society among the Irish in the United States, which he named the Fenian Brotherhood, after Finn, the hero of Irish legend. This organization was opposed by the Catholic clergy, but grew despite their opposition, its members becoming numerous and its funds large.

Its leader in Ireland was James Stephens, and its organ the *Irish People* newspaper. But there were traitors in the camp and in 1865 the paper

The Fenian Brotherhood was suppressed and the leaders were arrested. Stephens escaped from prison ten days after his arrest and made his way to America. The revolutionary activity of this association was small. There were some minor outbreaks and an abortive attempt to seize Chester Castle, and in September, 1867, an attack was made on a police van in Manchester, and the prisoners, who were Fenians, were rescued. Soon after an attempt was made to blow down Clerkenwell Prison wall, with the same purpose in view.

The Fenians in the United States organized a plot in 1866 for a raid upon Canada, which utterly failed, and in 1871 the government of this country put a summary end to a similar expedition. With this the active existence of the Fenian organization ended, unless we may ascribe to it the subsequent attempts to blow down important structures in London with dynamite.

These movements, while ineffective as attempts at insurrection, had their influence in arousing the more thoughtful statesmen of England to the causes for discontent and need of reform in Ireland, and since that period the Irish question has been the most prominent one in Parliament. Such men

Land Holding Reform in Ireland as Mr. Gladstone and Mr. Bright took the matter in hand, Gladstone presenting a bill for the final abolition of Irish tithes and the disestablishment of the English Church in Ireland. This was adopted in 1868, and the question of the reform of land holding was next taken up, a series of measures being passed to improve the condition of the Irish tenant farmer. If ejected, he was to be compensated for improvements he had made, and a Land Commission was formed with the power to reduce rents where this seemed necessary, and also to fix the rent for a term of years. At a later date a Land Purchase Commission was organized, to aid tenants in buying their farms from the landlords, by an advance of a large portion of the purchase money, with provision for gradually repayment.

These measures did not put an end to the agitation. Numerous ejections from farms for non-payment of rent had been going on, and a fierce struggle was raging between the peasants and the agents of the absentee landlords. The disturbance was great, and successive Coercion Acts were passed. The peasants were supported by the powerful Land League, while the old question of Home Rule was revived again, under the active leadership of Charles Stewart Parnell, who headed a small but very determined body in Parliament. The succeeding legislation for Ireland, engineered by Mr. Gladstone, to the passage in the House of Commons of the Home Rule Bill of 1893, has been sufficiently **The Home Rule Agitation** described in the preceding chapter, and need not be repeated here. It will suffice to say in conclusion, that the demand for Home Rule still exists, and that, in spite of all efforts at reform, the position of the Irish peasant is far from being satisfactory, the most prolific crop in that long-oppressed land seemingly being one of beggary and semi-starvation.

CHAPTER XVII.

England and Her Indian Empire.

IN 1756, in the town of Calcutta, the headquarters of the British in India, there occurred a terrible disaster. A Bengalese army marched upon and captured the town, taking prisoner all the English who had not escaped to their ships. The whole of these unfortunates, 146 in number, **The Black Hole of Calcutta** were thrust into the "black hole," a small room about eighteen feet square, with two small windows. It was a night of tropical heat. The air of the crowded and unventilated room soon became unfit to breathe. The victims fought each other fiercely to reach the windows. The next morning, when the door was opened, only twenty-three of them remained alive. Such is the famous story of the "black hole of Calcutta."

In the following year (1757) this barbarism was avenged. On the battlefield of Plassey stood an army of about 1,000 British and 2,100 Sepoys, with nine pieces of artillery. Opposed to them were 50,000 native infantry **Clive and the Battle of Plassey** and 18,000 cavalry, with fifty cannon. The disproportion was enormous, but at the head of the British army was a great leader, Robert Clive, who had come out to India as a humble clerk, but was now commander of an army. A brief conflict ended the affair. The unwieldy native army fled. Clive's handful of men stood victorious on the most famous field of Indian warfare.

This battle is taken as the beginning of the British Empire in India. It is of interest to remember that just one hundred years later, in 1857, that empire reached the most perilous point in its career, in the outbreak of the great Indian mutiny. Plassey settled one question. It gave India to the English in preference to the French, in whose interest the natives were fighting. The empire which Clive founded was organized by Warren Hastings, the ablest but the most unscrupulous of the governors of India. At the opening of the nineteenth century the British power in India was firmly established.

Wellesley's Career in India In 1798 the Marquis of Wellesly—afterwards known as Lord Wellington—was made governor Even there he had his future great antagonist to guard against, for Napoleon was at that time in Egypt, and was thought to have the design of driving the

268

British from India and restoring that great dominion to France. Wellesley's career in India was a brilliant one. He overthrew the powerful Marhatta Confederacy, gained victory after victory over the native chiefs and kings, captured the great Mogul cities of Delhi and Agra, and spread the power of the British arms far and wide through the peninsula.

In the succeeding years war after war took place. The warlike Marhattas rebelled and were again put down, other tribes were conquered, and in 1824 the city of Bhartpur in Central India, believed by the natives to be impregnable, was taken by storm, and the reputation of the British as indomitable fighters was greatly enhanced. Rapidly the British power extended until nearly the whole peninsula was subdued. In 1837 the conquerors of India began to interfere in the affairs of Afghanistan, and a British garrison was placed in Cabul, the capital of that country, in 1839.

Two years they stayed there, and then came to them one of the greatest catastrophes in the history of the British army. Surrounded by hostile and daring Afghans, the situation of the garrison grew so perilous that it seemed suicidal to remain in Cabul, and it was determined to evacuate the city and retreat to India through the difficult passes of the Himalayas. In January, 1842, they set out, 4,000 fighting men and 12,000 camp followers. Deep snows covered the hills and all around them swarmed **The Terrible** the Afghans, savage and implacable, bent on their utter de- **Retreat** struction, attacking them from every point of vantage, cutting **from Cabul** down women and children with the same ruthless cruelty as they displayed in the case of men. One terrible week passed, then, on the afternoon of January 13th, the sentinels at the Cabul gate of Jelalabad saw approaching a miserable, haggard man, barely able to sit upon his horse. Utterly exhausted, covered with cuts and contusions, he rode through the gate, and announced himself as Dr. Brydan, the sole survivor of the army which had left Cabul one week before. The remainder, men, women, and children,—except a few who had been taken prisoners,—lay slaughtered along that dreadful road, their mangled bodies covering almost every foot of its blood-stained length.

The British exacted revenge for this terrible massacre. A powerful force fought its way back to Cabul, defeated the Afghans wherever met, and rescued the few prisoners in the Afghan hands. Then the soldiers turned their backs on Cabul, which no British army was to see again for nearly forty years.

Three years afterwards the British Empire in India was seriously threatened by one of the most warlike races in the peninsula, the Sikhs, a courageous race inhabiting the Punjab, in northern India, their capital the

15

city of Lahore.   In 1845 a Sikh army, 60,000 strong, with 150 guns, crossed
the Sutléj River and invaded British territory.   Never before
**The War With
the Sikhs**
had the British in India encountered men like these.   Four
pitched battles were fought, in each of which the British lost
heavily, but in the last they drove the Sikhs back across the Sutléj and captured Lahore.

That ended the war for the time being, but in 1848 the brave Sikhs
were in arms again, and pushing the British as hard as before.   On the field
of Chilianwala the British were repulsed, with a loss of 2,400 men and the
colors of three regiments.   This defeat was quickly retrieved.   Lord Gough
met the enemy at Guzerat and defeated them so utterly that their army was
practically destroyed.   They were driven back as a shapeless mass of fugitives, losing their camp, their standards, and fifty-three of their cherished
guns.   With this victory was completed the conquest of the Punjab.   The
Sikhs became loyal subjects of the queen, and afterwards supplied her armies
with the most valorous and high-spirited of her native troops.

Thus time went on until that eventful year of 1857, when the British
power in India was to receive its most perilous shock.   For a long time
there had been a great and continually increasing discontent in India.
Complaints were made that the treaties with native princes were not kept,
that extortion was practised by which officials grew rapidly and mysteriously
wealthy, looking upon India as a field for the acquisition of riches, and that
the natives were treated by the governing powers with deep contempt,
**The Causes of
the Mutiny**
while every license was granted to the soldiery.   The hidden
cause of the discontent, however, lay in the deep hatred felt by
the natives, Hindu and Mussulmen alike, for the dominant
race of aliens to whom they had been obliged to bow in common subjection;
and the fanaticism of the Hindus caused the smouldering elements of discontent to burst out into the flames of insurrection.   A secret conspiracy was
formed, in which all classes of the natives participated, its object being
to overthrow the dominion of the English.   It had been prophesied among
the natives that the rule of the foreign masters of India should last only for
a hundred years; and a century had just elapsed since the triumph of Clive
at Plassey.

Small *chupatties*, cakes of unleavened bread, were secretly passed from
hand to hand among the natives, as tokens of comradeship in the enterprise.   This conspiracy was the more dangerous from making
**The Greased
Cartridges**
its way into the army, for India was a country governed by
the sword.   A rumor ran through the cantonments of the
Bengal army that cartridges had been served out greased with the fat of

animals unclean to Hindu and Mussulman alike, and which the Hindus could not bite without loss of caste, the injunction of their religion obliging them to abstain from animal food under this penalty. After this nothing could quiet their minds; fires broke out nightly in their quarters; officers were insulted by their men; all confidence was gone, and discipline became an empty form.

The sentence of penal servitude passed upon some of the mutineers became the signal for the breaking out of the revolt. At Meerut, on the Upper Ganges, the Sepoys broke into rebellion, liberated their comrades who were being led away in chains, and marched in a body to Delhi, the ancient capital of India and former seat of the Mogul empire. Here they took possession of the great military magazine and **The Old Emperor Akbar** seized its stores. Those among the British inhabitants who did not save themselves by immediate flight were barbarously put to death; and the decrepit Akbar, the descendant of the Moguls, an old man of ninety, who lived at Delhi upon a pension granted to him by the East India Company, was drawn from his retirement and proclaimed Emperor of Hindostan by the rebels, his son, Mirza, being associated with him in the government.

The mutiny spread with terrible rapidity, and massacres of the English took place at Indore, Allahabad, Azimghur, and other towns. Foremost in atrocity stands the massacre perpetrated at Cawnpore by Nana Sahib, the adopted son of the last Peishwa of the Marhattas, who, after **The Frightful Massacre at Cawnpore** entering into a compact with General Wheeler, by which he promised a free departure to the English, caused the boats in which they were proceeding down the river to be fired upon. The men were thus slain, while the women and children were brought back as prisoners to Cawnpore. Here they were confined for some days in a building, into which murderers were sent who massacred them every one, the mutilated corpses being thrown down a well.

In Oude, the noble-minded Sir Henry Lawrence defended himself throughout the whole summer in the citadel of Lucknow against the rebels under Nana Sahib with wonderful skill and bravery, until he was killed by the bursting of a bomb, on the 2d of July. The distress of the besieged, among whom were many ladies and children, was now extreme. But the little garrison held out for nearly three months longer against the greatest odds and amid the most distressing hardships. At length came that **The Scotch Slogan at Lucknow** eventful day, when, to the keen ears of one of the despairing sufferers, a Scotch woman, came from afar a familiar and most hopeful sound. "Dinna ye hear the pibroch?" she cried, springing to her feet in the ecstacy of hope renewed.

Those near her listened but heard no sound, and many minutes passed before a swell of wind bore to their ears the welcome music of the bagpipe, playing the war-march of the Highlanders of her native land. It came from the party of relief led by General Havelock, which had left Calcutta on the first tidings of the outbreak, and was now marching in all haste to imperilled Lucknow.

On his way Havelock had encountered the mutineers at Futtipur and gained a brilliant victory. Three days later Cawnpore was reached. There the insurgent Sepoys fought with desperation, but they were defeated, and the British entered the town, but not in time to rescue the women and chil-

The March of Havelock dren, whose slaughter had just taken place. What they saw there filled the soldiers with the deepest sentiments of horror and vengeance. The sight was one to make the blood run cold. "The ground," says a witness of the terrible scene, "was strewn with clotted blood, which here and there lay ankle deep. Long locks of hair were scattered about, shreds of women's garments, children's hats and shoes, torn books and broken playthings. The bodies were naked, the limbs dismembered. I have seen death in all possible forms, but I could not gaze on this terrible scene of blood."

The frightful slaughter was mercilessly avenged by the infuriated soldiers on the people of Cawnpore and on the prisoners they had taken. Havelock then crossed the Ganges and marched into Oude. Fighting its way through the difficulties caused by inclement weather and the continual onslaughts of the enemy, Havelock's regiment at last effected a coalition with the reinforcements under General Outram, and together they marched towards Lucknow, which was reached at the end of September.

An especial act of heroism was achieved during the siege of Lucknow by Mr. Kavanagh, an official, who offered, disguised as a native, to penetrate through a region swarming with enemies, to communicate with the general of the approaching relieving force. He happily accomplished his dangerous exploit, from which he obtained the honorable nickname of "Lucknow Kavanagh."

As the army of relief drew near, the beleaguered people heard with ears of delight the increasing sounds of their approach, the roar of distant guns reaching their gladdened ears. Yet the enterprise was a desperate one and its success was far from assured. Havelock and Outram had

The Relief of Lucknow no more than 2,600 men, while the enemy was 50,000 strong. Yet as the sound of the guns increased there were evidences of panic among the natives. Many of the town people and of the Sepoys took to flight, some crossing the river by the bridge, some by swimming.

At two o'clock the smoke of the guns was visible in the suburbs and the rattle of musketry could be heard. At five o'clock heavy firing broke out in the streets, and in a few minutes more a force of Highlanders and Sikhs turned into the street leading to the residency, in which the besieged garrison had so long been confined. Headed by General Outram, they ran at a rapid pace to the gate, and, amid wild cheers from those within, made their way into the beleaguered enclosure, and the first siege of Lucknow was at an end.

The garrison had fought for months behind slight defences and against enormous odds. They were well supplied with food and water, but they had been exposed to terrible heat and heavy and incessant rains. The Sepoys had been drilled by British officers, were well supplied with arms and ammunition, and from the housetops of the town kept up an incessant fire that searched every corner of the defended fortress. Sickness raged in the crowded and underground rooms in which shelter was sought against the constant musketry, and death had reaped a harvest among the gallant and unyielding few who had so long held that almost untenable post. **The Suffering at Lucknow**

Havelock's men were able to do no more than reinforce the garrison. After fighting their way with heavy losses into the citadel, they found that it was impossible, with their small army, to force a retreat through the ranks of the enemy with the women, children and invalids, surrounded by the swarms of rebels who surged round the walls like a foaming sea. They were compelled, therefore, to shut themselves up, and await fresh reinforcements. Provisions, however, now began to diminish, and they were menaced with the horrors of starvation; but matters did not reach this last extremity. Sir Colin Campbell, the new commander-in-chief, with 7,000 well-equipped troops, was already on the way. He arrived at Lucknow on the 14th of November, made a bold and successful attack on the fortifications, and liberated the besieged. Unable to hold the town, he left it to the enemy, being obliged to content himself with the rescue of the people in the residency. Eight days afterwards Havelock died of cholera. His memory is held in high esteem as the most heoric figure in the war of the mutiny. **The Coming of Campbell**

Meanwhile Delhi was under siege, which began on June 8th, just one month after the original outbreak. It was, however, not properly a siege, for the British were encamped on a ridge at some distance from the city. They never numbered more than 8,000 men, while within the walls were over 30,000 of the mutineers. General Nicholson arrived with a reinforcement in middle August, and on **Siege and Capture of Delhi**

September 14th an assault was made. The city was held with desperation by the rebels, fighting going on in the streets for six days before the Sepoys fled. Nicholson fell at the head of a storming party, and Hodson, the leader of a corps of irregular horse, took the old Mogul emperor prisoner, and shot down his sons in cold blood.

It was not until three months and a half after the release of the garrison at Lucknow that Sir Colin Campbell, having dealt out punishment to the mutineers at many of the stations where they still kept together, and having received large reinforcements of men and artillery from home, prepared for the crowning attack upon that place. On the 4th of February he advanced from Cawnpore, with three divisions of infantry, a division of cavalry, and fifteen batteries, and on the 1st of March operations began ; General Outram, with a force of 6,000 men and thirty guns, crossing the Goomtee, and reconnoitering the country as far as Chinhut. On the following day

Final Operations Against Lucknow he invested the king's race-house, which he carried the next day by assault, and on the 9th Sir Colin Campbell's main force captured, with a slight loss, the Martinière, pushed on to the bridges across the river, and carried, after some hard fighting, the Begum's palace. Two days later the Immaumbarra, which had been converted into a formidable stronghold and was held by a large force, was breached and stormed, and the captors followed so hotly upon the rear of the flying foe that they entered with them the Kaiserbagh, which was regarded by the rebels as their strongest fortress. Its garrison, taken wholly by surprise, made but a slight resistance. The loss of these two positions, on which they had greatly relied, completely disheartened the enemy, and throughout the night a stream of fugitives poured out of the town.

The success was so unexpected that the arrangements necessary for cutting off the retreat of the enemy had not been completed, and very large numbers of the rebels escaped, to give infinite trouble later on. Many were cut down by the cavalry and horse artillery, which set out the next morning in pursuit ; but, to the mortification of the army, a con-

The Storming of the Fortresses siderable proportion got away. The next day a number of palaces and houses fell into the hands of the advancing troops without resistance, and by midnight the whole city along the river bank was in their possession. In the meantime Jung Bahadoor, the British ally, was attacking the city with his Goorkhas from the south, and pushed forward so far that communications were opened with him halfway across the city. The following day the Goorkhas made a further advance, and, fighting with great gallantry, won the suburbs adjacent to the Charbach bridge.

The hard fighting was now over; the failure to defend even one of the fortresses upon which for months they had bestowed so much care, completely disheartened the mutineers remaining in the city. Numbers effected their escape; others hid themselves, after having got rid of their arms and uniforms; some parties took refuge in houses, and defended themselves desperately to the end. The work was practically accomplished on the 21st, and Lucknow, which had so long been the headquarters of the insurrection, was in British hands, and that with a far smaller loss than could have been expected from the task of capturing a city possessing so many places of strength, and held by some 20,000 desperate men fighting with ropes round their necks.

The city taken, the troops were permitted to plunder and murder to their hearts' content. In every house were dead or dying, and the corpses of Sepoys lay piled up several feet in height. The booty which the soldiers carried off in the way of jewels and treasures of every kind was enormous. The widowed queen of Oude set out for England, to proclaim the innocence of her son "in the dark countries of the West," and to preserve to her house the shadow of an independent monarchy. **The Booty of the Soldiers** She never saw her sunny India again, however; on the return journey she died of a broken heart. Though the rebellion gradually lost force and cohesion after this period, the vengeance continued for a year longer. But the chief rebel, Nana Sahib, and the two heroic women, the Begum of Oude and the Ranee of Jansee, escaped to Nepaul. In the course of the year 1858, peace and order again returned to the Anglo-Indian Empire, and the government was able to consider means of reconciliation. By a proclamation of the queen all rebels who were not directly implicated in the murder of British subjects, and would return to their duty and allegiance by January, 1859, were to obtain a complete amnesty. **The East India Company Abolished** This proclamation also announced that the queen, with the consent of Parliament, had determined to abolish the East India Company, to take the government into her own hands, and to rule India by means of a special secretary of state and council. The Indian Empire, both within and without, had assumed such gigantic proportions that it could no longer be properly ruled by a mercantile company, and came properly under the control of the crown. In 1876 Queen Victoria assumed, by act of Parliament, the title of Empress of India. The most recent important event, in the acquisition of territory in this part of the world, was the invasion of Burmah in 1885, and **Victoria is Made Empress of India** its capture after a short and decisive campaign. The Indian Empire of Victoria has now grown enormous in extent, its borders extending to the

Himalayas on the north, where they are in contact with the boundaries of the great imperial dominion which Russia has acquired in Asia. Whether the two great rivals will yet come into conflict on this border is a question which only the future can decide.

India possesses a population only surpassed by that of China, amounting at the census of 1896 to 221,172,952. This excludes the native and partially independent states, the population of which numbers 66,050,479, making a total for the whole empire, including Burmah, of 287,223,431. Under British control the country has been greatly developed, and abundantly supplied with means of internal communication, its railroad lines covering a length of about 27,000 miles, and its telegraphs of over 45,000 miles, while the telephone has also been widely introduced. Its commerce amounts in round numbers to nearly $500,000,000 annually.

This great country has long been subject to devastating disasters. In 1876 a terrible tidal wave drowned thousands of the people and destroyed millions in value of property. In 1897 much of the country suffered frightfully from famine, being the fifteenth occasion during the century. In the same year a plague broke out in the crowded city of Bombay and caused dreadful ravages among its native population. For ages past India has been subject to visitations of this kind, which have hitherto surpassed the power of man to prevent. In the last named all the world came to the aid of the starving and science did its utmost to stay the ravages of the plague.

The famine of 1897 was followed in 1900 by another of equal gravity. Lack of rain caused a failure of the crops, a condition which could have but one effect in that overcrowded agricultural country, the people of a wide district being left without food. The war in South Africa interfered with British efforts for the relief of the destitute, but earnest efforts were made, and at one time as many as 6,000,000 of the starving people were being fed. Fortunately, there succeeded a season of copious rainfall, and the stringency of the dreadful situation was greatly relieved.

CHAPTER XVIII.

Thiers, Gambetta, and the Rise of the French Republic.

IT has been already told how the capitulation of the French army at Sedan and the captivity of Louis Napoleon were followed in Paris by the overthrow of the empire and the formation of a republic, the third in the history of French political changes. A provisional government was formed, the legislative assembly was dissolved, and all the court paraphernalia of the imperial establishment disappeared. The new government was called in Paris the " Government of Lawyers," most of its members and officials belonging to that profession. At its head was General Trochu, in command of the army in Paris ; among its chief members were Jules Favre and Gambetta. While upright in its membership and honorable in its purposes, it was an arbitrary body, formed by a *coup d'etat* like that by which Napoleon had seized the reins of power, and not destined for a long existence.

A Provisional Government

The news of the fall of Metz and the surrender of Bazaine and his army served as a fresh spark to the inflammable public feeling of France. In Paris the Red Republic raised the banner of insurrection against the government of the national defence and endeavored to revive the spirit of the Commune of 1793. The insurgents marched to the senate-house, demanded the election of a municipal council which should share power with the government, and proceeded to imprison Trochu, Jules Favre, and their associates. This, however, was but a temporary success of the Commune, and the provisional government continued in existence until the end of the war, when a national assembly was elected by the people and the temporary government was set aside. Gambetta, the dictator, " the organizer of defeats," as he was sarcastically entitled, lost his power, and the aged statesman and historian, Louis Thiers, was chosen as chief of the executive department of the new government.

Excitement in Paris

The treaty of peace with France, including, as it did, the loss of Alsace and Lorraine and the payment of an indemnity of $1,000,000,000, roused once more the fierce passions of the radicals and the masses of the great cities, who passionately denounced the treaty as due to cowardice and treason. The dethroned emperor added to the excitement by a manifesto, in which he protested against his deposition by the assembly and called for a fresh election. The final incitement to insurrection came when the assembly decided to hold its sessions at Versailles instead of in Paris, whose unruly populace it feared.

In a moment all the revolutionary elements of the great city were in a blaze. The social democratic "Commune," elected from the central committee of the National Guard, renounced obedience to the government and the National Assembly, and broke into open revolt. An attempt to repress the movement only added to its violence, and all the riotous populace of Paris sprang to arms. A new war was about to be inaugurated in that city which had just suffered so severely from the guns of the Germans, and around which German troops were still encamped.

Outbreak of the Commune

The government had neglected to take possession of the cannon on Montmartre ; and now, when the troops of the line, instead of firing on the insurrectionists, went over in crowds to their side, the supremacy over Paris fell into the hands of the wildest demagogues. A fearful civil war commenced, and in the same forts which the Germans had shortly before evacuated firing once more resounded ; the houses, gardens, and villages around Paris were again surrendered to destruction, and the creations of art, industry, and civilization, and the abodes of wealth and pleasure were once more transformed into dreary wildernesses.

The wild outbreaks of fanaticism on the part of the Commune recalled the scenes of the revolution of 1789, and in these spring days of 1871 Paris added another leaf to its long history of crime and violence. The insurgents, roused to fury by the efforts of the government to suppress them, murdered two generals, Lecomte and Thomas, and fired on the unarmed citizens who, as the "friends of order," desired a reconciliation with the authorities at Versailles. They formed a government of their own, extorted loans from wealthy citizens, confiscated the property of religious societies, and seized and held as hostages Archbishop Darboy and many other distinguished clergymen and citizens.

Outrages of the Insurgents

Meanwhile the investing troops, led by Marshal MacMahon, gradually fought their way through the defences and into the suburbs of the city, and the surrender of the anarchists in the capital became inevitable. This necessity excited their passions to the most violent extent, and, with the wild fury of savages, they set themselves to do all the damage to the historical monuments of Paris they could. The noble Vendôme column, the symbol of the warlike renown of France, was torn down from its pedestal and hurled prostrate in the street. The most historic buildings in the city were set on fire, and either partially or entirely destroyed. Among these were the Tuileries, a portion of the Louvre, the Luxembourg, the Palais Royal, the Elysée, etc. ; while several of the imprisoned hostages, foremost among them Darboy, Archbishop of Paris, and the universally respected minister Daguerry, were shot by the infuriated mob. Such crimes excited the Versailles troops to terrible vengeance, when they at last succeeded in repressing the rebellion. They went their way along a bloody course ; human life was counted as nothing ; the streets were stained with blood and strewn with corpses, and the Seine once more ran red between its banks. When at last the Commune surrendered, the judicial courts at Versailles began their work of retribution. The leaders and participators in the rebellion who could not save themselves by flight were shot by hundreds, confined in fortresses, or transported to the colonies. For more than a year the imprisonments, trials, and executions continued, military courts being established which excited the world for months by their wholesale condemnations to exile and to death. The carnival of anarchy was followed by one of pitiless revenge.

Punishment of the Commune

The Republican government of France, which had been accepted in an emergency, was far from carrying with it the support of the whole of the assembly or of the people, and the aged, but active and keen-witted Thiers had to steer through a medley of opposing interests and sentiments. His government was considered, alike by the Monarchists and the Jacobins, as only provisional, and the Bourbons and Napoleonists on the one hand and the advocates of "liberty, equality and fraternity" on the other, intrigued for its overthrow. But the German armies still remained on French soil, pending the payment of the costs of the war ; and the astute chief of the executive power possessed moderation enough to pacify the passions of the people, to restrain their hatred of the Germans, which was so boldly exhibited in the streets and in the courts of justice, and to quiet the clamor for a war of revenge.

The position of parties at home was confused and distracted, and a disturbance of the existing order could only lead to anarchy and civil war. Thiers was thus the indispensable man of the moment, and so much was he himself impressed by consciousness of this fact, that he many times, by the threat of resignation, brought the opposing elements in the assembly to harmony and compliance. This occurred even during the siege of Paris, when the forces of the government

President Thiers and the Assembly

were in conflict with the Commune. In the assembly there was shown an inclination to moderate or break through the sharp centralization of the government, and to procure some autonomy for the provinces and towns. When, therefore, a new scheme was discussed, a large part of the assembly demanded that the mayors should not, as formerly, be appointed by the government, but be elected by the town councils. Only with difficulty was Thiers able to effect a compromise, on the strength of which the government was permitted the right of appointment for all towns numbering over twenty thousand. In the elections for the councils the Moderate Republicans proved triumphant. With a supple dexterity, Thiers knew how to steer between the Democratic-Republican party and the Monarchists. When Gambetta endeavored to establish a "league of Republican towns," the attempt was forbidden as illegal ; and when the decree of banishment against the Bourbon and Orlean princes was set aside, and the latter returned to France, Thiers knew how to postpone the entrance of the Duc d'Aumale and Prince de Joinville, who had been elected deputies, into the assembly, at least until the end of the year.

The brilliant success of the national loan went far to strengthen the position of Thiers. The high offers for a share in this loan, which indicated the inexhaustible wealth of the nation and the solid credit of France abroad, promised a rapid payment of the war indemnity, the **The National Loan** consequent evacuation of the country by the German army of occupation, and a restoration of the disturbed finances of the state. The foolish manifesto of the Count de Chambord, who declared that he had only to return with the white banner to be made sovereign of France, brought all reasonable and practical men to the side of Thiers, and he had, during the last days of August, 1871, the triumph of being proclaimed "President of the French Republic."

The new president aimed, next to the liberation of the garrisoned provinces from the German troops of occupation, at the reorganization of the French army. Yet he could not bring himself to the decision of enforcing in its entirety the principle of general armed service, such as had raised Prussia from a state of depression to one of military regeneration. Universal military service in France was, it is true, adopted in name, and the army was increased to an immense extent, but under such conditions and limitations that the richer and more educated classes could exempt themselves from service in the army ; and thus the active forces, as before, consisted of professional soldiers. And when the minister for education, Jules Simon, introduced an educational law based on liberal principles, he experienced on the part of the clergy and their champion, Bishop Dupanloup, such violent opposition, that the government dropped the measure.

DREYFUS, HIS ACCUSERS AND DEFENDERS

Lawyer Labori ; Henry, the suicide ; Dreyfus, the prisoner ; Esterhazy, the confessed criminal ; General Mercier, chief accuser

THE DREYFUS TRIAL

Dreyfus in the act of declaring "*I am Innocent.*"

In order to place the army in the condition which Thiers desired, an increase in the military budget was necessary, and consequently an enhancement of the general revenues of the state. For this purpose a return to the tariff system, which had been abolished under the empire, was proposed, but excited so great an opposition in the assembly that six months passed before it could be carried. The new organization of the army, undertaken with a view of placing France on a level in military strength with her late conqueror, was now eagerly undertaken by the president. An active army, with five years' service, was to be added to a "territorial army," a kind of militia. And so great was the demand on the portion of the nation capable of bearing arms that the new French army exceeded in numbers that of any other nation.

Reorganization of the Army

But all the statesmanship of Thiers could not overcome the anarchy in the assembly, where the forces for monarchy and republicanism were bitterly opposed to each other. Gambetta, in order to rouse public opinion in favor of democracy, made several tours through the country, his extravagance of language giving deep offence to the monarchists, while the opposed sections of the assembly grew wider and more violent in their breach.

Gambetta as an Agitator

Indisputable as were the valuable services which Thiers had rendered to France, by the foundation of public order and authority, the creation of a regular army, and the restoration of a solid financial system, yet all these services met with no recognition in the face of the party jealousy and political passions prevailing among the people's representatives at Versailles. More and more did the Royalist reaction gain ground, and, aided by the priests and by national hatred and prejudice, endeavor to bring about the destruction of its opponents. Against the Radicals and Liberals, among whom even the Voltairean Thiers was included, superstition and fanaticism were let loose, and against the Bonapartists was directed the terrorism of court martial. The French could not rest with the thought that their military supremacy had been broken by the superiority of the Prusso-German arms; their defeats could have proceeded only from the treachery or incapacity of their leaders. To this national prejudice the Government decided to bow, and to offer a sacrifice to the popular passion. And thus the world beheld the lamentable spectacle of the commanders who had surrendered the French fortresses to the enemy being subjected to a trial by court-martial under the presidency of Marshal Baraguay d'Hilliers, and the majority of them, on account of their proved incapacity or weakness, deprived of their military honors, at a moment when all had cause to reproach themselves and endeavor to raise up a

Trial and Condemnation of the Generals

new structure on the ruins of the past.   Even Ulrich, the once celebrated commander of Strasburg, whose name had been given to a street in Paris, was brought under the censure of the court-martial.   But the chief blow fell upon the commander-in-chief of Metz, Marshal Bazaine, to whose "treachery" the whole misfortune of France was attributed.   For months he was retained a prisoner at Versailles, while preparations were made for the great court-martial spectacle, which, in the following year, took place under the presidency of the Duc d'Aumale.

The result of the party division in the assembly was, in May, 1873, a vote of censure on the ministry which induced them to resign.   Their resignation was followed by an offer of resignation on the part of Thiers, who

MacMahon Elected President

experienced the unexpected slight of having it accepted by the majority of the assembly, the monarchist MacMahon, Marshal of France and Duke of Magenta, being elected President in his place.   Theirs had just performed one of his greatest services to France, by paying off the last installment of the war indemnity and relieving the soil of his country of the hated German troops.

The party now in power at once began to lay plans to carry out their cherished purpose of placing a Legitimist king upon the throne, this honor being offered to the Count de Chambord, grandson of Charles X.   He, an old man, unfitted for the thorny seat offered him, and out of all accord with

The Count de Chambord and His Demand

the spirit of the times, put a sudden end to the hopes of his partisans by his mediæval conservatism.   Their purpose was to establish a constitutional government, under the tri-colored flag of revolutionary France ; but the old Bourbon gave them to understand that he would not consent to reign under the Tricolor, but must remain steadfast to the white banner of his ancestors ; he had no desire to be "the legitimate king of revolution."

This letter shattered the plans of his supporters.   No man with ideas like these would be tolerated on the French throne.   There was never to be in France a King Henry V.   The Monarchists, in disgust at the failure of their schemes, elected MacMahon president of the republic for a term of seven years, and for the time being the reign of republicanism in France was made secure.

While MacMahon was thus being raised to the pinnacle of honor, his former comrade Bazaine was imprisoned in another part of the palace at

Trial and Sentence of Bazaine

Versailles, awaiting trial on the charge of treason for the surrender of Metz.   In the trial, in which the whole world took a deep interest, the efforts of the prosecution were directed to prove that the conquest of France was solely due to the treachery of the

Bonapartist marshal. Despite all that could be said in his defence, he was found guilty by the court-martial, sentenced to degradation from his rank in the army, and to be put to death.

A letter which Prince Frederick Charles wrote in his favor only added to the wrath of the people, who cried aloud for his execution. But, as though the judges themselves felt a twinge of conscience at the sentence, they at the same time signed a petition for pardon to the president of the republic. MacMahon thereupon commuted the punishment of death into a twenty years' imprisonment, remitted the disgrace of the formalities of a military degradation, without cancelling its operation, and appointed as the prisoner's place of confinement the fortess on the island of St. Marguerite, opposite Cannes, known in connection with the "iron mask." Bazaine's wealthy Mexican wife obtained permission to reside near him, with her family and servants, in a pavilion of the sea-fortress. This afforded her an opportunity of bringing about the freedom of her husband in the following year with the aid of her brother. After an adventurous escape, by letting himself down with a rope to a Genoese vessel, Bazaine fled to Holland, and then offered his services to the Republican government of Spain.

In 1875 the constitution under which France is now governed was adopted by the republicans. It provides for a legislature of two chambers; one a chamber of deputies elected by the people, the other a senate of 300 members, 75 of whom are elected by the National Assembly **The New Constitution of France** and the others by electoral colleges in the departments of France. The two chambers unite to elect a president, who has a term of seven years. He is commander-in-chief of the army, appoints all officers, receives all ambassadors, executes the laws, and appoints the cabinet, which is responsible to the Senate and House of Deputies,—thus resembling the cabinet of Great Britain instead of that of the United States.

This constitution was soon ignored by the arbitrary president, who forced the resignation of a cabinet which he could not control, and replaced it by another responsible to himself instead of to the assembly. His act of autocracy roused a violent opposition. Gambetta moved that the representatives of the people had no confidence in a cabinet which was not free in its actions and not Republican in its principles. The sudden death of Thiers, whose last writing was a defence of the republic, **MacMahon Resigns and Grevy Elected** stirred the heart of the nation and added to the excitement, which soon reached fever heat. In the election that followed the Republicans were in so great a majority over the Conservatives that the president was compelled either to resign or to govern according to the constitution. He accepted the latter and appointed a cabinet composed

of Republicans.   But the acts of the legislature, which passed laws to prevent arbitrary action by the executive and to secularize education, so
exasperated the old soldier that he finally resigned from his high office.

Jules Grévy was elected president in his place, and Gambetta was
made president of the House of Deputies.   Subsequently he was chosen
presiding minister in a cabinet composed wholly of his own creatures.   His

Gambetta as Prime Minister   career in this high office was a brief one.   The Chambers
refused to support him in his arbitrary measures and he
resigned in disgust.   Soon after the self-appointed dictator,
who had played so prominent a part in the war with Germany, died from a
wound whose origin remained a mystery.

The constitution was revised in 1884, the republic now declared permanent and final, and Grévy again elected president.   General Boulanger,
the minister of war in the new government, succeeded in making himself highly
popular, many looking upon him as a coming Napoleon, by whose genius
the republic would be overthrown.

In 1887 Grévy resigned, in consequence of a scandal in high circles,
and was succeeded by Sadi Carnot, grandson of a famous general of the
first republic.   Under the new president two striking events took place.

The Career of Boulanger   General Boulanger managed to lift himself into great prominence, and gain a powerful following in France.   Carried
away by self-esteem, he defied his superiors, and when tried
and found guilty of the offence, was strong enough in France to overthrow
the ministry, to gain re-election to the Chamber of Deputies, and to defeat
a second ministry.

But his reputation was declining.   It received a serious blow by a duel
he fought with a lawyer, in which the soldier was wounded and the lawyer
escaped unhurt.   The next cabinet was hostile to his intrigues, and he fled to
Brussels to escape arrest.   Tried by the Senate, sitting as a High Court of Justice, he was found guilty of plotting against the state and sentenced to imprisonment for life.   His career soon after ended in suicide and his party disappeared.

The second event spoken of was the Panama Canal affair.   De Lesseps,
the maker of the Suez Canal, had undertaken to excavate a similar one
across the Isthmus of Panama, but the work was managed with such wild

The Panama Canal Scandal   extravagance that vast sums were spent and the poor in-
vestors widely ruined, while the canal remained a half-dug
ditch.   At a later date this affair became a great scandal,
dishonest bargains in connection with it were abundantly unearthed, bribery
was shown to have been common in high places, and France was shaken

to its centre by the startling exposure. De Lesseps, fortunately for him, escaped by death, but others of the leaders in the enterprise were condemned and punished.

In the succeeding years perils manifold threatened the existence of the French republic. A moral decline seemed to have sapped the foundations of public virtue, and the new military organization rose to a dangerous height of power, becoming a monster of ambition and iniquity which overshadowed and portended evil to the state. The spirit of anarchy, which had been so strikingly displayed in the excesses of the Parisian Commune, was shown later in various instances of death and destruction by the use of dynamite bombs, exploded in Paris and elsewhere. But its most striking example was in the murder of President Carnot, who was stabbed by an anarchist in the streets of Lyons. This assassination, and the disheartening exposures of dishonesty in the Panama Canal Case trials, stirred the moral sentiment of France to its depths, and made many of the best citizens despair of the permanency of the republic.

Anarchy in France and Murder of the President

But the most alarming threat came from the army, which had grown in power and prominence until it fairly overtopped the state, while its leaders felt competent to set at defiance the civil authorities. This despotic army was an outgrowth of the Franco-Prussian war. The terrible punishment which the French had received in that war, and in particular the loss of Alsace and Lorraine, filled them with bitter hatred of Germany and a burning desire for revenge. Yet it was evident that their military organization was so imperfect as to leave them helpless before the army of Germany, and the first thing to be done was to place themselves on a level in military strengh with their foe. To this President Thiers had earnestly devoted himself, and the work of army organization went on until all France was virtually converted into a great camp, defended by powerful fortresses, and the whole people of the country were practically made part and portion of the army.

The Reorganization of the Army

The final result of this was the development of one of the most complete and well-appointed military establishments in Europe. The immediate cause of the reorganization of the army gradually passed away. As time went on the intense feeling against Germany softened and the danger of war decreased. But the army became more and more dominant in France, and, as the century neared its end, the autocratic position of its leaders was revealed by a startling event, which showed vividly to the world the moral decadence of France and the controlling influence and dominating power of the members of the General Staff. This was the celebrated Dreyfus

Case, the *cause célèbre* of the end of the century.   This case is of such importance that a description of its salient points becomes here necessary.

Albert Dreyfus, an Alsatian Jew and a captain in the Fourteenth Regiment of Artillery of the French army, detailed for service at the Informa-

**The Opening
of the Drey-
fus Case**

tion Bureau of the Minister of War, was arrested October 15, 1894, on the charge of having sold military secrets to a foreign power.   The following letter was said to have been found at the German embassy by a French detective, in what was declared to be the handwriting of Dreyfus :

"Having no news from you I do not know what to do.   I send you in the meantime the condition of the forts.   I also hand you the principal instructions as to firing.   If you desire the rest I shall have them copied.   The document is precious.   The instructions have been given only to the officers of the General Staff.   I leave for the manœuvres."

For some time prior to the arrest of Dreyfus on the charge of being the author of this letter, M. Drumont, editor of the *Libre Parole*, had been carrying on a violent anti-Semitic agitation through his journal.   He raved about the Jews in general, declared Dreyfus guilty, and asserted that there was danger that he would be acquitted through the potent Juiverie, "the cosmopolite syndicate which exploits France."

Public opinion in Paris became much influenced by this journalistic assault, and under these circumstances Dreyfus was brought to trial before a military court, found guilty and condemned to be degraded from his military rank, and by a special act of the Chamber of Deputies was ordered to be imprisoned for life in a penal settlement on Devil's Island, off the coast of French Guiana, a tropical region, desolate and malarious in character.   The sentence was executed with the most cruel harshness.   During part of his detention Dreyfus was locked in a hut, surrounded by an iron cage, on the island.   This was done on the plea of possible attempts at rescue.   He was allowed to send and receive only such letters as had been transcribed by one of his guardians.

He denied, and never ceased to deny, his guilt.   The letters he wrote to his counsel after the trial and after his disgrace are most pathetic assertions of his innocence, and of the hope that ultimately justice would be done him.   His wife and family continued to deny his guilt, and used every influence to get his case reopened.

The first trial of Dreyfus was conducted by court-martial and behind closed doors.   Some parts of the indictment were not communicated to the accused and his lawyer.   The secrecy of the trial, the lack of fairness in its management, his own protestations of innocence, the anti-Jewish feeling, and the course of the government in the affair aroused a strong suspicion that Dreyfus, being a Jew, had been used as a scapegoat for some one else and had been unjustly convicted. Many eminent literary men of France, and even M. Scheurer-Kestner, a vice president of the Senate—none of them Jews—eventually advocated the revision of a sentence which failed to appeal to the sense of justice of the best element of France.

Belief in the Innocence of Dreyfus

It was asserted by some that Dreyfus had sold the plans of various strongly fortified places to the German government, and by others that the sale had been to the Italian government. It was also said that he had disclosed the plans for the mobilization of the French army in case of war, covering several departments, and especially the important fortress of Briançon, the Alpine Gibraltar near the Italian frontier.

The *bordereau*, the paper on which the charges against Dreyfus were based, was a memorandum of treasonable revelations concerning French military affairs. The *dossier* was the official envelope containing the papers relative to the case, which embraced facts alleged to be sufficient to prove the guilt of the accused officer. The bordereau was examined by five experts in handwriting, only three of whom testified that it could have been written by Dreyfus. The papers in the dossier were not shown to Dreyfus or his counsel, so that it was impossible to refute them. In fact, the court-martial was conducted in the most unfair manner, and many became convinced that some disgraceful mystery lay behind it, and that Dreyfus had been made a scapegoat to shield some one higher in office.

The Bordereau and the Dossier

It was in the early part of 1898 that the case was again brought prominently to public notice, after the wife of the unfortunate prisoner had, with the most earnest devotion for three years, used every effort to obtain for him a new trial. Lieutenant-Colonel Picquart, in charge of the secret service bureau at Paris, became familiar through his official duties with the famous case, and was struck with the similarity between the handwriting of the bordereau and that of Count Ferdinand Esterhazy, an officer of the French army and a descendant of the well-known Esterhazy family of Hungary. Shortly afterwards M. Scheurer-Kestner declared that military secrets had continued to leak out after the arrest of Dreyfus, that in consequence a rich and titled officer had been requested to resign, and that this officer was the real author of the bordereau. This man was Count Esterhazy, whose exposure was due to Picquart's fortunate discovery. Others took up this accusation, and the affair was so ventilated that Esterhazy was subjected to a secret trial by court-martial, which ended in an acquittal.

The Accusation of Esterhazy

At the close of the Esterhazy trial a new defender of Dreyfus stepped into the fray, Emile Zola, the celebrated novelist. He wrote an open letter to M. Faure, then President of France, entitled "*J'accuse*" ("I accuse"), which was published in the *Aurore* newspaper. In it he boldly charged that Esterhazy had been acquitted by the members of the court-martial on the order of their chiefs in the ministry of war, who were anxious to show that French military justice could not possibly make an error.

Zola's Letter and Accusation

This letter led to the arrest and trial of Zola and the manager of the paper, their trial being conducted in a manner specially designed to prevent the facts from becoming known. They were found guilty of libel against the officers of the court-martial and sentenced to heavy fines and one year's imprisonment. On appeal, they were tried again in the same unfair way, and received the same sentence. Zola took care, by absenting himself from France, that the sentence of a year's imprisonment should not be executed.

As time went on new evidence became revealed. Colonel Henry, who was one of the witnesses in the Zola trial, was confronted with a damaging fact, one of the most important papers in the secret dossier being traced to him. He confessed that he had forged it to strengthen the case against Dreyfus, was imprisoned for the offence, and committed suicide *in his cell*—or was murdered, as some thought. Picquart was punished by being sent to Africa, and afterwards imprisoned. He made the significant remark that if he should be found dead in his cell it would not be a case of suicide. Esterhazy was said to have acknowledged to a London editor that he was the author of the bordereau, and it was proved that the handwriting was identical with his and the paper on which it was written a peculiar kind which he had used in 1894. The papers in the secret dossier were also alleged to be a mass of forgeries.

Henry's Forgery and Suicide

The great publicity of this case, in which the whole world had taken interest,—the action of the French courts being universally condemned,—and the development of the facts just mentioned, at length goaded the officials of the French government to action. President Faure had the case considered by the cabinet, and finally forced a revision. In consequence the cabinet resigned and a new one was chosen. As a result the case was brought before the Court of Cassation, the final court of appeal, which, after full consideration, ordered a new trial of the condemned officer.

Captain Dreyfus was accordingly brought from Devil's Island, and on July 1, 1899, reached the city of Rennes, where the new court-martial was

THE BOMBARDMENT OF ALEXANDRIA

The Egyptian patriots of 1882, who rushed to arms at the call of Arabi Pasha for the expulsion of the hated British from their country,
made their most vigorous stand behind the strong fortifications of Alexandria, where they fought with much resolution.
But the cannon of the British fleet proved too heavy for their powers of defence, and the city fell into the hands
of the invaders. It was plundered and partly burned by the Egyptians in their retreat

BATTLE BETWEEN THE ENGLISH AND THE ZULUS, SOUTH AFRICA

Of all the natives encountered by the British in Africa, there were none more brave and daring than the Zulus of the South, who did not hesitate with spear and shield to charge against the death dealing rifles of their foes. Cetewayo, the leader of these valiant blacks, was a man who would have been a hero in civilized warfare. As a captive savage in London streets he compelled the respect of his enemies by the majestic dignity of his bearing, and won the right to return and die in his native land.

to be held.   It is not necessary to repeat the evidence given in this trial, which lasted from August 7th to September 7th, and with which the world is sufficiently familiar.   It will suffice to say that the evidence against Dreyfus was of the most shadowy and uncertain character, being largely conjectures and opinions of army officers, and seemed insufficient to convict a criminal for the smallest offence before an equitable court; that the evidence in his favor was of the strongest character; that the proceedings **A Second Condemnation** were of the loosest description; that much favorable evidence was ruled out by the judges, the presiding judge throughout showing a bias against the accused; and that the trial ended in a conviction of the prisoner, by a vote of five judges to two, the verdict being the extraordinary one of "guilty of treason, with extenuating circumstances"—as if any treason could be extenuated.

This is but an outline sketch of this remarkable case, which embraced many circumstances favorable to Dreyfus which we have not had space to give.   The verdict was received by the world outside of France with universal astonishment and condemnation.   The opinion was everywhere expressed that not a particle of incriminating evidence had been adduced, and that the members of the court-martial had acted virtually under the commands of their superior officers, who held that the "honor of the army" demanded a conviction.   Dreyfus was thought by many to have been made a victim to shield certain criminals of high importance in the army, which so dominated French opinion that the great bulk of the people pronounced in favor of the sacrifice of this innocent victim to the Moloch of the French military system.   It was widely **The World's Opinion** felt in foreign lands that the great development of militarism in France, and the vast influence of the general staff of the army, formed a threatening feature of the governmental system, which might at any time overthrow the republic and form a military empire upon its ruins.   Two republics have already been brought to an end in France through the supremacy of the army, and the safety of the third is far from assured.   The Dreyfus case has thrown a flood of light upon the volcanic condition of affairs in France.

The general condemnation of this example of French "justice" by the press of other nations, and very probably the recognition by the governing powers of France of the inadequacy of the evidence led, shortly after the conclusion of the court-martial, to the pardon of the condemned.   The sentence of the court in no sense affected his position before the world, he being looked upon everywhere outside of France as a victim of injustice instead of a criminal.   The severity of his imprisonment however, had seriously affected his health, and threatened to bring his life to an end before he could obtain the justice which he proposed to seek in the courts of France.

This remarkable case, which made an obscure officer of the French army the most talked-of and commiserated man among all the peoples of the earth, at the end of the nineteenth century, is of further interest from the light it throws upon the legal system of France as compared with that of Anglo-Saxon nations. Dreyfus, it is true, was tried by court-martial, but the procedure was similar to that of the ordinary French courts, in which trial by jury does not exist, the judge having the double function of deciding upon the guilt or innocence of the accused and passing sentence; while efforts are made to induce the prisoner to incriminate himself which would be considered utterly unjust in British and American legal practice. The French legal system is a direct descendant of that of ancient Rome. The British one represents a new development in legal methods. Doubtless both have their advantages, but the Dreyfus trial seems to indicate that the system of France opens the way to acts of barbarous injustice.

CHAPTER XIX.

Paul Kruger and the Struggle for Dominion in South Africa.

A T the close of the nineteenth century, not the least important among the international questions that were disturbing the nations was the controversy between the English and the Boers in South Africa, concerning the political privileges of the Uitlanders, or foreign gold miners of the Transvaal. A consideration of this subject obliges us to go back to the beginning of the century and review the whole history of colonization in South Africa.

That region belongs by right of settlement to the Dutch, who founded a colony in the region of Capetown as early as 1650, and in **The Dutch** the succeeding century and a half spread far and wide over **Settlement in** the territory, their farms and cattle ranches occupying a very **South Africa** wide area. The first interference with their peaceful occupation came in 1795, when the English took possession. In 1800, however, they restored the colony to Holland, which held it in peaceable ownership until the Congress of Vienna, in 1815, came to disturb the map of Europe, and in a measure that of the world. As part of the distribution of spoils among the great nations, Cape Colony was ceded to Great Britain. Since then that country, which has a great faculty of taking hold and a very **Great Britain in** poor faculty of letting go, has held possession, and has pushed **Cape Colony** steadily northward until British South Africa is now a terri- **and the Emi-** tory of enormous extent, stretching northward to the borders **gration of the** of the Congo Free State and to Lake Tanganyika. **Boers**

This vast territory has not been gained without active and persistent aggression, from which the Dutch settlers, known as Boers, and the African natives have alike suffered. In truth, the Boers found the oppression of British rule an intolerable burden early in the century, and in 1840 a great party of them gave up their farms and " treked " northward—that is, traveled with their ox-teams and belongings—eager to get away from British control. Here they founded a republic of their own on the river Vaal, and settled down again to peace and prosperity.

The country in which they settled was a huntsman's paradise.   On the great plains of the High Veldt or plateau (from 4,000 to 7,000 feet in height) antelopes of several species roamed in tens of thousands.   In the valleys and plains of the low country the giraffe, elephant,

A Huntsman's Paradise buffalo, lion and other large animals were plentiful.   The rivers were full of alligators and hippopotami.   Here the new-comers found abundance of food, and a land of such pastoral wealth that the farm animals they brought increased abundantly.   For years a steady stream of Boers continued to enter and settle in this land, deserting their farms in the British territory, harnessing their cattle to their long, lumbering wagons, and bringing with them food for the journey, and a good supply of powder and lead for use in their tried muskets.   Their active hunting experience brought them in time to rank among the best marksmen in the world.

They had not alone wild animals to deal with, but wild men as well. Fierce tribes of natives possessed the land, and with these the Boers were soon at war.   A number of sanguinary battles were fought, with much

The Boers Drive Out the Blacks slaughter on both sides, but in the end the black men were forced to give way to the whites and cross the Limpopo River into Matabeleland, to the north, which their descendants still occupy.   Others of the natives were subdued and continued to live with the Boers.   The latter were essentially pioneers.   They did not till the soil, but divided up the land into great grazing ranges, covered with their abundant herds.   And they had no instinct for trade, what little commerce the country possessed falling into British hands.

Two settlements were made, one between the Orange and the Vaal rivers, and the other north of the Vaal.   The former had much trouble with the British previous to 1854, in which year it was given its independence.   It is known as the Orange River Free State.   The latter was given

The South African Republic Founded the name of Transvaal, and originally formed four separate republics, but in 1860 these united into one under the title of the South African Republic.   The settlers were for a time covered with the shadow of British sovereignty, the claims of the British extending up to the 25th degree of latitude.   But this claim was only on paper, and in 1852 it was withdrawn, Great Britain formally renouncing all rights over the country north of the Vaal.   And for years afterwards the Boers lived on here free and undisturbed.

But their country possessed other wealth than that of pasture lands, and its hidden treasures were to yield them no end of trouble in the years to come.   Under their soil lay untold riches, which in time brought hosts of unruly strangers to disturb their pastoral peace. The trouble began in 1867, when diamonds were found in the vicinity of the Vaal River, and a rush of miners began to invade this remote district. But the diamond mines lay west of the borders of the **The Discovery of Diamonds** Transvaal, and brought rather a threatening situation than immediate disturbance to the Boer state. It was the later discovery of gold on Transvaal territory that eventually overthrew the quiet content of the pastoral community.

In 1877 the first intrusion came. The British were now abundant in Griqualand West, the diamond region, and on the Transvaal borders lay a host of native enemies, chief among them being the warlike Zulus, led by the bold and daring Cetewayo. Only fear of the British kept this truculent chief at rest. Meanwhile the Boer Republic had fallen into a financial collapse. Its frequent wars with the natives had exhausted its revenues and thrown it deeply into debt. A **Shepstone's** serious crisis seemed impending. On the plea of preventing **Annexation of** this, Sir Theophilus Shepstone, secretary of Natal, made his **the Transvaal** way to Pretoria, the capital of the republic, and issued a proclamation annexing the Transvaal country to Great Britain. The public treasury he found to be almost empty, it containing only twelve shillings and six pence, and even part of this was counterfeit coin. His act was arbitrary and unwarranted, and while the Boers submitted, they did so with sullen anger, quietly biding their time.

In the following year the Zulus, who had been threatening the Boers, broke out into war with the British, and with such energy that the whites were at first repulsed by the impetuous Cetewayo and his warlike followers. In this onset Prince Napoleon, son of the deposed emperor Louis Napoleon, who served as a volunteer in the British ranks, was killed. The British soon retrieved the disaster, and in the end decisively defeated **The Zulu War** the Zulus, capturing their king, who was taken as a prisoner to London. After the Zulu war Sir Garnet Wolseley led his troops into the Transvaal, telling the protesting Boers that "so long as the sun shone and the Vaal River flowed to the sea the Transvaal would remain British territory." Other acts of interference, and the attempt of the British officials to tax the Boers, added to their exasperation, and at the end of 1880 they resolved to fight for the independence of which they had been robbed. Wolseley had before this left the territory, and the troops had been reduced to a few detachments, scattered here and there.

The first hostile action took place on December 20, 1880, a detachment of the Ninety-fourth regiment, on its march to Pretoria, being waylaid by a

body of about 150 armed Boers, who ordered them to stop.   Colonel Ans-
truther curtly replied : " I go to Pretoria ; do as you like."   The Boers

War With the Boers

did more than he liked.   They closed in on his columns and
opened on them so deadly a fire that the British fell at a frightful rate.   Out of 259 in all, 155 had fallen dead or wounded
in ten minutes' time.   Then the colonel, himself seriously wounded, ordered
a surrender, and the Boers at once became as friendly as they had just been
hostile.   They had lost only two killed and five wounded.

As soon as news of this disaster reached Natal, Colonel Sir George
Colley, in command at Natal, marched against the Boers without waiting
for reinforcements, the force at his disposal being but 1,200 men.   He paid
dearly for his temerity and contempt of the enemy.   On January 28, 1881,
he was encountered by the Boers at a place called Lang's Nek, and met with
a bloody defeat.   In about a week afterwards another engagement took
place, in which the British lost 139 officers and men, while the whole Boer
loss was 14.   Practised hunters, their fire was so deadly that almost every
shot found its mark.

The war was going badly for the British.   It was soon to go worse.
Receiving reinforcements, Colley made a stand in an elevated position
known as Majuba Hill, whose summit was 2,000 feet above the positions

The Stand at Majuba Hill

held by the Boers and its ascent so steep and rugged that the
soldiers had to climb it in single file.   Near the top of the
ascent the grassy slopes were succeeded by boulders, crags,
and loose stones, over which the weary men had to drag themselves on hands
and knees.   In this way about 400 men gained the summit on the morning
of February 27th.   The top of the hill was a saucer-shaped plateau, about
1,200 yards wide, with an elevated rim within which the British were
posted.

The place seemed impregnable, but the daring Boers did not hesitate
in the attack.   A force of the older men were detailed to keep on the watch
below—picked shots ready to fire on any soldier who should appear on the rim
of the hill.   The younger men began to climb the slopes, under cover of the
shrub and stones.   The assault was made on every side, and the defenders,
too weak in numbers to hold the whole edge of the plateau, had to be moved
from point to point to meet and attempt to thwart the attacks of the Boers.
Slowly and steadily the hostile skirmishers clambered upwards from cover
to cover, while the supports below protected their movement with a steady
and accurate fire.   During the hours from dawn to noon the British did not
suffer very heavily, notwithstanding the accuracy of the Boer marksmanship.
But the long strain of the Boers' close shooting began to tell on the *morale* of

the British soldiers, and when the enemy at length reached the crest and opened a deadly fire at short range the officers had to exert themselves to the utmost in the effort to avert disaster. The reserves stationed in the central dip of the plateau, out of reach until then of the enemy's fire, were ordered up in support of the fighting line. Their want of promptitude in obeying this order did not augur well, and soon after reaching the front they wavered, and then gave way. The officers temporarily succeeded in rallying them, but the "bolt" had a bad effect. To use the expression of an eye-witness, a "funk became established."

It was struggled against very gallantly by the officers, who, sword and revolver in hand, encouraged the soldiers by word and by action. A number of men, unable to confront the deadly fire of the Boers, had huddled for cover behind the rocky reef crossing the plateau, and no **The Boers** entreaty or upbraiding on the part of their officers would **Storm the** induce them to face the enemy. What then happened one **British Camp** does not care to tell in detail. Everything connected with this disastrous enterprise went to naught, as if there had been a curse on it. Whatever may have been the object intended, the force employed was absurdly inadequate. Instead of being homogeneous, it consisted of separate detachments with no link or bond of union—a disposition of troops which notoriously has led to more panics than any other cause that the annals of regimental history can furnish. Fragments of proud and distinguished regiments fresh from victory on another continent shared in the panic of the Majuba, seasoned warriors behaving no better than mere recruits. To the calm-pulsed philosopher a panic is an academic enigma. No man who has seen it—much less shared in it—can ever forget the infectious madness of panic-stricken soldiers.

In the sad ending, with a cry of fright and despair the remnants of the hapless force turned and fled, regardless of the efforts of the officers to stem the rearward rush. Sir George Colley lay dead, shot through the head just before the final flight. A surgeon and two hospital attendants caring for the wounded at the bandaging place in the dip of the plateau were shot down, probably inadvertently. The elder **The Victory of** Boers promptly stopped the firing in that direction. But **the Boers** there was no cessation of the fire directed on the fugitives. On them the bullets rained accurately and persistently. The Boers, now disdaining cover, stood boldly on the edge of the plateau, and, firing down upon the scared troops, picked off the men as if shooting game. The slaughter would have been yet heavier but for the entrenchment which had been made by the company of the Ninety-second, left overnight on the Nek, between the Inquela and the Majuba. Captain Robertson was joined at dawn from camp by a company of the Sixtieth, under Captain Thurlow. Later there arrived at the entrenchment on the Nek a troop of the Fifteenth Hussars, under the command of Captain Sullivan. After midday the sound of the firing on the Majuba rapidly increased, and men were seen running down the hill towards the laager, one of whom brought in the tidings that the Boers had captured the position, that most of the troops were killed or prisoners, and that the general was dead with a bullet through his head.

Wounded men presently came pouring in, and were attended by Surgeon-Major Cornish. The laager was manned by the companies, and outposts were thrown out, which were soon driven in by large bodies of mounted Boers, under whose fire men fell fast Robertson dispatched the rifle company down the ravine towards the camp, and a little later followed with the company of the Ninety-second under a murderous fire from the Boers, who had reached and occupied the entrenchment. The Highlanders
A Panic Flight   lost heavily in the retreat, and Surgeon-Major Cornish was killed. The surviving fugitives from Majuba and from the laager finally reached camp under cover of the artillery fire from it, which ultimately stopped the pursuit. With the consent of the Boer leaders a temporary hospital was established at a farm-house near the foot of the mountain, and throughout the cold and wet night the medical staff never ceased to search for and bring in the wounded. Sir George Colley's body was brought into camp on March 1st, and buried there with full military honors.

Of 650 officers and men who took part in this disastrous affair the loss in killed, wounded, and prisoners was 283 ; the Boers had one man killed and five wounded. Majuba Hill was enough for the British, fighting as they were in an unjust cause. An armistice was agreed upon, followed by a treaty of peace on March 23d. Large reinforcements had been sent out, which would have given the British an army of 20,000 against the 8,000
Peace Declared   Boers capable of bearing arms ; but to fight longer in defence
with British   of an arbitrary invasion against such brave defenders of their
Suzerainty   homes and their rights, did not appeal to the conscience of Mr. Gladstone, and he lost no time in bringing the war to an end. By the terms of the treaty the Boers were left free to govern themselves as they would, they acknowledging the queen as suzerain of their country, with control of its foreign relations.

The next important event in the history of the Transvaal was the exploitation of its gold mines. Gold was discovered there soon after the opening of the diamond mines, but not under very promising conditions. It exists

THE BATTLE OF MAJUBA HILL, BETWEEN THE ENGLISH AND BOERS, SOUTH AFRICA

The greatest disaster ever experienced by the British in Africa was at Majuba Hill, in the South African Republic. In the war of 1880 81 with the Boers, a British force occupied the flat top of this steep elevation, but was driven out with great slaughter. The attempt to recapture the hill in the face of the skilled Boer marksmen was simply a climb to death, and the day ended in a serious defeat for the in aday

PAUL KRUGER
President of the South African Republic

JOSEPH CHAMBERLAIN
Colonial Secretary of England

in a conglomerate rock, whose beds extend over an area of seventy by forty miles, and through a depth of from two to twenty feet ; but years passed before the richness in metal of these rocks was discovered, **The Gold Dig-** and it was not until after the Boer war that mining fairly **gings of the** began. No one in his wildest dreams foresaw that these **Transvaal** "banket" beds would in time yield gold to the value of more than $80,000,-000 a year. The yield of the diamond mines was also enormous, and these two incitements brought a steady stream of new settlers to that region, destined before many years greatly to outnumber the sturdy farmers and herders of Dutch descent.

In the vicinity of the gold mines, not far from Pretoria, the Boer capital, rose the mining city of Johannesburg, which now has a population of more than 100,000 souls, of whom half are European miners and nearly all the remainder are natives. The great event in the history of the **The Career of** diamond mines was the advent thither of Cecil Rhodes. This **Cecil Rhodes** remarkable man, the son of a country parson in England, who was ordered to South Africa for the benefit of his failing lungs, displayed such enterprise and ability that he soon became the leading figure in the diamond mining industry, organizing a company that controlled the mines, and accumulating an immense fortune.

This accomplished, he entered actively into South African politics, and was not long in immensely extending the dominion of Great Britain in that region of the earth. He obtained from Lord Salisbury, prime minister of Great Britain, a royal charter giving him the right to occupy and govern the great territory lying between the Limpopo River on the south and the Zambesi on the north, and extending far to the north and the west of the South African Republic. With an expedition of a thousand men, volunteers from the Transvaal and the Cape Colony, Rhodes marched north through a country filled with armed Zulus,—the best fighting stuff in Africa,—and reached the spot where now stands the flourishing town of Fort Salisbury without firing a shot or losing a man. Here gold mines were opened, the resources of the country developed, and within three years as many important townships were founded and settled.

Not until July, 1893, did trouble with the natives arise. Then a rupture took place with the Matabele chief, Lobengula, who sent against the whites powerful bands of his dreaded Zulu warriors, numbering in **War With the** all over 20,000 armed blacks. These were met by Dr. Jameson, **Matabeles** the administrator of the chartered territory, and dealt with so vigorously and skilfully that in two months the power of the Matabeles was at an end, their army was practically annihilated, their great kraals were occupied and their king was driven from his capital into the desert, where he died two months later. Thus Cecil Rhodes added to the dominion of Great Britain a territory as large as France and Germany, very fertile and healthful, and rich in gold and other metals.

Zambesia—or Rhodesia, as it is often called—now extends far to the

The Domain of the South African Company north of the Zambesi River, being bordered on the north by the Congo Free State and Lake Tanganyika, and on the east by Lake Nyassa, and embracing the heart of South Africa. This territory was chartered in 1889 by the British South Africa Company, with Cecil Rhodes, then premier of the Cape Colony, as its managing director and practical creator.

The rapid development of British interests in South Africa, the acquisition of territory in great part surrounding the South African Republic,—which was completely cut off from the sea by British and Portuguese territory,—and the growth of a large foreign population on the soil of the republic itself, could not fail to be a source of great annoyance to the Boers, who deeply mistrusted their new neighbors. Their effort to get away from the British had been a failure. They were surrounded and overrun by them. It is true, the coming of the gold miners had been a great boon to

What the Foreigners Brought to the Transvaal the Boer in one way. From having an empty treasury, he had now an overflowing one. The tax on the gold product had made the government rich. The foreigners had also brought the railway, the electric light, the telegraph, cheap and abundant articles of every-day use, newspapers, schools, and other appendages of civilization, but it is doubtful if these were as welcome to the Boers as the cash contribution, since they tended to break up their simple, patriarchal style of living and destroy their time-honored customs.

The question that particularly troubled the Boer mind was a political one. Paul Kruger, the president of the republic, was a man of remarkable character, an astute statesman, a shrewd politician, with an iron will and keen judgment, a personage strikingly capable of dealing with a disturbing situation. While ignorant in book lore, he had associated with him as secretary of state an educated Hollander, Dr. Leyds by name, one of the ablest and shrewdest statesmen in South Africa. The pair of them were a

Paul Kruger and the Uit-landers close match for the bold and aspiring Cecil Rhodes, then premier of the Cape Colony. The difficulty they had to deal with was the following: The *Uitlander* (Outlander or foreign) element in the republic had grown so enormously as far to outnumber the Dutch. The country presented the anomaly of a minority of 15,000 ignorant and unprogressive Dutch burghers ruling a majority of four or five times their number of educated, wealthy and prosperous aliens, who, while possessing the most valuable part of the territory, were given no voice in its government. They were not only deprived of legislative functions in the country at large, but also of municipal functions in the city of their own creation, and they demanded in vain a charter that would enable them to control and improve their own city. President Kruger, fearing to have his government overwhelmed by these Anglo-Saxon strangers, sternly determined that they should have no political foothold in his state until after a long residence, forseeing that if they were given the franchise on easy terms they would soon control the state. In this sense the gold which was making them rich seemed a curse to the Boers, since it threatened to bring them again under the dominion of the hated Englishman.

In 1895 the state of affairs reached a critical point. The British in Matabeleland, north of the Transvaal, were in warm sympathy with their brethren in Johannesburg, and between them a plot was laid to overthrow Kruger and his people. An outbreak took place in Johannesburg, led by Colonel F. W. Rhodes, brother of Cecil Rhodes, by whom it was thought to have been instigated. It was quickly followed by an invasion from Matabeleland, led by Dr. L. S. Jameson, Cecil Rhodes' lieutenant in that region. The movement was a hasty and ill-considered one. The invaders were met by the bold Boers, armed with their unerring rifles, were surrounded and forced to surrender, and their leaders were put on trial for their lives.

The Jameson Raid

Paul Kruger, however, was shrewd enough not to push the matter to extremities. Jameson and his confederates were set at liberty and allowed to return to England, where they were tried, convicted of invading a friendly country and imprisoned—Cecil Rhodes going free. This daring man soon after suppressed an extensive revolt of the Matabeles, and gained the reputation of designing to found a great British nationality in South Africa. At a later date he devised the magnificent scheme of building a railroad throughout the whole length of Africa, from Cairo to Cape Colony, and threw himself into this ambitious enterprise with all his accustomed energy and organizing capacity.

The victory of the Boers over Jameson and his raiders did not bring to an end the strained relations in Johannesburg. The demand of the Uitlanders for political rights and privileges grew more earnest and insistant as time went on, and the British government, on the basis of its suzerainty, began to take a hand in it. The right to vote, under certain stringent conditions as to period of residence and declaration of intention to become citizens, was accorded

The Demands of the Uitlanders

by the Boer government, but was far from satisfactory to the foreign residents, who demanded the suffrage under less rigorous conditions.

In 1899 the state of affairs became critical, England taking a more decided stand, and strongly pressing her claim to a voice in the status of British residents under her suzerainty—despite the fact that the latter gave her no right to interfere in the domestic affairs of the state.   Joseph Chamberlain, secretary of state for the colonies, demanded a more equitable arrangement than that existing, and his insistence led to a conference between the Boer authorities and those of Cape Colony.   But President Kruger refused to yield to the full demands made upon him, while the concessions which he offered were not satisfactory to the British cabinet.

Negotiations went on during the summer and early autumn of 1899, but at the same time both sides were actively preparing for war, and Great Britain had begun to send large contingents of troops to South Africa.   The state of indecision came to a sudden end on October 10th.   President Kruger apparently fearing that Joseph Chamberlain, who conducted the negotiations, was deceiving him, and seeking delay until he could land an overwhelming force in South Africa, sent a sudden ultimatum to the British cabinet.   They were bidden to remove the troops which threatened the borders of his state before five o'clock of the next day or accept war as the alternative.

Such a mandate from a weak to a strong state was not likely to be complied with.   The troops were not removed, and the Boers promptly crossed the borders into Natal on the east and Cape Colony on the west.   The Orange River Free State had joined the South African Republic in its attitude of hostility, and the British on the borders found themselves outnumbered and outgeneraled.   The towns of Mafeking and Kimberley on the west were closely besieged, and on the east the outlying troops were driven back on Ladysmith, where General White, the British commander, met with a severe repulse, losing two entire regiments as prisoners.

Meanwhile General Buller, the British commander-in-chief, had reached Cape Town and a powerful army was on the ocean, and it was widely felt that the successes of the Boers were but preliminaries to a desperate struggle whose issue only time could decide.

General White had made a serious tactical error in seeking to hold Ladysmith instead of falling back to the coast to await reinforcements.   The neatly devised plan of operations of the British army was greatly deranged, and General Buller, who had counted on a triumphal march to the Transvaal border, found himself held fast at the Tugela River, whose group of steep and rugged hills served the Boers as so many natural forts, from which the

British found it impossible to dislodge them. It had been supposed that the Boers were adapted only to warfare of the guerilla character, that of bold raids, sudden dashes and swift retreats, but this event proved them to be skillful in investment, stubborn in defence, and fertile in expedients.

An attempt to cross the Tugela at Colenso proved a sanguinary failure, the troops being repulsed and a battery of guns lost. Buller met with other defeats, the most serious being that on the hilltop called Spion Kop. Meanwhile General White held on obstinately to Ladysmith, though he had to contend, not only against the guns of the **General White's Operations** enemy, but against sparse food, unwholesome water, and threatening pestilence. Despite all these he defended himself with unflinching courage against the guns and the assaults of the enemy for four long months, at the end of which time he was rewarded by a sudden disappearance of the foe, and the welcome entrance of Lord Dundonald and his troop of cavalry. Operations elsewhere had forced the brave Joubert to give up the siege and withdraw with his men. Those distant operations now demand our attention.

Far away from Ladysmith, on the opposite side of the Orange Free State, lies the town of Kimberley, the centre of the diamond mining industry. Among its inmates was Cecil Rhodes, the diamond magnate, and the investing Boers were even more eager to capture their hated foe than to fall heir to the rich products of the diamond mines. To the relief of Kimberly came Lord Methuen, with a strong force, hastening by rail from Capetown north. From the Orange to the Modder River he made his way by dint of a succession of fierce skirmishes, in which the Boers gave a very good account of themselves. His misfortunes culminated at Magersfontein, on the Modder River, where his army fell into a Boer trap and was defeated with a loss of nearly 1,100 men. This was the most serious battle of the war.

By this time the government of Great Britain was thoroughly alarmed. Instead of the easy victory that had been looked for, it began to appear as if the courage, skill, and military resources of the **An Unexpected Contingency** Boers might yield them an eventual triumph, and Kruger and Joubert be able to drive the invaders from their native soil. This was a contingency which British pride could not accept. Strenuous efforts were made to raise and equip a great force, and early in 1900 Field-Marshal Lord Roberts and the gallant General Kitchener, the two most famous soldiers that England possessed, were sent to the front, Lord Roberts as commander-in-chief. Under them was the largest army which Great Britain had ever dispatched to a foreign soil.

It was too powerful a force for the small population of the Boer republics successfully to oppose. The abundant cavalry under Lord Roberts enabled him to flank his opponents at every point, and the stubborn resistance of the Boers was changed to a rapid retreat. A sudden dash of General French and his light cavalry freed Kimberley, and the diamond capital was entered by the swift horsemen on February 16th, much to the relief of Cecil Rhodes and the distressed people, who had suffered severely during the siege.

General Cronje, at the head of the Boer besieging force, hurried away as fast as his slow-moving ox teams would permit, but the pursuit was so hot and rapid that he was headed off and forced to take refuge in a dry river bed. Here he made a vigorous fight for life. For ten days he desperately held out, with a gallant persistance that won the plaudits of the world, and surrendered only when death stared him and his followers in the face. It was this surrender that forced Joubert to raise the siege of Ladysmith.

From this point Roberts' great army swept resistlessly onward, the enemy vanishing before it, and on March 13 it made a triumphant entry into Bloemfontein, the capital of the Orange River Free State. Two days afterwards the town of Mafeking, in which the valiant Colonel Baden-Powell and his gallant followers had made one of the most memorable defences of modern times, was relieved— none too soon, for starvation was almost at hand.

The Transvaal Entered

In early June the final great success was won. In May Roberts put his men again in motion, the Vaal River was passed and the Transvaal entered, and the mining city of Johannesburg fell without a blow. With it the gold mines, the impelling motive of the war, and which it was feared would be blown up and destroyed, were won. Finally Pretoria, the Transvaal capital, which was said to be strongly fortified and abundantly provisioned, and where the last dying struggle of Paul Kruger and his countrymen was looked for, fell into British hands, the Boers and their government taking precipitately to flight.

This conquest practically closed the drama of the war. Some daring raids on the British lines were made, but the Boer armies had vanished and there was every indication that their power of resistance was almost at an end. The great British army rapidly closed in on them, and little remained but to let fall the curtain of fate on the Boer republics, and raise it again over a British colony extending without a break from Capetown in the south to the Congo Free State in the north.

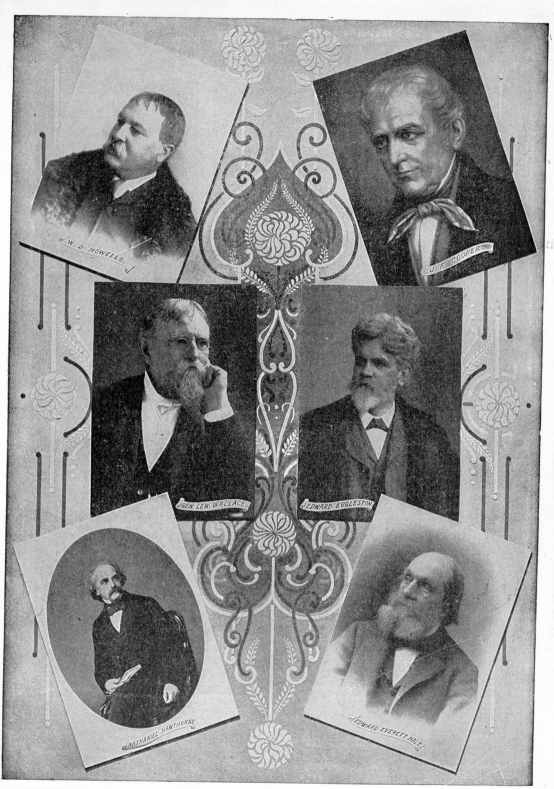

TYPICAL AMERICAN NOVELISTS

LI HUNG CHANG, THE GRAND OLD MAN OF CHINA   EMILIO AGUINALDO, LEADER OF THE FILIPINOS

TWO POWERFUL MEN IN THE ORIENT

CHAPTER XX

The Rise of Japan and the Decline of China.

ASIA, the greatest of the continents and the seat of the earliest civilizations, yields us the most remarkable phenomenon in the history of mankind. In remote ages, while Europe lay plunged in the deepest barbarism, certain sections of Asia were marked by surprising activity in thought and progress. In three far-separated regions—China, India, and Babylonia—and in a fourth on the borders of Asia—Egypt **Asia the Original Seat of Civilization** —civilization rose and flourished for ages, while the savage and the barbarian roamed over all other regions of the earth. A still more extraordinary fact is, that during the more recent era, that of European civilization, Asia has rested in the most sluggish conservatism, sleeping while Europe and America were actively moving, content with its ancient knowledge while the people of the West were pursuing new knowledge into its most secret lurking places.

And this conservatism is an almost immovable one. For a century England has been pouring new thought and new enterprise into India, yet the Hindoos cling stubbornly to their remotely ancient beliefs and customs. For half a century Europe has been hammering upon the gates of China, but the sleeping nation shows little signs of waking up to the fact that the world is moving around it. As regards the other early civili- **The Sluggishness of Modern Asia** zations—Babylonia and Egypt — they have been utterly swamped under the tide of Turkish barbarism and exist only in their ruins. Persia, once a great and flourishing empire, has likewise sunk under the flood of Arabian and Turkish invasion, and to-day, under its ruling Shah, is one of the most inert of nations, steeped in the self-satisfied barbarism that has succeeded its old civilization. Such was the Asia upon which the nineteenth century dawned, and such it remains to-day except in one remote section of its area, in which alone modern civilization has gained a firm foothold.

The section referred to is the island empire of Japan, a nation the people of which are closely allied in race to those of China, yet which has displayed a progressiveness and a readiness to avail itself of the resources of modern civilization strikingly diverse from the obstinate conservatism of its densely settled neighbor. The development of Japan has taken place within the

The Seclusion of China and Japan past half century. Previous to that time it was as resistant to western influences as China. They were both closed na· tions, prohibiting the entrance of modern ideas and peoples, proud of their own form of civilization and their own institutions, and sternly resolved to keep out the disturbing influences of the restless west. As a result, they remained locked against the new civilization until after the nineteenth century was well advanced, and China's disposition to avail itself of the results of modern invention was not manifested until the century was near its end.

China, with its estimated population of nearly 400,000,000, attained to a considerable measure of civilization at a very remote period, but has made almost no progress during the Christian era, being content to retain its old ideas, methods and institutions, which its people look upon as far superior

The Opening of China to those of the western nations. Great Britain gained a foothold in China as early as the seventeenth century, but the persistent attempt to flood the country with the opium of India, in disregard of the laws of the land, so annoyed the emperor that he had the opium of the British stores at Canton, worth $20,000,000, seized and destroyed. This led to the "opium war" of 1840, in which China was defeated and was forced to accept a much greater degree of intercourse with the world, five ports being made free to the world's commerce and Hong Kong ceded to Great Britain. In 1856 an arbitrary act of the Chinese authorities at Canton, in forcibly boarding a British vessel in the Canton River, led to a new war, in which the French joined the British and the allies gained fresh concessions from China. In 1859 the war was renewed, and Peking was occupied by the British and French forces in 1860, the emperor's summer palace being destroyed.

These wars had their effect in largely breaking down the Chinese wall of seclusion and opening the empire more fully to foreign trade and intercourse, and also in compelling the emperor to receive foreign ambassadors at his court in Peking. In this the United States was among the most successful of the nations, from the fact that it had always maintained friendly relations with China. In 1876 a short railroad was laid, and in 1877 a telegraph line was established. During the remainder of the century the telegraph service was widely extended, but the building of railroads was strongly opposed, and not until the century had reached its end did the Chinese awaken to the importance of this method of transportation. They did, however, admit steam traffic to their rivers, and purchased some powerful ironclad naval vessels in Europe.

The isolation of Japan was maintained longer than that of China, trade with that country being of less importance, and foreign nations knowing and caring less about it. The United States has the credit of breaking down its long and stubborn seclusion and setting in train the **How Japan Was** remarkably rapid development of the Japanese island empire. **Opened to** In 1854 Commodore Perry appeared with an American fleet **Commerce** in the bay of Yeddo, and, by a show of force and a determination not to be rebuffed, he forced the authorities to make a treaty of commercial intercourse with the United States. Other nations quickly demanded similar privileges, and Japan's obstinate resistance to foreign intercourse was at an end.

The result of this was revolutionary in Japan. For centuries the Shogun, or Tycoon, the principal military noble, had been dominant in the empire, and the Mikado, the true emperor, relegated to a position of obscurity. The entrance of foreigners disturbed conditions so greatly—by developing parties for and against seclusion—that the Mikado was enabled to regain his long-lost power, and in 1868 the ancient form of government was restored.

Meanwhile the Japanese began to show a striking activity in the acceptance of the results of western civilization, both in regard to objects of commerce, inventions, and industries, and to political organization. The latter advanced so rapidly that in 1889 the old despotic government **Great Develop-** was, by the voluntary act of the emperor, set aside and a lim- **ment of Japan** ited monarchy established, the country being given a constitution and a legislature, with universal suffrage for all men over twenty-five. This act is of remarkable interest, it being doubtful if history records any similar instance of a monarch decreasing his authority without appeal or pressure from his people. It indicates a liberal spirit that could hardly have been looked for in a nation so recently emerging from semi-barbarism. To-day, Japan differs little from the nations of Europe and America in its institutions and industries, and from being among the most backward, has taken its place among the most advanced nations of the world.

The Japanese army has been organized upon the European system, and armed with the most modern style of weapons, the German method of drill and organization being adopted. Its navy consists of over fifty war vessels, principally built in the dock-yards of Europe and America, and of the most advanced modern type, while a number of still more powerful ships are in process of building. Railroads have been widely extended; telegraphs run everywhere; education is in an advancing stage of development, embracing an imperial university at Tokio, and institutions in which foreign languages and science are taught; and in a hundred ways Japan is progressing at a rate which is one of the greatest marvels of the nineteenth century.   This is particularly notable in view of the obstinate adherence of the neighboring empire of China to its old customs, and the slowness with which it is yielding to the influx of new ideas.

As a result of this difference in progress between the two nations, we have to describe a remarkable event, one of the most striking evidences that

A Remarkable Event

could be given of the practical advantage of modern civilization.   Near the end of the century war broke out between China and Japan, and there was shown to the world the singular circumstance of a nation of 40,000,000 people, armed with modern implements of war, attacking a nation of 400,000,000—equally brave, but with its army organized on an ancient system—and defeating it as quickly and completely as Germany defeated France in the Franco-German War.   This war, which represents a completely new condition of events in the continent of Asia, is of sufficient interest and importance to speak of at some length.

Between China and Japan lies the kingdom of Corea, separated by rivers from the former and by a strait of the ocean from the latter, and claimed as a vassal state by both, yet preserving its independence as a state against the pair.   Japan invaded this country at two different periods in the past, but failed to conquer it.   China has often invaded it, with the same result.   Thus it remained practically independent until near the end of the nineteenth century, when it became a cause of war between the two rival empires.

Corea long pursued the same policy as China and Japan, locking its ports against foreigners so closely that it became known as the Hermit

Corea Opened to Foreign Intercourse

Nation and the Forbidden Land.   But it was forced to give way, like its neighbors.   The opening of Corea was due to Japan.   In 1876 the Japanese did to this secluded kingdom what Commodore Perry had done to Japan twenty-two years before.   They sent a fleet to Seoul, the Corean capital, and by threat of war forced the government to open to trade the port of Fusan.   In 1880 Chemulpo was made an open port.   Later on the United States sent a fleet there which obtained similar privileges.   Soon afterwards most of the nations of Europe were admitted to trade, and the isolation of the Hermit Nation was at an end.   Less than ten years had sufficed to break down an isolation which had lasted for centuries.   In less than twenty years after—in the year 1899—an electric trolley railway was put in operation in the streets of Seoul—a remarkable evidence of the great change in Corean policy.

Corea was no sooner opened to foreign intercourse than China and Japan became rivals for influence in that country—a rivalry in which Japan showed itself the more active. The Coreans became divided into two factions, a progressive one that favored Japan, and a conservative one that favored China. Japanese and Chinese soldiers were sent to the country, and the Chinese aided their party, which was in the ascendant among the Coreans, to drive out the Japanese troops. War was threatened, but it was averted by a treaty in 1885 under which both nations agreed to withdraw their troops and to send no officers to drill the Corean soldiers.

The war, thus for the time averted, came nine years afterwards, in consequence of an insurrection in Corea. The people of that country were discontented. They were oppressed with taxes and by tyranny, and in 1894 the followers of a new religious sect broke out in open revolt. **Insurrection in Corea** Their numbers rapidly increased until they were 20,000 strong, and they defeated the government troops, captured a provincial city, and put the capital itself in danger. The Min (or Chinese) faction was then at the head of affairs in the kingdom and called for aid from China, which responded by sending some two thousand troops and a number of war vessels to Corea. Japan, jealous of any such action on the part of China, responded by surrounding Seoul with soldiers, several thousands in number.

Disputes followed. China claimed to be suzerain of Corea and Japan denied it. Both parties refused to withdraw their troops, and the Japanese, finding that the party in power was acting against them, advanced on the capital, drove out the officials, and took possession of the palace and the king. A new government, made up of the party that favored Japan, was organized, and a revolution was accomplished in a day. The new authorities declared that the Chinese were intruders and requested the aid of the Japanese to expel them. War was close at hand.

China was at that time under the leadership of a statesman of marked ability, the famous Li Hung Chang, who, from being made viceroy of a province in 1870, had risen to be the prime minister of the empire. At the head of the empire was a woman, the Dowager Empress Tsu Tsi, who had usurped the power of the young emperor and ruled the state. **Li Hung Chang and the Empress** It was to these two people in power that the war was due. The dowager empress, blindly ignorant of the power of the Japanese, decided that these "insolent pigmies" deserved to be chastised. Li, her right-hand man, was of the same opinion. At the last moment, indeed, doubts began to assail his mind, into which came a dim idea that the army and navy of China were not in shape to meet the forces of Japan. But the empress was resolute. Her sixtieth birthday was at hand and she proposed to celebrate it magnificently ; and what better decorations could she display than the captured banners of these insolent islanders ? So it was decided to present a bold front, and, instead of the troops of China being removed, reinforcements were sent to the force at Asan.

There followed a startling event. On July 25th three Japanese men-of-war, cruising in the Yellow Sea, came in sight of a transport loaded with Chinese troops and convoyed by two ships of the Chinese navy. The **The Sinking of the Chinese Transport** Japanese admiral did not know of the seizure of Seoul by the land forces, but he took it to be his duty to prevent Chinese troops from reaching Corea, so he at once attacked the war ships of the enemy, with such effect that they were quickly put to flight. Then he sent orders to the transport that it should put about and follow his ships.

This the Chinese generals refused to do. They trusted to the fact that they were on a chartered British vessel and that the British flag flew over their heads. The daring Japanese admiral troubled his soul little about this foreign standard, but at once opened fire on the transport, and with such effect that in half an hour it went to the bottom, carrying with it one thousand men. Only about one hundred and seventy escaped.

On the same day that this terrible act took place on the waters of the **Declaration of War** sea, the Japanese left Seoul en route for Asan. Reaching there, they attacked the Chinese in their works and drove them out. Three days afterwards, on August 1, 1894, both countries issued declarations of war.

Of the conflict that followed, the most interesting events were those that took place on the waters, the land campaigns being an unbroken series of successes for the well-organized and amply-armed Japanese troops over the mediæval army of China, which went to war fan and umbrella in hand, with antiquated weapons and obsolete organization. The principal battle was **The War on Land** fought at Ping Yang on September 15th, the Chinese losing 16,000 killed, wounded and captured, while the Japanese loss was trifling. In November the powerful fortress of Port Arthur was attacked by army and fleet, and surrendered after a two days' siege. Then the armies advanced until they were in the vicinity of the Great Wall, with the soil and capital of China not far before them.

With this brief review of the land operations, we must return to the performances of the fleets, which were of high interest as forming the second occasion in which a modern ironclad fleet had met in battle—the first being that already described in which the Austrians defeated the Italians at

Lissa. Backward as the Chinese were on land, they were not so on the sea. Li Hung Chang, progressive as he was, had vainly attempted to introduce railroads into China, but he had been more successful in regard to ships, and had purchased a navy more powerful than that of Japan. The heaviest ships of Japan were cruisers, whose armor consisted of deck and interior lining of steel. The Chinese possessed two powerful battle- **The Chinese** ships, with 14-inch iron armor and turrets defended with 12- **and Japanese** inch armor, each carrying four 12-inch guns. Both navies had **Fleets** the advantage of European teaching in drill, tactics, and seamanship. The *Ting Yuen*, the Chinese flagship, had as virtual commander an experienced German officer named Van Hanneken; the *Chen Yuen*, the other big iron-clad, was handled by Commander M'Giffen, formerly of the United States navy. Thus commanded, it was expected in Europe that the superior strength of the Chinese ships would ensure them an easy victory over those of Japan. The event showed that this was a decidedly mistaken view.

It was the superior speed and the large number of rapid-fire guns of the Japanese vessels that gave them the victory. The Chinese guns were mainly heavy Krupps and Armstrongs. They had also some machine guns, but only three quick-firers. The Japanese, on the contrary, had a few heavy armor-piercing guns, but were supplied with a large number of quick-firing cannon, capable of pouring out shells in an incessant stream. Admiral Ting and his European officers expected to come at once to close quarters and quickly destroy the thin armored Japanese craft. But the shrewd Admiral Ito, commander of the fleet of Japan, had no intention of being thus dealt with. The speed of his craft enabled him to keep his distance and to dis-tract the aim of his foes, and he proposed to make the best use of this ad-vantage. Thus equipped the two fleets came together in the month of Sep-tember, and an epoch-making battle in the history of the ancient conti-nent of Asia was fought.

On the afternoon of Sunday, September 16th, Admiral Ting's fleet, consisting of 11 warships, 4 gunboats, and 6 torpedo boats, anchored off the mouth of the Yalu River. They were there as escorts to some trans-ports, which went up the river to discharge their troops. Admiral Ito had been engaged in the same work farther down the coast, and early on Monday morning came steaming towards the Yalu in search of the **The Fleets off** enemy. Under him were in all twelve ships, none of them **the Yalu River** with heavy armor, one of them an armed transport. The swiftest ship in the fleet was the *Yoshino*, capable of making twenty-three knots, and armed with 44 quick-firing Armstrongs, which would discharge nearly 4,000 pounds weight of shells every minute. The heaviest guns were long 13-inch cannon, of which four ships possessed one each, protected by 12-inch shields of steel.   Finally, they had an important advantage over the Chinese in being abundantly supplied with ammunition.

With this formidable fleet Ito steamed slowly to the north-westward. Early on Monday morning he was off the island of Hai-yun-tao.   At seven A.M. the fleet began steaming north-eastward.   It was a fine autumn morning.   The sun shone brightly, and there was only just enough of a breeze to ripple the surface of the water.   The long line of warships cleaving their way through the blue waters, all bright with white paint, the chrysanthemum of Japan shining like a golden shield on every bow, and the same emblem flying in red and white from every masthead, must have been a grand spectacle.   Some miles away to port rose the rocky coast and the blue hills of Manchuria, dotted with many an island, and showing here and there a little bay with its fishing villages.   On the other side, the waters of the wide Corean Gulf stretched to an unbroken horizon.   Towards eleven o'clock the hills at the head of the gulf began to rise. Ito had in his leading ship, the *Yoshino*, a cruiser that would have made a splendid scout.   In any European navy she would have been steaming some miles ahead of her colleagues with, perhaps, another quick ship between her and the fleet to pass on her signals.   Ito however seems to have done no scouting, but to have kept his ships in single line ahead, with a small interval between the van and the main squadron.   At half-past eleven smoke was seen far away on the starboard bow, the bearing being east-north-east.   It appeared to come from a number of steamers in line, on the horizon.   The course was altered and the speed increased.   Ito believed that he had the Chinese fleet in front of him.   He was right. The smoke was that of Ting's ironclads and cruisers anchored in line, with steam up, outside the mouth of the Yalu.

The Cruise of Admiral Ito's Fleet

On Monday morning the Chinese crews had been exercised at their guns, and a little before noon, while the cooks were busy getting dinner ready, the lookout men at several of the mastheads began to call out that they saw the smoke of a large fleet away on the horizon to the south-west. Admiral Ting was as eager for the fight as his opponents.   At once he signalled to his fleet to weigh anchor, and a few minutes later ran up the signal to clear for action.

A similar signal was made by Admiral Ito half-an-hour later, as his ships came in sight of the Chinese line of battle.   The actual moment was five minutes past noon, but it was not until three-quarters of an hour later that the fleets had closed sufficiently near for the fight to begin at long range.   This three-quarters of an hour was a time of anxious and eager expectation for both Chinese and Japanese. Commander McGiffen of the *Chen Yuen* has given a striking description of the scene when " the deadly space" between the two fleets was narrowing, and all were watching for the flash and smoke of the first gun :—" The twenty-two ships," he says, "trim and fresh-looking in their paint and their bright new bunting, and gay with fluttering signal-flags, presented such a holiday aspect that one found difficulty in realizing that they were not there simply for a friendly meeting. But, looking closer on the *Chen Yuen*, one could see beneath this gayety much that was sinister. Dark-skinned men, with queues tightly coiled round their heads, and with arms bared to the elbow, clustered along the decks in groups at the guns, waiting impatiently to kill or be **The Chinese** killed. Sand was sprinkled along the decks, and more was **on the " Chen** kept handy against the time when they might become slip- **Yuen "** pery. In the superstructures, and down out of sight in the bowels of the ship, were men at the shell whips and ammunition hoists and in the torpedo room. Here and there a man lay flat on the deck, with a charge of powder —fifty pounds or more—in his arms, waiting to spring up and pass it on when it should be wanted. The nerves of the men below deck were in extreme tension On deck one could see the approaching enemy, but below nothing was known, save that any moment might begin the action, and bring in a shell through the side. Once the battle had begun they were all right ; but at first the strain was intense. The fleets closed on each other rapidly. My crew was silent. The sub-lieutenant in the military foretop was taking sextant angles and announcing the range, and exhibiting an appropriate small signal-flag. As each range was called, the men at the guns would lower the sight-bars, each gun captain, lanyard in hand, keeping his gun trained on the enemy. Through the ventilators could be heard the beats of the steam pumps ; for all the lines of hose were joined up and spouting water, so that, in case of fire, no time need be lost. Every man's nerves were in a state of tension, which was greatly relieved as a huge cloud of white smoke, belching from the *Ting Yuen's* starboard barbette, opened the ball."

The shot fell a little ahead of the *Yoshino*, throwing up a tall column of white water. Admiral Ito, in his official report, notes that this first shot was fired at ten minutes to one. The range, as noted on the *Chen Yuen*, was 5,200 yards, or a little over three and a half miles. The heavy barbette and bow guns of the *Chen Yuen* and other ships **The Opening of** now joined in, but still the Japanese van squadron came on **the Battle** without replying. For five minutes the firing was all on the side of the Chinese. The space between the Japanese van and the hostile line had diminished to 3,000 yards—a little under two miles. The *Yoshino*, the leading ship, was heading for the centre of the Chinese line, but obliquely, so as to pass diagonally along the front of the Chinese right wing. At five minutes to one her powerful battery of quick-firers opened on the Chinese, sending out a storm of shells, most of which fell in the water just ahead of the *Ting* and *Chen Yuen*. Their first effect was to deluge the decks, barbettes and bridges of the two ironclads with the geysers of water flung up by their impact with the waves. In a few minutes every man on deck was soaked to the skin. One by one the other ships along the Japanese line opened fire, and then, as the range still diminished, the Chinese machine-guns, Hotchkisses and Nordenfelts added their sharp, growling reports to the deeper chorus of the heavier guns.

The armored barbettes and central citadels of the two Chinese battle-ships were especially the mark of the Japanese fire. Theoretically they ought to have been pierced again and again, but all the harm they received were some deep dents and grooves in the thick plates. But through the thin lined hulls of the cruisers the shells crashed like pebbles through glass, the only effect of the metal wall being to explode the shells and scatter their fragments far and wide.

The Chinese admiral had drawn up his ships in a single line, with the large ones in the centre and the weaker ones on the wings. Ito's ships came up in column, the *Yoshino* leading, his purpose being to take advantage of the superior speed of his ships and circle round his adversary. Past the Chinese right wing swept the swift *Yoshino*, pouring in the shells from her rapid-fire guns on the unprotected vessels there posted, one of which, the *Yang Wei*, was soon in flames. The ships that followed tore the woodwork of the *Chao Yung* with their shells, and she likewise burst into flames. The slower vessels of the Japanese fleet lagged behind their speedy leaders, particularly the little *Heijei*, which fell so far in the rear as to be exposed to the fire of the whole Chinese fleet. In this dilemma its captain displayed a daring spirit. Instead of following his consorts, he dashed straight for the line of the enemy, passing between two of their larger vessels at 500 yards distance. Two torpedoes were launched at him, but missed their mark. But he was made the target of a heavy fire, and came through with his craft in flames. At 2.23 the blazing *Chao Yung* went to the bottom with all on board.

As a result of the Japanese evolution, their ships finally closed in on the Chinese on both sides and the action reached its most furious phase. The two flag-ships, the Japanese *Matsushima* and the Chinese *Ting Yuen*,

Admiral Ito's Strategy

The Daring Act of the "Heijei"

battered each other with their great guns, the wood-work of the latter being soon in flames, while a heap of ammunition on the *Matsushima* was exploded by a shell and killed or wounded eighty men. The Chinese flag-ship would probably have been destroyed by the flames but that her consort came to her assistance. By five o'clock the Chinese fleet was in the greatest disorder, several The "Matsushima" and the "Ting Yuen" of its ships having been sunk or driven in flames ashore, while others were in flight. The Japanese fire was mainly concentrated on the two large ironclads, which continued the fight, their thick armor resisting the heaviest guns of the enemy.

Signals and signal halyards had been long since shot away, and all the signalmen killed or wounded; but the two ships conformed to each other's movements, and made a splendid fight of it. Admiral Ting had been insensible for some hours at the outset of the battle. He had stood too close to one of his own big guns on a platform above its muzzle, and had been stunned by the upward and backward concussion of the air; but he had recovered consciousness, and, though wounded by a burst shell, was bravely commanding his ship. Von Hanneken was also wounded in one of the barbettes. The ship was on fire forward, but the hose kept the flames under. The *Chen Yuen* was almost in the same plight. Her commander, McGiffen, had had several narrow escapes. When at last the lacquered woodwork on her forecastle caught fire, and the men declined to go forward and put it out unless an officer went with them, he led the party. He was stooping down to move something on the forecastle, when a McGiffen's Terrible Danger shot passed between his arms and legs, wounding both his wrists. At the same time he was struck down by an explosion near him. When he recovered from the shock he found himself in a terrible position. He was lying wounded on the forecastle, and full in front of him he saw the muzzle of one of the heavy barbette guns come sweeping round, rise, and then sink a little, as the gunners trained it on a Japanese ship, never noticing that he lay just below the line of fire. It was in vain to try to attract their attention. In another minute he would have been caught in the fiery blast. With a great effort he rolled himself over the edge of the forecastle, dropping on to some rubbish on the main deck, and hearing the roar of the gun as he fell.

The battle now resolved itself into a close cannonade of the two ironclads by the main body of the Japanese fleet, while the rest of the ships kept up a desultory fight with the three other Chinese ships and the gunboats. The torpedo boats seem to have done nothing. Commander McGiffen says that their engines had been worn out, and their fittings shaken to pieces, by their being recklessly used as ordinary steam launches in the weeks before the battle. The torpedoes fired from the tubes of the battleships were few in number, and all missed their mark, one, at least, going harmlessly under a ship at which it was fired at a range of only fifty yards. The Japanese used no torpedoes. It is even said that, by a mistake, they had sailed without a supply of these weapons. Nor was the ram used anywhere. Once or twice a Chinese ship tried to run down a Japanese, but the swifter and handier vessels of Ito's squadron easily avoided all such attacks. The Yalu fight was from first to last an artillery battle.

And the end of it came somewhat unexpectedly. The *Chen Yuen* and the *Ting Yuen* were both running short of ammunition. The latter had been hit more than four hundred times without her armour being pierced, and the former at least as often. One of the *Chen Yuen's* heavy guns had its mountings damaged, but otherwise she was yet serviceable. Still, she had been severely battered, had lost a great part of her crew, and her slow fire must have told the Japanese that she was economizing her ammunition, which was now all solid shot. But about half-past five Ito signalled to his

The End of the Battle

fleet to retire. The two Chinese ironclads followed them for a couple of miles, sending an occasional shot after them; then the Japanese main squadron suddenly circled round as if to renew the action, and, towards six o'clock, there was a brisk exchange of fire at long range. When Ito again ceased fire, the *Chen Yuen* had just three projectiles left for her heavy guns. If he had kept on for a few minutes longer the two Chinese ships would have been at his mercy.

Just why Ito retired has never been clearly explained. Probably exhaustion of his crew and the perils of a battle at night with such antag-

Lessons from the Yalu Sea-Fight

onists had much to do with it. The next morning the Chinese fleet had disappeared. It had lost four ships in the fight, two had taken to flight, and one ran ashore after the battle and was blown up. Two of the Japanese ships were badly damaged, but none were lost, while their losses in killed and wounded were much less than those of the Chinese. An important lesson from the battle was the danger of too much wood-work in ironclad ships, and another was the great value in naval warfare of rapid-firing guns. But the most remarkable characteristic of the battle of the Yalu was that it took place between two nations which, had the war broken out forty years earlier, would have done their fighting with fleets of junks and weapons a century old.

Capture of Wei Hai Wei

In January, 1895, the Japanese fleet advanced against the strongly fortified stronghold of Wei Hai Wei, on the northern coast of China. Here a force of 25,000 men was landed successfully, and attacked the fort in the rear, quickly capturing its landward defences. The stronghold was thereupon abandoned by its garrison and occupied by the Japanese. The Chinese fleet lay in the harbor, and surrendered to the Japanese after several ships had been sunk by torpedo boats.

China was now in a perilous position. Its fleet was lost, its coast strongholds of Port Arthur and Wei Hai Wei were held by the enemy, and its capital city was threatened from the latter place and by the army north of the Great Wall. A continuation of the war promised to bring about the complete conquest of the Chinese empire, and Li Hung Chang, who had been degraded from his official rank in consequence of the disasters to the army, was now restored to all his honors and sent to Japan to sue for peace. In the treaty obtained China was compelled to acknowledge the independence of Corea, to cede to Japan the island of For- **The Treaty of** mosa and the Pescadores group, and that part of Manchuria **Peace** occupied by the Japanese army, including Port Arthur, also to pay an indemnity of 300,000,000 taels and open seven new treaty ports. This treaty was not fully carried out. The Russian, British, and French ministers forced Japan, under threat of war, to give up her claim to the Liau Tung peninsula and Port Arthur.

The story of China during the few remaining years of the century may be briefly told. The evidence of its weakness yielded by the war with Japan was quickly taken advantage of by the great powers of Europe, **The Impending** and China was in danger of going to pieces under their attacks, **Partition of** which grew so decided and ominous that rumors of a partition **China** between these powers of the most ancient and populous empire of the world filled the air.

In 1898 decided steps in this direction were taken. Russia obtained a lease for ninety-nine years of Port Arthur and Talien Wan, and is at present in practical possession of Manchuria, through which a railroad is to be built connecting with the Trans-Siberian road, while Port Arthur affords her an ice-free harbor for her Pacific fleet. Great Britain, jealous of this movement on the part of Russia, forced from the unwilling hands of China the port of Wei Hai Wei, and Germany demanded and obtained the cession of a port at Kiau Chun, farther down the coast. France, not to be outdone by her neighbors, gained concessions of territory in the south, adjoining her Indo-China possessions, and Italy, last of all, came into the Eastern market for a share of the nearly defunct empire.

How far this will go it is not easy to say. The nations **A Palace** are settling on China like vultures on a carcass, and perhaps **Revolution** may tear the antique commonwealth to pieces between them. Within the empire itself revolutionary changes have taken place, the dowager empress having deprived the emperor of power and held him a palace prisoner at Peking. In this action she was sustained by the conservative party of the empire, which was disturbed by the emperor's attempt to reform the administration. For the events that succeeded see a subsequent chapter.

Meanwhile one important result has come from the recent war. Li Hung Chang and the other progressive statesmen of the empire, who have long been convinced that the only hope of China lies in its being thrown open to Western science and art, have now become able to carry out their plans, the conservative opposition having seriously broken down. The result of this is seen in a dozen directions. Railroads, long almost com-

Progress in China

pletely forbidden, have now gained free "right of way," and before many years promise to traverse the country far and wide. Steamers plough their way for a thousand miles up the Yang-tse-Kiang ; engineers are busy exploiting the coal and iron mines of the Flowery Kingdom ; great factories, equipped with the best modern machinery, are springing up in the foreign settlements ; foreign books are being translated and read ; and the emperor and the dowager empress have even gone so far as to receive foreign ambassadors in public audience and on a footing of outward equality in the "forbidden city" of Peking, long the sacredly secluded centre of an empire locked against the outer world.

All this is full of significance. The defeat of China in 1895 may prove its victory, if it starts it upon a career of acceptance of Western civilization which shall, before the twentieth century has far advanced, raise it to the level of Japan. It must be borne in mind that the extraordinary progress of the island empire has been made within about forty years. China is a larger body and in consequence less easy to move, but its people are innately

What the Future May Bring to China

practical and the pressure of circumstances is forcing them forward. Within the next half century this great empire, despite its thousands of years of unchanging conditions, may take a wonderful bound in advance, and come up to Japan in the race of political and industrial development. In such a case all talk of the partition of China must cease, and it will take its place among the greatest powers of the world.

CHAPTER XXI.

The Era of Colonies.

SINCE civilization began nations have endeavored to extend their dominions, not alone by adding to their territory by the conquest of adjoining countries, but also by sending out their excess population to distant regions and founding colonies that served as aids to and feeders of the parent state. In the ancient world the active commercial nations, Phœnicia and Greece, were alert in this direction, some of their colonies,— Carthage, for instance,—becoming powerful enough to gain the status of independent states. In modern times the colonial era began with the discovery of America in 1492 and the circumnavigation of Africa immediately afterwards. Spain and Portugal, the leaders in enterprise at that period, were quick to take advantage of their discoveries, while France, Great Britain and Holland came into the field as founders of colonies at a later date.

At the opening of the nineteenth century Spain and Portugal still held the great dominions they had won. They divided between them the continent of South America, while Spain held a large section of North America, embracing the whole continent south of Canada and west of the Mississippi River, together with the peninsula of Florida. Portugal held, in addition to Brazil, large territories in east and west Africa and minor possessions elsewhere. As regards the remaining active colonizing nations,—Great Britain, France, and Holland,— **Progress in Colonization** some striking transformations had taken place. Great Britain, while late to come into the field of colonization, had shown remarkable activity and aggressiveness in this direction, robbing Holland of her settlement on the Atlantic coast of America, and depriving France of her great colonial possessions in the east and the west.

France had shown a remarkable activity in colonization. In the east she gained a strong foothold in India, which promised to expand to imperial dimensions. In the west she had settled Canada, had planted **French Activity in Founding Colonies** military posts along the great Mississippi River and claimed the vast territory beyond, and was extending into the Ohio Valley, while the British still confined themselves to a narrow strip along the Atlantic coast. The war which broke out between the English and French colonists in 1754 put an end to this grand promise.   When it ended France had lost all her possessions in America and India, Great Britain becoming heir to the whole of them with the exception of the territory west of the Mississippi, which was transferred to Spain.   As regards Holland, she had become the successor of Portugal in the east, holding immensely valuable islands in the Malayan archipelago.

The colonial dominion of Great Britain, however, suffered one great loss before the end of the eighteenth century.   It failed to recognize the spirit of Anglo-Saxon colonists, and by its tyranny in America gave rise to an insurrection which ended in the freedom of its American colonies.   It still held Canada and many of the West India Islands, but the United States was free, and by the opening of the nineteenth century had fairly begun its remarkable development.

Such was the condition of colonial affairs at the beginning of the century with which we are concerned.   Spain and Portugal still held the greatest colonial dominions upon the earth, France had lost nearly the whole of her colonies, Holland possessed the rich spice islands of the eastern seas, and Great Britain was just entering upon that activity in colonization which forms one of the striking features of nineteenth century progress.

At the close of the century a remarkable difference appears.   Spain had lost practically the whole of her vast colonial empire.   She had learned no

**Spain's Colo-
nial Decline**
lesson from England's experience with her American colonies, but maintained a policy of tyranny and oppression until these far-extended colonial provinces rose in arms and won their independence by courage and endurance.   Her great domain west of the Mississippi, transferred by treaty to France, was purchased by the United States.   Florida was sold by her to the same country, and by the end of the first quarter of the century she did not own a foot of land on the American continent.   She still held the islands of Cuba and Porto Rico in the West Indies, but her oppressive policy yielded the same result there as on the continent.   The islanders broke into rebellion, the United States came to their aid, and she lost these islands and the Philippine Islands in the East.   At the end of the century all she held were the Canary Islands and some small possessions elsewhere.

Portugal had also suffered a heavy loss in her colonial dominions, but in a very different manner.   The invasion of the home state by Napoleon's armies had caused the king and his court to set sail for Brazil, where they established an independent empire, while a new scion of the family of Braganza took Portugal for his own.   Thus, with the exception of Canada,

Guiana, and the smaller islands of the West Indies, no colonies existed in America at the end of the century, all the former colonies having become independent republics.

The active powers in colonization within the nineteenth century were the great rivals of the preceding period, Great Britain and France, though the former gained decidedly the start, and its colonial empire **The Colonial** to-day surpasses that of any other nation of mankind. It is **Development** so enormous, in fact, as to dwarf the parent kingdom, which **of Great** is related to its colonial dominion, so far as comparative size **Britain** is concerned, as the small brain of the elephant is related to its great body.

Other powers, not heard of as colonizers in the past, have recently come into this field, though too late to obtain any of the great prizes. These are Germany and Italy, the latter to a small extent. But there is a great power still to name, which in its way stands as a rival to Great Britain, the empire of Russia, whose acquisitions in Asia have grown enormous in extent. These are not colonies in the ordinary sense, but rather results of the expansion of an empire through warlike aggression, but **Other Coloniz-** they are colonial in the sense of absorbing the excess popula- **ing Powers** tion of European Russia. The great territory of Siberia was gained by Russia before the nineteenth century, but within recent years its dominion in Asia has greatly increased, and it is not easy to tell just when and where it will end.

With this preliminary review we may proceed to consider the history of colonization within the century. And first we must take up the results of the colonial enterprise of Great Britain, as much the most important of the whole. Of this story we have already described some of the leading features. A chapter has been given to the story of the Indian empire of Great Britain, far the largest of her colonial possessions, and another to that of South Africa. In addition to Hindostan, in which the **Growth of the** dominion of Great Britain now extends to Afghanistan and **British** Thibet in the north, the British colony now includes Burmah **Colonies** and the west-coast region of Indo-China, with the Straits Settlements in the Malay peninsula, and the island of Ceylon, acquired in 1802 from Holland.

In the eastern seas Great Britain possesses another colony of vast dimensions, the continental island of Australia, which, with its area of nearly 3,000,000 square miles, is three-fourths the size of Europe. The first British settlement was made here in 1788, at Port Jackson, the site of the present thriving city of Sydney, and the island was long maintained as a penal settlement, convicts being sent there as late as 1868. It was the discovery of gold in 1851 to which Australia owed its great progress. The

18

incitement of the yellow metal drew the enterprising thither by thousands,
until the population of the colony is now more than 3,000,000,
and is growing at a rapid rate, it having developed other
valuable resources besides that of gold. Of its cities, Melbourne, the capital of Victoria, has more than 300,000 population ; Sydney,
the capital of New South Wales, probably 250,000, while there are other
cities of rapid growth. Australia is the one important British colony
obtained without a war. In its human beings, as in its animals generally,
it stood at a low level of development, and it was taken possession of
without a protest from the savage inhabitants.

Australia and New Zealand

The same cannot be said of the inhabitants of New Zealand, an important group of islands lying east of Australia, which was acquired by Great
Britain as a colony in 1840. The Maoris, as the people of these islands call
themselves, are of the bold and sturdy Polynesian race, a brave, generous,
and warlike people, who have given their new lords and masters no little
trouble. A series of wars with the natives began in 1843 and continued
until 1869, since which time the colony has enjoyed peace. It can have no
more trouble with the Maoris, since there are said to be few more Maoris.
They have vanished before the " white man's face." At present this colony
is one of the most advanced politically of any region on the face of the
earth, so far as attention to the interests of the masses of the people is concerned, and its laws and regulations offer a useful object lesson to the remainder of the world.

In addition to those great island dominions in the Pacific, Great Britain
possessess the Fiji Islands, the northern part of Borneo, and a large section
of the extensive island of Papua or New Guinea, the remainder of which is
held by Holland and Germany. In addition there are various
coaling stations on the islands and coast of Asia. In the
Mediterranean its possessions are Gibraltar, Malta, and Cyprus,
and in America the great colony of Canada, a considerable number of the
islands of the West Indies, and the districts of British Honduras and British
Guiana. Of these, far the most important is Canada, to which a chapter
will be devoted farther on in our work.

Other British Colonies

We have here to deal with the colonies in two of the continents, Asia
and Africa, of which the history presents certain features of singularity.
Though known from the most ancient times, while America was quite unknown until four centuries ago, the striking fact presents itself that at the
beginning of the nineteenth century the continents of North and South
America were fairly well known from coast to centre, while the interior of
Asia and Africa remained in great part unknown. This fact in regard to

Asia was due to the hostile attitude of its people, which rendered it very dangerous for any European traveler to attempt to penetrate its interior. In the case of Africa it was due to the inhospitality of nature, which had placed the most serious obstacles in the way of those who sought **The Interior** to penetrate beyond the coast regions. This state of affairs **of Africa** continued until the latter half of the century, within which **and Asia** period there has been a remarkable change in the aspect of affairs, both continents having been penetrated in all directions and their walls of isolation completely broken down.

Africa is not only now well known, but the penetration of its interior has been followed by political changes of the most revolutionary character. It presented a virgin field for colonization, of which the land-hungry nations of Europe hastened to avail themselves, dividing up the continent between them, so that, by the end of the century, the partition of Africa was practically complete. It is one of the most remarkable circumstances in the history of the nineteenth century that a complete continent **Early Colonies** remained thus until late in the history of the world to serve as **in Africa** a new field for the outpouring of the nations. The occupation of Africa by Europeans, indeed, began earlier. The Arabs had held the section north of the Sahara for many centuries, Portugal claimed—but scarcely occupied—large sections east and west, and the Dutch had a thriving settlement in the south. But the exploration and division of the bulk of the continent waited for the nineteenth century, and the greater part of the work of partition took place within the final quarter of that century.

In this work of colonization Great Britain was, as usual, most energetic and successful, and to-day the possessions and protectorates of this active kingdom in Africa embrace 2,587,755 square miles; or, if we add Egypt and the Egyptian Soudan—practically British territory—the area occupied or claimed amounts to 2,987,755 square miles. France comes **The Partition** next, with claims covering 1,232,454 square miles. Germany **of Africa** lays claim to 920,920; Italy, to 278,500; Portugal, to 735,304; Spain, to 243,877; the Congo Free State, to 900,000; and Turkey (if Egypt be included), to 798,738 square miles. The parts of Africa unoccupied or unclaimed by Europeans are a portion of the Desert of Sahara, which no one wants; Abyssinia, still independent though in danger of absorption; and Liberia, a state over which rests the shadow of protection of the United States.

Of the British colonial possessions in Africa we have already sufficiently described that in the south, extending now from Cape Town to Lake Tanganyika, and forming an immense area, replete with natural resources, and capable of sustaining a very large future population.   On the east coast is another large acquisition, British East Africa, extending north to Abyssinia and the Soudan and west to the Congo Free State, and including part of the great Victoria Nyanza.   Further north a large slice

British Colonies in Africa

has been carved out of Somaliland, facing on the Gulf of Aden.   The remainder of this section of Africa is claimed— though very feebly held—by Italy, whose possessions include Somaliland and Eritrea, a coast district north of Abyssinia.   Great Britain, in addition, lays claim to Sierra Leone and the Ashantee country on the west coast and an extensive region facing on the Gulf of Guinea, and extending far back into the Soudan.

Next to Great Britain in activity in the acquisition of African territory comes France, which within the recent period has enormously extended its claims to territory in this continent.   Of these the most difficult in acquire- ment was Algeria, on the Mediterranean, which France first invaded in 1830, but did not obtain quiet possession of for many years and then only at the cost of long and sanguinary wars.   At a later date the adjoining

African Colonies of France

Moorish kingdom of Tunis was added, and since then the claims of France have been extended indefinitely southward, to include the greater part of the western half of the Sahara—the Atlantic coast district of the Sahara being claimed by Spain.   Of this great desert region almost the whole is useless to any nation, and France holds it mainly as a connecting link between her possessions in Algeria and the Soudan.

French Soudan has had a phenomenal growth, the French displaying the same enterprise here as they did in America in the rapid extension of their Canadian province.   Claiming, as their share in the partition of Africa, the Atlantic coast region of Senegal and an extensive district facing on the Gulf of Guinea and the South Atlantic, and known as French Congo, they have made an enormous spread, northward from the latter, westward from Sene- gal, and southward from Algeria, until now their claims cover nearly the whole of the Soudan—a vast belt of territory stretching from the Atlantic nearly across the continent and bordering on the Egyptian Soudan in the east.   The French claim, indeed, extended as far as the Nile, being based on Major Marchand's journey to the river in 1898.   But the English con- quests in that region barred out the French claim, and it has been abandoned. In addition to the territories here named, France has taken possession of a portion of the coast region of Abyssinia, between the Italian and the British regions, and completely shutting out that ancient kingdom from the sea.

The latest of the nations to develop the colonizing spirit were Italy and Germany.   We have described Italy's share in Africa.   Germany's is far larger and more imporant. In East Africa it holds a large and valuable region of territory, on the Zanzibar coast, between British East Africa and Portuguese Mozambique, and extending westward to German and Lake Nyassa and Tanganyika and the Congo Free State, Italian and northward to the Victoria Nyanza. It cuts off British Colonies territory from an extension throughout the whole length of Africa, and if Cecil Rhodes' Cairo to Cape Town Railway is ever completed, some hundreds of miles of it will have to run through German territory.

In South Africa Germany has seized upon a broad region left unclaimed by Great Britain, the Atlantic coast section of Damaraland and Great Namaqualand, and also an extensive section on the right of the Gulf of Guinea, stretching inward like a wedge between British and French possessions in this region. On the Gold Coast it has also a minor territory, lying between British Ashantee and French Dahomey.

The broad interior of the continent, the mighty plateau region watered by the great Congo River and its innumerable affluents, first traversed by the daring Stanley not many years in the past, has been The Congo erected into the extensive and promising Congo Free State, Free State under the suzerainty of the king of Belgium. It is the most populous and agriculturally the richest section of Africa, while its remarkable extension of navigable waters gives uninterrupted communication through its every part. It has probably before it a great future.

Off the east coast of Africa lies the great island of Madagascar, now a French territory. France has had military posts on its coast for more than two hundred years, and in 1883 began the series of wars The French which resulted in the conquest of the island. The principal Conquest of war of invasion began in 1895 and ended in a complete over- Madagascar throw of the native government, Madagascar being declared a French colony in June, 1896.

Of these European possessions in Africa, all are held with a strong hand except those of Portugal, which unprogressive state may soon give up all claim to her territories of Angola and Mozambique. Great Britain and Germany have been negotiating with Portugal for the purchase of these territories—to be divided between them. But the Boer War has seriously interfered with this negotiation, and Great Britain's desire to gain possession of the Portuguese harbor of Delagoa Bay seems unlikely to be realized. Wars in Africa

This division of Africa between the European nations, with the subsequent taking possession of the acquired territories, has not been accomplished without war and bloodshed; England, France, and Italy having had to fight hard to establish their claims. In only two sections, Abyssinia and the Egyptian Soudan, have the natives been able to drive out their invaders, and the wars in these regions call for some fuller notice.

The first war in Abyssinia occurred in 1867, when England, irritated by an arbitrary action of the Emperor Theodore, declared war against him, and invaded his rocky and difficult country. The war ended in the conquest of Magdala and the death of Theodore. In 1889 Italy aided Menelek in gaining the throne, and was granted the large district of Eritrea on the Red

Defeat of the Italians in Abyssinia Sea, with a nominal protectorate over the whole kingdom. Subsequently Menelek repudiated the treaty, and in 1894 the Italians invaded his kingdom. For a time they were successful, but in March, 1896, the Italian army met with a most disastrous defeat, and in the treaty that followed Italy was compelled to acknowledge the complete independence of Abyssinia. It was the one case in Africa in which the natives were able to hold their own against the ambitious nations of Europe.

In Egypt they did so for a time, and a brief description of the recent history of this important kingdom seems of interest. Egypt broke loose in large measure from the rule of Turkey during the reign of the able and ambitious Mehemet Ali, who was made viceroy in 1840. In 1876 the independence of Egypt was much increased, and its rulers were given the title of khedive, or king. The powers of the khedives steadily increased, and in

The Expansion of Egypt 1874-75 Ismail Pasha greatly extended the Egyptian territory, annexing the Soudan as far as Darfur, and finally to the shores of the lately discovered Victoria Nyanza. Egypt thus embraced the valley of the Nile practically to its source, presenting an aspect of immense length and great narrowness.

Soon after, the finances of the country became so involved that they were placed under European control, and the growth of English and French influence led to the revolt of Arabi Pasha in 1879. This was repressed by Great Britain, which bombarded Alexandria and defeated the Egyptians, France taking no part. As a result the controlling influence of France ended, and Great Britain became the practical ruler of Egypt, which position she still maintains.

In 1880 began an important series of events. A Mohammedan prophet arose in the Soudan, claiming to be the Mahdi, a Messiah of the Mussulmans.

The Rise of the Mahdi A large body of devoted believers soon gathered around him, and he set up an independent sultanate in the desert, defeating four Egyptian expeditions sent against him, and capturing El Obeid, the chief city of Kordofan, which he made his capital in 1883.

Then against him Great Britain dispatched an army of British and Egyptian soldiers, under an English leader styled in Egypt Hicks Pasha. These advanced to El Obeid, where they fell into an ambush prepared by the Mahdists, and, after a desperate struggle, lasting three days, were almost completely annihilated, scarcely a man escaping to tell the disastrous tale. "General Hicks," said a newspaper correspondent, "charged at the head of staff. They galloped towards a sheikh, supposed by the The Massacre of Egyptians to be the Mahdi. Hicks rushed on him with his **Hicks Pasha** sword and cut his face and arm; this man had on a Darfur **and His Army** steel mail-shirt. Just then a club thrown struck General Hicks on the head and unhorsed him. The chargers of the staff were speared but the English officers fought on foot till all were killed. Hicks was the last to die."

Other expeditions of Egyptians troops sent against Osman Digna ("Osman the Ugly"), the lieutenant of the Mahdi in the Eastern Soudan, met with a similar fate, while the towns of Sinkat and Tokar were invested by the Mahdists. To relieve these towns Baker Pasha advanced with a force of 3,650 men. There was no more daring or accomplished officer in the British army than Valentine Baker, but his expedition met with the same fate as that of his predecessor. Advancing into the desert from Trinkitat, a town some distance south of Suakim, on the Red Sea, the force was met by a body of Mahdists, and the Egyptian soldiers at once broke into a panic of terror. The Mahdists were only some 1,200 strong, but they surrounded and butchered the unresisting Egyptians in a frightful slaughter.

"Inside the square," said an eyewitness, "the state of affairs was almost indescribable. Cavalry, infantry, mules, camels, falling baggage and dying men were crushed into a struggling, surging mass. The Egyptians were shrieking madly, hardly attempting to run **The Battles** away, but trying to shelter themselves one behind another." **Near Suakim** "The conduct of the Egyptians was simply disgraceful," said another officer. "Armed with rifle and bayonet, they allowed themselves to be slaughtered, without an effort at self-defence, by savages inferior to them in numbers and armed only with spears and swords."

Baker and his staff officers, seeing that affairs were hopeless, charged the enemy and cut their way through to the shore, but of the total force two-thirds were left dead or wounded on the field. Such was the "massacre" of El Teb, which was followed four days afterwards by the capture of Sinkat and slaughter of its garrison. This butchery was soon after avenged. General Graham was sent from Cairo with reinforcements of British troops, which advanced on Osman's position, and in two bloody engagements subjected him to disastrous defeat. The last victory was a crushing one, the total British loss being about 200, while, of the Arab loss, the killed alone numbered over 2,000.

In the same year in which these events took place (1884) General Charles Gordon—Chinese Gordon, as he was called, from his memorable exploits in the Flowery Kingdom—advanced by the Nile to Khartoum, the

Gordon Goes to Khartoum

far-off capital of the Mohammedan Soudan, of which he had been governor-general in former years. His purpose was to relieve the Egyptian garrison of that city—in which design he failed. In fact, the Arabs of the Soudan flocked in such multitudes to the standard of the Mahdi that Khartoum was soon cut off from all communication with the country to the north, and Gordon and the garrison were left in a position of dire peril. It was determined to send an expedition to his relief, and this was organized under the leadership of Lord Wolseley, the victor in the Ashantee and Zulu wars.

The expedition was divided into two sections, a desert column which was to cross a sandy stretch of land with the aid of camels, from Korti to Metamneh, on the Nile, thus cutting off a wide loop in the stream ; and a river column for whose transportation a flotilla of 800 whale boats was sent out from England. The desert column found its route strongly disputed.

To the Rescue of Gordon

On the 7th of January, 1885, it was attacked by the Arabs in overwhelming force and fighting with the ferocity of tigers, some 5,000 of them attacking the 1,500 British drawn up in square, round which the fanatical Mahdists raged like storm-driven waves. The peril was imminent. Among those who fell on the British side was Colonel Burnaby, the famous traveler. The battle was a remarkably brief one, the impetuous rush of the Arabs being repulsed in about five minutes of heroic effort, during which there was imminent danger of their penetrating the square and making an end of the British troops. As it was the Arabs lost

The Desert Fights

1,100 in dead and a large number of wounded, the British less than 200 in all. A few days afterwards the Arabs attacked again, but as before were repulsed with heavy loss. On the 19th of January the river was reached, and the weary troops bivouacked on its banks.

Here they were met by four steamers which Gordon had sent down the Nile, after plating their hulls with iron as a protection against Arab bullets. Various circumstances now caused delay, and several days passed before General Wilson, in command of the expedition, felt it safe to advance on Khartoum. At length, on January 24th, two of the steamers, with a small force of troops, set out up the river, but met with so many obstacles that it was the 28th before they came within sight of the distant towers of Khartoum. From the bank came a shout to the effect that Khartoum had been taken and Gordon killed two days before. As they drew nearer there came evidence that the announcement was true. No British flag was seen flying ; not a shot came from the shore in aid of the steamers. Masses of the enemy could be seen in all directions. A storm of musketry beat like hail on the iron sides of the boats. Wilson, believing the attempt hopeless, gave the order to turn and run at full speed down the river. They did so amid a rattle of bullets and bursting of shells from the artillery of the enemy.

The news they brought was true. The gallant Gordon was indeed dead. The exact events that took place are not known. Some attributed the fall of the town to the act of a traitor, some to the storming of the gates. It does not matter now ; it is enough to know that the famous Christian soldier had been killed with all his **Death of General Gordon** men—about 4,000 persons being slaughtered, in a massacre that continued for six hours. That was the end of it. The British soon after withdrew and left Khartoum and the Soudan in the undisputed possession of the Arabs. The Mahdi had been victorious, though he did not live long to enjoy his triumph, he dying some months later.

And so matters were left for nearly twelve years, when the British government, having arranged affairs in Egypt to its liking, and put the country in a prosperous condition, decided to attempt the reconquest of the Soudan, and avenge the slaughtered Gordon. An expedition was sent out in 1896, which captured Dongola in September and defeated the dervish force in several engagements. The progress continued, slowly but surely, up the Nile. In 1897 other advantages were gained. But it was not until 1898 that the Anglo-Egyptian force, under Sir Herbert Kitchener, known under his Egyptian title of the Sirdar, reached the vicinity of Khartoum. The Egyptian soldiers under him were of other **The Advance of the British and Recapture of the Soudan** stuff than those commanded by Baker Pasha. From a mob with arms in hand they had been drilled into brave and steady soldiers, quite capable of giving a good account of themselves. At Omdurman, near Khartoum, the dervishes were met in force and a fierce and final battle was fought. The Arabs suffered a crushing defeat, losing more than 10,000 men, while the British loss was only about 200. This brilliant victory ended the war on the Nile. The fight was taken out of the Arabs. The Soudan was restored to Egypt by British arms, fourteen years after it had been lost to the Mahdi.

Asia has been invaded by the nations of civilization almost as actively as Africa, and to-day, aside from the Chinese and Japanese Empires, far the greater part of that vast continent is under foreign control, the only important independent sections being Turkey, Arabia, Persia, and Afghanistan. As matters now look, all of these, China included, before the twentieth century is very old may be in European hands, and the partition of Asia become as complete as that of Africa. The nations active in this work have been Great Britain, Russia, and France, while Holland is in possession of Java, Sumatra, and others of the valuable spice islands of the eastern seas. Of the enterprise of Great Britain in extending her colonial dominion in Hindostan and Burmah we have already spoken. The enterprise of France here demands attention.

The Partition of Asia

France has always been remarkably active in her colonizing enterprises. In America she surpassed Great Britain in the rapid extension of her dominion, though she fell far behind in the solidity of her settlements. It has been the same in Africa. France has spread out with extraordinary rapidity over the Soudan, while England has moved much more slowly but far more surely. The enterprises of the one are brilliant, those of the other are solid, and it is the firmness with which the Anglo-Saxon race takes hold that makes it to-day the dominant power on the earth. The French have the faculty of assimilating themselves with foreign peoples, accepting their manners and customs and becoming their friends and allies. The British, on the contrary, are too apt to treat their colonial subjects as inferior beings, but they combine their haughtiness with justice, and win respect at the same time as they inspire distrust and fear.

French and British Methods of Colonization

The colonizing enterprise of France in Asia, after the French had been ousted from India by Great Britain, directed itself to the peninsula of Indo-China. This was the only region of the Asiatic coast land which was at once safe to meddle with and worth the cost and trouble. In 1789 the emperor of Annam accepted French aid in the conquest of the adjoining states of Cochin China and Tonquin. The wedge of French influence, thus entered, was not removed. Missionaries sought those far-off realms, and in time found themselves cruelly treated by the natives. As usual in such cases, this formed a pretext for invasion and annexation, and in 1862 a portion of Cochin China was seized upon by France, the remainder being annexed in 1867. Meanwhile, in 1863, the "protection" of France was extended over the neighboring state of Cambodia.

Operations of France in Indo-China

North of Cochin China lies Annam, and farther north, bordering on China, is the province of Tonquin, inhabited largely by Chinese. The four states mentioned constitute the eastern half of Indo-China. The western portion is formed by the kingdom of Burmah, now a British possession. Between these lies the contracted kingdom of Siam, the only portion of the peninsula that retains its independence.

The attention of France was next directed to Tonquin, the northern province of the Annamite Empire, which was invaded in 1873, and its capital city, Hanoi, captured. Here the French found foeman worthy of their steel. After the suppression of the Taiping rebellion in China certain bands of the rebels took refuge in Tonquin, where they won themselves a new home by force of arms, and in 1868 held the valley of the Red River as far south as Hanoi. These, known as the " Black Flags," were bold, restless, daring desperadoes, who made the conquest of the country a difficult task for the French. By their aid the invading French were driven from Hanoi and forced back in defeat.

The Black Flags

The French resumed their work of conquest in 1882, again taking the city of Hanoi, and in December, 1883, a strong expedition advanced up the Red River against the stronghold of Sontay, which, with the neighboring Bac Ninh, was looked upon, in a military sense, as the key to Tonquin. The enterprise seemed a desperate one, the expeditionary force consisting of but 6,000 soldiers and 1,350 coolies, while behind the strong works of the place were 25,000 armed men, of whom 10,000 were composed of the valiant Black Flags. But cannon served the place of men. The river defences were battered down and preparations made to storm the citadel. During the succeeding night, however, the French ran imminent risk of a disastrous repulse. At one o'clock at night, when all but the sentries were locked in slumber, a sudden shower of rockets was poured on the thatched roofs of the huts in which the soldiers lay asleep, and with savage yells the Chinese rushed from their gates and into the heart of the camp, firing briskly as they came. The French troops, fatigued with the hard fighting of the preceding day, and demoralized by the suddenness of the attack and the pluck and persistent energy of the assailants, were thrown almost into panic, and were ready to give way when the Chinese trumpets sounded the recall and the enemy drew off. As it appeared afterwards this attack was made by only 300 men. It would undoubtedly have stampeded the invading forces but for the vigilance of the sentinels.

The Siege of Sontay

A Night Attack

On the next day, December 16th, the fort was stormed, and taken after a desperate resistance. There is but one incident of the assault that we need relate. As the French rushed across the bridge that spanned the wide ditch and approached the gate of the citadel, there was seen an instance of cool and devoted bravery hardly excelled by that which was displayed by the famous " captain of the gate " who held the Tiber bridge against the Tuscan host. There, told off to guard the narrow passage between the stockade and the wall, stood a gallant Black Flag soldier. His Winchester repeating rifle was in his hand, its magazine filled with cartridges. Although half the French force were at the gate, he quailed not. Shot after shot he fired, deliberately and calmly, and each bullet found its billet. Down went brave Captain Méhl, leader of the Foreign Legion, with a ball through his heart, and other attackers were slain ; and when the stormers rushed in at last the heroic Black Flag, true to his trust, died with his face to the foe, as a soldier should die. The French, quick to recognize bravery either in friend or enemy, buried him with military honors when the day's fight was over, at the gate which he defended so well.

The Storming of the Citadel

The capture of this town, followed by that of Bac-Ninh, which was similarly taken by storm, completed the work of conquest and firmly established the French in their occupation of Tonquin.

They had, however, still the Chinese to deal with. China claimed a suzerainty over this region and protested against the French invasion, and in 1885 went to war for the expulsion of the foreign conquerors. During the previous year the Black Flags had engaged in murderous raids on the French mission stations, in which they massacred nearly 10,000 native Christians. In the war with China, they, with other Chinese troops, held the passes above Tuyen-Kivan for nearly a month against repeated assaults by the French, and were still in possession of their posts when peace was declared. China had yielded the country to France.

France in Possession

In 1895 France gained the right to extend a railway from Annam into China, a concession which was protested against by Great Britain, then in possession of the adjoining province. In 1896 a treaty was made between these two powers, which fixed the Mekong or Cambodia River as their dividing line. As a result those powers now hold all of Indo-China except the much diminished kingdom of Siam. France has permitted the form of the old government to continue, the Emperor of Annam still reigning— though he does not rule, since the real power is in the hands of the French governor-general at Hanoi.

While Great Britain and France were thus establishing themselves in the south, Russia was engaged in the conquest of the north and centre of the continent. The immense province of Siberia, crossing the whole width of the continent in the north, was acquired by Russia in the seventeenth century, after which the progress of Russia in Asia ceased until the nineteenth century, within which the territory of the Muscovite empire in that continent has been very greatly extended. Two provinces were wrested from Persia in 1828, as the prize of a victorious war, and in 1859 the conquest of the region of the Caucasus was completed **The Advance of Russia in Asia** by the capture of the heroic Schamyl. In 1858 the left bank of the great Amur River was gained by treaty with China, after having been occupied by force.

Soon after this period, Russia began the work of conquest in the region of Turkestan, that long-mysterious section of Central Asia, inhabited in part by fierce desert nomads, who for centuries made Persia the spoil of their devastating raids, and in part by intolerant settled tribes, among whom no Christian dared venture except at risk of his life. It remained in great measure a *terra incognita* until the Russians forced their way into it arms in hand.

The southern border of Siberia was gradually extended downward over the great region of the Mongolian steppes until the northern limits of Turkestan were reached, and in 1864 Russia invaded this region, sub-duing the oasis of Tashkend after a fierce war. In 1868 the march of invasion reached Bokhara, and in 1873 the oasis of Khiva was conquered and annexed. In 1875–76 Khokand was con- **The Invasion of Turkestan** quered after a fierce war, and annexed to Russia. This completed the acquisition of the fertile provinces of Turkestan, but the fierce nomads of the desert remained unsubdued, and the oasis of Merv and the country of the warlike Tekke Turcomans were still to conquer. This, which was accomplished in 1880–81, merits a fuller description.

A broad belt of desert lands stretches across the continent of Asia from Arabia, in the southwest, to the rainless highlands of Gobi, or Shamo, in the far east. This desert zone is here and there broken by a tract of steppe land that is covered with grass for a portion of the year, while more rarely a large oasis is formed where the rivers and streams, descending from a mountain range, supply water to a fertile region, before losing them-selves in the sands of the desert beyond.

Eastward of the Caspian, and south of the Aral, much of the waste land is a salt desert, and the shells, mixed with the surface sand, afford further evidence that it was in times not very remote part of the bottom of a large inland sea, of which the land- **The Deserts of Central Asia** locked waters of Western Asia are a survival.

Along the Caspian the steppe and desert sink gradually to the water-level, and the margins of the sea are so shallow that, except where extensive dredging works have been carried out, and long jetties constructed, ships have to discharge their cargoes into barges two or three miles from the shore.

This desert region marked for many years the southern limit of the Russian empire in Central Asia. A barren waste is a more formidable obstacle to an European army than the ocean itself; and the Turkoman tribes of the oases not only refused to acknowledge the dominion of the White Czar, but successfully raided up to the very gates of his border forts in the spring, when the grass of the steppe afforded forage for their horses. The first successful advance across the desert zone was made by Kaufmann, whose expeditions followed the belt of fertile land which breaks the desert where the Amu Daria (the Oxus of classical times) flows down from the central highlands of Asia to the great lake of the Aral Sea. But in 1878 the Russians began another series of conquests, starting not from their forts on the Oxus, but from their new ports on the southwestern shore of the Caspian.

In this direction the most powerful of the Turkoman tribes were the Tekkes of the Akhal oasis. Between their strongholds and the Caspian there was a desert nearly 150 miles wide, and then the ridge of the Kopet Dagh Mountains. The desert, which stretches from the northern shore of the Atrek River, is partly sandy waste, partly a tract of barren clayey land, baked hard by the sun; broken by cracks and crevices in the dry season, and like a half-flooded brickfield when it rains. The water of the river is scanty, and not good to drink. It flows in a deep channel between steep banks, and so closely does the desert approach it that for miles one might ride within a hundred yards of its clay-banked cañon without suspecting that water was so near. Where the Sumber River runs into the Atrek the Russians had an advanced post— the earthwork fort of Tchad, with its eight-gun battery. Following the Sumber, one enters the arid valleys on the south of the Kopet Dagh range. On this side the slopes rise gradually; on the other side of the ridge there is a sharp descent, and sometimes the mountains form for miles a line of precipitous rocky walls. At the foot of this natural rampart lay the fortified villages of the Tekke Turkomans.

Numerous streams descend from the Kopet Dagh, flowing to the northeastward, and after a few miles losing themselves in the sands of the Kara Kum desert. Between the mountain wall and the desert the ground thus watered forms a long, narrow oasis—the land of Akhal—to which a local Mussulman tradition says that Adam betook himself when he was driven forth from Eden. No doubt much of the praise that has been given to the beauty and fertility of this three-hundred-mile strip of well-watered garden ground comes from the contrast between its green enclosures and the endless waste that closes in the horizon to the north-eastward. Corn and maize, cotton and wool, form part of the wealth of its people. They had the finest horses of all Turkestan, and great herds and flocks of cattle, sheep and camels. **The Herds and** The streams turned numerous mills, and were led by a net- **Villages of** work of tunnels and conduits through the fields and garden. **the Tekkes** The villages were mud-walled quadrangles, with an inner enclosure for the cattle ; the kibitkas, or tents, and the mud huts of the Tekkes filling the space between the inner and outer walls, and straggling outside in temporary camps that could be rapidly cleared away in war time. The people were over 100,000 strong—perhaps 140,000 in all—men, women and children. They were united in a loose confederacy, acknowledged the lordship of the Khan of Merv, who had come from one of their own villages. They raided the Russian and Persian borders successfully, these plundering expeditions filling up the part of the year when they were not busy with more peaceful occupations. Along their fertile strip of land ran the caravan track from Merv by Askabad to Kizil Arvat and the Caspian, and when they were not at war the Tekkes had thus an outlet for their surplus productions, among which were beautiful car- **The Akhal** pets, the handiwork of their women. In war they had proved **Warriors** themselves formidable to all their neighbors. United with the warriors of Merv, the men of Akhal had cut to pieces a Khivan army in 1855 and a host of Persians in 1861.

The conquest of Akhal had long been a subject of Russian ambition. It was not merely that they were anxious to put an end once for all to the raids of the Turkomans of the great oasis, but they regarded the possession of this region as a great step towards the consolidation of their power in Asia. From Baku, the terminus of their railways in the Caucasus, it was easy to ferry troops across the Caspian. What they wanted was a secure road from some port on its eastern shore to their provinces on the Upper Oxus, and anyone who knew the country must have felt that this road would eventually run through the Akhal and the Merv oases.

The first effort to subdue the Akhal warriors proved a **Repulse of** complete failure. As soon as peace was concluded with **Lomakine** Turkey, after the war of 1877-78, General Lomakine was **and the** **Russians** sent with a strong force to the Caspian, whence he made his way by the caravan route over the desert to the strong nomade fortress of Geok Tepe ("blue hills"), at the foot of the mountain range mentioned. We shall say nothing more concerning this expedition than that the attempt to take the fort by storm proved a complete failure, and the Russians were forced to retreat in disorder.

To retrieve this disaster General Skobeleff, the most daring of the Russian generals, who had gained great glory in the siege of Plevna, was selected, and set out in 1880. On the 1st of January, 1881, he came in sight of the fort, with an army of 10,000 picked troops, and fifty-four cannon. Behind the clay ramparts lay awaiting him from 20,000 to 30,000 of valiant nomades, filled with the pride of their recent victory. The first bat-

Skobeleff and the Siege of Geok Tepe teries opened fire on the 8th, and the siege works were pushed so rapidly forward that the Russians had gained all the outworks by the 17th. This steady progress was depressing to the Turkomans, who were not used to such a method of fighting. The cannonade continued resistlessly, the wall being breached on the 23d and the assault fixed for the next day. Two mines had been driven under the rampart, one charged with gun-powder and one with dynamite, and all was ready for the desperate work of the storming parties.

Early the next day all the Russian guns opened upon the walls, and a false attack was made on the west side of the fort, the men firing incessantly to distract the attention of the Turkomans, while the actual column of attack was formed and held ready on the east. Another column, 2,000 strong, waited opposite the south angle, the soldiers ready and eager for the assault.

A little after eleven the mines were fired. The explosion caused momentary panic among the garrison, and in the midst of the confusion the two storming columns rushed for the breaches. But before they could climb

The Fort Carried by Storm the heaps of smoking *débris* the Tekkes were back at their posts, and it was through a sharp fire of rifles and muskets that the Russians pushed in through the first line of defence. The fight in and around the breaches was a close and desperate struggle; but as the stormers in front fell, others clambered up to replace them, and at the same time Haidaroff, converting his false attack into a real one escaladed the southern wall.

"No quarter!" had been the shout of the Russian officers as they dashed forward at the head of the stormers. The Tekkes expected none. They

A Frightful Massacre fought in desperate knots, back to back, among the huts and tents of the town, but at last they were driven out by the east side. Skobeleff did not make Lomakine's mistake of blocking their way. He let them go; but once they were out on the plain the Cossack cavalry was launched in wild pursuit, and for ten long miles sword and spear drank deep of the blood of the fugitives. Women as well as men were cut down or speared as the horses overtook them. More than 8,000 Tekkes fell in the pursuit. Asked a year after if this was true, Skobeleff said that he had the slain counted, and that it was so. Six thousand five hundred bodies were buried inside the fortress; eight thousand more strewed the ten miles of the plain.

Skobeleff looked on the massacre as a necessary element in the conquest of Geok Tepe. "I hold it as a principle," he said, "that in Asia the duration of peace is in direct proportion to the slaughter you inflict on the enemy. The harder you hit them the longer they will keep quiet after it." No women, he added, were killed by the troops under his immediate command, and he set at liberty 700 Persian women who were captives in Geok Tepe. After ten miles the pursuit was stopped. There was no further resistance. Not a shot was fired on either side after that terrible day. The chiefs came in and surrendered. The other towns in the eastern part of the oasis were occupied without fighting; nay, more, within a month of Geok Tepe Skobeleff was able to go without a guard into the midst of the very men who had fought against him. We in America **Submission of the Turkomans** cannot understand the calm submission with which the Asiatic accepts as the decree of fate the rule of the conqueror whose hand has been heavy upon him and his. The crumbling ramparts of Geok Tepe remain a memorial of the years of warfare which it cost the Russians, and the iron track on which the trains steam past the ruined fortress shows how complete has been the victory.

Skobeleff looked upon his triumph as only the first step to further conquests. But within eighteen months of the storming of Geok Tepe he died suddenly at Moscow. Others have built on the foundations which he laid; and, for good or ill, the advance which began with the subjugation of the Tekke Turkomans has now brought the Russian outposts in Central Asia in sight of the passes that lead across the mountain barriers of the Indian frontier.

This conquest was quickly followed by the laying of a railroad across the desert, from the Caspian to the sacred Mohammedan city of Samarcand, the former capital of the terrible Timur the Tartar, and the iron horse now penetrates freely into the heart of that once unknown land, its shrill whistle perhaps disturbing Timur in his tomb. Across the broad stretch of Siberia another railroad is being rapidly laid, and extended downward through Manchuria to the borders of China, a stupendous enterpise, the road being thousands of miles in length. Manchuria, the native land of the Chinese emperors, is now held firmly by Russia, and the ancient empire of Persia, on the southern border of Turkestan, is threatened with absorption. When and where the advance of Russia in Asia will end no man can say, **Great Development of Russia in Asia** perhaps not until Hindostan is torn from British hands and the empire of the north has reached the southern sea. While Russia in Europe comprises about 2,000,000 square miles, Russia in Asia has attained an area of 6,564,778 square miles, and the total area of this colossal empire is nearly equal to that of the entire continent of North America.

The final step in colonization—if we may call it by this name—belongs to the United States, which at the end of the century laid its hand on two island groups of the Eastern Seas, acquiring Hawaii by peaceful annexation and the Philippine Islands by warlike invasion. What will be the result of this acquisition on the future of the United States it is impossible to say, but it brings the American border close to China, and when the destiny of that great empire is settled, the republic of the West may have something to say.

At the end of the nineteenth century the work of the colonizing powers was fairly at an end. Nearly all the available territory of the earth had **The Future of Colonizing Enterprise** been entered upon and occupied. But the work, while in this sense completed, was in a fuller sense only begun. It was left for the twentieth century for those great tracts of the earth to be brought properly under the dominion of civilization, their abundant resources developed, peace and prosperity brought to their fertile soils, and their long turbulent population taught the arts of peaceful progress and civilized industry.

CHAPTER XXII.

How the United States Entered the Century.

HITHERTO our attention has been directed to the Eastern Hemisphere, and to the stirring events of nineteenth century history in that great section of the earth. But beyond the ocean, in North America, a greater event, one filled with more promise for mankind, one destined to loom larger on the horizon of time, was meanwhile taking place, the development of the noble commonwealth of the United States of America. To this far-extending Republic of the West, a nation almost solely an outgrowth of the nineteenth century, our attention The Great needs now to be turned. Its history is one full of great steps Republic of of progress, illuminated by a hundred events of the highest the West promise and significance, and it stands to-day as a beacon light of national progress and human liberty to the world, "the land of the brave and the home of the free."

A hundred years ago the giant here described was but a babe, a new-born nation just beginning to feel the strength of its limbs. It is with this section of its history that we are here concerned, its days of origin and childhood. Two events of extraordinary significance in human history rise before us in the final quarter of the eighteenth century, the French Revolution and the American Declaration of Independence and its results. The first of these revolutionary events we have dealt with; the second remains to be presented.

There is one circumstance that impresses us most strongly in this great event, the remarkable group of able men who laid the foundation of the American commonwealth. Among those whose hands gave The Great Men the first impulse to the ship of state were men of such noble who Founded proportions as George Washington, the greatest man of the our Nation century not only in America but in the whole world; Benjamin Franklin, who came closely to the level of Washington in another field of human greatness; Patrick Henry, whose masterpieces of oratory still stir the soul like trumpet-blasts; Thomas Jefferson, to whose genius we owe the inimitable "Declaration of Independence;" Thomas Paine, whose pen had the point of a sword and the strength of an army; John Paul Jones, the hero of the most brilliant feat of daring in the whole era of naval warfare, and Alexander Hamilton, whose financial genius saved the infant state in one of the most critical moments of its career.   These were not the whole of that surpassing coterie, but simply in their special fields the greatest, and it is doubtful if the earth ever saw an abler group of statesmen than those to whom we owe the Constitution of the United States.

It is not our purpose to tell the story of the American Revolution. That lies back of the borders of time within which this work is confined. But some brief statement of its results is in order, as an introduction to the nineteenth century record of the United States.

It was a country in almost an expiring state when it emerged from the fierce death struggle of the Revolution.   It had been swept by

Weakness of the States After the Revolution
fire and sword, its resources destroyed, its industries ruined, its government financially bankrupt, its organization in a state of tottering weakness, little left it but the courage of its people and the aspirations of its leaders.   But in courage and aspiration safety and progress lie, and with those for its motive forces the future of the country was assured.

The weakness spoken of was not the only or the worst weakness with which the new community had to contend.   Though named the United States, its chief danger lay in its lack of union.   The thirteen recent colonies—now states—were combined only by the feeblest of bonds, one calculated to carry them through an emergency, not to hold them together under all the contingencies of human affairs.   Practically they were thirteen distinct nations, not one close union ; a group of communities with a few ties of common self-interest, but otherwise disunited and distinct.

"Articles of Confederation and Perpetual Union" had been adopted in 1777 and ratified by the agreement of all the states in 1781.   But the Confederation was not a union.   Each state claimed to be a sovereign commonwealth, and little power was given to the central government.   The

The Articles of Confederation
weak point in the Articles of Confederation was that they gave Congress no power to lay taxes or to levy soldiers.   It could merely ask the states for men and money, but must wait till they were ready to give them—if they chose to do so at all.   It could make treaties, but could not enforce them ; could borrow money, but could not repay it ; could make war, but could not force a man to join its armies ; could recommend, but had no power to act.

The states proposed to remain independent except in minor particulars. They were jealous of one another and of the general Congress.   "We are," said Washington, "one nation to-day and thirteen to-morrow."   That well expressed the state of the case; no true union existed; the states were free to join hands more closely or to drift more widely asunder.

The time from the revolt against the stamp duties in 1775 to the inauguration in 1789 of the National Government under which we live has been called the critical period of American history. It was a period which displayed the inexperience of the Americans in sound financiering. There is hardly an evil in finances that cannot be illustrated by some event in American affairs at that time. The Americans began the war without any preparation, they conducted it on credit, and at the end of fourteen years three millions of people were five hundred millions of dollars or more in debt. The exact amount will never be known. Congress and the State Legislatures issued paper currency in unlimited quantities and upon no security. The Americans were deceived themselves in believing that their products were essential to the welfare of Europe, and that all European nations would speedily make overtures to them for **False Ideas in Finance** the control of American commerce. It may be said that the Americans wholly over-estimated their importance in the world at that time; they thought that to cut off England from American commerce would ruin England; they thought that the bestowal of their commerce upon France would enrich France so much that the French king, for so inestimable a privilege, could well afford to loan them, and even to give them, money.

The doctrine of the rights of man ran riot in America. Paper currency became the infatuation of the day. It was thought that paper currency would meet all the demands for money, would win American independence. Even so practical a man as Franklin, then in France, said: "This effect of paper currency is not understood on this side the water; and, indeed, the whole is a mystery even to the politicians, how we have been able to continue a war four years without money, and how we could pay with paper that had no previously fixed fund appropriated specifically to redeem it. This currency, as we manage it, is a wonderful machine: it performs its office when we issue it; it pays and clothes troops and provides victuals and ammunition, and when we are obliged to issue a quantity excessive, it pays itself off by depreciation."

If the taxing power is the most august power in government, the abuse of the taxing power is the most serious sin government can commit. No one will deny that the Americans were guilty of committing most grievous financial offenses during the critical period of their history. They abused liberty by demanding and by exercising the rights of nationality and at the same time neglecting or refusing to burden themselves with the taxation necessary to support nationality.

The inability of the Congress of the Confederation to legislate under the provisions of the Articles compelled their amendment; for while the exigencies of war had forced the colonies into closer union,—a "perpetual

Constitutions of Colonies and Confederated States

league of friendship,"—they had also learned additional lessons in the theory and administration of local government; for each of the colonies, with the exception of Connecticut and Rhode Island, had transformed colonial government into government under a constitution. The people had not looked to Congress as a central power; they considered it as a central committee of the States. The individualistic tendencies of the colonies strengthened when the colonies transformed themselves into commonwealths.

The struggle, which began between the thirteen colonies and the imperial Parliament, was now transformed into a struggle between two tendencies in America, the tendency toward sovereign commonwealths and the tendency toward nationality. The first commonwealth constitutions did not acknowledge the supreme authority of Congress; there was yet lacking that essential bond between the people and their general government, the power of the general government to address itself directly to individuals. Interstate relations in 1787 were scarcely more perfect than they had been fifteen years before. The understanding of American affairs was more common, but intimate political association between the commonwealths was still unknown. The liberty of nationality had not yet been won. A peculiar tendency in American affairs from their beginning is seen in the succession of written constitutions, instruments peculiar to America. The commonwealths of the old Confederation demonstrated the necessity for a clearer definition of their relations to each other and of the association of the American people in nationality.

A sense of the necessity for commercial integrity led to the calling of the Philadelphia Convention to amend the old Articles, but when the Convention assembled it was found that an adequate solution of the large problem of nationality could not be found in an amendment of the old "Articles of Confederation," but called for a new and more vigorous Con-

The Constitutional Convention and its Work

stitution. This Convention combined the associated states into a strongly united nation, possessed of all the powers of nationality, civil, financial and military. It organized a tripartite government, consisting of Supreme Executive, Supreme Legislative, and Supreme Judicial departments, each with all the power "necessary to make it feared and respected." While the Upper House of Congress still represented the states as separate commonwealths, the Lower House represented the people as individuals; it standing, not for a group of distinct communities, but for a nation of people. And to this House was given the sole power "to lay and collect taxes, duties, imposts and excises, and to pay the debt, and provide for the common defence and general welfare of the United States."

With this Constitution the United States of America first came into existence; a strong, energetic and capable nation; its government possessed of all the powers necessary to the full control of the states, and full ability to make itself respected abroad; its people possessed of all the civil rights yet known or demanded.

Yet the people, in their political privileges, were still controlled by the constitutions of the states, and these fixed close restrictions on the right of suffrage, the electorate being confined to a small body whose ownership of real estate and whose religious opinions agreed with the ideas existing in colonial times. The property each voter was required to possess differed in different commonwealths. In New Jersey he must have property to the value of fifty pounds, in Maryland and the Carolinas an estate of fifty acres, in Delaware a freehold **Restrictions on the Right of Suffrage** estate of known value, in Georgia an estate of ten dollars or follow a mechanic trade; in New York, if he would vote for a member of Assembly he must possess a freehold of twenty pounds, and if he would vote for State Senator, it must be a hundred. Massachusetts required an elector to own a freehold estate worth sixty pounds or to possess an annual income of three pounds. Connecticut was satisfied if his estate was of the yearly value of seven dollars, and Rhode Island required him to own the value of one hundred and thirty-four dollars in land. Pennsylvania required him to be a freeholder, but New Hampshire and Vermont were satisfied with the payment of a poll-tax.

The number of electors was still further affected by the religious opinions required of them. In New Jersey, in New Hampshire, in Vermont, in Connecticut, and in South Carolina, no Roman Catholic could vote; Maryland and Massachusetts allowed "those of the Christian religion" to exercise the franchise, but the "Christian religion" in Massa- **Religious Qualifications of Voters** chusetts was of the Congregational Church. North Carolina required her electors to believe in the divine authority of the Scriptures; Delaware was satisfied with a belief in the Trinity and in the inspiration of the Bible; Pennsylvania allowed those, otherwise qualified, to vote who believed "in one God, in the reward of good, and the punishment of evil, and in the inspiration of the Scriptures." In New York, in Virginia, in Georgia, and in Rhode Island, the Protestant faith was predominant, but a Roman Catholic, if a male resident, of the age of twenty-one years or over, could vote in Rhode Island.

The property qualifications which limited the number of electors were higher for those who sought office. If a man wished to be governor of New Jersey or of South Carolina, his real and personal property must amount to ten thousand dollars; in North Carolina to one thousand pounds; in Georgia to two hundred and fifty pounds or two hundred and fifty acres

**Property Quali-
fications of
Officials**
of land; in New Hampshire to five hundred pounds; in Maryland to ten times as much, of which a thousand pounds must be of land; in Delaware he must own real estate; in New York he must be worth a hundred pounds; in Rhode Island, one hundred and thirty-four dollars; and in Massacusetts a thousand pounds. Connecticut required her candidate for governor to be qualified as an elector, as did New Hampshire, Vermont, Pennsylvania, and Virginia. In all the commonwealths the candidate for office must possess the religious qualifications required of electors.

From these statements it is evident that the suffrage in the United States was greatly limited when, after the winning of American independence, the Constitution of the United States was framed and the commonwealths had adopted their first constitutions of government. It may be said that in 1787 the country was bankrupt, and America was without credit,

**Condition of the
Country in
1787**
and that of a population of three million souls, who, by our present ratio, would represent six hundred thousand voters, less than one hundred and fifty thousand possessed the right to vote. African slavery and property qualifications excluded above four hundred thousand men from the exercise of the franchise. It is evident, then, that at the time when American liberty was won American liberty had only begun; the offices of the country were in the possession of the few, scarcely any provision existed for common education, the roads of the country may be described as impassable, the means for transportation, trade, and commerce as feeble. If the struggle for liberty in America was not to be in vain, the people of the United States must address themselves directly to the payment of their debts, to the enlargement of the franchise, to improvements in transportation, and to the creation, organization, and support of a national system of common taxation. It is these great changes which

**Payment of
Debt and Ex-
tension of
Suffrage**
constitute the history of this country during the nineteenth century.

All these have been gained since the adoption of the Constitution. The remarkable financial operations of Alexander Hamilton—by which the crushing load of debt of the new nation was funded for payment in after years, a customs tariff established as a means of obtaining revenue, and provision made for paying the claims of the soldiers of the Revolution—saved the credit and secured the honor of the nation. As regards the franchise, it was greatly extended during the nineteenth century. By the time the Erie canal was excavated property qualifications for suffrage had disappeared in nearly all the states, and by the middle of the century such qualifications had been abandoned in them all. Those of a religious character had vanished thirty years earlier.

As yet, however, the right to vote was limited to "free, white, male citizens." Twenty years afterwards, on March 30, 1870, a further great extension of the right of suffrage was made, when, in accordance with the Fifteenth Amendment to the Constitution, it was proclaimed by Hamilton Fish, Secretary of State, that the right of citizens of this country to vote could not be denied or abridged by the United States or by any State on account of race, color, or previous condition of servitude.

Universal suffrage, so far as male citizens were concerned, thus became the common condition of American political life in 1870. But the struggle for liberty in this direction was not yet ended. Female citizens, about the middle of the century, gave voice to their claim to the same right, and with such effort that they had gained the right to vote at all elections in four of the States—Wyoming, Colorado, Utah, and Idaho—by the end of the century, and partial rights of suffrage in a majority of the States. The outlook is that before many years universal suffrage in its fullest sense will be established in the United States.

With the westward movements of the millions of human beings who have occupied the North American continent have gone the institutions and constitutions of the east, modified in their journey westward by the varying conditions of the life of the people. The brief constitutions of 1776 have developed into extraordinary length by successive changes and additions made by the more than seventy Constitutional Conventions which have been held west of the original thirteen States. These later consti- **Development in State Constitutions** tutions resemble elaborate legal codes rather than brief statements of the fundamental ideas of government. But these constitutions, of which those of the Dakotas and of Montana and Washington are a type, express very clearly the opinions of the American people in government at the present time. The earnest desire shown in them for an accurate definition of the theory and the administration of government proves how anxiously the people of this country at all times consider the interpretation of their liberties, and with what hesitation, it may be said, they delegate their powers in government to legislatures, to judges, and to governors.

The struggle for liberty will never cease, for with the progress of civilization new definitions of the wants of the people are constantly forming in the mind. The whole movement of the American people in government, from the simple beginnings of representative government in Virginia, when the little parliament was called, to the present time, when nationality is enthroned and mighty commonwealths are become the component parts of the "more perfect union," has been toward the slow but constant realization of the rights and liberties of the people. Education, for which no commonwealth made adequate provision a century ago, is now the first care of the State. Easy and rapid transportation, wholly unknown to our fathers, is now a necessary condition of daily life. Trade has so prospered that the accumulated wealth of the country is more than sixty billions of dollars. Newspapers, magazines, books and pamphlets are now so numerous as to make it impossible to contain them all in hundreds of libraries, and the American people have become the largest class of readers in the world.

Progress in the United States

A century ago there were but six cities of more than eight thousand people in this country ; the number is now more than five hundred. Three millions of people have become seventy-five millions. The area of the original United States has expanded from eight hundred and thirty thousand square miles to four times that area. With expansion and growth and the amelioration in the conditions of life, the earnest problems of government have been brought home to the people by the leaders in the State, by the clergy, by the teachers in schools and colleges, and by the press.

But though we may be proud of these conquests, we are compelled in the last analysis of our institutions, to return to a few fundamental notions of our government. We must continue the representative idea based upon the doctrine of the equality of rights and exercised by representative assemblies founded on popular elections ; and after our most pleasing contemplation of the institutions of America, we must return to the people, the foundation of our government. Their wisdom and self-control, and these alone, will impart to our institutions that strength which insures their perpetuity

CHAPTER XXIII.

Expansion of the United States from Dwarf to Giant.

IN 1775, when the British colonies in America struck the first blow for independence, they were of dwarfish stature as compared with the present superb dimensions of the United States. Though the war with France had given them possession of the great Ohio Valley, the settled portion of the country lay between the Alleghanies and the Atlantic, and the thirteen confederated States were confined to a narrow strip along the ocean border of the continent.

But before and during the Revolutionary War pathfinders and pioneers were at work. Chief among them was the noted hunter Daniel Boone, the explorer and settler of the "Dark and Bloody Ground" of Kentucky. Before him daring men had crossed the mountains, and after him came others, so that by the end of the Revolution the hand of civilization was firmly laid on the broad forest land of Kentucky and Tennessee. The rich country north of the Ohio, where the British possessed a number of forts, was captured for the United States by another daring adventurer, George Rogers Clark, who led a body of men down the Ohio, took and held the British forts, and saved the northwest to the struggling States. The boundaries of the United States in 1800, as established by the treaty of peace with Great Britain, extended from the Atlantic Ocean to the Mississippi, and from the Great Lakes on the north to Florida on the south. Florida, then held by Spain, included a strip of land extending to the Mississippi River, so that the new republic was cut off from the Gulf of Mexico by domain belonging to a foreign country. The area thus acquired by the new nation was over 827,000 square miles. It was inhabited in 1800 by a population of 5,300,000.

The vast and almost wholly unknown territory west of the Mississippi, claimed by France, in virtue of her discoveries and settlements on the great river, until 1763, when it was ceded to Spain, was held by that country in 1800. This cession gave Spain complete control of the lower course of the Mississippi, since her province of Florida extended to the east bank of the stream. And she held it in a manner that proved deeply annoying to the American settlers in the west, to whom free navigation of the Mississippi was of great and growing importance.

These settlers were increasing in numbers with considerable rapidity. The daring enterprise of Daniel Boone and other fearless pioneers had opened up the fertile lands of Kentucky and Tennessee. The warlike boldness of Colonel Clark had gained the northwest territory for the new nation. Into this new country pioneer settlers poured, over the mountains and down the Ohio, and by the opening of the century villages and towns had been built in a hundred places, and farmers were widely felling the virgin woods and planting their grain in the fertile soil. Kentucky and Tennessee had already been organized as states, and their admission was quickly followed by that of Ohio, which entered the Union in 1803. In the same year an event of the highest importance took place, the acquisition of the great Louisiana territory by the United States.

The Settlement of the West

It has been stated above that the action of Spain gave great annoyance to the settlers in the country west of the Alleghanies. To these the natural commercial outlet to the sea was the Mississippi River, and the free use of this stream was forbidden by Spain, through whose country ran its lower course. Spain was so determined to retain for herself the exclusive navigation of the great river that in 1786 the new American republic withdrew all claim upon it, agreeing to withhold any demand for navigation of the Mississippi for twenty-five years.

Spain Closes the Mississippi to Traffic

This action proved to be hasty and unwise. The West filled up with unlooked-for rapidity, and the settlers upon the Mississippi soon began to insist on free use of its waters, their irritation growing so great that the United States vainly sought in 1793 to induce Spain to open the stream to American craft. This purpose was attained, however, in 1795, when a treaty was made which opened the Mississippi to the sea for a term of three years, with permission for Americans to use New Orleans as a free port of entry, and place goods there on deposit.

Five years later (1800), by an article in a secret treaty between Spain and France, the vast province of Louisiana, extending from the source to the mouth of the Mississippi River, and westward to the Rocky Mountains, was ceded by Spain to France, from which country Spain had received it in 1763. Towards the end of 1801 Napoleon Bonaparte, then at the head of French affairs, sent out a fleet and army ostensibly to act against San Domingo, but really to take possession of New Orleans.

France Obtains Louisiana

When the secret of this treaty leaked out, as it soon did, there was great excitement in the United States, the irritation being increased by a

Spanish order which withdrew the right of deposit of American merchandise in New Orleans. granted by the treaty of 1795, and failed to substitute any other place for that city, in accordance with the terms of the treaty. So strong was the feeling that a Pennsylvania Senator introduced a resolution into Congress, authorizing President Jefferson to call out 50,000 militia and occupy New Orleans. But Congress wisely decided that it would be better and cheaper to buy it than to fight for it, and in January, 1803, made an appropriation of $2,000,000 for its purchase. The President thereupon sent James Monroe to Paris to co-operate with Robert R. Livingston, United States Minister to France, in the proposed purchase.

Fortunately for the United States a new war between England and France was then imminent, in the event of which Napoleon felt that he could not long hold his American acquisition against the powerful British navy. Not only New Orleans, but the whole of Louisiana, would probably be lost to him, and just then money for his **The Louisiana Purchase** wars was of more consequence than wild lands beyond the sea. Therefore, to the surprise of the American Minister, he was asked to make an offer for the entire territory. This was on April 11th. On the 12th Monroe reached Paris. The two commissioners earnestly debated on the offer. They had no authority to close with such a proposition, but by the time they could receive fresh instructions from Washington the golden opportunity might be lost, and Great Britain deprive us of the mighty West. An ocean telegraph cable would have been to them an invaluable boon. As it was, there was no time to hesitate, and they decided to close with the offer, fixing the purchase price at $10,000,000. Napoleon demanded more, and in the end the price fixed upon was $15,000,000, of which $3,750,000 was to be paid to American citizens who held claims against Spain. A treaty to this effect was signed April 30, 1803.

The news fell upon Spain like a thunderbolt. She filed a protest against the treaty—based, probably, on a secret condition of her cession of Louisiana to France, to the effect that it should not be parted with by that country. But Napoleon was not the man to pay any attention to a protest from a power so weak as Spain, and the matter was one with which the United States was not concerned. President Jefferson highly **How the Purchase Was Received** approved of the purchase, and called an extra session of the Senate for its consideration. It met with some vigorous opposition in that body, based upon almost absolute ignorance of the value of the territory involved; but it was ratified in October, 1803, and Louisiana became ours. The territory thus easily and cheaply acquired added about 920,000 square miles to the United States, more than doubling its area. It is now divided up into a large number of States, and includes much of the most productive agricultural land of the United States.

The members of the Senate who opposed the ratification of the treaty of purchase were in a measure justified in their doubt. Almost nothing was known of the country involved, and many idle legends were afloat concerning it. Hunters and trappers had penetrated its wilds, but the stories told by them had been transformed out of all semblance of truth. In order to **Ignorance of the Country** dispel this ignorance and satisfy these doubts, the President determined to send an exploring expedition to the far West, with the purpose of crossing the Rocky Mountains, seeking the head-waters of the Columbia River, and following that stream to its mouth. The men chosen to lead this expedition were William Clark— brother of George Rogers Clark, of Revolutionary fame—and Merriwether Lewis. Both of these were army officers, and they were well adapted for the arduous enterprise which they were asked to undertake.

Lewis and Clark left St. Louis in the summer of 1803. They encamped for the winter on the bank of the Mississippi opposite the mouth of the **The Lewis and Clark Expedition** Missouri River. The company included nine Kentuckians, who were used to Indian ways and frontier life, fourteen soldiers, two Canadian boatmen, an interpreter, a hunter and a negro boatman. Besides these, a corporal and guard with nine boatmen were engaged to accompany the expedition as far as the territory of the Mandans.

The party carried with it the usual goods for trading with the Indians— looking-glasses, beads, trinkets, hatchets, etc., and such provisions as were necessary for the sustenance of its members. While the greater part of the command embarked in a fleet of three large canoes, the hunters and pack-horses followed a parallel route along the shore. In this way, in the spring of 1804, the ascent of the Missouri was commenced. In June the country of the Osages was reached, then the lands occupied by the Ottawa tribes, and finally, in the fall, the hunting grounds of the Sioux. Here the leaders of the expedition ordered cabins to be constructed, and camped for the winter among the Mandans, in latitude 27 degrees 21 minutes north. They found in that country plenty of game, buffalo and deer being abundant; but the weather was intensely cold and the expedition was hardly prepared for the severity of the climate, so that its members suffered greatly.

In April a fresh start was made and the party continued to ascend the Missouri, reaching the great falls by June. Here they named the tributary waters and ascended the northernmost, which they called the Jefferson River, until further navigation was impossible; then Captain Lewis with three companions left the expedition in camp and started out on foot toward the mountains, in search of the friendly Shoshone Indians, from whom he expected assistance in his projected journey across the mountains.

On the 12th of August he discovered the source of the Jefferson River in a defile of the Rocky Mountains and crossed the dividing ridge, upon the other side of which his eyes were gladdened by the discovery of a small rivulet which flowed toward the west. Here was proof irrefutable "that the great backbone of earth" had been passed. The intrepid explorer saw with joy that this little stream danced out toward the setting **The Head-** sun—toward the Pacific Ocean. Meeting a force of Sho- **Waters of the** shones and persuading them to accompany him on his return **Columbia** to the main body of the expedition, Captain Lewis sought his companions once more. Captain Clark then went forward to determine their future course, and coming to the river which his companion had discovered, he named it the Lewis River.

A number of Indian horses were procured from their red-skinned friends and the explorers pushed on to the broad plains of the western slope. The latter part of their progress in the mountains had been slow and painful, because of the early fall of snow, but the plains presented all the charm of early autumn. In October the Kaskaskia River was reached, and, leaving the horses and whatever baggage could be dispensed with in charge of the Indians, the command embarked in canoes and descended to the mouth of the Columbia River, upon the south bank of which, four hundred miles from their starting point upon **Descending the** this stream, they passed the second winter. Much of the **Columbia** return journey was a fight with hostile Indians, and the way proved to be much more difficult than it had been found while advancing toward the west. Lewis was wounded before reaching home, by the accidental discharge of a gun in the hands of one of his force.

Finally, after an absence of two years, the expedition returned to its starting point, the leaders reaching Washington while Congress was in session. Grants of land were immediately made to them and to their subordinates. Captain Lewis was rewarded also with the governorship of Missouri. Clark was appointed brigadier-general for the territory of Upper Louisiana, and in 1813 was made governor of Missouri. When this Territory became a State he was appointed superintendent of Indian affairs, which office he filled till his death.

The second acquisition of territory by the United States embraced the peninsula of Florida. The Spanish colony of Florida was divided into two sections, known as Eastern and Western Florida, the latter extending from the Appalachicola River to the Mississippi River, and cutting off the Americans of Florida and Alabama from all access to the Gulf. Spain set up a customhouse at the mouth of the Alabama River, and levied heavy duties on goods to or from the country up that stream.

Spain's Irritating Action

The United States was not willing to acknowledge the right of Spain to this country. It claimed that the Louisiana purchase included the region east of the Mississippi as far as the Perdido River,—the present western boundary of Florida—and in 1810 a force was sent into this country which took possession of it, with the exception of the city of Mobile. That city was occupied by General Wilkinson, commander-in-chief of the army, in 1813, leaving to Spain only the country between the Perdido and the Atlantic Ocean and south of Georgia.

Western Florida Occupied

Throughout these years the purpose had grown in the southern states to gain this portion of the Spanish dominion, as well as Western Florida, for the United States. On January 15 and March 3, 1811, the United States Congress passed in secret—and its action was not made known until 1818—acts which authorized the President of the United States to take "temporary possession" of East Florida. The commissioners appointed under these acts, Matthews and Mitchell, both Georgians, stirred up insurrection in the coveted territory, and, when President Madison refused to sustain them, the state of Georgia formally pronounced Florida needful to its own peace and welfare, and practically declared war on its private account. But its expedition against Florida came to nothing. In 1814, General Andrew Jackson, then in command of United States forces at Mobile, made a raid into Pensacola, and drove out a British force which had been placed there. He afterwards restored the place to the Spanish authorities and retired. Four years after, during the Seminole war, Jackson, annoyed by Spanish assistance given to the Indians, again raided Eastern Florida, captured St. Marks and Pensacola, hung Arbuthnot and Ambruster, two Englishmen who were suspected of aiding the Seminoles, as "outlaws and pirates," and again demonstrated the fact that Florida was at the mercy of the United States.

General Jackson Invades Eastern Florida

The action of Jackson was unauthorized by the government, and his hanging the Englishmen without taking the trouble to make sure of their guilt caused a feeling of hostile irritation in England. But it had by this time grown quite evident to Spain, both that it could not hold Florida in peace and that this colony was of very little value to it. In consequence it agreed to sell the peninsula to the

The Purchase of Florida

United States for the sum of $5,000,000, the treaty being signed February 22, 1819. By this treaty Spain also gave up all claim to the country west of the Louisiana purchase, extending from the Rocky Mountains to the Pacific Ocean. The purchase of Florida added 59,268 square miles to the United States, and the way was cleared for the subsequent acquisition of the Oregon country.

The next accession of territory came in 1845, when Texas was added to the dominion of the United States. This country had, since 1821, been one of the states of the Mexican Republic. But American frontiersmen, of the kind calculated to foment trouble, soon made their way across the borders, increasing in numbers as the years passed on, until Texas had a considerable population of United States origin. Efforts were made to purchase this country from Mexico, $1,000.000 being offered in 1827 and $5,000,000 in 1829. These were declined, and in 1833 Texas adopted a constitution as a state of the Mexican republic. Two years later Santa Anna, the president of Mexico, was made dictator, and all state constitutions were abolished. Irritated by this, the American inhabitants declared the independence of Texas in 1836, and after a short war, marked by instances of savage *Texas Gains Freedom and is Annexed to the United States* cruelty on the part of the Mexicans, gained freedom for that country. Texas was organized as a republic, but its people soon applied for annexation to the United States. This was not granted until 1845. The territory added to this country by the admission of Texas amounted to 376,133 square miles.

In the following year another large section of territory was added to the rapidly growing United States. The Louisiana purchase ran indefinitely westward, but came to be considered as bounded on the west by the Rocky Mountains, Spain retaining a shadowy claim over the country west of that range. This exceedingly vague claim was abandoned in the Florida purchase treaty, and the broad Oregon country was left without an owner. The United States, indeed, might justly *The Oregon Country* have claimed ownership on the same plea advanced for new regions elsewhere—namely, that of discovery and exploration. Captain Grey, in his ship, the *Columbia*, carried the starry flag to its coast in 1792, and was the first to enter and sail up its great river, which he named after his vessel. In 1805 the country was traversed and explored by Lewis and Clark. In 1811 John Jacob Astor founded the settlement of Astoria at the mouth of the Columbia, and sent hunters in search of furs through the back country. And in 1819 the vague right over the country held by Spain was transferred by treaty to the United States.

These various circumstances would have established a prescriptive right to the country concerned as against other countries, had any thought of claiming such a right been entertained. But no man, statesman or commoner, thought the country worth the value of even a paper claim, and it was left unconsidered and unthought of until the century was well advanced. Then, after the Hudson Bay Company had gained control of Astoria, and had begun to fill the country with fur hunters, a living sense of the value of this great region came to the mind of one man.

This was Dr. Marcus Whitman, a missionary physician among the Indians of the Columbia River region. He discovered that the Hudson Bay Company was making efforts to bring permanent settlers there, and that it proposed to claim the country for Great Britain. At once the energetic doctor set out for Washington, crossing the vast stretch of country from the Pacific to the Atlantic on horseback and traversing the Rocky Mountains in the dead of winter. It was a long and terrible journey, full of perils and hardships, but he accomplished it in safety, and strongly urged the government at Washington to lay claim to the country. Even then it was hard to arouse an interest in the statesmen concerning this far-off territory, so the brave pioneer went among the people, told them of the beauty of the country and the fertility of its soil, and on his return, in 1843, took with him an emigrant train of nearly a thousand persons. This settled the question. The newcomers formed a government of their own. Others followed, and the question of ownership was practically settled. In 1845 there were some 7,000 Americans in Oregon and only a few British. By that time a stern determination had arisen in the people of this country to retain Oregon. A claim was made on the whole western region up to the parallel of 54 degrees 40 minutes, the southern boundary of Russian America, and the political war-cry of that year was "fifty-four forty or fight." In 1846 the question was settled by treaty with Great Britain, the disputed country being divided at the forty-ninth parallel. The northern portion became British Columbia, the southern Oregon. In this way it was that the United States spanned the continent and established its dominion from ocean to ocean. The tract acquired measured about 255,000 square miles. It now constitutes the States of Oregon, Washington and Idaho.

Whitman's Ride

Oregon Is Acquired

The United States grew with extraordinary rapidity in the decade with which we are now concerned, the acquisition of Texas and Florida being followed in 1848 by another great addition of territory, much larger than either. This came as the result of the annexation of Texas.

Mexico had never acknowledged the independence of the "Lone Star Republic," and was deeply dissatisfied at its acquisition by the United States, which it looked upon as an unwarranted interference in its private affairs. The strained relations between the two countries were made more stringent by a dispute as to the western boundary of Texas, both countries claiming the strip of land between the Rio Grande and **War With Mexico and Its Results** Nueces Rivers. The result was a war, the description of which must be left for a later chapter. It will suffice here to say that the American troops marched steadily to victory, and at the end of the war held two large districts of northern Mexico, those of New Mexico and California. The occupation of these Mexican states gave this country a warrant to claim them as the prizes of victory.

But there was no disposition shown to despoil the defeated party without compensation. An agreement was made to pay Mexico $15,000,000 for New Mexico and California, and to assume debts owed by Mexico to United States citizens amounting to about $3,000,000. The territory thus acquired was 545,783 square miles in extent. Of its immense **California and New Mexico Purchased** value we need scarce speak. It will suffice to say that it gave the United States the gold mines of California and the silver mines of Nevada, together with the still more valuable fertile fields of the California lowlands. Five years afterwards, to settle a border dispute, another tract of land, south of New Mexico, 45,535 square miles in extent, was purchased for the sum of $10,000,000. This is known as the Gadsden purchase, the treaty being negociated by James Gadsden. Thus in less than ten years the United States acquired more than 1,220,000 square miles of territory, increasing its domain by nearly three-fourths. These new acquisitions carried it across the continent in a broad band, giving it a coast line on the Pacific nearly equal to that on the Atlantic, and adding enormously to its mineral and agricultural wealth.

Still another extensive acquisition remained to be made. Long before, when the daring pioneers of Russia overran Siberia, parties of them crossed the narrow Bering Strait and took possession of the northwestern section of the American continent. This territory, long known as Russian America, embraced the broad peninsular extension west of the 141st degree of west longitude, and a narrow strip of land stretching down the coast **The Acquisition of Russian America** as far south as the parallel of 54 degrees 40 minutes. It included also all the coast islands and the Aleutian Archipelago, with the exception of Copper and Bering Islands on the Siberian coast. This territory was of little value or advantage to Russia, and in 1867 that country offered to sell it to the United States for $7,200,000. The offer was accepted without hesitation, the result being an addition of 577.000 square miles to our territory.

As regards the value of this acquisition something more remains to be said. The active Yankee prospectors have found Alaska—as the new territory was named—far richer than its original owners dreamed of. It was like the story of California repeated. First were the valuable fur seals. which haunted certain islands of Bering Sea. Then were the fur animals of the mainland. To these must be added the wealth of the rivers, which were found to swarm with salmon and other food fishes Next may be named the forests, which cover the coast regions for hundreds of square

The Wealth of Alaska miles. Finally, the country proved to be rich in mineral wealth, and especially in gold. The recently discovered gold deposits lie principally on the British side of the border, the Klondike diggings—developed in 1897—being in Canada. But gold has been mined in Alaska for years, and probably exists on most of the tributaries of the Yukon River, so that the country may yet prove to be a second California in its golden treasures. .

The final acquisition of territory by the United States came in 1899, as a result of the Spanish-American War of 1898. The treaty of peace gave to this country a series of highly fertile tropical islands, consisting of Porto Rico in the West Indies, and the Philippine Archipelago in the Asiatic Seas. To these must be added a temporary protectorate over, and possibly the future ownership of, the broad and fertile West Indian Island of Cuba. In 1898 there came by peaceful means another accession of territory, the Hawaiian group of islands in the Central Pacific. These, with some islands of minor importance—including Guam, in the Ladrone group, also acquired from Spain—constitute the recent island accessions of the United States.

Island Acquisitions Their areas are: Porto Rico, 3,530; Hawaii, 6,564; and the Philippines, 116,000 square miles; making a total of about 126,000 square miles. As a consequence of those various accessions of territory, the United States now has an area of, in round numbers, 3,732,000 square miles, more than four times its area in 1800. As a result of these several acquisitions this country has grown from one of the smaller nations to nearly the largest nation in area, on the earth, while its population has increased from 5,300,000 in 1800 to about 75,000,000 in 1900. Its few small cities at the beginning of the century have been replaced by a considerable number of large ones, three of them with more than 1,000,000 inhabitants each, while New York, the largest, is now the second city in population on the earth.

CHAPTER XXIV.

The Development of Democratic Institutions in America.

MODERN democracy is often looked upon as something peculiarly secular, unreligious, or even irreligious in its origin. In truth, however, it has its origin in religious aspirations quite as much as modern art or architecture or literature. To the theology of Calvin, the founder of the Republic of Geneva, grafted upon the sturdy independence of English and Scotch middle classes, our American democracy owes its birth. James I. well appreciated that the principles of uncompromising Protestantism were as incompatible with monarchy as with the hierarchy which they swept aside. Each man by his theology was brought into direct personal responsibility to his God, without the intervention of priest, bishop, or pope, and without any allegiance to his king except so far as it agreed with his allegiance to the King of kings. Macaulay has struck this note of Puritan republicanism when he says that the Puritans regarded themselves as " Kings by the right of an earlier creation ; priests by the interposition of an Almighty hand." As John Fiske says, James Stuart always treasured up in his memory the day when a Puritan preacher caught him by the sleeve and called him " God's silly vassal." " A Scotch Presbytery," cried the king, " agrees as well with monarchy as God and the devil. Then Jack and Tom and Will and Dick shall meet, and at their pleasure censure me and my council and all our proceedings ! "

The Religious Origin of Modern Democracy

But the democracy which was founded in New England as the logical outcome of the religious principles for which the Puritans left Old England was not democracy as we know it to-day. The Puritans, for the most part, believed as much in divinely appointed rulers as the monarchs against whom they rebelled · but these divinely appointed rulers were to be the " elect of God "—those who believed as they did, and joined with their organizations to establish His kingdom on earth. For this reason we find the Massachusetts Colony as early as 1631 deciding that, " no man shall be admitted to the freedom of this body politic but such as are members of some of the churches within the limits of the same." The government, in short, was simply a democratic theocracy, and, as the colony grew in numbers, the power came to be lodged in the hands of the minority.   There were, however, among the clergy of Massachusetts men who believed in democracy as we understand it to-day.   Alexander Johnson, in his history of Connecticut, says with truth that Thomas Hooker, who led from Massachusetts into

The Political Conceptions of the Puritans Connecticut the colony which established itself at Hartford, laid down the principle upon which the American nation long generations after was to be established.   When Governor Winthrop, in a letter to Hooker, defended the restriction of the suffrage on the ground that " the best part is always the least, and of that best part the wiser part is always the lesser," the learned and generous-hearted pastor replied :   " In matters which concern the common good, a general council, chosen by all to transact business which concerns all, I conceive most suitable to rule, and most safe for the relief of the whole."   The principles of our republicanism were never better stated until Lincoln in his oration at Gettysburg made his appeal that this nation might be consecrated anew in the fulfillment of its mission, and that government "from the people, for the people, by the people " might not perish from the earth.   Both Hooker and Lincoln had a supreme belief in the wisdom of the plain people in the matters which affect their own lives.   The rank and file of the people have the surest instinct as to what will benefit or injure the rank and file of the people, and when upon them is placed the responsibility of determining what their government shall be, they are educated for self-government.   In the colony which Thomas Hooker founded upon these principles there was found at the time of the Revolution more political wisdom, more genius for self-government, and more devotion to the patriotic cause, than in any other of the thirteen colonies.

At the time of the Revolution, however, there was another democracy besides that of New England which enabled the colonies successfully to resist the Government of George III.   This was the democracy of the planters of the South.   The democracy of the Southern colonies was not, like that

Democracy in the South of New England, the democracy of collective self-government, but the democracy of individual self-government, or, rather, of individual self-assertion.   In fact, it would hardly be too much to say that many of the Virginia planters who espoused so warmly and fought so bravely in the cause of liberty were not inspired by the spirit of democracy at all, but rather by the spirit of an aristocracy which could brook no control.   These southern planters were the aristocrats of the American Revolution.   In New York City, and even in Boston and Philadelphia, the wealthiest merchants were strongly Tory in their sympathies.   In New

York it was affirmed by General Greene that two-thirds of the land belonged to men in sympathy with the English and out of sympathy with their fellow countrymen. In these cities it was the plain people and the poorer classes who furnished most of the uncompromising patriots, but in the South men of fortune risked their fortunes in the cause of independence. These men were slave owners, and the habit of mastery made them fiercely rebellious when George III. attempted in any way to tyrannize over them. Many of them were the descendants of the English nobility, and as such they acknowledged no superiors. Naturally, then, in the struggle for liberty they furnished the leaders of the colonists, both North and South; and the agricultural classes, whether rich or poor, were naturally on the side of self-government, for their isolation had from the first compelled them to be self-governing.

The first half century of the political history of the United States consisted rather in the development of the political rights of the individual citizen than of the loyalty which all owed to the American nation. Nothing is so difficult as to keep in mind that the government of the colonies at the close of the Revolution was not what it is to-day, and that democracy as we know it was regarded as the dream of theorists. Some of the members of the Federal Convention deeply distrusted the common people. Elbridge Gerry, of Massachusetts, declared that "The people do not want suffrage, but are the dupes of pretended patriots;" and those who were at all in sympathy with him prevented, as they imagined, the election of the President by the people themselves, and did prevent the election of the United States Senators by the people. Some of them were even opposed to the election of the House of Representatives directly by the people; but, fortunately, even Hamilton sided with Madison and Mason, when they urged that our House of Commons ought to have at heart the rights and interests of, and be bound, by the manner of their election, to be the representatives of every class of people. But by "every class of people" the framers of the Constitution from the more conservative of the States meant simply every class of freeholders.

What Was Thought of Democracy in the Federal Convention

In Virginia none could vote except those who owned fifty acres of land. In New York, to vote for Governor or State Senator, a freehold worth $250 clear of mortgage was necessary, and to vote for Assemblymen a freehold of $50 or the payment of a yearly rent of $10 was necessary. Even Thomas Jefferson, who was the Democratic philosopher of the Revolutionary period, did not strenuously insist that the suffrage must be universal, and it was not for a half century

Property Qualifications for Suffrage

that it became universal, even among white males.   In the State of New York these restrictions existed until the adoption of the Constitution of 1821, and even this Constitution merely reduced the privileges of land owners.   Old Chancellor Kent, the author of "Kent's Commentaries," declared in this convention that he would not "bow before the idol of uni-

Chancellor Kent's Views on Universal Suffrage versal suffrage," the theory which he said had "been regarded with terror by the wise men of every age," and whenever tried had brought "corruption, injustice, violence, and tyranny."

" If universal suffrage were adopted," he declared, "prosperity would deplore in sackcloth and ashes the delusion of the day."   The horrors of the French Revolution were always held up by conservatives to show that the people could not be trusted, and the learned author of the " Commentaries," which every lawyer has pored over, maintained that, if universal suffrage should be adopted, " The radicals of England, with the force of that mighty engine, would sweep away the property, the laws, and the people of that island like a deluge."   Not until between 1840 and 1850 did universal suffrage among the whites come to be accepted in the older States.

During the first half century of our history it was the Democratic party, the party of Jefferson, which was on the side of these extensions of popular rights.   The principle of this party was that each State ought to legislate for itself, with the least possible control from the central government ; that each locality ought to have its freedom of local government extended ; and that each individual should be self-governing, with the same rights and privileges for all.   As regards foreign affairs, it was characterized by a "passion for peace," and an abiding hostility toward a costly army and navy.   Jefferson believed that the way to avoid wars, and the way to be strong, should war become inevitable, was by the devotion of the people to productive industry, and not by burdening them to rival the powers of Europe in the strength of their armaments.   In the year 1800, the party which rallied to his support—then called the Republican party, but generally spoken of as the Democratic party—triumphed over the Federalists.

In New England alone did Federalism remain strong at the close of

Federalism and Democracy in New England Jefferson's first administration.   In that section the calvinistic clergy, who had done so much for the establishment of American democracy, fought fiercely against its extension.   Jefferson's followers demanded the separation of Church and State and the abolition of the religious qualifications for office holding, which were then almost as general as property qualifications.   He was known to be in sympathy with the French revolution, and was therefore denounced as a Jacobin, both in religion and in politics. We cannot wonder, therefore, that in the section in which the clergy were the real rulers, Jeffersonian democracy was regarded with hatred and contempt. Vermont alone, among the New England States, was from the first thoroughly democratic, and this was because in Vermont there was no established aristocracy, either of education or of wealth. In Connecticut, which under clerical leadership had once been the stronghold of advanced democracy, we find President Dwight expressing a sentiment common not only to the clergy but to the educated classes generally, when he declared that "the great object of Jacobinism, both in its political and moral revolution, is to destroy every race of civilization in the world." " In the triumph of Jeffersonianism," he said, "we have now reached a consummation of democratic blessings ; we have a country governed by blockheads and knaves."

But the ideas which in New England were at first received only by the poor and the ignorant, were in the very air which Americans breathed. The new States which were organized at the West were aggressively democratic from the outset. In the Northwest Territory the inequalities **New Ideas in** against which Jeffersonian democracy protested never gained **the New** a foothold. Here, where the State of Ohio was organized **West** during Jefferson's first administration, the union of Church and State was not thought of, and no religious qualifications whatever for the office of Governor were exacted. Property qualifications were almost as completely set aside. While in some of the older States the Governor had to possess £5,000, and even £10,000, Ohio's Governor was simply required to be a resident and an owner of land. As regards inheritances, the English law of primogeniture which remained unaltered in some of the older States, and in New England generally took the form of a double portion to the oldest son, was completely set aside, and all children of the same parents became entitled to the same rights. That Ohio thus led the way in the democratic advance was due to the fact that its constitution was framed when these ideas had already become ascendant in the hearts of the people, and the failure of the clergy of New England was due to their trying to keep alive institutions which were the offspring of another age, and could not long survive it.

For its distrust of the new democracy New England Federalism paid heavily in the isolation, defeat, and destruction which shortly awaited it. When the new democratic administration had fully reduced Federal taxation and shown its capacity for government, the more liberal-minded of the Federalists went over to the Democrats. Even Massachusetts gave a majority for Jefferson in 1804, and when the extreme Federalists became

The Decay and Disappearance of Federalism

more extreme through the loss of their Liberal contingent, and called the Hartford Convention, in 1814, Federalism died of its own excesses. The policy of the democratic administration toward England may not have been wise, but the proposal of secession in order to resist it made Federalism almost synonymous with toryism and disloyalty.

For a number of years after the close of the war of 1812 there was really only one political party in the United States. In 1824, when the contest was so close between Jackson, Adams and Clay, each of these contestants was a " Democratic Republican," and it would have been hard to tell what questions of policy divided their followers ; though Jackson's followers, as a rule, cared most for the extension of the political rights of the poorer classes, and least for that policy of protection which the war had made an important issue, by cutting off commerce and thus calling into being exten-

A Period Without a Party

sive manufacturing interests. That the followers of Clay finally voted for Adams may have been due to sympathy upon this question of the tariff. In 1828 something akin to party lines were drawn upon the question of the national bank, and the victory of Jackson provoked the hostility of the masses toward that institution, which certainly enriched its stockholders to such an extent as to make them a favored class. The Tariff Act, passed in 1828, made the tariff question thenceforth the dividing question in our national politics until slavery took its place.

Most of the absolute free-traders were supporters of Jackson, but when South Carolina passed its Nullification Act as a protest against the "tariff of abominations," as it was called, President Jackson promptly declared that " the Union must and shall be preserved," and forced the recalcitrant State to renew its allegiance to the National Government. By the end of Jackson's administration there were again two distinct parties in the United States; the one advocating a high tariff and extensive national improvements by the Federal Government, and the other advocating a low tariff and the restriction of national expenditures to the lowest possible limit. The former party—the Whig—was, of course, in favor of a liberal construction of the Constitution and the extension of powers to the National Government, while the latter advocated " strict construction " and " State rights."

Jackson belonged to the latter party, and in 1836 was able to transfer the succession to Van Buren. But in 1840 the Whigs swept the country electing Harrison and Tyler after the most picturesque Presidential campaign ever known in America. All the financial ills from which the country was suffering were for the time attributed to Van Buren's economic policy, and his alleged extravagance at the White House enabled the Whigs to arouse the enthusiasm of the poor for their candidate, who was claimed to live in a log cabin and drink hard cider. During the next four years, however, there **Rise of the Democratic and Whig Parties** was a reaction, and in 1844 Polk was elected upon the platform on which Van Buren had stood. It is true that in Pennsylvania the Democratic campaign cry was, "Polk, Dallas and the tariff of '42," which was a high tariff; but in most of the country Democracy meant "free trade and sailors' rights."

From this time on, the Whig party grew weaker and the Democratic party stronger. It is true that the Whigs elected General Taylor in 1848. The revenue tariff law passed by the Democrats in 1846 was not changed until the still lower tariff of 1857 was enacted. By 1852 the Whig party had so declined that it was hardly stronger than the old Federalist party at the close of Jefferson's first term. But just as the Democratic party became able to boast of its strength, a new party came into being which adopted the principles of the free-soil wing of the old Democratic party, chose the name of "Republican Party," swept into its ranks the remnants of various political organizations of the past, and in its second national campaign elected Abraham Lincoln to the presidency. In this readjustment of parties the pro-slavery Whigs went over to the Democrats and the anti-slavery Democrats went over to **The Origin and Character of the Republican Party** the Republicans. The bolting Democrats claimed, with truth, to maintain the principles held by their party from the time of Jefferson down, but the party as a whole followed the interests of its most powerful element instead of the principles of its founder. In the States from Ohio west, where upon economic questions the Democratic party had swept everything by increasing majorities since 1840, the bolting element was so great that all of these States were landed in the Republican column. One great Church—the Methodist—which before had been, as a rule, Democratic in politics, now became solidly Republican.

From time to time, in the succeeding years, a variety of political organizations, of minor importance, rose and declined. But none of national significance were added to the two great parties until the Presidential campaigns of 1892 and 1896, when a new organization, known as the People's party, came into prominence. The principles distinguishing it from the old Democratic and Republican parties were its demand for a currency issued by the general Government only, without the intervention of banks of issue, and the free and unrestricted coinage of **The People's Party and Its Principles** silver and gold at the ratio of 16 to 1, regardless of foreign nations.   It demanded further that the Government, in payment of its obligations, should use its option as to the kind of lawful money in which they were to be paid ; should establish and collect a graduated income tax ; and should own and operate the railroads and telegraph lines in the interests of the people.   Its general tendency was to favor what is known as " Paternalism in government," the existing form in America of what is known as Socialism in Europe.   This party found its chief strength among the farmers, who believed it possible and right for the Government to pass laws to suppress " trusts " and monopolies, and also to favor the agricultural and laboring classes.

The history of American politics up to the time of the introduction of the new economic questions by the labor unions in the East, and the farmer's unions in the West and South, has been the history of the gradual extension of political rights.   The Federalist party gave us the Constitution ; the old Democratic party gave us white manhood suffrage ; the Republican party gave us universal suffrage.   What the People's party may give us remains for the future to demonstrate.   The glory of America's past is that she has been continually progressing ; that she has proven to the world the capacity of the whole people for self-government.

CHATPER XXV

America's Answer to the British Claim of the Right, of Search.

BY their first war with Great Britain our forefathers asserted and maintained their right to independent national existence; by their second war with Great Britain, they claimed and obtained equal consideration in international affairs. The War of 1812 was not based on a single cause; it was undertaken from mixed motives,—partly political, partly commercial, partly patriotic. It was always unpopular with a great number of the American people; it was far from logical in some of its positions; it was perhaps precipitated by party clamor. But, despite all these facts, it remains true that this war established once for all the position of the United States as an equal power among the powers. Above all—clearing away the petty political and partisan aspects of the struggle—we find that in it the United States stood for a strong, sound, and universally beneficial principle, that of the rights of neutral nations in time of war. "Free ships make free goods" is a maxim of international law now universally recognized, but at the opening of the century it was a theory, supported, indeed, by good reasoning, but practically disregarded by the most powerful nations. It was almost solely to the stand taken by the United States in 1812 that the final settlement of this disputed principle was due.

The Causes of the War of 1812

The cause of the War of 1812, which appealed most strongly to the patriotic feelings of the common people, though, perhaps, not in itself so intrinsically important as that just referred to, was unquestionably the impressment by Great Britain of sailors from American ships. No doubt great numbers of English sailors did desert from their naval vessels and avail themselves of the easier service and better treatment of the American merchant ships. Great Britain, in the exigencies of her desperate contest with Napoleon, was straining every nerve to strengthen her already powerful navy, and the press-gang was constantly at work in English seaports. Once on board a British man-of-war, the impressed sailor was subject to overwork, bad rations, and the lash. That British sailors fought as gallantly as they did under

British Impressment of American Seamen

this regime will always remain a wonder. But it is certain that they deserted in considerable numbers, and that they found in the rapidly-growing commercial prosperity of our carrying trade a tempting chance of employment.

Great Britain, with a large contempt for the naval weakness of the United States, assumed, rather than claimed, the right to stop our merchant vessels on the high seas, to examine their crews, and to take as her own any British sailors among them. This was bad enough in itself, but the way in which the search was carried out was worse. Every form of insolence and overbearing was exhibited. The pretense of claiming British deserters covered what was sometimes barefaced and outrageous kidnapping of Americans. The British officers went so far as to lay the burden of proof of nationality in each case upon the sailor himself ; if he were without papers proving his identity he was at once assumed to be a British subject. To such an extent was this insult to our flag carried, that our Government had the record of about forty-five hundred cases of impressment from our ships between the years of 1803 and 1810 ; and when the War of 1812 broke out the number of American sailors serving against their will in British war vessels was variously computed to be from six to fourteen thousand. It is even recorded that in some cases American ships were obliged to return home in the middle of their voyages because their crews had been so diminished in number by the seizures made by British officers that they were too short-handed to proceed. In not a few cases these depredations led to bloodshed.

Outrages Upon American Ships and Sailors

The greatest outrage of all, and one which stirred the blood of Americans to the fighting point, was the capture of an American war vessel, the *Chesapeake*, by the British man-of-war, the *Leopard*. The latter was by far the more powerful vessel, and the *Chesapeake* was quite unprepared for action ; nevertheless, her commander refused to accede to a demand that his crew be overhauled in search for British deserters. Thereupon the *Leopard* poured broadside after broadside into her until her flag was struck. Three Americans were killed and eighteen wounded ; four were taken away as alleged deserters ; of these, three were afterwards returned, while in one case the charge was satisfactorily proved and the man was hanged. The whole affair was without the slightest justification under the law of nations and was in itself ample ground for war. Great Britain, however, in a quite ungracious and tardy way, apologized and offered reparation. This incident took place six years before the actual declaration of war. But the outrage rankled during all that time, and nothing did more to fan the anti-British feeling which was

The Affair of the " Chesapeake " and the "Leopard"

already so strong in the rank and file of Americans, especially in the Democratic (or, as it was then often called, the Republican) party. It was such deeds as this that led Henry Clay to exclaim, " Not content with seizing upon all our property which falls within her rapacious grasp, the personal rights of our countrymen—rights which must forever be sacred—are tramped on and violated by the impressment of our seamen. What are we to gain by war? What are we not to lose by peace? Commerce, character, a nation's best treasure, honor !"

The interference with American commerce was also a serious threat to the cause of peace. In the early years of the century Great Britain was at war not only with France, but with other European countries. Both Great Britain and France adopted in practice the most extreme **The Era** theories of non-intercourse between neutral and hostile **of Paper** nations. It was the era of "paper blockades." In 1806 **Blockades** England, for instance, declared that eight hundred miles of the European coast were to be considered blockaded, whereupon Napoleon, not to be outdone, declared the entire Kingdom of Great Britain to be under blockade.

Up to a certain point the interruption of the neutral trade relations between the countries of Europe was to the commercial advantage of America. Our carrying trade grew and prospered wonderfully. Much of this trade consisted in taking goods from the colonies of European nations, bringing them to the United States, then trans-shipping them and conveying them to the parent nation. This was allowable under the international law of the time, although the direct carrying of goods by the neutral ship from the colony to the parent nation (the latter, of course, being at war) was forbidden. But by her famous "Orders in Council" Great Britain absolutely forbade this system of trans-shipment as to nations with whom she was at war. American vessels engaged in this form of trade were seized and condemned by English prize courts. Naturally, France followed Great Britain's example and even went further. Our merchants, who had actually been earning double freights under the old system, now found that their commerce was woefully restricted. At first it was thought that the unfair restriction might be punished by retaliatory measures, and a quite illogical analogy was drawn from the effect produced on Great Britain before the Revolution by the refusal of the colonies to receive goods on which a tax had been imposed. So President Jefferson's administration resorted to the most unwise measure that could be thought of—an absolute embargo on our own ships, which were prohibited from leaving port.

This measure was passed in 1807, and its immediate result was to reduce the exports of this country from nearly fifty million dollars' worth to nine million dollars' worth in a single year. This was evidently anything but profitable, and the act was changed so as to forbid only commercia

Jefferson and the Embargo intercourse with Great Britain and France and their colonies with a proviso that the law should be abandoned as regards either of these countries which should repeal its objectionable decrees. The French government moved in the matter first, but only con ditionally. Our non-intercourse act, however, was after 1810 in force only against Great Britain. That our claims of wrong were equally, or nearly so, as great against France in this matter cannot be doubted. But the popular feeling was stronger against Great Britain; a war with England was popular with the mass of the Democrats; and it was the refusal of England to accept our conditions which finally led to the declaration of war By a curious chain of circumstances it happened, however, that between the time when Congress declared war (June 18, 1812) and the date when the

War Declared Against Great Britain news of this declaration was received in England, the latter country had already revoked her famous "Orders in Council." In point of fact, President Madison was very reluctant to declare war, though the Federalists always took great pleasure in speaking of this as "Mr. Madison's war." The Federalists throughout considered the war unnecessary and the result of partisan feeling and unreasonable prejudice.

It is peculiarly grateful to American pride that this war, undertaken in defence of our maritime interests and to uphold the honor of our flag upon the high seas, resulted in a series of naval victories brilliant in the extreme It was not, indeed, at first thought that this would be chiefly a naval war President Madison was at one time strongly inclined to keep our war vessels in port; but, happily, other counsels prevailed. The disparity between the American and British navies was certainly disheartening. The United States had seven or eight frigates and a few sloops, brigs, and gunboats while the sails of England's navy whitened every sea, and her ships cer tainly outnumbered ours by fifty to one. On the other hand, her hands were tied to a great extent by the stupendous European war in which she was involved. She had to defend her commerce from formidable enemies

The British and American Navies Compared and could spare but a small part of her naval strength for battle with the new foe. That this new foe was despised by the great power which claimed, not without reason, to be the mistress of the seas, was not unnatural. But soon we find a lament raised in Parliament about the reverses of its navy, which were such as "English officers and English sailors had not before been used to particularly from such a contemptible navy as that of America had alway been held to be." The fact is, that the restriction of American commerce had made it possible for our naval officers to take their pick of a remarkably fine body of native American seamen, naturally brave and intelligent, and thoroughly well trained in all seamanlike experiences. These men were in many instances filled with a spirit of resentment at British insolence, having either themselves been the victims of the aggressions which we have described, or having seen their friends compelled to submit to these insolent acts. The very smallness of our navy, too, was in a measure its strength; the competition for active service among those bearing commissions was great, and there was never any trouble in finding officers of proved sagacity and courage.

At the outset, however, the policy determined on by the administration was not one of naval aggression. It was decided to attack England from her Canadian colonies. This plan of campaign, however reasonable it might seem to a strategist, failed wretchedly in execution. The first **The War on** year of the war, so far as regards the land campaigns, showed **the Canada** nothing but reverses and fiascoes. There was a long and **Border** thinly settled border country, in which our slender forces struggled to hold their own against the barbarous Indian onslaughts, making futile expeditions across the border into Canada, and resisting with some success the similar expeditions by the Canadian troops. One of the complaints which led to the war was that the Indian tribes had been incited against our settlers by the Canadian authorities and had been promised aid from Canada. It is certain that after war was declared British officers not only employed Indians as their allies, but, in some instances at least, paid bounties for the scalps of American settlers.

The Indian war planned by Tecumseh had just been put down by General (afterward President) Harrison. No doubt Tecumseh was a man of more elevated ambition and more humane instincts than one often finds in an Indian chief. His hope to unite the tribes and to drive the whites out of his country has a certain nobility of purpose and breadth of view. But this scheme had failed, and the Indian warriors, still inflamed for war, were only too eager to assist the Canadian forces in a desultory but bloody border war. The strength of our campaign against Canada was dissipated in an attempt to hold Fort Wayne, Fort Harrison, and other garrisons against Indian attacks. Still more disappointing was the complete **Hull and the** failure of the attempt, under the command of General Hull, **Surrender of** to advance from Detroit into Canada. He was easily driven **Detroit** back to Detroit, and, while the nation was confidently waiting to hear of a bold defence of that place, it was startled by the news of Hull's surrender

21

without firing a gun, and under circumstances which seemed to indicate either cowardice or treachery. Hull was, in fact, court-martialed and condemned to death, and was only pardoned on account of his services in the war of 1776.

The mortification that followed the land campaign of 1812 was forgotten in the joy at the splendid naval victories of that year. Pre-eminent among these was the famous sea-duel between the frigates *Constitution* and *Guerrière*. Every one knows of the glory of *Old Ironsides*, and this, though the greatest, was only one of many victories through which the name of the *Constitution* became the most famed and beloved of all that have been associated with American ships. She was a fine frigate, carrying forty-four guns, and though English journals had ridiculed her as "a bunch of pine boards under a bit of striped bunting," it was not long before they were busily engaged in trying to prove that she was too large a vessel to be properly called a frigate, and that she greatly out-classed her opponent in

The "Constitu- metal and men. It is true that the *Constitution* carried six
tion" and the more guns and a few more men than the *Guerrière*, but all
"Guerrière" allowances being made, her victory was a naval triumph of the

first magnitude. Captain Isaac Hull, who commanded her, had just before the engagement proved his superior seamanship by escaping from a whole squadron of British vessels, out-sailing and out-manœuvring them at every point. It was on August 19, 1812, that he descried the *Guerrière*. Both vessels at once cleared for action and came together with the greatest eagerness on both sides for the engagement. Though the battle lasted but half an hour, it was one of the hottest in naval annals. At one time the *Constitution* was on fire, and both ships were soon seriously crippled by injuries to their spars. Attempts to board each other were thwarted on both sides by the close fire of small arms. Here, as in later sea-fights of this war, the accu-

The Glorious racy and skill of the American gunners were something mar-
Victory of the velous. At the end of half an hour the *Guerrière* had lost
Frigate "Con- both mainmast and foremast, and floated as a helpless hulk in
stitution" the open sea. Her surrender was no discredit to her officers,

as she was almost in a sinking condition. It was hopeless to attempt to tow her into port, and Captain Hull transferred his prisoners to his own vessel and set fire to his prize.

In this engagement the American frigate had only seven men killed and an equal number wounded, while the British vessel had as many as seventy-nine men killed or wounded. The conduct of the American seamen was throughout gallant in the highest degree. Captain Hull put it on record that "From the smallest boy in the ship to the oldest seaman not a look of fear was seen.   They all went into action giving three cheers and requesting to be laid close alongside the enemy." The effect of this victory in both America and England was extraordinary.   English papers long refused to believe in the possibility of the well-proved facts, while in America the whole country joined in a triumphal shout of joy, and loaded well-deserved honors on vessel, captain, officers, and men.

The chagrin of the English public at the unexpected result of this sea-battle was changed to amazement and vexation when, one after another, there followed no less than six combats of the same duel-like character, in all of which the American vessels were victorious.   The first was between the American sloop *Wasp* and the English brig *Frolic*, which was convoying a fleet of merchantmen.   The fight was one of the most desperate in the war ; the two ships were brought so close together that their gunners could touch the sides of the opposing vessels with their rammers.   Broadside after broadside was poured into the *Frolic* by the *Wasp*, which obtained the superior position ; but her sailors, too excited to await the victory which was sure to come from the continued raking of the enemy's vessel, rushed upon her decks without orders and soon overpowered her.   Again the British loss in killed and wounded was large ; that of the Americans very small.   It in no wise detracted from the glory of this victory that both victor and prize were soon captured by a British man-of-war of immensely superior strength.

The "Wasp" Captures the "Frolic"

Following this action, Commodore Stephen Decatur, in the frigate *United States*, attacked the *Macedonian*, a British vessel of the same class, and easily defeated her, bringing her into New York harbor on New Year's Day, 1813, where he received an ovation equal to that offered Captain Hull.   The same result followed the attack of the *Constitution*, now under the command of Commodore Bainbridge, upon the British *Java*.   The latter had her captain and fifty men killed and about one hundred wounded, and was left such a wreck that it was decided to blow her up, while the *Constitution* suffered so little that she was in sport dubbed *Old Ironsides*, a name now ennobled by a poem which has been in every school-boy's mouth.   Other naval combats resulted, in the great majority of cases, in the same way ; in all unstinted praise was awarded by the nations of the world, even including England herself, to the admirable seamanship, the wonderful gunnery, and the personal intrepidity of our naval forces.   When the second year of the war closed our little navy had captured twenty-six warships, armed with 560 guns, while it had lost only seven ships, carrying 119 guns.

The "United States" and the "Macedonian"

But, if the highest honors of the war were thus won by our navy, the most serious injury materially to Great Britain was in the devastation of her commerce by American privateers. No less than two hundred and fifty of these sea guerrillas were afloat, and in the first year of the war they captured over three hundred merchant vessels, sometimes even attacking and overcoming the smaller class of warships. The privateers were usually schooners armed with a few small guns, but carrying one long cannon mounted on a swivel so that it could be turned to any point of the horizon, and familiarly known as Long Tom. Of course, the crews were influenced by greed as well as by patriotism. Privateering is a somewhat doubtful mode of warfare at the best ; but international law permits it, and, though it is hard to dissociate from it the aspect of legalized piracy, it is recognized to this day. In the most recent war, however, the Spanish-American, neither of the belligerent nations indulged in this relic of barbarism.

American Privateers and Their Work

If privateering were ever justifiable it was in the war now under consideration. As Jefferson said, there were then tens of thousands of seamen cut off by the war from their natural means of support and useless to their country in any other way, while by "licensing private armed vessels, the whole naval force of the nation was truly brought to bear on the foe." The havoc wrought on British trade was widespread indeed ; altogether between fifteen hundred and two thousand prizes were taken by the privateers. To compute the value of these prizes is impossible, but some idea may be gained from the single fact that one privateer, the *Yankee*, in a cruise of less than two months captured five brigs and four schooners, with cargoes valued at over half a million dollars. The men engaged in this form of warfare were bold to recklessness, and their exploits have furnished many a tale to American writers of romance.

The naval combats thus far mentioned were almost always of single vessels. For battles of fleets we must turn from the salt water to the fresh, from the ocean to the great lakes. The control of the waters of Lake Erie, Lake Ontario, and Lake Champlain was obviously of vast importance, in view of the continued land-fighting in the West and of the attempted invasion of Canada and the threatened counter-invasions. The British had the great advantage of being able to reach the lakes by the St. Lawrence, while our lake navies had to be constructed after the war began. One such little navy had been built at Presque Isle, now Erie, on Lake Erie. It comprised two brigs of twenty guns and several schooners and gunboats. It must be remembered that everything but the lumber needed for the vessels had to be brought through

The Fleets on the Lakes

the forests by land from the eastern seaports, and the mere problem of transportation was a serious one. When finished, the fleet was put in command of Oliver Hazard Perry. Watching his time (and, it is said, taking advantage of the carelessness of the British commander, who went on shore to dinner one Sunday, when he should have been watching Perry's movements), the American commander drew his fleet over the bar which had protected it while in harbor from the onslaughts of the British fleet. To get the brigs over this bar was a work of time and great difficulty; an attack at that hour by the British would certainly have ended in the total destruction of the fleet. This feat accomplished, Perry, in his flagship, the *Lawrence*, headed a fleet of ten vessels, fifty-five guns and four hundred men. Opposed to him was Captain Barclay with six ships, sixty-five guns, and also about four hundred men. The British for several weeks avoided the conflict, but in the end were cornered and forced to fight. It was at the beginning of this battle that Perry displayed the flag bearing Lawrence's famous dying words, "Don't give up the ship!" No less famous is his dispatch announcing the result in the words, "We have met the enemy and they are ours." The victory was indeed a complete and decisive one; all six of the enemy's ships were captured, and their loss was nearly double that of Perry's forces. The complete control of Lake Erie was assured; that of Lake Ontario had already been gained by Commodore Chauncey.

Perry's Great Victory on Lake Erie

Perry's memorable victory opened the way for important land operations by General Harrison, who now marched from Detroit with the design of invading Canada. He engaged with Proctor's mingled body of British troops and Indians, and by the battle of the Thames drove back the British from that part of Canada and restored matters to the position in which they stood before Hull's deplorable surrender of Detroit—and, indeed, of all Michigan—to the British. In this battle the Indian chief, Tecumseh, fell, and about three hundred of the British and Indians were killed on the field. The hold of our enemies on the Indian tribes was greatly broken by this defeat.

The Battle of the Thames

Previous to this the land campaigns had been marked by a succession of minor victories and defeats. In the West a force of Americans under General Winchester had been captured at the River Raisin, where there took place an atrocious massacre of prisoners by the Indians, who were quite beyond restraint from their white allies. On the other hand, the Americans had captured the city of York, now Toronto, though at the cost of their leader, General Pike, who, with two hundred of his men, was destroyed by the explosion of a magazine. Fort George had also been captured by the Americans and an attack on Sackett's Harbor had been gallantly repulsed. Following the battle of the Thames, extensive operations of an aggressive kind were planned, looking toward the capture of Montreal and the invasion of Canada by way of Lakes Ontario and Champlain. Unhappily, jealousy between the American Generals Wilkinson and Hampton resulted in a lack of concert in their military operations, and the expedition became a complete fiasco.

One turns for consolation from the mortifying record of Wilkinson's expedition to the story of the continuous successes which accompanied the naval operations of 1813. Captain Lawrence, in the *Hornet*, won a complete victory over the English brig *Peacock;* our brig, the *Enterprise*, captured the *Boxer*, and other equally welcome victories were reported. One distinct defeat marred the record—that of our fine brig, the *Chesapeake*, commanded by Captain Lawrence, which was captured after one of the most hard-fought contests of the war by the British brig, the *Shannon*.

Lawrence's Famous Saying, "Don't Give Up the Ship." Lawrence himself fell mortally wounded, exclaiming as he was carried away, "Tell the men not to give up the ship, but fight her till she sinks." It was a paraphrase of this exclamation which Perry used as a rallying signal in the battle on Lake Erie. Despite his one defeat, Captain Lawrence's fame as a gallant seaman and high-minded patriot was untarnished, and his death was more deplored throughout the country than was the loss of his ship.

In the latter part of the war England was enabled to send large reinforcements both to her army and navy engaged in the American campaigns. Events in Europe seemed in 1814 to insure peace for at least a time. Napoleon's power was broken ; the Emperor himself was exiled at Elba ; and Great Britain at last had her hands free. But before the reinforcements reached this country, our army had won greater credit and had shown more military skill by far than were evinced in its earlier operations. Along the line of the Niagara River active fighting had been going on. In the battle of Chippewa, the capture of Fort Erie, the engagement at Lundy's Lane, and the defence of Fort Erie the troops, under the command of Generals Winfield Scott and Brown, had more than held their own against superior forces, and had won from British officers the admission that they fought as well under fire as regular troops. More encouraging still

Macdonough's Victory on Lake Champlain was the total defeat of the plan of invasion from Canada undertaken by the now greatly strengthened British forces. These numbered twelve thousand men and were supported by a fleet on Lake Champlain. Their operations were directed against Plattsburg, and in the battle on the lake, usually called by the name of that town, the American flotilla, under the command of Commodore Macdonough, completely routed the British fleet. As a result the English army also beat a rapid and undignified retreat to Canada. This was the last important engagement to take place in the North.

Meanwhile expeditions of considerable size were directed by the British against our principal Southern cities. One of these brought General Ross with five thousand men, chiefly the pick of the Duke of Wellington's army, into the Bay of Chesapeake. Nothing was more discreditable in the military strategy of our administration than the fact that at this time Washington was left unprotected, though in evident danger. General Ross marched straight upon the capital, easily defeated at Bladensburg an inferior force of raw militia—who fought, however, with much courage—seized the city, and carried out his intention of destroying the public buildings and a great part of the town. Most of the public archives had been removed. Ross's conduct in the burning of Washington, though of a character common enough in modern warfare, has been condemned as semi-barbarous by many writers. The achievement was greeted with enthusiasm by the English papers, but was really of much less importance than they supposed. Washington at that time was a straggling town of only eight thousand inhabitants; its public buildings were not at all adequate to the demands of the future; and an optimist might even consider the destruction of the old city as a public benefit, for it **The Burning of the American Capital** enabled Congress to adopt the plans which have since led to the making of the most beautiful city of the country, if not of the world.

A similar attempt upon Baltimore was less successful. The people of that city made a brave defence and hastily threw up extensive fortifications. In the end the British fleet, after a severe bombardment of Fort McHenry, was driven off. The British admiral had boasted that Fort McHenry would yield in a few hours; and two days after, when its flag was still flying, Francis S. Key was inspired by its sight to compose our far-famed national ode, the "Star Spangled Banner."

A still larger expedition of British troops soon after landed on the Louisiana coast and marched to the attack of New Orleans. Here General Andrew Jackson was in command. He had already distinguished himself during the war by putting down with a strong hand the hostile Creek Indians, who had been incited by English envoys to warfare against our southern settlers; and in April, 1814, William Weathersford, the halfbreed chief, had surrendered in person to Jackson. General Packenham, who commanded the five thousand British soldiers sent against New Orleans, expected as easy a victory as that of Gen- **Jackson and the Creek Indians** eral Ross at Washington. But Jackson had summoned to his aid the stalwart frontiersmen of Kentucky and Tennessee—men used from boyhood to the rifle, and who made up what was in effect a splendid force of sharp-shooters. Both armies threw up rough fortifications; General Jackson made great use for that purpose of cotton bales, Packenham employing the still less solid material of sugar barrels. As it proved neither of these were suitable for the purpose, and they had to be replaced by earthworks. Oddly enough, the final battle, and really the most important one of the war, took place after the treaty of peace between the two countries had been signed. The British were repulsed again and again in persistent and

Jackson's Famous Great Victory at New Orleans gallant attacks on our fortifications. General Packenham himself was killed, together with many of his officers and seven hundred of his men. One British officer pushed to the top of our earthworks and demanded their surrender, whereupon he was smilingly asked to look behind him, and turning saw, as he afterwards said, that the men he supposed to be supporting him "had vanished as if the earth had swallowed them up." Of the Americans only a few men were killed.

The treaty of peace, signed at Ghent, December 24, 1814, has been ridiculed because it contained no positive agreement as to many of the questions in dispute. Not a word did it say about the impressment of American sailors or the rights of neutral ships. Its chief stipulations were the mutual restoration of territory and the appointing of a commission to determine our northern boundary line. The truth is that both nations were tired of the war; the circumstances that had led to England's aggressions no longer existed; both countries were suffering enormous commercial loss to no avail; and, above all, the United States had emphatically justified by its deeds its claim to an equal place in the council of nations.

The Results of the War Politically and materially, further warfare was illogical. If the two nations had understood each other better in the first place; if Great Britain had treated our demands with courtesy and justice instead of with insolence; if, in short, international comity had taken the place of international ill-temper, the war might have been avoided altogether. Its undoubted benefits to us were incidental rather than direct. But though not formally recognized by treaty, the rights of American seamen and of American ships were in fact no longer infringed upon by Great Britain.

One political outcome of the war must not be overlooked. The New England Federalists had opposed it from the beginning, had naturally fretted at their loss of commerce, and had bitterly upbraided the Democratic administration for currying popularity by a war carried on mainly at New England's expense. When, in the latter days of the war, New England ports were closed, Stonington was bombarded, Castine in Maine was seized, and serious depredations were threatened everywhere along the northeastern coast, the Federalists complained that the administration taxed them for the war but did not protect them. The outcome of all this discontent was the Hartford Convention. In point of fact it was a quite harmless conference which proposed some constitutional amendments, protested against too great centralization of power, and urged the desirability of peace with honor. But **The Hartford Convention** the most absurd rumors were prevalent about its intentions; a regiment of troops was actually sent to Hartford to anticipate treasonable outbreaks; and for many years good Democrats religiously believed that there had been a plot to set up a monarchy in New England with the Duke of Kent as king. Harmless as it was, the Hartford Convention caused the death of the Federalist party. Its mild debates were distorted into secret conclaves plotting treason, and, though the news of peace followed close upon it, the Convention was long an object of opprobrium and a political bugbear.

CHAPTER XXVI.

The United States Sustains Its Dignity Abroad.

IF the reader will look at any map of Africa he will see on the northern coast, defining the southern limits of the Mediterranean, four States, Morocco, Algeria, Tunis, and Tripoli, running east and west a distance of 1800 miles. These powers had for centuries maintained a state of semi-independency by paying tribute to Turkey. But this did not suit Algeria, the strongest and most warlike of the North African States; and in the year 1710 the natives overthrew the rule of the Turkish Pasha, expelled him from the country, and united his authority to that of the Dey, the Algerian monarch. The Dey subsequently governed the country by means of a **The Piratical** Divan or Council of State chosen from the principal civic **States of** functionaries. The Algerians, with the other "Barbary **North Africa** States," as the piratical States were called, defied the powers of Europe; their armed vessels sweeping the waters of the Mediterranean, committing a thousand ravages upon the merchant vessels of other nations, and almost driving commerce from its waters. France alone resisted these depredations, and this only partially, for after she had repeatedly chastised the Algerians, the strongest of the piratical States, and had induced the Dey to sign a treaty of peace, the Corsairs would await their opportunity and after a time resume their depredations. Algiers in the end forced the United States to resort to arms in the defence of its commerce, and the long immunity of the pirates did not cease until the great republic of the West took them in hand.

The truth is, this conflict was no less irrepressible than that greater conflict which a century later deluged the land in blood. Before the Constitution of the United States had been adopted, two American vessels, flying the flag of thirteen stripes and thirteen stars, instead of the forty-five stars which now form our national constellation, while sailing the Mediterranean had fallen a prey to the swift, heavily-armed Algerian cruisers. The vessels were confiscated, and their crews, to the number of twenty-one persons, were held for ransom, for which an enormous sum was demanded.

This sum our Government was by no means willing to pay, as to do so would be to establish a precedent not only with Algeria, but also with Tunis,

Tripoli, and Morocco, for each of these African piratical States was in league with the others, and all had to be separately conciliated.

But, after all, what else could the Government do? The country had no navy. It could not undertake in improvised ships to go forth and fight the powerful cruisers of the African pirates—States so strong that the commercial nations of Europe were glad to win exemption from their depredations by annual payments. Why not, then, ransom these American captives by the payment of money and construct a navy sufficiently strong to resist their encroachments in the future? This feeling on the part of the Government was shared by the people of the country, and as a result Congress authorized the building of six frigates, and by another act empowered President Washington to borrow a million of dollars for purchasing peace. Eventually the ransom money was paid to the piratical powers, and it was hoped all difficulty was at an end. But, as a necessary provision for the future, the work of constructing the new warships was pushed with expedition. As will be seen, this proved to be a wise and timely precaution. *The War with the Pirates of Tripoli*

We are now brought to the year 1800. Tripoli, angry at not receiving as much money as was paid to Algiers, declared war against the United States. Circumstances, however, had changed for the better, and the republic was prepared to deal with the oppressors of its seamen in a more dignified and efficient manner than that of paying ransom. For our new navy, a small but most efficient one, had been completed, and a squadron consisting of the frigates *Essex*, Captain Bainbridge, the *Philadelphia*, the *President*, and the schooner *Experiment*, was in Mediterranean waters. Two Tripolitan cruisers lying at Gibraltar on the watch for American vessels were blockaded by the *Philadelphia*. Cruising off Tripoli, the *Experiment* fell in with a Tripolitan cruiser of fourteen guns, and after three hours' hard fighting captured her, the Tripolitans losing twenty killed and thirty wounded. This brilliant result had a marked effect in quieting the turbulent pirates, who for the first time began to respect the United States. A treaty was signed in 1805, in which Tripoli agreed no longer to molest American ships and sailors.

This war was marked by a striking evidence of American pluck and readiness in an emergency. During the contest the frigate *Philadelphia*, while chasing certain piratical craft into the harbor of Tripoli, ran aground in a most perilous situation. Escape was impossible, she was under the guns of the shore batteries and of the Tripolitan navy, and after a vain effort to sink her, all on board were forced to surrender as prisoners of war. Subsequently *The Famous Incident of the "Philadelphia"* the Tripolitans suceeded in floating the frigate, brought her into port in triumph, and began to refit her as a welcome addition to their navy. This state of affairs was galling to American pride, and, as the vessel could not be rescued, it was determined to make an effort to destroy her.   One night a Moorish merchantman (captured and fitted for the purpose) entered the harbor and made her way close up to the side of the *Philadelphia*.   Only a few men, dressed in Moorish garb, were visible, and no suspicion of their purpose was entertained.   As these men claimed to have lost their anchor, a rope was thrown them from the vessel, and they made fast.   In a minute more a startling change took place.   A multitude of concealed Americans suddenly sprang into sight, clambered to the deck of the *Philadelphia*, and drove the surprised Moors over her sides.   The frigate was fairly recaptured. But she could not be taken out, so the tars set her on fire, and made their escape by the light of her blazing spars and under the guns of the Tripolitan batteries, not a ball from which reached them.   It was a gallant achievement, and gave fame to Decatur, its leader.

But peace was not yet assured.   In 1815, when this country had just ended its war with Great Britain, the Dey of Algiers unceremoniously dismissed the American Consul and declared war against the United States, on the plea that he had not received certain articles demanded under the tribute treaty.

War Declared by Algiers   This time the government was well prepared for the issue.   The population of the country had increased to over eight millions. The military spirit of the nation had been aroused by the war with Great Britain, ending in the splendid victory at New Orleans under General Jackson.   Besides this, the navy had been increased and made far more effective.   The administration, with Madison at its head, decided to submit to no further extortions from the Mediterranean pirates, and the President sent in a forcible message to Congress on the subject, taking high American ground.   The result was a prompt acceptance of the Algerian declaration of war.   Events succeeded each other in rapid succession. Ships new and old were at once fitted out.   On May 15, 1815, Decatur sailed from New York to the Mediterranean.   His squadron comprised the frigates *Guerriere*, *Macedonian* and *Constellation*, the new sloop of war *Ontario*, and four brigs and two schooners in addition.

The Dey Sues for Peace   On June 17th, the second day after entering the Mediterranean, Decatur captured the largest frigate in the Algerian navy, having forty-four guns.   The next day an Algerian brig was taken, and in less than two weeks after his first capture Decatur, with his entire squadron, appeared off Algiers.   The end had come.   The Dey's courage, like that of Bob Acres, oozed out at his fingers' ends.   The terrified Dey sued for peace, which Decatur compelled him to sign on the quarter-deck of the *Guerriere*.   In this treaty it was agreed by the Dey to sur-render all prisoners, pay a heavy indemnity, and renounce all tribute from America in the future.   Decatur also secured indemnity from Tunis and Tripoli for American vessels captured under the guns of their forts by British cruisers during the late war.

This ended at once and forever the payment of tribute to the piratical States of North Africa.   All Europe, as well as our own country, rang with the splendid achievements of our navy ; and surely the stars and stripes had never before floated more proudly from the masthead of an American vessel—and they are flying as proudly to-day.

One further example of the readiness of this country to defend itself upon the seas in its weak, early period may be related, though it slightly antedated the beginning of the century.   This was a result of American indignation at the ravages upon its commerce by the warring nations of Europe.   About 1798 the depredations of France **A Naval War with France** upon our merchantmen became so aggravating that, without the formality of a declaration, a naval war began.   The vessels of our new navy were sent out, "letters of marque and reprisal" were granted to privateers, and their work soon began to tell.   Captain Truxton of the *Con-stellation* captured the French frigate *L'Insurgente*, the privateers brought more than fifty armed vessels of the French into port and France quickly de-cided that she wanted peace.   This sort of argument was not quite to her taste.

Seventeen years after the close of the trouble with Algiers, in 1832, one of the most interesting cases of difficulty with a foreign power arose. As with Algeria and Tripoli, so now our navy was resorted to for the pur-pose of exacting reparation.   This time the trouble was with the kingdom of Naples, in Italy, which had been wrested from Spain by Napoleon, who placed successively his brother Joseph and his brother-in-law Murat on the throne of Naples and the two Sicilies.   During the years 1809–12 the Nea-politan government, under Joseph and Murat successively, had confiscated numerous American ships with their cargoes.   The total amount of the American claims against Naples, as filed in the State department when Jackson's administration assumed control, was $1,734,994.   They were held by various insurance companies and by citizens, principally of Baltimore. Demands for the payment of these claims had from time to time been made by our government, but Naples had always refused to settle them.

Jackson and his cabinet took a decided stand, and determined that the Neapolitan government, then in the hands of Ferdinand II.—subsequently nicknamed Bomba because of his cruelties—should make due reparation for the losses sustained by American citizens. The Hon. John Nelson, of Frederick, Maryland, was appointed Minister to Naples, and required to insist upon a settlement. Commodore Daniel Patterson, who had aided

The Claim Against Naples in the defense of New Orleans in 1815, was put in command of the Mediterranean squadron and ordered to co-operate with Minister Nelson in enforcing his demands. But Naples persisted in her refusal to render satisfaction, and a warlike demonstration was decided upon, the whole matter being placed, under instructions, in the hands of Commodore Patterson.

The entire force under his command consisted of three fifty-gun frigates and three twenty-gun corvettes. In order not to precipitate matters too hastily, the plan adopted was that these vessels should appear in the Neapolitan waters one at a time, and instructions were given to that effect. The *Brandywine*, with Minister Nelson on board, went first. Mr. Nelson made his demand for a settlement and was refused. There was nothing in the appearance of a Yankee envoy and a single ship to trouble King Bomba and his little kingdom. The *Brandywine* cast anchor in the harbor and the humbled envoy waited patiently for a few days. Then

How King Bomba was Brought to Terms another American flag appeared on the horizon, and the frigate *United States* floated into the harbor and came to anchor. Mr. Nelson repeated his demands, and they were again refused. Four days slipped away, and the stars and stripes once more appeared off the harbor. King Bomba, looking out from his palace windows, saw the fifty-gun frigate *Concord* sail into the harbor and drop her anchor. Then unmistakable signs of uneasiness began to show themselves. Forts were repaired, troops drilled, and more cannon mounted on the coast. The demands were reiterated, but the Neapolitan government still declined to consider them. Two days later another war-ship made her way into the harbor. It was the *John Adams*. When the fifth ship sailed gallantly in, Nelson sent word home that he was still unable to collect the bill. The end was not yet. Three days later, and the sixth American sail showed itself on the blue waters of the peerless bay. It was the handwriting on the wall for King Bomba, and his government announced that they would accede to the American demands. The negotiations were promptly resumed and speedily closed, the payment of the principal in installments with interest being guaranteed. Pending negotiations, from August 28th to September 15th the entire squadron remained in the Bay of Naples, and then the ships sailed away and separated. So, happily and bloodlessly, ended a difficulty which at one time threatened most serious results.

Another demonstration, less imposing in numbers but quite as spirited, and, indeed, more intensely dramatic, occurred at Smyrna in 1853, when Captain Duncan N. Ingraham, with a single sloop-of-war, trained his broadsides on a fleet of Austrian warships in the harbor. The episode was a most thrilling one, and our record would be incomplete were so dramatic an affair left unrecorded on its pages. This is the story:

Captain Ingraham and the Koszta Affair

When the revolution of Hungary against Austria was put down, Kossuth, Koszta, and other leading revolutionists fled to Smyrna, and the Turkish government, after long negotiations, refused to give them up. Koszta soon after came to the United States, and in July, 1852, declared under oath his intention of becoming an American citizen. He resided in New York city a year and eleven months.

A year after he had declared his intention to assume American citizenship, Koszta went to Smyrna on business, where he remained for a time undisturbed. He had so inflamed the Austrian government against him, however, that a plot was formed to capture him. On June 21, 1853, while he was seated on the Marina, a public resort in Smyrna, a band of Greek mercenaries, hired by the Austrian Consul, seized him and carried him off to an Austrian ship-of-war, the *Huzzar*, then lying in the harbor. Archduke John, brother of the emperor, is said to have been in command of this vessel. Koszta was put in irons and treated as a criminal. The next day an American sloop-of-war, the *St. Louis*, commanded by Captain Duncan N. Ingraham, sailed into the harbor. Learning what had happened, Captain Ingraham immediately sent on board the *Huzzar* and courteously asked permission to see Koszta. His request was granted, and the captain assured himself that Koszta was entitled to the protection of the American flag. He demanded his release from the Austrian commander. When it was refused, he communicated with the nearest United States official, Consul Brown, at Constantinople. While he was waiting for an answer six Austrian warships sailed into the harbor and came to anchor in positions near the *Huzzar*. On June 29th, before Captain Ingraham had received any answer from the American Consul, he noticed unusual signs of activity on board the *Huzzar*, and before long she began to get under way. The American captain made up his mind immediately. He put the *St. Louis* straight in the *Huzzar's* course and cleared his guns for action. The *Huzzar* hove to, and Captain Ingraham went on board and demanded the meaning of her action.

The "St. Louis" and the "Huzzar"

"We propose to sail for home," replied the Austrian. "The consul has ordered us to take our prisoner to Austria."

You will pardon me," said Captain Ingraham, "but if you attempt to leave this port with that American on board I shall be compelled to resort to extreme measures."

The Austrian glanced around at the fleet of Austrian war-ships and the single American sloop-of-war. Then he smiled pleasantly, and intimated that the *Huzzar* would do as she pleased.

Captain Ingraham bowed and returned to the *St. Louis*. He had no sooner reached her deck than he called out : "Clear the guns for action !"

The Archduke of Austria saw the batteries of the *St. Louis* turned upon him, and suddenly realized that he was in the wrong. The *Huzzar* was put about and sailed back to her old anchorage. Word was sent to Captain Ingraham that the Austrian would await the arrival of the note from Mr. Brown.

The consul's note, which came on July 1st, commended Captain Ingraham's course and advised him to take whatever action he thought the situation demanded. At eight o'clock on the morning of July 2d, Captain Ingraham sent a note to the commander of the *Huzzar*, formally demanding the release of Mr. Koszta. Unless the prisoner was delivered on board the *St. Louis* before four o'clock the next afternoon, Captain Ingraham would take him from the Austrians by force. The Archduke sent back a formal refusal. At eight o'clock the next morning Captain Ingraham once more

Koszta is Given Up to Ingraham ordered the decks cleared for action and trained his batteries on the *Huzzar*. The seven Austrian war vessels cleared their decks and put their men at the guns.

At ten o'clock an Austrian officer came to Captain Ingraham and began to temporize. Captain Ingraham refused to listen to him.

"To avoid the worst," he said, "I will agree to let the man be delivered to the French Consul at Smyrna until you have opportunity to communicate with your government. But he must be delivered there, or I will take him. I have stated the time."

At twelve o'clock a boat left the *Huzzar* with Koszta in it, and an hour later the French Consul sent word that Koszta was in his keeping. Then several of the Austrian war-wessels sailed out of the harbor. Long negotiations between the two governments followed, and in the end Austria admitted that the United States was in the right, and apologized.

Scarcely had the plaudits which greeted Captain Ingraham's intrepid course died away, when, the next year, another occasion arose where our government was obliged to resort to the show of force. This time Nicaragua was the country involved. Various outrages, as was contended, had been committed on the persons and property of American citizens dwelling in that country. The repeated demands for redress were not complied with. Peaceful negotiations having failed, in June, 1854, Commander Hollins, with the sloop of war *Cyane*, was ordered to proceed to the town of San Juan, or Greytown, **The Trouble with Nicaragua** which lies on the Mosquito coast of Nicaragua, and to insist on favorable action from the Nicaraguan government.

Captain Hollins came to anchor off the coast and placed his demands before the authorities. He waited patiently for a response, but no satisfactory one was offered him. After a number of days he made a final appeal and then proceeded to carry out his instructions. On the morning of July 13th he directed his batteries on the town of San Juan and opened fire. Until four o'clock in the afternoon the ship poured out broadsides as fast as its guns could be loaded. By that time the greater part of the town was destroyed. Then a party of marines was put on shore, and completed the destruction of the place by burning the houses.

A lieutenant of the British navy commanding a small vessel of war was in the harbor at the time. England claimed a species of protectorate over the settlement, and the British officer raised violent protest against the action taken by America's representative. Captain Hollins, however, paid no attention to the interference and carried out his instructions. The United States government later sustained Captain Hollins in everything he had done, and England thereupon thought best to let the matter drop. In this that country was unquestionably wise.

At this time the United States seems to have entered upon a period of international conflict; for no sooner had the difficulties with Austria and Nicaragua been adjusted than another war-cloud appeared on the horizon. Here again only a year from the last conflict had elapsed, for in 1855 an offense was committed against the United States by Paraguay. To explain what it was we shall have to go back three years. **In Paraguayan Waters** In 1852 Captain Thomas J. Page, commanding a small light-draught steamer, the *Water Witch*, by direction of his government started for South America to explore the River La Plata and its large tributaries, with a view to opening up commercial intercourse between the United States and the interior States of South America. We have said that the expedition was ordered by our government; it also remains to be noted that it was undertaken with the full consent and approbation of the countries having jurisdiction over those waters. Slowly, but surely, the little steamer pushed her way up the river, making soundings and charting the river as she proceeded. All went well until February 1, 1855, when the first sign of trouble appeared.

It was a lovely day in early summer—the summer begins in February in that latitude—and nothing appeared to indicate the slightest disturbance The little *Water Witch* was quietly steaming up the River Paraná, which forms the northern boundary of the State of Corrientes, separating it from Paraguay, when suddenly, without a moment's warning, a battery from Fort Itaparu, on the Paraguayan shore, opened fire upon her, immediately killing

The Assault on the "Water Witch" one of her crew, who at that time was at the wheel. The *Water Witch* was not fitted for hostilities; least of all could she assume the risk of attempting to run the batteries of the fort. Accordingly, Captain Page put the steamer about, and was soon out of range. It should here be explained that at that time President Carlos A. Lopez was the autocratic ruler of Paraguay, and that he had previously received Captain Page with every assurance of friendship. A few months previous, however, Lopez had been antagonized by the United States consul at Ascencion. This gentleman, in addition to his official position, acted as agent for an American mercantile company of which Lopez disapproved and whose business he had broken up. He had also issued a decree forbidding foreign vessels of war to navigate the Paraná or any of the waters bounding Paraguay, which he clearly had no right to do, as half the stream belonged to the country bo dering on the other side.

Captain Page, finding it impr cticable to prosecute his exploration any further, at once returned to the Ur ted States, where he gave the Washington authorities a detailed account of the occurrence. It was claimed by our government that the *Water Witch* was not subject to the jurisdiction of Paraguay, as the channel was the equal property of the Argentine Republic. It was further claimed that, even if she had been within the jurisdiction of Paraguay, she was not properly a vessel of war, but a government boat employed for scientific purposes. And even were the vessel supposed to be a war vessel, it was contended that it was a gross violation of international right and courtesy to fire shot at the vessel of a friendly power without first esorting to more peaceful means. At that time William L. Marcy, one of the oremost statesmen of his day, was Secretary of State. Mr. Marcy at once

Marcy Demands Reparation wrote a strong letter to the Paraguayan government, stating the facts of the case, declaring that the action of Paraguay in firing upon the *Water Witch* would not be submitted to, and demanding ample apology and compensation. All efforts in this direction, however, proved fruitless. Lopez refused to give any reparation; and not only so, but declared that no American vessel would be allowed to ascend the Paraná for the purpose indicated.

The event, as it became known, aroused not a little excitement; and while there were some who deprecated a resort to extreme measures, the general sentiment of the country was decidedly manifested in favor of an assertion of our rights in the premises. Accordingly, President Pierce sent a message to Congress, stating that a peaceful adjustment of the difficulty was impossible, and asking for authority to send such a naval force to Paraguay as would compel her arbitrary ruler to give the full satisfaction demanded.

To this request Congress promptly and almost unanimously gave assent, and one of the strongest naval expeditions ever fitted out by the United States up to that time was ordered to assemble at the mouth of La Plata River. The fleet was an imposing one for the purpose, and comprised nineteen vessels, seven of which were steamers specially **A Powerful** chartered for the purpose, as our largest war vessels were of **Fleet Sent to** too deep draught to ascend the La Plata and Paraná. The **Paraguay** entire squadron carried 200 guns and 2,500 men, and was commanded by flag officer, afterward rear-admiral, Shubrick, one of the oldest officers of our navy, and one of the most gallant men that ever trod a quarter-deck. Flag Officer Shubrick was accompanied by United States Commissioner Bowlin, to whom was intrusted negotiations for the settlement of the difficulty.

Three years and eleven months had now passed since the *Water Witch* was fired upon, and President Buchanan had succeeded Franklin Pierce. The winter of 1859 was just closing in at the north; the streams were closed by ice, and the lakes were ice-bound, but the palm trees of the south were displaying their fresh green leaves, like so many fringed banners, in the warm tropical air when the United States squadron assembled at Montevideo. The fleet included two United States frigates, the *Sabine* and the *St. Lawrence;* two sloops-of-war, the *Falmouth* and the *Preble;* three brigs, the *Bainbridge,* the *Dolphin* and the *Perry;* seven steamers especially armed for the occasion, the *Memphis,* the *Caledonia,* the *Atlanta,* the *Southern Star,* the *Westernport,* the *M. W. Chapin,* and the *Metacomet;* two armed store-ships, the *Supply* and the *Release;* the revenue steamer, *Harriet Lane;* and, lastly, the little *Water Witch* herself, no longer defenceless, but in fighting trim for hostilities.

On the 25th of January, 1859, within just one week of four years from the firing up the *Water Witch,* the squadron got under way and came to anchor off Ascencion, the capital of Paraguay. Meanwhile **The Ships** President Urquiza, of the Argentine Republic, who had **Anchor off** offered his services to mediate the difficulty, had arrived at **Ascencion** Ascencion in advance of the squadron. The negotiations were reopened, and

Commissioner Bowlin made his demand for instant reparation. All this time Flag Officer Shubrick was not idle. With such of our vessels as were of suitable size he ascended the river, taking them through the difficulties created by its currents, shoals and sand bars, and brought them to a position above the town, where they were made ready for action in case of necessity to open fire. The force within striking distance of Paraguay consisted of 1,740 men, besides the officers, and 78 guns, including 23 nine-inch shell guns and one shell gun of eleven inches.

Ships and guns proved to be very strong arguments with Lopez. It did not take the Dictator-President long to see that the United States meant business, and that the time for trifling had passed and the time for serious work had come. President Lopez's cerebral processes worked with remarkable and encouraging celerity. By February 5th, within less than two weeks of the starting of the squadron from Montevideo, Commissioner Bowlin's demands were all acceded to. Ample apologies were made for **President Lopez** firing on the *Water Witch*, aud pecuniary compensation was **Brought to** given to the family of the sailor who had been killed. In **Terms** addition to this, a new commercial treaty was made, and cordial relations were fully restored between the two governments.

A period of more than thirty years now elapsed before any serious difficulty occurred with a foreign power. In 1891 an event took place that threatened to disturb our relations with Chili and possibly involve the United States in war with that power. Happily the matter reached a peaceful settlement. In January, of that year, civil war had broken out in Chili, the cause of which was a contest between the legislative branch of the government **The Civil War** and the executive, for the control of affairs. The President of **in Chili** Chili, General Balmaceda, began to assert authority which the legislature, or "the Congressionalists," as the opposing party was called, resisted as unconstitutional and oppressive, and they accordingly proceeded to interfere with Balmaceda's Cabinet in its efforts to carry out the president's despotic will.

Finally matters came to a point where appeal to arms was necessary. On the 9th of January the Congressional party took possession of the greater part of the Chilian fleet, the navy being in hearty sympathy with them, and the guns of the warships were turned against Balmaceda,— Valparaiso, the capital, and other ports being blockaded by the ships. For a time Balmaceda maintained control of the capital and the southern part of the country. The key to the position was Valparaiso, which was strongly fortified, Balmaceda's army being massed there and placed at available points.

At last the Congressionalists determined to attack Balmaceda at his capital, and on August 21st landed every available fighting man at their disposal at Concon, about ten miles north of Valparaiso. They were attacked by the Dictator on the 22d, there being twenty thousand men on each side. The Dictator had the worst of it. Then he rallied his shattered forces, and made his last stand at Placillo, close to Valparaiso, on the 28th. The battle was hot, the carnage fearful; neither side asked for or received quarter. The magazine rifles, with which the revolutionists were armed, did wonders. The odds were against Balmaceda; both his generals quarreled in face of the enemy; his army became divided and demoralized. In a later battle both of his generals were killed. **The Overthrow of Balmaceda** The valor and the superior tactics of General Canto, leader of the Congressional army, won the day. Balmaceda fled and eventually committed suicide, and the Congressionalists entered the capital in triumph.

Several incidents meantime had conspired, during the progress of this war, to rouse the animosity of the stronger party in Chili against the United States. Before the Congressionalists' triumph the steamship *Itata*, loaded with American arms and ammunition for Chili, sailed from San Francisco, and as this was a violation of the neutrality laws, a United States war vessel pursued her to the harbor of Iquique, where she surrendered. Then other troubles arose. Our minister at Valparaiso, Mr. Egan, was charged by the Congressionalists, then in power, with disregarding international law in allowing the American Legation to be made an asylum for the adherents of Balmaceda. Subsequently these refugees were permitted to go aboard American vessels and sail away. Then Admiral Brown, of the United States squadron, was, in Chili's opinion, guilty of having acted as a spy upon the movements of the Congressionalists' fleet at Quinteros, and of bringing intelligence of its movements to Balmaceda at Valparaiso. This, however, the Admiral stoutly denied.

The strong popular feeling of dislike which was engendered by these charges culminated on the 16th of October, in an attack upon American seamen by a mob in the streets of the Chilian capital. Captain Schley, commander of the United States cruiser *Baltimore*, had given shore-leave to a hundred and seventeen petty officers and seamen, some of **An Attack on** whom, when they had been on shore for several hours, were **the Men of** set upon by Chilians. They took refuge in a street car, from **the "Baltimore"** which, however, they were soon driven and mercilessly beaten, and a subordinate officer named Riggen fell, apparently lifeless. The American sailors, according to Captain Schley's testimony, were sober and conducting themselves with propriety when the attack was made. They were not armed, even their knives having been taken from them before they left the vessel.

The assault upon those in the street car seemed to be only a signal for a general uprising; and a mob which is variously estimated at from one thousand to two thousand people attacked our sailors with such fury that in a little while these men, whom no investigation could find guilty of any breach of the peace, were fleeing for their lives before an overwhelming crowd, among which were a number of the police of Valparaiso. In this affray eighteen sailors were stabbed, several dying from their wounds.

Of course the United States government at once communicated with the Chilian authorities on the subject, expressing an intention to investigate the occurrence fully. The first reply made to the American government by Signor Matta, the Chilian minister of foreign affairs, was to the effect that Chili would not allow anything to interfere with her own official investigation.

An examination of all the facts was made on our part. It was careful and thorough, and showed that our flag had been insulted in the persons of American seamen. Yet, while the Chilian court of inquiry could present

An Investigation Demanded no extenuating facts, that country refused at first to offer apology or reparation for the affront. In the course of the correspondence Minister Matta sent a note of instruction to Mr. Montt, Chilian representative at Washington, in which he used the most offensive terms in relation to the United States, and directed that the letter should be given to the press for publication.

After waiting for a long time for the result of the investigation at Valparaiso, and finding that, although no excuse or palliation had been found for the outrage, the Chilian authorities seemed reluctant to offer apology, the President of the United States, in a message to Congress, made an extended statement of the various incidents of the case and its legal aspect, and stated that on the 21st of January he had caused a peremptory communication to be presented to the Chilian government by the American minister at Santiago, in which severance of diplomatic relations was threatened if our demands for satisfaction, which included the withdrawal of Mr. Matta's insulting note, were not complied with. At the time that this message was delivered no reply had been sent to the note.

Mr. Harrison's statement of the legal aspect of the case, upon which the final settlement of the difficulty was based, was that the presence of a warship of any nation in a port belonging to a friendly power is by virtue of a general invitation which nations are held to extend to each other; that

Commander Schley was invited, with his officers and crew, to enjoy the hospitality of Valparaiso; that while no claim that an attack which an individual sailor may be subjected to raises an international The American question, yet where the resident population assault sailors of Case Presented another country's war vessels, as at Valparaiso, animated by an animosity against the government to which they belong, that government must act as it would if the representatives or flag of the nation had been attacked, since the sailors are there by the order of their government.

Finally an ultimatum was sent from the State department at Washington, on the 25th, to Minister Egan, and was by him transmitted to the proper Chilian authorities. It demanded the retraction of Mr. Matta's note and suitable apology and reparation for the insult and injury Chili Offers an sustained by the United States. On the 28th of January, Apology and Reparation 1892, a dispatch from Chili was received, in which the demands of our government were fully acceded to, the offensive letter was withdrawn, and regret was expressed for the occurrence. In his relation to this particular case, Minister Egan's conduct received the entire approval of his government.

While the United States looked for a peaceful solution of this annoying international episode, the proper preparations were made for a less desirable outcome. Our naval force was put in as efficient a condition as possible, and the vessels which were then in the navy yard were got ready for service with all expedition. If the Chilian war-scare did nothing else, it aroused a wholesome interest in naval matters throughout the whole of the United States, and by focusing attention upon the needs of this branch of the public service, showed at once how helpless we might become in the event of a war with any first-class power. We may thank Chili that to-day the United States Navy is in a better condition than at any time in our history.

When the great Napoleon was overthrown, France, Russia, Prussia and Austria formed an alliance for preserving the "balance of power" and for suppressing revolutions within one another's dominions. This has been spoken of in a preceding chapter as the "Holy Alliance." At the time the Spanish South American colonies were in revolt, and the alliance had taken steps indicating an intention to aid in their reduction. George Canning, the English secretary of state, proposed to our country that we should unite with England in preventing such an outrage against civilization. It was a momentous question, and President The Monroe Monroe consulted with Jefferson, Madison, Calhoun and Doctrine John Quincy Adams, the secretary of state, before making answer. The decision being reached, the President embodied in his annual message to Congress in December, 1823, a clause which formulated what has ever since been known as the " Monroe Doctrine." It was written by John Quincy Adams, and, referring to the intervention of the allied powers, said that we "should consider any attempt on their part to extend their system to any portion of this hemisphere as dangerous to our peace and safety;" and further, "that the American continents, by the free and independent condition which they have assumed and maintain, are henceforth not to be considered as subjects for future colonization by any European powers."

By the Monroe Doctrine the United States formally adopted the position of guardian of the weaker American States, and since its promulgation there have been few aggressions of European nations in America, and none in which the United States has not decisively warned them off. The most striking instances may be stated. When, during the troubles in Cuba, France and Great Britain suggested an alliance with the United States to look after affairs in that quarter, they were given plainly to understand that this country would attend to that matter itself and would brook no interference on the part of foreign powers. It also intimated that, in the event of Spain giving up her authority in Cuba from any cause, the United States proposed to act as the sole arbiter of the destinies of the island. Since that date no European power has shown any inclination to interfere in Cuban affairs.

The Case of Cuba

The only decided effort to set at naught the Monroe Doctrine was made by France during the American Civil War. Taking advantage of the difficulties under which our government then labored, France landed an army in Mexico, overthrew the republic, established an empire, and placed Maximilian, a brother of the Emperor of Austria, upon its throne. All went well with the new emperor until after the close of our Civil War; then all began to go ill. The Monroe Doctrine raised its head again, and the French were plainly bidden to take their troops from Mexico if they did not want trouble. Napoleon III. was quick to take the hint, and to withdraw his army. Maximilian was advised to go with it, but he unwisely declined, fancying that he could maintain his seat upon the Mexican throne. He was quickly undeceived. The liberals sprang to arms, defeated with ease his small army, and soon had him in their hands. A few words complete the story. He was tried by court martial, condemned to death, and shot. Thus ended in disaster the most decided attempt to set at naught the Monroe Doctrine of American guardianship.

France in Mexico and the Fate of Maximilian

A second effort, less piratical in its character, was the attempt of Great Britain to extend the borders of British Guiana at the expense of Venezuela. To a certain degree Great Britain seems to have had right on its side in this movement, but its methods were those used by strong nations when dealing with weak ones, the demand of Venezuela for arbitration was scornfully ignored, **The Venezuelan Boundary and the Monroe Doctrine** and force was used to support a claim whose justice no effort was made to show. These high-handed proceedings were brought to a quick termination by the action of the United States, which offered itself as the friend and ally of Venezuela in the dispute. President Cleveland insisted on an arbitration of the difficulty in words that had no uncertain ring, and the statesmen of Great Britain, convinced that he meant just what he said, submitted with what grace they could. A court of arbitration was appointed, the boundary question put into its hands to settle, and peace and satisfaction reigned again. The Monroe Doctrine had once more decisively asserted itself. By the decision of the court of arbitration each country got the portion of the disputed territory it most valued, and both were satisfied. Thus peace has its triumphs greater than those of war.

These are not offered as the only occasions in which the United States has come into hostile relations with foreign powers and has sustained its dignity with or without war, but they are the most striking ones, unless we include in this category the Mexican war. Various disputes of a minor character have arisen, notably with Great Britain, the latest being that concerning the Alaskan boundary; but those given are the only instances that seem to call for attention here.

CHAPTER XXVII.

Webster and Clay and the Preservation of the Union.

DURING the first half of the nineteenth century a number of great questions came up in American politics and pressed for solution. There was abundance of hostilities—wars with Great Britain, the Barbary states, Mexico and the Indians—and international difficulties of various kinds. The most important of these we have described. We have now to consider questions of internal policy, problems arising in the development of the nation which threatened its peace and prosperity, and to deal with which called for the most earnest patriotism and the highest statesmanship in the political leaders of the commonwealth. Among these leaders two men loomed high above their contemporaries, Daniel Webster, the supreme orator and staunch defender of the Union, and Henry Clay, the great peace-maker, whose hand for years stayed the waves of the political tempest and more than once checked legislative hostilities in their early stage. It was not until Clay had passed from the scene that one of the national problems alluded to plunged the country into civil war and racked the Union almost to the point of dissolution.

Questions of In-
—ternal Policy

Of these great political questions, danger to the Union arose from two, the problem of the tariff and the dispute over the institution of slavery. There were others of minor importance, prominent among them those of internal improvement at government expense, and of state rights, or the degree of independence of the states under the Federal Union, but it was the first two only that threatened the existence of the nation, and in dealing with which the noblest statesmanship and the most fervid and convincing oratory were called into play. The subject of slavery in particular gloomed above the nation like a terrible thunder cloud. All other questions of domestic policy—tariff, currency, internal improvements, state rights—were subordinate to the main question of how to preserve the Union under this unceasing threat. Some, like Calhoun, were ready to abandon the Union that slavery might be saved; others, like Garrison, were ready to abandon the Union that slavery might be destroyed. Between these extremes stood many able and patriotic

Danger to the
Union

statesmen, who, to save the Union, were ready to make any sacrifice and join in any compromise. And high among these, for more than fifty years, stood the noble figure of Henry Clay.

Not often does a man whose life is spent in purely civil affairs become such a popular hero and idol as did Clay—especially when it is his fate never to reach the highest place in the people's gift. "Was there ever," says Parton, "a public man, not at the head of a state, so be- loved as he? Who ever heard such cheers, so hearty, distinct **Clay's Great** and ringing, as those which his name evoked? Men shed **Popularity** tears at his defeat, and women went to bed sick from pure sympathy with his disappointment. He could not travel during the last thirty years of his life, but only make *progresses.* When he left home the public seized him and bore him along over the land, the committee of one state passing him on to the committee of another, and the hurrahs of one town dying away as those of the next caught his ear."

Born a poor boy, who had to make his way up from the lowest state of frontier indigence, he was favored by nature with a kindly soul, the finest and most effective powers of oratory, and a voice of the most admirable character; one of deep and rich tone, wonderful volume, and sweet and tender harmony, which invested all he said with majesty, and swept audiences away as much by its musical and swelling cadences as by the logic and convincing nature of his utterances.

After years of active and useful labor in Congress, it was in 1818 that Clay first stepped into the arena for the calming of the passions of Con- gress and the preservation of the Union, a duty to which he devoted him- self for the remainder of his life. In the year named a petition for the admission of Missouri into the Union was presented in Congress, and with it began that long and bitter struggle over slavery which did not end until the surrender of Lee at Appomattox in 1865.

For years the sentiment in favor of slavery had been growing stronger in the South. At one time many of the wisest southern statesmen and planters disapproved of the institution and proposed its aboli- **The Slavery** tion. But the invention of the cotton gin by Eli Whitney, in **Sentiment** 1793, and the subsequent great development of the cotton culture had decidedly changed the situation. By 1800 the value of the cotton product had advanced to $5,700.000. In 1820 it had made another great advance, and was valued at nearly $20,000,000. There was now no thought of doing away with the use of slaves, but a strong sentiment had arisen in the South in favor of extending the area in which slave labor could be employed.

In the North a different state of feeling existed.   Slavery was believed to be a wrong and an injury to American institutions, though no movement for its abolition had been started.   Many people thought it ought to and would disappear in time, but there was no idea of taking steps to enforce its disappearance.   But when, in the bill for the admission of Missouri, there was shown a purpose of extend-ing the area of slavery, northern sentiment became alarmed and a strong opposition to this project developed in Congress.

The Admission of Missouri

It was the sudden revelation of a change of feeling in the South which the North had not observed in its progress.   "The discussion of this Missouri question has betrayed the secret of their souls," wrote John Quincy Adams.   The slaveholders watched with apprehension the steady growth of the free states in population, wealth and power.   In 1790 the population of the two sections had been nearly even.   In 1820 there was a difference of over 600,000 in favor of the North in a total of less than ten millions. In 1790 the representation of the two sections in Congress had been about evenly balanced.   In 1820 the census promised to give the North a prepon-derance of more than thirty votes in the House of Representatives.   If the South was to retain its political equality in Congress, or at least in the Senate, it must have more slave states, and there now began a vigorous struggle with this object in view.   It was determined, if possible, to have as many states as the North, and it was with this purpose that it fought so hard to have slavery introduced into Missouri.

The famous "Missouri Compromise," by which the ominous dispute of 1820 was at last settled, included the admission of one free state (Maine) and one slave state (Missouri) at the same time, and it was enacted that no other slave state should be formed out of any part of the Louisiana territory north of thirty-six degrees thirty minutes, which was the southern boundary line of Missouri.   The assent of opposing parties to this arrangement was secured largely by the patriotic efforts of Clay, who, says Schurz, "did not confine himself to speeches, * * * but went from man to man, expostulating, beseeching, persuading, in his most winning way. * * * His success added greatly to his reputation and gave new strength to his influence."   The result, says John Quincy Adams, was "to bring into full display the talents and re-sources and influence of Mr. Clay."   He was praised as "the great pacifi-cator"—a title which was confirmed by the deeds of his later life.

The Missouri Compromise

Clay served as secretary of state during the administration of John Quincy Adams, but in 1829, when Jackson, his bitter enemy, succeeded to the presidency, he retired for a short season to private life in his beautiful

Kentucky home. But he was not long to remain there; in 1831 he was again elected to the Senate, where he remained until 1842. They were stormy years. In South Carolina the opposition to the protective tariff had led to the promulgation of the famous "nullification" theory—the doctrine that any state had the power to declare a law of the United States null and void. Jackson, whose anger was thoroughly aroused, dealt with the revolt in summary fashion, threatening that if any resistance to the government was attempted he would instantly have the leaders arrested and brought to trial for treason. Nevertheless, to allay the discontent of the South, Clay devised his Compromise Tariff of 1833, under which the duties were to be gradually reduced, until they should reach a minimum of twenty per cent. In 1832 he allowed himself, very unwisely, to be a candidate for the presidency, Jackson's re-election being a foregone conclusion. In 1836 he declined a nomination, and Van Buren was elected. Then followed the panic of 1837, which insured the defeat of the party in power, and the election of the Whig candidate at the following presidential election; but the popularity of General Jackson had convinced the party managers that success demanded a military hero as a candidate; and accordingly General Harrison, "the hero of Tippecanoe," was elected, after the famous "Log Cabin and Hard Cider campaign" of 1840. This slight was deeply mortifying to Clay, who had counted with confidence upon being the candidate of the party. "I am the most unfortunate man in the history of parties," he truly remarked; "always run by my friends when sure to be defeated, and now betrayed for a nomination when I, or any one else, would be sure of an election."

In 1844, however, Clay's opportunity came at last. He was so obviously the Whig candidate that there was no opposition. The convention met at Baltimore in May, and he was nominated by acclamation, with a shout that shook the building. Everything appeared to indicate success, and his supporters regarded his triumphant election as certain.

Clay as a Presidential Candidate

But into the politics of the time had come a new factor—the "Liberty party." This had been hitherto considered unimportant; but the proposed annexation of Texas, which had become a prominent question, was opposed by many in the North who had hitherto voted with the Whig party. Clay was a slaveholder; and though he had opposed the extension of slavery, his record was not satisfactory to those who disapproved of the annexation of Texas. In truth, the opposition to slavery in the North was rapidly gaining political strength, while the question of the annexation of Texas was looked upon as one for the extension of the "peculiar institution," since Texas would, under the Missouri Compromise, fall into line as a slave state, and was large enough, if Congress should permit, to be cut up into a number of slave states. Clay was between two fires. He was distrusted in the South; while his competitor, Polk, was pledged to support the annexation of Texas. He was doubted in the North as a slaveholder. His old enemy, Jackson, used his influence strongly against him. The contest finally turned upon the vote of New York, and that proved so close that the suspense became painful. People did not go to bed, waiting for the delayed returns. The contest was singularly like that of Blaine and Garfield, forty years later, when the result again turned upon a close vote in the State of New York. When at last the decisive news was received, and the fact of Clay's defeat was assured, the Whigs broke out in a wail of agony all over the land. "It was," says Nathan Sargent, "as if the first-born of every family had been stricken down." The descriptions we have of the grief manifested are almost incredible. Tears flowed in abundance from the eyes of men and women. In the cities and villages the business places were almost deserted for a day or two, people gathering together in groups to discuss in low tones what had happened. The Whigs were fairly stunned by their defeat, and the Democrats failed to indulge in demonstrations of triumph, it being widely felt that a great wrong had been done. It was the opinion of many that there would be no hope thereafter of electing the great statesmen of the country to the presidency, and that this high office would in future be attained only by men of second-rate ability.

The Contest of 1844

The last and greatest work of the life of Henry Clay was the famous Compromise of 1850, which has been said to have postponed for ten years the great Civil War. At that period the sentiment against slavery was rapidly increasing in the North and had gained great strength. Though the number of free and slave states continued equal, the former were fast surpassing the latter in wealth and population.

The Compromise of 1850

It was evident that slavery must have more territory or lose its political influence. Shut out of the northwest by the Missouri Compromise, it was supposed that a great field for its extension had been gained in Texas and the territory acquired from Mexico. But now California, a part of this territory which had been counted upon for slavery, was populated by a sudden rush of northern immigration, attracted by the discovery of gold; and a state government was organized with a constitution excluding slavery, thus giving the free states a majority of one. Instead of adding to the area of slavery, the Mexican territory seemed likely to increase the strength of freedom. The South was both alarmed and exasperated. Threats of disunion were freely made. It was clear that prompt measures must be taken to allay the prevailing excitement, if disruption were to be avoided. In such an emergency it was natural that all eyes should turn to the "great pacificator," Henry Clay.

When, at the session of 1849–50, he appeared in the Senate to assist, if possible, in removing the slavery question from politics, Clay was an infirm and serious, but not sad, old man of seventy-two. He never lost his cheerfulness or faith, but he felt deeply for his distracted country. During that memorable session of Congress he spoke seventy times. Often extremely sick and feeble, scarcely able, with the assistance of a friend's arm, to climb the steps of the Capitol, he was never absent on the days when the compromise was to be debated. On **An Orator of Seventy-two** the morning on which he began his great speech, he was accompanied by a clerical friend, to whom he said, on reaching the long flight of steps leading to the Capitol, " Will you lend me your arm, my friend ? for I find myself quite weak and exhausted this morning." Every few steps he was obliged to stop and take breath. " Had you not better defer your speech ?" asked the clergyman. " My dear friend," said the dying orator, " I consider our country in danger ; and if I can be the means, in any measure, of averting that danger, my health or life is of little consequence." When he rose to speak it was but too evident that he was unfit for the task he had undertaken. But as he kindled with his subject, his cough left him, and his bent form resumed all its wonted erectness and majesty. He may, in the prime of his strength, have spoken with more energy, but never with so much pathos or grandeur. His speech lasted two days ; and though he lived two years longer, he never recovered from the effects of the effort. The thermometer in the Senate chamber marked nearly 100 degrees. Toward the close of the second day, his friends repeatedly proposed an adjournment ; but he would not desist until he had given complete utterance to his feelings. He said afterwards that he was not sure, if he gave way to an adjournment, that he should ever be able to resume.

Never was Clay's devotion to the Union displayed in such thrilling and pathetic forms as in the course of this long debate. On one occasion allusion was made to a South Carolina hot-head, who had publicly proposed to raise the flag of disunion. When Clay retorted **Clay's Tribute to the Union** by saying, that, if Mr. Rhett had really meant that proposition, and should follow it up by corresponding acts, he would be a *traitor*, and added, "and I hope he will meet a traitor's fate," thunders of applause broke from the crowded galleries. When the chairman succeeded in restoring silence, Mr. Clay made that celebrated declaration which was so frequently quoted in 1861 : " If Kentucky to-morrow shall unfurl the banner of resistance unjustly, I will never fight under that banner. I owe paramount allegiance to the whole Union, a subordinate one to my own state." Again : " The senator speaks of Virginia being my country. This Union, sir, is my country ; the thirty states are my country ; Kentucky is my country, and Virginia, no more than any state in the Union." And yet again : " There are those who think that the Union must be preserved by an exclusive reliance upon love and reason. That is not my opinion. I have some confidence in this instrumentality ; but, depend upon it, no human government can exist without the power of applying force, and the actual application of it in extreme cases."

The compromise offered by Clay became known as the "Omnibus Bill," from the various measures it covered. It embraced the following provisions : 1. California should be admitted as a free state. 2. New Mexico and Utah should be formed into territories, and the question of the admission of slavery be left for their people to decide. 3. Texas should give up part of the territory it claimed, and be paid $10,000,000 as a recompense. 4. The slave-trade should be prohibited in the District of Columbia. 5. A stringent law for the return of fugitive slaves to their masters should be enacted.

The Omnibus Bill

The question concerning Texas was the following : Texas claimed that its western boundary followed the Rio Grande to its source. This took in territory which had never been part of Texas, but the claim was strongly pushed, and was settled in the manner above stated. The serious question, however, in this compromise was that concerning the return of fugitive slaves. When an effort was made to enforce the Fugitive Slave Law great opposition was excited, on account of the stringency of its provisions. The fugitive, when arrested, was not permitted to testify in his own behalf or to claim trial by jury, and all persons were required to assist the United States marshal, when called upon for aid. To assist a fugitive to escape was an offence punishable by fine and imprisonment. In the last two respects the law failed ; and its severe provisions added greatly to the strength of the anti-slavery party, and thus had much to do in bringing on the Civil War.

Effect of the Fugitive Slave Law

Side by side with Clay in the senate stood another and greater figure, the majestic presence of Daniel Webster, one of the greatest orators the world has ever known, a man fitted to stand on the rostrum with Demosthenes, the renowned orator of Greece, or with Chatham, Burke, or Gladstone of the British parliament.

THE PRESERVATION OF THE UNION 405

In the hall of the United States Senate, on January 26, 1830, occurred what may be considered the most memorable scene in the annals of Congress. It was then that Daniel Webster made his famous "Reply to Hayne,"—that renowned speech which has been declared the greatest oration ever made in Congress, and which, in its far-reaching effect upon the public mind, did so much to shape the future destiny of the American Union. That speech was Webster's crowning work, and the event of his life by which he will be best known to posterity.

The "Reply to Hayne"

Nothing in our history is more striking than the contrast between the Union of the time of Washington and the Union of the time of Lincoln. It was not merely that in the intervening seventy-two years the republic had grown great and powerful; it was that the popular sentiment toward the Union was transformed. The old feeling of distrust and jealousy had given place to a passionate attachment. It was as though a puny, sickly, feeble child, not expected by its parents even to live, had come to be their strong defense and support, their joy and pride. A weak league of states had become a strong nation; and when in 1861 it was attacked, millions of men were ready to fight for its defence. What brought about this great change? What was it that stirred the larger patriotism that gave shape and purpose to this growing feeling of national pride and unity? It was in a great degree the work of Daniel Webster. It was he who maintained and advocated the theory that the Federal Constitution created, not a league, but a nation; that it welded the people into organic union, supreme and perpetual. He it was who set forth in splendid completeness the picture of a great nation, inseparably united, commanding the first allegiance and loyalty of every citizen; and who so fostered and strengthened the sentiment of union that, when the great struggle came, it had grown too strong to be overthrown.

No description of Daniel Webster is complete or adequate which fails to describe his extraordinary personal appearance. In face, form and voice nature did her utmost for him. So impressive was his presence that men commonly spoke of this man of five feet ten inches in height and less than two hundred pounds in weight as a giant. He seemed to dwarf those surrounding him. His head was very large, but of noble shape, with broad and lofty brow, and strong but finely cut features. His eyes were remarkable. They were large and deep-set, and in the excitement of an eloquent appeal they glowed with the deep light of the fire of a forge. His voice was in harmony with his appearance. In conversation it was low and musical; in debate it was high but full. In moments of excitement it rang out like a clarion, whence it would sink into

Webster's Personal Appearance

notes of the solemn richness of organ tones, while the grace and dignity of
Voice and Personal Magnetism of Webster his manner added greatly to the impressive delivery of his words. That wonderful quality which we call personal magnetism, the power of impressing by one's personality every human being who comes near, was at its height in Mr.
Webster. He never punished his children. It sufficed, when they did wrong, to send for them and look at them in silence. The look, whether of sorrow or anger, was rebuke and punishment enough.

As an orator, Mr. Webster's most famous speeches were the Plymouth Rock address, in 1820; the Bunker Hill Monument address, in 1825; and his orations in the Senate in 1830 in reply to Hayne, and in 1850 on Clay's Compromise Bill. Greatest among these was the speech in reply to Robert Y. Hayne, of South Carolina, on the 26th of January, 1830. The Union was threatened, and Webster rose to the utmost height of his
The Question of Nullification impassioned genius in this thrilling appeal for its preservation and endurance. The question under debate was the right of a state to nullify the acts of Congress. Hayne, in sustaining the affirmative of this dangerous proposition, had bitterly assailed New England, and had attacked Mr. Webster by caustic personalities, rousing "the giant" to a crushing reply.

"There was," says Edward Everett, "a very great excitement in Washington, growing out of the controversies of the day, and the action of the South; and party spirit ran uncommonly high. There seemed to be a preconcerted action on the part of the southern members to break down the northern men, and to destroy their force and influence by a premeditated onslaught.

"Mr. Hayne's speech was an eloquent one, as all know who ever read it. He was considered the foremost southerner in debate, except Calhoun, who was vice-president and could not enter the arena. Mr. Hayne was the champion of the southern side. Those who heard his speech felt much alarm, for two reasons; first, on account of its eloquence and power, and second, because of its many personalities. It was thought by many who heard it, and by some of Mr. Webster's personal friends, that it was impossible for him to answer the speech.

'I shared a little myself in that fear and apprehension," said Mr. Everett. "I knew from what I heard concerning General Hayne's speech that it was a very masterly effort, and delivered with a great
Hayne's Speech in the Senate deal of power and with an air of triumph. I was engaged on that day in a committee of which I was chairman, and could not be present in the Senate. But immediately after the adjournment,

I hastened to Mr. Webster's house, with, I admit, some little trepidation, not knowing how I should find him. But I was quite re-assured in a moment after seeing Mr. Webster, and observing his entire calmness. He seemed to be as much at ease and as unmoved as I ever saw him. Indeed, at first I was a little afraid from this that he was not quite aware of the magnitude of the contest. I said at once ·

"'Mr. Hayne has made a speech?'

"'Yes, he has made a speech.'

"'You reply in the morning?'

"'Yes,' said Mr. Webster, 'I do not propose to let the case go by default, and without saying a word.'

"'Did you take notes, Mr. Webster, of Mr. Hayne's speech?'

"Mr. Webster took from his vest pocket a piece of paper about as big as the palm of his hand, and replied, 'I have it all: that is his speech.'

Webster Prepares for Reply

"I immediately arose," said Mr. Everett, "and remarked to him that I would not disturb him longer; Mr. Webster desired me not to hasten, as he had no desire to be alone; but I left."

"On the morning of the memorable day," writes Mr. Lodge, "the Senate chamber was packed by an eager and excited crowd. Every seat on the floor and in the galleries was occupied, and all the available standing-room was filled. The protracted debate, conducted with so much ability on both sides, had excited the attention of the whole country, and had given time for the arrival of hundreds of interested spectators from all parts of the Union, and especially from New England.

"In the midst of the hush of expectation, in that dead silence which is so peculiarly oppressive because it is possible only when many human beings are gathered together, Mr. Webster arose. His personal grandeur and his majestic calm thrilled all who looked upon him. With perfect quietness, unaffected apparently by the atmosphere of intense feeling about him, he said, in a low, even tone:

"'Mr. President: When the mariner has been tossed for many days in thick weather and on an unknown sea, he naturally avails himself of the first pause in the storm, the earliest glance of the sun, to take his latitude and ascertain how far the elements have driven him from his true course. Let us imitate this prudence; and

The Opening of a Great Speech

before we float farther on the waves of this debate, refer to the point from which we departed, that we may, at least, be able to conjecture where we are now. I ask for the reading of the resolution before the Senate.'

"This opening sentence was a piece of consummate art. The simple and appropriate image, the low voice, the calm manner, relieved the strained excitement of the audience, which might have ended by disconcerting the speaker if it had been maintained. Every one was now at his ease; and when the monotonous reading of the resolution ceased, Mr. Webster was master of the situation, and had his listeners in complete control."

With breathless attention they followed him as he proceeded. The strong, masculine sentences, the sarcasm, the pathos, the reasoning, the burning appeals to love of state and country, flowed on unbroken. As his feelings warmed the fire came into his eyes; there was a glow in his swarthy cheek; his strong right arm seemed to sweep away resistlessly the whole phalanx of his opponents, and the deep and melodious cadences of his voice sounded like harmonious organ tones as they filled the chamber with their music. Who that ever read or heard it can forget the closing passage of that glorious speech?

"When my eyes shall be turned to behold for the last time the sun in heaven, may I not see him shining on the broken and dishonored fragments of a once glorious Union; on states dissevered, discordant, belligerent; on a land rent with civil feuds, or drenched, it may be, in fraternal blood! Let

A Magnificent Peroration

their last feeble and lingering glance behold rather the glorious ensign of the republic, now known and honored throughout the earth, still full high advanced, its arms and trophies streaming in their original lustre, not a stripe erased or polluted, not a single star obscured; bearing for its motto no such miserable interrogatory as, *What is all this worth?* or those other words of delusion and folly, *Liberty first, and Union afterwards;* but everywhere, spread all over in characters of living light, blazing on all its ample folds, as they float over the sea and over the land, that other sentiment, dear to every true American heart,— LIBERTY AND UNION, NOW AND FOREVER, ONE AND INSEPARABLE!"

As the last words died away into silence, those who had listened looked wonderingly at each other, dimly conscious that they had heard one of the grand speeches which are landmarks in the history of eloquence; and the men of the North and of New England went forth full of the pride of victory, for their champion had triumphed, and no assurance was needed to prove to the world that this time no answer could be made.

Calhoun, the Advocate of Slavery

The great supporter of the doctrine which Hayne advocated and which Webster tore into shreds and fragments, the indefatigable sustainer of the institution of slavery in the United States Congress, was John C. Calhoun. That this man was sincere in his conviction that slavery was morally and politically right, and beneficial

THOMAS JEFFERSON. (1743-1826)

ANDREW JACKSON. (1767-1845)

JOHN QUINCY ADAMS. (1767-1848)

ZACHARY TAYLOR. (1784-1850)

PATRICK HENRY.   HENRY CLAY   DANIEL WEBSTER.

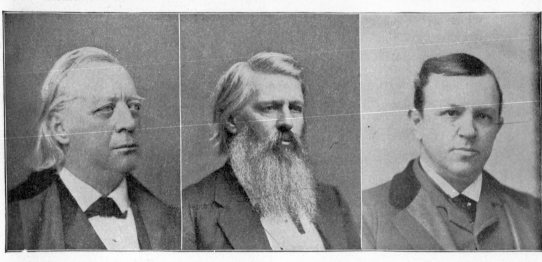

HENRY WARD BEECHER.   JOHN B. GOUGH.   HENRY W. GRADY.

CHAUNCEY M. DEPEW.   WENDELL PHILLIPS.   EDWARD EVERETT

alike to white and black, to North and South, no one has questioned. He was one of the most upright of men ; one devoid of pretence or concealment ; a man of pure honesty of purpose and great ability, and in consequence of immense influence. His own state followed his lead with unquestioning faith, and it is not too much to say that the slavery conflict was in great measure due to the doctrines which he unceasingly advocated for a quarter of a century.

Calhoun is equally well known for his state rights championship and in connection with the effort of South Carolina to secede from the Union, as a consequence of the tariff bill of 1828. This measure, which considerably increased the duties on imports, aroused bitter opposition in the South, where it was styled the " Tariff of Abominations." On its passage Calhoun prepared a vigorous paper called the " South Carolina Exposi- The South tion," in which he maintained that the Constitution limited the   Carolina Exright of Congress to exact tariff charges to the purpose of   position revenue ; that protective duties were, therefore, unconstitutional ; and that any state had the right to declare an unconstitutional law null and void, and forbid its execution in that state. Such was the famous doctrine of " nullification."

This paper was issued in 1828, Calhoun being then Vice-President under Jackson, and as such president of the senate. In 1829, the long debate on the question : " Does the Constitution make us one sovereign nation or only a league of separate states ? " reached its height. Its climax came in January, 1830, in the remarkable contest between Webster and Hayne, above described. Webster showed that an attempt to nullify the laws of the nation was treason, and would lead to revolution, in the employment of armed force to sustain it.

To such a revolutionary measure South Carolina proceeded. After the presidential election of 1832, Calhoun, who had resigned the vice-presidency, called a convention of the people of the state, which The Ordinance passed the famous Ordinance of Nullification, declaring   of Nullificathe 1828 tariff null and void in that state.   tion

The passage of the ordinance created intense excitement throughout the states. Everywhere the dread of civil war and of the dissolution of the Union was entertained. Fortunately there was a Jackson, and not a Buchanan, in the presidential chair. Jackson was not a model President under ordinary circumstances, but he was just the man for an emergency of this character, and he dealt with it much as he had dealt with the Spaniards in Florida. On December 10, 1832, came out his vigorous proclamation against nullification. The governor of South Carolina issued a counter

proclamation, and called out twelve thousand volunteers. A crisis seemed
at hand. Congress passed a "Force Bill" to provide for the

Jackson and Nullification collection of the revenue in South Carolina, though Calhoun
—then in the Senate—opposed it in the most powerful of his
speeches. It is said that Jackson warned him that, if any resistance to the
government was made in South Carolina, he would be at once arrested on
a charge of treason.

The President made prompt preparations to suppress the threatened
revolt by force of arms, troops and naval vessels being sent to Charleston.
But at the same time Congress made concessions to South Carolina and the
crisis passed. It was through the efforts of Henry Clay as already specified
that this warcloud was dissipated. The tariff question settled,

Calhoun Seeks to Force the Issue of Slavery the slavery issue grew prominent. The agitation of this question, from 1835 to 1850, was chiefly the work of one man, John C.
Calhoun. Parton says that "the labors of Mr. Garrison and
Mr. Wendell Phillips might have borne no fruit during their lifetime, if Calhoun had not made it his business to supply them with material. 'I mean
to force the issue on the North,' he once wrote; and he did force it.

This chapter cannot be more fitly closed than with a quotation from
Harriet Martineau, in whose "Retrospect of Western Travel" we find the
following pen-picture of the three great statesmen above treated: "Mr.
Clay sitting upright on the sofa, with his snuff-box ever in his hand, would

A Pen Picture of Three Great Orators discourse for many an hour in his even, soft, deliberate tone,
on any one of the great subjects of American policy which
we might happen to start, always amazing us with the moderation of estimate and speech which so impetuous a nature has been able to
attain. Mr. Webster, leaning back at his ease, telling stories, cracking
jokes, shaking the sofa with burst after burst of laughter, or smoothly dis-
coursing to the perfect felicity of the logical part of one's constitution, would
illuminate an evening now and then. Mr. Calhoun, the cast-iron man, who
looks as if he had never been born and could never be extinguished, would
come in sometimes to keep our understanding on a painful stretch for a
short while, and leave us to take to pieces his close, rapid, theoretical, illustrated talk, and see what we could make of it. We found it usually more
worth retaining as a curiosity, than as either very just or useful.

"I know of no man who lives in such utter intellectual solitude. He
meets men and harangues by the fireside as in the Senate; he is wrought
like a piece of machinery, set going vehemently by a weight, and stops
while you answer; he either passes by what you say, or twists it into a
suitability with what is in his head, and begins to lecture again."

CHAPTER XXVIII.

The Annexation of Texas and the War with Mexico.

WE have spoken, in Chapter xxiii, of the revolt of Texas from Mexico and the annexation of the newly formed republic to the United States. In the present chapter it is proposed to deal more fully with this subject and describe its results in the war with Mexico. In the year 1821, after more than ten years of struggle for freedom, **Mexico Gains Its Independence** Mexico won its independence from Spain, and soon after founded a constitutional monarchy, with Augustin de Iturbide, the head of the revolutionary government, as emperor. This empire did not last long. General Santa Anna proclaimed a republic in 1823, and the emperor was obliged to resign his crown. In the following year he returned to Mexico with the hope of recovering his lost crown ; but, on the contrary, was arrested and shot as a traitor. Mexico is not a good country for emperors. About forty years afterward, a second emperor, sent there by France, was disposed of in the same manner.

The establishment of the republic was followed by earnest efforts in favor of the settlement and development of the unoccupied territory of the country, and Texas, a large province in its northeastern boundary, began to be settled by immigrants, very largely from the United States. **The Settlement of Texas** By 1830 the American population numbered about 20,000, being much in excess of that of Mexican origin. These people were largely of the pioneer class, bold, unruly, energetic frontiersmen, difficult to control under any government, and unanimous in their detestation of the tyranny of Mexican rule. Their American spirit rose against the dominance of those whom they called by the offensive title of "greasers," and in 1832 they broke into rebellion and drove all the Mexican troops out of the country.

It was this revolt that brought the famous Samuel Houston to Texas. The early life of this born leader had been spent on the Tennessee frontier, and during much of his boyhood he had lived among the Cherokee Indians, who looked up to him as to one of their head chiefs. He fought under

Jackson in the war of 1812, and was desperately wounded in the Creek War. He subsequently studied law, was elected to Congress, and in 1827

The Career became governor of Tennessee. An unhappy marriage brought
of General to an end this promising part of his career. A separation
Houston from his wife was followed by calumnies on the part of her friends, which became so bitter that Houston, in disgust, left the state and proceeded to Arkansas, where for three years he lived with his boyhood friends, the Cherokees. The outbreak in Texas offered a promising opportunity to a man of his ambitious and enterprising disposition, and he set out for that region in December, 1832.

For two years after Houston joined fortunes with Texas there was comparative quiet ; but immigration went on in a steadily increasing stream, and the sentiment for independence grew stronger every day. The Mexican government, in fear of the growing strength of Texas, ordered that the

War in Texas people should be disarmed—a decree which aroused instant rebellion. A company of Mexican soldiers sent to the little town of Gonzales, on the Guadalupe, to remove a small brass six-pounder, was met a few miles from the town by one hundred and eighty Texans, who fell upon them with such vigor that they turned and fled, losing several men. No Texan was killed. This battle was called "the Lexington of Texas."

Then war broke out again more furiously than ever. The Mexican soldiers, who were under weak and incompetent commanders, were again dispersed and driven out of the country. But now Santa Anna himself, the Mexican dictator, an able general, but a false and cruel man, took the field. With an army of several thousand men, he crossed the Rio Grande, and marched against the Texans.

The town of Bexar, on the San Antonio River, was defended by a garrison of about one hundred and seventy-five men. Among them were two whose names are still famous—David Crockett, the renowned pioneer, and Colonel James Bowie, noted for his murderous "bowie-knife," his duels, and his deeds of valor and shame. The company was commanded by Colonel W. Barrett Travis, a brave young Texan. On the approach of Santa Anna, they took refuge in the Alamo, about half a mile to the north of the town.

The Alamo was an ancient Franciscan mission of the eighteenth century. It covered an area of about three acres, surrounded by walls three feet thick and eight feet high. Within the walls were a stone church

The Massacre and several other buildings. For two weeks it withstood
of the Alamo Santa Anna's assaults. A shower of bombs and cannon-balls
and Goliad fell incessantly within the walls. At last, after a brave defense by the little garrison, the fortress was captured, in the early morning

of Sunday, March 6, 1836. After the surrender, Travis, Bowie and Crockett, with all their companions, were by Santa Anna's especial command massacred in cold blood.

But this was not the worst; a few days afterwards a company of over four hundred Texans, under Colonel Fannin, besieged at Goliad, were induced to surrender, under Santa Anna's solemn promises of protection. After the surrender they were divided into several companies, marched in different directions a short distance out of the town, and shot down like dogs by the Mexican soldiers. Not a man escaped.

While these horrible events were taking place, Houston was at Gonzales, with a force of less than four hundred men. Meetings were held in the different settlements to raise an army to resist the Mexican invasion; and a convention of the people issued a proclamation declaring Texas a free and independent republic. It was two weeks before General Houston received intelligence of the atrocious massacres at Bexar and Goliad, and of Santa Anna's advance. The country was in a state of panic. Settlers were everywhere abandoning their homes, and fleeing in terror at the approach of the Mexican soldiers. Houston's force of a few hundred men was the only defense of Texas; and even this was diminished by frequent desertion from the ranks. The cause of Texan freedom seemed utterly hopeless.

In order to gain time, while watching his opportunity for attack, Houston slowly retreated before the Mexican army. After waiting two weeks for reinforcements, he moved toward Buffalo Bayou, a deep, narrow stream connecting with the San Jacinto River, about twenty miles **General Houston** southeast of the present city of Houston. Here he expected **and Santa** to meet the Mexican army. The lines being formed, General **Anna** Houston made one of his most impassioned and eloquent appeals to his troops, firing every breast by giving as a watchword, "REMEMBER THE ALAMO."

Soon the Mexican bugles rang out over the prairie, announcing the advance guard of the enemy, almost eighteen hundred strong. The rank and file of the patriots was less than seven hundred and fifty men. Their disadvantages only served to increase the enthusiasm of the soldiers; and when their general said, "Men, there is the enemy; do you wish to fight?" the universal shout was, "We do!" "Well, then," he said, "remember it is for liberty or death; *remember the Alamo!*"

At the moment of attack, a lieutenant came galloping up, his horse covered with foam, and shouted along the lines, "I've cut down Vince's bridge." Each army had used this bridge in coming to the battle-field, and General Houston had ordered its destruction, thus preventing all hope of escape to the vanquished.

Santa Anna's forces were in perfect order, awaiting the attack, and reserved their fire until the patriots were within sixty paces of their works. Then they poured forth a volley, which went over the heads of the at-

The Battle of San Jacinto tackers, though a ball struck General Houston's ankle, inflicting a very painful wound. Though suffering and bleeding, General Houston kept his saddle during the entire action. The patriots held their fire until it was given to the enemy almost in their very bosoms, and then, having no time to reload, made a general rush upon the foe, who were altogether unprepared for the furious charge. The patriots not having bayonets, clubbed their rifles. About half-past four the Mexican rout began, and closed only with the night. Seven of the patriots were killed and twenty-three were wounded ; while the Mexicans had six hundred and thirty-two killed and wounded, and seven hundred and thirty, among whom was Santa Anna, made prisoners.

The victory of San Jacinto struck the fetters forever from the hands of Texas, and drove back the standard of Mexico beyond the Rio Grande, never to return except in predatory and transient incursions. General Houston became at once the leading man in Texas, almost universal applause following him. As soon as quiet and order were restored, he was made the first President of the new republic, under the Constitution adopted in November, 1835.

In 1837 the republic of Texas was acknowledged by the United States, and in 1840 by Great Britain, France and Belgium. The population was overwhelmingly of American origin, and these people had in no sense lost their love for their former country, a sentiment in favor of the annexation of the "Lone Star State" to the United States being from the first enter-

Texas Applies for Admission to the Union tained. In 1837 a formal application for admission as a state of the American Union was made. This proposition found many advocates and many opposers in this country, it being strongly objected to by northern Congressmen and favored by those from the South. The controversy turned upon the question of the extension of the area of slavery, which was a matter of importance to the South, while others who supported it held large tracts of land in Texas' which they hoped would increase in value under United States rule.

As a result of the opposition, the question remained open for years, and was prominent in the presidential campaign of 1844, in which Henry Clay, the Whig candidate, was defeated, and James K. Polk, the Democratic candidate, was elected on the annexation platform. This settled the dispute. The people had expressed their will and the opposition yielded. Both Houses of Congress passed a bill in favor of admitting Texas as a

state, and it was signed by President Tyler in the closing hours of his administration. The offer was unanimously accepted by the legislature of Texas on July 4, 1845, and it became a state of the American Union in December of that year.

In admitting Texas, Congress had opened the way to serious trouble. Though Mexico had taken no steps to recover its lost province, it had never acknowledged its independence, and stood over it somewhat like the dog in the manger, not prepared to take it, yet vigorously protesting against any other power doing so. Its protest **Mexico Protests** against the action of the United States was soon followed by a more critical exigency, an active boundary dispute. Texas claimed the Rio Grande River as her western boundary. Mexico held that the Nueces River was the true boundary. Between these two streams lay a broad tract of land claimed by both nations, and which both soon sought to occupy. War arose in consequence of this ownership dispute.

In the summer of 1845 President Polk directed General Zachary Taylor to proceed to Corpus Christi, on the Nueces, and in the spring of 1846 he received orders to march to the Rio Grande. As soon as this movement was made, the Mexicans claimed that their territory had been invaded, ordered Taylor to retire, and on his **A Disputed Boundary** refusal sent a body of troops across the river. Both countries were ripe for war, and both had taken steps to bring it on. A hostile meeting took place on April 24th, with some loss to both sides. On receiving word by telegraph of this skirmish, the President at once sent a message to Congress, saying : " Mexico has passed the boundary of the United States, and shed American blood upon American soil. * * * War exists, notwithstanding all our efforts to avoid it."

The efforts to avoid it had not been active. There was rather an effort to favor it. Abraham Lincoln, then a member of **War Declared** Congress, asked pointedly if special efforts had not been **Against** taken to provoke a war. But Congress responded favorably **Mexico** to the President's appeal, declared that war existed " by the act of Mexico " and called for fifty thousand volunteers.

The declaration of war was dated May 13, 1846. Several days before this, severe fights had taken place at Palo Alto and Resaca de la Palma, on the disputed territory. The Mexicans were defeated, and retreated across the Rio Grande. They were quickly followed by Taylor, who took possession of the town of Matamoras. The plan of war laid out embraced an invasion of Mexico from four quarters. Taylor was to march southward from his position on the Rio Grande, General Winfield Scott to advance on the capital by the way of Vera Cruz, General Stephen W. Kearny to invade New Mexico, and California was to be attacked by a naval expedition, already despatched.

Taylor was quick to act after receiving reinforcements. He advanced on September 5th, and on the 9th reached Monterey, a strongly fortified interior town. The Mexicans looked upon this place as almost impregnable, it being surrounded by mountains and ravines, difficult to pass and easy of defense. Yet the Americans quickly penetrated to the walls, and were soon within the town, where a severe and bloody conflict took place. The stormers made their way over the house roofs and through excavations in the adobe walls, and in four days' time were in possession of the town which the Mexicans had confidently counted upon stopping their march.

The Storming of Monterey

Some months passed before Taylor was in condition to advance again, his force being much depleted by reinforcements sent to General Scott. It was February, 1847, when he took the field once more, reaching a position south of Monterey known as Buena Vista, a narrow mountain pass, with hills on one side and a ravine on the other. This bold advance of an army not more than 5,000 strong seemed a splendid opportunity to Santa Anna, then commander-in-chief of the Mexican army, who marched on the small American force with 20,000 men. The battle that followed was the most interesting and hard fought one in the war. Santa Anna hoped to crush the Americans utterly, and would perhaps have done so but for the advantage of their position and the effective service of their artillery.

Taylor at Buena Vista

"You are surrounded by twenty thousand men, and cannot, in all human probability, avoid suffering rout and being cut to pieces with your troops." Such were the alarming words with which the Mexican general accompanied a summons to General Taylor to surrender within an hour. Taylor's answer was polite but brief. "In answer to your note of this date summoning me to surrender my forces at discretion, I beg leave to say that I decline acceeding to your request."

General Taylor, or "Rough and Ready" as he was affectionately called by his men, had long before—he was now sixty-three years old—won his spurs on the battlefield. He was short, round-shouldered, and stout. His forehead was high, his eyes keen, his mouth firm, with the lower lip protruding, his hair snow-white, and his expression betokened his essentially humane and unassuming character. No private could have lived in simpler fashion. When he could escape from his uniform he wore a linen roundabout, cotton trousers, and a straw hat, and, if it rained, an old brown overcoat. In battle

BATTLE OF RESACA DE LA PALMA

Captain May leaped his steed over the parapets, followed by those of his men whose horses could do a like feat, and was among the gunners the next moment, sabering them right and left. General La Vega and a hundred of his men were made

JOHN L. MOTLEY

WM·H·PRESCOTT

GEO. BANCROFT

JOHN B. McMASTER

JAMES PARTON

GREAT AMERICAN HISTORIANS AND BIOGRAPHERS

he was absolutely fearless, and invariably rode a favourite white horse, altogether regardless of attracting the enemy's attention. The old hero never wavered when he heard of the approach of the dreaded Santa Anna. He quietly went to work, and, having strongly garrisoned Saltillo, placed his men so as to seize all the advantages the position offered.

Imagine a narrow valley between two mountain ranges. On the west side of the road a series of gullies or ravines, on the east the sheer sides of precipitous mountains. Such was the Pass of Angostura, which, at one spot three miles from Buena Vista, could be held as easily as Horatius kept the bridge in the brave days of old; and here was placed Captain Washington's battery of three guns, with two companies as a guard. Up the mountain to the eastward the rest of the American army was ranged, more especially on a plateau so high as to command all the ground east and west, and only approachable from the south or north by intricate windings formed by ledges of rock.

The Field of Battle

At nine o'clock on the morning of the 22d of February the advance pickets espied the Mexican van, and General Wool sent in hot haste to Taylor, who was at Saltillo. The Mexican army dragged its slow length along, its resplendent uniforms shining in the sun. With much the same feelings as Macbeth saw Birnam Wood approach, must many of the Americans have watched the coming of this forest of steel. Two hours after the pickets had announced the van, a Mexican officer came forward with a white flag. He bore the imperious message from the dictator the opening words of which have already been quoted.

The fight on that day was confined to an exchange of artillery shots, and at nightfall Taylor returned to Saltillo, seeing that the affair was over for the time. But during the night the Mexicans made a movement that put the small American force in serious peril. While the Americans bivouacked without fires in the bitter chill of the mountain height, some 1,500 Mexicans gained the summit under cover of the darkness, and when the mists of morning rose the Americans, to their surprise and chagrin, saw everywhere before them the batallions of the enemy.

Up the pass soon came heavy force, in the face of Captain Washington's battery, while a rush, that seemed as if it must be irresistable, was made for the plateau. The fight here was desperate. The soldiers of neither army had had any experience in battle, and an Indiana regiment retreated at the command of its colonel, and could not be rallied again. This imperilled the safety of all who remained, many of them being killed, while only the active service of the artillery prevented the loss of the plateau, upon whose safe keeping

The Mexican Cavalry Charge

depended the issue of the day.   So fierce was the Mexican charge that every cannonier of the advanced battery fell beside his gun, and Captain O'Brien was obliged to fall back in haste, losing his guns.   He replaced them by two six pounders, borrowed from Captain Washington, who had repulsed the attack in the pass.   Meanwhile, more American artillery on O'Brien's left was driving the Mexicans back upon the cavalry opposed to the gallant captain.   The Mexican lancers charged the Illinois soldiers—"the very earth did shake."   It was not until the lancers were within a few yards of O'Brien that he opened fire.   This gave the Mexicans pause, but with cries of "God and Liberty!" on they came.   Once more the deadly cannonade—

O'Brien's Battery
another pause.   O'Brien determined to stand his ground until the hoofs of the enemy's horses were upon him, but the recruits with him, only few of whom had escaped from being shot down, had no stomach left for fighting.   The intrepid captain again lost his pieces, but he had saved the day.

At this point the leisurely General Taylor, on his white horse, so easily recognisable, came from Saltillo to the field of battle.   North of the chief plateau was another, where the Mississippi Rifles, under Colonel Davis—who, although early wounded, kept his horse all day—stood at bay, formed into a V-shape with the opening towards the enemy.   Nothing loth, the Mexican lancers rushed on, and the riflemen did not fire until they were able to recognize the features of their foe and to take deliberate aim at their eyes.   This coolness was too great to be combated.

For hours the active and deadly struggle went on.   The Mexican lancers made an assault on Buena Vista, where were the American baggage and supply train, but were driven off after a sharp contest.   At a later hour of the day the brunt of the fight was being borne by the Illinois regiment and the Second Kentucky Cavalry, who were in serious straits when Taylor sent to their relief a light battery under Captain Bragg.   It was quickly in peril.   The Mexicans captured the foremost guns and repulsed the infantry support.

Bragg appealed for fresh help.   "I have no reinforcements to give you," "Rough and Ready" is reported to have replied, "but Major Bliss and I will support you"; and the brave old man spurred his horse to the

The Work of Captain Bragg
spot beside the cannon.   Unheeding, the Mexican cavalry rode forward—the day was now theirs for a certainty, "God and Liberty!" their proud cry again rang out.   Their horses galloped so near to Captain Bragg's coign of vantage that their riders had no time in which to pull them up before the battery opened fire with canister.   As the smoke cleared, the little group of Americans saw the terrible

work they had done in the gaps in the enemy's ranks, and heard it in the screams of men and horses in agony. They reloaded with grape. The Mexicans pressed on; their courage at the cannon's mouth was truly marvelous. This second shower of lead did equal, if not greater, mischief. A third discharge completely routed the enemy, who, being human, fled in headlong haste over the wounded and the dead—no matter where. The American infantry pursued the flying foe, with foolish rashness, beyond safe limits. The Mexicans, all on an instant, turned about, the hounds became the hare, and had it not been for Washington's cannon checking the Mexican cavalry, who had had enough grape and canister for one day, they would have been annihilated.

At six o'clock, after ten hours of fierce and uninterrupted fighting, the battle came to an end, both armies occupying the same positions as in the morning, though each had lost heavily during the day. General Taylor expected the battle to be renewed in the morning, but with daylight came the welcome news that the enemy had disappeared. The five thousand had held their own against four times their number, and the victory that was to make General Taylor President of the United States had been won.

Meanwhile General Scott, the hero of Chippewa and Lundy's Lane in 1814, had sailed down the Gulf with a considerable force to the seaport city of Vera Cruz, which was taken after a brief bombardment. From here an overland march of two hundred miles was made to the Mexican capital. Scott reached the vicinity of the City of Mexico with a force 11,000 strong, and found its approaches *Scott's Advance Against the City of Mexico* strongly fortified and guarded by 30,000 men. Yet he pushed on almost unchecked. Victories were won at Contreras and Churubusco, the defences surrounding the city were taken, and on September 13th the most formidable of them all, the strong hill fortress of Chapultepec, was carried by storm, the American troops charging up a steep hill in face of a severe fire and driving the garrison in dismay from their guns.

This ended the war in that quarter. The next day the star and stripes waved over the famous "Halls of the Montezumas" and the city was ours. On February 2, 1848, a treaty of peace was signed at the village of Guadalupe Hidalgo, whose terms gave the United States an accession of territory that was destined to prove of extraordinary value.

New Mexico, a portion of this territory, had been invaded and occupied by General Kearny, who had taken Santa Fé after a thousand miles' march overland. Before the fleet sent to California could reach there, Captain John C. Fremont, in charge of a surveying party in Oregon, had invaded that country. He did not know that war had been declared, his purpose being to protect the American settlers, whom the Mexicans threatened to expel. Fremont was one of the daring pioneers who made their way over the mountains and plains of the West in the days when Indian hostility and the difficulties raised by nature made this a very arduous and perilous enterprise. Several conflicts with the Mexicans, in which he was aided by the fleet, and later by General Kearny, who had crossed the wild interior from Santa Fé, gave Fremont control of that great country, which was destined almost to double the wealth of the United States. Whatever be thought of the ethics of the acquisition of Texas and the Mexican war, their economical advantages to the United States have been enormous, and the whole world has been enriched by the product of California's golden sands and fertile fields.

New Mexico and California

CHAPTER XXIX.

The Negro in America and the Slavery Conflict.

WHEN, over two hundred and eighty years ago (it is in doubt whether the correct date is 1619 or 1620) a few wretched negroes, some say fourteen, some say twenty, were bartered for provisions by the crew of a Dutch man-of-war, then lying off the Virginia coast, it would have seemed incredible that in 1900 the negro population of the Southern States alone should reach very nearly eight million souls. African negroes had, indeed, been sold into slavery among many nations for perhaps three thousand years ; but in its earlier periods slavery was rather the outcome of war than the deliberate subject of trade, and white captives no less than black were ruthlessly thrown into servitude. It has been estimated that in historical times some forty million Africans have been enslaved. The Spaniards found the Indian an intractable slave, and for the arduous labors of colonization soon began to make use of negro slaves, importing them in great numbers and declaring that one negro was worth, as a human beast of burden, four Indians. Soon the English adventurers took up the traffic. It is to Sir John Hawkins, the ardent discoverer, that the English-speaking peoples owe their participation in the slave trade. He has put it on record, as the result of one of his famous voyages, that he found "that negroes were very good merchandise in Hispaniola and might easily be had on the coast of Guinea." For his early adventures of this kind he was roundly taken to task by Queen Elizabeth. But tradition says that he boldly faced her with the argument that the Africans were an inferior race, and ended by convincing the Virgin Queen that the slave trade was not merely a lucrative but a perfectly philanthropic undertaking. Certain it is that she acquiesced in future slave trading, while her successors Charles II. and James II. chartered four slave trading companies and received a share in their profits. It is noteworthy that both Great Britain and the United States recognized the horrors of the slave trade as regards the seizing and transportation from Africa of the unhappy negroes, long before they could bring themselves to deal with the problem of slavery as a domestic institution. Of those horrors nothing can be said in exaggeration.

Beginning of the Slave Traffic

Increase in Numbers

The institution of slavery, introduced as we have seen into Virginia, grew at first very slowly. Twenty-five years after the first slaves were landed the negro population of the colony was only three hundred. But the conditions of agriculture and of climate were such that, once slavery **Colonial Laws** obtained a fair start, it spread with continually increasing **About** rapidity. We find the Colonial Assembly passing one after **Slavery** another a series of laws defining the condition of the negro slave more and more clearly, and more and more pitilessly. Thus, a distinction was soon made between them and Indians held in servitude. It was enacted that "all servants not being Christians imported into this colony by shipping shall be slaves for their lives; but what shall come by land shall serve, if boyes or girles, until thirty years of age; if men or women, twelve years and no longer." And before the end of the century a long series of laws so encompassed the negro with limitations and prohibitions, that he almost ceased to have any criminal or civil rights and became a mere personal chattel.

In some of the northern colonies slavery seemed to take root as readily and to flourish as rapidly as in the South. It was only after a considerable time that social and commercial conditions arose which led to its gradual **Slavery in** abandonment. In New York a mild type of negro slavery **Early** was introduced by the Dutch. The relation of master and **New York** slave seems in the period of the Dutch rule to have been free from great severity or cruelty. After the seizure of the government by the English, however, the institution was officially recognized and even encouraged. The slave trade grew in magnitude; and here again we find a series of oppressive laws forbidding meetings of negroes, laying down penalties for concealing slaves, and the like. When the Revolution broke out there were not less than fifteen thousand slaves in New York— a number greatly in excess of that held by any other northern colony.

Massachusetts, the home in later days of so many of the most eloquent abolition agitators, was from the very first, until after the war with Great Britain was well under way, a stronghold of slavery. The records of 1633 tell of the fright of Indians who saw a "Blackamoor" in a treetop, whom they took for the devil in person, but who turned out to be an escaped **Slavery in** slave. A few years later the authorities of the colony offici- **Massachu-** ally recognized the institution. To quote Chief Justice Par- **setts** sons, "Slavery was introduced into Massachusetts soon after its first settlement, and was tolerated until the ratification of the present constitution in 1780." The curious may find in ancient Boston newspapers no lack of such advertisements as that, in 1728, of the sale of "two **very** likely negro girls," and of "A likely negro woman of about nineteen years and a child about seven months of age, to be sold together or apart." A Tory writer before the outbreak of the Revolution sneers at the Bostonians for their talk about freedom when they possessed two thousand negro slaves. Even Peter Faneuil, who built the famous "Cradle of Liberty," was himself, at that very time, actively engaged in the slave trade. There is some truth in the once common taunt of the pro-slavery orators that the North imported slaves, the South only bought them.

As with New York and Massachusetts, so with the other colonies. Either slavery was introduced by greedy speculators from abroad or it spread easily from adjoining colonies. In 1776 the slave Negro Soldiers population of the thirteen colonies was almost exactly half a in the Revolu- million, nine-tenths of whom were to be found in the southern tion states. In the War of the Revolution the question of arming the negroes raised bitter opposition. In the end a comparatively few were enrolled, and it is admitted that they served faithfully and with courage. Rhode Island even formed a regiment of blacks, and at the siege of Newport and afterwards at Point's Bridge, New York, this body of soldiers fought not only without reproach but with positive heroism.

From the day when the Declaration of Independence asserted "That all men are created equal, that they are endowed by their Creator with certain inalienable rights; that among these are life, liberty and the pursuit of happiness," the peoples of the new, self-governing states could not but have seen that with them lay the responsibility. There is ample evidence that the fixing of the popular mind on liberty as an ideal bore results immediately in arousing anti-slavery sentiment. Such sentiment existed in the South as well as in the North. Even North Carolina in 1786 declared the slave trade of "evil consequences and highly impolitic." All the northern states abolished slavery, beginning with Vermont Slavery Abol- in 1777, and ending with New Jersey in 1804. It should be ished in the added, however, that many of the northern slaves were not North freed, but sold to the South. The agricultural and commercial conditions in the North were such as to make slave labor less and less profitable, while in the South the social order of things, agricultural conditions, and climate were gradually making it seemingly indispensable.

When the Constitutional debates began the trend of opinion seemed strongly against slavery. Many delegates thought that the evil would die out of itself. One thought the abolition of slavery already rapidly going on and soon to be completed. Another asserted that "slavery in time will not be a speck in our country." Mr. Jefferson, on the other hand, in view of the retention of slavery, declared roundly that he trembled for his country when he remembered that God was just. And John Adams urged again and again that "every measure of prudence ought to be assumed for the eventual total extirpation of slavery from the United States." The obstinate states in the convention were South Carolina and Georgia. Their delegates declared that their states would absolutely refuse ratification to the Constitution unless slavery were recognized. The compromise sections finally agreed upon, avoided the use of the words slave and slavery, but clearly recognized the institution, and even gave the slave states the advantage of sending representatives to Congress on a basis of population determined by adding to the whole number of free persons "three-fifths of all other persons." The other persons referred to were, it is almost needless to add, negro slaves.

The entire dealing with the question of slavery, at the framing of the Constitution, was a series of compromises. This is seen again in the failure definitely to forbid the slave trade from abroad. Some of the southern **Compromises in the Constitution** states had absolutely declined to listen to any proposition which would restrict their freedom of action in this matter, and they were yielded to so far that Congress was forbidden to make the traffic unlawful before the year 1808. As that time approached, President Jefferson urged Congress to withdraw the country from all "further participation in those violations of human rights which have so long been continued on the unoffending inhabitants of Africa." Such an act was at once adopted, and by it heavy fines were imposed on all persons fitting out vessels for the slave trade and also upon all actually engaged in the trade, while vessels so employed became absolutely forfeited. Twelve years later another act was passed declaring the importation of slaves to be actual piracy. The latter law, however, was of little practical value, as it was not until 1861 that a conviction was obtained under it. Then, at last, when the whole slave question was about to be settled forever, a shipmaster was convicted and hanged for piracy in New York for the crime of being engaged in the slave trade. In despite of all laws, however, the trade in slaves was continued secretly, and the profits were so enormous that the risks did not prevent continual attempts to smuggle slaves into the territory of the United States.

The first quarter of a century of our history, after the adoption of the Constitution, was marked by comparative quietude in regard to the future of slavery. In the North, as we have seen, the institution died a natural death, but there was no disposition evinced in the northern states to interfere with it in the South. The first great battle took place in 1820 over the so-called Missouri compromise. Now, for the first time, the country was divided, sectionally and in a strictly political way, upon issues which involved the future policy of the United States as to the extension or restriction of slave territory. State after state had been admitted **The Slave Trade** into the Union, but there had been an alternation of slave and free states, so that the political balance was not disturbed. Thus Ohio was balanced by Lousiana, Indiana by Mississippi, Illinois by Alabama. Of the twenty-two states admitted before 1820, eleven were slave and eleven free states.

Immediately after the admission of Alabama, of course as a slave-holding state, Maine and Missouri applied for admission. The admission of Maine alone would have given a preponderance to the free states, and for this reason it was strongly contended by southern members that Missouri should be admitted as a slave state. But the sentiment of opposition to the extension of slavery was growing rapidly in the North, and many members from that section opposed this proposition. They had believed that the ordinance of 1787, adopted simultaneously with the Constitution, and which forbade slavery to be established in the territory northwest of the Ohio, had settled this question definitely; but this ordinance did not apply to territory west of the Mississippi, so that the question really remained open. A fierce debate was waged through two sessions of Congress, and in the end it was agreed to permit the introduction of slavery into Missouri, but to prohibit it forever in all future states lying north of the parallel of 36 degrees 30 minutes, the **The Missouri Compromise** southern boundary of Missouri. This was a compromise, satisfactory only because it seemed to dispose of the question of slavery in the territories once and forever. It was carried mainly by the great personal influence of Henry Clay. It did, indeed, dispose of slavery as a matter of national legislative discussion for thirty years.

But this interval was distinctively a period of popular agitation. Anti-slavery sentiment of a mild type had long existed. The Quakers had, since revolutionary times, held anti-slavery doctrines, had released their own servants from bondage, and had disfellowshiped members who refused to concur in the sacrifice. The very last public act of Benjamin Franklin was the framing of a memorial to Congress in which he deprecated the existence of slavery in a free country. In New York the **The Anti-slavery Sentiment** Manumission society had been founded in 1785, with John Jay and Alexander Hamilton, in turn, as its presidents. But this early writing and speaking were directed against slavery in a general way, and with no tone of aggression. Gradual emancipation and colonization were the only remedies suggested. It was with the founding of the *Liberator* by William Lloyd Garrison, in 1831, that the era of aggressive abolitionism began. Garrison and his society maintained that slavery was a sin against God and man; that immediate emancipation was a duty; that slave owners had no claim to compensation; that all laws upholding slavery were, before God, null and void. Garrison exclaimed: " I am in earnest. I will not equivocate—I will not excuse—I will not retreat a single inch. And I will be heard." His paper bore conspicuously the motto " No union with slaveholders."

The Abolitionists were, in numbers, a feeble band; as a party they never acquired strength, nor were their tenets adopted strictly by any political party; but they served the purpose of arousing the conscience of the nation. They were abused, vilified, mobbed, all but killed. Garrison was dragged through the streets of Boston with a rope around his neck— through those very streets which, in 1854, had their shops closed and hung in black, with flags Union down and a huge coffin suspended in mid-air, on the day when the fugitive slave, Anthony Burns, was marched through them on his way back to his master, under a guard of nearly two thousand men. Mr. Garrison's society soon took the stand that the union of states with slavery retained was "an agreement with hell and a covenant with death," and openly advocated secession of the non-slaveholding states. On this issue the Abolitionists split into two branches, and those who threw off

Leading Opponents of Slavery

Garrison's lead maintained that there was power enough under the Constitution to do away with slavery. To the fierce invective and constant agitation of Garrison were, in time, added the splendid oratory of Wendell Phillips, the economic arguments of Horace Greeley, the wise statesmanship of Charles Sumner, the fervid writings of Channing and Emerson, and the noble poetry of Whittier. All these and others, in varied ways and from different points of view, joined in bringing the public opinion of the North to the view that the permanent existence of slavery was incompatible with that of a free republic.

In the South, meanwhile, the institution was intrenching itself more and more firmly. The invention of the cotton gin and the beginning of the reign of cotton as king made the great plantation system a seeming commercial necessity. From the deprecatory and half apologetic utterances of early southern statesmen, we come to Mr. Calhoun's declaration that slavery " now preserves in quiet and security more than six and a half million human beings, and that it could not be destroyed without destroying the peace and prosperity of nearly half the states in the Union." The Abolitionists were regarded in the South with the bitterest hatred. Attempts were even made to compel the northern states to silence the anti-slavery orators, to prohibit the circulation through the mail of anti-slavery speeches, and to refuse a hearing in Congress to anti-slavery petitions. The influence of the South was still dominant in the North. Though the feeling against slavery spread, there co-existed with it the belief that an open quarrel with the South meant commercial ruin ; and the anti-slavery sentiment was also neutralized by the nobler feeling that the Union must be preserved at all hazards, and that there was no constitutional mode of interfering with the slave system. The annexation of Texas was a distinct gain to the slave power, and the Mexican war was undertaken, said John Quincy Adams, in order that "the slave-holding power in the government shall be secured and riveted." **Southern Hatred of Abolitionists**

The actual condition of the negro over whom such a strife was being waged differed materially in different parts of the South, and, under masters of different character, in the same locality. It had its side of cruelty, oppression and atrocity ; it had also its side of kindness on the part of master and of devotion on the part of slave. Its dark side has been made familiar to readers by such books as " Uncle Tom's Cabin," Dickens' "American Notes," and Edmund Kirk's "Among the Pines;" its brighter side has been charmingly depicted in the stories of Thomas Nelson Page, Joel Chandler Harris, and Harry Edwards. On the great cotton plantations of Mississippi and Alabama the slave was often overtaxed and harshly treated ; in the domestic life of Virginia, on the other hand, he was as a rule most kindly used, and often a relation of deep affection sprang up between him and his master. **The Literature of Slavery**

With this state of public feeling North and South, it was with increased bitterness and developed sectionalism that the subject of slavery in new states was again debated in the Congress of 1850. The Liberty party, which held that slavery might be abolished under the Constitution, had been merged in the Free Soil party, whose cardinal principle was, " To secure free soil to a free people," and, while not interfering with slavery in existing states, to insist on its exclusion from territory so far free. The proposed admission of California was not affected by the Missouri Compromise. Its status as a future free or slave state was the turning point of the famous debates in the Senate of 1850, in which Webster, Calhoun, Douglas and Seward won fame—debates which have never been equaled in our history for eloquence and acerbity. It was in the course of these debates that Mr. Seward, while denying that the Constitution recognized property in man, struck out his famous dictum, " There is a higher law than the Constitution." The end reached was a compromise which allowed California to settle for itself the question of slavery, forbade the slave trade in the District of Columbia, but enacted a strict fugitive slave law. To the Abolitionists this fugitive slave law, sustained in its most extreme measures by the courts in the famous—or as they called it, infamous—Dred Scott case, was as fuel to fire. They defied it in every possible way. The "Underground Railway" was the outcome of this defiance. By it a chain of secret stations was established, from one to the other of which the slave was guided at night until at last he reached the Canada border. The most used of these routes in the East was from Baltimore to New York, thence north through New England; that most employed in the West was from Cincinnati to Detroit. It has been estimated that not fewer than thirty thousand slaves were thus assisted to freedom.

The Fugitive Slave Law and Underground Railroad

Soon the struggle was changed to another part of the western territory, which was now growing so rapidly as to demand the formation of new states. The Kansas-Nebraska Bill introduced by Douglas was in effect the repeal of the Missouri Compromise, in that it left the question as to whether slavery should be carried into the new territories to the decision of the settlers themselves. As a consequence immigration was directed by both the anti-slavery and the pro-slavery parties to Kansas, each determined on obtaining a majority enabling it to control the proposed State Constitution. Then began a series of acts of violence which almost amounted to civil war. "Bleeding Kansas" became a phrase in almost every one's mouth. Border ruffians swaggered at the polls and attempted to drive out the assisted emigrants sent to Kansas by the Abolition societies. The result of the election of the Legislature on its face made Kansas a slave state, but a great part of the people refused to accept this result; and a convention was held at Topeka which resolved that Kansas should be free even if the laws formed by the Legislature should have to be "resisted to a bloody issue."

The Outbreak in Kansas

Prominent among the armed supporters of free state ideas in Kansas was Captain John Brown, a man whose watchword was at all times action. "Talk," he said, "is a national institution; but it does no good for the slave." He believed that slavery could only be coped with by armed force. His theory was that the way to make free men of slaves was for the slaves themselves to resist any attempt to coerce them by their masters. He was undoubtedly a fanatic in that he did not stop to measure probabilities or to take account of the written law. His attempt at Harper's Ferry was without reasonable hope, and as

John Brown at Harper's Ferry

he intended beginning of a great military movement was a ridiculous fiasco. To attempt to make war upon the United States with twenty men was utter madness, and if the hoped for rising of the slaves had taken place might have yielded horrible results. The execution of John Brown, that followed, was the logical consequence of his hopeless effort.

But there was that about the man which none could call ridiculous. Rash and unreasoning as his action seemed, he was still, even by his enemies, recognized as a man of unswerving conscience, of high ideals, of deep belief in the brotherhood of mankind. His offense against law and peace was cheerfully paid for by his death and that of others near and dear to him. Almost no one at that day could be found to applaud his plot, but the incident had an effect on the minds of the people altogether out of proportion to its intrinsic character. More and more as time went on he became recognized as a martyr in the cause of human liberty.

Events of vast importance to the future of the negro in America now hurried fast upon each other's footsteps: the final settlement of the Kansas dispute by its becoming a free state; the formation and rapid growth of the Republican party; the division of the Democratic party into northern and southern factions; the election of Abraham Lincoln; the secession of South Carolina, and, finally, the greatest civil war the world has known. Though that war would never have been waged were it not for the negro, and though his fate was inevitably involved in its result, it must be remembered that it was not undertaken on his account. Before the struggle began Mr. Lincoln said: "If there be those who would not save the Union unless they could at the same time save slavery, I do not agree with them. If there be those who would not save the Union unless they could at the same time destroy slavery, I do not agree with them. My paramount object is to save the Union, and not either to destroy or to save slavery." And the northern press emphasized over and over again the fact that this was "a white man's war." But the logic of events is inexorable. It seems amazing now that Union generals should have been puzzled as to the question whether they ought in duty to return runaway slaves to their masters. General Butler settled the controversy by one happy phrase when he called the fugitives "contraband of war." Soon it was deemed right to use these contrabands, to employ the new-coined word, as the South **Slaves "Contraband of War"** was using the negroes still in bondage, to aid in the non-fighting work of the army—on fortification, team-driving, cooking, and so on. From this it was but a step, though a step not taken without much perturbation, to employ them as soldiers. At Vicksburg, at Fort Pillow, and in many another battle, the negro showed beyond dispute that he could fight for his liberty.   No fiercer or braver charge was made in the war than that upon the parapet of Fort Wagner by Colonel Shaw's gallant colored regiment, the Massachusetts Fifty-fourth.

In a thousand ways the negro figures in the history of the war.   In its literature he everywhere stands out picturesquely. He sought the flag with the greatest avidity for freedom ; flocking in crowds, old men and young,

Behavior of Slaves During the Civil War women and children, sometimes with quaint odds and ends of personal belongings, often empty-handed, always enthusiastic and hopeful, almost always densely ignorant of the meaning of freedom and of self-support. But while the negro showed this avidity for liberty, his conduct toward his old masters was often generous, and almost never did he seize the opportunity to inflict vengeance for his past wrongs.   The eloquent southern orator and writer, Henry W. Grady, said ; " History has no parallel to the faith kept by the negro in the South during the war. Often five hundred negroes to a single white man, and yet through these dusky throngs the women and children walked in safety and the unprotected homes rested in peace. . . A thousand torches would have disbanded every southern army, but not one was lighted."

It was with conditions, and only after great hesitation, that the final step of emancipating the slaves was taken by President Lincoln in September, 1862.   The proclamation was distinctly a war measure, but its reception by the North and by the foreign powers and its immediate effect upon the contest were such that its expediency was at once recognized.   Thereafter there was possible no question as to the personal freedom of the negro

The Emancipation Proclamation in the United States of America. With the Confederacy, slavery went down once and forever.   In the so-called reconstruction period which followed, the negro suffered almost as much from the over-zeal of his political friends as from the prejudice of his old masters. A negro writer, who is a historian of his race, has declared that the government gave the negro the statute book when he should have had the spelling book ; that it placed him in the legislature when he ought to have been in the school house, and that, so to speak, "the heels were put where the brains ought to have been."

A quarter of a century and more has passed since that turbulent period began, and if the negro has become less prominent as a political factor, all the more for that reason has he been advancing steadily though slowly in the requisites of citizenship.   He has learned that he must, by force of circumstances, turn his attention, for the time at least, rather to educational, industrial and material progress than to political ambition. And the record of his advance on these lines is promising and hopeful. In

Mississippi alone, for instance, the negroes own one-fifth of the entire property in the state. In all, the negroes of the South to-day possess two hundred and fifty million dollars' worth of property. Everywhere throughout the South white men and negroes may be found working together.

The promise of the negro race to-day is not so much in the development of men of exceptional talent, such as Frederick Douglas or Senator Bruce, as in the general spread of intelligence and knowledge. **Progress of the Negroes of the South** The southern states have very generally given the negro equal educational opportunities with the whites, while the eagerness of the race to learn is shown in the recently ascertained fact that while the colored population has increased only twenty-seven per cent. the enrollment in the colored schools has increased one hundred and thirty-seven per cent. Fifty industrial schools are crowded by the colored youth of the South. Institutions of higher education, like the Atlanta University, the Hampton Institute of Virginia, and Tuskegee College are doing admirable work in turning out hundreds of negroes fitted to educate their own race. Honors and scholarships have been taken by colored young men at Harvard, at Cornell, at Phillips Academy and at other northern schools and colleges of the highest rank. The fact that a young negro, Mr. Morgan, was, in 1890, elected by his classmates at Harvard as the class orator has a a special significance. Yet there is greater significance, as a **Educational Development of the Negro Race** negro newspaper writes, in the fact that the equatorial telescope now used by the Lawrence University of Wisconsin was made entirely by colored pupils in the School of Mechanical Arts of Nashville, Tenn. In other words, the Afro-American is finding his place as an intelligent worker, a property owner, and an independent citizen, rather than as an agitator, a politician or a race advocate. In religion, superstition and effusive sentiment are giving way to stricter morality. In educational matters, ambition for the high-sounding and the abstract is giving place to practical and industrial acquirements. It will be many years before the character of the negro, for centuries dwarfed and distorted by oppression and ignorance, reaches its normal growth, but that the race is at last upon the right path, and is being guided by the true principles cannot be doubted.

CHAPTER XXX.

Abraham Lincoln and the Work of Emancipation.

AMONG the men who have filled the office of President of the United States two stand pre-eminent, George Washington and Abraham Lincoln, both of them men not for the admiration of a century but of the ages, heroes of history whose names will live as the chief figures among the makers of our nation. To the hand of Washington it owed its freedom, to that of Lincoln its preservation, and the name of

Washington and Lincoln

the preserver will occupy a niche in the temple of fame next to that of the founder. But our feeling for Lincoln is different from that with which we regard the "Father of his Country." While we venerate the one, we love the other. Washington was a stately figure, too dignified for near approach. He commanded respect, admiration and loyalty; but in addition to these Lincoln commands our affection, a feeling as for one very near and dear to us.

The fame of Lincoln is increasing as the inner history of the great struggle for the life of the nation becomes known. For almost two decades after that struggle had settled the permanence of our government, our vision was obscured by the near view of the pygmy giants who "strutted their brief hour upon the stage;" our ears were filled with the loud claims of those who would magnify their own little part, and, knowing the facts concerning some one fraction of the contest, assumed from that knowledge to proclaim the principles which should have governed the whole. Time is

A Great Man and His Critics

dissipating the mist, and we are coming better to know the great man who had no pride of opinion, who was willing to let Seward or Sumner or McClellan or any one imagine himself to be the guiding spirit of the government, if he were willing to give that government the best service of which he was capable. We see more clearly the real greatness of the leader who was too slow for one great section of his people, and too fast for another, too conservative for those, too radical for these; who refused to make the contest merely a war for the negro, yet who saw the end from the beginning, and led, not a section of his people, but the whole people, away from the Egyptian plagues of slavery and disunion, and brought them, united in sentiment and feeling,

436

to the borders of the promised land. We are coming to appreciate that the "Father Abraham" who in that Red Sea passage of fraternal strife was ready to listen to every tale of sorrow, and who wanted it said that he "always plucked a thistle and planted a flower when he thought a flower would grow," was not only in this sense the father of his people ; but that he was a truly great statesman, who, within the limits of human knowledge and human strength, guided **The Character of Lincoln** the affairs of state with a wisdom, a patience, a courage which belittle all praise, and make him seem indeed a man divinely raised up, not only to set the captive free, but in order that "government of the people, by the people, and for the people, shall not perish from the earth."

It is not our purpose to tell the story of Lincoln's boyhood—his days of penury in the miserable frontier cabins of his father in Kentucky and Indiana, his struggles to obtain an education, his pitiful necessity of writing his school exercises with charcoal on the back of a wooden shovel, his efforts to make a livelihood when he had become a tall and ungainly, but strong and vigorous, youth, his work at farming, rail-splitting, clerking, boating, and in other occupations. A journey on a flat-boat to New **Lincoln's First Experience of Slavery** Orleans gave him his first acquaintance with the institution of slavery, with which he was thereafter to have so much to do. Here he witnessed a slave auction. The scene was one that made a deep and abiding impression on his sympathetic mind, and he is said to have declared to his companion, "If I ever get a chance to hit that institution, *I'll hit it hard.*" Whether this is legend or fact, it is certain that he did get a chance to hit it, and did "hit it hard."

Difficult as it was to obtain an education on the rude frontier and in the extreme poverty in which Lincoln was reared, he succeeded by persistent reading and study in making himself the one man of learning among his farming fellows, and one who was not long content with the occupations of rail-splitting, flat-boating, or even that of keeping country store, which he tried without success. He was too devoted to his books to attend very carefully to his business, which left him seriously in debt, and he soon chose the law as his vocation, supporting himself meanwhile by serving as land surveyor in the neighboring district.

Lincoln's political career began in 1834, when his neighbors, who admired him for his learning and ability, elected him to represent them in the Illinois legislature. His knowledge was only one of the elements of his popularity. He had acquired a reputation as a teller of quaint and humorous stories ; he was a champion wrestler, and could fight well if forced to ; and he was beginning to make his mark as a ready and able orator. In the legislature he became prominent enough to gain twice the nomination of his party for speaker. His principal service there was to advocate a system of public improvements, whose chief result was to plunge Illinois deeply in debt. A significant act of his at this early day in his career was to join with a single colleague in a written protest against the passage of resolutions in favor of slavery. The signers based their action on their belief that "the institution of slavery is founded on both injustice and bad policy." It needed no little moral courage to make such a protest in 1837 in a community largely of southern origin, but moral courage was a possession of which Lincoln had an abundant store.

In the Illinois Legislature

In the meantime Lincoln had been admitted to the bar, and in 1837 he removed to Springfield, where he formed a partnership with an attorney of established reputation. He became a successful lawyer, not so much by his knowledge of law, for this was never great, as by his ability as an advocate, and by reason of his sterling integrity.   He would not be a party to misrepresentation, and more than once refused to take cases which involved such a result.   He even was known to abandon a case which brought him unexpectedly into this attitude, making in his first case before the United States Circuit Court the unusual statement that he had not been able to find any authorities supporting his side of the case, but had found several favoring the opposite, which he proceeded to quote.

Lincoln as a Lawyer

The very appearance of such an attorney in any case must have gone far to win the jury ; and, when deeply stirred, the power of his oratory, and the invincible logic of his argument, made him a most formidable opponent. "Yes," he was overheard to say to a would-be client, "we can doubtless gain your case for you ; we can set a whole neighborhood at loggerheads ; we can distress a widowed mother and her six fatherless children, and thereby get for you the six hundred dollars to which you seem to have a legal claim, but which rightfully belongs, it appears to me, as much to the woman and her children as it does to you. You must remember that some things legally right are not morally right. We shall not take your case, but will give you a little advice for which we will charge you nothing. You seem to be a sprightly, energetic man ; we would advise you to try your hand at making six hundred dollars in some other way."

In the United States Congress

In 1846 he accepted a nomination to Congress and was triumphantly elected, being the only Whig among the seven representatives from his state. As a member of the House his voice was always given on the side of human freedom, he voting in favor of considering the petitions for the abolition of slavery and supporting the doctrines of the Wilmot proviso, which opposed the extension of slavery to the territory acquired from Mexico.

As yet Lincoln had not made a striking figure as a legislator. He was admired by those about him for his sterling honesty and integrity, but his name was hardly known in the country at large, and there was no indication that he would ever occupy a prominent position in the politics of the nation. It was the threatened repeal of the Missouri Compromise, in 1854, an act which would open the western territory to the admission of slavery, that first fairly wakened him up and laid the foundation of his remarkable career. The dangerous question which Henry Clay had set aside for years, but which was now brought forward again, absorbed his attention, and he grew constantly more bold and powerful in his denunciation of the encroachments of the slave power. He became, therefore, the natural champion of his party in the campaigns in which Senator Douglas undertook to defend before the people of his state his advocacy of "squatter sovereignty," or the right of the people of each territory to decide whether it should be admitted as a slave or a free state, and of the Kansas-Nebraska bill, by which the "Missouri Compromise" was repealed.

The first great battle between these two giants of debate took place at the State Fair at Springfield, in October, 1854. Douglas made a great speech to an unprecedented concourse of people, and was the lion of the hour. The next day Lincoln replied, and his effort was such as to surprise both his friends and his opponents. It was probably the first occasion in which he reached his full power. In the words of a friendly editor: "The Nebraska bill was shivered, and like a tree of the forest was torn and rent asunder by the hot bolts of truth. . . . At the conclusion of this speech every man and child felt that it was unanswerable."

The Great Lincoln and Douglas Debate

But it was the campaign of 1858 that made Lincoln famous. In this contest he first fully displayed his powers as an orator and logician, and won the reputation that made him President. Douglas, his opponent, was immensely popular in the West. His advocacy of territorial expansion appealed to the patriotism of the young and ardent; his doctrine of popular sovereignty was well calculated to mislead shallow thinkers; and his power in debate was so great that he became widely known as the "Little Giant." But he found a worthy champion of the opposite in Abraham Lincoln, who riddled and ventilated many of his specious arguments, and succeeded in inducing him to make a statement that proved fatal to his hopes of the Presidency.

When Lincoln proposed to press upon his opponent the question whether there were lawful means by which slavery could be excluded from a territory before its admission as a state, his friends suggested that

Douglas's Fatal Answer

Douglas would reply that slavery could not exist unless it was desired by the people, and unless protected by territorial legislation, and that this answer would be sufficiently satisfactory to insure his re-election. But Lincoln replied, "I am after larger game. If Douglas so answers, he can never be President, and the battle of 1860 is worth a hundred of this." Both predictions were verified. The people of the South might have forgiven Douglas his opposition to the Lecompton Constitution of Kansas, but they could not forgive the promulgation of a doctrine which, in spite of the Dred Scott decision (a Supreme Court decision to the effect that a master had the right to take his slave into any state and hold him there as "property"), would keep slavery out of a territory; and so, although Douglas was elected and Lincoln defeated, the Democracy was divided, and it was impossible for Douglas to command southern votes for the presidency.

The campaign had been opened with a speech by Lincoln which startled the country by its boldness and its power. It was delivered at the Republican convention which nominated him for Senator, and had been previously submitted to his confidential advisers. They strenuously opposed the introduction of its opening sentences. He was warned that they would be fatal to his election, and, in the existing state of public feeling, might permanently destroy his political prospects. Lincoln could

Lincoln Takes His Stand

not be moved. "It is *true*," said he, "and I *will* deliver it as written. I would rather be defeated with these expressions in my speech held up and discussed before the people than be victorious without them." The paragraph gave to the country a statement of the problem as terse and vigorous and even more complete than Seward's "irrepressible conflict," and as startling as Sumner's proposition that "freedom was national, slavery sectional." "A house divided against itself," said Lincoln, "cannot stand. I believe this government cannot endure permanently half slave and half free. I do not expect the Union to be dissolved; I do not expect the house to fall; but I expect it will cease to be divided. It will become all one thing or all the other. Either the opponents of slavery will arrest the farther spread of it, and place it where the public mind shall rest in the belief that it is in the course of ultimate extinction, or its advocates will push it forward till it shall become alike lawful in all the states,—old as well as new, North as well as South."

Never had the issues of a political campaign seemed more momentous; never was one more ably contested. The triumph of the doctrine of "popular sovereignty," in the Kansas-Nebraska bill, had opened the territories to slavery, while it professed to leave the question to be decided by the people. To the question whether the people of a territory could exclude slavery Douglas had answered, "That is a question for the courts to decide," but the Dred Scott decision, practically holding that the Federal Constitution guaranteed the right to hold slaves in the territories, seemed to make the pro-slavery cause triumphant. The course of Douglas regarding the Lecompton Constitution, however, had made it possible for his friends to describe him as "the true champion of freedom," while Lincoln continually exposed, with merciless force, the illogical position of his adversary, and his complete lack of political morality.

The "Champion of Freedom"

Douglas claimed that the doctrine of popular sovereignty "originated when God made man and placed good and evil before him, allowing him to choose upon his own responsibility." But Lincoln declared with great solemnity: "No; God did not place good and evil before man, telling him to take his choice. On the contrary, God did tell him that there was one tree of the fruit of which he should not eat, upon pain of death." The question was to him one of right, a high question of morality, and only upon such a question could he ever be fully roused. "Slavery is wrong," was the keynote of his speeches. But he did not take the position of the abolitionists. He even admitted that the South was entitled, under the Constitution, to a national fugitive slave law, though his soul revolted at the law which was then in force. His position, as already cited, was that of the Republican party. He would limit the extension of slavery, and place it in such a position as would insure its ultimate extinction. It was a moderate course, viewed from this distance of time, but in the face of a dominant, arrogant, irascible pro-slavery sentiment it seemed radical in the extreme, calculated, indeed, to fulfill a threat he had made to the governor of the state. He had been attempting to secure the release of a young negro from Springfield who was wrongfully detained in New Orleans, and who was in danger of being sold for prison expenses. Moved to the depths of his being by the refusal of the official to interfere, Lincoln exclaimed: "By God, governor, I'll make the ground of this country *too hot for the foot of a slave.'*

Lincoln's Views on the Slavery Question

Douglas was re-elected. Lincoln had hardly anticipated a different result, and he had nothing of the feeling of defeat. On the contrary, he felt that the **corner-stone of victory** had been laid. He had said of his

25

opening speech : " If I had to draw a pen across my record, and erase my whole life from sight, and I had one poor gift or choice left as to what I should choose to save from the wreck, I should choose that speech, and leave it to the world unerased."

The great debate had made Lincoln famous.   In Illinois his name was a household word.   His stand for the liberty of the slave was on the lips of the advocates of human freedom through all the country.   Deep and wide-

The Cooper Institute Speech

spread interest was felt in the East for this prairie orator, and when, in 1860, he appeared by invitation to deliver an address in the Cooper Institute, of New York, he was welcomed by an audience of the mental calibre of those who of old gathered to hear Clay and Webster speak.

It was a deeply surprised audience.   They expected to be treated to something of the freshness, but much of the shallowness, of the frontier region, and listened with astonishment and admiration to the dignified, clear, and luminous oration of the prairie statesman.   It is said that those who afterwards published the speech as a campaign document were three weeks in verifying its historical and other statements, so deep and abundant was the learning it displayed.

He had taken the East by storm.   He was invited to speak in many places in New England, and everywhere met with the most flattering reception, which surprised almost as much as it delighted him.   It astonished him to hear that the Professor of Rhetoric of Yale College took notes of his speech and lectured upon them to his class, and followed him to Meriden the next evening to hear him again for the same purpose.   An intelligent

A Tour in New England

hearer spoke to him of the remarkable " clearness of your statements, the unanswerable style of your reasoning, and especially your illustrations, which are romance and pathos, fun and logic, all welded together."   Perhaps his style could not be better described.   He himself said that it used to anger him, when a child, to hear statements which he could not understand, and he was thus led to form the habit of turning over a thought until it was in language any boy could comprehend.

It is not necessary to tell in detail what followed.   Lincoln had attained the high eminence of being considered as a suitable candidate for President, and when the Republican Convention of 1860 met in Chicago, he found himself looked upon as the man for the West.   Seward was a prominent candidate, but his candidacy sank before that of the choice of the westerners, who were roused to a frenzy of enthusiasm when some of the rails which Lincoln had split were borne into the hall.   He was nominated on the third ballot.

amid the wildest acclamations. In the campaign that followed Lincoln and Hamlin were the triumphant candidates, winning their seats by a majority of fifty-seven in the electoral college. The poor rail-splitter of Illinois had lifted himself, by pure force of genius, to be President of the United States of America. From that time forward the life of Abraham Lincoln is the history of the great Civil War. His task was such as few men had ever faced before. The mighty republic of the West, the most promising experiment in self-government by the people that the world had ever known, seemed about to end in failure. No man did more to save it from destruction and start it on its future course of greatness and renown than this western prodigy of genius and rectitude.

The Rail-splitter Made President

Mr. Lincoln called to his cabinet the ablest men of his party, two of whom, Seward and Chase, had been his competitors for the nomination, and the new administration devoted itself to the work of saving the Union. Every means was tried to prevent the secession of the border states, and the President delayed until Fort Sumter had been fired upon before he began active measures for the suppression of the rebellion and called for seventy-five thousand volunteers.

The great question, from the start, was the treatment of the negro. The advanced anti-slavery men demanded decisive action, and could not understand that success depended absolutely upon the administration commanding the support of the whole people. And so Mr. Lincoln incurred the displeasure and lost the confidence of some of those who had been his heartiest supporters, by keeping the negro in the background and making the preservation of the Union the great end for which he strove. He repeatedly declared that, if he could do so, he would preserve the Union *with slavery*, and further said, "I could not feel that, to the best of my ability, I had even *tried* to preserve the Constitution, if, to save slavery or for any minor matter, I should permit the wreck of government, country and Constitution, all together." Only when it became evident that the North was in accord with him in his detestation of slavery did the President venture to strike the blow which was to bring that perilous system to an end.

The Great Question of the Civil War

In the dark days of 1862, when the reverses of the Union arms cast a gloom over the North, and European governments were seriously considering the propriety of recognizing the Confederacy, it seemed to Mr. Lincoln that the time had come, that the North was prepared to support a radical measure, and that emancipation would not only weaken the South at home, but would make it impossible for any European government to take the attitude toward slavery which would be involved in recognizing the Confederacy. Action was delayed until a favorable moment, and after the victory of Antietam the President called his cabinet together and announced

The Proclama-
tion of Eman-
cipation
that he was about to issue the Proclamation of Emancipation. It was a solemn moment. The President had made a vow— "I promised my God," were his words—that if the tide of invasion should be mercifully arrested, he would set the negro free. The final proclamation, issued three months later, fitly closes with an appeal which indicates the devout spirit in which the deed was done : " And upon this act, sincerely believed to be an act of justice, warranted by the Constitution upon military necessity, I invoke the considerate judgment of mankind, and the gracious favor of Almighty God."

The question of slavery was only one of the many with which Lincoln had to contend. Questions of foreign policy, of finance, of the conduct of the war, of a dozen different kinds pressed upon him for solution, while dissensions in his cabinet and incompetence in the army made his task anything but a pleasant one. His personal advisers, Stanton, Seward, Chase, and others, were strong and able men, but above them was a stronger man, who held firmly in his own hands the reins of government, and would not yield them to any of his ambitious subordinates, nor change his fixed policy at the bidding of irresponsible critics and fault-finders.

Upon what Lincoln called " the plain people "—the mass of his countrymen—he could always depend, because he, more than any other political

Lincoln and
the " Plain
People "
leader in our history, understood them. Sumner, matchless advocate of liberty as he was, distrusted the President, and was desirous of getting the power out of his hands into stronger and safer ones. But suddenly the great Massachusetts senator awoke to the fact that he could not command the support of his own constituency, and found it necessary to issue an interview declaring himself not an opponent, but a supporter, of Lincoln. The President's grasp of questions of state policy was, indeed, stronger than that of any of his advisers. The important dispatch to our minister in England, in May, 1861, outlining the course to be pursued towards that power, has been published in its original draft, showing the work of the Secretary of State and President

An Able
Diplomatist
Lincoln's alterations. Of this publication the editor of the *North American Review* says : " Many military men, who have had access to Lincoln's papers, have classed him as the best general of the war. This paper will go far toward establishing his reputation as its ablest diplomatist." It would be impossible for any intelligent person to study the paper thus published, the omissions, the alterations,

ABRAHAM LINCOLN. (1809-1865)

ULYSSES SIMPSON GRANT. 1822-1885)

ROBERT EDMUND LEE. (1807-1870)

WILLIAM T. SHERMAN. (1820-1891)

THE ATTACK ON FORT DONELSON

This memorable battle of February, 1862, was the first serious blow to the Confederate cause. It was also Grant's first victory of importance, and marks the beginning of his rise to fame. Fifteen thousand prisoners were taken. Grant generously allowed the Confederates to retain their personal baggage, and the officers to keep their side arms. General Buckner expressed his thanks for this chivalrous act, and later in life became Grant's personal friend.

the substitutions, without acknowledging that they were the work of a master mind, and that the raw backwoodsman, not three months in office, was the peer of any statesman with whom he might find it necessary to cope.   He was entirely willing to grant to his secretaries and to his generals the greatest liberty of action ; he was ready to listen to any one, and to accept advice even from hostile critics ; and his readiness made them think, sometimes, that he had little mental power of his own, and brought upon him the charge of weakness ; but, as the facts have become more fully known, it has grown more and more evident that he was not only the "best general" and the "ablest diplomatist," but the greatest man among all the great men whom that era of trial brought to the rescue of our country.

And when the end came, after four years of desperate conflict ; when Lee had surrendered and the work of saving the Union seemed complete ; when the liberator was made, by the assassin's hand, the martyr to that great cause which he had carried to its glorious termina- **The Assasina-** tion, a depth of pathos was added to our memory of America's **tion of Lincoln** noblest man, insuring him a fame that was worth dying for, that crown of human sympathy which lends glory to martyrdom.

The story of the end need hardly be told.   On the evening of April 14, 1865, Abraham Lincoln was shot by a half-crazed sympathizer with the South, John Wilkes Booth.   The President had gone, by special invitation, to witness a play at Ford's Theatre, and the assassin had no difficulty in gaining entrance to the box, committing the dreadful deed, and leaping to the stage to make his escape.   The story of his pursuit and death while resisting arrest is familiar to us all.   Mr. Lincoln lingered till the morning, when the little group of friends and relatives, with members of the cabinet, stood with breaking hearts about the death-bed.

Sorrow more deep and universal cannot be imagined than enveloped our land on that 15th of April.   Throughout the country every household felt the loss as of one of themselves.   The honored remains lay for a few days in state at Washington, and then began the funeral journey, taking in backward course almost the route which had been followed four years before, when the newly-elected President went to **The Grief of the** assume his burdens of his high office.   Such a pilgrimage of **People** sorrow had never been witnessed by our people.   It was followed by the sympathy of the whole world until the loved remains were laid in the tomb at Springfield, Illinois.   Over the door of the state house, in the city of his nome, where his old neighbors took their last farewell, were these lines :

"He left us borne up by our prayers ;
He returns embalmed in our tears."

Abraham Lincoln was in every way a remarkable man. Towering above his fellows, six feet four inches in height, his giant figure, with its inclination to stoop, of itself attracted attention. While possessed of gigantic strength, he was diffident and modest in the extreme. The expression of his face was sad, and that sadness deepened as the war dragged on and causes for national depression increased. Melancholy was hereditary with him, and it is doubtful if his mind was ever free from a degree of mental dejection. On certain occasions he was almost overwhelmed by it. Yet with all this he was one of the readiest inventors and gatherers of amusing stories, which were inimitable as told by him. He opened the cabinet meeting in which he announced his purpose to issue the Emancipation Proclamation by reading to his dignified associates a chapter from Artemus Ward. His jokes were usually for a purpose. He settled more than one weighty question by the wit of a homely "yarn," that told better than hours of argument would have done. A signal illustration of his method is the telling aphorism by which he once settled the question of changing the generals in command : " It is a bad plan to swap horses crossing a stream."

A Man of Melancholy and of Wit

His gift of expression was only equaled by the clearness and firmness of his grasp upon the truths which he desired to convey ; and the beauty of his words, upon many occasions, is only matched by the goodness and purity of the soul from which they sprung. His Gettysburg speech will be remembered as long as the story of the battle for freedom shall be told ; and of his second inaugural it has been said : " This was like a sacred poem. No American President had ever spoken words like these to the American people. America never had a President who found such words in the depth of his heart." The following were its closing words, and with them we may fitly close this imperfect sketch :

" Fondly do we hope, fervently do we pray, that this mighty scourge of war may speedily pass away. Yet if God wills that it continue until all the wealth piled by the bondman's two hundred and fifty years of unrequited toil shall be sunk, and until every drop of blood drawn with the lash shall be paid by another drawn with the sword ; as was said three thousand years ago, so still it must be said, ' The judgments of the Lord are true and righteous altogether.' With malice toward none, with charity for all, with firmness in the right as God gives us to see the right, let us strive on to finish the work we are in ; to bind up the nation's wounds ; to care for him who shall have borne the battle, and for his widow and his orphan ; to do all which may achieve and cherish a just and lasting peace among ourselves and with all nations."

The Great Gettysburg Oration

CHAPTER XXXI.

Grant and Lee and the Civil War.

IN several of the preceding chapters the causes which led the United States into its great fratricidal war have been given. In the present we propose to deal with the war itself; not to describe it in detail,—that belongs to general history,—but to speak of its great soldiers and its leading events, which form the chosen topics of this work. Of the statesmen brought into prominence by the war, President Lincoln was the chief, and we have given an account of his life. Of its famous soldiers two stand pre-eminent, Ulysses S. Grant and Robert E. Lee, and around the careers of these two men the whole story of the war revolves. They did not stand alone; there were others who played leading parts,—Thomas, Sherman, Sheridan, McClellan and others, on the Union side; Jackson, Johnston and others on the Confederate,—but this is not a work of biographical sketches, and our main attention must be centred upon the two leading figures in the war, the mighty opponents who linked arms in the desperate struggle from the Wilderness to Appomattox.

The Great Leaders of the Civil War

Grant was a modest and retiring man. While others were strenuously pushing their claims to command, he, an experienced soldier of the Mexican war, held back and was thrust aside by the crowd of enterprising incompetents, doing anything that was offered him, the coming Napoleon of the war performing services suitable for a drill sergeant. But gradually men of experience in war began to find their appropriate places, and in August, 1861, Grant was made brigadier-general and given command of a district including southeast Missouri and western Kentucky. He soon set out to meet the Confederates, and found them at Belmont, Missouri, where he drove them back in a hard four hours' fight. Then they were reinforced and advanced in such strength that Grant and his men were in danger of being cut off from the boats in which they had come.

Grant Takes Command

"We are surrounded," cried the men, in some alarm.

"Well, then," said Grant, "we must cut our way out, as we cut our way in," and they did. It was the only retreat in Grant's career.

Meanwhile, in the East, the battle of Bull Run had been fought, to the dismay of the Union side, the triumph of the Confederate. There followed an autumn and winter of weary waiting, which severely tried the patience of North and South alike, both sides being eager for something to be done. Early in the following year something was done, but not in the region where the people looked for it. While attention was chiefly concentrated upon the Potomac, where McClellan was organizing and drilling that splendid army which another and a greater commander was to lead to final victory; while the only response to the people's urgent call, "On to Rich-

All Quiet on the Potomac

mond!" was the daily report, "All quiet on the Potomac;" Grant, an obscure and almost unknown soldier, was pushing forward against Forts Henry and Donelson, eleven miles apart, on the Tennessee and the Cumberland, near where these rivers cross the line dividing Kentucky and Tennessee.

He had obtained from his commander, Halleck, a reluctant consent to his plan for attacking these important posts with a land force, co-operating at the same time with a fleet of gunboats under Commodore Foote. It was the month of February and bitterly cold. Amid sleet and snow the men pushed along the roads, arriving at Fort Henry just after it had been captured, as the result of a severe bombardment, by the gunboats. Grant immediately turned his attention to Fort Donelson, which had been reinforced by a large part of the garrison that had escaped from Fort Henry. It was held by Generals Buckner, Floyd and Pillow with 20,000 men. For three days a fierce attack was kept up. Buckner, who had been at West Point with Grant, and doubtless knew that he was, as his wife designated him, "a very obstinate man," sent on the morning of the fourth day, under a flag of truce, to ask what terms of surrender would be granted. In reply Grant sent

The Surrender of Fort Donelson

that brief, stern message which thrilled throughout the North, stirring the blood in every loyal heart: "No terms but unconditional and immediate surrender can be accepted. I propose to move immediately upon your works."

Buckner protested against the terms; but he was obliged to accept them and to surrender unconditionally. With Fort Donelson were surrendered 15,000 men, 3,000 horses, sixty-five cannon, and a great quantity of small arms and military stores. It was the first victory for the North, and the whole country was electrified. Grant's reply to Buckner became a household word, and the people of the North delighted to call him, " Unconditional Surrender Grant." He was made a major-general of volunteers, his commission bearing date of February 16, 1862, the day of the surrender of Fort Donelson.

On April 6th, less than two months afterwards, another of Grant's great battles was fought, at Shiloh, or Pittsburg Landing, in **The Terrible Struggle at Pittsburg Landing** Mississippi. In this battle Sherman was Grant's chief lieutenant, and the two men tested each other's qualities in the greatest trial to which either had as yet been exposed. The battle was one of the turning-points of the war. The Confederates, 50,000 strong, under Albert Sidney Johnston, one of their best generals, attacked the Union force of 40,000 men at Shiloh Church. All day on Sunday the battle raged. The brave Johnston was killed; but the Union forces were driven back, and at night their lines were a mile in the rear of their position in the morning. Grant came into his headquarters' tent that evening, when, to any but the bravest and most sanguine, the battle seemed lost, and said: "Well, it was tough work to-day, but we will beat them out of their boots to-morrow." "When his staff and the generals present heard this," writes one of his officers, "they were as fully persuaded of the result of the morrow's battle as when the victory had actually been achieved."

The next day, after dreadful fighting, the tide turned in favor of the Union forces, which had been strongly reinforced by General Buell during the night. In the afternoon Grant himself led a charge against the Confederate lines, under which they broke and were driven back. Night found the Union army in possession of the field, after one of the severest battles of the war.

A man who wins victories is apt to become a fair foil for criticism from those who lose them. "Grant is a drunkard," said his opponents. This charge came to the President's ears. "Grant drinks too much whisky," some fault-finder said. Lincoln replied, with his dry humor. "I wish you would tell me what brand of whisky General Grant uses; I should like to send some of it to our other generals."

It would doubtless have been better if this general, who drank a fighting brand of whisky, had been brought to the East, where the war was proceeding in a manner far from satisfactory. For six days **The War in the East** the armies of Lee and McClellan met in desperate battle before Richmond, the Union army being driven from all its positions, and forced to seek a new base on the James River. This disaster was followed by a second conflict at Bull Run, which ended in one of the most sanguinary defeats of the Union side during the war. The repulse was in a measure retrieved by McClellan at Antietam, yet affairs did not look very bright for the Union cause, and in the winter of 1862–63 there was much depression in the North. The terrible defeats at Fredericksburg and Chancellorsville added to the anxiety of the people, and the necessity of some signal success seemed urgent. Such a success came in double measure in the following summer, at Gettysburg and at Vicksburg.

On a high bluff on the east bank of the Mississippi River, which pursues a winding course through its fertile valley, stands the town of Vicksburg. From this point a railroad ran to the eastward, and from the opposite shore another ran westward through the rich, level country of Louisiana. The town was strongly fortified, and from its elevation it commanded the river in both directions. So long as it was held by the Confederate armies, the Mississippi could not be opened to navigation; and the line of railroad running east and west kept communication open between the western and eastern parts of the Confederacy. How to capture Vicksburg was a great problem; but it was one which General Grant determined should be solved.

The Vicksburg Problem

For eight months he worked at this problem. He formed plan after plan, only to be forced to abandon them. Sherman made a direct attack at the only place where a landing was practicable, and failed. Weeks were spent in cutting a canal across the neck of a peninsula formed by a great bend in the river opposite Vicksburg, so as to bring the gunboats through without their passing under the fire of the batteries; but a flood destroyed the work. Meanwhile great numbers of the troops were ill with malaria or other diseases, and many died. There was much clamor at Washington to have Grant removed, but the President refused. He had faith in Grant, and determined to give him time to work out the great problem,—how to get below and in the rear of Vicksburg, on the Mississippi River.

This was at last accomplished. On a dark night the gunboats were successfully run past the batteries, although every one of them was more or less damaged by the guns. The troops were marched across the peninsula, and then taken down the river on the side opposite the town; and on April 30th the whole force was landed on the Mississippi side, on high ground, and at a point where it could reach the enemy.

The railroad running east from Vicksburg connected that city with Jackson, the state capital, which was an important railway centre, and from which Vicksburg was supplied. Grant made his movements with great rapidity. He fought in quick succession a series of battles by which Jackson and several other towns were captured; then, turning westward, he attacked the forces of Pemberton, drove him back into Vicksburg, cut off his supplies, and laid siege to the place.

Passing the Batteries

The eyes of the whole nation were now centred on Vicksburg. More than two hundred guns were brought to bear upon the place, besides the batteries of the gunboats. In default of mortars, guns were improvised by boring out tough logs, strongly bound with iron bands, which did good service. The people of Vicksburg took shelter in cellars and caves to escape the shot and shell. Food of all kinds became very scarce; flour was sold at five dollars a pound, molasses at twelve dollars a gallon. The endurance and devotion of the inhabitants were wonderful. But the siege was so rigidly and relentlessly maintained that there could be only one end. On July 3d, at ten o'clock, flags of truce were displayed on the works, and General Pemberton sent a message to Grant asking for an armistice, and proposing that commissioners should be appointed to arrange terms of capitulation.

The Siege of Vicksburg

On the afternoon of the same day, Grant and Pemberton met under an oak between the lines of the two armies and arranged the terms of surrender. It took three hours for the Confederate army to march out and stack their arms. There were surrendered 31,000 men, 250 cannon, and a great quantity of arms and munitions of war. But the moral advantage to the Union cause was far beyond any material gain. The fall of Vicksburg carried with it that of Port Hudson, a few miles below, which surrendered to Banks a few days later; and at last the great river was open from St. Louis to the sea.

The news of this great victory came to the North on the same day with that of Gettysburg, July 4, 1863. The rejoicing over the great triumph is indescribable. A heavy load was lifted from the minds of the President and his cabinet. The North took heart, and resolved again to prosecute the war with energy. The name of Grant was on every tongue. It was everywhere felt that he was the foremost man of the campaign. He was at once made a major-general in the regular army, and a gold medal was awarded him by Congress.

The Great Victories and Their Effect

Grant's next striking victory was at Chattanooga, an important railway centre in the valley of the Tennessee River, near where it enters Alabama. South of the town the slope of Lookout Mountain rises to a height of 2000 feet above sea-level. Two miles to the east rises Missionary Ridge 500 feet high. Both Lookout Mountain and Missionary Ridge were occupied by the army of General Bragg, and his commanding position, strengthened by fortifications, was considered by him impregnable.

The disastrous battle of Chickamauga, in September, 1863, had left the Union armies in East Tennessee in a perilous situation. General Thomas, in Chattanooga, was hemmed in by the Confederate forces, his line of supplies was endangered, and his men and horses were almost starving. The army was on quarter rations.

Chickamauga and Chattanooga

Ammunition was almost exhausted, and the troops were short of clothing. Thousands of army mules, worn out and starved, lay dead along the miry roads. Chattanooga, occupied by the Union army, was too strongly fortified for Bragg to take by storm, but every day shells from his batteries upon the heights were thrown into the town.   This was the situation when Grant, stiff and sore from a recent accident, arrived at Nashville, on his way to direct the campaign in East Tennessee.

"Hold Chattanooga at all hazards. I will be there as soon as possible," he telegraphed from Nashville to General Thomas.   "We will hold the town until we starve," was the brave reply.

Grant's movements were rapid and decisive. He ordered the troops to be concentrated at Chattanooga; he fought a battle at Wauhatchie, in Lookout Valley, which broke Bragg's hold on the river below Chattanooga and shortened the Union line of supplies; and by his prompt and vigorous preparation for effective action he soon had his troops lifted out of the demoralized condition in which they had sunk after the defeat of Chickamauga.   One month after his arrival were fought the memorable battles of Lookout Mountain and Missionary Ridge, by which the Confederate troops **Lookout Mount-** were driven out of Tennessee, their hold on the country was **ain and Mis-** broken up, and a large number of prisoners and guns were cap- **sionary Ridge** tured.   Nothing in the history of war is more inspiring than the impetuous bravery with which the Union troops fought their way up the steep mountain sides, bristling with cannon, and drove the Confederate troops out of their works at the point of the bayonet.   An officer of General Bragg's staff afterward declared that they considered their position perfectly impregnable, and that when they saw the Union troops, after capturing their rifle-pits at the base, coming up the craggy mountain toward their headquarters, they could scarcely credit their eyes, and thought that every man of them must be drunk.   History has no parallel for sublimity and picturesqueness of effect, while the consequences, which were the division of the Confederacy in the East, were inestimable.

After Grant's success in Tennessee, the popular demand that he should be put at the head of all the armies became irresistible.   In Virginia the **Grant Made** magnificent Army of the Potomac, after two years of fighting, **Lieutenant-** had been barely able to turn back from the North the tide of **General and** Confederate invasion, and was apparently as far as ever from **Commander-** capturing Richmond.   In the West, on the other hand, **in-Chief** Grant's armies had won victory after victory, had driven the opposing forces out of Kentucky and Tennessee, had taken Vicksburg, opened up the Mississippi, and divided the Confederacy in both the West

GENERAL LEE'S INVASION OF THE NORTH

The Confederate army under General Lee twice invaded the North. The first invasion was brought to a disastrous end by the Battle of Antietam, September 17, 1862. The second invasion ended with greater disaster at Gettysburg, July 1-3, 1863. Gettysburg was the greatest and Antietam the bloodiest battles of the war.

THE SINKING OF THE "ALABAMA," THE MOST FAMOUS OF ALL CONFEDERATE CRUISERS

The battle between the *Kearsarge* and the *Alabama* took place off the coast of France, June, 1864. The famous cruiser was going down, and the boats of the *Kearsarge* were hurriedly sent to help the drowning men. The stern settled, the bow rose high in the air, the immense ship plunged out of sight, and the career of the *Alabama* was ended forever.

and the East.   In response to the call for Grant, Congress revived the grade
of lieutenant-general, which had been held by only one commander, Scott,
since the time of Washington ; and the hero of Fort Donelson, Vicksburg,
and Chattanooga was nominated to this rank by the President, confirmed
by the Senate, and placed in command of all the armies of the nation.

The relief of President Lincoln at having such a man in command was
very great.   " Grant is the first *general* I've had," he remarked to a friend.
' You know how it has been with all the rest.   As soon as I put a man in
command of the army, he would come to me with a plan, and about as much
as say, 'Now, I don't believe I can do it, but if you say so I'll try it on,' and
so put the responsibility of success or failure upon me.   They all wanted
me to be the general.   Now, it isn't so with Grant.   He hasn't told me what
his plans are.   I don't know, and I don't want to know.   I am glad to find a
man who can go ahead without me."

Never were the persistent courage, the determined purpose, which formed
the foundation of Grant's character, more clearly brought out than in the Virginia campaign of 1864, in which he commanded ; and never   **The Virginia**
were they more needed.   Well did he know that no single   **Campain of**
triumph, however brilliant, would suffice.   He saw plainly that   **1864-65**
nothing but " hammering away " would avail.   The stone wall of the Confederacy had too broad and firm a base to be suddenly overturned ; it had
to be slowly reduced to powder.

During the anxious days which followed the battle of the Wilderness,
Frank B. Carpenter, the artist, relates that he asked President Lincoln,
" How does Grant impress you as compared with other generals ? "

" The great thing about him," said the President, " is cool persistency
of purpose.   He is not easily excited, and he has the grip of a bull-dog.
When he once gets his teeth in, nothing can shake him off."

His great opponent, Lee, saw and felt the same quality.   When, after
days of indecisive battle, the fighting in the Wilderness came to a pause, it
was believed in the Confederate lines that the Union troops were falling
back.   General Gordon said to Lee,—

" I think there is no doubt that Grant is retreating."

The Confederate chief knew better.   He shook his head.

" You are mistaken," he replied earnestly,—" quite mistaken.   Grant is
not retreating ; *he is not a retreating man.*"

The battles of Spottsylvania and North Anna followed, and then came
the disastrous affair at Cold Harbor.   Then Grant changed his base to James
river and attacked Petersburg.   Slowly but surely the Union lines closed
in.   " Falling back " on the Union side had gone out of fashion.   South or

North, all could see that now a steady resistless force was back of the Union armies, pushing them ever on toward Richmond.

Grant's losses in the final campaign were heavy, but Lee's slender resources were wrecked in a much more serious proportion; and for the Confederates no recruiting was possible. Their dead, who lay so thickly beneath the fields, were the children of the soil, and there were none to replace them. In some cases whole families were destroyed; but the survivors still fought on. In the Confederate lines around Petersburg there was often absolute destitution. An officer who was there testified, shortly after the end of the struggle, that every cat and dog for miles around had been caught and eaten. Grant was pressing onward; Sherman's march through Georgia and the Carolinas had proved that the Confederacy was an egg-shell; Sheridan's splendid cavalry was ever hovering round the last defenders of the bars and stripes. Grant saw that all was over, and on April 7, 1865, he wrote that memorable letter calling upon Lee to surrender and bring the war to an end. Lee, whose army was cut off beyond possibility of escape, was obliged to consent, and the terrible four years' conflict ceased.

The End of The War

We have told the chief incidents in the career as a soldier of the great Union general; we have now to deal with that of his equally great opponent in the final year of the war, the brilliant commander of the Confederate forces, General Robert E. Lee.

Of all the men whose character and ability were developed in the Civil War, there was perhaps not one in either army whose greatness is more generally acknowledged than that of the man just named. His ability as a soldier and his character as a man are alike appreciated; and while it is natural that men of the North should be unwilling to condone his taking up arms against the government, yet that has not prevented their doing full justice to his greatness. It is not too much to say that General Lee is recognized, both North and South, as one of the greatest soldiers, and one of the ablest and purest men, that America has produced.

Character of General Lee

Lee, like Grant, was a graduate of West Point and had seen service in the Mexican war, in which he won high honor. It was he who, when John Brown made his raid against Harper's Ferry, was despatched with a body of troops for his capture. The raiders had entrenched themselves in the engine house of the arsenal, but Lee quickly battered down the door, captured them, and turned them over to the civil authorities.

Lee, the son of "Light Horse Harry Lee," a famous general of the Revolutionary War, cherished an attachment to the Union which his father had helped him to form, and at the breaking out of the Civil War was in great doubt as to what course he should take. He disapproved of secession, but was thoroughly pervaded with the idea of loyalty to his state,—an idea which was almost universal in the South, though not entertained by the people of the North. He had great difficulty **Lee's Devotion to His State** in arriving at a decision; but when at last Virginia adopted an ordinance of secession, he resigned his commission in the United States army. Writing to his sister, he said, " Though I recognize no necessity for this state of things, and would have forborne and pleaded to the end for redress of grievances, yet in my own person I had to meet the question whether I should take part against my native state. With all my devotion to the Union, and the feeling of loyalty and duty as an American citizen, I have not been able to make up my mind to raise my hand against my relatives, my children, my home. I have therefore resigned my commission in the army, and, save in defence of my native state, I hope I may never be called upon to draw my sword."

It was not a case in which a soldier who believed in state supremacy could long hesitate. Virginia was invaded, and Lee drew his sword " in defence of his native state," his first service being as brigadier-general in Northwestern Virginia, where he was opposed to General Rosecrans. Here no important battle was fought, and in the latter part of **Lee in Command at Richmond** 1861 he was sent to the coast of North Carolina, where he planned the defences which were held good against Union attack until the last year of the war. After the wounding of General J. E. Johnston at Fair Oaks, Lee was called to the command of the forces at Richmond, and on June 3, 1862, took charge of the army defending the Confederate capital.

The task before him was no light one. McClellan lay before Richmond with a powerful and well-appointed army, and that city was in considerable danger of capture. But the generals opposed to each other were of very different calibre. McClellan was of the cautious and deliberate order; Lee was one of those ready to dare all " on the hazard of a die." On June 26th he made a vigorous assault on the Union army, and continued it with unceasing persistence day after day for six days, driving **The Six Day's Fight** McClellan and his men steadily backward. On the final day, July 1st, the Union army, strongly posted on Malvern Hill, defeated Lee, who suffered heavy loss. But McClellan continued to retreat until the James River was reached and the siege of Richmond abandoned.

A few months passed, and then, with a sudden and rapid sweep north, Lee fell upon the large army which had been gathered under General Pope,

on the old battlefield of Bull Run.   Here a terrible struggle took place,
ending in the disastrous defeat of Pope.   In this bloody battle the Unionists
lost 25,000 men, of whom 9,000 were made prisoners.   The Confederates
lost about 15,000.   As the defeated army had fallen back on Washington,
that city was safe against assault, and on September 4th, with another of
his brilliant and rapid movements, Lee marched his army into Maryland,
hoping that this State would rise in his support.

He was disappointed in this; the Marylanders proved staunch for the
Union ; but one great advantage was gained in the capture of Harper's
Ferry by Stonewall Jackson, with nearly 12,000 prisoners and immense
quantities of munitions of war.   It was a bloodless victory, as valuable in its
results for the Confederacy as had been the sanguinary battle of Bull Run.
A few days later, on September 17th, the two late opponents, McClellan and
Lee, met in conflict at Antietam, in the most bloody battle, for
the numbers engaged, of the war.   Lee had taken a dangerous
risk in weakening his army to despatch Jackson against
Second Bull Run and Antietam
Harper's Ferry.   But the alert Jackson was back again, and the Confederates
had 70,000 men to oppose to the 80,000 under McClellan.   The result was in
a measure a drawn battle, but Lee was so severely handled that he did not
deem it safe to wait for a renewal of the conflict, and withdrew across the
Potomac.   The failure of McClellan to pursue with energy brought his
career to an end.   He was removed from command by the government and
replaced by General Burnside.

It cannot be said that the change of commanders was a successful one.
Burnside attacked the vigilant Lee at Fredericksburg, on December 13th,
and met with one of the most disastrous defeats of the war, losing nearly
14,000 men to a Confederate loss of 5,000.   General Hooker, who succeeded
him, met with a similar defeat.   Supplied with a splendid
army, over 100,000 strong, he attacked Lee at Chancellorsville
Fredericksburg And Chancellorsville
on May 3, 1863, and met with a terrible repulse, through a
brilliant flank movement executed by Stonewall Jackson, losing over 17,000
men.   The Confederates had a loss, not less severe, this being the death of
Jackson, their most brilliant leader after Lee.

His great successes at Fredericksburg and Chancellorsville led Lee to
venture upon a daring but dangerous movement, an invasion of the North ;
one which, if successful, might have placed Philadelphia, Baltimore, and
Washington in his hands, but which, if unsuccessful, would leave him in a
very critical position.

It was, as all readers know, unsuccessful. General Meade, who replaced
Hooker in command, followed the Confederates north with the utmost

haste, and placed himself across their path at Gettysburg, in western Pennsylvania. On July 1st, the advance columns of the two armies
met, and engaged in a preliminary struggle, which ended in a   The Armies at
repulse of the Union forces. These fell back and took up a   Gettysburg
strong position on Cemetery Ridge, where during the night they were
strongly reinforced by the troops hurrying up from the south. During the
next two days the Union army fought on the defensive, Lee making vigorous ouslaughts upon it and fighting desperately but unsuccessfully to break
Meade's line or seize some commanding point. The end of this fierce
struggle—which is ranked among the decisive battles of the world—came
on the 3d, when Lee launched a powerful column, 15,000   The Union Vic-
strong, under General Pickett, against the Union centre. It   tory at Get-
ended in a repulse, almost an annihilation, of the charging   tysburg
force, and the great battle was at an end. The next day Lee retreated.
He had lost in all about 30,000 men. The Union loss aggregated about
23,000.

The 4th of July, 1863, was in its way as great a day for the American
Union as the 4th of July, 1776, for it was the great turning point in the
war. On this day Grant took possession of Vicksburg, with 30,000
prisoners, and cut the Confederacy in two. And on the same day Lee
began his retreat, disastrously beaten in his last act of offensive warfare.
During the remainder of his career he was to stand on the
defence, until driven to bay and forced to surrender by the   The 4th of July,
hammer-like blows of "Unconditional surrender Grant."   1863

But while brilliant in offensive war, Lee was in his true element in
defence, and never has greater skill and ability, or more indomitable resis-
ance, been shown than in his struggle against his vigorous adversary.
Grant was appointed commander-in-chief of the Union armies, on March 1,
1864. Having sent Sherman to conduct a campaign in the South, he himself,
on May 4 and 5, crossed the Rapidan River for a direct advance on Richmond. A campaign of forty-three days followed, in which more than 100,000
men, frequently reinforced, were engaged on either side. Grant   The Great
came first into encounter with Lee in the Wilderness, near the   Struggle for
scene of Hooker's defeat a year before. Here, after two days   Richmond
of terrible slaughter, the battle ended without decided advantage to either
side, though the Union loss was double that of the Confederates.

Finding Lee's position impregnable, Grant advanced by a flank movement to Spottsylvania Court House. Here, on May 11th, Hancock, by a
desperate assault, captured Generals Johnson and E. H. Stewart, with 3000
men and 30 guns, while Lee himself barely escaped. But no fighting, how-

ever desperate, could carry Lee's works. Sheridan with his cavalry now made a dashing raid toward Richmond. He fought the Confederate cavalry, killed their ablest general, J. E. B. Stuart, and returned having suffered little damage, to Grant. On May 17th, Grant, having executed another flank movement, reached the North Anna River. But Lee had fallen back with his usual celerity, and the advancing army found itself again in face of strong entrenchments. As a vigorous attack failed to carry Lee's works, Grant made a third flank march, which brought him to the vicinity of Richmond.

Here once more he found his indefatigable opponent in his front, very strongly posted at Cold Harbor. Grant, perhaps incensed at seeing this man always blocking up his road, hurled his tried troops upon the impregnable works of the enemy. It was a vain effort, leading only to dreadful slaughter. The Unionists lost in this hopeless affair over 10,000 in killed and wounded, while the Confederates escaped practically without loss.

Grant now executed the most promising of his flank movements. He secretly crossed the James River about June 15th and made a dash on **Grant's March on Petersburg** Petersburg, hoping to seize the railroads leading south and to cut the line of supply of Richmond. But unforeseen delays and strong resistance enabled Lee to throw a force of his veterans into the town, and the movement failed. And now for months it was a question of attack and defence. Both sides threw up entrenchments of enormous strength, and the following fall and winter were occupied in an incessant artillery duel, marked by a few assaults, which had little effect other than that of loss of life.

But during all this time Lee's army was weakening, while that of Grant was kept in full strength. At the end of March, 1865, the final events of the great struggle were at hand. Grant sent Warren and Sheridan to the south of Petersburg, to cut the Danville and Southside Railroads, Lee's avenues of supply. On April 1st the Confederate right wing was encountered and defeated at Five Forks, and on the following day the whole line of works defending Petersburg was successfully assailed.

Richmond could no longer be held. Lee evacuated it that night, and **The End of the Conflict** retreated towards Danville with about 35,000 men. But the Union cavalry under Sheridan pursued with such celerity that escape was cut off, and the Confederates were surrounded at Appomattox Court House, and forced to surrender on April 9, 1865.

Lee had made for himself a world-wide reputation. While the bull-dog persistence of Grant had enabled him to crush army after army of the

Confederacy, Lee had shown himself one of the most brilliant of generals, successful in all his assaults except at Gettysburg, and almost without a peer in defensive warfare. Only the utter exhaustion of the country behind him and the slow grinding of his army into fragments brought final success to his opponents.

We can only refer briefly to the careers of some of the abler subordinate commanders in the war. First among them was Sherman, whose exploits in great measure place him on a level with Grant and Lee. In truth, there was no more brilliant operation in the entire war than his famous " March through Georgia."

This striking event was the culmination of a series of successful battles and flank movements, by which Johnston was gradually forced back from Chattanooga to Atlanta. Here the able Johnston was removed and replaced by the dashing but reckless Hood, who attacked Sherman **Sherman's** fiercely, but only to meet a disastrous repulse. A final flank **March on** movement, which cut off Hood's sources of supply, forced him **Atlanta** to evacuate Atlanta, which Sherman occupied on September 1, 1864. It was the most brilliant success of the year, and Sherman became the hero of the hour. Hood, finding that he could do nothing there, made a dash into Tennessee, hoping to draw Sherman after him for the defence of Nashville.

Sherman had no intention of doing anything of the kind. The removal of Hood from his vicinity was just what he wanted, and he remarked in a chuckling tone, " If Hood will go to Tennessee I will be glad to furnish him with rations for the trip." What he had in view was something very different; namely, to abandon his long line of supplies, march across Georgia to Savannah, nearly three hundred miles away, and live upon the country as he went, while destroying one of the richest sources of Confederate supply.

The Confederate generals did not dream of a movement of such unusual boldness, and left the field clear for Sherman's march. For a month he and his men simply disappeared. No one knew **Marching** where they were, or if they were not annihilated. They had **Through** plunged into the heart of the Confederacy, far away from all **Georgia** means of communication, and the people of the North could only wait and hope. " I know which hole he went in at," said Lincoln to anxious inquirers, " but I know no more than you at which hole he will come out."

He came out at Savannah. He had cut a great swath, thirty miles wide, through Georgia, his soldiers living off the country and rendering it incapable of furnishing supplies for the Confederate armies, and on December 23d he sent Lincoln a despatch that carried joy throughout the

North: "I beg to present you as a Christmas gift the city of Savannah, with one hundred and fifty guns and plenty of ammunition, and about twenty-five thousand bales of cotton."

The remainder of Sherman's movement may be briefly told. Marching northward, he took Charleston, which had so long defied Union assault, without a shot. Reaching North Carolina, he found himself opposed again

Sherman Marches North to Johnston, but before much fighting took place the news of Lee's surrender came, and nothing was left for Johnston except to yield up his force. Meanwhile, Thomas, who had saved the army at Chickamauga, hurried to Nashville to meet the hard-fighting Hood, and there defeated him so utterly and dispersed his army so completely that it never came together again.

There is only one further exploit of the Union generals that calls here for special mention, that of Sheridan's famous ride. In 1864 Lee sent General Early with 20,000 men to the Shenandoah Valley, recently cleared

General Early's Raid on Washington of its defenders, the purpose being to threaten Washington and possibly oblige Grant to weaken his forces for its defence. Success attended Early's movement. He invaded Maryland, defeated Lew Wallace near Frederick, and reached the suburbs of Washington, which an immediate attack might have placed in his hands. Not venturing, however, to attack the capital, he soon returned, with large spoils in horses and cattle, to the Valley, where he defeated General Crook at Winchester.

In one respect this movement had failed. Grant was not induced to weaken his forces to any important extent. Had it been Stonewall Jackson in the Valley it might have been different, but he contented himself with sending Sheridan to take care of Early. Sheridan bided his time, despite the growing impatience in the country. Grant visited him, intending to propose a plan of operations, but he found that Sheridan was in full touch with the situation, and left him to his own devices.

At length, in September, Early incautiously divided his command, and Sheridan, who was closely on the watch, attacked him, flanked him right and left, broke his lines in every direction, and sent him, as he telegraphed

"Whirling Through Winchester." to Washington, "Whirling through Winchester." "I have never since deemed it necessary to visit General Sheridan before giving him orders," said Grant afterwards. Sheridan again attacked and defeated Early at Fisher's Hill, driving him out of the valley and into the gaps of the Blue Ridge.

Sometime afterwards took place the most famous event in Sheridan's career. During an absence at Washington his camp at Cedar Creek was surprised by Early, the men were driven back in disorderly rout, and eighteen

SURRENDER OF GENERAL LEE TO GENERAL GRANT AT APPOMATTOX COURTHOUSE, APRIL 9, 1865

The two generals met at the house of Major McLean, in the hamlet of Appomattox Courthouse, where Lee surrendered all that remained of the Confederate Army, which for nearly four years had beaten back every attempt to capture Richmond. Grant's terms, as usual, were generous. He did not ask for Lee's sword, and demanded only that he and his men should agree not again to bear arms against the Government of the United States.

THE ELECTORAL COMMISSION WHICH DECIDED UPON THE ELECTION OF PRESIDENT HAYES

Composed of three Republican and two Democratic Senators, three Democratic and two Republican Representatives, three Republican and two Democratic Justices of the Supreme Court; total, eight Republicans and seven Democrats. By a strict party vote the decision was given in favor of Mr. Hayes, who, two days later, March 4, 1877, was inaugurated President of the United States.

guns and nearly a thousand prisoners were lost. Sheridan, on his way back from the capital, had stopped for the night at Winchester. On his way to the front the next morning the sound of distant guns came to his ears. Perceiving that a battle was in progress, he rode forward at full speed. Soon he began to meet frightened fugitives, and guessed what had happened. Taking off his hat, he swung it in the air as he dashed onward at a gallop, shouting, "Face the other way, boys; face the other way. We're going back to lick them out of their boots!"

His words were electrical. The fugitives did "face the other way." As he came nearer and met the retreating companies and regiments, he rallied them with the same inspiring cry. The men turned back. The Confederates, who were rifling their camp, were astounded to find a routed army charging upon them. Dismay spread through their ranks, they were thrown into disorder, and were soon in full flight, having lost all the captured guns and twenty-four more, with a heavy loss in killed, wounded, and prisoners. Since that day "Sheridan's ride" has been celebrated in song and story as the most dramatic incident of the war.

Sheridan's Ride

We have told some of the exciting events of the conflict from the Union side. The Confederates also had their dashing generals and thrilling deeds of valor. But this chapter is already so extended that we must confine ourselves to an account of but one in addition to Lee, the renowned Stonewall Jackson. It is well known how Thomas J. Jackson got this title of honor. In the battle of Bull Run his men stood so firm amid the disordered fragments of other corps, that General Bee called attention to them: "Look at those Virginians! They stand like a stone wall." The title of "Stonewall" clung to their leader until his death. His most famous work was done in the Shenandoah Valley. In March, 1862, he retreated before Banks some forty miles, then suddenly turned and with only 3,500 men drove him back in dismay. But his most brilliant exploit was in April, when he whipped Milroy, Banks, Shields, and Fremont, one after another, in the Valley, and then suddenly turned, marched to Lee's aid, and helped to defeat McClellan at Gaines's Mills, the first victory in the memorable six days' fight.

Stonewall Jackson and His Exploits

In August, 1862, he drove Pope back from the Rappahannock, and by stubborn fighting held him fast until Longstreet could get up to aid in the victory of the second Bull Run. We have told of his striking exploit at Harper's Ferry, and how he won the day at Chancellorsville. Here he was wounded by a mistaken volley from his own men, was soon after attacked with pneumonia, and died on May 10, 1863. Thus fell the ablest man, after Lee, that the great contest developed on the Confederate side.

CHAPTER XXXII.

The Indian in the Nineteenth Century

THE relation of the American people to the Indians, since the first settlement of this country, has been one of conflict, which has been almost incessant in some sections of the land. By the opening of the nineteenth century the red men had been driven back in great measure from the thirteen original states, but the tribes in the west were still frequently **The Relation of** hostile, and stood sternly in the way of our progress westward. **Whites and** We propose in this chapter to describe the various relations, **Indians** both peaceful and warlike, which have existed between the whites and the red men during the century with which we are here concerned.

The close of the Revolutionary War brought only a partial cessation of the Indian warfare. The red man was by no means disposed to give up his country without a struggle, and throughout the interior, in what is now Indiana, Illinois, and Wisconsin, and along the Ohio River, there were constant outbreaks, and battles of great severity. The conflict in Indiana brought forward the services of a young lieutenant, William Henry Harrison, who for many years had much to do with Indians, both as military officer and as governor of the Indian territory. In 1811 appeared one of those great Indian chiefs whose abilities and influence are well worth attention and study. Tecumseh, a mighty warrior of mixed Creek and Shawnee blood, was one who dreamt the dream of freeing his people. With eloquence and courage he urged them on, by skill he combined the tribes in a new alliance, and, encouraged by British influence, he looked forward to a great success. While he was seeking to draw the Southern Indians into his scheme, his brother rashly joined battle with General Harrison, and was utterly defeated in the fight which gained for Harrison the title of Old Tippecanoe. Disappointed and disheartened at this destruction of his life-work, Tecumseh threw all his great influence on the British side in the War of 1812, in which he dealt much destruction to the United **Harrison and** States troops. At Sandusky and Detroit and Chicago, and at **Tecumseh** other less important forts, the Indian power was severely felt; but at Terre Haute the young captain Zachary Taylor met the savages with such courage and readiness of resources that they were finally repulsed.

But rarely did a similar good fortune befall our troops ; and it was not until after Commodore Perry won victory for us at Lake Erie, that Tecumseh himself was killed, and the twenty-five hundred Indians of his force were finally scattered, in the great fight of the Thames River, where our troops were commanded by William Henry Harrison and Richard M. Johnson, afterward President and Vice-President of the United States. For a little time the Northwest had peace. But in the South the warfare was not over. Tecumseh had stirred up the Creeks and Seminoles against the whites, and throughout Alabama, Georgia, and Northern Florida the Creek War raged with all its horrid accompaniments until 1814 ; even the redoubtable Andrew Jackson could not conquer the brave Creeks until they were almost extermi-nated, and then a small remnant remained in the swamps of Florida to be heard of at a later time.

Before the new government of the United States was fully upon its feet it recognized the necessity and duty of caring for its Indian population. In 1775, a year before the Declaration of Independence, the Continental Congress divided the Indians into three departments, northern, middle and southern, each under the care of three or more commissioners, among whom we find no less personages than Oliver Wolcott, Philip Schuyler, Patrick Henry and Benjamin Franklin. As early as 1832 the young nation found itself confronted with a serious Indian problem, **National Period** created a separate bureau for the charge of the red men, and inaugurated a definite policy of treatment. Speaking in general, we have altered this policy three times. As a matter of fact, we have altered its details, changed its plans, and adopted new methods of management as often as changing administrations have changed the administrators of our Indian affairs. But in the large, there have been three great steps in our Indian policy, and these have to some extent grown out of our changing conditions. The first plan was that of the reservations. Under that system, as the Indian land was wanted by the white population, the red man was removed across the Mississippi and pushed step by step still further west ; and as time went on and the population followed hard after, he was eventually confined to designated tracts. Yet despite the fact **Government Policy** that these tracts were absolutely guaranteed to him, he was driven off them again and again as the farmer or the miner demanded the land. In time a new policy was attempted, or rather an old policy was revived, that of concentrating the whole body of Indians into one state or territory, but the obvious impossibility of that scheme soon brought it to an end. Less than thirty years ago the present plan took its place, that of education and eventual absorption.

In 1830 the country seemed to stretch beyond any possible need of the young nation, lusty as it was, and the wide wilderness of the Rocky Mountains promised to furnish hunting grounds for all time. The Mississippi Valley and the Northwest were still unsettled, but in the South the Five Nations were greatly in the way of their white neighbors, and the work of the removal of the latter beyond the Mississippi was begun. Under President Monroe several treaties were made with those tribes—the Creeks, Cherokees, Choctaws, Chickasaws and Seminoles—by which, one after another, **Removal of the Southern Tribes** they ceded their lands to the government, and took in exchange the country now known as the Indian Territory. They were already somewhat advanced in civilization, with leaders combining in blood and brain the Indian astuteness and the white man's experience and education. John Ross, a half-breed chief of the Cherokees, of unusual ability, brought about the removal under conditions more favorable than often occurred. He was bitterly opposed by full half the Indians, and it was not without sufferings and losses of more than one kind that the great southern league was removed to the fair and fertile land set aside for them in the far-off West. It was owing to the sagacity of John Ross and his associates that this land was secured to them, in a way in which no other land has ever been secured to an Indian tribe. They hold it to-day by patent, as secure in the sight of the law as an old Dutch manor house or a Virginia plantation, and all the learning of the highest tribunals has not yet found the way to evade or disregard these solemn obligations. To these men, too, and to the missionaries who long taught their tribes, do they owe an effective form of civilization, and a governmental **War with the Seminoles** polity which preserves for them alone, among all the red men, the title and the state of nations. The Seminoles, who were of the Creek blood, were divided, some of them going west with their brethren, the larger number of them remaining in Florida. With these—about 4,000 in all—under their young and able chief, Osceola, the government fought a seven years' war, costing many lives and forty millions in money, and did not then succeed in removing all the Seminoles from their much-loved home.

A similar state of affairs attended the removals in the north. The savages bitterly opposed giving up their native soil, there being in every case two parties in the tribe, one that sorrowfully yielded to the necessity of submission, and one that indulged in the hopeless dream of successful resistance. Thus the Sac and Fox tribe of Wisconsin was divided, and although Keokuk and one band went peaceably to their new home among the Iowas, Black Hawk and his followers were slow to depart, and were removed by force. The Indian Department failed to furnish corn enough for the new settlement, and, going to seek it among the Winnebagoes, the Indians came into collision with the government. Thereafter ensued a series of misunderstandings, and consequent fights, resulting in great alarm among the whites and destruction to the Indians. The story is the same story, almost to details, that has been frequently seen since that time. After the fashion above described all the removals have proceeded, the cause ever the same, the white man's greed and the ferocity of the wronged and infuriated savage.

Hostilities with Northern Tribes

It is useless and impossible to give the details of all the various tribes that have been pushed about in the manner described. In 1830 the East was already crowding toward the West, and every succeeding decade saw the frontier moved onward with giant strides. Everywhere the Indian was an undesirable neighbor, and when, in 1849, the discovery of gold began to create a new nation on the Pacific slope, a pressure began from that side also, and the intervening deserts became a thoroughfare for the pilgrims of fortune and the lovers of adventure. From year to year the United States made fresh treaties with the tribes; those in the East were gone already, those in the interior were following fast, and there had arisen the new necessity of dealing with those in the far West. One tribe after another would be planted on a reservation millions of acres in extent and apparently far beyond the home of civilization, and almost in a twelvemonth the settler would be upon its border, demanding its broad acres. The reservations were altered, reduced, taken away altogether, at the pleasure of the government, with little regard to the rights or wishes of the Indian. Usually this brought about fighting, and it produced a state of permanent discontent that wrought harm for both settler and savage. The Indian grew daily more and more treacherous and constantly more cruel. The white settler was daily in greater danger, and constantly more eager for revenge.

Treatment of the Western Indians

A new complication entered into the problem. The game was fast disappearing, and with it the subsistence of the Indian. It became necessary for the government to furnish rations and clothes, lest he should starve and freeze. Cheating was the rule and deception the every-day experience of these savages. In 1795 General Wayne gained the nickname of General To-morrow, so slow was the government to fulfill his promises; and thus for more than a hundred years it was to-morrow for the Indian. Exasperated beyond endurance, he was ever ready to retaliate, and the horrors of an Indian war constantly hung over the pioneer. During all this period we treated the Indian tribes as if they

General " To-morrow "

were foreign nations, and made solemn treaties with them, agreeing to furnish them rations or marking the reservation bounds. We have made more than a thousand of these treaties, and General Sherman is the authority for the statement that we have broken every one of them. Day by day the gluttonous idleness, the loss of hope, the sense of wrong, and the bitter feeling of contempt united to degrade the red man as well as to madden him.

The fighting did not cease, for all the promises or the threats of the government. But always, it is credibly declared, the first cause of an Indian outbreak was a wrong inflicted upon some tribe. And always, in the latter days as in the earlier period, it has meant one more effort on the part of the old warriors to regain the power they saw slipping away so fast.

The Sioux War of 1862

Both these causes entered into the awful Sioux War in Minnesota in 1862. Suffering from piled-up wrongs, smarting under the loss of power, and conscious that the Civil War was their opportunity, a party of one hundred and fifty Sioux began the most horrid massacre known for fifty years; the beginning of a struggle which lasted more than a year, and which was remarkable for the steadfast fidelity of the Christian Indians, to whose help and succor whole bodies of white men owed their lives. Four years later, in 1866, the discovery of gold in Montana caused the invasion of the Sioux reservation, and Red Cloud set about defending it. Scarcely more than thirty years old, but no mean warrior, he fought the white man long and desperately and with the cunning of his race.

This outbreak was scarcely quieted when another occurred. As was its wont, the government forgot the promises of its treaty of peace, and a small band of the Cheyennes retaliated with a raid upon their white neighbors. General Sheridan made this the occasion he was seeking for a war of extermination, and in November, 1868, Lieutenant Custer fell upon Black Kettle's village and after a severe fight destroyed the village, killing more than a hundred warriors and capturing half as many women and children. The next year General Sheridan ordered the Sioux and Cheyennes off the hunting grounds the treaty had reserved to them, but these were the strongest

Massacre of General Custer's Command

and bravest of the tribes and they resisted the order. A number of Civil War heroes, Crook, Terry, Custer, Miles and McKenzie, led our troops, and among the chiefs whom they met in a long and desperate struggle were Crazy Horse and Spotted Tail, notable warriors both. At the battle of the Big Horn, by some misunderstanding or mismanagement, General Custer was left with only five companies to meet nearly three thousand savage Sioux. He fought desperately until the last, but he was killed and his command so utterly des-troyed that not a single man was left alive. The attempt to remove the Modocs from California to Oregon in 1872 was the signal for a new war; and a year or two afterwards similar results followed when it was attempted to push the Nez Perces from the homes they had sought in Oregon to a new reservation in Idaho. This tribe, under its famous leader, Chief Joseph, was hard to conquer. The military organization, the civilized method of warfare, and the courage and skill of the tribe were publicly complimented by Gen-erals Sherman, Howard and Gibbons, who declared Chief Joseph to be one of the greatest of modern warriors.

In 1877, discouraged by the failure of our efforts to hold the Indians in check, it was determined by Secretary Schurz, then in charge of the Depart-ment of the Interior, to remove them all to the western part of the Indian Territory, where the tribes in possession agreed to cede the necessary land. It was hoped to create there an Indian commonwealth, but trouble arose from the attempt to carry out the well-meant effort. A single story, the story of the Northern Cheyennes, will illustrate the wrongs the Indian suffered, as well as those he inflicted. The Cheyennes, as has been seen, were a tribe of valiant warriors some of them at home in the hills of the North, some residing in the hills of the South. The Cheyennes, Arapahoes, Kiowas and Comanches were banded together in a close and common bond, and, at first the friends of the government, had become frequently its enemies, by reason of broken faith, cruel treatment, injustice, and downright wrong. That chronicle of misery, "A Century of Dishonor," contains forty pages of facts taken from the government records, which relate the **Barbarous** inexcusable and indefensible treatment of the Cheyenne tribe **Treatment of** by the government, and their vain endurance of wrongs, inter- **the Cheyennes** spersed with savage outbreaks, when human nature could endure no longer. It includes the account of a massacre of helpless Indian women and children under a flag of truce ; a war begun over ponies stolen from the Indians, and sold in the open market by the whites in a land where the horse thief counts with the murderer ; another incited by a rage against a trader who paid one dollar bills for ten dollar bills ; and tells of whole tracts of land seized with-out compensation by the United States itself.

The Northern Cheyennes had been taken by force to the Indian Terri-torry, and in its severe heat, with scant and poor rations, a pestilence came npon them. Two thousand were sick at once, and many died because there was not medicine enough. At last three hundred braves, old men and young, with their women and children, broke away and, making a raid through Western Kansas, sought their Nebraska home. This was not a mild and peaceable tribe. It was fierce and savage beyond most, and its people were wild with long endured injustice and frantic with a nameless terror. Three

How the Cheyennes were Subdued times they drove back the troops who were sent to face them, and, living by plunder, they made a red trail all through Kansas, until they were finally captured in Nebraska in December. They refused to go back to the Indian Territory, and the department ordered them to be starved into submission. Food and fuel were taken from the imprisoned Indians. Four days they had neither food nor fire—and the mercury froze at Fort Robinson in that month! And when at last two chiefs came out under a flag of truce, they were seized and imprisoned. Then pandemonium broke loose inside. The Indians broke up the useless stoves, and fought with the twisted iron. They brought out a few hidden arms, and, howling like devils, they rushed out into the night and the snow. Seven days later they were shot down like dogs.

Experiences like this soon ended the attempt to gather together all our Indian wards, and we returned to the old plan of the reservations, but with little more certainty of peace than before. Again and again starvation was followed by fighting, nameless outrages upon the Indian by cruel outrages upon the white man. Whether Apaches under Geronimo in New Mexico, or Sioux in Dakota, it was the old story over again. Thus, with constant danger menacing the white settler from the infuriated savage Indian, and constant outrage upon the red man by rapacious and cruel whites, the

President Grant Adopts a New System government found a new policy necessary. This policy was inaugurated by a strange and unusual sequence of events. In 1869 a sharp difference arose between the two Houses of Congress over the appropriations to pay for eleven treaties then just negotiated, and the session closed with no appropriation for the Indian service. The necessity for some measure was extreme; the plan was devised of a bill which was passed at an extra session, putting two millions of dollars in the hands of President Grant, to be used as he saw fit for the civilization and protection of the Indian. He immediately called to his aid a commision composed of nine philanthropic gentlemen to overlook the affairs of the Indian and advise him thereupon. This commission served without salary and continues to this day its beneficent work. Another valuable measure followed. At the next Congress a law was enacted forbidding any more treaties with Indians, and thenceforth they became our wards; not foreigners and rivals, as practically the case before.

The war of 1877 had indirectly another beneficent result, most far-reaching in its consequences. Among the brave men who had fought the Cheyennes and Kiowas and Comanches, was Captain Richard H. Pratt, who was

JAMES G. BLAINE

WILLIAM McKINLEY

GROVER CLEVELAND

WILLIAM J. BRYAN

GREAT AMERICAN POLITICAL LEADERS, LAST QUARTER OF THE NINETEENTH CENTURY

HORACE GREELEY.   MURAT HALSTEAD.   ALBERT SHAW.

LYMAN ABBOTT.   CHAS. A. DANA.   HENRY W. WATTERSON.

WHITELAW REID.   JULIAN HAWTHORNE.   RICHARD HARDING DAVIS.

NOTED AMERICAN JOURNALISTS AND MAGAZINE CONTRIBUTORS.

put in charge of the prisoners who had been sent to Fort Marion, Florida, as a punishment worse than death. They were the wildest and fiercest warriors, who had fought long and desperately. On their way East they killed their guard, and repeatedly tried, one and another, to kill themselves. But Captain Pratt was a man of wonderful executive ability, of splendid courage and great faith in God and man. By firmness and patience and wondrous tact he gradually taught the savages to read and to work, and when after three years the government offered to return them to their homes, twenty-three of them refused to go. Captain Pratt appealed to the government to continue their education, and **Captain Pratt and his Captives** General Armstrong, with his undying faith in human beings as children of one Father and his sublime enthusiasm for humanity, received most of them at Hampton Institute, the rest being sent to the North under the care of Bishop Huntington, of New York. In the end these men returned to their tribes Christian men, and, with the seventy who returned directly from Florida, they became a power for peace and industry in their tribe. Out of this small beginning grew the great policy of Indian education, and the long story of death and destruction began to change to the bright chronicle of peace and education.

What, then, is the condition of the Indian to-day? In number there are scarcely more than two hundred and forty thousand in the whole country. Of these less than one-fifth depend upon the government for support. All told, they are fewer than the inhabitants of Buffalo or Cleveland or Pittsburg, yet they are *not* dying out, but rather steadily increasing. They are divided and subdivided into many tribes of different characteristics and widely different degrees of civilization. Some are Sioux—these are brave and able and intelligent; they live in wigwams or tepees, and are dangerous and often hostile. Some are Zunis, who live in houses and make beautiful pottery, and are mild and peace- **How the Indians Live** able, and do not question the ways of the Great Father at Washington. Some are roving bands of Shoshones, dirty, ignorant, and shiftless—the tramps of their race—who are on every man's side at once. Some are Chilcats or Klinkas, whose Alaskan homes offer new problems of new kinds for every day we know them. And some are Cherokees, living in fine houses, dressed in the latest fashion, and spending their winters in Washington or Saint Louis.

Yet these, and many of other kinds, are all alike Indians. They have their own governments, their own unwritten laws, their own customs. As a race they are neither worthless nor degraded. The Indian is not only brave, strong, and able by inheritance and practice to endure, but he is patient under wrong, ready and eager to learn, and willing to undergo much privation for that end; usually affectionate in his family relations, grateful to a degree, pure and careful of the honor of his wife and daughter; and he is also patriotic to a fault. He has a genius for government, and an unusual interest in it. He is full of manly honor, and he is strongly religious. His history and traditions have only recently been traced, to the delight and surprise of scientific students. His daily life is a thing of elaborate ceremonial, and his national existence is as carefully regulated as our own, and by an intricate code. It is true that our failure to comprehend his character and our neglect to study his customs have bred many faults in him and have fostered much evil. Our treatment of him, moreover, has produced and increased a hostility which has been manifested in savage methods for which we have had little mercy.

But we have not always given the same admiration to warlike virtues when our enemy was an Indian that we have showered without stint upon ancient Gaul or modern German. The popular idea of the Indian not only misconceives his character, but to a large degree his habits also.

Indian Character and Habits Even the wildest tribes live for the most part in huts or cabins made of logs, with two windows and a door. In the middle is a fire, sometimes with a stovepipe and sometimes without. Here the food is cooked, mostly stewed, in a kettle hung gypsy-fashion, or laid on stones over the fire. Around the fire, each in a particular place of his own, lies or sits the whole family. Sometimes the cooking is done out of doors, and in summer the close cabin is exchanged for a tepee or tent. Here they live, night and day. At night a blanket is hung up, partitioning the tent for the younger women, and if the family is very large, there are often two tents, in the smaller of which sleep the young girls in charge of an old woman. These tents or cabins are clustered close together, and their inhabitants spend their days smoking, talking, eating, or quarreling, as the case may be. Sometimes near them, sometimes miles away, is the agent's house and the government buildings. These are usually a commissary building where the food for the Indians is kept, a blacksmith shop, the store of the trader, school buildings, and perhaps a saw-mill. To this place the Indians come week by week for their food. The amount and nature of the rations called for by treaties vary greatly among different

The Indian Agencies tribes. But everywhere the Indian has come into some sort of contact with the whites, and usually he makes some shift to adopt the white man's ways. A few are rich, some own houses, and almost universally, at present, government schools teach the children something of the elements of learning as well as the indispensable English.

The immediate control of the reservation Indian is in the hands of the agent, whose power is almost absolute, and, like all despotisms, may be very good or intolerably bad according to the character of the man. The agencies are visited from time to time by inspectors, who report directly to the Commissioner of Indian Affairs,—an officer of the Interior Department and responsible to the secretary, who is, of course, amenable to the President. In each house of Congress is a committee having charge of all legislation relating to Indian affairs. Besides these officials there is the Indian Commission already mentioned. The National Indian Rights Association and the Women's National Indian Association are the unofficial and voluntary guardians of the Indian work. It is their task to spread correct information, to create intelligent interest, to set in motion public and private forces which will bring about legislation, and by public meetings and private labors to prevent wrongs against the Indian, and to further good work of many kinds. While the Indian Rights Association does the most public and official work for the race and has large influence over legislation, the Women's Indian Association concerns itself more largely with various philanthropic efforts in behalf of the individual, and thus the two bodies supplement each other.

The Indian Rights Association

Hopeless and impossible as it seemed to many when this effort began to absorb the Indian, to-day we see the process well under way and in some cases half accomplished; and in this work the government, philanthropy, education and religion have all had their share, and so closely have these worked together that neither can be set above nor before the others. We began to realize, it is true, that our duty and our safety alike lay in educating the Indians as early as 1819, when Congress appropriated $10,000 for that purpose, and still earlier President Washington declared to a deputation of Indians his belief that industrial education was their greatest need; but it is only within recent years that determined efforts have been made or adequate provision afforded. Beginning with $10,000 in 1819, we had reached only $20,000 in 1877; but the appropriation for Indian education is now over $2,500,000. With this money we support great industrial training schools established at various convenient points. In them several thousand children are learning not only books, but all manner of industries, and are adding to study the training of character. There are more than 150 boarding schools on the various reservations teaching and training these children of the hills and plains, and many gather daily at the three hundred little day schools which dot the prairies, some of them appearing to the uninitiated to be miles away from any habitation. This does not include the mission schools of the various churches.

Appropriations for Education

But all together it is hoped that in the excellent government schools now provided, in the splendid missionary seminaries, and in the great centres of light like Hampton and Carlisle and Haskell Institute, we shall soon do something for the education of nearly or quite all the Indian children who can be reached with schools. At present the daily school attendance is over 20,000.

The two great training schools at the East, Hampton and Carlisle,

Hampton and Carlisle Indian Schools have proved object lessons for the white man as well as the Indian, and the opposition they constantly encounter from those who do not believe that the red man can ever receive civilization is in some sort a proof of their value. In the main, they and all their kind have one end—the thorough and careful training in books and work and home life of the Indian boy and girl—and their methods are much alike. Once a year the superintendents or teachers of these schools go out among the Indians and bring back as many boys and girls as they can persuade the fathers and mothers to send. At first these children came in dirt and filth, and with little or no ideas of any regular or useful life, but of late many of them have gained some beginnings of civilization in the day schools. They are taught English first, and by degrees to make bread and sew and cook and wash and keep house if they are girls; the trade of a printer, a blacksmith, a carpenter, etc., if they are boys. They study books, the boys are drilled, and from kind, strong men and gentle, patient women they learn to respect work and even to love it, to turn their hands to any needed effort, to adapt themselves to new situations.

It is charged that the Indian educated in these schools does not remain civilized, but shortly returns to his habits and customs. A detailed examination into the lives of three hundred and eighteen Indian students who have

The Effect of Education gone out from Hampton Institute has shown that only thirty-five have in any way disappointed the expectations of their friends and teachers, and only twelve have failed altogether; and the extraordinary test of the last Sioux war, in which only one of these students, and he a son-in-law of Sitting Bull, joined the hostiles, may well settle the question. A recent statement says that 76 per cent. of the school graduates prove "good average men and women, capable of taking their place in the great body politic of our country."

In 1887 a new step was taken for the advancement of the Indian, in the passage of the Severalty Act, by which homesteads of 160 acres were set aside for each head of a family willing to accept the proffer, and smaller homesteads for other members of the family. These were to be free from taxation and could not be sold for twenty-five years. They might be selected on the reservation of the tribe or anywhere else on the public domain. This allotment of land carried with it all the rights, privileges and immunities of American citizenship. In case the Indian should not care to take up a homestead, he could still become **The Severalty Act** a citizen if he took up his residence apart from the tribe and adopted civilized habits. The purpose was to break up the tribal organization which had stood so greatly in the way of the beneficent purposes of the government, and to convert each Indian into an individual citizen of the United States.

The effort has been attended with highly encouraging success. Within twelve years after the law was passed 55,467 Indians had taken up homesteads, aggregating in all 6,708,628 acres. Of these agriculturists, more than 15,000 were heads of families, around whose farms were gathered the smaller ones of the other members of the family. The change to the independence and responsibilites of United States citizenship **The Homestead Indians** was so sudden as to prove a severe strain to the Indian, accustomed to consider himself a fraction of a tribe and lacking the full sense of individuality. Yet the failures have been very few, and we begin to see our way clear to a final disposal of the long-existing Indian question.

As regards the effect of religious training upon the Indians, it may be said to be quite encouraging. Of the 33,000 Sioux, for instance, 8,000 are now church members. The Presbyterian Church numbers nearly 5,000 Indian members and 4,000 Sunday-school pupils; while the total number of church communicants among the Indians is nearly 30,000.

Thus, with the close of the nineteenth century, there is good reason to hope for the end of a serious difficulty that has confronted the whites since their first settlement in this country nearly three hundred years ago. War, slaughter, injustice, wrongs innumerable have attended its attempted solution, which long seemed as if it would be reached only when all the red men had been exterminated. Fortunately it was justice, not slaughter, that was needed, and the moment our government awoke fully to this fact and began to practice justice the difficulty began to disap- **The Outcome of Indian Policy.** pear. To-day just treatment, education, religious training are rapidly overcoming the assumed ineradicable savageness of the Indian, while the breaking up of the tribal system promises before many years to do away with the political aggregation of the Indians, and distribute them among the other citizens of our country as members of the general body politic. Thus has the nineteenth century happily disposed of an awkward problem that threatened seriously the successful development of our nation a century ago.

CHAPTER XXXIII.

The Development of the American Navy.

IN scarcely any department of human industry are the changes produced by the progress of civilization more strikingly seen than in the navy. When America was discovered the galleon and the caravel were the standard warships of the world—clumsy wooden tubs, towering high in the air, propelled by sails and even oars, with a large number of small cannons, and men armed with muskets and cross-bows. Such was the kind of vessels that made up the famous Armada, "that great fleet invincible," which was vanquished by the smaller and lighter crafts of Britain. Three hundred years have passed, and what is the warship of to-day? A low-lying hulk of iron and steel; armed with a few big guns, each one of which throws a heavier shot than a galleon's whole broadside; driven resistlessly through the water by mighty steam engines; lighted and steered by electric apparatus, and using an electric search-light that makes midnight as bright as day. All the triumphs of science and mechanic arts have contributed to the perfection of these dreadful sea monsters, a single one of which could have destroyed the whole Armada in an hour, and laughed to scorn the might of Nelson at Trafalgar.

Development in Naval Architecture

And in the development of this modern warship no other nation on earth has won as much credit as the United States, the whole career of which upon the sea has been one of glory and success, while its inventors and engineers have gained as much renown as its admirals and sailors, in their development of new ideas in naval architecture and warfare. Of all ocean exploits in history that of John Paul Jones in the *Bon Homme Richard* ranks first. Lord Nelson himself scarcely showed such indomitable pluck and intrepidity. And in the war of 1812 American ships and sailors took from Great Britain the credit of being the mistress of the seas, winning gallantly in every conflict where the forces engaged were at all near equality.

American Sailors and Their Doings

This good work of the sailors was aided by that of the shipwrights, the Americans winning battles largely because they had better ships than their opponents. But their success was also in great measure due to the superiority of their ordnance and the better service of their guns. It was

482

THE "OREGON," A TYPE OF THE MODERN BATTLESHIP

One of the most renowned ships of the American Navy is the mighty Battleship "Oregon." Her famous run from San Francisco around Cape Horn to take part in the Battle of Santiago has never been equalled by any battleship in the world's history. After she won fame in the destruction of Cervera's fleet she was ordered to Manila by Admiral Dewey "for political reasons," and remained there throughout the Philippine War

IN THE WAR ROOM AT WASHINGTON.

The above illustration shows President McKinley, Secretary Long, Secretary Alger, and Major General Miles consulting map during the progress of the Spanish-American War. It is in this room that the plans of conducting the war, by land and sea, are formulated, and the commands for action are wired to the fleet and the army.

to the careful sighting of the pieces that our sailors owed much of their victorious career. While most of the British shot were wasted on the sea and in the air, nearly all the American balls went **American Marksmanship** home, carrying death to the British crews and destruction to their hulls and spars, while the American ships and sailors escaped in great measure unharmed.

As regards the work of our naval inventors, it will suffice to say, that the Americans, while not the first to plate vessels with iron, were the first to do so effectively and to prove the superiority of the ironclad in naval warfare. The memorable contest in Hampton Roads between the *Monitor* and the *Merrimac* made useless in a day all the fleets of all the nations of the world, and caused such a revolution in naval architecture and warfare as the world had never known.

The fleet with which the United States entered the nineteenth century was due to the depredations on American ships and commerce of the war vessels of France and Great Britain. This roused great indignation, particularly against France. While England contented herself with stopping American ships on the high seas and impressing sailors claimed to be of British birth, France seized our ships themselves, under the pretext that they had British goods on board, and if she found an American seaman on a British ship—even if impressed—she treated him as a **The Early American Navy** pirate instead of as a prisoner of war. Protection was felt to be necessary, and preparations for war were made. The small navy of the Revolution had practically disappeared, and a new one was built. In July, 1798, the three famous frigates, the *Constellation*, the *United States*, and the *Constitution*—the renowned *Old Ironsides*—were completed and sent to sea, and others were ordered to be built. Actual hostilities soon began. French piratical cruisers were captured, and an American squadron sailed for the West Indies to deal with the French privateers that abounded there, in which work it was generally successful. In January, 1799, Congress voted a million dollars, for building six ships of the line and six sloops. Soon after, on February 9, occurred the first engagement between vessels of the American and **The Naval War with France** French navies. The *Constellation*, Captain Truxton, overhauled *L'Insurgente* at St. Kitts, in the West Indies, and after a fight of an hour and a quarter forced her to surrender. The *Constellation* had three men killed and one wounded; *L'Insurgente* twenty killed and forty-six wounded.

Again, on February 1, 1800, Truxton with the *Constellation* came up, at Guadeloupe, with the French Frigate *La Vengeance*. After chasing her two days he brought on an action.   The two ships fought all night.   In the morning, *La Vengeance*, completely silenced and greatly shattered, drew away and escaped to Curaçoa, where she was condemned as unfit for further service.   The *Constellation* was little injured save in her rigging.   For his gallantry, Truxton received a gold medal from Congress.   Later in that year there were some minor engagements, in which the American vessels were successful.

By the spring of 1801, friendly relations with France were restored. The President was accordingly authorized to dispose of all the navy, save thirteen ships, six of which were to be kept constantly in commission, and to dismiss from the service all officers save nine captains, thirty-six lieutenants, and one hundred and fifty midshipmen.   At about this time ground was purchased and navy-yards were established at Portsmouth, Boston, New York, Philadelphia, Washington and Norfolk, and half a million dollars were appropriated for the completion of six seventy-four gun ships.

Nothing needs to be said here concerning our conflicts with the pirates of the Mediterranean or of the remarkable exploits of the small American navy in the second war with Great Britain.   These have already been dealt with in chapters xxv. and xxvi.   In the interval between that period and the Civil War there was little demand upon the American navy. The naval operations during the Mexican war were of no great importance. Some vessels were used in scientific exploration, and the dignity of America had to be asserted on some occasions, but the most important service rendered by the navy was the opening up of Japan to the commerce of the world.   After some fruitless efforts at intercourse with the

The Opening up of Japan

island realm, Commodore Perry was sent thither in 1852, and by a resolute show of force he succeeded in obtaining a treaty of commerce from Japan.   That treaty opened Japan to the world, and was the first step in its remarkable recent career.

At the beginning of the Civil War the United States was very poorly provided with ships of war.   There were only forty-two vessels in commission, nearly all of which were absent in distant parts of the world.   Others were destroyed in southern ports, and for a time there was actually only one serviceable warship on the North Atlantic coast.   This difficulty was soon overcome by buying and building, and by the end of 1861 there were 264 vessels in commission, and all the ports in the South were under blockade.   These vessels were a motley set,—ferry boats, freight steamers, every sort of craft—but they served to tide over the emergency.

With all this we are not particularly concerned, but must turn our attention to the great naval events of the war, those conflicts which served

REAR-ADMIRAL WILLIAM T. SAMPSON

ADMIRAL GEORGE DEWEY

REAR-ADMIRAL JOHN CRITTENDEN WATSON

REAR-ADMIRAL WINFIELD SCOTT SCHLEY

LEADING COMMANDERS OF OUR NAVY IN THE SPANISH-AMERICAN

MAJOR-GENERAL NELSON APPLETON MILES.

MAJOR-GENERAL FITZHUGH LEE.

MAJOR-GENERAL WESLEY MERRITT.

MAJOR-GENERAL WILLIAM R. SHAFTER.

COMMANDERS OF OUR ARMY IN THE SPANISH-AMERICAN WAR.

as turning points in nineteenth century warfare. And first and greatest among these was the remarkable naval battle in Hampton Roads on March 9, 1862.

The use of iron for plating the hulls of ships was not first adopted in American war. This device was employed by England and France in the Crimean war in attacks on the Turkish forts. The idea, however, was American. As early as 1813 Colonel John Stevens, of New York, made plans for an ironclad ship somewhat resembling the *Monitor* in type. His son Edwin afterwards performed experiments with cannon balls against iron plate, and in 1844 Robert L. Stevens began the construction of a vessel to be plated with 4½-inch iron for the government. It was never finished, though in all nearly $2,000,000 were spent upon it. New invention rendered it obsolete before it could be completed, yet to it belongs the credit of inaugurating the era of the ironclad navy. After the Crimean war France and England both built ironclad ships, the French *La Gloire* being the first ironclad ever constructed. It was followed by the British *Warrior*, launched in January, 1861. Yet despite this enterprise, the fact remains that the first conception of an ironclad ship belongs to the United States, and the first hostile meeting of two ironclads took place in American waters.

> The Idea of Ironplating of American Origin

> Early Ironclads of Great Britain and France

At the opening of the American Civil War this idea was in the air, and it was soon made evident that the era of wooden warships was near its end. It is interesting to learn that the Confederates were the first to adopt the new idea, the earliest ironclad of the war being produced by them on the lower Mississippi. A large double-screw tugboat was employed, whose deck was covered with a rounded roof, plated with bar iron one and a half inches thick. This craft—named the *Manassas* after the first Confederate victory—made its appearance at the mouth of the Mississippi on the night of October 31, 1861, and created a complete panic in the blockading fleet at that point. The *Manassas* wrecked one of her engines in attempting to ram the flagship *Richmond*, and crept slowly back, at the same time as the alarmed fleet was hastening away with all speed over the waters of the gulf.

> The Ironclad "Manassas"

While this event was taking place, two ironclads of more formidable description were being built elsewhere, the meeting of which subsequently was the most startling revelation to the nations of the earth ever shown in naval warfare. The United States steam frigate *Merrimac* had been set on fire at the Gosport Navy Yard, when hastily abandoned by the Federal navy officers at the outbreak of the war. It was burned to the water's edge and sunk, but soon after the Confederates raised the hull, which was seriously damaged—its engines being in reasonably good condition—and they hurriedly undertook the work of converting it into an ironclad. A

The Plating of the " Merrimac " powerful prow of cast iron was attached to its stem, a few feet under water and projecting sufficiently to enable it to break in the side of any wooden vessel. A low wooden roof two feet thick was built at an incline of about 36 degrees, and this was plated with double iron armor, making a four-inch iron plating. Under this protection were mounted two broadside batteries of four guns each, and a gun at the stem and stern. The government was soon advised of the raising of the hull of the *Merrimac*, and without having detailed information on the subject, knew that a powerful ironclad was being constructed. A board of naval officers had been selected by the government to consider the various suggestions for the construction of ironclad vessels, and although, as a rule, naval officers had little faith in the experiment, Congress coerced them into action by the appropriation of half a million dollars for the work. The Naval Board recommended a trial of three of the most acceptable plans presented, and ships on these plans were put under contract.

Among those who pressed the adoption of light ironclads, capable of penetrating our shallow harbors, rivers, and bayous, was John Ericsson.

Ericsson and the " Monitor " He was a Swede by birth, but had long been an American citizen, and exhibited uncommon genius and scientific attainments in engineering. The vessel he proposed to build was to be only 127 feet in length, 27 feet in width, and 12 feet deep, to be covered by a flat deck rising only one or two feet above water. The only armament of the vessel was to be a revolving turret, about 20 feet in diameter and nine feet high, made of plated wrought iron aggregating eight inches in thickness, with two eleven-inch Dahlgren guns. The guns were so constructed that they could be fired as the turret revolved, and the port-hole would be closed immediately after firing. The size of the *Merrimac* was well known to the government to be quite double the length and breadth of the *Monitor*, but it had the disadvantage of requiring nearly double the depth of water in which to manœuvre it. Various sensational reports were received from time to time of the progress made on the *Merrimac*, the name of which was changed by the Confederates to *Virginia*, and as there were only wooden hulls at Fortress Monroe to resist it, great solicitude was felt for the safety of the fleet and the maintenance of the blockade. While the government hurried the construction of the new ironclads to the utmost, little faith was felt that so fragile a vessel as the *Monitor* could cope with so powerful an engine of war as the *Merrimac*. The most formidable vessels of the navy, including the *Minnesota*, the twin ship of the original *Merrimac*, the *St. Lawrence*, the *Roanoke*, the *Congress* and the *Cumberland*, were all in Hampton Rhoads waiting the advent of the *Merrimac*.

On Saturday, the 8th of March, the *Merrimac* appeared at the mouth of the Elizabeth River and steamed directly for the Federal fleet. All the vessels slipped cable and started to enter the conflict, but the heavier ships soon ran aground and became helpless. The *Merrimac* hurried on, and, after firing a broadside at the *Congress*, crashed into the sides **The Coming of** of the *Cumberland*, whose brave men fired broadside after **the " Mer-** broadside at their assailant only to see their balls glance from **rimac "** its mailed roof. An immense hole had been broken into the hull by the prow of the *Merrimac*, and in a very few minutes the *Cumberland* sank in fifty feet of water, her last gun being fired when the water had reached its muzzle, while the whole gallant crew went to the bottom with their flag still flying from the masthead. The *Merrimac* then turned upon the *Congress*, which was compelled to flee from such a hopeless struggle, and was finally grounded near the shore; but the *Merrimac* selected a position where her guns could rake her antagonist, and, after a bloody fight of **The Fate of** more than an hour, with the commander killed and the ship **the " Con-** on fire, the *Congress* struck her flag, and was soon blown up **gress " and** by the explosion of her magazine. Most fortunately for the **the " Cum-** **berland "** Federal fleet, the *Merrimac* had not started out on its work of destruction until after midday. Its iron prow was broken in breaching the *Cumberland*, and, after the fierce broadsides it had received from the *Congress* and the *Cumberland*, with the other vessels firing repeatedly during the hand-to-hand conflict, the *Merrimac's* captain was content to withdraw for the day, and anchor for the night under the Confederate shore batteries on Sewall's Point.

The night of March 8th was one of the gloomiest periods of the war. The *Merrimac* was sure to resume its work on the following day, and, with the fleet destroyed and the blockade raised, Washington, and even New York, might be at the mercy of this terrible engine of war. But deliverance was at hand. The building of the *Monitor* had been hurried with all speed, and this little vessel,—"a cheese box on a raft," as it was contemptuously termed—was afloat and steaming in all haste **The Monitor in** to Hampton Roads. . It entered there that night, and took up **Hampton** a position near the helpless *Minnesota* in bold challenge to the **Roads** *Merrimac*. On Sunday morning, March 9th, the Confederate ironclad came out to finish its work of destruction, preparatory to a cruise against the northern ports.

The little *Monitor* steamed boldly out to meet it.   The history of that conflict need not be repeated.   To the amazement of the commander of the *Merrimac*, the *Monitor* was impervious to its terrible broadsides, while its lightness and shallow draft enabled it to out-manœuvre its antagonist at every turn ; and while it did not fire one gun to ten from its adversary, its aim was precise and the *Merrimac* was materially worsted in the conflict.   After three hours of desperate battle the defiant and invincible conqueror of the day before found it advisable to give up the contest and retreat to Norfolk.

The First Battle of Ironclads

It was this naval conflict, and the signal triumph of the little *Monitor*, that revolutionized the whole naval warfare of the world in a single day, and from that time until the present the study of all nations in aggressive or defensive warfare has looked to the perfection of the ironclad.   To the people of the present time the ironclad is so familiar, and its discussion so common, that few recall the fact that less than fifty years ago it was almost undreamed of as an important implement of war.   It is notable that neither of those vessels which inaugurated ironclad warfare, and made it at once the accepted method for naval combat for the world, ever afterward engaged in battle during the three years of war which continued.   The *Merrimac* was feared as likely to make a new incursion against our fleet, but her commander did not again venture to lock horns with the *Monitor*.   Early in May the capture of Norfolk by General Wool placed the *Merrimac* in a position of such peril that on the 11th of that month she was fired by her commander and crew and abandoned, and soon after was made a hopeless wreck by the explosion of her magazine. The fate of the *Monitor* was even more tragic.   The following December, when being towed off Cape Hatteras, she foundered in a gale and went to the bottom with part of her officers and men ; but she had taught the practicability of ironclads in naval warfare, and when she went down a whole fleet was under construction after her own model, and some vessels already in active service.

Fate of the First Ironclads

While these events were taking place in the waters of the coast, a fleet of ironclad boats was being built for service on the rivers of the West, seven of these being begun in August, 1861, by James B. Eads, the famous engineer of later times.   These were light-draught, stern paddle-wheel river steamers, plated with 2½-inch iron on their sloping sides and ends.   These, and those that followed them, saw much service in the western rivers, bombarding Forts Henry and Donelson, running through the fire of the forts on Island No. 10, and daring the terrible bombardment from the Vicksburg batteries.

But the most famous event in river warfare during the conflict was the exploit of the daring Farragut in running past Forts St. Philip and Jackson on the Mississippi with his fleet of wooden vessels, breaking their iron chain, dispersing their gun-boats, and driving ashore the ironclad *Manassas.* The Confederates had also an ironclad battery, **Farragut on the** the *Louisiana,* but it proved of little service, and Farragut **Mississippi** sailed triumphantly through the hail of fire of the forts, and on the same afternoon reached the wharves of New Orleans.

The most famous exploit of Farragut was the passing of the forts at Mobile. It is worth a brief relation, for in this the resources of ironclad warfare, as then developed, were fully employed, while the bottom of the channel was thickly sown with torpedoes, a mechanism in naval warfare to become of great importance in the following years. Farragut's main fleet, indeed, was of wooden ships, but he had four monitors; while the Confederates, in addition to their forts and gunboats, had the ironclad ram *Tennessee*, the most powerful floating battery ever built by them. This formidable craft—for that period—was plated with six inch iron armor in front and five inch elsewhere; and, while carrying only six guns, these were 6- and 8-inch rifled cannon.

The torpedoes, of which no fewer than 180 were sown in the channel, were not quite ineffective, since one of them exploded under the monitor *Tecumseh*, and she went down head first with nearly all her crew. The *Brooklyn*, following in her track, halted as this disaster was seen, her recoil checking all the vessels in her rear. Farragut **Farragut and** had taken his famous stand in the shrouds, just under the **the Torpedoes** maintop, and hailed the *Brooklyn* as he came up in the *Hartford.* "What is the matter?" he demanded. "Torpedoes," came back the reply. "Damn the torpedoes!" cried Farragut, in a burst of noble anger. "Follow me." As the *Hartford* passed on the percussion caps of the torpedoes were heard snapping under her keel. Fortunately they were badly made, and no other explosion took place.

The story of the battle we may briefly complete. The ships dashed almost unharmed through the fire of the forts, driving the Confederate gunners from their pieces with a shower of grape and canister; and the contest ended with an attack upon the *Tennessee*, whose stern-port shutters were jammed and her steering gear shot away. Rendered helpless, she was forced to surrender, and the fight was at an end.

The Confederates were singularly unfortunate with their ironclads. With the exception of the temporary advantage gained by the *Merrimac*, all their labor and expense proved of no avail. The last of these war-monsters.

the *Albemarle*, built in Roanoke River, and causing some alarm in the
blockading fleet on the coast, was sent to the bottom by a daring young
officer, Lieutenant Cushing, in one of the most gallant exploits of the war.

Lieutenant Cushing and the " Albemarle "
He and a few men, in a steam launch carrying a large torpedo,
sailed up the stream at night to where the ironclad lay in her
dock at Plymouth. A protecting raft of logs guarded the
Albemarle, but Cushing daringly drove his launch up on the
slimy logs, exploded the torpedo as it touched the sides of the ship, and
leaped with his men into the stream. The *Albemarle* sank to a muddy bed
in the river's bottom, and Cushing escaped to the blockading fleet, after a
series of thrilling adventures.

But the most important thing achieved in this war was the entire transformation effected in naval science. Previously the warship had been of the
type of an armed merchantship, propelled by sails or, latterly, by steam, and
carrying a large number of small guns. Modern inventiveness made it, after

The Type of the New Navies
the duel of the *Monitor* and *Merrimac*, a floating fortress of iron
or steel, carrying a few enormously heavy guns. The glory
of the old line-of-battle ship, with three or four tiers of guns
on each side and a big cloud of canvas overhead, firing rattling broadsides,
and manœuvring to get and hold the weather-gauge of the enemy—all that
was relegated to the past forever. In its place came the engine of war,
with little pomp and circumstance, but with all the resources of science shut
within its ugly, black iron hull.

John Paul Jones, with his *Bon Homme Richard*, struck the blow that
made universal the law of neutrals' rights. Hull, with the *Constitution*,
sending a British frigate to the bottom, showed what Yankee ingenuity in
sighting guns could do. Ericsson and Worden, with the *Monitor*, sent
wooden navies to the hulk-yard and ushered in the era of iron and steel
fighting-engines. These were the great naval events of a century.

Yet the American navy was greatly neglected in the years succeeding the
Civil War, while foreign nations, quick to learn the lesson taught at Hampton
Roads, were straining every nerve to build powerful fleets of iron and
steelclad ships, and to develop the breech-loading rifled cannon into an

Beginning of the Modern American Fleet
implement of war capable of piercing through many inches
of solid steel. It was not until after 1880 that our government awoke to the need of a navy on the new lines, and
began to take advantage of the lessons that had been learned abroad. It
is not our purpose to speak in detail of the results. The steelclad battleship and cruiser, the armor-piercing breech-loader, the quick-firing gun, the
machine gun, the submarine torpedoboate, the anchored mine, the auto-

mobile torpedo, and other devices have come to make the naval warfare of our day a wonderfully different thing from that of the past.

The United States began late to build a modern navy, but has made highly encouraging progress, and while still far in the rear of Great Britain and France in the number of her ships, possesses some of the finest examples of naval architecture now afloat upon the waters. The "Columbia" and the *Columbia* and the *Minnea-* "Minnea-polis", with their respective trial speeds of 22.81 and 23.07 "Minnea-polis" knots, stand beyond any rivals to-day in the navies of Europe, while the inventive naval engineering of the Americans is exemplified in the double turrets of the *Kearsarge* and *Kentucky*, two additions to our navy of original formation, and likely to give an excellent account of themselves should any new war occur.

Of modern fleets, however, far the most powerful one is that of Great Britain, the government of which island shows a fixed determination to keep its naval force beyond rivalry. This stupendous fleet forms the most striking example of naval destructiveness the world has ever The Powerful seen, and the nations of the world are entering the twentieth Fleet of Great century with powers of warfare developed enormously beyond Britain those with which they entered the nineteenth. We can only hope that this vast development both in army and navy may prove to exert a peace-compelling influence, and that every new discovery in the art of killing and destroying may be a nail in the coffin of Mars, the god of war.

CHAPTER XXXIV.

America's Conflict With Spain.

A THIRD of a century passed after the great struggle of the United States for the existence of the Union, and then, in almost the closing year of the nineteenth century, came another war, this time fought in the interests of humanity. It was not a war for gain or conquest; the thought of territorial acquisition did not enter into the motives leading to it, despite the fact that this country gained new territory as one of its results; in its inception humane feeling, the sentiment of sympathy with the oppressed and starving people of Cuba, alone prevailed, and the nineteenth century fitly reached its end with a war entered into for humanity's sake alone, it being one of the very few instances in the history of the world in which a nation has gone to war from purely philanthropic motives.

A War in the Cause of Humanity

It is not necessary here to repeat the story of Spain's tyranny in Cuba. It is too well known to need telling again, and simply carried out the colonial policy of Spain from the time of the discovery of America. The successful rebellion of her colonies on the American continent failed to teach that country the lesson which England learned from a similar occurrence, and in Cuba was continued the same system of tyranny and official oppression which had driven the other colonies to revolt. The result was the same, Cuba blazed into rebellion, and for years war desolated that fair island.

The United States, however, sedulously avoided taking any part in the affair until absolutely driven to interfere by the horrible inhumanity displayed by Captain-General Weyler. It was the awful policy of "reconcentration" that stretched the forbearance of the people of this country to the breaking point. Not content with fighting the rebels in arms, the brutal Weyler extended the war against the people in their homes, burning their houses, destroying the crops in their fields, driving them in multitudes into the cities and towns, and holding them there in the most pitiable destitution and misery until they died by thousands the terrible death of starvation. It was not until word came to this country that not less than 200,000 of the helpless people had perished

General Weyler and His Policy

SENOR MONTERO RIOS

President of the Spanish Peace Commission whose painful
duty required him to sign away his country's
colonial possessions.

GENERAL RAMON BLANCO

Who succeeded Weyler as Captain-General of Cuba in 1897.
He was formerly Governor-General of the
Philippine Islands.

ADMIRAL CERVERA

Commander of Spanish Fleet at Santiago

SAGASTA

Premier of Spain during the Spanish-American War.

GENERAL JOSEPH WHEELER

RICHMOND PEARSON HOBSON

THEODORE ROOSEVELT

MAJOR-GENERAL ELWELL S. OTIS

POPULAR HEROES OF THE SPANISH-AMERICAN WAR

in this horrible manner, and that there seemed no hope of alleviation of the frightful situation, that there arose a general demand for the government to interfere. Spain was asked to fix a date in which the war should be brought to an end, with the intimation that if the contest was not concluded or the independence of the island conceded by that date, this country would feel obliged to take decisive steps.

No satisfactory answer was received, and anticipations of war filled all minds, though many hoped that this dread ultimatum might be avoided, when, in the last week of January, 1898, the battleship *Maine* was ordered to proceed from Key West to the harbor of Havana. Her visit was ostensibly a friendly one, but there had been riots in Havana which imperilled the safety of American residents, to whom the Spanish inhabitants of that city were bitterly hostile, and it was felt that some show of force in that harbor was imperative.

A terrible disaster succeeded. In one fatal instant, on the night of February 15th, the noble ship was hurled to destruction and her crew into eternity. This frightful event took place about 9.45 in the evening, while the ship lay quietly at anchor in the place selected for her by the Spanish authorities. Intense darkness prevailed in the harbor, Captain Sigsbee was writing in his cabin, the men were in their quarters below, when of a sudden came a terrible explosion that **The Sinking of the " Maine "** tore the vessel asunder and killed most of her crew. So violent was the shock that the whole water-front of the city was shaken as by an earthquake, telegraph poles were thrown down and the electric lights extinguished. The wrecked vessel sank quickly into the mud of the harbor's bottom, and a great flame broke from her upper works that illuminated the whole harbor. Of three hundred and fifty-three men in the ship's company only forty-eight escaped unhurt, and the roll-call of the dead in the end reached two hundred and sixty-six.

This terrible event was the immediate cause of the war. It intensified the feeling of the people and of their representatives in Congress to such an extent that no other solution of the difficulty now seemed possible. The popular indignation was increased when the court of inquiry announced that, in its opinion, "the *Maine* was destroyed by a submarine mine." It was universally felt that the disaster was another instance of Spanish malignity, the war-fever redoubled, and Congress unanimously voted an appropriation of $50,000,000 "for the national **Preparations for War** defense." The War and Navy Departments hummed with the activity of recruiting, the preparations of vessels and coast defenses, and the purchase of war material and vessels at home, while agents were sent to Europe to procure all the warships that could be purchased. Unlimited capital was at their command, and the question of price was not an obstacle. When hostilities impended the United States was unprepared for war, but by amazing activity, energy and skill the preparations were pushed and completed with a rapidity that approached the marvelous.

Negotiations went on, it is true, but they were principally with the purpose of gaining time to permit American citizens to leave Cuba. Consul-general Lee left Havana on April 11th, and on the same day President McKinley sent a message to Congress in which he described in earnest terms the situation in Cuba, reciting the dreadful results of Weyler's heartless policy and asking for power to intervene. "In the name of humanity, in the name of civilization," he said, "the war in Cuba must stop." On April 18th, Congress responded with a series of resolutions that were virtually a declaration of war, and on the 22d war actually began, **War is Declared** the fleet which had gathered at Key West being despatched to Cuba with orders to blockade Havana and some other leading ports. On the following day a call was issued for 125,000 volunteers to serve in the coming conflict.

While it seems important to give the preliminary events that led to the war, we do not propose to tell the story of the war itself, but to confine ourselves to a description of its more important incidents, in accordance with the plan of this work. It may be said here, however, that the war was in great part a naval one, and gave rise to naval operations of intense interest and great importance, so that this chapter will fitly round out the preceding one, which deals with the progress in naval warfare during the century. We there described the contests of ironclad ships during the Civil War. In other chapters have been told the stories of the fight between Austrian and Italian ironclads at the battle of Lissa and of the Japanese and Chinese **Progress in** ironclad fleets at the battle of the Yalu. We have now to tell **Naval War-** the final events in naval warfare of the century, the epoch-**fare** making contest in Manila Bay, and the desperate flight and fight off Santiago harbor. If these examples of ocean warfare be contrasted with those between the *Constellation* and the French frigates *L'Insurgente* and *Vengeance* a century before, they will place in striking clearness the immense advance in naval warfare within the hundred years involved.

Of these two events the greatest was that which took place in Manila Bay. War, it must be remembered, is governed by a different system of ethics from that operative in peace. Though inhumanity in Cuba was the cause of the war, to strike the enemy wherever he could be found was the demand of prudence and military science. Spain had an important posses-

THE SURRENDER OF SANTIAGO, JULY 17, 1898

After a little ceremony the two commanding generals faced each other, and General Toral, speaking in Spanish, said: "Through fate I am forced to surrender to General Shafter the city and strongholds of the city of Santiago." General Shafter in reply said: "I receive the city in the name of the Government of the United States."

THE UNITED STATES PEACE COMMISSIONERS OF THE SPANISH WAR.

Appointed September 9, 1898. Met Spanish Commissioners at Paris, October 1st. Treaty of Peace signed by the Commissioners at Paris, December 10th. Ratified by the United States Senate at Washington, February 6, 1899.

sion in the eastern seas, the Philippine Islands, off the southeastern coast of Asia. There, in the bay of Manila, near the large city of that name, lay a Spanish fleet, which, if left unmolested, might seek our Pacific Coast and commit terrible depredations. In the harbor of Hong Kong lay a squadron of American war-vessels under Commodore Dewey. **The Mission of Dewey** Prudence dictated but one course under the circumstances. There was flashed to Dewey under sea and over land the telegraphic message to "find the Spanish fleet and capture or destroy it." How Dewey obeyed this order is the circumstance with which we are now concerned.

He lost no time. Leaving port in China on April 27th, he arrived off the entrance to Manila Bay on the night of the 30th. An island lay in the neck of the bay, with well-manned batteries on its shores. It was probable that torpedoes had been planted in the channel. But George Dewey had been a pupil of Farragut in the Civil War, and was inspired **How Dewey** with the spirit of that hero's famous order, "Damn the tor- **Entered** pedoes! Follow me!" Past Corregidor Island in the dark- **Manila Bay** ness glided the great ships, several of them being out of range of its batteries before the alarm was taken. Then some shots were fired, but the return fire from the squadron silenced the Spanish guns and the ships passed safely into Manila Bay.

About five o'clock on the morning of May 1st Dewey's fleet swept in battle-line past the front of the city of Manila, and soon after rounded up in face of the Spanish fleet, which extended across the mouth of Bakoor Bay, within which lay the naval station of Cavité. There were ten of the Spanish ships in all, with shore batteries to add to their defensive force, while the effective American ships consisted of six, the cruisers *Olympia*, *Baltimore*, *Raleigh*, *Boston*, and the gunboats *Petrel* and *Concord*. The Spaniards had two large and four small cruisers, three gunboats and an armed transport. They were not equal in size or weight of metal to the American vessels, but their fixed position, their protection by shore batteries, and the acquaintance of their officers with **The Opposing Fleet** the waters in which they lay gave them an important advantage over the Americans, which was added to by their possession of torpedo boats and by the mines which they had planted in the track of an attacking fleet. Dewey and his men were, in fact, in a position of great peril, and if the Spaniards knew how to work their guns none of them might leave that bay alive. Fortunately for them the Spaniards did not know how to work their guns.

On swept the gallant squadron of assault, the *Olympia* leading with Dewey on the bridge. He had a look-out place protected by steel armor, but he preferred to stand in the open and dare all peril from the Spanish guns. The mines were there. As the flagship drove onward two of them exploded in her path. Luckily the nervous hands at the electric wires set them off too soon. Heedless of such perils as this Dewey pursued his course, and at 5.40 A.M. opened fire, followed by the remainder of his ships.

The Deadly Work of the American Guns From that moment the fire was deadly and continuous, the boom of the great guns seconded by the rattle of the rapid fire pieces until the air seemed full of the roar of ordnance. The Spanish returned as hot a fire, but by no means so effective. While most of their shot were wasted on the waves, the bulk of those from the American ships found a goal, and death and destruction reigned in the Spanish ships while their opponents moved on almost unharmed.

Back and forth across the Spanish lines swept Dewey's ships, five times in all, at first at 5,000 yards distance, then drawing in to a distance of 2,000 yards. And during all this time the great guns roared their message and the small guns poured out their fiery hail, rending the Spanish hulls and carrying death to their crews, while the flames that shot up from their decks told that another element of destruction was at work. Early in the fight two torpedo boats darted out towards the *Olympia*, but were met with a torrent of fire that sent one to the bottom and drove the other hastily to the beach. Then, with an instinct of desperation, Admiral Montojo drove gallantly out in his flagship, the *Reina Christina,* with the purpose of engaging the *Olympia* at shorter

The Fate of the Spanish Flag-ship range. At once Dewey turned his entire battery upon her, and poured in shot and shell at such a frightful rate that the Spaniard hastily turned and fled for the shelter of Bakoor Bay. But the deadly baptism of fire with which she had been met proved the end of her career. Swept from stern to stem by shells as she fled, she burst into flames, which continued to burn until she sank to a muddy death.

Meanwhile the Spanish ships and batteries returned the fire vigorously, but with singular lack of effect. While they were being riddled and sunk, the American ships escaped almost unhurt, and while hundreds of their crews fell dead or wounded, not an American was

The Destruction of the Spanish Fleet killed and seven men alone were slightly wounded. What little skill in aiming the Spaniards possessed was utterly disconcerted by the incessant and deadly American fire, and their balls and shells screamed uselessly through the air to plunge into the waves.

At the hour of 7.35 Dewey withdrew from the fight, that he might see how all things stood on his ships and give the men an interval of rest and an opportunity for breakfast. He knew very well that the Spaniards must await his return. Fight and flight were alike taken out of them. When he came back to the attack, shortly after 11 o'clock, nearly all the Spanish ships were in flames and some rested on the bottom of the bay. For an hour longer the firing continued on both sides. At the end of that time the batteries were silenced and the ships sunk, burned, and deserted. The great battle was at an end, and Dewey had made himself the hero of the war.

When the news of the result reached Europe, the naval powers of the nations heard with utter astonishment of the fighting prowess and skill of the Yankees. Anything so complete in the way of a naval victory the century had not seen before, and it was everywhere recognized that a new power had to be dealt with in the future counsels of the nations. Americans, previously looked upon almost with contempt from a mili- **How the Nation** tary point of view, suddenly won respect, and Dewey took **Rewarded** rank among the great ocean fighters of the century. His **Dewey** nation hastened to honor him with the title of rear-admiral, and finally with that of admiral, its highest naval dignity, and on his return home in autumn of the following year he was received with an ovation such as few Americans had ever been given before. To his fellow citizens he was one of the chief of their heroes, and they could not do him honor enough.

The second notable naval event of which we have spoken took place off the harbor of Santiago, a city on the southern coast of Cuba, at a date after that just described.

The finest fleet possessed by Spain, that under the command of Admiral Cervera, consisted of four cruisers, the *Christobal Colon*, plated with a complete belt of 6-inch nickel steel, and with a deck armor of steel 2 to 6 inches thick, and the *Vizcaya*, the *Almirante Oquendo*, and the *Infanta Maria Teresa*, each of 6890 tons, with 10- to 12-inch armor and power- **The Fleet of** ful armament. They were all of high speed, and were the **Admiral Cer-** only vessels of which any dread was felt in the United States. **vera** With them were three torpedo boats, the *Terror*, the *Furor* and the *Pluton*, among the best of their class, and dangerous enemies to deal with.

This fleet lay in the Cape Verde Islands at the opening of the war. From there, in May, it set sail, causing doubt and dread in American coast cities while its destination remained unknown, and yielding relief when the news came that it had reached some of the lower islands of the West Indies. On May 21st it was learned that the dreaded squadron had reached Santiago and was safely at anchor in its harbor.

The Atlantic fleet of the United States meanwhile had been partly engaged in blockading the Cuban ports, partly in searching for Cervera's fleet, and there was a decided sensation of relief when the tidings from Santiago were confirmed. Thither from all quarters the great ships of the

The Spanish Fleet at Santiago fleet hastened at full speed, battleships, cruisers, monitors, gunboats, and craft of other kinds, and soon they hung like grim birds of war off the harbor's mouth, determined that the Spanish fleet should never leave that place of refuge except to meet destruction. To the battleships of the fleet was soon added the *Oregon*, which had made an admirable journey of many thousand miles around the continent of South America, and barely touched land in Florida before it was off again to take part in the great blockade.

The story that follows is, if given in all its details, a long one, but we must confine ourselves to its salient points. Admiral Sampson, in command of the American fleet, at first sought to lock up the Spaniards in their harbor of refuge, by sinking a coaler, the *Merrimac*, in the narrow channel of Santiago Bay. The work was gallantly and ably done by Lieutenant Hob-

The Sinking of the "Merrimac" son and his daring crew, but proved a failure through causes beyond his control. The *Merrimac* sank lengthwise in the channel, and the passage remained open. This being recognized, the most vigilant watch was kept up, battle-ships, cruisers, and gunboats lying off the harbor's mouth in a wide semicircle, with their lookouts ever closely on the watch.

On the morning of Sunday, July 3d, the long-looked for alarm came, in a yell from the sentinel on the *Brooklyn*, "There is a big ship coming out of the harbor!" A like alarm was given on other ships, and Commodore Schley, on the *Brooklyn*, hastened to signal the fleet and to give the order, "Clear ship for action." Almost in an instant the lazily swinging fleet awoke to life and activity, and the men sprang from their listless Sunday rest into the most enthusiastic readiness for duty.

Admiral Sampson, unfortunately for him, was absent, having gone up the coast in the cruiser *New York*, and the direction of affairs fell to Commodore Schley. He was capable of meeting the emergency. It was soon

The Flight of the Spanish Ships evident that Cervera's fleet was coming out, the flagship, *Infanta Maria Teresa*, in the lead, the others following. On clearing the harbor headland they turned west, and the Americans at once set out in pursuit, firing as they went. "Full speed ahead; open fire, and don't waste a shot," shouted Schley. The *Oregon* had already opened fire from her great 13-inch guns, and was followed by the battleships *Texas, Indiana, and Iowa.* The *Brooklyn* joined in with her 8- and 5-inch batteries, and soon a rain of shells was pouring upon the devoted fugitive ships. The *Maria Teresa* ran towards the *Brooklyn* as if with intention to ram her, but the danger was avoided by a quick swerve of the helm, and Cervera's flagship turned again and sped away in flight.

The fugitive ships soon found themselves the centre of the most terrific fire any war vessels had ever endured, with the exception of those at Manila. Big guns and little guns joined in the frightful concert, shot after shot telling, while the response of the Spaniards was little more effective than that of their compatriots in Manila Bay. One man killed on the *Brooklyn* was the sole loss of life on the American side, while the unfortunate Spaniards were swept down by hundreds.

A Hot Chase Down the Cuban Coast

The first ship to succumb to this hail of shells was the *Maria Teresa*, which quickly burst into flames, and soon after ran ashore. Then the *Brooklyn*, *Oregon* and *Indiana* concentrated their fire on the *Almirante Oquendo*, which was similarly beached in flames. Next the *Vizcaya* drew abeam of the *Iowa*, which turned its fire from the *Oquendo* to this new quarry, pouring in shells that tore great rents in her side, while the *Vizcaya* fired back hotly but uneffectively. As the Spaniard drew ahead of the *Iowa*, the fire of the *Oregon* and *Texas* reached her, and an 8-inch shell from the *Brooklyn* raked her fore and aft. The next moment a great shell exploded in her interior, killing eighty men. She was clearly out of the race, and ran in despair for the beach.

The Fate of the Spanish fleet

Meanwhile the *Christobal Colon* was running at great speed along the beach, pursued by the American ships. Of these the *Oregon* and *Brooklyn* alone were able to keep within hopeful distance. For an hour the chase kept up, then the *Oregon* tried a 13-inch shell, which struck the water close astern of the *Colon*, four miles away. Another was tried and reached its mark. Soon after a shell from the *Brooklyn* pierced the *Colon* at the top of her armor belt. Then she too gave up and ran for the beach, Admiral Sampson, on the *New York*, reaching the scene in time only to receive the surrender of her officers.

Perhaps the most telling work of the day was that done by the little *Gloucesier*, a yacht turned into a gunboat, which was commanded by Richard Wainwright, one of the surviving officers of the *Maine*. Two torpedo-boat destroyers had followed the Spanish ships from the harbor, and these were gallantly attacked and sunk by Wainwright in his little craft, thus finally disposing of the second Spanish fleet with which the Yankees came into contact.

The "Gloucester" and Her Work

The annals of naval history record no more complete destruction of an enemy's fleet than in the two cases we have described, and never has such work been done with so little loss—only one man being killed and a few wounded in both American fleets.   It taught the world a new **The Lesson of the War** lesson in the art of naval warfare, and admonished the nations that the United States was a power to be gravely considered in the future in any question of war.

We have told the only incidents of this short war with which we are concerned.   In the conflict on land there was nothing of special character. An American army landed near Santiago and fought its fight to a quick finish in the capture of that city ; and a similar story is to be told of Manila ; while the attempted conquest of Porto Rico was cut short in the middle by the signing of a peace protocol.   In December a treaty of peace was signed in which Spain abandoned her colonies of Cuba and Porto Rico, the latter being ceded to the United States, while the Philippine Islands, the scene of Dewey's great victory, were likewise ceded to this country.   The latter, however, was not to the pleasure of the island people, who took up arms to fight for freedom from the dominion of the whites.

Brief as was the war, it had the effect of radically changing the position of the United States, which for the first time in its history became a **The United States Made a Colonial Power** colonial power, and acquired an interest in that troublesome Eastern Question which reached, at the end of the century, a highly critical stage.   Into what complication this new political relation is likely to lead the republic of the West it is impossible to say, but this country will certainly play its part in the shaping of the future destiny of the East.

CHAPTER XXXV.

The Dominion of Canada.

OCCUPYING the northern section of the western hemisphere lies Great Britain's most extended colony, the vast Dominion of Canada, which covers an immense area of the earth's surface, surpassing that of the United States, and nearly equal to the whole of Europe. Its population, however, is not in accordance with its dimensions, being less than 5,000,000, while the bleak and inhospitable character of much the greater part of its area is likely to debar it from ever having any other than a scanty nomad population, fur **The Area and Population of Canada** animals being its principal useful product. It is, however, always unsafe to predict. The recent discovery of gold in a part of this region, that traversed by the Klondike River, has brought miners by the thousands to that wintry realm, and it would be very unwise to declare that the remainder of the great northern region contains no treasures for the craving hands of man.

It is the development of Canada during the nineteenth century with which we are here concerned, and we must confine ourselves, as in the case of the other countries treated, to its salient points, those upon which the problem of its progress turns. First settled by the French in the seventeenth century, this country came under British control in 1763, as a result of the great struggle between the two active colonizing powers for dominion in America. The outcome of this conquest is the fact that Canada, like the other colonies of Great Britain, possesses **Canada's Early History** a large alien population, in this case of French origin ; and it may further be said that the conflict between England and France in America is not yet at an end, since political warfare, varied by an occasional act of open rebellion, has been maintained throughout the century by the French Canadians.

The revolution of 1775 in the colonies to the south failed to gain adherents in Canada, which remained loyal to Great Britain and repelled every attempt to invade its territory. It met invasion in the war of 1812 in the same spirit, and despite the fact that there has long been a party favoring annexation to the United States, the Canadians as a whole are to-day among the most loyal colonial subjects of the home government of Great Britain.

At the opening of the nineteenth century the population of Canada was small, and its resources were only slightly developed. Its people did not reach the million mark until about 1840, though since then the tide of immigration has flowed thither with considerable strength and the population has grown with some rapidity. In 1791 the original province of Quebec was divided into Upper and Lower Canada, a political separation which by no means gave satisfaction, but led to severe political conflicts. As a result an act of union took place, the provinces being reunited in 1840.

Upper Canada, at the opening of the century, was only slightly developed, the country being a vast forest, without towns, without roads, and practically shut out from the remainder of the world. The sparse population endured much suffering, which, in 1788, deepened into a destructive famine, long remembered as a terrible visitation. But it began to grow with the new century, numbers crossed the Niagara River from the States to the fertile lands beyond, immigrants crossed the waters from Great Britain and France, Toronto was made the capital city, and the population of the province soon rose to 30,000 in number. Lower Canada, however, with its old cities of Quebec and Montreal, and its flourishing settlements along the St. Lawrence River, continued the most populous section of the country, though its people were almost exclusively of French origin. The strength of the British population lay in the upper province.

Upper and Lower Canada

These historical particulars are desirable as a statement of the position and relations of Canada at the opening of the nineteenth century, though in the succeeding history of the country only an occasional event occurred of sufficiently striking character to fit into our plan. We have already detailed the events of the war of 1812 on the Canada frontier, in which the capture and burning of York (now Toronto) served as an excuse for the subsequent indefensible burning of Washington by the British. Battles were fought on Canadian soil in 1814 at Chippewa and Lundy's Lane—the latter the bloodiest battle of the war. But though the Americans were victorious in these engagements, they soon after withdrew from Canada—to which they have never since returned in a hostile way. Many political complications have arisen between the two countries, and at times sharp words have been spoken, but all the questions have been amicably settled and the two countries remain fairly good friends, with only such disputes as too close neighborhood is apt to provoke.

The War of 1812

The leader of public opinion in Canada during the three years' struggle with the United States was a clergyman of the English church John Strachan, rector of York. Though a clergyman of the English establishment, Strachan was by birth a Scotchman, and a decidedly pugnacious and determined character, a man of courage, persistence, cunning and political skill, whose ambition drove him forward, until, with his party, he formed in 1820 what was long known as the "Family Compact," which for years ruled the country in an autocratic way. The governor and council were the tools of Strachan **John Strachan and the Family Compact** and his allies; they filled the public offices with their favorites, and went so far as to drive Robert Gourlay, an honest and capable business man, from the country, because he was so presumptuous as to reflect on the character of their administration.

In 1824 their power was for a time overturned. William Lyon Mackenzie, a Scotchman of impetuous disposition, started the *Colonial Advocate* newspaper, which opposed the "Compact" so vigorously as to arouse the hatred of its adherents. The office of the *Advocate* was gutted by a mob, but Mackenzie recovered large damages, an opposition Assembly was elected, and the Family Compact fell from power. Strachan however, was only temporarily defeated. A religious quarrel arose which lasted for thirty years, and in which he played the leading **A Religious Quarrel** part. This turned upon the use of what was known as the "clergy reserve fund," an allotment of one-seventh of the crown lands for the support of a Protestant clergy. A portion of this fund was demanded by a Scotch Presbyterian congregation, but Strachan, who had a controlling voice in its disposition, claimed it all for the English Established Church, and entered into this new fight with all his old energy. He gained strong support, was promoted to the dignity of a bishop, founded King's College from part of the fund, and, in 1853 obtained a transfer of the fund—which had been placed at the disposal of the British Parliament for religious purposes—to Canada. The controversy was finally settled in 1854, an act being passed which secured their life interests to the clergy already enjoying them, while the remainder of the fund was devoted to public education.

Thus for forty years and more John Strachan made himself the most prominent and powerful figure in Upper Canada. Meanwhile a strained condition of affairs existed in Lower Canada, due to the rivalry and struggle for power of the inhabitants of French and British descent. The strife became so intense as in 1837 to lead to open rebellion.

The great supremacy of the French in numbers gave them a decided majority in the Assembly, and for years Louis Papineau was elected by

them speaker of that body, though bitterly opposed by the British popula·
tion. When Lord Dalhousie, the governor-general, refused to recognize
him in this position, sufficient influence was brought to bear upon the home
French Suprem- government to have the autocratic lord transferred to India,
acy in Lower and the French retained their control of the Assembly. A
Canada reform in the government of the province was recommended
by a committe of the British Parliament, which resulted in 1832 in giving
the Assembly control of the local finances.

This gave the French Canadians a perilous power, and they endeavored
to rid themselves of the English judges and civil officials by a process of
financial starvation. Salaries were unpaid and the government was blocked
through lack of funds. The sharpness of the strife was added to by resolutions in the British Parliament which condemned the Canadian legislature
and supported the council—an arbitrary body under the governor's control,
and in the British interest.

The strife eventually deepened into revolt. Both provinces vigorously
demanded that the council should be chosen by the votes of the people, and
thus truly represent the country. Lower Canada became violently excited
on this question; funds known as "Papineau tribute" were collected; the
liberty cap was worn; imported goods were replaced by homespun clothes,
and military training soon began. These movements were followed by
hostile acts, the English "Constitutionalists" and the French "Sons of
Liberty" coming into warlike contact. But Sir John Colborne, the governor,
was a man of energy and decision, and quickly brought the
The Revolt of incipient rebellion to an end. The insurgents were attacked
1837 and dispersed wherever they showed themselves, Dr. Nelson,
one of their leaders, was captured, and Papineau, the head of the revolt, was
obliged to escape across the border.

This movement in Lower Canada was accompanied by a similar revolt
in Uppe1 Canada under the leadership of William Lyon Mackenzie, the
former opponent of the Family Compact. He, as a leader of the opposition
forces, had continued bitterly to oppose the oligarchy which controlled
Canadian affairs. Three times he was elected to the Assembly of Upper
Canada, and three times expelled by the tyrannical majority. The law
officers of Great Britain pronounced his expulsion illegal, and he was re-
elected by a large majority, but the arbitrary Assembly again refused to
admit him.

The result of this unlawful action was to make him highly popular, he
was elected the first mayor of Toronto, and the struggle went on more
bitterly than ever. An unlucky expression he had used—"The baneful

domination of the mother country"—was now quoted against him as evidence of disloyalty, and Mackenzie, exasperated by the acts of his enemies, lost his self-control and entered into rebellion. He made a compact with Louis Papineau to head a rising in Toronto on the same day with the insurgent rising in Montreal. In furtherance **Mackenzie's Rebellion** of this he proclaimed a "Provisional Government of the State of Upper Canada," gathered a force of eight hundred men, and threatened Toronto with capture. But hesitation was fatal to his cause, his men were attacked and dispersed, and he was forced to flee. On Navy Island he flung the flag of rebellion to the breeze, but he had lost his one opportunity and the flag soon went down. Lack of prudence and patience had put an end to a promising political career.

The suppression of this rebellion was followed in 1840 by the Act of Union of the two provinces already mentioned. The population now began to grow with considerable rapidity. From about 1,100,000 in 1840, it grew to nearly 2,000,000 in 1850, and 2,500,000 in 1860. And the **Growth of** people were spreading out widely northward and westward, **Population** settling new lands, and stretching far towards the Pacific **and Industry** border. The industries of Canada, which had been greatly depressed by the adoption of free trade in Great Britain, were revived by a treaty of reciprocity in trade with the United States, and prosperity came upon the country in a flood.

But political troubles were by no means at an end, and much irritation arose from acts of citizens of the United States during the Civil War. Refugees and conspirators from the south sought the Canadian cities, and endeavored to involve the two countries in hostile relations. Fenian raids were attempted from the United States, and there was much alarm, though nothing of importance arose from the disturbed condition of affairs.

In time the confederation which existed between the two larger provinces of Canada became too narrow to serve the purposes of the entire colony. The maritime provinces began to discuss the question of local federation, and it was finally proposed to unite all British North America into one general union. This was done in 1867, the British Parliament passing an act which created the "Dominion of Canada." **Organization of** The new confederation included Ontario (Upper Canada), **the Dominion** Quebec (Lower Canada), New Brunswick and Nova Scotia. **of Canada** Four years later Manitoba and British Columbia were included, and Prince Edward's Island in 1874. A parliament was formed consisting of a Senate of life members chosen by the prime minister and an Assembly elected by the people. The formation of the dominion was soon followed by trouble, this time arising in the Indian country, over which the Canadian people had rapidly extended their authority.   Louis Riel, son of the leader of the Metés (half-breed) Indians, headed a rebellion in 1869 and established a

The Riel Revolts provisional governmei.t at Fort Garry.   In the following year the revolt collapsed on the arrival of General Wolseley at this fort.   Twice in later years Riel attempted rebellion, the second time in 1885.   He was finally captured and executed, and the rebellious sentiment vanished with his death.

Shortly after the formation of the dominion, Sir John Macdonald became a conspicuous figure in Canadian politics and for many years served as prime minister of the country.   He took part in the treaty of Washington, which referred to arbitration of the Alabama claim and other questions between Great Britain and the United States, and came near defeat in consequence, since the parts of the treaty which referred to Canada were very unpopular in that country.   He was defeated in 1873 on the question of the Canadian Pacific Railway, concerning which a great scandal had arisen, with suspicion of wholesale bribery.   In 1878 Macdonald returned to the premiership, which he continued to hold until his death in 1891.

Despite the scandal attending the Pacific Railway bill, that enterprise was pushed forward with much energy, and, after desperate financial struggles, was completed in 1886.   It need scarcely be said that it has since played a highly important part in the development of Canada.   Under the

The Canadian Pacific Railway liberal ministry of Alexander Mackenzie (1873–78) the country prospered greatly for a time, but a period of financial stringency followed, and the people demanded commerical protection.   This was given by the Conservatives, under Macdonald, in 1879, a protective tariff being adopted as a measure of defence against the commerical enterprise of the United States.   The result was a rapid revival of trade and wide-spread prosperity.   In 1880, by an act of the British Parliament, the control of all the British possessions in Canada—except Newfoundland, which had not joined the Union—was transferred to the Dominion Parliament, and the country became in large measure an independent nation.

The important questions which have since that time arisen in Canada have had largely to do with its relations to the United States and its people.   One of the most troublesome of these has been the question of

The Fishery Difficulties the fisheries on the banks of Newfoundland and the coasts of Nova Scotia and New Brunswick.   For years the problem of the rights of American fishermen on the Canadian coast excited controversy.   In 1877 the Halifax Fishery Commission awarded

$5,500,000 to Great Britain, to pay for the privileges granted to the United States, and in 1888 a treaty was signed for the settlement of this vexatious question.

The temporary removal of this difficulty was followed by the development of a still more serious fishery controversy between the two countries, that relating to the fur-seal fishery of Alaska. The fur-seals, frequenting the Pribylof Islands of the Bering Sea for breeding purposes, belonged to the United States, which rented out the right of killing seals on these islands to the Alaska Commercial Company, whose killing privileges were restricted to 100,000 yearly. But these seals had a wide range of excursion at sea, and Canadian fishermen began to prey upon them in the open waters. These depredations, beginning in 1886, reduced the herds by 1890 to such an extent that the Alaska Company could secure **The Fur=Seal Question** only 21,000 skins in that year. There was serious danger of the extermination of the animals, and the United States took active measures to prevent poaching on its preserves, as it regarded the work of the Canadians. The controversy on this question became strenuous as time went on, and it was seriously thought at one time that the easiest way out of the difficulty would be to kill all the seals at once and so put an end to the problem. Finally the two nations concerned agreed to submit the question to arbitration, and a decision was rendered in 1893, establishing a "protected zone" of sixty miles around the Pribylof Islands. Unfortunately the ocean range of the seals is much wider than this, and the diminution of the herd has still gone on. The difficulty, therefore, remains unsettled.

Sir John Macdonald died in 1891 and Sir John S. D. Thompson, a man of marked ability, became premier in 1892. He lived, however, only until 1894 and for a brief interval Sir Charles Tupper filled the office. Before the end of the year he resigned, and Sir Wilfred Laurier became premier, he being the first French Canadian to hold that high office. The most important questions rising under his administration were those springing from the discovery of gold on the Klondike River. This find was made in the autumn of 1896, and as reports quickly spread **The Gold of the Klondike** of the richness of the diggings, a rush of miners, mainly Americans, took place during the following year. But it was quickly perceived that the region was not in Alaska, as at first supposed, but in Canadian territory, and mining laws were imposed by the Canadian government, including heavy fees and royalties, which were bitterly objected to by the American miners.

But the chief question arising from the find was that concerning the true boundary between the two countries. This had never been clearly decided upon for the southern section of Alaska, and the natural desire of Canada to obtain an ocean outing for the new gold district, which was being very rapidly settled, soon stirred up a very active controversy.

The claim of Russia, transferred by purchase to the United States, called for a strip of land ten leagues wide from the coast backward. This would have been definite enough had it been quite clear what constituted the coast. The sea line of Alaska is marked by deep indentations, some of which are open to question as to whether they should be considered oceanic or inland waters. Such a one is Lynn Canal, which affords the natural waterway to the mountain passes leading to the upper Yukon, by whose waters the gold district can be most easily reached. This inlet, running sixty miles into the land, is less than six miles wide at its mouth; and while the United States claimed that it was part of the open sea, the Canadian government looked upon it as territorial water, and demanded that the coast line should be drawn across its mouth. This would have given Canada control of its upper waters and the access to the sea from the Klondike region over its own territory which it so urgently needed. It would also have given it possession of Dyea and Skagua, two mining towns built and peopled by Americans at the head of the canal, and whose people would have bitterly opposed being made citizens of Canada.

A Boundary Question

As will be perceived from the above statement a number of international questions had arisen between the United States and Canada, of which only the most urgent have here been mentioned. In 1898 an earnest attempt was made to adjust these annoying problems, by the appointment of an International Commission, whose sessions began in the city of Quebec, August 23, 1898. On the part of Great Britain and Canada the membership consisted of Lord Herschell, ex-Lord Chancellor of England, chairman, Sir Wilfred Laurier, the Premier of Canada, Sir Richard J. Cartwright, Minister of Trade and Commerce, Sir Louis H. Davies, Minister of Marine and Fisheries, John Charlton, M. P., and Sir James T. Winter, Premier of Newfoundland. The American members were Charles W. Fairbanks, United States Senator from Indiana, chairman, George Gray, Senator from Delaware, Nelson Dingley, Representative from Maine, John W. Foster, former Secretary of State and ex-Minister to Spain, Russia and Mexico, John A. Kasson, former Minister to Germany and Austria, and T. Jefferson Coolidge, former Minister to France. Senator Gray resigned in September, to take part in the Peace Commission on the Spanish War, and was succeeded by Senator Charles J Faulkner, of West Virginia.

An International Commission

The principal questions that came before this Commission for consideration were the following: The adjustment of the difficulties concerning the Atlantic and Pacific coast fisheries and those still arising in reference to the fur-seals; the establishment of a fixed boundary between Alaska and Canada; provision for the transit of merchandise to or from either country across territory of the other, or to be delivered at points in either country beyond the frontier; the questions of labor laws and mining rights affecting the subjects of either country within the territory of the other; a mutually satisfactory readjustment of customs duties; an understanding concerning the placing of war vessels on the great lakes; arrangements to define and mark the frontier line; provision for the conveyance of accused persons by officers of one country through the territory of the other; and reciprocity in wrecking and salvage rights.

The Questions at Issue

As will be perceived from this list of subjects to be considered, the High Commission had abundance of work mapped out for it. While some of the questions were of minor importance and might be settled with comparative ease, others were of high significance and likely to prove very difficult to adjust. In fact, they proved beyond the powers of the commission. Adjourning from Quebec to meet in Washington in November, the members continued in session there for several months longer, but adjourned finally in the spring of 1899 without having been able to come to a decision on the difficult matters involved.

The Failure of the Commission

Several of these questions, indeed, were of the most complex and vexatious character, particularly that relating to the fisheries, which had been a source of trouble and conflict through most of the century. As respects the transport of goods of one country over the territory of the other, it is a matter of much importance to Canada, which sends great quantities of goods over United States territory for shipment abroad, six times more Canadian grain, for instance, going by way of Buffalo, than *via* Montreal and the St. Lawrence. The problem of reciprocal customs regulations is also one of much importance to Canada, which imports more merchandise from the United States than is sent by that country to all the remainder of the American Continent, amounting in all to about $70,000,000 annually. In return its exports to the United States amount to about $50,000,000, the total commerce being of importance enough to call for special tariff regulations between the two countries.

Commerce of Canada with the United States

After the adjournment of the commission, efforts were made to adjust the boundary question, so far as Lynn Canal was concerned, through an understanding between the two governments. The United States, in consideration of the needs of Canada in the Klondike region, showed a disposition to concede temporarily to that country a tidewater port in the Lynn Canal. But decided protests from commercial ports on the Pacific seaboard caused the withdrawal of the proposed concession. A temporary adjustment of the question was subsequently made, a line being drawn by officials of the two countries which followed the mountian summits and cut off Canada from access to the sea except across United States territory.

The progress of Canada during the past quarter of a century has been very great, while her population has increased in that period by nearly one-half. Railways have spread like a network over the rich agricultural territory along the southern border land of the dominion, from

Railway Progress in Canada ocean to ocean, and are now pushing into the deep forest land and rich mineral regions of the interior and the northwest, their total length in 1899 being over 17,000 miles, a large mileage for a population of 5,000,000. The most recent railway projected is one to the Klondike region, which already has a large population, and possesses in Dawson City a thriving and enterprising headquarters of the mining region. Canada has also been active in canal building, and has now under consideration a project of the highest importance, namely, the excavation of a ship-canal from Lake Huron to the St. Lawrence. This great enterprise, if carried into effect, will shorten the distance of commercial navigation by hundreds of miles and be of untold advantage to the Canadian commonwealth. It is proposed also to deepen the existing canals, so as to permit the conveyance of ocean freight without breaking bulk.

In manufacturing industry almost every branch of production is to be found, the progressive enterprise of the people of the Dominion being great, and a large proportion of the goods they need being

Manufacturing Enterprise made at home. The best evidence of the enterprise of Canada in manufacture is shown by the fact that she exports many thousand dollars worth of goods annually more than she buys—England being her largest customer and the United States second on the list. In addition to her manufactured products, Canada is actively agricultural, and possesses vast natural wealth in the products of her rich mines, vast

The Yield of Precious Metals forests and prolific fisheries. The most recent of these sources of wealth are her mines of the precious metals, which yielded over $6,000,000 in gold and $7,000,000 in silver in 1897, shortly after the discovery of the Klondike deposits. The yield of those has since very greatly increased.

Not only is the outside world largely ignorant of the importance of Canada, but few of her own people realize the greatness of the country they possess. Its area of more than three and one-half millions of square miles —one-sixteenth of the entire land surface of the earth—is great enough to include an immense variety of natural conditions and products. This area constitutes forty per cent. of the far extended British empire, while its richness of soil and resources in forest and mineral wealth are as yet almost untouched, and its promise of future yield is immense. The dimensions of the dominion guarantee a great variety of natural attractions. There are vast grass-covered plains, thousands of square miles of untouched forest lands, multitudes of lakes and rivers, great and small, and **Extent and Resources of the Dominion** mountains of the wildest and grandest character, whose natural beauty equals that of the far-famed Alpine peaks. In fact, the Canadian Pacific Railway is becoming a route of pilgrimage for the lovers of the beautiful and sublime, its mountain scenery being un- rivaled upon the continent.

The population of Canada varies in character according to location. In Ontario the people are generally English. In Quebec, and many other portions of what was formerly called Lower Canada, the original settlers were French, and their descendants are still in the majority and retain many of the habits and customs of their mother country—so much so, in fact, that, though England has ruled the land for about one hundred and fifty years, the French language is still almost exclusively spoken. Even in the cities of Montreal and Quebec the prevalence of the language makes the visitor from Toronto feel that he is in a foreign city.

In the west, until a few years ago, the prevailing population was the original Indian and the half-breed. But this element, though still numerous, is fast being swallowed up or hidden by the throng of immigrants, who are now pouring into that vast and resourceful region. These immigrants, unlike those of the older eastern provinces, are made up of all **The Character of the Canadian Population.** the nationalities of northern Europe, the British Isles, however, being well represented. Out of this mixture a new people, combining the good and progressive elements of various nations, is springing up. In this respect the Canadians of the northwest are much like the inhabitants of the northwestern United States.

Population at present is densest on the southern borders of the country, along the Great Lakes and the shores of the St. Lawrence. The interior is very sparsely settled, and as the latitude increases the cold of winter, except where the country is warmed by the winds of the Pacific, becomes more intense, until, in the northern part of the dominion, it is practically impossible for the Caucasian race to live in comfort. Much of this unbroken wilderness is covered with gigantic forests, which make lumbering the chief industry of that section, as agriculture is of the lower latitudes. In fact, lumbering and agriculture are the chief industries of all sections except the sea-coasts, where fishing interests are of great importance, and certain portions of the great northwest, like the Yukon districts, where mining is predominant. On the whole, Canada has before it a great future, and what its political destiny will be no man can foresee.

In several conditions the people of Canada, while preserving the general features of English society, are much more free and untrammeled. The caste system of Great Britain has gained little footing in this new land, where nearly every farmer is the owner of the soil which he tills, and the people have a feeling of independence unknown to the agricultural population of European countries. There has been great progress also in many social questions. The liquor traffic, for instance, is subject to the local option of restriction ; religious liberty prevails ; education is practically free and un-sectarian ; the franchise is enjoyed by all citizens ; members of the parliament are paid for their services ; and though the executive department of the government is under the control of a governor-general appointed by the queen, the laws of Canada are made by its own statesmen, and a state of practical independence prevails. Recognizing this, and respecting the liberty-loving spirit of the people, Great Britain is chary in interfering with any question of Canadian policy, or in any sense in attempting to limit the freedom of her great Transatlantic Colony.

RT. HON. SIR JOHN A. MACDONALD, G. C. B.
Prime Minister of Canada, 1878-1891.

RT. HON. J. S. D. THOMPSON, K. C. M. G.
Prime Minister of Canada, 1892-1894.

RT. HON. SIR WILFRID LAURIER,
Prime Minister of Canada, 1896.

SIR CHARLES TUPPER.

ILLUSTRIOUS SONS OF CANADA

DAVID LIVINGSTONE.

HENRY M. STANLEY.

DR. FRITHIOF NANSEN.

LIEUT. R. E. PEARY.

GREAT EXPLORERS IN THE TROPICS AND ARCTICS.

CHAPTER XXXVI.

Livingstone, Stanley, Peary, Nansen and Other Great Discoverers and Explorers.

A T the beginning of the nineteenth century, long as man had previously existed upon the earth, much more than half its surface was unknown to the most civilized nations. Of the extensive continent of Africa, for instance, only the coast regions had been explored, while the vast interior could fairly be described as the " Great Unknown." The immense continent of Asia was known only in outline. With its main features men had some acquaintance, but its details were as little known as the mountains of the moon. With America men were little better acquainted than with Africa. The United States itself had been explored only as far west as the Mississippi, and that but imperfectly. The vast space between that great stream and the Pacific almost wholly awaited discovery. The remainder of the continent was divided into national domains, which were thinly inhabited and very imperfectly known. Of the continental island of Australia only a few spots on the border had been visited, and still less was known of the broad region of the North Polar zone.

Ignorance of the Earth's Surface at the Beginning of the Century

At the end of the century a very different tale could be told. The hundred years had been marked by an extraordinary activity in travel, adventure, and discovery; daring men had penetrated the most obscure recesses of continents and islands, climbed the most difficult mountains, ventured among the most savage tribes, studied the geographical features and natural productions of a thousand regions before unknown, and learned more about the conditions of the earth than had been learned in a thousand years before. The work of the century has no parallel in history except the fifteenth and sixteenth centuries, when America was discovered and the East Indies were explored, and the horizon of human knowledge was immensely extended.

Great Activity of Explorers in the Nineteenth Century

The great achievements of the century with which we have to deal were performed by a large number of adventurous men, far too numerous even to be named in this review.

29

523

In fact it would need a volume, and one of considerable extent, to tell, even in epitome, the story of travel and exploration within the nineteenth century. Such a story, given in any fulness, would far transcend our purpose, which is confined to the description of the great events of the century, those of epoch-making significance, and which played leading parts in the progress of the period with which we are concerned. In this review, there-

The Notable
Fields of
Nineteenth
Century
Travel

fore, we may fairly confine ourselves to records of travel in two regions of the earth, the continent of Africa and the Arctic Zone, of both of which little was known at the opening of the century, while the story of their exploration has been of startling interest and importance. The interior of Asia and America, while presenting problems to be solved, were not unknown in the sense in which we speak of Africa, over which rested a pall of darkness as black as the complexion of its inhabitants. Australia alone was unknown in a similar sense. But the interior of that great island is practically a desert, and its exploration possesses nothing of the interest which attaches to that of Africa, a land which for many centuries has attracted the active attention and aroused the vivid curiosity of mankind, while a satisfactory acquaintance with it has been left for the latter half of the nineteenth century.

Of the great travelers to whom we are indebted for our present knowledge of this continent two stand pre-eminent, David Livingstone and Henry M. Stanley, and we may deal with their careers as the pivots around which the whole story of African exploration revolves.

The first of modern travelers to penetrate the interior of western

Famous African
Travelers

Africa to any considerable depth was the justly celebrated Mungo Park, whose first journey to the Niger was made in 1795–96, and the second in 1805. He traced that important stream through a large part of its upper course—finally losing his life as a result of his intrepid daring. On the east coast, at a somewhat earlier date (1768–73) the equally famous James Bruce penetrated Abyssinia to the headwaters of the Blue Nile, which he looked upon as the source of the great river of Egypt. About the same time the French traveler Vaillant entered the continent at Cape Town and journeyed north for more than three hundred miles, into the country of the Bushmen.

Such was the state of African exploration at the beginning of the century under consideration. The travelers named, and others of minor importance, had not penetrated far from the coast, and the vast interior of the continent remained almost utterly unknown. In fact the century was half gone before anything further of consequence was discovered, the first journey of Dr. Livingstone being made in 1849.

David Livingstone, an enterprising man, of Scotch birth, left England in 1840 to devote his life to missionary work in Africa. He had studied medicine and theology, and was well equipped in every way for the arduous and difficult work he had undertaken. Landing at Port Natal, he became associated with the Rev. Robert Moffat, a noted African missionary, whose daughter he afterwards married, and for years he labored perseveringly as an agent of the London Missionary Society. He studied the languages, habits, and religious beliefs of a number of tribes, and became one of the most earnest and successful of missionaries, his subsequent journeys being undertaken largely for the advance of his religious labors.

Dr. Livingstone's Missionary Labors

His experience in missionary work convinced him that success in this field of duty was not to be measured by the tale of conversions—of doubtful character—which could be sent home every year, but that the proper work for the enterprising white man was that of pioneer research. He could best employ himself in opening up and exploring new fields of labor, and might safely leave to native agents the duty of working these out in detail.

This theory he first put into effect in 1849, in which year he set out on a journey into the unknown land to the north, the goal of his enterprise being Lake Ngami, on which no white man's eyes had ever fallen. In company with two English sportsmen, Mr. Oswell and Mr. Murray, he traversed the great and bleak Kalahari Desert,—which he was the first to describe in detail,—and on the 1st of August the travelers were gladdened by the sight of the previously unknown liquid plain, the most southerly of the great African lakes.

Discovery of Lake Ngami

Two hundred miles beyond this body of water lived a noted chief named Sebituane, the chief of the Makololo tribe, whose residence Livingstone sought to reach the following year, bringing with him on this journey his wife and children. But fever seized the children and he was obliged to stop at the shores of the lake. Nothing daunted by this failure, he set out again in 1851, once more accompanied by his family, and with his former companion, Mr. Oswell, his purpose being to settle among the Makololos and seek to convert to Christianity their great chief. He succeeded in reaching the tribe, but the death of Sebituane, shortly after his arrival, disarranged his plans, and he was obliged to return. But before doing so he and Mr. Oswell made an exploration of several hundred miles to the northeast, their journey ending at the Zambesi, the great river of South Africa, which he here found flowing in a broad and noble current through the centre of the continent.

The subsequent travels of Livingstone were performed more for purposes of exploration than for religious labors, though to the end he considered himself a missionary pioneer. Sending his family to England, he left Capetown in June, 1852, and reached Linyanti, the capital of the

Livingstone's Journey from the Zambesi to the West Coast

Makololo, in May, 1853, being received in royal style by the chief and his people, by whom he was greatly esteemed. He next ascended the Zambesi, in search of some healthy high land for a missionary station. But everywhere he found the tsetse fly, an insect deadly to animals, and, annoyed by the ravages of this insect among his cattle, he determined to leave that locality and enter upon the greatest journey ever yet undertaken in Africa, one through the unknown interior to the west coast.

The start was made from Linyanti on November 11, 1853, the party ascending the Leeba to Lake Dilolo, which was reached in February, 1854. Finally, on the 31st of May, they came to the coast town of St. Paul de Loanda, in Portuguese West Africa. Their long and dangerous journey had been attended by numberless hardships, and Livingstone reached the coast nearly worn out by fever, dysentery and semi-starvation. But nothing could deter the indefatigable traveler. He set out again after a few months, reached Lake Dilolo on June 13, 1855, and Linyanti in September. After a brief interval of rest he left this place with a determination to follow the broad-flowing Zambesi to its mouth in the eastern sea.

A fortnight after his start he made the most notable of his discoveries, the one with which his name is most intimately associated in popular

The Discovery of the Great Victoria Falls

estimation, that of the great Victoria Falls of the Zambesi, a cataract which has no rival upon the earth except the still mightier one of the Niagara. Here an immense cleft or fissure in the earth cuts directly across the channel of the river, which pours in an enormous flood down into the cavernous abyss, whence "the smoke of its torrent ascendeth forever." The country surrounding seems to be a great basin-shaped plateau, surrounded by a ring of mountains, the depression having probably at one time been filled with an immense lake whose waters were drained off when the earth split asunder across its bed.

On went the untiring traveler, and on May 20, 1856, he reached the east coast at the Portuguese town of Quillimane, at the mouth of the Zambesi, in a frightfully emaciated condition. He had, in two and a half years of travel, performed one of the most remarkable journeys ever made up to

The First Crossing of the Continent

that time. First proceeding north from the Cape to Loanda, through twenty-five degrees of latitude, he had for the first time in history, crossed the continent of Africa from ocean to ocean, through as many degrees of longitude, while his discoveries in the geography and natural history of the region traversed had been immense.

Livingstone returned to England in the latter part of the year and was received with the highest enthusiasm, being welcomed as the first to break through that pall of darkness which had so long enveloped the interior of Africa. The Royal Geographical Society had already conferred upon him its highest token of honor, its gold medal, and now honors and compliments were showered upon him until the modest traveler was over-whelmed with the warmth of his reception.

The desire to complete his work was strong upon him, and after pub-lishing an account of his travels, in a work of modest simplicity, he returned to Africa, reaching the mouth of the Zambesi in May, 1858. In 1859 his new career of discovery began in an exploration of the Shire, **Livingstone** a northern affluent of the Zambesi, up which he journeyed to **Discovers** the great Lake Nyassa, another capital discovery. For several **Lake Nyassa** years he was engaged in exploring the surrounding region and in furthering the interests of missionary enterprise among the natives. In one of his journeys his wife, who was his companion during this period of his travels, died, and in 1864 he returned home, worn out with his extraordinary labors in new lands and desiring to spend the remainder of his days in quiet and repose.

But at the suggestion of Murchison, the famous geologist and his staunch friend, he was induced to return to Africa, one of his main purposes being to take steps looking to the suppression of the Arab slave trade, whose horrors had long excited his deepest sympathies. Landing at the mouth of the Rovuma River—a stream he had previously explored—on March 22, 1866, he started for the interior, rounded Lake Nyassa on the south, and set off to the northeast for the great Lake Tanganyika—which had mean-while been discovered by Barton and Speke, in 1857.

After his departure Livingstone vanished from sight and knowledge. and for five years was utterly lost in the deep interior of the continent. From time to time vague intimations of his movements reached the world of civilization, but the question of his fate became so exciting a one that in 1871 Henry M. Stanley was dispatched, at the expense of the proprietor of the *New York Herald*, to penetrate the continent and seek to discover the long-lost traveler. Stanley found him at Ujiji, on the **Stanley** northeast shore of Tanganyika, on October 18, 1871, the great **in Search of** explorer being then, in his words, "a ruckle of bones." Far **Livingstone** and wide he had traveled through Central Africa, discovering a host of lakes and streams, and finding many new tribes with strange habits. Among his notable discoveries was that of the Lualaba River—The Upper Congo —which he believed to be the head-waters of the Nile. His work had been enormous, and the "Dark Continent" had yielded to him a host of its long hidden mysteries.   Not willing yet to give up his work, he waited at Ujiji for men and supplies sent him by Stanley from the coast, and then started

The Death of the Great Explorer

south for Lake Bangweolo, one of his former discoveries. But attacked again by his old enemy, dysentery, the iron frame of the great traveller at length yielded, and he was found, on May 1, 1873, by his men, dead in his tent, kneeling by the side of his bed. Thus perished in prayer the greatest traveler in modern times.

For more than thirty years Livingstone had dwelt in Africa, most of that time engaged in exploring new regions and visiting new peoples.   His travels had covered a third of the continent, extending from the Cape to near the equator, and from the Atlantic to the Indian Ocean, his work being all done leisurely and carefully, so that its results were of the utmost value to geographical science.   He had also aroused a sentiment against the Arab slave-trade which was to give that frightful system its death-blow.

The work of Livingstone stirred up an enthusiasm for African travel, and many adventurous explorers set out for that continent during his career.   After the discovery of Lake Tanganyika by Burton and Speke, in 1857, the latter started to the northeast, and reached the head-waters of the great Victoria Nyanza, the largest body of water on the continent.   Subsequently this traveler, accompanied by Mr. Grant, journeyed to the White Nile, north of this lake, while Samuel Baker, another adventurous traveler, accompanied by his heroic wife, reached in 1864 a great lake west of the Victoria, which he named the Albert Nyanza.

Further north Dr. Barth, as early as 1850, set out on a journey across the Sahara to the Soudan, and at a later date various travelers explored

Other African Travelers

this northern section of the continent, while in 1874–75 Lieutenant Cameron repeated Livingstone's feat of crossing the continent from sea to sea.   But the greatest of African travelers after Livingstone was Henry M. Stanley, with whose work we are next concerned.

While a reporter in the *New York Herald*, this enterprising man had been sent to Crete to report upon the revolution in that island, to Abyssinia during the British invasion, and to Spain during the revolution in that country.   While in Spain, in 1869, James Gordon Bennett sent him the brief order to "find Livingstone."   This was enough for Stanley, who proceeded at once to Zanzibar, organized an expedition, and did "find Livingstone," as above stated.

Next, filled with the spirit of travel, Stanley set out to "find Africa," now as joint agent for the *Herald* and the London *Daily Telegraph*.

Setting out from Zanzibar in November, 1874, he proceeded, with a large expedition, to the Victoria Nyanza, which he circumnavigated; and then journeyed to Tanganyika, whose shape and dimension he similarly ascertained.   From these he proceeded westward to the Lualaba, **Stanley's Journey to the Victoria Nyanza** the stream which Livingstone had supposed to be the Nile. How Stanley made his way down this great stream, overcoming enormous difficulties and fighting his way through hostile tribes, is too long a story to be told here.   It must suffice to say that he soon found that he was not upon the Nile, but upon a westward flowing stream, which he eventually identified as the Congo—a great river whose lower course only had been previously known.   For ten months the daring traveler pursued his journey down this stream, assailed by treachery and hostility, and finally reached the ocean, having traversed the heart of that vast "unexplored territory" which long occupied so wide a space on all maps of Africa.   He had learned that the interior of the continent is a mighty plateau, watered by the Congo and its many large **The Descent of the Great Congo River** affluents and traversed in all directions by navigable waters. Politically this remarkable journey led to the founding of the Congo Free State, which embraces the central region of tropical Africa, and which Stanley was sent to establish in 1879.

In 1887 he set out on another great journey.   The conquest of the Egyptian Soudan by the Mahdi, described in a preceding chapter, had not only greatly diminished the territory of Egypt, but had cut off Emin Pasha (Dr. Edward Schnitzler), governor of the Equatorial Province of Egypt, leaving him stranded on the Upper Nile, near the Albert Nyanza.   Here Emin maintained himself for years, holding his own against his foes, and actively engaging in natural history study.   But, cut off as he was from civilization, threatened by the Mahdi, and his fate unknown in Europe, a growing anxiety concerning him prevailed, and Stanley was sent to find him, as he had before found Livingstone.

Organizing a strong expedition at Zanzibar, the traveler sailed with his officers, soldiers and negro porters for the mouth of the Congo, which river he proposed to make the channel of his exploration. Setting out **Stanley Goes to the Rescue of Emin Pasha** from this point on March 18, 1887, by June 15th the expedition had reached the village of Yambuya, 1,300 miles up the stream. Thus far he had traversed waters well known to him.   From this point he proposed to plunge into the unknown, following the course of the Aruwimi, a large affluent of the Congo which flowed from the direction of the great Nyanza lake-basins.

It was a terrible journey which the expedition now made. Before it spread a forest of seemingly interminable extent, peopled mainly by the curious dwarfs who form the forest-folk of Central Africa. The difficulties before the traveler were enormous, but no hardship or danger could daunt his indomitable courage, and he kept resolutely on until he met the lost Emin on the shores of Albert Nyanza, as he had formerly met Livingstone on those of Lake Tanganyika.

Three times in effect Stanley crossed that terrible forest, since he returned to Yambuya for the men and supplies he had left there and journeyed back again. Finally he made an overland journey to Zanzibar, on the east coast, with Emin and his followers, who had been rescued just in time to save them **A Terrible Forest Journey** from imminent peril of overthrow and slaughter by the fanatical hordes of the Mahdi. This second crossing of the continent by Stanley ended December 4, 1889, having continued little short of three years. The discoveries made were great and valuable, and on his return to Europe the explorer met with a reception almost royal in its splendor. Among the large number of travelers who during the latter half of the century have contributed to make the interior of Africa as familiar to us as that of portions of our own continent, Livingstone and Stanley stand pre-eminent, the most heroic figures in modern travel : Livingstone as the missionary explorer, who won the love of the savage tribes and made his way by the arts of peace and gentleness ; Stanley as the soldierly explorer, who fought his way through cannibal hordes, his arts being those of force and daring. They and their successors have performed one of the greatest works of the nineteenth century, that of lifting the cloud which for so many centuries lay thick and dense over the whole extent of interior Africa.

Leaving this region of research, we must now seek another which has been the seat of as earnest efforts and terrible hardships and has aroused **The Exploration of the Arctic Zone** as ardent a spirit of investigation, the Arctic Zone. At no point in the story of the nineteenth century do we find a greater display of courage and resolution, a more patient endurance of suffering, and a more unyielding determination to extend the limits of human knowledge, than in this region of ice and snow, the delving into whose secrets has actively continued during the latter half of the century.

A number of voyages were made to the Arctic regions in former centuries, and Henry Hudson as early as 1607 sailed as far north as the latitude of 81 degrees 30 minutes in the vicinity of Spitzbergen. With the opening of the nineteenth century exploration grew more active, and voyage after voyage was made ; but the distance north reached by Hudson two centuries before was not surpassed until 1827, when Parry reached 82 degrees 40 minutes north latitude in the same region of the sea. Beyond these efforts to penetrate the ice barrier, and the discovery of some islands in the Arctic Ocean, nothing of special interest occurred until the date of Sir John Franklin's expedition, which left England in 1845 and disappeared in the icy seas, every soul on board perishing. This expedition was made famous by the many search parties which were sent out in quest of the lost mariners. **Early Expeditions to the Far North**

By one of these parties the northwest passage from ocean to ocean, around the Arctic coast of America, was traversed in 1854. The fate of Franklin and his men was not fully solved until 1880, when an American expedition, under Lieutenant Schwatka, found the last traces left by the unfortunate explorers.

As famous and as disastrous as the Franklin expedition was the " Lady Franklin Bay Expedition," conducted by Lieutenant Greely, of the United States army, which set out in 1881. This expedition was not sent for purposes of polar research, but in pursuance of a plan to conduct a series of circumpolar meteorological observations. The relief party of 1883, dispatched to the rescue of the explorers, was unfortunately put under the control of military men, who not only failed to reach their destination, but even to leave a supply of food where Greely and his men might justly expect to find one.

As a result of this failure, the explorers were obliged to abandon their ships and make their way southwards over almost impassable ice. In October they reached Cape Sabine, one of the bleakest spots in the Arctic zone. If food had been left there for them all would have been well. But they looked in vain for the expected supplies, and when, in June, 1884, Commodore Schley reached them with a new relief ship, starvation had almost completed its work. Of the whole party only six men survived, and a day or two more of delay would have carried them all away. Among the survivors was their leader, Lieutenant Greely. **The Dreadful Fate of the Greely Party**

A disaster as fatal in character attended the *Jeannette* expedition, sent out by the *New York Herald*, in 1879, under Commander DeLong, to push north by way of Bering Strait. The vessel was crushed by the ice in 1882, and the crew made their way over the frozen surface past the New Siberian Islands to the mouth of the Lena River, on the north coast of Siberia. Here starvation attacked them, and DeLong and many of his men miserably perished, their bodies being **The Fatal " Jeannette " Expedition** found by Engineer Melville, one of their companions, who had pushed south to the Siberian settlements and secured aid, with which he heroically returned for the rescue of the unfortunate mariners.

Another expedition calling for attention was that of Adolf Erik Nordenskjöld, a Swedish scientist. The purpose of this enterprise was to discover, if possible, a practical commercial route through the waters north of Europe and Asia, the long sought-for Northeast Passage. In 1878 **Expedition of Prof. Nordenskjöld** Nordenskjöld set out in the *Vega*, commanded by Captain Pallander, of the Swedish Navy. The party succeeded in making the long journey round the northern coasts of Europe and Asia, wintering in Bering Strait and reaching Japan in 1879. This vessel was the first one to round the northernmost point of Asia, and Nordenskjöld was rewarded by being made a baron and a commander of the order of the Pole Star in his own country, and by marks of distinction from several others of the courts of Europe.

Since 1890 the work of polar exploration has taken new forms. In 1870 Nordenskjöld made a journey into Greenland, and a second one in 1883, penetrating that island more than 100 miles and reach- **Land Journeys in Greenland** ing a snow-clad elevation of 7,000 feet. In 1886 Lieutenant Robet E. Peary, of the United States Navy, made a similar journey, and in 1888 Dr. Frithjof Nansen, a Norwegian explorer, crossed the southern part of the island on snowshoes from east to west.

In 1891 Peary proceeded with a small party to McCormick Bay, a locality far up on the west coast of Greenland, whence he set out in the following spring with a single companion for a sledge journey over the northern section of the island. After a remarkable journey of 650 miles he reached the northeast coast of Greenland, at 81°, 37″ N. latitude, but the appearance of an area of broken stones impassable by sledges cut off his progress **Peary Crosses North Greenland** to the far north. In 1895 Peary repeated this journey, but failed to make farther progress northward.

During the final decade of the century polar expeditions became numerous. Walter Wellman, a young American journalist, attempted in 1894 to reach the pole by sledge and boat over the Spitzbergen route, but his supporting vessel was crushed in the ice, and he was forced to retreat when near the 81st parallel. He made a second "dash for the pole" in 1898–99, but was disabled by an accident, and again obliged to return without success. In 1894 Frederick G. Jackson, an English explorer, visited Franz Joseph Land, an island region discovered by an Austrian expedition in 1872–74, and whose northern extension was not known. He remained on this island three years, carefully exploring it, and in 1896 stood on its northern extremity, near the 81st parallel, and in view of an open expanse of polar waters. Jackson's most notable service to science was the rescue of the daring explorer Nansen, whose expedition needs next to be described.

Frithjof Nansen, whose crossing of Greenland has been mentioned, soon after projected an enterprise of a new character. There was excellent reason to suppose that a strong ocean current crossed the polar area, flowing from the coast of the Eastern hemisphere across to Greenland and down both shores of that island. By trusting to the drift influence of this current a vessel might be carried past the pole and the long baffling mystery solved. Nansen accordingly had a vessel constructed adapted to resist the most powerful crushing force, and so formed that a severe ice pressure would lift it to the surface of the floe. In this vessel, the *Fram*, he set out in June, 1893, sailed east to the vicinity of the New Siberia Islands, and there made fast his ship to an ice floe, with the hope that the current would slowly carry ice and ship across the polar area.

Nansen and His Enterprise

For three years Nansen and his crew were lost to all knowledge of man, in these frozen seas, and all hopes of his return had nearly vanished when he triumphantly reappeared, having achieved a marvelous success, even though short of that which he had desired. For more than a year the *Fram* had drifted slowly northward, and on Christmas eve, 1894, the latitude of 83 degrees 24 minutes, reached by the Greely expedition, and the highest yet attained, was passed. In March, 1895, Nansen left the ship, dissatisfied with its slow progress, and with one companion started on a sledge journey to the north. But the ice grew so difficult to cross and his dog teams so depleted in number, that, after a desperate effort, he was obliged to give up the enterprise on April 7th. He had then reached latitude 86 degrees 14 minutes, being 200 miles nearer the pole than former explorers had gone, and within 300 miles of that "farthest north" point. The vessel which he had left continued to drift north until it reached 85 degrees 57 minutes, when it turned southward. Here the sea was found to be deep, and the belief that the pole might be surrounded by a land area was disproved. It lies probably in a sea region of over 10,000 feet in depth.

Nansen's "Farthest North"

Nansen and Johansen, his companion, finally reached the coast of Franz Joseph Land, where they drearily spent the winter of 1895-96, living on the flesh of bears and walrusses, which they shot. In the spring they set out to cross the ice to Spitzbergen, and after two unsucessful attempts had the good fortune to meet Dr. Jackson on the shores of Franz Joseph Land.

The incident was one of the most notable in the history of research, it seeming next to impossible that almost the only human beings in the vast area of the frozen north should have the remarkable fortune to come together. The voyagers completed their journey home in Jackson's supply ship, the *Windward*, their arrival in the realms of civilization being one of the most striking events of the century. In 1897 Jackson returned, having explored and mapped Franz Joseph Land.

The Rescue of Nansen

The final years of the century were very active in polar research. A new explorer of Swedish birth, S. A. Andrée, devised a plan of reaching the pole as original as that of Nansen, and thought by many to be more hopeful. This was the taking advantage of the currents of air, instead of those of water. Mr. Andrée was an aëronaut of experience, and found it possible, by aid of a rope drag and a rubber sail, to direct the motion of a balloon somewhat aside from the course of the wind. A balloon seemingly suitable for his enterprise was constructed, and in the summer of 1897 he set out for the north with two companions, and with ardent hopes of returning successful in a few months. Unhappily, accident or miscalculation interfered with the plans of the adventurous aëronaut, and he and his companions have failed to return. They have in all probability fallen victims to the terrible conditions of the northern zone.

Andrée's Fatal Balloon Venture

In 1898 Lieutenant Peary set out again for the scene of his former triumph, now equipped for a continued effort to solve the problem of the pole. He proposed to establish depots of provisions at successive points in the north, and to continue the enterprise for years if necessary, finally dashing polar-ward from his farthest north station. In the same year the Norwegian Captain Sverdrup proceeded to the same locality in the famous *Fram*, with purposes analogous to those of Peary. In 1899 the adventurous Italian Prince Luigi, set out for Franz Joseph Land, well equipped for a journey north, and proposing to devote several years to the enterprise.

Thus there is room for hope that the pole may be reached by the end of the nineteenth century, or before the twentieth century is many years advanced. Meanwhile the enterprise of South Polar exploration, long neglected, has been actively revived. Several expeditions have recently visited that region, and active steps are being taken for its exploration on a larger scale.

CHAPTER XXXVII.

Robert Fulton, George Stephenson, and the Triumphs of Invention.

IN no direction has the nineteenth century been more prolific than in that of invention, and its fame in the future is likely to be largely based on its immense achievements in this field of human activity. It has been great in other directions,—in science, in exploration, in political and moral development, but it is perhaps in invention and the industrial adaptation of scientific discovery that it stands highest and has done most for the advancement of mankind. And it is a fact of great interest that much the most striking and important work in this direction has been done by the Anglo-Saxon race, in many respects the most **Anglo-Saxon Activity in Invention** enterprising and progressive race upon the face of the earth. For the beginning of this work, during the eighteenth century, credit must be given to Great Britain; and especially for the notable invention of the steam engine, which forms the foundation stone of the whole immense edifice. But to the development of the work, during the nineteenth century, we must seek the United States, whose inventive activity and the value of its results have surpassed those of any other region of the earth.

We cannot confine ourselves to the nineteenth century in considering this subject, but must go back to the eighteenth, and glance at the epoch-making discovery of James Watt, the famous Scottish engi- **James Watt and** neer, to whom we owe the great moving force of nineteenth **the Steam** century industry and progress, and whose life extended until **Engine** 1819, well within the century. There exists an interesting legend that his attention was first attracted to the power of steam when a boy, when sitting by the fireside and observing the lid of his mother's tea-kettle lifted by the escaping steam. It is not, however, to the discovery, but to the useful application of steam power that his fame is due. The use of steam as a motive power had been attempted long before, and steam pumps used almost a century before Watt's great invention. What he did was to produce the first effective steam engine, the parent machine upon which the multitudinous improvements during the succeeding century were based.

While the eighteenth century is notable for the discovery of the steam engine and for the first stages in the production of labor-saving machinery, the great triumphs in the latter field of invention were made in the succeeding century, during which era the powers of human production were **Nineteenth Century Invention** developed to an extent not only unprecedented, but almost incredible, the powers of man, aided by steam and electricity, being increased a hundred-fold during a century of time. It would need a volume devoted to this subject alone to tell, even in epitome, all that has been done in this direction, and here we must confine ourselves to a rapid review of the leading results of inventive genius.

Both in Great Britain and in America notable triumphs in the invention of labor-saving machines were accomplished in the closing period of the eighteenth century. These include the famous British inventions of the spinning jenny of James Hargreaves, the spinning frame of Sir Richard Arkwright, and the power loom of Dr. Cartwright, the first notable aids in cotton manufacture. These were rendered available by the cotton-gin of Eli Whitney, the American inventor, by whose genius the production of cotton fibre was enormously cheapened. Other celebrated American inventors of this period were John Fitch, to whose efforts the first practical steamboat was due, and Oliver Evans, who revolutionized milling machinery, **Labor-saving Machinery of the Eighteenth Century** his devices in flour and grist mills being in use for half a century after his death. He was also the first to devise a steam carriage, and in 1804 built a steam dredger, which propelled itself through the streets of Philadelphia and afterwards was moved as a stern-wheel steamboat on the Schuylkill River. Another famous invention of this period was the nail machine of Jacob Perkins, patented in 1795, though not fully developed until 1810. At that time nails were all hand-wrought, and cost twenty-five cents a pound. By this machine the ancient hand process was speedily brought to an end and the price of nails has since been reduced to little more than that of the iron of which they are made. Another famous American inventor of early date was Thomas Blanchard, the most notable of whose many inventions was the Blanchard lathe, developed in 1819, for the turning of irregular forms, a contrivance of the utmost value in doing away with slow and costly methods of labor.

Of early inventions of the nineteenth century, however, the most **The Steamboat and Locomotive** notable were the steamboat and the locomotive, the later development of which has been of extraordinary value to mankind. Previous to the century under review, for a period of several thousand years, the horse had been depended on for rapid land travel, the sail for rapid motion on the water. The inventions of Fulton and

Stephenson brought these ancient systems to an end, and within a single century produced a magical change in the ability of man to make his way over the surface of land and sea.

The application of steam to the movement of boats had been tried by several inventors in Great Britain and America in the eighteenth century, the most successful being John Fitch, whose steamboat was used for months on the Delaware about 1790. But the earliest inventor to produce a commercially successful steamboat was Robert Fulton, another American, whose boat, the *Clermont*, was given its trial trip on the Hudson in 1807.

This boat, in which was employed the principle of the side paddle-wheel, and which used a more powerful engine than John Fitch could command, was completed in August, 1807, and excited a great degree of public interest, far more than had been given to the pioneer steamboat. Monday, September 11, 1807, the time set for sailing, came, and expectation was at its highest pitch. The friends of the inventor were in a state of feverish anxiety lest the enterprise should come to grief, and the scoffers on the wharf were ready to give vent to shouts of derision. Precisely at the hour of one the moorings were thrown off, and the *Clermont* moved slowly out into the stream. Volumes of smoke rushed forth from her chimney, and her wheels, which were uncovered, scattered the spray far behind her. The spectacle was certainly novel to the people of those days, and some of the crowd on the wharf broke into shouts of ridicule. Soon, however, the jeers grew silent, for it was seen that the steamer was increasing her speed. Soon she was fairly under way, and making a steady progress up the stream at the rate of five miles per hour. The incredulity of the spectators had been succeeded by astonishment, and now this feeling gave way to undisguised delight, and cheer after cheer went up from the vast throng. In a little while, however, the boat was observed to stop, and the enthusiasm at once subsided. The scoffers were again in their glory, and unhesitatingly pronounced the enterprise a failure. But to their chagrin, the steamer, after a short delay, once more proceeded on her way, and this time even more rapidly than before. Fulton had discovered that the paddles were too long, and took too deep a hold on the water, and had stopped the boat for the purpose of shortening them.

This defect remedied, the *Clermont* continued her voyage during the rest of the day and all night, without stopping, and at one o'clock the next day ran alongside the landing at Clermont, the seat of Chancellor Livingston. She lay there until nine the next morning, when she continued her voyage toward Albany, reaching that city at five in the afternoon. On her return trip, she reached New York in thirty hours running time—exactly five miles per hour.

The river was at this time navigated entirely with sailing vessels. The surprise and dismay excited among the crews of these vessels by the

The Effect of the Steam- boat on River Men

appearance of the steamer was extreme. These simple people beheld what they supposed to be a huge monster, vomiting fire and smoke from its throat, lashing the water with its fins, and shaking the river with its roar, approaching rapidly in the face of both wind and tide. Some threw themselves flat on the decks of their vessels, where they remained in an agony of terror until the monster had passed, while others took to their boats and made for the shore in dismay, leaving their vessels to drift helplessly down the stream.

The introduction of the steamboat gave a powerful impetus to the internal commerce of the Union. It opened to navigation many important rivers whose swift currents had closed them to sailing craft, and made rapid and easy communication between the most distant parts of the country practicable. The public soon began to appreciate this, and orders came in rapidly for steamboats for various parts of the country. Fulton executed these as fast as possible, several among the number being for boats on the Ohio and Mississippi rivers.

The subsequent history of this important invention need but be glanced at here. The first steamship to cross the ocean was the *Savannah*, which set out from the city of that name in 1819, and reached Liverpool by the combined aid of wind and steam in twenty-eight days. The first to cross entirely by steam power was the *Royal William*, a Canadian-built vessel, in 1833. A year or two later the *Great Britain*, the first iron ocean steamer— 322 feet long by 31 feet beam—crossed the ocean in fifteen days. Since then the development of steam navigation, alike on inland and ocean waters, has been enormous, and an extraordinary increase has been made in the size and speed of steam vessels. Forty years ago the fastest ocean steamer took more than nine days to cross from New York to Queenstown. This

Development of Ocean Steamers

journey can be made now in a little over five days. As regards size, the great *Oceanic*, whose first voyage was made in 1899, surpasses any other boat ever built. This sea- monster is 704 feet long, and has a displacement of 28,000 tons, while it is capable of steaming around the earth at twelve knots an hour with- out recoaling. Its engine power is enormous, and its carrying capacity unprecedented. This leviathan considerably outranks in dimensions the *Great*

GEORGE STEPHENSON.

THE INVENTORS OF THE LOCOMOTIVE AND THE ELECTRIC TELEGRAPH

Stephenson's genius enabled men to travel 1000 miles in a day. Morse's genius enabled men to send a message around the world in less than one hour.

SAMUEL F. B. MORSE.

EDISON PERFECTING THE FIRST PHONOGRAPH

The phonograph, one of the most wonderful discoveries of the nineteenth century, was, in a measure, the result of chance, that of Edison's accidentally perceiving a vibration due to an electric current. But it was one of the chances of which only great minds avail themselves. By its aid the words and voices of this century may be heard ten or twenty centuries in the future.

Eastern, the former ocean marvel, and fitly typifies the progress of the century. As will be remembered the *Great Eastern* proved a failure, while the *Oceanic* is a pronounced success.

Important as has been the invention of the steamboat, it is much surpassed by that of the locomotive and the railroad, which have increased the ease, cheapness, and rapidity of land travel and freight transportation far more than steam navigation has increased traffic by water. While the sailing vessel falls short of the steamship as an aid to commerce, the difference between the two is very much less than that between the horse and the locomotive, the iron rail and the ordinary road, and the railroad has achieved a revolution in transportation equal to that made by the steam engine in manufacture.

The motor engine is, aside from the work of Oliver Evans, already mentioned, solely a result of nineteenth century enterprise. The railroad came earlier, first in the form of tramways of wood; the earliest iron rails being laid in England about 1767. But it was not until after 1800 that an attempt was made to replace the horse by the steam carriage on these roads. Of those who sought to solve this problem, George Stephenson, a poor English workingman, stands decidedly first. While serving as fireman in a colliery, and later as engineer, he occupied himself earnestly in the study of machinery, and as early as 1814 constructed for the colliery a traction engine with two cylinders. This was seated on a boiler mounted on wheels, which were turned by means of chains connected with their axles. It drew eight loaded cars at a speed of four miles an hour. This was a clumsy affair, weak in power, and inefficient in service, but it was much superior to any other engine then in use, and was improved on greatly by his second engine, built the following year, and in which he used the steam blast-pipe. These early engines were not much esteemed, and the horse con- **George Stephen-** tinued to be employed in preference, the first passenger rail- **son and the** road, the Stockton and Darlington, opened in 1825, being run **Locomotive** by horse-power. Meanwhile Stephenson continued to work on the locomotive, improving it year after year, until his early ventures were far surpassed in efficiency by his later. A French engineer, M. Seguin, in 1826, successfully introduced locomotives in which improved appliances for increasing the draught were employed. At that time, indeed, inventors seem to have been actively engaged on this problem, and when the Liverpool and Manchester Railway, begun in 1825, offered premiums for the best engines to be run at high speed, a number of applicants appeared. The premium was easily won, in 1830, by Stephenson's "Rocket," the most effective locomotive yet produced. This antediluvian affair, as it would appear to-day, weighed only 4¼ tons, but was able to draw a load of 17 tons at an average speed of fourteen miles an hour, sometimes reaching seventeen miles. When

The Perform- ance of the "Rocket" run alone it attained thirty miles an hour, to the amazement and admiration of the public. It is to George Stephenson we owe the locomotive as an effective piece of mechanism. "He found it inefficient," says Smiles, "and he made it powerful, efficient and useful."

While these events were taking place in England and France, the new idea had taken root in America, and the inventors and engineers of the United States set themselves to the development of the problem. Short lines of railway, for horse traction, were laid at early dates, the first locomotive, the "Stourbridge Lion," being imported from England and placed on a short line at Honesdale, Pa., in 1829. The Baltimore and Ohio, the first passenger railroad in the United States, was begun in 1830, and on it was tried the earliest American-built locomotive, the production of Peter Cooper, the celebrated philanthropist of later years. This was a toy affair,

First American Railroads and Locomotives with a three and a half inch cylinder, an upright tubular boiler made of old gun barrels, and a fan blower to increase the draught. Its weight was two and a half tons. Yet it did not lack speed, making the run from Baltimore to Ellicott's Mills, twenty-seven miles, in an hour. But the first serviceable American locomotive was the "Best Friend," built at West Point, N. Y., and run on the Charleston and Hamburg Road, in South Carolina, in 1830, shortly after Stephenson's "Rocket" had been tried. The "Best Friend" could make more than thirty miles an hour, and could draw a train of four or five coaches, with forty to fifty passengers, at twenty miles an hour. It was inferior to the "Rocket," however, in design, and its career came to a sudden end through the zeal of a negro fireman, who sat on the safety valve to stop the escape of steam. The fireman shared the fate of the locomotive.

Such was the railroad as it began,—a microscopic event. To day it is of telescopic magnitude. At the end of 1831 there were less than a hundred miles of railroad in the United States, and probably still fewer

Development of The Railroad elsewhere. At the end of the century this country alone had over 180,000 miles of railroad, while there were single railroad systems with more than 8000 miles of track. In the whole world there were about 450,000 miles of road,—only two and a half times the mileage of the United States.

As for the development of the locomotive, the railroad carriage, the track, etc., it has been enormous, and sixty miles an hour for passenger trains is now a common speed, while the numbers of people and tons of freight transported annually by the railroads of the world are incredibly great. We cannot here undertake to describe the notable feats of engineering which have carried railroads over rivers and chasms, over mountains impassable otherwise except by sure-footed mules, across deserts too hot and dry even for mule trains. "No heights seem too great to-day, no valleys too deep, no cañons too forbidding, no streams too wide; if commerce demands it the engineer will respond and the railways will be built." The railroad bridges of the country would make a continuous structure from New York to San Francisco, and include many of the boldest and most original, as well as the longest and highest, bridges in the world. The pioneer railroad suspension bridge at Niagara Falls was as remarkable in its day for boldness and originality as for dimensions and success. **Great Railroad Bridges** A single span of 821 feet, supported by four cables, carried the track 245 feet above the river that rushed beneath. The cables were supported by masonry towers, whose slow disintegration gave occasion for an engineering feat even more notable than the original construction of the bridge. The first railroad bridge across the Ohio was at Steubenville, completed in 1866; the first iron bridge over the Upper Mississippi was the Burlington bridge of 1869. The first great bridge across the Mississippi was Eads' magnificent structure at St. Louis, whose beautiful steel arches of over 500 feet span each give no hint of the difficult problems that had to be solved before a permanent bridge was possible at that point. It was completed in 1874. Since then the great river has been frequently bridged for railroads, while its great branch, the Missouri, has been crossed by bridges in a dozen places.

The steam railroad has been supplemented by the electric street railway, which at the close of the century was being extended at a highly promising rate. Passenger travel in cities by aid of the horse railway was inaugurated about the middle of the century, the horse beginning to be replaced by the electric motor in 1881, when the first railway of this character was laid in Berlin. A second was laid in Ireland in 1883. But the electric steel railway has made its greatest progress in the United States, where the first line went into operation at Richmond, Va., in 1888. This adopted the overhead trolly system, since so widely employed, and the length of line had increased to over 3,000 miles in 1892 and 15,000 miles in 1897. Since that date the progress of electric **The Electric Steel Railway** railways has been enormous, they being extended from the cities far into the country, where they come into active competion with the steam roads. Electric locomotives are also in use, and the twentieth century is likely to see a development of electric traction which will have the whole earth for its field, and may perhaps displace the steam road, the great triumph in transportation of the nineteenth century.

Other recent devices for swift travel are the bicycle, which came extraordinarily into use during the last quarter of the century, and the automobile carriage, whose era only fairly began as the century reached its end. It is

The Bicycle and the Automobile

in the direction of the latter and of aërial travel that the twentieth century will perhaps achieve its most notable triumphs in this field. As for the horse, man's most useful servant at the beginning of the century, it was rapidly being displaced at the end, and may during the century to come cease to be employed in the service of man.

The story of railroading leads naturally to that of progress in iron and steel work generally, which has been extraordinary during the century. Of inventions in this direction perhaps the most notable is the Bessemer steel-making process, which converts iron into steel by the direct addition of the necessary quantity of carbon, and has had the important result of making steel cheaper to-day than iron was not very many years ago. In iron-working machinery the progress has been very great, and in no other field has the genius of the American inventor been more conspicuously dis-

Marvels in Iron and Wood-working

played. The same may be said of wood-working machinery, in which the most clever mechanism is employed. The result is that many articles in metal and wood, of the most varied and useful kinds, formerly almost unattainable by the rich, are now within the easy reach of the poor, and the comfort and convenience of common life to-day are enormously in advance of those enjoyed by our ancestors of a century ago.

As it is impossible to name all the inventions which conduce to this increase in convenience, it will perhaps suffice to name one alone, the friction match, that most useful of small contrivances, which has relegated into the museum of antiquities the slow and clumsy flint and steel to which the world was for centuries confined. This invention, gradually developed in various countries, owes its cheapness largely to the invention of an American, whose patent, taken out in 1836, first made possible the production of phosphorus matches on a large scale.

Mention of the friction match opens to us one broad vista of nineteenth century progress, too great to be more than glanced at. This embraces the replacement of wood by coal for heating purposes, the development of the stove, the furnace, the coal-burning grate, and various conveniences of like character. As regards the tallow candle, which was in common use during the first third of the century, it seems as antiquated now as the pyramids. Various kinds of oil succeeded it as illuminants, until the discovery of petroleum set them all aside, and gave the world one of its most useful natural products. Then came the illuminating gas, and finally the wonderful electric light, whose brilliant glow lighted up the threshold of the twentieth century. Petroleum, gas and electricity are also beginning to replace coal for heating and cooking purposes,—as coal replaced wood,—and an outlook into the future seems to reveal to us the marvelous electric energy performing these and a thousand other services; this energy yielded, not as now, by costly fuel dug from the earth, but by power derived from falling water, from moving air, from swelling tides and flowing currents, and even from the direct light and heat of the sun. **Progress in Illumination and Heating**

We cannot undertake to describe in detail the inventions of the century, even all those of great service to mankind. A mere inventory of these would more than fill this chapter, and we must confine ourselves to the notable ones of American origin. Among the most important of these may be named the sewing machine, a device gradually approached through a century of effort, but not made workable until a poor mechanic named Elias Howe attacked the problem, and worked it out through years of penury and disappointment. It was **Howe and the Sewing Machine** the lock-stitch and shuttle to which he owed his success, but these devices, patented by him in 1846, were pirated by wealthy corporations, and years of litigation were necessary before he gained his rights. He finally obtained a royalty of five dollars for each machine made up to 1860, and, after the renewal of his patent in that year, one dollar for each machine. The numbers produced were sufficient to make him very wealthy, and by the time the original patents expired, in 1877, over six million machines had been produced and sold by American manufacturers alone. Aside from the vast number of sewing machines now used in families, those used in factories are estimated to give employment, throughout the world, to over 20,000,000 women.

Another American invention of the greatest utility is that of vulcanized India-rubber, the production of a poor man named Charles Goodyear, who, like Howe, spent years of his life and endured semi-starvation while persistently experimenting. Beginning in 1834, it was 1839 before, after innumerable failures, he discovered the secret of vulcanizing the rubber by means of sulphur. Before that date **Goodyear and the Vulcanization of Rubber** the softening effect of heat rendered rubber practically useless, but the vulcanized rubber produced by Goodyear was, before his death in 1860, applied to nearly five hundred purposes, and gave employment to 60,000 persons in Europe and the United States. Since then its utility has very greatly increased, and its recent employment for bicycle and carriage tires opens up a new field for its use which must enormously increase the demand.

Another of the famous inventions of the century, the electric telegraph, usually attributed to Samuel Finley Morse, should really be credited to the labors of several scientists both in Europe and America. The merit

Morse and the Telegraph

of Morse lay, not in the discovery of the principle of electric telegraphy, but in his simplified telegraphic alphabet, which has nearly driven out all other devices and has made its way throughout the world. Morse's first line, completed in 1844, was the pioneer of a development analogous to that of the railroad. To-day the telegraph runs over all continents and under almost all seas, the length of the telegraph lines in the world at the end of the century being over 5,000,000 miles, of which more than half were in America. The telephone—the marvelous talking telegraph—invented by Alexander Bell and developed in the final quarter of the century, now has over half a million miles of wire in the United States.

The mention of the telegraph and telephone calls to our attention one of the ablest and most prolific of American inventors, the indefatigable Thomas Alva Edison, to whom are due important discoveries in multiplex telegraphy—the sending of various messages at once over a single wire—in

The Inventions of Edison

telephony, in the incandescent electric light, and other fields of research. Most surprising of his many discoveries is the marvelous phonograph, by which the sounds of the human voice may be put on permanent record, to speak again in their original tones years or centuries hence.

Other inventors have been active in this field, and extraordinary progress has been made in systems of telegraphy, some of the new inventions being capable of remarkable feats in the rapid sending of messages, while it is possible now to transmit pictures as well as words over the telegraphic wire.

So vast, indeed, has been the advance in this field of practical science, so many the applications and devices employed, and so wonderful the results, that it seemed as if the powers of telegraphy must be exhausted, when, at the very end of the century, one of its most remarkable results was announced, as the discovery of a young Italian named Marconi. This was the method of "wireless telegrapy," the sending of messages through the air without the aid of connecting wires. This discovery, like most others, cannot be credited to one man alone.   A number of scientists were experimenting with it simultaneously, but to Marconi is due the honor of a successful and practical solution of the problem.   It has long been known that electric energy can produce effects through space by the influence known as induction, in which a moving current causes a reverse **Marconi and** current to appear in a neighboring wire.   By aid of the **Wireless** very powerful currents now produced this effect may be shown **Telegraphy** at a considerable distance.   Whether the action in wireless telegraphy is the result of induction, or of a direct passage of electricity through space, must be left for scientists to decide, but the results are astonishing, messages having been sent and received over distances of many miles.   It is not well to state how many miles, since the system is still in its infancy, and before many years have elapsed, for all that can now be affirmed to the contrary, a message may be sent in this manner from America to Europe.

Wireless telegraphy is a combination of science and invention.   Scientifically the electric waves appear to flow out through the air in all directions from the powerful currents employed.   Mechanically a lofty pole seems necessary, and it may become possible, by a directive contrivance, to send the waves in a fixed course.   In the Marconi contrivance, the electric waves, when received, are made to pass through a vial containing metal filings, which are caused to cohere so as to furnish a direct line of passage for the current. Marconi's special invention is a small tapper which strikes the vial of filings and causes them to fall asunder, thus breaking the current.   The public at large, however, is likely to be more interested in results than methods, and in the system of wireless telegraphy there is promise of a development that may supplant all existing telegraphic systems during the century upon whose threshold we stand.

In no field of effort have inventors been more active or their results more useful than in the production of labor-saving devices in agriculture. In these we have to do with the yield of food, the very corner-stone of life itself, and whatever seems to increase the product of the fields, **Labor=saving** or to cheapen the necessaries of life, is of the most direct and **Agricultural** immediate utility to mankind.   This subject, therefore, one of **Implements** vital interest to all the farmers of our country, calls for special notice here.

Great inventions are not necessarily large or costly.   The scythe is a simple and inexpensive tool ; yet the practical perfecting of it by Joseph Jenks, almost at the outset of farm-life in New England, formed an epoch-mark in agriculture.   It was the beginning of a new order of things.   Putting curved fingers to the improved scythe-blade and snath did for the harvester what had been done for the grass-cutter, gave him an implement which doubled or trebled his efficiency at a critical season, and furnished in

Early Farming Tools the American grain cradle a farm-tool perfect of its kind, and likely to hold its place as long as grain is grown on uneven ground. For the great bulk of grain and grain-cutting, the scythe and the cradle have been displaced by later American inventions,— mowers and harvesters, operated by animal or steam power,—still they are likely to remain forever a part of every farm's equipment. Their utility is beyond computation.

The plow supplied to the Colonial farmers, was as venerable as the reaping-hook. It had been substantially unimproved for four thousand years. The moment our people were free to manufacture for themselves, they set about its improvement in form and material, the very first patent granted by the National Patent Office being for an improved plow of cast-iron. The best plow then in use was a rude affair, clumsily made, hard to guide, and harder to draw. It had a share of wrought iron, roughly shaped by the roadside black-smith, a landside and standard of wood, and an ill-shaped mould-board plated with tin, sheet iron, or worn-out saw-plates. Only a stout man could hold it, and a yoke of oxen was needed for work that a colt can do with a modern plow. Its improvement engaged the attention of many inventors, notably President Jefferson, who experimented with various forms and made a mathematical investigation of the shape of the mould-board, to determine the form best suited for the work. He was the first to discover the importance of straight lines from the sole to the top of the share and mould-board. Pinckney discovered the value of a straight line from front to rear. Jethro Wood discovered that all lines, from front to rear, should be straight. The method of drafting the lines, on a plane surface, in designing plows, is due to Knox. The discovery of the importance of the centre-draught, and the practical means of attaining it by the

The Development of the American plow inclination of the landside inward, is credited to Mears. Governor Holbrook, of New Hampshire, devised the method of making plows of any size symmetrical, so as to ensure the complete pulverization of the soil. Col. Randolph, Jefferson's son-in-law, "the best farmer in Virginia," invented a side-hill plow. Smith was the first to hitch two plows together; and Allen, by combining a number of small plow-points in one implement, led the way to the production of the infinite variety of horse-hoes, cultivators, and the like, for special use. But Jethro Wood, of New York, in 1819 and after, probably did more than any other man to perfect the cast-iron plow, and to secure its general use in place of the cumbrous plows of the earlier days. His skill as an inventor, and his pluck as a fighter against stolid ignorance and prejudice, for the advancement of sensible plowing, cost him—what they ought to have gained for him—a fortune. The use of cast-iron plows had become general by 1825.

The construction of plows has since been taken up by a multitude of inventors, the most valuable of improvements, probably, coming through the use of chilled iron, and the most promising from the application of steam-power to plowing. The increase in the working power of the farmer, from American improvements in plows, may be estimated from the fact that two million plowmen, with as many teams, would need to work every day in the year with **Increase of Working Power of the Farmer** the primitive plow to prepare the soil annually under cultivation in this country. It would be impossible, under the ancient system, to do this work within the brief plowing season.

The era of agricultural machinery began about 1825, its earliest phase appearing in the application of horse-power to the threshing and cleaning of grain. Already the American tendency to seek practical results by the simplest means, and to make high-priced labor profitable by increasing its efficiency, had been shown in the improvement of a wide range of farmer's tools, almost everything they had to use being made lighter, neater, and more serviceable. The same improving, practical sense was displayed in devising more complicated labor-saving machines, which made it possible to do easily and directly what had been previously difficult or quite impossible to do. Too often, however, the early inventor was defeated by the lack of skilled labor and proper machine tools for making his improvements commercially successful. As soon as the mechanic arts had been sufficiently perfected and extended—largely by American genius—the development and production of agricultural machinery became rapid and profitable.

Washington had tried a sort of threshing machine as early as 1798; and one of the first patents issued by the Patent Office was for an improved thresher; yet the flail held the field until after 1825. In the following twenty-five years over two hundred patents were granted for improvements in threshers, and since then the patents have numbered thousands. By 1840, most of the grain was threshed by horse-driven machinery. In 1853, when a famous trial of rival threshers was held in England, the American machine did **Threshing Machines and Their Performance** three times as much as the best English machine, and did it better. In a subsequent trial in France, the average work of experts with the flail being reckoned as one, that of the best French machine was twenty-five; of the best English machine, forty-one; while Pitt's American machine did the work of seventy-four. The application of steam-power greatly increased the efficiency of threshing machines, raising the output from perhaps 2,000 bushels a day to six or seven thousand for a single machine.

Still more significant and important have been the victories of American inventors in connection with mowers and reapers. The circumstance that reaping by machinery is as old as the Christian era, and that a multitude of comparatively modern attempts have been made, particularly in England, to apply horse-power to the cutting of grass and grain, only added to the merit of inventors like Hussey and McCormick, who practically solved the problems involved by means so simple and efficient that they have not been and are likely never to be entirely displaced.

The American Reapers and Mowers Hussey's mowing machine of 1833 had reciprocating knives working through slotted fingers, a feature not only new but essential to all practical grass and grain cutters, except the special type known as lawn-mowers. McCormick patented a combination reaper and mower in 1834, which he subsequently so improved as to make it the necessary basis of all reapers. In competitive trials at home and abroad, the American mowers and reapers have never failed to demonstrate their superiority over all others.

The first great victory, which gave these machines the world-wide fame they have so successfully maintained, was won in London in 1851. In the competitive trial near Paris, in 1855, the American machine cut an acre of oats in twenty-two minutes; the English in sixty-six minutes; the French in seventy-two. In the later competition, local and international, their superior efficiency has been not less signally manifested. By increasing the efficiency of the harvester twenty-fold (and twice that by the self-binders), these products of American invention have played a part second only to railroads in opening up the West to profitable cultivation, rapidly converting a wilderness into the granary of the world. Devices for binding grain as it was cut began to be developed about 1855.

Harvesters and Self-binders The first machine used wire binders; the later twine. The combination of reapers and threshers in one machine has been most largely developed in California. The largest in use there weighs eight tons; and, pushed by thirty mules, cuts a swath twenty-two feet wide and eighteen miles long in a day—over forty-eight acres, yielding about as many tons of wheat, which is cut, threshed, cleaned and deposited in 700 sacks. The machine employs a driver, a shearer, a knife-tender, and a sack-lowerer —four men, costing eight dollars a day for wages.

Less important individually, yet in the aggregate of incalculable assistance to agriculture, have been a multitude of American inventions intended to expedite and lighten the farmer's work—stump and stone extractors for clearing the ground, ditching machines for drainage systems, fencing devices, particularly the barbed wire fence, special plows for breaking up new ground, harrows of many types, seeders, planters, culti- **The Great** vators, horse rakes, hay tedders and hay loaders, potato and **Variety of** rock diggers, corn huskers and shellers, cotton pickers, and **Agricultural** **Implements** countless other labor-saving tools and devices. In most cases these improved appliances enable one man to do easily the work of several working with primitive tools. With the help of machine planters and seeders the farmer's work is made at least five times more efficient; with cultivators, ten times; with potato diggers, twenty; with harrowers, thirty; with mowers and harvesters, from twenty to fifty; with corn huskers and shellers, a hundred. The latest cotton harvester, employing a team, a driver, and a helper, does the work of forty hand-pickers.

These agricultural machines, by greatly cheapening all food products, have had a wider influence, probably, than any other group of American inventions. In connection with improvements in means of transportation— largely of American origin—they have changed the food conditions of half the world, making food more abundant, more varied, more wholesome, more secure, and vastly cheaper than ever before. At the same time they have lightened the farmer's labor, shortened his hours of toil, increased his gains, and quite transformed his social and industrial position.

The marvelous evolution in the nineteenth century, of which we have mentioned only some of the more notable particulars, the whole story being far too voluminous to deal with here, has had the result of immensely increas- ing the wealth of the world and the cheapness and rapid distribution of pro- ducts, and of placing within the ready control of mankind hundreds of articles of art and utility scarcely dreamed of a century ago. In textile production, in metal working, in the making of furniture, clothing and other articles of ordinary use, in heating and illumination, in travel and transporta- tion of goods, farm operations, engineering, mining and **Productive** excavation, and the production of the tools of peace and the **Activity of the** weapons of war, in ways, indeed, too numerous to mention, the **Nineteenth** **Century** inventive activity and the industrial energy of the nineteenth century have added enormously to the variety and abundance of useful objects at man's disposal, increased his wealth to an extraordinary extent, and enabled him to move over land and sea with marvelous ease and speed, and to send information around the world with a rapidity that almost annihilates time and space.

Not the least among the results of modern mechanical progress is the vast development in commerce, and particularly in that of the Anglo-Saxon people—the inhabitants of Great Britain and the United States—the commercial enterprise of which countries is nowhere else equalled. The ocean commerce of the United States, for instance, has nearly doubled within thirty years, and now amounts to nearly $2,000,000,000 worth of goods annually, two-thirds of which are articles of export. But this great sum **Commerce of the** is far from indicating the actual commerce of this country, **United States** since it is greatly surpassed by its interior commerce, the movement of goods by aid of river, canal, and railroad from part to part of the vast area of the United States, the extent of which commerce it is impossible even to estimate.

The statement of a single fact will suffice to put in striking prominence the result of this in increasing the value of property and the wealth of the people of this country. In the year 1801, the opening year of the century, the ideas entertained of riches differed remarkably from what they do now. At that time it is doubtful if there was a person in this country worth more than a quarter million of dollars. Thirty years afterwards, Stephen Girard, with an estate of about nine million dollars, was looked upon as a prodigy of wealth, and his reputation as a man of immense riches spread round the world. In 1900, the closing year of the century, there were single estates worth more than two hundred million dollars, and the number of millionaires in the United States could be counted **Wealth and its** by the hundreds. As regards the largest estates possessed **Sources** in 1801, there are thousands among us with greater wealth to-day, while the general average of property possessed by our citizens has very greatly advanced.

If it be asked in what this wealth consists, it may be said that the railroad property of the country alone suffices to account for a considerable proportion of it. The assets of the railroads of the United States are valued at over $12,000,000,000, and the annual profits of their business amounts to a very great sum. Another immense source of wealth is the landed property of the United States, the annual product of which alone is worth over $3,000,000,000. A third great element of wealth consists in the dwellings and other buildings of cities and towns; and a fourth in the buildings and machinery of manufacturing enterprises, whose annual products alone are valued at more than $10,000,000,000. It will suffice here to name a fifth great source of wealth, our mines and their productions, particularly those of coal, iron and precious metals. The annual yield of coal alone is worth more than $200,000,000; that of iron more than $90,000,000; those of gold and silver more than $100,000,000. To these may be added an annual production of nearly $60,000,000 worth of copper, and as much of petroleum and its products—each of which nearly equals gold in value,—$12,000,000 worth of lead, and large values of other minerals; the grand total being over $750,000,000.

If these figures should be extended to cover the world, the total sum of values would be something astounding. What we are principally concerned with here is the fact that this vast total of wealth is **Expansion of** very largely the result of nineteenth century enterprise, and **Values During** mainly as applied in Europe and the northern section of North **the Century** America. What the percentage of increase in value has been it is quite impossible to state, but the wealth of the world as a whole is probably more than double what it was a century ago, while that of such expanding countries as the United States has increased in a vastly greater proportion. That this growth in wealth will go on during the twentieth century cannot be doubted, but that the proportionate rate of increase will equal that of the century now at its end may well be questioned, the inventive activity and application of nature's forces within this century having reached a development which seems to preclude as great a future rate of progress. The nineteenth may, therefore, perhaps remain the banner century in material progress.

CHAPTER XXXVIII.

The Evolution in Industry and the Revolt Against Capital.

INDUSTRY in the past centuries was a strikingly different thing from what it has been in the recent period. For a century it has been passing through a great process of evolution, which has by no means reached its culmination, and whose final outcome no man can safely predict.

For a long period during the mediæval and the subsequent centuries industry existed in a stable condition, or one whose changes were few and **The Conditions of Mediæval Industry** none of them revolutionary. Manufacture was in a large sense individual. The great hive of industry known as a factory did not exist, workshops being small and every expert mechanic able to conduct business as a master. Employees were mainly apprentices, each of whom expected to become a master mechanic, or, if he chose to work for a master, did so with an independence that no longer exists. The workshop was usually a portion of the dwelling, where the master worked with his apprentices, teaching them the whole art and mystery of his craft, and giving them knowledge of a complete trade, not of a minor portion of one as in our day.

The trade-union had its prototype in the guild. But this was in no sense a combination of labor for protection against capital, but of master workmen to protect their calling from being swamped by invasion from without. In truth, when we go back into the past centuries, it is to find ourselves in another world of labor, radically different from that which surrounds us to-day.

It was the steam-engine that precipitated the revolution. This great invention rendered possible labor-saving machinery. From working directly upon the material, men began to work indirectly through the **The Cause of the Revolution in the Labor System** medium of machines. As a result the old household industries rapidly disappeared. Engines and machines needed special buildings to contain them and large sums of money to purchase them, the separation of capital and labor began, and the nineteenth century opened with the factory system fully launched upon the world.

The century with which we are concerned is the one of vast accumulations of capital in single hands or under the control of companies, the concentration of labor in factories and workshops, the extraordinary development of labor-saving machines, the growth of monopolies on the one hand and of labor unions on the other, the revolt of labor against the tyranny of capital, the battle for shorter hours and higher wages, the coming of woman into the labor field as a rival of man, the development of economic theories and industrial organizations, and in still **Present Aspect** other ways the growth of a state of affairs in the world of **of the Labor** industry that had no counterpart in the past, and which we **Question** hope may not extend far into the future, since it involves a condition of anarchy, injustice, and violence that is certainly not calculated to advance the interests of mankind.

In past times wealth was largely accumulated in the hands of the nobility, who had no thought of using it productively. Such of it as lay under the control of the commonalty was applied mainly for commercial purposes and in usury, and comparatively little was used in manufacture. This state of affairs came somewhat suddenly to an end with the invention of the steam-engine and of labor-saving machinery. Capital was largely diverted to purposes of manufacture, wealth grew **A Revolution** rapidly as a result of the new methods of production, the **In Industry** making of articles cheaply required costly plants in buildings and machinery which put it beyond the reach of the ordinary artisan, the old individuality in labor disappeared, the number of employers largely diminished and that of employees increased, and the mediæval guild vanished, the workmen finding themselves exposed to a state of affairs unlike that for which their old organizations were devised.

A radically new condition of industrial affairs had come, and the industrial class was not prepared to meet it. Everywhere the employers became supreme and the men were at their mercy. Labor was dismayed. Its unions lost their industrial character and resumed their original form of purely benevolent associations. Such was the state of affairs in the early years of the nineteenth century. Industry was in a stage of transition, and inevitably suffered from the change. It was only at a later date that the idea of mutual aid in industry revived, and the trade union—a new form of association adapted to the new situation—arose as the lineal successor of the old society of artisans.

The trade union resembles the old industrial association in general character, and in modes of action, but is much more extensive and concentrated in organization and far-seeing in management, in accordance with the vast expansion of industries and the changed relations of the workingman. The new form of association was not welcomed by the employers, who scented danger afar. They attacked it in the press, in the **The Trade Union** legislature, and by every means at their command. But the trade union had come to stay, hostile legislation failed to destroy it, and the opposition of employers to check its growth. It slowly, but steadily advanced, increased in strength and unity of purpose, gained legislative recognition, and in time became a legally protected institution and one of the powerful forces in modern industry.

The trade union had its origin in England, in which country the modern conditions of industry rapidly gained a great development. It appeared in a crude form near the end of the eighteenth century, one of the earliest societies known being the "Institution," established by the cloth-workers of Halifax in 1796. Many other unions were formed during the first twenty years of the nineteenth century, in spite of persecution and attempts at repression. It was not until 1825, however, that they gained legal recognition, and not until 1871 that they obtained permanent protection for their property and funds. Some of the earlier unions still survive, though many changes have taken place in their constitution.

In 1850 a new departure was taken, in the formation of the Amalgamated Society of Engineers, one of the most perfect types of a trade union in the world. It is organized for the mutual benefit of its members as well as for protection against oppression by employers, and the annual tax upon **Progress and** its members for various purposes amounts to as much as **Purpose of** $15.00 per year, often more. Others of the same character **the Unions** followed, and in all there are about 2,000 trade unions in Great Britain and Ireland, with a membership of nearly 2,250,000, and an annual income of about $10,000,000.

The purposes of the union are various. The mutual aid and benefit feature is secondary to the protective purpose, which is to secure the most favorable conditions of labor that can be obtained. This includes efforts to raise wages and to prevent their fall, reduction of hours of labor and prevention of their increase, the regulation of apprentices, overtime, piecework, and many other difficulties which arise in the complicated relations of labor and capital.

It is generally acknowledged that the trade union has reached its highest state of organization and power in Great Britain, and that the British workman, in consequence, controls the situation more fully than in any other country. This form of organization has only of late years appeared on the continent of Europe, freedom to combine having been denied

THE HERO OF THE STRIKE, COAL CREEK, TENN.

In 1892 a period of great labor agitation began, lasting for several years.   One of the most heroic figures of those troublesome times is Colonel Anderson, under a flag of truce, meeting the infuriated miners at Coal Creek.

ARBITRATION

The relations of capital and labor—both selfish and often unjust—have caused serious trouble in the past decade of the world's history. Fair and equitable arbitration seems to be the only safe and just way of settling disputes of this character.

to workmen in most countries until late in the century. There are excellent unions in the Australian colonies, both these and those of the mother country being superior in organization and influence to the trade unions of the United States, though those of the latter country have gained much in power and cohesion in recent years.

The first great combination of all trades was the International Workingmen's Association, founded in London in 1847, and intended to combine the industrial classes throughout Europe. Dr. Karl Marx gave it a definite organization on the continent in 1864, but it was there warped widely from its original purpose, became a field for anarchists, and came to an end in 1872. In the United States a general organization called the Knights of Labor was formed in 1869, and at one time had a membership of a million, but has now greatly decreased, being largely replaced by the American Federation of Labor, an association of trade unions of very large membership. Of single trade organizations probably the most powerful in this country is the Brotherhood of Carpenters and Joiners, with more than 60,000 members. The International Typographical Union, the oldest in America, has a membership of over 40,000, and there are many others of great strength.

The International Workingmen's Association

The weapon of offense with which the labor organization seeks to gain its ends is the strike, in which the artisans quit work for the purpose of forcing employers to grant their demands, and endeavor to prevent others from taking their place. The reverse of this is the lock-out, an expedient adopted by capitalists for the purpose of obliging workmen to yield to their demands.

During the century under consideration strikes have been very numerous both in England and America, many of them of great dimensions and serious results. It must suffice to speak of some of the more important of those within the United States. In 1803 occurred a strike of sailors in New York, often spoken of as the first strike in this country, though there seem to have been several in the preceding century. A strike of Philadelphia shoemakers took place in 1805 and one of New York cordwainers in 1809, while as time went on strikes became frequent, with varying results of success and failure. Violence was at times resorted to, and in the early days strikers were tried for conspiracy. As population increased and labor associations became stronger, strikes grew greatly in dimensions, and were frequently attended with bloodshed and destruction. Such was the case with the famous railroad strike of 1877, which interrupted traffic over great part of the country for a week, and resulted in acts of sanguinary violence at

The System of the Strike

Pittsburg.   There a lawless mob joined the strikers, the militia were
attacked and lives were lost, and the railroad buildings
Great American and cars were burned, the total loss being estimated at
Strikes $5,000,000.   The coal miners of Pennsylvania joined the
strike, and in all about 150,000 men stopped work.

Since that date strikes have been very numerous and some of them of
great proportions.   Among these, one of the most notable was that which
began in Chicago on May 1, 1886, in which fully 40,000 men took part.   On
the 4th, when the disorder was at its height, a meeting of Anarchists was held,
in the streets, which the police attempted to disperse on account of the violent
and threatening language used.   While doing so a dynamite bomb was
thrown in their midst, which killed several and wounded about sixty of the
officers.   This action was denounced by workingmen throughout the
country and excited general horror and detestation.

Another serious strike took place at the Carnegie Steel-Works, at
Homestead, Pa., in 1892, which was also attended with bloodshed, the
workmen firing on a force of detectives hired to protect the works.   The
disturbance became so great that the whole military force of Pennsylvania
had to be called out.   Two years afterwards Chicago was the scene of a great
railroad strike, directed against the Pullman Car Works of that city.   The
movement of trains was greatly interfered with, and in the end President
Cleveland sent United States troops to Chicago to maintain order and protect the movement of the mails.

That the difficulty between capital and labor will ever be settled by the
strike and the lock-out cannot be expected, though these methods of warfare
have had the effect of producing some degree of wholesome fear on both
sides, and of rendering each more likely to offer concessions
Arbitration and than to indulge in a costly and doubtful strife.   A disposition
Profit Sharing to replace violent measures by peaceful arbitration is growing up, while in some instances employers have agreed to share a portion of
their profits with their employees.   This system of profit sharing, origi-
nating in France, has been extended to other countries, and appears to have
proved very generally successful.   Workmen act as if they were real
partners in the business, and had their own interests to serve.   They do
more and better work, and are more careful in the use of tools and materials, so that in some instances the increased profit arising from their
carefulness and diligence has covered their share of the proceeds, leaving
that of their employers undiminished.   Strikes have almost ceased to exist
in such institutions, and the future of profit-sharing is full of promise.

But expedients which leave the existing system practically unchanged can have only a temporary and partial utility. The cause of the difficulty appears to lie deeper and to call for more radical changes. It is not easy to believe that a system of perpetual protest and frequent strife is a natural one, and it seems as if it must in the future be replaced by some more peaceful and satisfactory relation between capital and labor. During the nineteenth century the labor problem has given rise to a number of experiments and theories looking towards its solution, an account of which is here in place.

Experiments and Theories in Economics

The chief of the experiments alluded to is that of co-operation, the association of workingmen as producers, a democratic organization of labor calculated, if successfully instituted, to bring the present system to an end, and replace it by one in which the division into employer and employee, capitalist and artisan, will cease to exist, each workman embracing both of these in his single person, the combined property of the group representing the capital of the concern and the profits being equitably divided. This seemingly promising solution of the problem has not hitherto proved satisfactory in practice. In most cases experience and skill in management have been wanting, and the placing of ambitious and influential members of the association in the positions of business manager and financier, regardless of their adaptation to these duties, has wrecked more than one promising co-operative concern.

But while most of such manufacturing associations of workingmen have failed, some have succeeded, and the story of the latter seems to show that there is nothing false in the principle, the failure being due to the results of injudicious management, as above indicated. The successful associations have accumulated large capital, pay good dividends, and are noted for the honesty of their operations and the unusual industry of their members, each of whom feels that the profit from increased or superior product will come to himself. Of

Co-operative Associations

co-operative institutions now in existence, the most famous is that of the Rochdale Pioneers, founded at Rochdale, England, in 1844. This association, organized by twenty-eight poor weavers with a capital of twenty-eight pounds, at first as a distributive enterprise, is now a rich and flourishing institution, which adds manufacturing to its distributive interests.

At first these poor pioneers, who had very slowly collected their small capital of one pound each, opened a store to supply themselves with provisions, having only four articles to sell—flour, butter, sugar and oatmeal. They limited interest on shares to five per cent., and divided profits among members in proportion to their purchases, a system which proved highly advantageous. From the first this organization was successful, and by 1857 it had 1,850 members, a capital of £15,000, and annual sales of £80,000. Since then its growth has continued rapid, and it is now in a high state of prosperity.

There were co-operative societies in Great Britain long before the date of this, and many have been started since, nearly all of them being in the form of co-operative stores, of which the Army and Navy Stores are among the most flourishing. There are now in that country probably over 1,500 of these associations, with a million of members, a capital of more than £10,000,000, and profits of over £3,000,000 annually. In 1864 there was founded at Manchester a Wholesale Society to supply goods to these stores, and a second at Glasgow in 1869—the two being now practically one institution. This society purchases and forwards goods, and owns a number of steamships of its own, which traffic with cities on the continent. Its manufacturing industries are also large, including boot and shoe factories at Leicester, soap works at Durham, woolen-cloth mills at Batley, and other factories elsewhere. There are in addition mills and factories carried on by retail societies, the annual production by these associations being probably considerably over £5,000,000. It will be perceived from the above statement that the workmen's co-operative enterprises in Great Britain comprise one of the important institutions of the country, one that has become firmly established during the latter half of the nineteenth century, and may grow enormously in importance during the twentieth. It is likely to play a prominent part in the solution of the labor question.

In no other country has this form of association flourished. In France profit-sharing has made a much greater progress, and ordinary co-operation has met with slight success. In Germany and Austria co-operation has **Co-operation in Europe and the United States** taken the form of people's banks. These originated in 1849 at the little town of Delitzsch, in Saxony, and have flourished greatly, there being several thousand societies in the German states, with probably two million members and a very large business. There are also in Germany a considerable number of productive associations and co-operative dairies, while the latter have greatly flourished in Denmark. In Italy the people's banks have made marked progress, and there are several hundred co-operative dairies, bakeries and other enterprises

Co-operation has made no decided progress in the United States, it being most developed in New England, where it takes the form of associations of fishermen, of creameries and banks. In Philadelphia co-operative building societies have provided workmen with more than 100,000 homes.

The co-operative store has not flourished, and associated manufacture has made little progress, though profit-sharing has been introduced into many large stores and factories.

Such is the status of the experimental development in associated manufacturing and distributive enterprise. The theoretical phase of this question has gone much further, and has given rise to an extensive popular movement whose final outcome it is not easy to predict. This is really, in its way, an extension of the co-operative idea, being an attempt to make co-operation national, the entire nation becoming one great co-operative association, and the functions of government being extended to cover production and distribution of the necessaries of life, in addition to its present duties. This theory is most commonly known as **The Theories of** Socialism, though also entitled Nationalism and Collect- **Socialism and** ivism. Its main purpose is industrial reform, but it seeks to **Anarchism** produce by political means what the trade union has attempted to do by non-political agitation. An opposite doctrine, which has many adherents, is known as Anarchism, whose platform contemplates the overthrow of existing institutions and the rebuilding of society from its elements upon the basis of local grouping. This doctrine has attracted to itself much of the ignorant and violent element of the European populations, and has been seriously discredited by the outrages committed by its members. Prominent examples of these were the massacre of the police in Chicago, already mentioned, the excesses of the Commune in Paris, and the acts of violence of the Russian Nihilists. The theory itself is philosophical, even if impracticable, and has been advocated by a number of able men who cannot be charged with its excesses.

Returning to the doctrines of Socialism, it may be said that it was preceded by the conception of Communism, or equal distribution of the proceeds of labor among the members of a community. This has long since passed from the stage of belief to that of experiment, many Communistic societies having been founded in both **Communistic** ancient and modern times. The Essenes, prominent in Pales- **Societies** tine in the time of Christ, were one of the ancient examples. In modern times the United States has been a favorite field for the founding of Communistic societies, probably from the reason that they were less likely to come into conflict with existing institutions than in Europe.

The best known of those societies of a religious character comprise the Dunkers, founded at Ephrata, Pennsylvania, in 1713; the Harmony Society, established in 1824, and still in existence at Economy, near Pittsburg; the Separatist Community, established at Zoar, Ohio, in 1817; the Shakers, first organized at Watervliet, N. Y., in 1774; and the Perfectionists, founded by John H. Noyes, at Putney, Vermont, in 1837. Several others, less well known, might be named, but it must be said that the persistence of several of these organizations has been mainly due to the religious enthusiasm of their members, and is in no sense a proof of the economic correctness of their principle. Many of them require celibacy of their members, while the Perfectionist Society practiced free love until broken up by the strong disapproval of the community.

In addition to these religious experiments in Communism, a number of secular communistic societies have been founded in this country. Prominent among these was that established by Robert Owen, in 1824, at New **Secular Com-** Harmony, Indiana. Every effort was made to promote the **munistic** success of this enterprise, and ten other communities on the **Experiments** same principle were organized elsewhere, but they all failed in a few years, and the Owenite movement came to an end in this country by 1832.

A second example was the celebrated Brook Farm enterprise, first suggested by Dr. Channing, and founded at West Roxbury, Mass., in 1841. It included the most remarkable group of men and women ever embraced in such an undertaking, among its members being Emerson, Hawthorne, Dana, Ripley, Alcott, and other well known literary men. Its business management was anything but practical, and it came to an end in 1847. The form of community suggested by Fourier, the French theorist, was abundantly tried in the United States, where thirty-three communities or "phalanxes" were founded in the years 1842–53. They had all failed by 1855.

The result of these efforts to establish societies where everything shall be in common between the members, of which hundreds have been founded and none persisted for more than a few years, except where sustained by religious fanaticism, does not speak well for the practical nature of communism. The mass of the people have always kept away from it, and its abrogation of the principle of personal reward for personal effort seems likely to prevent its ever becoming successful.

Socialism was originally similar to Communism, but as now understood and advocated differs essentially from it, since the principle of equal division of property or products is no longer maintained. **Development of** Nationalism, or the ownership of all productive property and **Socialism** all manufactures and their products by the nation, with the complete distribution of profits among the people, on the basis of the value to the community of the labor or service of each person, is the existing form of Socialism. Originated and developed within the nineteenth century, it has now become one of the prominent social and political movements of the age, and some brief description of it is here in order.

France is the birth place of Socialism in its primary form. Two writers, Mably and Morelly, advanced a scheme for a communistic reorganization of society about the middle of the eighteenth century, and in 1796 a communistic conspirary to revolutionize the government, organized by a man named Babeuf, at the head of a society called the Equals, was discovered and suppressed. Later arose Robert Owen in England, with his communistic scheme, and St. Simon and Fourier in France, whose plans were only in part communistic. A more properly Socialistic movement was attempted by Louis Blanc in Paris during the revolution of 1848, when national workshops for the industrial classes of France were established. In Paris 150,-000 workmen were employed in these shops, but they were closed after a brief trial. Their failure, it is claimed, was largely the result of bad management. Of recent English Socialistic movements may be named that of Maurice and Kingsley, the originators of Christian Socialism, which continues to exercise an important influence.

After 1850 the socialistic movement temporarily declined in France and Great Britain, but it gained a great impetus in Germany, under the teachings of certain able and skillful advocates. German Socialism first became active in 1863, through the efforts of Ferdinand Lasalle, though it had earlier supporters. He proposed to establish a German workman's republic, with himself as president; but ended his **Lasalle and Karl Marx** career in the following year, being killed in a duel. After his death his system of "social democracy" fell under the control of the notable Karl Marx, a writer of original genius, to whom Socialism as it exists to-day is largely due. The International Association of Workingmen, as reorganized by him in 1864, changed its purpose from an industrial to a political one, and soon became a threatening compound of dangerous elements. It was socialistic in aim, having, below its declared purpose of the protection and emancipation of the working classes, schemes for the abolition of the wages system, the state control of all property, and the grading of compensation for labor on the basis of time occupied, instead of on the more logical basis of ability and industry shown and value of product.

Karl Marx's famous work "Capital," is the ablest and most logical exposition of the socialistic theory yet produced, and has exerted a powerful influence on recent thought. It set in motion a great political and social movement which has grown with extraordinary rapidity, in spite of

repressive laws against it, and has given rise to a large number of volumes
dealing with the subject, some of which have had a phenom-
The Literature enal sale.   The popular little volume entitled " Merrie Eng-
of Socialism   land " is said to have sold to the number of considerably
more than a million copies, while Bellamy's " Looking Backward," which
advocates a communistic organization of society, has had a sale of several
hundred thousands.

In recent years Socialism has spread upward from the working classes
and gained many advocates among the leaders of thought.   It has had a considerable development in all western Europe, and particularly in Germany, in
which country the Socialists form a powerful political party, which as early
as 1887 polled eleven per cent. of the total vote, and gained a considerable
membership in the Reichstag.   By 1890 its vote had so largely increased
that liberalism obtained a majority in the Reichstag.   At the end of the
Growth of the century the Social Democrat party had 56 members in the
Socialist   Reichstag as contrasted with 54 members of the German
Party in   Conservatives.   The remainder of the 396 members were
Germany
divided among a number of parties, the Clericals or Centre
being the strongest, with 104 members.   As will be seen from these figures,
Socialism has made a remarkable advance in that country, having within
less than forty years become a power in Parliament.   The time may come
in the near future when it will be the controlling party in legislature and
government.

In the United States Socialism has grown with less rapidity, yet within
recent years it has sprung into political importance in the rapid growth of
the Populist party, organized in 1892.   This new organization gained five
senators and eleven representatives in Congress in the year of its
origin.   In 1896, while its success was no greater, it had the striking effect
of gaining the adhesion of the Democratic party, not only to the Free Silver
plank in its platform, but to some of its more socialistic features.   There are
The Populist   probably very many citizens of this country of strongly social-
Party in the   istic views who are opposed to the radical measures advocated
United States by the Populists, and the real strength of Socialism in the
United States may be much greater than is commonly supposed.   It is shown
in other directions than that of party affiliation, and at the end of the
century was particularly indicated in the movement for the municipal
ownership of street railways, gas works, and other forms of what are known
as public utilities.   This movement has gone farther in Europe than in this
country, several nations owning their railway and telegraph plants, while
municipal control of street railways and other public utilities is becoming

general. In short, it would be difficult to point to a popular movement in the history of the world that has made a more rapid and substantial advance than has Socialism within the past forty years.

As the nineteenth century approached its end a new element in the economic situation, which had been displaying itself in some measure for a considerable number of years, suddenly assumed a striking prominence in the United States, and remarkably transformed the industrial situation. This was the element of the combination of distributive and manufacturing enterprises, shown at first in the growth of the department stores and the pooling of manufacturing **The Development of the Trust** interests, and later in the formation of trusts and monopolies, powerful corporations of industrial interests, which assumed gigantic proportions in 1898 and the succeeding years.

Several of these great organizations, absorbing all the factories or plants of the special trades concerned into single vast corporations, have been in existence for years. Most prominent of these are the Sugar Trust and the Standard Oil Company, which have eliminated the element of competition from those industries and accumulated their profits in the hands of a few great capitalists.

The complete control of important productive interests gained by these groups of capitalists has instigated those connected with other lines of production to similar methods, and the formation of trusts has gone on at an accelerating ratio, until all the great and many of the minor industries of the country have formed trust organizations, while a large number of establishments have been closed, and thousands of workmen and other employees dismissed.

The result of all this has been to produce a state of affairs in which competition, so long considered the life of trade, is practically eliminated from many branches of industry, while the opportunities for individual enterprise, which have been active for so many centuries, have in great part vanished. An economic situation **Probable Effect of Trusts** seems at hand in which the mass of the community will be obliged to assume the position of employees, the class of employers being reduced to a few very rich men, absorbing the profits of industry and holding the remainder of the community in a condition of galling servitude.

Such an undesirable condition of industrial affairs as is here threatened has naturally aroused a strong feeling of opposition, and the forces of the community are being marshalled to prevent such a radical revolution in industry. Just how the brake is to be applied is not clear. It is not easy to prevent capital from pooling its forces, and legislation may fail to find a remedy which will reach the root of the disease. Yet a cure must come, in one way or the other—the trust movement being either reversed or carried forward to its logical conclusion. It is being widely recognized and acknowledged, even by some of the trust potentates themselves, that the movement thus inaugurated is likely to hasten the advent of socialistic institutions.

To What the Trust Must Lead The abolition of individual enterprise under the trust must eventually become almost as extreme as it would be in a socialistic community, and if the trust movement continues the principal objection to socialism will be removed. It must be evident to all that the tyranny of a group of irresponsible and grasping capitalists, ambitious to obtain enormous wealth, will be much greater than that of officials chosen as the servants of the people, and subject to removal at their will, can ever become.

The Roman despot wished that all the Roman people had but one neck, that he might cut it off with a single blow. Capital is in a measure reducing itself to this condition, and the people may in time cut off its head in a similar manner. It is easier to deal with the few than with the many, and the relation into which capital and labor has now come can have, sooner or later, only one or the other of two endings. As above said, the evolution now in operation must go forward or go backward; go backward until the former state of affairs is regained, or go forward until industrial slavery grows complete, in which case the people will, in the end, inevitably rebel. It is impossible for such a movement to stop half way, one result or the other must inevitably come, either a return to individualism or a progress to collectivism. Which it shall be depends upon the people themselves. The power is in their hands the moment they elect

An Industrial Revolution to cast aside their differences and act in concert, and the presence of a great danger or an intolerable situation is the one thing to bring them to this common action. In such a case it will rest with themselves which status of industry they prefer, the old state of individualism and competition or a new state of collectivism and industrial alliance. Though it is but dimly recognized, the world of industry is in the throes of a revolution, the final result of nineteenth century development, and it must be left for the twentieth century to decide what the outcome of this revolution is to be.

CHAPTER XXXIX.

Charles Darwin and the Development of Science.

SCIENCE by no means belongs to the nineteenth century. It has been extant upon the earth ever since man began to observe and consider the marvels of the universe. We can trace it back to an age possibly ten thousand years remote, when men began to watch and record the movements of the stars in the heavens above the broad Babylonian plain. It grew active among the Greeks of Alexandria in that too brief period before the hand of war checked for centuries the progress of mankind. It rose again in Europe during the mediæval period, and became active during the later centuries of this period. In the centuries immediately preceding the nineteenth numbers of great scientists arose, and many highly important discoveries were made, while theoretical science achieved a remarkable progress, its ranks being adorned by such names as those of Copernicus, Kepler, Galileo, Newton, and various others of world-wide fame that might be given. Thus at the dawn of the nineteenth century there existed a great groundwork of scientific facts and theories upon which to build the massive future edifice.

Progress of Scientific Discovery in the Past

This building has been going on with extraordinary rapidity during the present century, and to-day our knowledge of the facts of science is immensely greater than that of our predecessors of a century ago ; while of the views entertained and theories promulgated previous to 1800, the great sum have been thrown overboard and replaced by others founded upon a much wider and deeper knowledge of facts.

Scientific Activity of the Nineteenth Century

New and important theoretical views of science have been reached in all departments. Recent chemistry, for instance, is a very different thing from the chemistry of a century ago. Geology has been largely transformed within the century. Heat, once supposed to be a substance, is now known to be a motion ; light, formerly thought to be a direct motion of particles, is now believed to be a wave motion ; new and important conceptions have been reached concerning electricity and magnetism ; and our knowledge of the various sciences that have to do with the world of life is extraordinarily advanced. As for the practical applications of science, it may suffice to present the startling fact that the substance of the atmosphere, scarcely known a century ago, can now be reduced to a liquid and carried about like water in a bucket.

In view of the facts here briefly stated it might almost be said that science, as it exists to-day, is a result of nineteenth century thought and observation ; since that of the past was largely theoretical and the bulk of its theories have been set aside, while the scientific observations of former times were but a drop in the bucket as compared with the vast multitude of those of the past hundred years. As regards the utilization of scientific facts, their application to the benefit of mankind, this is almost solely the work of the century under review, and in no direction has invention produced more wonderful and useful results.

Alfred Russell Wallace, one of the most distinguished scientists of recent times, in his work entitled " The Wonderful Century," has made a

Wallace's "Wonderful Century" careful inventory of the discoveries and inventions to which the progress of mankind is mainly due, and he divides them into two groups, the first embracing all the epoch-making discoveries achieved by men previous to the present century, and the second taking in the steps of progress of equal importance which have been made in the nineteenth century. In the first list he finds only fifteen items of the highest rank, and the claims of some even of these to a separate place are not beyond question, since they may not really be of epoch-making character. He puts first in the list the following, viz. : Alphabetic writing and the Arabic notation, which have always been powerful engines of knowledge and discovery. Their inventors are unknown, lost in the dim twilight of prehistoric times. As the third great discovery of ancient times he names the development of geometry. Coming after a vast interval to the fourteenth century A. D., we find the mariner's compass, and in the fifteenth the printing press, both of which beyond question are of the same character and rank as alphabetic writing. From the sixteenth century we get no physical invention or discovery of leading importance, but it witnessed an amazing movement of the human mind, which in good time gave rise to the

Epoch-Making Discoveries of Past Times great catalogue of advances of the seventeenth century. To this he credits the invention of the telescope, and, though not of equal rank, the barometer and thermometer (which he classes as one discovery), and in other fields the discovery of the differential calculus, of gravitation, of the laws of planetary motion, of the circulation of the blood, and the measurement of the velocity of light. To the eighteenth century he refers the more important of the earlier steps in the evolution of the steam engine and the foundation of both modern chemistry and electrical science.   This completes the list.   To the above many would add Jenner's discovery of vaccination and probably several others.   Each writer, in making up such a list, would be governed in a measure by his personal range of studies, but no one would be likely to deviate widely from the above list.

Now what has been the record since 1800?   How does the nineteenth cetury compare with its predecessors?   In Wallace's view it is not to be compared, as regards scientific progress and dis- covery, with any single century, but with all past time.   In fact, it far outstrips the entire progress of mankind in the ages preceding 1800.

Great Dis=
coveries of
the Nine=
teenth Cen=
tury

Estimating on the same basis as that which he previously adopted, Wallace finds twenty-four discoveries and inventions of the first class that have had their origin in the nineteenth century, against the fifteen enumer- ated from all previous time.

Of the same rank with Newton's theory of gravitation, which comes from the seventeenth century, stands out the doctrine of the correlation and conservation of forces, one of the widest and most far reaching general- izations that the mind of man has yet reached.   Against Kepler's laws of planetary motions from the seventeenth century we can set the nebular theory of the nineteenth.   The telescope of the seventeenth is matched by the spectroscope of the nineteenth.   If the first reveals to us myriads of suns, otherwise unseen, scattered through the illimitable fields of space, the second tells us what substances compose these suns and maintain their distant fires, and, most wonderful of all, the direction and the rate in which each is moving.   Harvey's immortal discovery of the seventeenth century finds a full equivalent in the germ theory of disease of the nineteenth. The mariner's compass of the fourteenth century easily yields first place to the electric telegraph of the nineteenth, while the barometer and thermometer of the seventeenth century are certainly less wonderful, though perhaps not less serviceable, than the telephone and phonograph and the Röntgen rays of our own day.

We may more briefly enumerate the remaining discoveries cited by Wallace, partly, as will be perceived, mechanical, but mainly results of scientific research.   Early in the century came the inestima- ble inventions of the railway engine and the steamboat, and somewhat later the minor but highly useful discoveries of the lucifer match and of gas illumination.   These were quickly followed by the wonderful discovery of photography, than which few things have added more to the enjoyment of man.   Equally important in relation

Useful and
Scientific
Steps of
Progress

to his relief from suffering are the remarkable discoveries of anæsthetics and the antiseptic method in surgery. Another of the great discoveries of the age is that of the electric light, with its remarkably rapid development and utilization.

More purely scientific in character are Mendeljeff's discovery of the periodic law in chemistry, the molecular theory of matter, the direct measurement of the velocity of light, and the remarkable utility of floating dust in meteorology. The list concludes with the geological theory of the glacial age, the discovery of the great antiquity of man, the cell theory and the doctrine of embryological development, and last, but, in pure science, perhaps the greatest, Darwin's famous theory of organic evolution—developed by Spencer into universal evolution.

It is quite possible that other nineteenth century scientists would be tempted to expand this list, and perhaps add considerably to Wallace's twenty-four epoch-making discoveries. Indeed, since his book was written, a twenty-fifth has arisen, in the discovery of wireless telegraphy, the scientific marvel of the end of the century, too young as yet for its vast possibilities to be perceived. We might also mention the electric motor and liquid air as of equal importance with some of those enumerated.

An interesting review of the advances made in science during the nineteenth century was offered by Sir Michael Foster, President of the British Association in its 1899 meeting, from which we may quote. He first touched upon chemistry. The ancients, he said, thought that but four

Foster's Views on Recent Progress
elements existed—fire, air, earth, and water. Anything like a correct notion of the composition of matter dates from the latter part of the eighteenth century, when Priestley and Lavoisier revealed to the world the nature of oxygen, and thus led to a long series of fruitful discoveries.

The whole history of electricity as a servant of man is confined to the last sixty or seventy years, and really springs from Volta's invention of the galvanic battery. Frictional electricity had long been known, but nothing beyond curious laboratory experiments were conducted with it. The investigations and discoveries of Oersted and Faraday, which made possible the telegraph, dynamo, trolley car and telephone, followed Volta's discovery of the means of producing a steady current of electricity—first announced in 1799.

Geology, too, he states to be a new born science. Although numerous ingenious theories were entertained in regard to the origin and significance of the rock strata, it was only at the close of the eighteenth century that men began to recognize that the earth's crust, with its various layers of rock, was a vast book of history, each leaf of which told of periods of thousands or millions of years. The slow processes of formation, and the embedding of the remains of the animal and vegetable life of those ancient times, were only interpreted aright after Hutton, Playfair and Cuvier had wrestled with the problem.

With these interesting views of prominent scientists, we may proceed to a more detailed consideration of the scientific triumphs of the century. To present anything other than the headlights of its progress, in the space at our command, would be impossible, in view of the extraordinary accumulation of facts made by its many thousands of observers, and the multitude of generalizations, of the most varied character, offered by the thinkers in the domain of science. These generalizations **Headlights of** vary in importance as much as they do in character. Many of **Progress** them are evidently temporary only, and must fall before the future progress of discovery; others are founded upon such a multitude of significant facts, and are of such inherent probability, that they seem likely to be as permanent as the theories of Galileo, Kepler, Newton, and others of the older worthies.

Beginning with astronomy, the oldest and noblest of the sciences, we could record a vast number of minor discoveries, but shall confine ourselves to the major ones. Progress in astronomy has kept in close pace with development in instruments. The telescope of the end of the century, for instance, has enormously greater space-penetrating and star-defining powers than that used at the beginning, and has added extraordinarily to our knowledge of the number of stars, the character of their groupings, and the constitution of solar orbs and nebulæ. These results have been greatly addded to by the use of the camera in astronomy, the photo- **Discoveries in** graph revealing stellar secrets which could never have been **Astronomy** learned by the aid of the telescope alone. This has also the great advantage of placing on record the positions of the stars at any fixed moment, and thus rendering comparatively easy the detection of motions among them.

But it is to a new instrument of research, the spectroscope, that we owe our most interesting knowledge of the stars. This wonderful instrument enables us to analyze the ray of light itself, to study the many lines by which the vari-colored spectrum is crossed and discover to what substances certain groups of lines are due. From studying with this instru- **Revelations of** ment the substances which compose the earth, science has taken **the Spectro-** to studying the stars, and has found that not only our sun, **scope** but suns whose distance is almost beyond the grasp of thought, are made up largely of chemical substances similar to those that exist in the earth.

A second result of the use of this instrument has been to prove that there are true nebulæ in the heavens, masses of star dust or vapor not yet gathered into orbs, and that there are dark suns, great invisible orbs, which have cooled until they have ceased to give off light. A third result is the power of tracing the motions of stars which are passing in a direct line to or from the earth. By this means it has been found that many of the double or multiple stars are revolving around each other. A late discovery in this direction, made in 1899, is that the Polar star, which appears single in the most powerful telescope, is really made up of three stars, two of which revolve round each other every four hours, while the two circle round a more distant companion.

Late astronomy has revealed to us many marvels of the solar system. Before the nineteenth century it was not known that any planetary bodies existed between Mars and Jupiter. On the first day of the century—January 1, 1801—Ceres, the first of the asteroids or planetoids, was discovered. **New Facts in the Solar System** Three others were soon discovered, and later on smaller ones began to be found in multitudes, so that by the end of the century not less than four hundred and fifty of these small planetary bodies were known. Of other discoveries we may briefly refer to the new facts discovered concerning comets and meteors, planets and satellites, the condition of the sun's surface, the detailed knowledge of the surface conditions of Mars and the Moon, the character of Saturn's rings, the discovery of the planet Neptune, etc., all due to nineteenth century research.

In the group of sciences known under the general title of Physics —chemistry, light, heat, electricity, and magnetism—the progress has been equally decided and many of the discoveries of almost startling signifiance. Chemistry, as it exists to-day, is almost wholly a child of the century. Many chemical substances were known in the past, but their number sinks into insignificance as compared with those of late discovery. Of chemical conceptions of earlier date, Dalton's theory of atoms is the only one of importance that still exists. The view long maintained—until **The Advance of Chemistry** late in the nineteenth century, in fact—that organic and inorganic chemistry are separated from each other by a wide gap, is no longer held. Hundreds of organic substances, some of them of great complexity, have been made in the chemist's laboratory, and can now be classed as properly with inorganic as with organic substances. The gap has been closed, and there is now but one chemistry. Only the most intricate chemical compounds still lie beyond the chemist's grasp, and the isolation of these may be at any time overthrown. Organic chemistry has become simply the chemistry of carbon-compounds.

BARON F. H. ALEXANDER von HUMBOLDT.

LOUIS AGASSIZ.

CHARLES DARWIN.

THOMAS H. HUXLEY.

ILLUSTRIOUS MEN OF SCIENCE, 19TH CENTURY

PASTEUR IN HIS LABORATORY

The discovery of the mission of the exceedingly minute organisms known as bacteria in producing disease ranks among the greatest and most beneficent of our age. By it the art of the physician was first raised to the rank of a science. The honor of this discovery belongs to Louis Pasteur, the eminent French chemist and biologist.

One chemical theory of recent date, the vortex atom theory of Lord Kelvin, has quickly met its fate, being abandoned by its author himself, but the study of it has been rich in results. It is now widely held that the universe is made up of two great basic elements, ether and matter, or perhaps one only, since it seems highly probable that the atom of matter is a minute, self coherent mass of ether. It is further held as doubtful that atoms ever exist alone, they being combined by their attractions into small bodies known as molecules, which are in incessant motion, and to whose activity the physical force of the universe is largely due.

One of the most important chemical discoveries of the century was that of the "periodic law" of the chemical elements, advanced by the Russian scientist Mendeljeff, under which the weights of the atoms of the elements were for the first time placed in harmony with each other, and a fixed numerical relation shown to exist between them. We may conclude this brief glance at the science by mention of the very high temperature which the electric furnace has now placed at the command of chemists, and the equally great refrigeration now attainable, by which the air itself can easily be liquified and even frozen into a solid mass.

Light, naturally one of the earliest of the phenomena of nature to attract the attention of man, was little understood until after the advent of the nineteenth century. It was of old supposed to be a substance of so rapid motion as to be practically instantaneous   **Light and Its Phenomena** in its movement through space. Even Newton looked upon it as a substance given off by shining bodies, and it remained for Young, in the beginning of the nineteenth century, to prove that light is not a substance but a motion, a series of rapid waves or undulations in a substance extending throughout space, and known as the lumeniferous ether. The idea that light is instantaneous in its motion also vanished when Roemer discovered, by observing the eclipses of Jupiter's moons, that it takes about eight minutes for the ray of light to travel from the sun to the earth. A cannon ball moving at the rate of 1,700 feet per second would take about nine years to make the same journey, the wave of light traveling at the extraordinary speed of over 186,000 miles in a second. Yet immensely rapid as is this rate of movement, we do not need to go to the sun and planets to measure the speed of light, but can now do so, by the use of delicate instruments, on a few miles of the earth's surface. This is one of the great discoveries enumerated by Wallace.

The discoveries in relation to the constitution and characteristics of light made during the century have been so numerous that we must confine ourselves to those of major importance. Much might be said about the phenomena of polarization, refraction, diffraction, photography, and the development of the power of lenses, to which the great advance in telescopic and microscopic observation is due. Among these steps of progress perhaps

Late Discoveries in Optics the most interesting is the development of instantaneous photography, a striking result of which is the power, by aid of photographs taken in rapid succession, of portraying objects in motion—living pictures, as they are called—an exhibit now so common and so marvelous. But among all the advances in the science of optics the most important are spectrum analysis and the Röntgen ray. The remarkable discoveries made in astronomy by the former of these have been already stated. The Röntgen ray, which has the power of rendering ordinarily opaque substances transparent, has become of extraordinary value in surgery, as showing the exact location of foreign substances within the body, the position and character of bone fractures, etc.

Heat, once looked upon as a substance, and known by the now obsolete name of Caloric, has been demonstrated to be, like light, a motion, the incessant leaping about of the molecules of matter, this motion being readily transferable from one substance to another, and forming the great substratum of power in the universe. This theory, first promulgated by Count Rumford, an American by birth, was fully worked out by others, and put in

Heat as a Mode of Motion popular form by Professor Tyndall, an English scientist, in his "Heat Considered as a Mode of Motion," published in 1862. Radiant heat is identical with light, being a vibration of the ether. It may be further said in relation to heat phenonema that remarkable power in producing very high and extremely low temperatures is now possessed. By the former the most refractory substances may be vaporized. By the latter the most volatile gases may be liquified and even frozen. The point of absolute zero, that in which all heat motion would disappear, is estimated to be at the temperature of 274 degrees 6 minutes centigrade below the freezing point of water. A degree of cold within some forty degrees of this has been reached in the liquefaction of hydrogen. In 1889 the climax in this direction was reached in the reduction, by Professor Dewar, of the very volatile element hydrogen to the solid state.

Electricity, formerly, like heat and light, looked upon as a substance, is now known to be a motion, being, in fact, identical in origin with light

Conservation and Correlation of Forces and radiant heat. All these forces are considered to be motions of the lumeniferous ether, their principal distinction being in length of wave. In fact, it is easy to convert one of them into the other, and the great doctrine of the conservation and correlation of forces means simply that heat, light and electricity may be mutually transformed, and that no loss of motion or force takes place in these changes from one mode of motion to another. In the operation of the electric trolley car, to offer a familiar example, the heat power of coal is first transformed into engine motion, then into electricity, then again into light and heat within the car, then into mass motion in the motor, and finally passes away as electricity. No better example of the "correlation of forces" than this familiar instance could be adduced.

As regards the nature of electricity, though innumerable observations have been made during the nineteenth century and a vast multitude of facts put upon record, we know little more than is above stated. But if we turn to the practical applications of electric power, it is to find these standing high among the great advances of the century. To it we owe the highly important discoveries of the telegraph and the telephone; the conversion of engine power into electricity by the dynamo and the use of this in moving cars, carriages and machinery; the storage **Applications of Electricity** battery, with its similar applications; the use of electricity in lighting and heating, the latter remarkably exemplified in the electric furnace, which yields the highest temperature known on the earth; the welding of metals by electricity; the electrotype and electro-plating; the conversion of water power into electric force and its transportation by wire for long distances; the therapeutic uses of the electric current, and other applications too numerous to mention.

In regard to the magnet, the handmaid of electric power, we know little other than that the force displayed by it seems to be a result of some mode of rotation in the atoms or molecules of matter, since all the effects of magnetism can be produced by the rotary motion of the electric current in spirals of wire. From this it is thought that the molecular motion to which magnetism is due may be of an electric **The Principles of Magnetism** character, though the permanence of the magnetic force renders this very doubtful. It seems most probable that magnetism is a result of some special condition of the ordinary, inherent motions of atoms —not their fluctuating heat activities, but those fixed motions upon which their organization and persistence depend. The readiness with which soft iron can be magnetized and demagnetized by the use of the electric current is of extraordinary value in the practical applications of electricity. To this fact we owe the dynamo and the electric motor, with all their varied uses.

With this passing glance at the physical forces, we may proceed to the consideration of the great science of geology, which, as above stated by Foster, is a new-born science, almost wholly of nineteenth century development. Geology as it now exists may be said to date from 1790, when

William Smith published his "Tabular View," in which he showed the proper succession of the rock strata and pointed out that each group of rocks is marked by fossils peculiar to itself. With his work began that great series of close observations which still continue, and which have laid the constitution of the earth's crust open before us in many of its intimate details.

Among the many geologists of the century Sir Charles Lyell stands prominent, his "Principles of Geology" (1830–33) forming an epoch in the advance of the science. Before his time the seeming breaks in the series of the rocks were looked upon as the results of mighty catastrophes, vast upheavals or depressions in the surface, which worked widespread destruction among animals and plants, these cataclysms being followed by new creations in the world of life. Lyell contended that the forces

Progress in Geology

now at work are of the same type as those which have been always at work; that catastrophes have always been local, as they are now local; that general forces have acted slowly, and that there has been no world-wide break, either in rock deposits or the progress of human beings.

His views gave rise to a conception of the unbroken continuity of organic life which was greatly strengthened by the publication of Charles Darwin's "Origin of Species," which went far to do away with the old belief that each new life-form has arisen through special creation, and to replace it by the theory now widely held that all new forms of life arise through hereditary descent, with variation, from older forms. In this conception we have the basis of the recent theory of evolution, so thoroughly worked out and widely extended since Darwin's time—a theory including the doctrine that man himself is a result of descent, and not of special creation.

With geology is closely connected the Nebular Hypothesis of Kant and Laplace, of eighteenth century origin, to the effect that all the spheres of space originated in the condensation and rotation of immense volumes of nebulous vapor, similar to the nebulæ now known to exist in the heavens, and that each planet began its existence as a great gaseous globe, its evolution being due to the gradual process of cooling and condensing, by which its surface, and perhaps its whole mass, were in time converted

The Nebular and Meteoric Hypotheses

into solid matter. This interesting doctrine of world evolution does not remain unquestioned. A new hypothesis was advanced by Professor Lockyer in the final decade of the nineteenth century, to the effect that spheral evolution is not due to the condensation of gaseous nebulæ, but of vast aggregations of those meteoric stones with which space seems filled, and which are drawn together by their mutual attractions, become intensely heated through their collisions, and are converted into liquids and gases through the heat thus evolved. It is possible that the visible nebulæ, like the comets, are great volumes of such meteors. This is the meteoric theory referred to in Wallace's category of great discoveries. It is still, however, far from being established.

Meteorology, the study of the atmosphere and its phenomena, is another science to which much attention was given during the century under review. A vast number of facts have been learned concerning the atmosphere, its alternations of heat and cold, of calm and storm, of pressure, of diminution of density and loss of heat in **The Science of Meteorology** ascending, and of its fluctuations in humidity, with the variations of sunshine and cloud, fog, rain, snow, hail, lightning and other manifestations.

The study of the winds has been a prominent feature in the progress of this science, and our knowledge of the causes and character of storms has been greatly developed. The theory that storms are due to great rotary movements in the atmosphere, immense cyclonic whirls, frequently followed by reverse, or anti-cyclonic, movements, has gone far to clear up the mystery of the winds, while the destructive tornado, the terrific local whirl in the winds, has been closely studied, though not yet fully understood. These close observations of atmospheric changes have given rise to the Weather Bureau, by which the kind of weather to be looked for is predicted for the United States. Similar observations and predictions have been widely extended among civilized nations. This is a practical application in meteorology which has been of immense advantage, particularly in the field of navigation.

Of the sciences with which the nineteentn century has had much to do, those relating to organic life, classed under the general title of biology, stand prominent, which includes botany and zoology. Sub- **Progress in the Biological Sciences** siduary to these are the sciences of anatomy, physiology, embryology, psychology, anthropology, and several others of minor importance. We have, here laid out before us a very large subject, which has made remarkable progress during the past hundred years, much too great to handle except in brief general terms.

In botany and zoology alike, the development of the cell theory is one of the most conspicuous advances of the century. It has been shown clearly that all plants and animals are made up of minute cells, semi-fluid in consistency, and principally made up of a highly organized chemical compound known as protoplasm, which Huxley has denominated the "physical basis of life." These cells are the laboratories of the system. Motions and changes take place within them. They increase in size and divide in a peculiar manner, thus growing in number.   Many of them have self-motion like that of the low forms known as amœbæ.   Various chemical substances are elaborated in them, such as the osseous structure of animals, the wood-fibre of plants, and others which are given off into the sap or the blood.   In short, they are the foundation stones of life, and the physical operations of the highest beings are made up of the combined and harmonized activities of these myriads of minute cells.

It would be impossible, unless we should devote a volume to the subject, to do justice to the progress of botany and zoology in the nineteenth century.   This progress consists largely in observation and description of a vast multitude of varied forms, with the consequent study of their **Classification of** affinities, and their classification into family groups, ranging **Plants and** from species and varieties to orders and classes, or from minor **Animals** and local to major and general groups.   Both plants and animals have been divided up into a number of great orders, ranging in the former instance from the microscopic bacteria to the great and highly organized exogens, and in the latter from the minute unicellular forms to the mammalia.   We have here, aside from the cell-theory, and the great progress in classification, nothing of epoch-making significance to offer, and are obliged to dismiss these subjects with this brief retrospect.

There are, however, two fields in which an important accumulation of facts in reference to organic life has been made, those of embryology and palæontology.   The study of the organic cell by the microscope is one of the basic facts of embryology, since living operations take place within this cell.   The network of minute fibres, of which it is largely made up, is seen **Division of the** to gather into two star-shaped forms with a connecting spindle **Cell** of fibres, the division of which in the centre is followed by the division of the cell into two.   This is the primary fact in reproduction, new cells being thus born.   In higher production two cells, arising from opposite sexes, combine, and their growth and division give rise to the organs and tissues of a new living being.   It is the development of these organs and tissues that constitutes the science of embryology.

The observation, under the microscope, of the stages of this development, has been of the highest value in the study of animal origin, and has aided greatly in the classification of animals.   Many old ideas died out when it was clearly shown that all life begins in a single cell, from which the organs of the new being gradually arise.   The most important lesson taught by embryology is that the embryo in its development passes through various stages of its ancestry, resembling now one, now another, of the lower animals, and gains for a brief time organs which some of its ancestors possessed permanently. Of these facts the most significant is that the embryo of man develops gill-slits like those which the fish The Sciences of uses in breathing. These are of no use to it and soon disap- the Embryo pear, but their appearance is very strong evidence that the and the Fossil fish form lay in the line of man's ancestry, and that man has developed through a long series of the lower animals.

In palæontology, or the study of fossil forms of animals and plant life, we have the embryology of races as contrasted with that of individuals. The study of the multitude of these forms which has been collected within the past century has enabled man to fill many of the gaps which formerly appeared to divide animal forms, and has furnished very strong arguments in favor of the descent of new species from older ones. One of the most striking of these facts is that in relation to the horse, of which a practically complete series of ancestral forms have been found, leading from a small five-toed animal, far back in geological time, through forms in which the toes decrease in number and the animal increases in size until the large single-toed horse is reached.

Two other organic sciences, those of anatomy and physiology, have added enormously to our knowledge of animated nature. Anatomy, which is of high practical importance from its relation to surgery, is a science of ancient origin, many important facts concerning it having been discovered by the physicians of old Greece and Rome. This study continued during later centuries, and by the opening of the nineteenth the gross anatomy of the human frame was fairly well known, and many facts in its finer anatomy had been traced. In later anatomical work the microscope has played an active part, and has yielded numbers of important revelations.

What is known as comparative anatomy has formed perhaps the most important field of nineteenth century study in this domain of science. Though this branch of anatomical study is as old as Comparative Aristotle, little was done in it from his time to that of Cuvier, Anatomy who was the founder of the science of palæontology, and the first to show that the forms and affinities of fossil forms could be deduced from the study of existing animals. If a fossil jaw were found, for instance, with the teeth of a ruminant, it could be taken for granted that it came from an animal whose feet had hoofs instead of claws. It is often said that Cuvier could construct an animal from a single bone, and though this is saying much more than the facts bear out, he did make some marvelous predictions of this kind.

A notable triumph of the science of comparative anatomy was the prediction made by Cope, Marsh, and Kowalewsky, from the fact that specialized forms are preceded by others of more generalized structure, that an animal must once have existed with affinities, on the one hand, with hoofed animals, and on the other with the carnivores and the lemurs

Predictions Concerning Fossil Animals

This prediction was fulfilled in the discovery of the fossil Phenacodus in the Eocene deposits of the western United States. The study of comparative anatomy, particularly in its application to fossil forms, has aided greatly in the acceptance of the doctrine of evolution, and has been specially valuable in classification, as showing how nearly animals are related to each other. To classify animals and plants, in short, may be simply stated as a method of sorting them over and placing together those which have similar characters, just as in arranging a library we keep together books which relate to similar subjects. We may, for instance, make one general branch of history, a smaller branch of American history, and yet others relating to states, to counties, to cities and towns, and, most special of all, to particular families.

The science of physiology differs from that of anatomy in dealing with the functions of life instead of with its forms. The study of these functions has gone on for many centuries, covering the various

Discoveries in Physiology

operations of motion, nutrition, respiration, nervous action, growth, and reproduction, with the many minor functions included under these. Though many of the facts of physiology were discovered in earlier centuries, the scientists of the nineteenth have been busy in adding to the list, and a number of important discoveries have been made. Prominent among these is that of anæsthesia, the discovery that by the inhalation of certain gases a state of temporary insensibility can be produced, lasting long enough to permit surgical and dental operations to be performed without pain; and that of antiseptical surgery, in which, by the employment of other chemical substances, wounds can be kept free from the action of deleterious substances, and surgical operations be performed without the perils formerly arising from inflammation,—the disease-producing germs and poisons being kept out.

One of the great gains of the century, says Sir Michael Foster, from whom we have already quoted, is in our insight into nervous phenomena. "We now know that what takes place along a tiny thread we call a nerve fibre differs from that which takes place along its fellow threads;

Living Threads of the Brain

that differing nervous impulses travel along different nerve fibres; and that nervous and psychical events are the outcome of the clashing of nervous impulses as they sweep along the closely woven web of living threads, of which the brain is made. We have learned by experiment and observation that the pattern of the web determines the play of the impulses; and we can already explain many of the obscure problems, not only of nervous disease, but of nervous life, by an analysis, tracking out the devious and linked paths of the nervous threads."

This observation links together the sciences of physiology and psychology, the latter the science of mental phenomena, the exact study of which largely belongs to the nineteenth century. Broad as this subject is, and much as has been done in it, few facts stand out with sufficient distinctness to call for special mention here. The most famous psychical experiments are those made on the brains of some of the animals below man, and especially on that of the monkey, by which the functions of the several sections of the brain have been to some extent mapped out, the important fact being discovered that each function is confined to a fixed locality in the brain, and with it the accordant fact that certain regions of the brain control the muscular movements of certain parts of the body. In consequence, a particular affection of the hand, foot, or other region has often **Brain Surgery** been traced to a diseased condition of some known part of the brain, and the trouble has been removed by a surgical operation on that organ.

The sciences last named refer specially to man, in whom they have been particularly studied. Other sciences relating to him exclusively are those of ethnology and anthropology, which belong almost solely to the nineteenth century. Ethnology, the study of the races of mankind, has been carefully and widely studied, and though the problems relating to it have not yet been solved, a very fair conception has been gained of the diversities and relations of mankind. Anthropology, embracing, as it does, archæology, has been prolific in discoveries. Archæological research has laid out before us the pathway of man through **The Study of Man's Past** the ages and shown his gradual and steady development, through the successive periods of chipped stone and polished stone implements, of bronze and iron tools and weapons, with his gradual development of pottery, ornament, art, architecture, etc.

The most striking and notable fact in anthropological science is the total reversal of our ideas concerning the length of time man has dwelt upon the earth. The old limitation to a few thousand years, everwhere held at the beginning of the century, fails to reach back to a time when, as we now know, man had reached a considerable degree of civilization. Back of that we can trace him by his tools and his bones through a period many times more distant, leading back to the glacial age of geology and possibly to a much more remote era. Instead of man's residence upon the earth being restricted to some 6,000 years, it probably reached back not less than 60,000, and possibly to a much earlier period.

Among the minor sciences, there is one that has deserved that name only within the past thirty or forty years, the science of medicine. Formerly it was an art only, and by no means a satisfactory one. Nothing was known of the cause of the most virulent and destructive diseases—the infectuous

Development of the Science of Medicine fevers, the plague, cholera, etc. And the treatment of these, and in fact of nearly all diseases, was wholly empirical, depending solely upon experiment, not at all upon scientific principles. Experience showed that certain drugs and chemical compounds produced certain effects upon the system, and upon this physicians depended, with no conception of the cause of diseases and little knowledge of the physiological action of medicines.

This state of affairs was materially changed during the final third of the nineteenth century, as the result of an extensive series of observations, set in train in great part by Louis Pasteur, Professor of chemistry at the Sorbonne in Paris, who was in large measure the originator of the germ theory of disease. The discovery that the fermentation which produces alcohol is due to a microscopic organism, the yeast-plant, gave Pasteur the clue, and he soon was able to prove that other fermentations,—the lactic, acetic, and butyric,—are also due to the action of living forms. It had

Pasteur and His Discoveries further been found that the putrefaction of animal substance was caused in the same way, and it has since been abundantly demonstrated that if these minute organisms can be kept out of animal and vegetable substances these may be preserved indefinitely. This fact has given rise to one of the most important industries of the century, the keeping of fruits, meats, etc., by the process of air-tight canning.

Pasteur next extended his observations to the silkworm, which was subject to an epidemic disease that had almost ruined the silk industry in France. Others before him had discovered what were supposed to be disease germs in the blood of these worms. He proved positively that these bacteria, as they are called, are the cause of the disease, and that infection could be prevented by proper precautions. From the insect Pasteur proceeded to the higher animals, and investigated the cause of splenic fever, a dangerous epidemic among farm cattle. This he also proved to be caused by a minute-form of life, and that fowl cholera is due to still another form of micro-organism. At a later date he studied hydrophobia, which he traced to a similar cause, and for the cure of which he established the Pasteur Institute in 1886.

This was not the whole of Pasteur's work. He discovered not only the cause of these diseases, but a system of vaccination by which they could be cured or prevented. By "cultivating" the bacteria in various ways, he succeeded in decreasing their dangerous properties, so that they would give the disease in a mild form,—acting in the same way as vaccination does in the case of small-pox, by enabling the animals to resist virulent attacks of the disease.

Pasteur's work was performed largely on the lower animals. Others have devoted themselves to the infectuous diseases which attack the human frame, and with remarkable success. Robert Koch, a German physician, applied himself to the study of cholera, which he proved in **Koch and** 1883 to be due to a germ named by him, from its shape, the **the Comma** comma bacillus. He discovered about the same time the **Bacillus** bacterial organism which causes the fatal disease of tuberculosis, or consumption. Other investigators have traced typhoid and yellow fevers, diphtheria, and some other infectuous diseases to similar causes, and the study of diseases of this character has at last gained the status of a science.

Methods of cure are also becoming scientific. These minute organisms, once introduced within the body, tend to increase in number at an amazing rate, feeding on the blood and tissues, and giving off substances called toxines which in some cases are of highly poisonous character. To overcome their effect inoculation of anti-toxines is practiced. These are yielded by the same bacteria as produce the toxines, and inoculation with them enables the system to resist the action of the toxin poisons.

We must dismiss this broad subject with this brief consideration, saying further that it is still largely in the stage of experiment, and that many of its theories must be left to the twentieth century for proof. Its study, however, has been of inestimable value in another direction, that of antiseptic surgery, a mode of treatment of surgical wounds introduced **Antiseptic Sur-** by Sir Joseph Lister, and now used by all surgeons with the **gery** most beneficial effects. It being recognized that inflammation and putrefactive action in wounded tissues are due to the action of disease germs introduced by the air or by the hands and instruments of the operators, the greatest care is now taken, by the use of chemical substances fatal to those germs, to prevent their entrance. As a result many diseases once common in hospitals—pyæmia, septicæmia, gangrene and erysipelas—have almost disappeared, fever and the formation of pus are prevented, and healing is rapid and continuous, while surgeons now daringly and successfully undertake operations in the most secret recesses of the body, which formerly would have led to certain death.

A secondary result of the germ theory of disease is the great advance in hygiene, which, formerly almost non-existent, has now reached the status of a science.   It is still against these perilous germs that continuous battle is kept up, absolute cleanliness being the ultimatum at which

The Science of Hygiene physicians aim.   Disease germs lurk everywhere, and can only be combatted by incessant care.   The bacteria of cholera and typhoid fever, for example, are known to be conveyed in water, and the former epidemics of these diseases were in great measure due to the free use of polluted water for drinking.   Their ravages have been largely arrested by boiling, filtering or otherwise purifying drinking water, while the free use of carbolic acid and other antiseptics in hospitals has put an end to the reign of infection which once made those places hives of disease.

We may fitly conclude this chapter with reference to a subject several times referred to in its pages, and which is looked upon as the greatest scientific theory of the century, that of evolution.   The belief that new species of animals and plants arise through development from older ones is not of recent origin, but is at least as old as Aristotle.   It was taught by Harvey, Erasmus Darwin, Gœthe, and others in the eighteenth century, but the first attempt to develop a general theory of organic evolution was made by Lamarck, in the early part of the succeeding century.   Lamarck's view, however, that the variations in animals are the result of efforts on their part to gain certain results,—the neck of the giraffe, for instance growing longer through its attempt to browse on leaves just out of reach,— did not gain acceptance, and it was not until after the middle of the century that a more satisfactory theory was presented.

The theory of evolution, as now understood, was arrived at simulta-

Darwin and Natural Selection neously by Alfred Russell Wallace and Charles Darwin, it being fully worked out by the latter in his "Origin of Species by Means of Natural Selection," published in 1859.   This theory—that the changes in animals are due to the struggle for existence among vast multitudes, and the survival of those whose natural variations in form give them an advantage over their fellows in the battle of life—is now accepted by the great body of scientists, while the general idea of evolution has been extended to cover all changes in the universe, inorganic as well as organic.   This extension has been the work of Herbert Spencer and many other scientific and philosophical writers, and no domain of nature is now left outside of the range of evolutionary forces.   The argument which makes man himself a result of evolution, and not a product of special creation, was the final one presented by Darwin, and has given point to a multitude of observations in the science of anthropology made since his day.

BROWNING

WORDSWORTH

TENNYSON

SHELLEY

AUSTIN

THE GREAT POETS OF ENGLAND

WILLIAM CULLEN BRYANT

JAMES R. LOWELL

OLIVER W. HOLMES

H. W. LONGFELLOW

RALPH WALDO EMERSON

JOHN G. WHITTIER

SIX GREAT AMERICAN POETS

CHAPTER XL.

Literature and Art in the Nineteenth Century.

FOR ages the world has swarmed with writers. Almost since man first began to think he has been actively engaged in literary labor; long, indeed, before he had learned the art of writing, and when the work of his mind could be preserved only in his memory and that of his fellows. And the progress of man down the ages is starred with names that gleam like suns in the firmament of thought, those of such great magicians of the intellect as Homer, Virgil, Dante, Chaucer, Shakespeare, Milton, and a host besides. In this field of human effort, therefore, the **The Literary** nineteenth century has nothing peculiar to show. Its finest **Giants of For-** labors are surpassed by those of others who lived centuries or **mer Times** ages ago. Here, almost alone in the circle of human labors, the century we deal with stands on the level of many of its predecessors and below that of others. Its single claim to distinction is an extraordinary activity in literary production, and especially in the field of novelistic fiction, which it may in great measure claim as its own. The novel before the nineteenth century was a crude pioneer; within the century it has grown into a product of the most advanced culture.

What has been said about literature may be repeated about art. That, too, seemingly reached its culmination in the past, and the artists of to-day can merely seek to emulate, they cannot hope to surpass, those of former centuries. Sculpture, for instance, reached its highest **The Standing** stage of perfection in Greece, and painting in mediæval **of the Fine** Europe; and strive as our artists may, they seem incapable **Arts in the** of producing works of superior beauty and charm to those of **Past and the** the long ago. The architecture of to-day is largely a rescript **Present** of that of the past, the original ideas are few, nobler and more beautiful conceptions are wanting. Of the remaining fine arts, music and poetry— if we may class the latter in this category—the work of former centuries remains unsurpassed, and the best that can be done with the nineteenth century authors and artists is to mention their works and speak of their styles; it is impossible to place them on a pedestal overlooking that of their predecessors

Yet while what has been said is true as a whole, the literature of at least one country is almost wholly a product of the nineteenth century. This is the United States, which had writers, but little which fairly deserves the name of literature, prior to 1800. Aside from the famous papers of the *Federalist*, the work of the great statesmen of the Constitutional Convention, the writings of one or two authors of the Revolutionary period,

Early American Writers

and some of those of Benjamin Franklin, this country possessed hardly any literature, truly so-called, before the days of Washington Irving, whose polished " Sketch Book " essays, popular histories of Columbus and Mahomet, and humorous " History of New York," first taught the English critics that Americans could write as well as fight and work, and that a new world of thought was likely to arise beyond the waters   Irving was not alone.   Contemporary with him were a number of graceful poets, chief among them being William Cullen Bryant, whose " Thanatopsis," still an American classic, is perhaps unequalled in depth of reflection and grandeur of thought by the work of any other author of nineteen years of age.

Bryant, however, did not rise above this early effort, but rather declined, and he has been far surpassed in poetic fervor and richness of diction and conception by a number of his successors, notably Whittier, Longfellow and Lowell, men worthy to occupy a place beside the famous English poets of the century.   Of these, Longfellow has gained the widest reputation, not, however, through force of superior genius, but from the sweetness, grace and ease of his diction and the popular character of his themes

The Poets of the United States

and handling, which have fitted his verse to touch the heart of the people in all lands.   Lowell was not only a poet of rare depth of thought, but stands as the first of American satirists, his " Biglow Papers" being among the keenest and most humorous works of satire of the century, while they rank with the most purely national of American works.   Of other American poets, of whom many of fine powers might be named, we shall mention only Edgar Allan Poe, the most original in style and musical in tone of all our writers of verse ; the witty and genial Oliver Wendell Holmes ; and Ralph Waldo Emerson, whose verse, while lacking polish and smoothness, is rich in poetic thought.

It was rather in his philosophy than in his poetry that the rich imagination and fine powers of reflection of Emerson made themselves manifest, and his essays stand prominent among the finest thought products of the century.   They are expressed in telling apothems, of which many are little poems in themselves, while his works are instinct with the finest spirit of altruism and optimism, taking the most hopeful and cheerful views of the future of man and his institutions.

Among popular American novelists James Fenimore Cooper stands as the pioneer, his tales of ocean and Indian life, while of no superior merit as literature, holding a wide audience by their spirit of adventure and careful elaboration.   Most original of our writers is Nathaniel Hawthorne, whose " Scarlet Letter," " Marble Faun," and other novels stand in a field of their own among the productions of the century, and take rank with the best of European productions.   For the sensational and lurid tale Poe stands first, and his genius in this direction still brings him readers, despite the impossible incidents of many of his plots.   Of other novelists we may name Harriet Beecher Stowe, with her famous " Uncle Tom's   **American Novelists** Cabin ;" Howells, our leading naturalistic novelist ; Edward Everett Hale, made famous by his " Man Without a Country ;" Edward Eggleston, with the flavor of frontier life in his " Hoosier Schoolmaster," Lew Wallace, who touched a deep vein of popular approval in his " Ben Hur ;" Henry James, too scholarly perhaps to be highly popular, but of the finest literary skill ; Helen Hunt Jackson, whose " Ramona" depicts in thrilling idealism the wrongs of the Indians ; and—but we must stop here, for as we approach the present day novelists of merit so throng the field of view that we cannot venture even to name them.

Not the least notable field of American literature lies in the domain of history, in which the authors of our country hold their own with the best of those abroad.   Irving's graceful, though not critical, works of   **Historians of the United States** history we have mentioned.   Greatest in this field stands Bancroft, whose history of our country is a classic of worldwide fame.   Close beside him may be placed Prescott, with his glowing pictures of Spanish and Spanish-American life ; Motley, the skilled and popular historian of the Netherlands ; Parkman, who brilliantly pictures for us the romance of French enterprise in America ; McMaster, who may fairly pose as the historian of the American people ; and Parton, whose historical biographies are among the most readable of American books of this character.

Our greatest orators, men whose speeches have become literature, hold a place in the history of our country.   The famous Webster and Clay and Calhoun we have already described.   Close after those come Sumner, Seward and others who stood high in the stirring period of the Civil War and of reconstruction.   Aside from public speakers   **American Orators** devoted to statesmanship are many others of fame, including the eloquent Edward Everett ; the daring anti-slavery orator, Wendell Phillips ; the earnest platform apostle of temperance, John B. Gough ; the greatest of our pulpit orators, Henry Ward Beecher ; the advocate of the

"New South, Henry W. Grady; the most amusing of our recent orators, Chauncey M. Depew, and others of fine powers whom the need of brevity forbids our naming. The mention of Depew's vein of humor calls to mind this domain of literature, of which our country has had many popular representatives, chief among whom stands the rollicking and favorite Samuel L. Clemens (Mark Twain).

It has not been proposed here to present more than a passing review of the authors of the United States, or to attempt to name all those of leading merit. We might have named in political economy Henry C. Carey; in American history, John Fiske; in European church history, Henry C. Lea; and, in addition, eminent authors in legal lore, in science, in philosophy, in theology, and in other fields, all aiding to show the vast advance our people have made in this important direction since their feeble beginnings in the early days of the century.

Unlike the United States, Great Britain came to the nineteenth century with a great galaxy of famous writers, leading back through many centuries.

The Poets of Great Britain — The eighteenth century is rich in great names, including among its poets Pope, Burns, Cowper, Gray and Thompson; among its essayists, Addison, Swift and Johnson; among its novelists, Richardson, Fielding, Smollet, Sterne, and Goldsmith; among its historians Gibbon, Hume and Robertson. It crossed the portals of the nineteenth century with a galaxy of poets more brilliant than has appeared in any equal period of English literature, including the world-famous Byron, Wordsworth, Coleridge, Shelley, Moore, Keats, Scott and Campbell, a group of writers which, taken as a whole, it would be difficult to match in any age. These sweet singers have been followed by others who have kept up the standard of British poetry, including Tennyson, one of the rarest of artists in words, the two Brownings, Matthew and Edwin Arnold, William Morris, Swinburne, the Rossettis, and various others of lesser note, among whom we must include Alfred Austin, the latest though not the most admired poet-laureate. These are but the elder flight of singing birds of the century, many younger ones being on the wing, among whom at present Rudyard Kipling leads the way.

In the second field of imaginative literature, that of the novel, the British isles are abundantly represented, and by some of the most famous **British Novel- ists and Historians** names anywhere existing in this domain of intellectual activity. The names alone of these writers form a catalogue rarely equalled in the world's literature. It will suffice to name Scott, Thackeray, Dickens, Bulwer, Charlotte Bronte and Marion Evans as the most prominent among a multitude of able writers, containing many names high in merit and rich in variety of style. At the end of the century the field was crowded with writers of conspicuous skill.

History has reached a high level in the hands of some of the ablest writers in this field known in any age, including Macaulay, Freeman, Froude, Grote, Thirwall, Hallam, Merivale, Buckle, Leckey, Carlyle and Green. Two of these, Carlyle and Macaulay, have won as high a place in the field of criticism and biography as in that of history. In art criticism Ruskin occupies a unique position, while theological subjects and religious thought are represented by such able exponents as Cardinal Newman, Dean Stanley, Canon Liddon, Dean Farrar, Martineau, Whately, Drummond, Spurgeon and many others. The great reviewers include Jeffrey, Sydney, Smith, Hazlitt, De Quincey, Foster; the wits **Other British Writers** Sheridan, Hook, Jerrold, Smith and Hood; the philosophers Stewart, Bentham, Brown, Hamilton, Spencer and Stuart Mill; and the scientists Owen, Faraday, Murchison, Darwin, Huxley, Tyndall and various others.

The above named are merely some of the best known English writers of the century. If it were attempted to name all those of merit the list would be wearisomely long. The same may be said of the literary men of France, of whom many of world-wide fame flourished during the nineteenth century. At the beginning of the new age appeared the versatile Madame de Staël, and Chateaubriand with his famous "Genius of Christianity.'" These ushered in a host of able writers, of whom the leading lyric poets were Victor Hugo, Béranger, Lamartine and Alfred de Musset, and the most prominent novelists Hugo, Dumas, Sue, Balzac, Dudevant (George **French Novelists and Historians** Sand), succeeded in later years by the younger Dumas, Feuillet, Murger, Zola, About and a host besides. Dramatic writers have been little less numerous, and essayists and literary critics of merit might be named by the dozen, among them the well-known names of Renan, St. Beuve, Gautier, Taine, Girardin and Rémusat.

Perhaps the most successful branch of recent French literature is history, around which a brilliant galaxy of great names has gathered. Prominent among these are Guizot, Thierry and Thiers, to whom may be added, as able writers of the history of their country, Sismondi, Michelet, Martin, Barante and Mignet. Other workers in this field are Lamartine and Villemain, while in philosophy, sociology and the various branches of science the writers have been numerous, and many of them of high ability.

The writers of Germany have been as prolific as those of England and France, though the greatest names of that country, such giants of thought as Gœthe, Schiller, and Kant, belong to the closing period of the eighteenth century, and have found no equals in the nineteenth. Kant was succeeded

33

by three other great metaphysical philosophers, Fichte, Schelling, and Hegel, the four forming a group nowhere matched for depth of thought in any similar period of time.   In poetry, Goethe and Schiller

German Poets and Novelists

were succeeded by the song writers Körner, Arndt, Rückert, and Uhland, while of the poets of later date Heine undoubtedly ranks first.   Fiction was enormously developed during the century, Gustav Freytag being one of the most eminent novelists, while others of note were Hackländer, Spielhagen, Heyse, Ebers, Auerbach, and of women writers Ida von Hahn-Hahn, Fanny Lewald, Schopenhauer, and Marlitt.   Famous authors who have dealt with the mysterious agencies of nature are De la Motte Fouque, the author of the charming "Undine," Chamisso, with his fantastic "Peter Schlemihl," and Hoffmann, whose tales of wonder and fantasy are of the first merit.   Best known among fantastic and imaginative writers is Jean Paul Richter, whose satirical and humorous novels had a striking effect upon German thought at the beginning of the century.   Of German humorists, Fritz Reuter occupies perhaps the highest rank.

In the field of science and exploration the literature of Germany is rich.

German Scientists and Historians

Scientific travel was given a great impetus by the famous works of Alexander von Humboldt,—"Cosmos," "Views of Nature," etc.,—and his example has been abundantly followed. Among his more famous successors are Martins, the learned traveler in Brazil; Tschudi, in Peru; Lepsius and Brugsch, in Egypt; Gützlaff, in China; Barth, Vogel, and Schweinfurth, in Africa; and Leichhardt, in Australia.

In scientific literature of high value Germany is strong, its writers including Bessel, Encke, Mädler, and Struve, in astronomy; Müller, Ehrenberg, Liebig, Virchow, Vogel, Helmholtz, Haeckel, Kirchhoff, von Baer, and many others in natural science.   The historians are of unsurpassed critical excellence, and embrace Von Ranke, Curtius, Mommsen, von Müller, Heeren, Niebuhr, Neander, Menzel, and many more.   In philology and critical study may be named Wolf, Hermann, the brothers Grimm, Bopp, Benecke, and Haupt.   Critical essayists include the two Schlegels, von Hardenberg (Novalis), Tieck, Schelling, and Wilhelm von Humboldt.

This is by no means an exhaustive list of the prominent German authors of the nineteenth century, and we must deal still more briefly with the other nations of Europe.   Russia may fairly be ranked with the United

The Literature of Russia

States, as being, in a literary sense, largely confined to the nineteenth century.   It had some writers of merit of earlier date, largely poets and fabulists, but the first prose writer of excellence of style was Nicholas Karamzin, whose famous "History of the

Russian Empire" began to appear in 1815. Poetry also became more merit‑orious in this period, Alexander Pushkin, the greatest of Russian poets, giv‑ing to the world some charming narratives in verse. Ivan Kriloff won fame as a writer of fables, while other poets of merit appeared, among them Koltsov, the writer of Russian national songs.

In the field of fiction the first of special merit was Nicholai Gogol, one of the most powerful of Russian novelists ; but the first to gain a European fame was Ivan Turgeneff. Greatest among his successors is Count Leo Tolstoi, who entered this field with " War and Peace," the record of his experience in the Crimean war. His radical studies of the problems of social life have since led to a number of works of striking character, which have won him a world-wide fame. In romantic fiction Russian writers have gained much celebrity, and they include able authors in history, science and other fields.

The three Scandinavian nations, Denmark, Sweden and Norway, have been active in literary production, and possess many authors of national fame, and several who are read and admired throughout the world. Of high standing among the poets of Sweden is the popular poet Runeberg, born in Finland in 1804, who possessed a poetic genius of the highest quality. But the most celebrated poet of Sweden is Esaias Tegnér, whose " Frithiof's Saga " has won him a world-wide fame, it having been translated in‑to the principal modern languages, though with great loss of the beauty of the original. Almquist, a man of fine genius and **The Authors of Sweden** wide knowledge, was a poet and novelist of the romantic school, his novels including " Book of the Rose," " The Palace," etc. Stagnelius, another poet of eminence, obtained fame by his epic of " Wladimir the Great." The novelists include several well-known women writers, the productions of Fredrika Bremer and Emilie Carlén having gained popularity in English translations. Fredrika Runeberg, wife of the poet, was also a popular novelist, while favorite male writers of histori‑cal novels include Mellin, Sparre, Topelius, and Rydberg, the last also a popular poet. Wetterbergh (Uncle Adam) gained reputation by his humorous tales of Swedish home life.

Most famous of the poets of Norway is Wergeland, the Schiller of his country, his works including tragedies, poems and satires. Various later writers followed in his line, including Moe, Jensen, Kjerulf and Thomsen. Chief among Norwegian novelists is Björnson, the author of a series of charming studies of the peasant life of his country, all which are popular in English speaking countries. Others who have wrought in the same field are Thoresen and Lie. But most famous of the recent writers of Norway

is the dramatist Ibsen, a thorough playwright on historical and romantic
Literarure of themes, and on social problems.   It is the striking and radical
Sweden and character of his productions in the last named field, including
Norway " A Doll's House" and various others, to which he owes his
widespread fame, and the severe criticism with which his works have
been assailed.

The Danish literature of the nineteenth century opened with Jens
Baggesen, whose lyrics, mock-heroic poems, and " Comic Tales " are much
admired.   The great poet of Denmark, however, is Oehlenschläger, who
produced tragedies of the highest merit, while his splendid epic poem,
" The Gods of the North," is one of the noblest modern works of this
character.   Of the many other Danish writers of the century we shall name
only the famous Hans Christian Andersen, whose folk-tales are household
words throughout the world.

The literary fame of Spain rests with its authors of the past, there
being few of notable merit of recent date.   Much the same must be said in
regard to Italy, the latest of its great poets and dramatists, Alfieri, dying in
1803.   One of its most famous nineteenth century writers was Ugo Foscolo,
whose political romance, " Letters of Jacopo Ortis," published about 1800,
became immensely popular.   His finest work is considered to be " The
Monuments," an admirable lyric poem.   Count Leopardi also attained to
high eminence as a poet, and Manzoni as a novelist and
Writers of Italy dramatist, his " Betrothed Lovers " ("I Promessi Sposi "),
having a wide reputation as a vivid picture of Italian society of the seventeenth century.   We shall speak of only one other, Silvio Pellico, whose
work, " My Prisons," descriptive of his own sufferings in Austrian prisons, is
a classic of its kind and has been widely translated.

This rapid review by no means exhausts the meritorious nineteenth
century authors of Europe, whose smaller countries possess their writers of
fame.   Hungary, for instance, presents to us the prolific novelist Jokai, whose
works are read in all civilized lands.   Poland, no longer a country, merely a
people, has its famous novelists, chief among them being H. Sienkiewiez,
author of the popular " Quo Vadis."   The same may be said of the Netherlands and of Switzerland, to the latter of which the United States was
Other Cele- indebted for one of its most eloquent scientific writers, the
brated celebrated Louis Agassiz.   Of course, the literature of merit
Authors in the nineteenth century has not been confined to Europe and
the United States.   Canada, for instance, has produced able writers, and the
same may be said of the British colonies of Australia and South Africa,
while the nations of Spanish-America have also produced noted authors.

We have said in the beginning of this chapter that literature has made no recent advance, writers of conspicuous merit reaching far back into the past. The "Iliad" of Homer, for example, dates back some three thousand years, and Dante belongs to an early era of mediæval Europe. Yet this assertion is true only in a general sense, that of the comparative merit of authors in style and depth of thought, without regard to the character of their works. In a more special sense, that of the distinctive varieties of literature, we may credit the nineteenth century with several marked steps of progress. The most meritorious works of the past ages were in the fields of poetry, drama, philosophy, oratory, and other branches of imaginative and metaphysical thought. The practice of accurate observation and the literature arising from it are very largely of nineteenth century development. The literature of travel, for instance, is confined in great measure to the past century, and the same may be said of that of science, the comparatively few scientific treatises of the past having been replaced by a vast multitude of scientific works. These are in great measure confined to records of scientific observation and discovery. Theoretical science, while very active in the past century, has yielded no works of higher merit than those of such older writers as Aristotle, Copernicus, Kepler, Galileo, Newton and others of the older worthies. But the gathering of facts has been enormous, and great libraries of works of science to-day replace the scanty volumes of a century ago.

Merit of the Literature of the Past

Scientific and Historical Literature

A second field of nineteenth century advance is in the domain of history. The history of the past is largely the annals of kings and the story of wars. Thucydides, the philosophical historian of Greece, had few successors before the century in question, within which written history has greatly broadened its scope, reaching to heights and descending to depths unattempted before. Histories of the people have for the first time been written, and the outreach of historical research has been made to cover institutions, manners and customs, morals and superstitions, and a thousand things neglected by older authors. History, in short, has at once become philosophical and scientific, efforts being made in th , latter direction to sweep into its net everything relating to man, and in the former to discover the forces underlying the downward flow through time of the human race, and to trace the influences which have given rise to the political, social and other institutions of mankind.

A still more special field of nineteenth century literary development is that of the novel. Imaginative thought has existed for long ages, and fictitious tales are as old as civilization, but in the ancient world these were couched in the form of poetic and dramatic literature, of fable, fairy tale, and the like.   The first steps of approach towards the modern novel began in late Greek times, and the development of the tale continued through the

The Novel and Its Development   Middle Ages, though it failed to reach the level of what may be distinctively called the novel until the middle of the eighteenth century.   The novel, specially so called, is the character tale, the development of human personality under the guise of fiction. This was scarcely attempted in the prose works of the past, character drawing being then confined to the drama.   Abundant works of romance and adventure were written, but it was left to Richardson, Fielding, and the contemporary French authors to produce character novels, works of fiction peopled by individual men and women, instead of by speaking puppets, shows of man in the abstract, as in earlier years.

The novel attained some promising development in the latter part of the eighteenth century, but was still in a crude state at the opening of the nineteenth, when it was taken up by the powerful hand of Scott, whose remarkable works first fairly opened this new domain of intellectual enjoyment to mankind.   Since his time the literature of the novel has grown stupendous in quantity and remarkable in quality, reaching from the most worthless and degraded forms of literary production to the highest regions of human thought.   The novel, as now developed, covers almost the entire domain of intellectual production, embracing works of adventure, romance, literal and ideal pictures of life, humor, philosophy, religion, science,—forming indeed a great drag-net that sweeps up everything that comes in its way.

There is another field of literary production, more humble but not less useful than those named, which has had an immense development in the past century, that of the school text-book.   The text-books of earlier periods

The Text-Book and Progress in Education   were of the crudest and most imperfect character as compared with the multitude of works, admirably designed to smooth the pathway to knowledge, which now crowd our schools.   In connection with these may be named the great development in methods of education, and the spread of educational facilities, whose effect has been such that, whereas a century ago education was confined to the few, it now belongs to the many, and ignorance is being almost driven beyond the borders of civilized nations.   These who cannot read and write are becoming a degraded minority, while a multitude of colleges and universities are yielding the advantages of the higher education to a constantly increasing multitude.

By no means the least among the triumphs of the nineteenth century has been the enormous development of book-making.   The wide-spread education of the people in recent times has created an extraordinary demand for books, there being a thousand readers now to the one of a century or two ago. This demand has given rise to as extraordinary a supply, which is not offered in books alone, but in periodicals of the most varied character and scope, including a multitude of newspapers almost beyond **Vast Increase in** comprehension. The United States alone, in addition to its **Books and** numerous magazines, issues more than twenty thousand dif- **Newspapers** ferent newspapers, of which the aggregate circulation reaches daily far up into the millions.

The demand for reading matter could not have been a tenth part supplied with the facilities of a century ago, but man's powers in this direction have steadily increased. From the intellectual side, the advance in education has provided a great number of men competent to cater to the multitude of readers, as authors in various fields, editors, reporters, etc., an army of able men and women being enlisted in this work. From the mechanical side, invention has served a similar purpose ; the paper-making machinery, with the use of wood as raw material, the mechanical type-setters, the rapid printing-presses, and other inventions having not only enormously increased the ability to produce books and newspapers, but cheapened them to such an extent that they are now within the reach of the poorest. A century ago such a thing as an one-cent newspaper was not known. Now a daily that sells for more than a cent is growing rare. A century ago only a few dictionaries, encyclopedias, and other works of reference were **Wide=Spread** in existence, and those were within the reach only of the well- **Use of Books** to-do. Now works of this kind are very numerous, and they are being sold so cheaply and on such easy terms of payment, that they are widely spread through the families of artisans and farmers.

In truth, the number of books possessed by wage-earners and agriculturists to-day is very much greater than those classes could possess a century ago, and the character of these works has improved so greatly that they serve a highly useful purpose in the advancement of popular education. In addition to the actual ownership of books, there has been so great an increase in libraries, and such an improvement in methods of distribution, that books of all kinds are within the reach of the poorest of city people, and measures are being taken to place them at the disposal of country people as well.

At the opening of the century the free library was almost unknown. At its close there was not a large city in the United States without its free library, and many small ones were similarly provided. In truth, the great library development in this country has been within the latter half of the century. In 1850 there were only eighty-one libraries in the United States that contained over 5,000 volumes, and the total number of books in them was less than a million, a much smaller number than could be found **The Develop-** in the libraries of Paris alone. No single American library **ment of** at that date contained over 75,000 volumes. In 1900 there **Libraries** were more than a dozen with over 100,000 volumes each, some of these possessing considerably over half a million books. Thus the Boston Public Library contained over 600,000 volumes, while a still larger number was housed within the Congressional Library at Washington, in what is the finest and most magnificently decorated library building in the world, with room to accommodate as many as 4,000,000 volumes. The great libraries of the United States are far surpassed in number of books by those of the leading capitals of Europe, and particularly by that of Paris, which contains the enormous number of more than 2,500,000 volumes.

What has been said about literature can scarcely be repeated about art. The nineteenth century has developed no new species of fine art, and in its **Art in Past** productions in sculpture, painting, architecture and music has **Centuries** given us no works superior to those of the earlier centuries. Many names of artists of genius in this century could be given, if necessary, but as these names indicate nothing original in style or superior in merit there is no call to present them. The advance of the nineteenth century has been rather in the cheap production and wide dissemination of works of art than in any originality of conception.

In this direction the greatest advance has been made in pictorial art. Methods of engraving have been very greatly cheapened, and the photograph has supplied the world with an enormous multitude of faithful counterparts of nature. Among the many ways in which this form of art has been applied, one of the most useful is that of book illustration. The ordinary "picture-book" of the beginning of the century was an eye-sore of frightful **Great Progress** character, its only alleviation being that the cost of illustra- **in Pictorial** tions prevented many of them being given. The "half-tone" **Art** method of reproduction of photographs has made a wonderful development in this direction, pictures that faithfully reproduce in black and white scenes of nature or works of art being now made with such cheapness that book illustrations of superior character have grown very abundant, and it has become possible to illustrate effectively the daily newspaper, laying before us in pictorial form the scenes of events that happened only a few hours before.

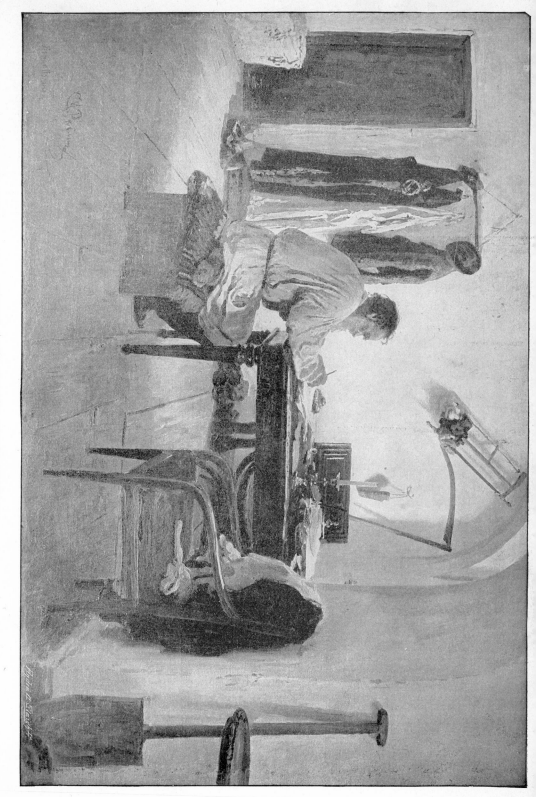

COUNT LYOF TOLSTOI IN HIS LIBRARY

Russia came late into the field of modern literature, yet it has produced a fair number of writers who have gained a high position in the temple of fame. Chief among these is Count Lyof Tolstoi, born in 1828, and to-day the most famous of Russian novelists and moralists. He is still better known for his ultra socialistic duties, he believing it the duty of the highest to place himself on a level in toil with the lowest. This theory he has carried out in his life, working like a common laborer on his estate.

THE NEW CONGRESSIONAL LIBRARY, WASHINGTON, D. C.

CHAPTER XLI.

The American Church and the Spirit of Human Brotherhood.

A S the century draws toward its end, and men make careful survey of the work it has wrought in the many and varied fields of human activity, it is natural that each observer should take a special interest in the department which constitutes his specialty. The statesman studies the social and political phenomena and forces of the age. The scientist, the educator, the manufacturer, the financier, the merchant, find in their respective spheres problems to be taken in hand and carefully investigated, that the experience of the past may become wisdom for the future. While this division of labor may tend to develop one-sidedness in the individual, it provides ample material for the true student of history, who, by collecting the data furnished by these various investigators, may make wide and wise generalizations, and thus contribute to a more **Division of Labor** complete study of human nature and human history. The increase of general interest among special observers and students will ensure in due time co-operation, increased intelligence, and enthusiasm in the promotion of the highest civilization.

As the procession of the years which form the most wonderful century of human history closes its solemn march, those who look on time as deriving its chief worth from its relations to eternity, and who estimate civilization as it bears upon the immortal character of man, will of necessity judge a century by its religious quality and results, asking : What place has religion held, what work has it wrought, what errors have weakened it, what are the tendencies which now dominate it, what are the opportunities which open before it ?

The American type of Christianity is in advance of all other Christian types, since it grows among and permeates political and **American Type of Christianity** social ideas and institutions which give it larger and fuller opportunities than it has ever before known, opportunities to develop humanity on all sides and in all relations. The American Church is made up of all individuals, classes, societies, and agencies which bear the Christian name or hold the Christian thought. It is not a "State Church."

It is not a " union Church"—constituted by the formal unification of diverse sects or denominations. It embraces all believers (and in a sense all citizens) without visible consolidation; it favors all without legislative interference; it gives freedom to all without partiality or discrimination.

The distinguishing feature of American life—which makes what we call "freedom" mean more and promise more than does the civil, political and religious freedom of any other land, and which therefore gives a distinctive character to the American Church—is that the liberty of the individual has large and unhampered opportunity for growth and action. Individual liberty here is actual liberty; unhindered by governmental provisions for privileged classes, who, by the accident of birth, leap into place and prerogative without merit of their own, and whose unearned advantage is detrimental to the well-being of the multitude. It is liberty which carries with it opportunity,—the liberty of the lowest in the nation to reach the rank of the highest; of the poorest to become the richest; of the most ignorant to become the most learned; of the most despised to become the

Distinguishing Feature of American Life most honored; the liberty of every man to know all that he can know, to be all that he can be, and do all that he pleases to do, so long as he does not interfere with the right of any other man to know all that he can know, to be all that he can be, and to do all that he pleases to do. It is the liberty among brothers, who, with all the prerogatives of individuality, need not forget the brotherhood of man, and who have every inducement not merely to guarantee to each other this regal right of full personal development, but who easily learn how to render mutual aid—every man helping every other man to know all that he can know, be all that he can be, and to do all that he pleases to do.

This, then, is the ideal of American civilization : A nation of equals, who are brothers. This is the doctrine of the closing American century; the root of the goodly tree that covers such ample area with its fruitful and bending branches; the vine which the right hand of the Lord our God hath planted; this the lesson running along the bars and shining out of the stars of our national flag. It is necessary that the race experiment with this great idea of freedom and fraternity. It is an idea that sounds well in rhyme and song, but it must stand the test of practice as well; and is it capable of this? May this large Gospel of the Christ be realized by a nation, and this nation become in spirit and fact a church? This is the glorious thought running through the civilization of our century, and this we believe to be the purpose of the God of nations.

The distinctive feature of the nineteenth century in America is the struggle for the recognition of these two noble ideas : The freedom of the individual and the brotherhood of the race. And this thought is thoroughly religious. It is pre-eminently Christian. It was taught, enforced, and illustrated by the Nazarene. It is asserting itself in our civilization. The work is now going on. It has not gone far, but it is bound to go on to the blessed end. The leaven is working every day. We are in the midst of the great experiment.

The American Church is not a State Church. It is supported not by law, but by love. No large subsidies corrupt it. No political complications weaken it. Church and State serve each other best when the only bond between them is one of individual conviction and mutual confi- **Development** dence. The beginnings of the Republic were made by religi- **of the Ameri-** ous men, who organized religious communities. They sought **can Church** our shores to secure religious liberty. Some of them may have been narrow, but they were true and brave. Some of the fetters that bound them had been severed, but some still remained. They had not yet conceived the idea of an emancipated and responsible individuality. Protestants fled from the severities of Roman rule, and Romans from the oppressions of Protestants. And it took a long time for Protestants to become free. But the founders and fathers of the Republic were religious and God-fearing men. They were simply pupils ("primary pupils" at that) in the school of human rights and human brotherhood. The lessons were long and hard. It has taken more than a century to get half through the "first reader," and there is ample work for the century ahead, but as a people we are coming to see the life of the Church in the aims and order of the State, and to learn that God is in all history, that His claims upon men extend to all social relations, sanctifying all secular and political life, and embracing charity, sympathy, and justice in the minutest details of life, as well as awe, reverence and worship.

Simultaneously with the rise of the Republic began the great Sunday-school system, which went everywhere with the open Bible and the living teacher, with inspiring Christian songs, attractive books for **The Sunday-** week-day reading, juvenile pictorial papers, social gatherings, **school System** and the stimulating power of friendly fellowship in religious life. It brought the people together, old and young, learned and unlearned, rich and poor. It did more to "level up" society than any other agency in the Republic. It made the adult who taught susceptible and affectionate childhood a better citizen. It prepared the children to be wiser, more conscientious, and more loyal citizens in the next generation. In the widely extended Methodist revival, and in the all-embracing Sunday-school movement, we see the hand of God fashioning the Nation and the Church, that they might be one in aim and spirit, and that through them might be promoted liberty, equality, and fraternity.

The various branches or denominations of the American Church are influenced by these ruling ideas of the century ; the freedom and unrestricted opportunity of the individual and the spirit of generous fraternity. The old warfare between the Protestant denominations has virtually ceased. Co-operation in religious and reformatory effort—the Young Men's Christian

Union Church Associations

Association, the Women's Christian Temperance Union, the Young People's Society of Christian Endeavor, the International Lesson system, the State and International Sunday-school Conventions, the Evangelical Alliance, the Chautauqua Assemblies, the exchange of pulpits, the frequent union revival meetings held by representative evangelists, the ease with which ministers pass from one denomination to another, the warm, personal friendships between representative leaders of the several Churches, the growth and enrichment of non-denominational periodical literature—these are some of the signs of the larger thought now controlling our people.

The American Church, which imposes no creed but the creed of the Republic, which knows no lines of division—sectarian, political, or territorial—but which seeks the well-being of the individual and

The Value of Religion in Politics

ritorial—but which seeks the well-being of the individual and the fellowship of all true citizens, will soon wield an immense influence in matters political. It will discuss great ethical questions ; it will carry conscientiousness and independence into political action ; it will dissipate the weak heresy that Christians are not to take part in national affairs. In the days of Christ and the Apostles, the governing powers, the rulers of this world, were beyond the touch and control of the people. It was for them humbly to serve and uncomplainingly to suffer. But now all this has been changed. The people to-day stand where Cæsar used to stand ; and to be a thoughtful, conscientious, active, consistent politician, is to be doing God's service. The church member who neglects political duty is guilty of sin against both God and the neighbor. The power of the people will be felt for good when the people begin to know and to defend the true and the good. They have during the century expressed the purpose of the American Church on the subject of slavery. At its declaration the shackles have fallen. They pronounced against and destroyed the Louisiana Lottery. Through the press, the ballot, and the authority of law, the moral force of the nation expresses itself and the base conspirators surrender. So must it be with the saloon, and with all political evil. If politicians carry moral questions into the political arena, the pulpit and all other agencies of the church must go with the question before the people, and lead them to consider it no less from the moral than from the political point of view.

Aside from the development of the Christian religion as distinctively displayed in the United States, its progress in the world at large has been great and encouraging. Particularly has the spirit of sectarianism, strongly manifested a century ago, decreased in force and fanaticism diminished, while the sentiment of union and brotherhood between churches of different sects has developed to a highly encouraging degree.

Outside of Christendom the influences of the religion of Christ have been widely spread by the active and enthusiastic labors of missionaries, who have carried the lessons of the Gospels to all lands, and established Christianity among numerous tribes formerly in the lowest stages of heathenism and idolatry. The success of these devoted men has been much less among peoples possessed of a religious faith of a higher grade, as the Mohammedans, Hindoos, and Chinese, and perhaps the most important results of their labors everywhere have been **Missionary Activity** those of education and civilization, necessary preliminaries, in the case of ignorant and undeveloped peoples, to a just comprehension of the principles of Christianity and the inculcation of advanced moral sentiments and the high standard of the Golden Rule.

The religious history of the century does not end with the relation of the progress of Christianity. There has indeed been some degree of reaction of heathenism upon Christian countries, particularly in the case of Buddhism, whose doctrines have made their way into Europe and America, and gained there a considerable body of adherents. This infiltration from without has developed into what is known as the Theosophical Society, which claims over 100,000 members in the United **New Religious Movements** States alone. In addition may be named various new religious outgrowths of home origin, including the Mormons, the Spiritualists, the Christian Scientists, and others of less prominence. Similar new sects have arisen in Mohammedan and Hindoo countries, such as the Babists in Persia and the Brahmo Somaj in India, these latter being distinctive reforms on the more ancient religious creeds and practices.

What has been said above does not show the full extent of the religious movement within the century. There has been an active spirit of progress within the lines of denominational religion itself, and liberal sentiment has made a marked and promising advance. The former insistance upon creed as the essential factor in religion has greatly weakened in favor of its ethical element, and the supremacy of conduct over creed is openly taught. Again, the old religion of fear is giving way before a new religion of love. The

doctrine of future punishment, and the attempt to swell the lists of church members by insistence upon the horrors of Hades, are rarely heard in **The Religion of** the pulpits of to-day, the old Hell-fire conception having be-
Fear and of come at once too preposterous and too alien to the character of
Love the All Wise and All Good to be any longer entertained except by the most ignorant of pulpit orators. In truth, the doctrines of the modern pulpit are rapidly rising towards the level of Christ's elevated teachings, and inculcating love and human brotherhood as the essential elements of the Christian faith.

The growing spirit of liberalism has given rise to a large body of moralists who repudiate the idea that faith in a creed is essential to salvation, and claim that moral conduct is the sole religious element that is likely to influence the future destiny of mankind. Persons of this class are specially numerous in the ranks of the scientists, whose habit of close
observation, and rigorous demand for established facts as the
The Spirit of basis of all theoretical views, unfit them for acceptance of any
Liberalism doctrines insusceptible of rigid demonstration from the scientific standpoint. This requirement of hard and fast evidence, appealing directly to the senses, and discarding all reliance upon the ideal or upon the broad consensus of ancient belief, has no doubt been carried too far, and has yielded a narrowness of outlook which will be replaced by broader conceptions as psychological science develops. That it exists now, however, cannot be denied, and its adherents constitute a very large and influential body. Yet it must be said that science and religion, for a time widely separated, are growing together, and that in all probability the final outcome of modern thought and research will be an alliance between these two great forces, a religion which science can accept and a science in full accord with religious views and principles.

If we now turn aside from religion as a whole, and consider only its ethical side, it is to find an immense advance within the nineteenth century.
The standard of right conduct may not have risen, but the
The Movement sentiment of human sympathy and of the brotherhood of man-
in Ethics kind has very greatly developed, and human charity and fellow feeling, a century or two ago largely confined within the limits of a nation or a city, are now coming to embrace all mankind.

There has been a great amelioration in manners and customs within the century, a great decrease in barbarity and cruelty. A few examples will suffice to point this out. The barbarous practices in regard to child labor which existed in 1800 and much later have often been depicted in lurid colors, the selfish greed of employers giving rise to a "massacre of the innocents" as

declared and even more cruel in its methods than that of the time of Christ.
Thousands of children in the days of our grandfathers were
simply tortured to death in dark and dank mines or gloomy   **Child Labor in**
and unhealthy workshops, at an age when they should have   **Factories**
been alternating between the useful confinement of the schools and the
healthful freedom of the playgrounds and the fields.   This state of affairs
happily no longer exists, and in the present condition of public sentiment
could not be reproduced.   The world has grown decidedly beyond the level
of such heartless cruelty.

The development of sympathy has not confined itself to a redress of
the wrongs of children, but has made itself manifest in attention to the
wrongs of workmen as a whole, factory inspection having put an end to
many unhealthful and oppressive conditions formerly prevailing, and saved
thousands of workmen from being poisoned in the midst of their daily
labors.   And not only human beings, but dumb animals, have been reached
by the awakened sympathy of modern communities.   A century ago the
noble and patient horse was frequently treated with the   **Prevention of**
utmost brutality, without a hand or a voice being raised in its   **Cruelty to**
defence.   This barbarity was accepted as a part of the estab-   **Animals**
lished and necessary order of things. and dismissed with a shrug or perhaps
without a thought.   To-day, in the more enlightened nations, this state of
things has ceased to exist.   Societies for the prevention of cruelty to
animals keep a close watch upon the brutally inclined, and have almost
put an end to cruel practices which formerly prevailed without a word of protest, domestic animals being now protected as carefully as human beings.

In no direction did the lack of kindly sentiment of a century ago
show itself more decisively than in prison management.   We do not mean
to say that philanthropy did not then exist, but that it was far from being
the active sentiment it has become to-day, and was largely without effect
upon legislators ; the condition alike of convicted criminals, of debtors, and
of those held for trial being in many cases almost indescribably horrible.
The first effective movement towards prison reform was made by John
Howard, in the latter part of the eighteenth century, but
public sentiment was so dulled towards the condition of   **Prison Reform**
prisoners that the horrors painted out by him were in great measure permitted to continue.   The legislators of England could not be awakened to
any active interest in the inmates of the gaols.

When Elizabeth Fry made her first visit to the female department of
Newgate, the city prison of London, in 1813, she found a state of affairs
whose horrors words are weak to convey.   The women inmates " were limited

to two wards and two yards, an area of about one hundred and ninety-two superficial yards in all, into which some three hundred women with their children were crowded, all classes together, felon and misdemeanant, tried and untried; the whole under the superintendence of an old man and his son. They slept on the floor, without so much as a mat for bedding. Many were

Prison Life a Century ago very nearly naked, others were in rags; some desperate from want of food, some savage from drink, foul in language, still more recklessly depraved in their habits and behavior. Everything was filthy beyond description. The smell of the place was quite disgusting."

The condition of affairs on the men's side, unless they were able to pay for better accommodations, was similar to that here described. Their treatment, indeed, depended largely on the amount of money they could pay the jail officials and they were fleeced without mercy. The practice of fettering them was so common that nearly every one wore irons, even the untried being often laden with fetters, while their limbs were chafed into sores by the weight of these useless instruments of torture.

The report of the Prison Discipline Improvement Society, at as late a date as 1818, shows the existence of an almost incredible state of things in English prisons. Many of the gaols were in the most deplorable condition, and crowded far beyond their powers of accommodation. All prisoners passed their time in absolute idleness, or spent it in gambling and loose conversation. The debtors were crowded into the narrowest quarters conceivable. Twenty men were forced to sleep in a space twenty feet long by six wide—accomplishing this seemingly impossible feat by "sleeping edgeways." In the morning the stench and heat were something terrible; "the smell on first opening the door was enough to knock down a horse." The jail hospitals were filled with infectious cases, and in one room, seven feet by nine, with closed windows, where a boy lay ill with fever, three other prisoners, at first perfectly healthy, were found lodged. It is no wonder that the deadly jail fever raged as an epidemic in such pest holes, and even communicated itself to the judges before whom these wretches were brought for trial.

We have by no means told all the horrors of prison life at that period, but will desist from giving any more of its painful details. It need scarcely

Improvement in Prison Life be said that an utterly different state of affairs now exists in all civilized lands, prisoners being treated as human beings instead of wild beasts; and so warm is the feeling of public sympathy with the wretched that any of the horrors here depicted would raise a universal cry of deprecation in the land. Kindness is now the rule in dealing with criminals of all grades, and every effort is made to supply them with employment, and to attend to the requirements of comfort and cleanliness. Prisons are rapidly developing into schools for reform, and with remarkable success where systems of this kind have been fully developed.

The laws of a century ago were barbarous almost beyond conception at the present day. Capital punishment, now confined to murderers, was then inflicted for some twenty-five separate crimes, including forgery, coining, sheep or horse stealing, burglary, cutting and maiming, rick-burning, robbery, arson, etc. There were, in fact some two hundred capital crimes on the statute books, but most of these had grown obsolete. Yet such a minor offence as stealing in a dwelling house was a crime punishable by hanging, and men were occasionally executed on *Capital Punishment in 1800* the gallows for a small theft that would now subject them to only a few months of imprisonment. It was not until after 1830 that an amelioration in these severe laws began, and with such effect that the number of persons sentenced to death in England decreased from 458 in 1837 to fifty-six in 1839. After 1841 the death penalty was inflicted only for murder, though seven other crimes remained capital by law until 1861.

The practice of public executions was another barbarous feature of the code, and the scenes around the gallows at Tyburn, on the occasion of the execution of any criminal of note, were so disgraceful that it seems incredible that they could exist in any civilized land. Other relics of the dark ages were the public exhibition of the *Public Executions* bodies of the executed, and hanging in chains on a gibbet, a practice in vogue until 1832. In one case mentioned, at that late date, "a sort of fair was held, gaming tables were set up, and cards were played under the gibbet, to the disturbance of the public peace and the annoyance of all decent people."

It will suffice to say here that this state of affairs has been reformed out of existence. Executions, restricted solely to murderers, now take place wholly in private, and so great is the public desire to prevent suffering to the condemned that the first electrical execution in New York raised a cry of horror when it was announced that life did not cease within the few seconds expected, but that the power of sensation continued for perhaps a minute. In truth, in this instance, there was something of a hyper-sensibility manifested, but one of a kind creditable to human nature.

The development of the spirit of sympathy with the poor and suffering is by no means confined to the instances stated, but has gained an extraordinary extension. The rapid progress of railroad and steamship communication, the enormous increase in travel, and the bringing of the ends of the earth together by means of the telegraph wire have made of all mankind

The Spirit of Sympathy

one great family, and the instinct of charity and benevolence reaches to the most remote quarters of the globe. Notable results of this feeling, of recent date, have been the efforts to ameliorate the suffering in India during the late famine, the war instigated by sympathy in Cuba, the earnest efforts to supply food to the starving in Porto Rico, and the fervent feeling aroused in favor of the unjustly punished Dreyfus.

In regard to charity at home, the instances of it are voluminous beyond our power to record. Hospitals, asylums, institutions of benevolence of the most varied character, have been everywhere instituted, alike in Europe and America, mainly through public donations, and there is no form of

The Growth of Charity

want or suffering which is not met by some attempt at allevia-tion. Homes for the afflicted of every kind are rising in all directions; charity is organized and active to a degree never before seen; the bettering of the condition of the poor by improved resi-dences, methods of recreation and instruction, and other acts of aid and kindness is actively going on, and in a hundred ways benevolence is striving to lift man from want and degradation into comfort and advanced conditions.

What is known as altruism, the sentiment of fellow feeling, is, in part, coming to be one of the active conditions of the age, and is among the most promising signs of the times. Selfishness, indeed, is abundantly prevalent still, yet altruistic feeling is rapidly on the increase, and gifts for benevolent purposes of all kinds are becoming remarkably abundant. Hundreds of instances might be named, but we shall confine ourselves to one, Andrew Carnegie's wise and kindly devotion of the income of his great fortune to the founding of public libraries, than which nothing could serve better to bring man into a condition of mind which will prevent him from becoming a willing object of charity.

Certainly the Golden Rule is bearing fruit in these later days, and men are widely doing unto others as they would wish to be done by. The old,

An Advanced Spirit of Benevolence

narrow idea of patriotism is being replaced by a growing senti-ment of the brotherhood of all mankind, and altruism is mak-ing its way upward through the dense mass of selfism which has so long dominated the world. It is still only in its pioneer stage, but the indications of its growth are encouraging, and we may look forward with hope to a day in which it will become the leading influence in the social world, and selfishness lose its long and strong hold upon the heart of man.

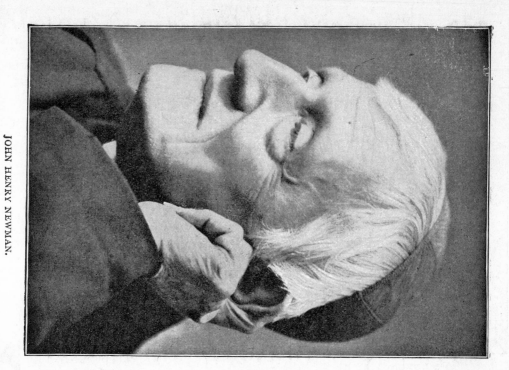

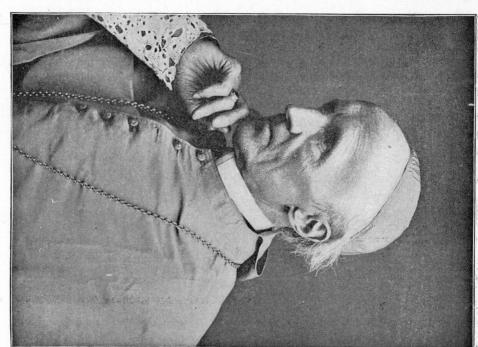

JOHN HENRY NEWMAN.

HENRY EDWARD MANNING.

LEARNED CARDINALS

HENRY DRUMMOND.

REV. JOHN WATSON (IAN MACLAREN).

CHARLES HADDON SPURGEON.

FREDERICK W. FARRAR.

WRITERS OF RELIGIOUS CLASSICS.

CHAPTER XLII.

The Dawn of the Twentieth Century.

THE nineteenth century saw the modern world in its making. At its opening the long mediæval era was just ceasing to exist. The French Revolution had brought it to a sudden and violent termination in France, and had sown the seeds of the new ideas of equality and fraternity and the rights of man widely over Europe. In the new world a great modern nation, instinct with the most advanced ideas of liberty and justice, had just sprung into existence, a nation without royalty or nobility, and whose leaders were the chosen servants, not the privileged masters, of the people.

The Nineteenth Century and the Era of Mediævalism

This grand political revolution, with which the century began, was paralleled with as notable an industrial revolution. The invention of the steam engine had brought to an end the mediæval system of industry. The old, individual, household era of labor, where every man could be his own master and supply his own capital, ceased to exist; costly labor-saving machines, needing large accumulations of capital, came into use; great buildings and the centralization of labor became necessary; and the factory system, which has had such an immense development in the nineteenth century, began its remarkable career.

With the opening and progress of the nineteenth century came other conditions of prime importance. Invention, which first became active near the end of the preceding century, now flourished until its results seemed rather the work of magic than of plain human thought and work. Science, which already had made some notable triumphs, gained an undreamed-of activity and hundreds of the deep secrets of the universe were unfolded.

The Century's Wonderful Stages of Progress

Discovery and exploration achieved surprising results. At the beginning of the century half the world was unknown. At its end only the frozen realms of the poles remained unexplored, and civilization was making its way into a hundred haunts of ancient savagery. Literature and art, while they can claim no works of acknowledged superiority as compared with the master pieces of past centuries, have displayed a remarkable activity, and the number of meritorious books now annually issued is one of the most extraordinary events of the century.

Not less important is the immense progress in education. The school-house forms the great mile-post on the highway of progress. It is every-where in evidence. Free schools extend throughout the civilized world, and reach upward to a plane far beyond the highest level of public educa-tion a century ago, linking the common school with the college, and forming a direct stepping stone to university education, which has widened out

Progress in Education

with similar activity. In methods of education a marked advance has been made, while the text-books of to-day are almost infinitely superior to those of the earlier period. And education is turning its attention in a highly encouraging degree towards practical subjects and away from that incubus of the dead languages which was so strenuously insisted upon in the past. Man is going back to nature in education, observation is supplementing book knowledge, and experiment taking the place of authority. In short, education, with its handmaids, the book and the newspaper, is making its way into the humblest of homes, and man is everywhere fitting himself for an intelligent discharge of his social, industrial and political duties.

As regards the development of the spirit of charity and human brother hood, it has been spoken of in the preceding chapter and does not need recapitulation here. Yet there is one stage of advance of which nothing has so far been said, but which is of high and significant importance, namely, the great progress made in the educational industrial and political position of woman.

In the beginning of the nineteenth century education, except of the most elementary character, was in great measure confined to boys. In 1788

The Education of Women

the village fathers of Northampton, Mass., where Smith's College for women is now situated, voted "not to be at the expense of schooling girls;" and in 1792 the selectment of Newburyport decided that "during the summer months, when the boys have diminished, the Master shall receive girls for instruction in grammar and reading, after the dismission of the boys in the afternoon, for an hour and a half." The site of this schoolhouse, to which, as is believed, women were first admitted on this continent to an education at public expense, is still shown with pride to visitors. The same town established in 1803 four girls' schools, the first on record, to be kept six months in the year, from six to eight in the morning and on Thursday afternoon.

Step by step the free school was opened to girls, and gradually institu-tions for the higher education of women were established, the pioneer college which opened its doors to the fair sex being Oberlin, in Ohio, in 1833. The advance since then has been great, and at the opening of the twentieth century there was not a college west of the Alleghanies which denied to woman the full advantages of education, while the same was the case in many of the older colleges of the East. In 1865 Matthew Vassar founded in Poughkeepsie, N. Y., the first college exclusively for women. To this is now added Smith, Wellesley and **Women's Colleges** Bryn Mawr Colleges, within whose doors the highest advantages of education are to be obtained. The distinction between boys and girls in education, in short, has nearly ceased to exist in this country, and is in a fair way of vanishing in Europe.

In industrial occupation the advance of woman has been as great. A century ago few avenues of labor were open to them outside the household, and such work as was performed was miserably paid for. At present there is not an industry which they desire or are suited to follow from which they are debarred, and the last census enumerated four thousand different branches of employment in which women were engaged. This was not only in the lower, but in many of the higher employments. Women physicians are numerous, women lawyers and preachers are coming into the field, women professors teach in schools and colleges, and women authors have given us some of the best books of the century.

Politically the progress, while not so great, has been encouraging. In the middle of the nineteenth century no woman had a right to vote, and the thought of woman suffrage was just being evolved. At the end of the century women possessed the fullest privileges of the suffrage in the four states of Colorado, Idaho, Wyoming and Utah, and partial suffrage in many other states, while a much wider extension of this privilege **Occupation and** seemed not far distant. In many European countries, and **Suffrage for** in the British colonies of Australia, New Zealand, Cape Colony, **Women** Canada, and parts of India, woman had won the right to vote, under various restrictions, for municipal and school officers. Such has been the progress in this direction of a half century.

What else shall be said of the state of affairs at the dawn of the twentieth century? Perhaps one of the most significant and promising movements of the time is that taken with the object of bringing war, which has raged upon the earth since the primitive days of mankind, **Peace Propositions of the** to an end. The movement in this direction, singularly **tions of the** enough, emanated from the monarch of the most unpro- **Emperor of** gressive of civilized lands, but one whose size and power give **Russia** prominence and influence to any proposition coming from its court. On August 24, 1898, Count Muravieff, Foreign Minister of Russia, by order of

the Emperor Nicholas II., handed to the representatives of foreign governments at St. Petersburg copies of a proposition of such importance, that we
give it below in full :

" The maintenance of general peace and the possible reduction of the
excessive armaments which weigh upon all nations present themselves in
existing conditions to the whole world as an ideal toward which the en-
deavors of all governments should be directed. The humanitarian and
magnanimous ideas of His Majesty the Emperor, my august master, have
been won over to this view in the conviction that this lofty aim is in con-
formity with the most essential interests and legitimate views of all the
powers ; and the Imperial Government thinks the present moment would be
favorable to seeking the means.

" International discussion is the most effectual means of insuring all
people's benefit—a real durable peace, above all, putting an end to the
progressive development of the present armaments.

" In the course of the last twenty years the longing for general appease-
ment has grown especially pronounced in the consciences of civilized nations ;
and the preservation of peace has been put forward as an object of international policy. It is in its name that great states have concluded between
themselves powerful alliances.

" It is the better to guarantee peace that they have developed in proportions hitherto unprecedented their military forces, and still continue to
increase them, without shrinking from any sacrifice.

" Nevertheless, all these efforts have not yet been able to bring about
the beneficient result desired—pacification.

" The financial charges following the upward march strike at the very
root of public prosperity. The intellectual and physical strength of the
nations' labor and capital are mostly diverted from the natural application,
and are unproductively consumed. Hundreds of millions are devoted to
acquiring terrible engines of destruction, which, though to-day regarded as
the last work of science, are destined to-morrow to lose all their value in
consequence of some fresh discovery in the same field. National culture,
economic progress, and the production of wealth are either paralyzed or
checked in development. Moreover, in proportion as the armaments of
each power increase, they less and less fulfil the object the governments
have set before themselves.

" The ecomomic crisis, due in a great part to the system of armaments
a l'outrance, and the continual danger which lies in this massing of war
material, are transforming the armed peace of our days into a crushing
burden which the peoples have more and more difficulty in bearing.

" It appears evident that if this state of things were to be prolonged it would inevitably lead to the very cataclysm it is desired to avert, and the horrors whereof make every thinking being shudder in advance.

" To put an end to these incessant armaments and to seek the means of warding off the calamities which are threatening the whole world—such is the supreme duty to-day imposed upon all states.

" Filled with this idea, His Majesty has been pleased to command me to propose to all the governments whose representatives are accredited to the Imperial Court the assembling of a conference which shall occupy itself with this grave problem.

" This conference will be, by the help of God, a happy presage for the century which is about to open. It would converge into one powerful focus the efforts of all states sincerely seeking to make the great conception of universal peace triumph over the elements of trouble and discord, and it would, at the same time, cement their agreement by a corporate consecration of the principles of equity and right whereon rest the security of states and the welfare of peoples."

This hopeful proposal did not, unfortunately, produce the result hoped for by its distinguished promulgator. Doubt of the honesty of the czar and his advisers, and mutual jealousies of the powers of Europe, stood in the way of an acceptance of the proposition to reduce the enormous armaments of the great nations. Yet, despite this, it was not without important results in the direction of doing away with the horrors of war and bringing about the reign of peace upon the earth. A peace conference of representatives of the nations, in accordance with the suggestion of the czar, was held at The Hague, the capital of the Netherlands, in the spring of 1899, and resulted in the adoption of a scheme of international arbitration which is full of promise for the future, as an important step in the direction of settling international disputes in the high courts of the nations instead of on the bloody field of war. It proposes to adopt in regard to the nations the principle long since in vogue in regard to their people, that of the legal in place of the violent redress of wrongs and settlement of disputes. A permanent court of arbitration is to be established, composed of men amply competent to deal with the questions likely to come before them, and enjoying the public confidence, to deal with national disputes which previously had no other ready arbiter but the sword. There is, it is true, no legal obligations upon nations to submit their differences of opinion to this tribunal, but there is a high moral obligation,

The Peace Conference at The Hague

The Court of Arbitration

whose force is sure to grow as the years pass on, and in the establishment of this court we have the most promising step yet taken towards the abolition of the barbaric custom of war.

With the question of the development of the peace sentiment comes that of the advance of industry, which has been one of the most important results of nineteenth century progress. This, as already indicated in these pages, has made an enormous advance within the century, the invention of labor-saving machinery having so enhanced man's powers of production that the results of each person's labor is very much greater than that of a century ago. Where slow hand processes then widely prevailed, now the whirr of

Labor Saving Machines

wheels, the intricate play of almost human-like machines, which need the eye rather than the hand of the mechanic, turn out products in astonishing profusion and phenomenal cheapness, while the "man with the hoe" of the past is everywhere making way for the man with the machine.

The rate of progress in this direction has been well shown in the successive fairs of the nations, of which, as we have already stated, the first was held in Paris in the first year of the century, while the last was held in 1900, the closing year of the century. Between these two dates a large number of fairs, international and national, have been held in Europe and America, each surpassing its predecessor in size and in the variety and originality of its exhibits, and each showing new and important steps of advance. It was the middle of the century before the ideas of mankind expanded to the conception of an international exhibition, or "world's fair," the first of which was

Industrial Expositions

held in London in 1851. Since then many others on this extended scale have been held, the first in the United States being the Centennial Exposition at Philadelphia in 1876. The Columbian Exposition, which followed at Chicago in 1893, was full of indications of great progress in the intervening seventeen years, especially in the department of electricity, which had made a remarkable advance in the interval. Still more significant, as showing the vast industrial progress of the United States, was the National Export Exposition at Philadelphia in 1899, a display of commercial products significant of the great development of American commerce in the final decade of the century, and justly held in the city which had established the first great commercial museum in the world.

As indicative of the progress in American commerce, a few statistics may be of importance. In 1873 the exports of the United States amounted to $522,479,922, a sum surpassed by that of the imports, which reached $642,136.210. In 1892 the exports had increased to $1,030,278,148; the imports reaching $827,402,462. In 1898 the total exports aggregated the great sum of $1,231,482,330; while the imports fell to a lower figure than in 1873, the total being $616,050,654, almost exactly one half the sum of the exports. It must further be said that these exports are **Development of** no longer predominately agricultural, as in the earlier period, **American** but that the mechanical products of the United States are being **Commerce** sent abroad in a constantly increasing ratio. And a significant fact in this relation is that of our growing sum of exports to England herself, long the dominant lord of manufacture and commerce. This is strikingly indicated in the shipment of locomotives for use on English railroads, and of iron bridges for English use by the British authorities in Egypt, the rapidity and cheapness with which American workshops can turn out their products being the ruling elements in this remarkable diversion of trade.

The progress in other fields of human endeavor, as indicated at the dawn of the twentieth century, has been equally pronounced. Science, for example, manifests a wonderful activity, and displays results of bewildering variety and great importance; while the **Progress in** rapid and varied applications of scientific discoveries to **Science** useful purposes is one of the most significant signs of the age. Striking recent examples of this have been the Röntgen ray and wireless telegraphy.

Politically the world has been by no means at rest during the century. In 1800 despotisms, of greater or less rigidness, controlled most of the countries of the world. The republic of the United Netherlands had been overthrown, that recently established in France was sinking under the autocracy of Napoleon, and the small mountain-girdled republic of Switzerland alone remained. Beyond the seas this was matched by a new republic, that of the United States, at that time small and of little importance in the councils of the world. In 1900 a vast change manifested itself. The whole double continent of America was occupied by republics, **Political** Canada being practically one under distant supervision, **Evolution** France had regained its republican institutions, and Great Britain had all the freedom of a republican form of government. Through all Western Europe autocracy had vanished, constitutional governments having succeeded the absolutism of the past, and the only strongholds of autocracy remaining in Europe were Russia and Turkey, in both of which the embers of revolution were smouldering, and might at any moment burst into flame.

These are not the only significant signs of progress which present themselves to us at the dawn of the twentieth century. In truth, in a hundred directions the world has been equipping itself for the new century, which seems to have before it a destiny unequalled in the history of the world. It is of special importance to observe how prominent the Anglo-Saxon peoples have been in the great advance which we have chronicled. Great Britain, and, following in her footsteps, the United States, have occupied the position of the leading manufacturing and commercial nations of the world. The contracted boundaries of the British Islands long since proved too narrow to contain a people of such expanding enterprise, and they have gone forth, "conquering and to conquer," settling and developing,

Great Development of Great Britain until, at the beginning of the twentieth century, the empire of Great Britain and its colonies covered an area of 11,336,806 square miles, inhabited by 381,037,374 human beings. This area is nearly one fourth that of the habitable land surface of the earth, and its population quite one fourth of all mankind. The East Indian possessions of this great empire are larger than all Europe without Russia, and the North American ones, if their water surface be included, are larger than the whole of Europe.

The other nations which have made a great advance in territory are Russia, with its 8,644,100 square miles of territory, and the United States with its 3,602,990. But in both the latter cases these are compact terri-

Territorial Progress of the Nations tories, held not as colonies, which at any time may break loose, but as integral parts of the national domain. This is particularly the case in the United States, whose territory is inhabited by a patriotic and largely homogenous population, and is not made up of a congeries of varied and dissatisfied tribes like those of Russia. The remaining great territorial nation is France, which, with its colonial acquisitions, covers 3,357,856 square miles of territory. But France herself is only 204,177 square miles in extent, and her immense colonial dominions in Africa are held by so weak and uncertain a tenure as to count for little at present in the strength of the nation.

A significant fact, in respect to the recent proposition to establish a universal language, is that the English form of speech, spoken in 1801 by 20,000,000 people, is now used by 125,000,000. Russian comes next, with

Probable Future of English Speech 90,000,000, German with 75,000,000, French with 55,000,000, Spanish with 45,000,000, and Italian with 35,000,000. The rate of increase in the use of English has far surpassed that of any other language, and it is said that two-thirds of the letters that pass through the post-offices of the world are written and sent by people who speak this cosmopolitan tongue.

This immense advance of the English form of speech is full of significance. If it goes on, the question as to which is to become the dominant language of the world will settle itself by a natural process, and the necessity of inventing a special form of speech will be obviated. English is to-day the chief commercial language of the world, and is fast becoming the polite tongue of Europe, a position held a century ago by French. By the end of the twentieth century it may well have become the only language besides their own which the peoples of the earth will find it necessary to learn. And its marked simplicity of grammatical form adapts it to this destiny beyond any other of the prominent languages of mankind.

To return to the subject under consideration, that of nineteenth century progress, it may be claimed as due to several influences, materially to the extended use of the forces of nature in mechanical processes, in which it went far beyond any of the earlier centuries; scientifically to the rapid extension of observation and the vast collection of facts. While there was no superior faculty of generalization, this accumulation of scientific facts added greatly to the probability of the *Influences Aiding Development* theoretical conclusions thence derived. Again, this activity in investigation, and the great increase of the numbers engaged in it, are legitimate results of the extension of education, and in a large measure of the replacement of classical by scientific instruction. The progress in ethical sentiment is doubtless largely due to the same cause, that of educational development. This has gone far to dispel the cloud of ignorance which formerly hung heavily over the nations, to ripen human intelligence, to broaden man's outlook, to extend his interest far beyond the range of his immediate surroundings, and, by increasing his information and widening his mental grasp, to develop his sympathies and enhance in him the sentiment of the universal brotherhood of mankind.

The intense activity of the human mind in those late days, and the quickness with which men take practical advantage of any new suggestion of workable character, are strikingly exemplified in an example that is well worth relating. In the famous sociological novel by Edward Bellamy, entitled "Looking Backward," in which the author describes an ideal community placed at a date near the end of the twentieth century, he pictures a number of advanced conditions which he evidently hopes will exist at that coming period. One of these is a newspaper on a new type, a spoken instead of a written paper. By aid of telephone connections running in all directions, the events of the day in all parts of the world are to be "phoned" to subscribers in their homes, while great orations, theatrical entertainments, concerts, etc., may be enjoyed without leaving their rooms.

Whether suggested by this imaginative picture or not, it is said that something of this kind has been already introduced, a century in advance of its appointed time. We are told that the city of Budapest, Hungary, has had for several years a spoken newspaper named the *Telephone Gazette*, in which all the news of the day are transmitted by telephone to the subscribers, who are constantly growing in numbers. It has a corps of forty reporters and literary men for the collecting and preparing of material, and sends its news to clubs, restaurants, cafés, public and private residences, the hours of publication beginning at 8.30 A.M., and continuing without interruption until 11 P.M. Each hour is devoted to some special class of news, beginning with telegraphic dispatches from abroad, following with local and provincial news, etc., while at 8 P.M. there are given concerts, lectures, recitations, or other forms of instruction or entertainment.

A Telephone Newspaper

We have hitherto dealt solely with the progress of the nineteenth century. Now, standing like Bellamy at the dawn of the twentieth, it may be well to take a long look ahead, and strive to trace some stages of the probable progress of the coming time, looking forward from this summit of the ages and stating what this outlook into the dim and distant future brings to our eyes.

Before making this effort there is one thing that needs to be said. The progress of the nineteenth century, great as it has been in various directions, must be considered as confined within comparatively narrow limits of space, its effects rapidly diminishing as we pass into the remoter lands of semi-civilization and barbarism. The United States, Western Europe, and such British colonies as Canada, Australia, and Cape Colony have been the seats of most active progress; Spanish America, Russia, and Southeastern Europe have played secondary parts in this movement; Asia, with the exception of Japan, has taken very little part in it; and Africa almost no part at all, except in a few of its European settlements.

Limits of Nineteenth Century Progress

This is one of the important directions in which we may look for a declared exercise of twentieth century activity, that of the planting of the results of recent civilization in all the regions of the earth. This work, as above said, has been done in Japan, whose people have responded with wonderful alacrity to the touch of the new civilization. In the great empire of China the response has been much less encouraging, not from lack of intellectual activity in its people, but from self-satisfaction in their existing institutions and culture. At the close of the nineteenth century, however, this resistance to the thought

Progress in China and Hindostan

and mechanical inventions of the West was rapidly giving way, and doubtless one of the triumphs of the twentieth century will be the rejuvenation of China, which we may look to see rivalling Japan on the path of progress.

Of the other great centre of intellectual activity in Asia, the populous land of Hindostan, its progress is likely to depend far more on its British overlords than on the people themselves. While as mentally active as the Chinese, the Hindoos are far less practical. The Chinaman is natively a man of business, and needs only to be convinced that some new method is to his advantage to take active hold of it. The Hindoo is a dreamer, remarkably lacking in the business instinct, and is so deeply imbued with the ancient religious culture of his land that it will not be easy to rouse him from the fatalistic theories in which his whole nature is steeped. National progress in that land must be the work of British energy. But it has already made such marked advance that India may be trusted to wheel into line with the West in the new century.

The future of the remainder of the world is less assured. The slow thinking peoples of the remainder of Asia, the fanatical populations of Mohammedan lands, the negroes of Africa, the natives of Brazil and Patagonia, the inhabitants of the islands of the Pacific, the peoples **Among the** of the tropics in general, all are likely to act as brakes upon **Dull=Minded** the wheels of progress, and the "white man's burden" with **Peoples** these tribes and races during the twentieth century is certain to prove an arduous one.

Yet it is not well to be too pessimistic in regard to this problem. It must be remembered that the work of the nineteenth century in these lands has been largely one of discovery. The labor of settlement and development has only fairly begun ; what the results will be it is not safe to predict. To make thinkers of these dull-minded savages and barbarians will perhaps be the work of many centuries. To make workers of them is a far easier task, and civilized processes may be active in all these lands long before the nations are in condition to appreciate them. One method of solving the problem is already under way. In the Hawaiian Islands the native population is rapidly disappearing and being replaced by a new one. In New Zealand it has in great measure disappeared and British immigrants have taken its place. The natives are diminishing in numbers elsewhere, as in Australia. The problem of civilization in many of the new lands is likely to be solved in this easy way. But in the thickly settled countries this radical solution of the problem is not to be looked for, and the white man has before him the burden of lifting these unprogressive populations into a higher state.

To come back to the question of the general advance of the world during the twentieth century, we find ourselves facing a difficult and varied problem. That the great progress of the nineteenth century will be continued cannot well be questioned, but the directions this progress will take is far from easy to decide. In some of its phases progress seems approaching its limiting point, in others its rapidity is likely to decrease, while in still others it may be enormously enhanced. It is by no means improbable that the development of human institutions during the century at hand will be in quite different lines from those of the century just closed, less mechanical perhaps and more moral, less scientific and more philosophical, less political and more industrial, less laborious and more artistic.

Conditions of Twentieth Century Development

In some branches of invention and discovery we seem approaching a termination. It is not easy to see, for instance, how telegraphy can advance in the future as it has in the past. Its powers seem nearing their ultimate measure of ease and rapidity. Yet it is dangerous to predict. Here at the end of the century comes wireless telegraphy, with untold powers. And by its side appears telepathy, mental telegraphy,—the direct action of mind upon mind in a manner analogous to that of telegraphing without wires—of which as yet we know little, yet which may have in it great possibilites of development.

Other discoveries which seem approaching their ultimate condition are telephony, photography, illumination, and apparently labor-saving machinery in some of its fields, since the performance of some machines appears to have practically reached perfection. Transportation may well be one of these. The rapidity of railroad travel will, no doubt, be increased, yet natural limitations must check its indefinite increase. The same may be said in regard to steamship travel, it appearing that any great future increase of speed must be at an increased ratio of cost so considerable as to bring development in this direction to a speedy termination.

Limitations to Progress

Of course, we are speaking only from our present point of view. It is quite possible that some new and luminous conceptions may break down the bars which now appear to be erected and open the way for new progress in all these directions. Yet it seems safe to assert, as a general principle, that development in any one direction can go on only unto a certain point, and that the limitations of nature must check it at that point.

We cannot, indeed, well conceive of a greater activity of invention and a more rapid unfoldment of new processes than we have had before us in the nineteenth century. But an equal activity may long continue. While

GREATER NEW YORK.

On January 1, 1898, Greater New York was created by the union of New York, Brooklyn, Long Island City, and Staten Island into one municipality. The city now covers nearly 318 square miles, contains over three and one-half million inhabitants, and, next to London, is the largest city in the world.

DELEGATES TO THE UNIVERSAL PEACE CONGRESS AT THE HAGUE, 1899

This memorable Congress, held in 1899, in the Summer Palace at the Hague, the capital of Holland, was called at the suggestion of the Czar of Russia for the purpose of promoting peace by a reduction of the great armaments of the nations. This purpose failed, but a system of International Arbitration was adopted, which may prove still more useful in the prevention of war.

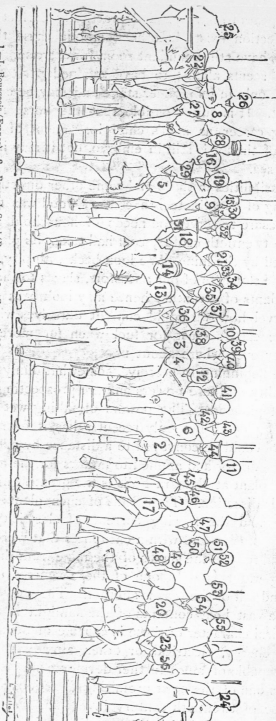

1.—L. Bourgeois (France). 2.—Baron de Staal (Russia). 3.—Comte de Munster (Germany). 4.—Chevalier de Karnebeek (Holland). 5.—General J. C. C. Den Beer Poortugael (Holland). 6.—A. Beernaert (Belgium). 7.—Phya Suriya (Siam). 8.—De Bille (Denmark). 9.—Comte Welsersheimb (Austria). 10.—A. D. White (United States). 11.—E. M. Rahusen (Holland). 12.—Baron Hayashi (Japan). 13.—Yang Yu (China). 14.—Hoo Wei-Teh (China). 15.—A. Roth (Switzerland). 16.—Sir J. Pauncefote (England). 17.—J. Motono (Japan). 18.—Comte de Grelle Rogier (Belgium). 19.—A. Beldiman (Roumania). 20.—Raffalovich (Russia). 21.—J. N. Papiniu (Roumania). 22.—Seth Low (United States). 23.—Baron d'Estournelles (France). 24.—A. G. Schimmelpenninck (Holland). 25.—Tadema (Holland). 26.—Von Schnack (Denmark). 27.—G. Merey de Kapos-mère (Austria). 28.—Phya Visuddha (Siam). 29.—Corragioni d'Orelli (Siam). 30.—S. Ardagh (England). 31.—Stanford Newel (United States). 32.—C. Coanda (Roumania). 33.—E. Rolin (Siam). 34.—H. Howard (England). 35.—C. Descamps (Belgium). 36.—C. de Selir (Portugal). 37.—Voishave Wejkovitch (Servia). 38.—Kreyer (China). 39.—V. de Khnepach (Austria). 40.—Abdullah-Pasha (Turkey). 41.—Louis Renault (France). 42.—A. Cœur (England). 43.—T. Mahan (United States). 44.—Guido Pompilj (Italy). 45.—Mourey Bey (Turkey). 46.—Mirza Rizakhan (Persia). 47.—Ovtchinnikow (Russia). 48.—A. de Castillo (Portugal). 49.—E. Odier (Switzerland). 50.—Miyatovitch (Servia). 51.—Uyehara (Japan). 52.—Comte de Villiers (Luxembourg). 53.—Nago Arigo (Japan). 54.—S. Heine (Russia). 55.—Comte Barantzew (Russia). 56.—A. Kunzli (Switzerland).

invention appears to have yielded practically perfect results in some fields, great imperfection exists in others, and in these the minds of inventors

Probable Lines of Future Activity have still abundant room for exercise. Thus while the bicycle seems almost to have attained perfection, the automobile is only in its pioneer stage and may be capable of extraordinary improvement. It is quite possible that the horse may in the near future end his long career as man's chief instrument of carriage and traction. Navigation of the air is still in embryo, but it may in time supplant travel on land and sea.

The possibilities in these and some other directions seem immense. At the beginning of the nineteenth century wood was the chief fuel, and had in great measure to serve the needs of household and workshop. At the dawn of the twentieth century coal had taken its place, and the forest had been replaced by the mine. We look back with pity, not unmixed with contempt, on the slowness of our ancestors, slaves to the axe and the firebrand. Our descendants of a century hence may look back with like feelings upon us, and marvel how we could content ourselves with delving in the deep rocks of the earth's crust for fuel when far more abundant and useful resources lay everywhere about us.

We are beginning to perceive, somewhat dimly still, the immensity and inexhaustibility of these powers and are prospecting among them with the footsteps of pioneers. The powers of falling water have long been em-

Employment of the Forces of Nature ployed, but only recently has it been discovered that they could be conveyed to a distance by means of the electric conductor and applied to motors for the movement of machinery. The electric plant at Niagara Falls is the greatest nineteenth century installation in this direction. Thousands of such plants may be installed in the near future, and the flowing currents of electricity yield light, heat and power in a profusion and with a cheapness that will quite throw coal out of the race, and release the slaves of the mine from their age-old fetters.

Falling water is only one of these sources of natural power. The tidal rise and fall of the seas is another. The movement of the winds is a third. The vast heat contents of the sunlight is a fourth. The variable and periodical character of these is capable of being overcome by methods of storing energy, electrical or other, already somewhat developed and doubtless capable of much further development.

This is one of the most promising directions that appear before us for the exercise of twentieth century invention. Yet, despite this and other fields of inventive activity, what we have said appears to hold good, that one by one each of the varied lines of invention will reach its ultimatum, and gradually the activity of man in this direction decrease. While the twentieth century may be as active in the development of mechanism as the nineteenth has been, it seems unlikely to be more so, and in succeeding centuries, inventive activity must decline for want of fields in which to exercise itself.

In some other fields of mental activity a similar slackening of energy may appear. Science has been as active as mechanics in the century just closed, but in some of its fields of exercise an approach towards a limiting point seems evident. Observational science has been phenomenally busy, and the multitude of facts collected has been extraordinarily great; so great indeed that in some lines the facts remaining to be observed have become limited.

Possible Decline in Mechanical and Scientific Progress

Such is the case in zoology and botany. The species of animals and plants are by no means all known, but only the inconspicuous and those existing in lands yet unexplored remain to be discovered. There is much room for work still in this field, but future labors must be more difficult and results less abundant. The same can be said of several other fields of scientific observation, such as chemistry, mineralogy, anatomy and physiology, and others that could be named. Doubtless there is still large room for observation, but it must be in the finer and less evident domains of science, the surface facts having been largely gathered in. In theoretical science great progress has also been made by such men as Copernicus, Kepler, Newton, Young, Darwin and a host of others. But many important problems remain to be solved, and human thought may profitably be exercised in this direction for a long time to come.

Yet it may be that the progress of the twentieth century will be directed most largely towards fields of research or improvement which have been secondary considerations, or have made only partial advance, in the century we have been considering. These will perhaps be intellectual rather than physical in character, and the advance social rather than material. Man has been struggling actively with inanimate substances and physical forces and adapting them to his ends. There lie before him the world of the animate and the forces of society

New Lines of Mental Activity

and the intellect, to be treated with similar activity. The political, moral, educational, and industrial problems of the day need to be taken hold of more decisively than ever before, and the reign of fraud, injustice, autocratic power, unnatural inequality, ignorance, unnecessary want and suffering, etc., brought to an end.

There has been, as above stated, very considerable political evolution during the recent century, but the political condition of the world remains very far from satisfactory, even in civilized lands, and there is abundant room for progress in this field. Man will not be satisfied until every vestige of autocratic power and hereditary rank is swept away and the rulers of the nations have become the chosen servants of the people, as in the republic of the United States, and what we may call the prime-ministry of Great Britain—for the so-called monarchy of that kingdom has sunk to a title without power. Nor will man be satisfied until the rule of the **Purity in Politics** political boss is similarly swept aside and honesty in office and in elective methods secured. This state of affairs cannot be reached under the present condition of public opinion. In the educational activities of the age political instruction is sadly needed. The masses need to be taught their duties and their rights. If they can once be brought to act together for their own interests and their own ideas of right and wrong, and cease to be led astray by the shibboleth of party or partisanship, there will be a rapid change in the state of public affairs, and men be chosen for official positions who can be trusted to act for the good of those who sent them there.

Advance in education is not alone needed for this, but its accompaniment, advance in moral standards, is equally requisite. The moral progress of mankind, which has been so marked during the past century, is sure to go on to higher levels, and with every step upwards there will doubtless be demanded a higher standard of action in those who are called upon to act as servants of the public. We have not mentioned in this work one of the great evils of the age, the vice of intoxication, which has done so much to degrade and pauperize mankind, and has been one of the leading influences in the retention of the unworthy in power. Legal enactments have failed to put an end to this indulgence in a debased appetite, but **The Vice of Intemperance** public opinion is beginning to succeed where law has failed. Drunkenness has ceased to be respectable, and as a result open intoxication among respectable people is growing more and more rare. At the same time the desire to be considered respectable is making its way downward among the people, and widening the field of its effect. Drinking in moderation is prevalent still. Drinking in excess is plainly on the decrease. And with every step in this direction the self-respect of the people must grow, pauperism decrease, and an enlightened conception of public duty develop. Whatever else the twentieth century brings about, we may reasonably look for a great revolution in the political status of the world.

There is one farther field of twentieth century progress to be reviewed, the industrial. The nineteenth century has reached its end leaving this great domain of human interests in a highly unsatisfactory condition. The progress of labor during the century under review has been considered in a preceding chapter, and brought down to its existing state. **Industry in the** What the character of its progress will be in the twentieth **Twentieth** century is open to conjecture. While nothing concerning it **Century** can be stated positively, some deductions from the present condition of things may be made.

Mankind for some thousands of years past has been subjected to tyrannies of various kinds, and in particular to those of physical force, of mental influence, and of material possessions; the first controlling him by the power of the sword, the second by that of superstition, the third by that of his daily needs. The control of the first two of these has **Physical Force,** long been rapidly slipping away. That of the autocrat of **Superstition** the sword has vanished in the most advanced lands, and the **and Money** political equality of all men is there assured. That of the tyrant of the mind has similarly vanished in these lands and is diminishing everywhere, liberty of thought being made secure. The autocratic dominion of wealth, on the contrary, has grown as the authority of its rivals has decreased, and it stands to-day as the great power in the most advanced communities, it being particularly dominant in the United States.

Shall this third of the great tyrants of the world retain its supremacy? Shall it not in its turn be overthrown, and liberty and equality in this direction be also attained? Certainly great progress is likely to be made in this direction, whatever the final outcome may be. For ages a state of protest against the control of the tyrants of man's body and mind prevailed. This state now exists in regard to the money power, the industrial classes of all lands struggling bitterly against it, and combining with a view to its overthrow. Such a state of revolt, bitter, persistent, unrelenting, indicates something innately wrong in the industrial situation, and cannot fail in the end to have its effect. We may safely look forward to an amelioration in the situation, even though we cannot tell how it is to be brought about.

The extraordinary activity of productive industry within the century is the cause of the state of affairs which now exists. The wealth of the world has increased enormously, and has fallen largely into the hands of individuals. A century ago there was not a millionaire in our land, and few in any land. Now they exist by the thousands, and million- **The Vast** aires two hundred fold multiplied are not unknown. This vast **Growth of** accumulation of wealth in single hands does not satisfy its **Wealth** owners. They are eager for more, and capital is widely combining into great corporations for the purpose of reducing expenses, so that the cost of manufacture may be decreased, and doing away with competition, so that prices of goods may be augmented. This is but one result of the trust combination. A second and highly important one is a great reduction of the opportunity for individual business operations, the tendency being to reduce the great mass of the community to the position of employees.

This problem has been already considered in Chapter xxxviii., with the suggestion there made that it is apt to strengthen the force of Socialism, the purpose of which, as there indicated, is to put an end to individualism in productive enterprises, and place all workshops, stores, railroads, etc., under government control, to be conducted for the good of the people as a whole, not for that of individual capitalists. A step in this direction some-what widely taken in Europe, is the control of railroads and telegraphs by **National and Municipal Ownership** the government. Another step is the control of all municipal functions, including street railways, electric lights, etc., by the city authorities. The latter system, adopted by many European cities, is being actively advocated in the United States, and is gathering to its support a vigorous public opinion which promises to be strong enough in the end to achieve its purpose.

Abroad the forces of Socialism are organizing themselves actively, and are gaining a political strength vigorous enough to create much alarm in the ruling powers. Whether this cult of Socialism has come to stay, and has in it sufficient force of growth to give it an eventual supremacy, or whether it is to be classed with the many popular movements which have played their parts for a time and passed away, is not for us to say, only the arbitrament of time can decide.

We might consider the question of the twentieth century progress from other points of view, such as agriculture, architecture, household art, litera-ture, medicine, surgery, social relations, etc., though in doing so we should be considering simply developments of existing conditions. Perhaps the most promising line of progress is in experimental psychology, the study of the brain and nervous system, the instruments of the mind from the scientific point of view, in distinction from the old, theoretical psy-chology. This, the latest of the sciences, has recently **The New Psychology** begun its development, and is full of **promise of** important discoveries concerning the conditions of mental phenomena. It must suffice here, however, to refer to it as one of the lines in which science has before it a broad field of research, and with this mention we shall bring to an end the long journey we have made in this work through the stirring history and marvelous events and discoveries of the wonderful nineteenth century.

CHAPTER XLIII.

The End of the Century and Its Events

AS the nineteenth century came in to the roll of the drum and the roar of the cannon, so it is going out to the same terror-inspiring sounds. People have dreamed of a coming time in which the war drum shall beat no longer and the banner of battle shall be furled. No doubt this happy time is coming, but it is still afar, and the Peace Conference of 1899 seems almost to have let loose the dogs of war. There is fighting in South Africa, fighting on the Guinea coast, fighting in the Philippines, fighting in Colombia, fighting in China, and threats of war in nearer quarters still; war vessels are building, armies drilling, workshops busy in making implements of war, and the labors of death tread close on the heels of the labors of life.

So swift has been the march of events that we could not keep pace with it in the foregoing chapters; momentous things happening even while we were writing, and it has become necessary to take up the ends of these dropped threads and carry them forward to the **Swift March of Progress** century's end. Here we can only offer the hope that the war flag may be furled before the twentieth century comes in, and peace smile propitious upon its advent.

The war of 1898 with Spain left the United States with several unsettled affairs upon its hands. Porto Rico and Hawaii had to be brought under the sheltering folds of the flag and a system of government given them, Cuba had to be launched on the waters of independence, and, most momentous of all, the war in the Philippines had to be fought out to the bitter end and peace restored to that populous and fertile group of islands. Great Britain had her household affair to settle by stretching the blanket of Cape Colony over the Boer states and getting full possession of the mines of diamonds and gold. And all the great civilized powers of the earth were concerned in the attempt of China to get rid of foreigners by the summary process of assassination and to close once more its doors against the world of the whites. These are the events with which we have now to deal, in order to round out the cycle of nineteenth century events.

Of the new possessions of the United States, the Hawaiian Islands were the most easily dealt with. These islands were already under American control, and the affairs went on there without a break. They were given the government of a Territory of the United States, with no tariff fence to keep out their sugar and other products.   This was not the case with Porto Rico. This island was taken in but its products were kept out, with the result that the people sank into destitution and misery, and many of them grew to hate the dominion they had at first warmly welcomed.   In the end the tariff wall

Hawaii, Porto Rico and Cuba was partly broken down and prosperity showed some signs of coming back, but the people were far from content, to be left half in and half out of the United States.   As for Cuba, it remained for a time a military ward of the United States, but that country kept its pledge of honor by inviting the Cubans to adopt a constitution for themselves, under which they could be safely launched upon the deep waters of self-government.

At the end of 1899 an old dispute was amicably settled.   For years the Samoan Islands had been under the joint control of Germany, Great Britain, and the United States, and there had been no small amount of intrigue and controversy.   The difficulty was now settled.   Germany got the islands of Apolu and Savaii, and the United States fell heir to Tutuila.   This is a small island, but it contains the splendid harbor of Pago-Pago, the finest in the South Pacific, if not in the whole Pacific Ocean.   Two other islands were obtained by the United States, the small island of Guam, in the Ladrones, which was ceded by Spain, and Wake Island, a lonely spot in the open ocean, which was taken in 1899 by hoisting the flag over it.   Those three small islands, far removed from each other, give the United States valuable places of call at points thousands of miles apart in that mighty ocean of the East.

Far the most valuable of all these new possessions of the great republic was the archipelago of the Philippines.   But this multitude of rich islands was not to be had for the asking.   Of its 8,000,000 of people, a host of those

Philippine Islands who had been in arms against Spain demanded their independence, and the United States had not long held possession of Manila before it had a new war on its hands.   Emilio Aguinaldo, the general in command of the Filipino army demanded more than the government at Washington was ready to grant, and as a result hostilities began.

Aguinaldo had been brought from Hong Kong to Manila in an American vessel.   On reaching there he called his old followers to arms, and besieged Manila on the land side while Dewey's fleet threatened it from the bay.   After the fall of Manila Aguinaldo became hostile to the Americans. He said that he had been promised independence as the price of his aid. When he found that the United States intended to take possession of the islands, in accordance with their treaty with Spain, his hostility increased, and led him, in February, 1899, to make a fierce attack on the American outposts at Manila.

This affair ended in the repulse of the native forces, which were driven back for several miles and suffered severe loss. But they were not to be subdued by a single defeat. Aguinaldo, who had been made president of the republic proclaimed by the Philippine leaders, now issued a declaration of war, and both sides prepared for an active campaign. This began, on the part of the Filipinos, in an attempt to burn the city of Manila, with the hope of driving out its garrison, but in which the natives were the principal sufferers, the fire sweeping widely over their residence quarter. Vigilant precautions were taken by the American leaders to prevent a renewal of this dangerous enterprise.

General Elwell S. Otis, then commander-in-chief in the Philippines, lost no time in putting an army of invasion in the field. The advance of the American forces began on March 25, 1899, and on the 31st Malolos, Aguinaldo's capital, was occupied. This was not accomplished without sharp fighting. The Filipinos had thrown up earthworks at every defensible point, and resisted the advance with some stubbornness, though in every instance without effect. The Americans pushed **The Spring Campaign in the Philippines** steadily forward, driving the natives from their works with resistless charges, swimming rivers in the face of a sharp rifle fire, and carrying everything before them. Calumpit, the second Filipino stronghold, was reached and carried near the end of April; San Fernando fell soon after, and General Lawton, whose long experience in Indian warfare admirably adapted him to this work, made his way northward through the foothills and occupied San Isidro, the second Filipino capital.

These and other successes were not gained without much hardship and loss of life. Marching through swampy rice-fields and thorny chapparal, facing well-built earthworks at every few miles, and at a hundred points encountering an active and persistent enemy, the soldiers of the States found their task a severe and annoying one, and their ranks were considerably depleted when the coming on of the rainy season, at the beginning of July, put an end to active operations for several months.

Meanwhile an effort had been made to bring the insurrectionists to terms by peaceful measures. A Philippine Commission, consisting of Admiral Dewey and General Otis, and the civilians Jacob G. Schurman, Dean Worcester, and Charles Denb, was appointed to consider and report on the situation, and began operations by issuing a proclamation in which the supremacy of the United States was declared, but the natives were offered a large measure of civil rights and local self-rule.   This proclamation proved of no avail, so far as the insurgent forces were concerned, Aguinaldo issuing counter-proclamations and calling on the people to accept no terms short of full independence.

In the summer of 1899 Admiral Dewey returned home.   On the 3d of March he had been promoted to the grade of full admiral, an exalted rank which before him had been borne only by Farragut and Porter; and during his journey home the whole world seemed eager to do him honor.

Dewey's Return Home   In his own country he met with an enthusiastic reception, the people everywhere greeting him as the most heroic figure of the recent war.   As a testimony of appreciation they purchased him a beautiful home in the city of Washington, in which, taking to himself a wife, the grateful recipient settled down to rest and comfort after his arduous labors.

With the close of the rainy season in Luzon the war began again, now with a larger army on the part of the Americans, who were also provided with a much-needed force of cavalry.   The Filipinos seemed to have lost heart through their reverses in the spring campaign, and fought with less courage than before, so that by the 1st of December they were in full flight for the mountains, pursued by Generals Lawton and Young with cavalry and scouts.   After this date the natives had nothing that could be called an army in the field.   The forces under Aguinaldo were broken and dispersed, and were capable only of guerilla warfare, which, though annoying, seemed likely only to delay the period of complete pacification.   During the succeeding period there were frequent collisions with detached bands, in one of which the brave Lawton was shot dead.   In the summer of 1900 President McKinley issued a proclamation of amnesty, of which many of the natives in arms took advantage.   Aguinaldo, however, refused

The Death of Lawton   to submit, and the costly guerilla warfare went on.   Hopeless as the cause of the Filipinos was held to be, they were not yet ready to submit, and the affair seemed as if it might be protracted for months to come.

A somewhat similar state of affairs existed in South Africa, where the British-Boer war appeared likely to outlive the century.   Here, too, organized resistance had largely degenerated into guerilla warfare, which was greatly aided by the broken and hilly character of the country.   Lord Roberts, after establishing himself in Pretoria, had spread his forces widely out, with the hope of taking in a net the scattered commandos still in arms in the Orange River Free State, before devoting himself to Paul Kruger and his fellows in the northern Transvaal.   But he found it much easier to set his net than to catch his fish. The Boers proved extraordinarily mobile. Though some of them surrendered, a strong force continued in the field, and not only defied the British but succeeded in capturing detached bodies of them. General De Wet, their leader, showed a remarkable ability in this kind of warfare, and escaped with ease and alertness every trap set for him, while striking his foes at unexpected points.

Meanwhile, Kruger and the Transvaal forces remained in the hill coun-try to the north, still defiant, and likely to give Lord Roberts no small trouble when he should be at liberty to attend to them. Though it was announced to the world that the struggle was practically at an end and the South African republics had ceased to exist, the indications were that the British empire had a costly and troublesome war still before it, and that the twentieth century would dawn before the Boers were subdued. The situations in the Transvaal and the Philippines were thus closely analogous, and the Anglo-Saxons of the East and the West alike were ending the century with an annoying and protracted guerilla war on hand, the final outcome of which could not be foreseen.

Guerilla War in the Transvaal

As the summer of 1900 approached there appeared indications of trouble in a new quarter, which threatened to overshadow these minor oper-ations and involve the whole civilized world in a conflict which might assume gigantic proportions. The vast empire of China, with its 400,000,-000 of population, suddenly showed a violent hostility to foreigners, which endangered the lives not only of the missionaries scattered far and wide throughout the land, but even of the representatives of the Powers at Pekin—high dignitaries whose lives and liberty are held sacred by all civilized nations alike in peace and war.

We must go back and trace the course of events leading to this lament-able state of affairs. For many years Europe had been heaping up "vials of wrath" in China. In the "opium war," the French and English advance on Peking, and other hostile relations of China with the powers, that ancient nation had been treated with an injustice and a supercilious disregard of its rights and susceptibilities which could not fail to produce a widespread feeling of indignation. The pride of China lay in its ancient learning, it had never been a military nation and it was quite incapable of main-taining itself against these fighting foreigners, but it was abundantly capable of indignation for affronts to its dignity, and it was growing evident to far-seeing critics of world affairs that the time might come when the densely peopled old nation would turn on its enemies and exact ample retribution for its insults and injuries.

How England and France Treated China

The turn in the tide came with the Japano-Chinese war. This had the double effect of showing the incapacity of the Chinese to cope in war with modern powers, and of vividly demonstrating to themselves these defects. The logical result followed. The nations of Europe, perceiving the weakness of the ancient empire, began to descend upon it like wolves upon their prey. What they did has been stated in an earlier chapter. Russia, England, Germany, and France alike took forcible possession of ports and territory of the feeble old Oriental realm, and the newspapers were full of threats of a partition of the whole empire between the land-hungry nations, in utter disregard of the ethical aspect of the question.

While this spirit of greed was displayed by the European nations, the statesmen of China were awakening to a perception of the urgency of the situation and the need of taking radical steps if they wished to save their empire from a total collapse. A spirit of reform began to show itself. Railroads had long been practically forbidden, but now concessions for the building of hundreds of miles of railroad were granted. Modern implements and munitions of war were purchased in great quanti**Reform in the Chinese Empire** ties, and European officers were engaged to drill and discipline the imperial army. European books were eagerly sought for, perhaps with the sentiment that they might contain the secret of European strength. The great nation was stirring in its sleep of centuries and beginning to awake.

The reformers gained the ear of the youthful emperor and infected him with their new ideas, with the result that radical changes were ordered in the administration—revolutionary ones, indeed, when attempted in a so stringently conservative nation as China. The result was one that might have been expected. The party of ancient prejudice and conservatism—a powerful party in China—took the alarm. The empress-dowager, who had recently laid down the reins of power as regent, took them up again, under the support of this dominant party, seized and practically dethroned the emperor, executed all his advisers upon whom she could lay hands, and restored the methods of the old administration in every respect except that of military discipline.

This palace reaction made itself felt throughout the country. Hatred of foreigners, which had been growing for years in the Chinese populace, reached a perilous climax under this seeming sanction from the palace authorities in Peking, and in the spring of 1900 a murderous attack against the missionaries began. A secret society of Chinese athletes, known in English phrase as "The Boxers," rose in arms and made an onslaught upon the missionaries, a class of foreigners who were immediately exposed to their attacks, and whom they seem to have hated as virulently as the Filipinos hated the Spanish friars. The insurrection spread with extraordinary rapidity, many of the missionaries were murdered, and the Boxers quickly appeared in multitudes in the capital, where, joined by many of the soldiers, they made a violent assault on the foreign legations and put the lives of the ministers and their attendants in imminent peril.

When tidings of this state of affairs reached the Western world there was a wide-spread alarm. The ministers were cut off from all communication with their governments; stories of their massacre, with details of terrible tortures, were sent abroad; the murder of **The Boxer Outbreak** the German Minister and a Japanese official was confirmed; there was much reason to believe that the government favored and its soldiers aided the Boxer hosts, and for the first time in history the great nations of Europe and America joined their forces in an attempt to avert a common danger. The United States had kept apart from all seizure of Chinese territory and all schemes of partition of China. It contented itself with demanding freedom of commerce—an "open door" to the Chinese market—and sedulously avoided interference with the national affairs of the empire. But its minister, Edwin H. Conger, was in equal peril with those of other nations, and in this critical exigency it sent a hasty contingent of troops to China and joined the European powers in the work of rescue.

We can give only an epitome of the events that followed. A small force, made up of marines and soldiers of various nations, under Admiral Seymour of the British navy, made a hasty advance upon Peking. But they found the railroad torn up, and their route invested with an overwhelming force of enemies, and were forced to retreat, barely escaping entire destruction. About the same time the allied fleets made an attack on the Chinese forts at Taku. In this the United States vessels took no part, Admiral Remey declaring it to be uncalled for and un- **Attack on the Taku Forts** wise, an opinion which the succeeding events appeared to substantiate, since the Chinese government made this assault a pretext for active war against the allied forces.

As an act of reprisal, a strong force of Boxers and soldiers made an attack on the foreign quarter of the city of Tien Tsin, fighting with a skill, courage and persistence which they had never shown before. They were well armed with rifles and cannon of the best types, which they used with effect, while they stubbornly resisted the efforts of the foreign forces to dislodge them. It needed a fierce struggle to effect this and give the allies control of the city. Never before, had the Chinese fought the Europeans with such stubborn courage, and serious doubts of the final result began to be felt.

The nations hurried troops to the point of danger as rapidly as possible, Japan, which was in full accord with the Western powers, sending the largest force. The United States sent troops from the Philippines, Great Britain from India, and Russia from her posts to the north; but all this took time, and the month of July passed before there was a sufficient force to justify a second advance. Meanwhile the danger of the ministers in Peking was daily growing more imminent and the mystery that surrounded them more pronounced. Gathered within the stout walls of the British legation, they fought off the ravening multitudes that clamored for their blood, while for weeks their people at home were in distressing doubt as to whether they were alive or dead.

At length, early in August, the advance began, the army, about 16,000 strong made up of Japanese, Russians, British, and Americans. The French and Germans, who were as yet in small numbers, were left on guard at Tien Tsin. What degree of opposition would be encountered was not known. There were several strongly fortified towns on the way, and there was reason to believe that the lowlands would be flooded from the Peiho River, along whose banks the march took place. The midsummer heat of the climate added to the difficulties of the way, and the ability of the small army to reach Pekin was far from assured.

As it proved, the Chinese had shown their greatest courage at Tien Tsin, and their opposition to the advance of the allies was half-hearted and ineffective. They made a strong stand at Peitsang, a native town **The Rescue of the Ministers** on the Peiho, but were driven from their works, and from that point the allies marched to Peking with only feeble efforts to check their advance. The triple-walled city was reached on the 14th of August. On the 15th an assault was made on several of its gates. Here there was a resistance, but not a very vigorous one, and before nightfall the foreign forces were in the streets of the populous Chinese capital, the Americans and British the first. Marching in haste to the legations, they had the high gratification of finding the beleaguered officials alive, and of rescuing them from a siege which had lasted for weeks, and which, in a few days more, would probably have ended in assassination, as their powers of resistance were almost at an end.

The joy of the wearied and almost hopeless men and women of the legations on seeing the stars and stripes and the union jack borne side by side to their rescue, can be better imagined than described. There soon followed the banners of Russia and Japan, and as the allied troops marched in triumph into the legation the cheers of the troops woke a responsive throb in the hearts of those whose hands they clasped and drew tears of joy to eyes that had long looked only on the dread form of fear and the threatened horror of death by torture. The situation, thus happily ended, was one that had rarely, if ever, presented itself before in the history of the world.

The rescue of the ministers at Peking ended all the concern of the United States in the issue. The government had practically pledged itself to withdraw its troops as soon as its embassy was safe and its relations with China properly adjusted, whatever course the other nations might pursue. It had no land hunger to gratify, like its European allies, and had no ends to gain by remaining. In fact, it had quite a surfeit of new possessions in the Philippines. These distant islands were proving a serious trouble not only abroad but at home. A party in opposition to the policy of the administration had arisen, which accused the government of imperialistic purposes, and called upon it to abandon the Philippines and permit their people to govern themselves.

This party grew in strength as the war dragged on into its second year at a serious cost in money and lives, and by the summer of 1900 it had gained such power as to make its demand the dominant issue in the Presidential campaign of that year. Of all the home affairs of the nations in the closing year of the century this campaign was the most prominent and important event, and the only one which here calls for attention at our hands. It is true, a startling affair had **Work of the Anarchists** taken place in Europe. King Humbert of Italy had been shot dead by an assassin, and his son, Victor Emanuel III., was now king of that disturbed land. An attempt had also been made to assassinate the Shah of Persia, during his visit to the Paris Exposition of the closing century. The Anarchists were abroad, Europe seemed seething with plots of royal murder, and the monarchs trembled on their thrones. But in the broad United States the one great question at issue was that of obtaining a new ruler by ballot instead of by bullet, or of reseating President McKinley for another four years.

The Republican National Convention met at Philadelphia in June, and nominated as its candidate for President the ruling incumbent of the office, Willliam McKinley, and for Vice-President Theodore Roosevelt, the governor of New York, and the hero of the battle of San Juan. The Democratic National Convention met at Kansas City in July, and nominated for President its standard bearer of four years before, William Jennings Bryan, and for Vice-President, Adlai E. Stevenson, who has already served one term in this honorable office. So far as the presidential nominees were concerned, it was a renewal of the contest of 1896, McKinley being again pitted against Bryan.   But as regards the principles to be fought for, the war cries of the campaign, there was a radical change, the old issues of the parties largely vanishing, and new issues being presented to the alert minded people of the United States.

One old issue was revived, that of the Republican insistence on the gold standard of coinage and the Democratic demand for "the free and unlimited coinage of silver at the ratio of 16 to 1." But this **The Political** issue sank in great part out of sight in the campaign, as did **Campaign** that of the tariff, which had been the bone of contention **of 1900** between the parties during many preceding campaigns.   In this last year of the century two distinctly new questions were presented; that of the Trust, the monopolistic combination of great business concerns; and that of Imperialism, the Republican administration being accused of the purpose of converting the republic into an empire, so far as the control of its new possessions were concerned.   The question of the Trusts was only a minor issue.   Both parties condemned them in their platforms. The great question at issue, however, was that of Imperialism *versus* Anti-imperialism, and on this the result of the campaign seemed to depend, the orators speaking in ringing tones in favor or denunciation of the policy of the McKinley administration in this regard.

William McKinley had come to the helm of the ship of state in 1897 in a period of profound peace and advancing prosperity.   But his whole term had been one of war and turmoil, not only in the United States but in various other parts of the world.   The war with Spain in 1898 had been followed by the acquisition of new territory and the development of new problems.   Then in 1899 and 1900 came the insurrection of the Philippines and the British-Boer war in South Africa; to be followed in 1900 by the outbreak against foreigners in China, and the invasion of that ancient realm by the allied forces of all the great powers.   Such a turmoil of the nations could not fail to bring important political questions to the front, and of these the great problem in America was that of Imperialism.   Anti-**War in the** imperialism expanded from the war-cry of a minor faction to **McKinley Ad-** the declared policy of one of the two great political parties **ministration** of the country, and the main question at issue in the Presidential campaign of 1900 was whether the United States should continue its work of subduing the Philippine insurgents, or should be withdrawn from the islands and leave the natives free to govern and control themselves. With this issue inscribed on their banners the two parties marched forward to the great war of the ballots at the end of the nineteenth century.